Abuse of Process in
Criminal Proceedings

To my wife, Caroline
David Young

For Sophia and Thomas
Mark Summers

To my wife, Louise
David Corker

Abuse of Process in Criminal Proceedings

Third edition

David Young BA (Hons), LLM (Lond)
of the Middle Temple, Barrister
9 Bedford Row

Mark Summers LLB (Hons)
of the Inner Temple, Barrister
Matrix Chambers, London

David Corker MA
Oriel College, Oxford and the University of Sheffield
Solicitor, Corker Binning

With (on chapter 11)

Martin Evans BA (Sussex), Dip Law (City)
of the Middle Temple, Barrister
Chambers of Andrew Mitchell QC, 33 Chancery Lane

Tottel
publishing

Tottel Publishing, Maxwelton House, 41–43 Boltro Road, Haywards Heath, West Sussex, RH16 1BJ

© Tottel Publishing Ltd 2009

A CIP Catalogue record for this book is available from the British Library.

ISBN: 978 1 84592 234 4

Typeset by Columns Design Limited, Reading
Printed and bound in Great Britain by Athenæum Press, Gateshead, Tyne and Wear

Foreword

It is a pleasure to be asked to write the foreword for this third edition of *Abuse of Process in Criminal Proceedings*. The authors are to be congratulated on maintaining the high standards which made the previous two editions of the work so successful.

An application to stay proceedings as an abuse of the process of the court has the potential to arise in any trial however minor, serious or complex and in whatever trial venue. Although not on the scale of the dramatic expansion of the doctrine of abuse of process during the 1990s, developments in recent years have been significant. There is no doubt that the appellate courts were uneasy at the volume of applications to stay proceedings and that recent years have seen the courts striving to refine the principles (eg in relation to reneging on promises (Chapter 2); ensure their consistent application (eg on the destruction or loss of evidence (Chapter 3)) and effectively eliminate some categories of abuse (as with adverse publicity after *Abu Hamza*, see Chapter 9). The authors have responded by incorporating discussion of all these developments and of the areas in which abuse of process continues to expand more dramatically. Thus, the chapter on extradition has been extensively rewritten, and there is a valuable new chapter on confiscation reflecting the recent case law on that subject (Chapter 11).

The work is renowned for its comprehensive and up-to-date coverage and this edition does not disappoint. The authors have included several hundred cases decided since the last edition, many of them unreported, as well as the relevant ECHR case law. The accessibility of the work is also to be commended. The busy practitioner ought to be able to locate relevant information easily and swiftly. However, the text offers more than simply a catalogue of cases and relevant principles. Within each chapter, the authors have placed the discussion in context. For example, the examination of delay in Chapter 1 is preceded by explanation of the dominant ECHR jurisprudence on which that head of abuse has developed. Similarly, the analysis of publicity in Chapter 9 includes an outline of contempt of court, and confiscation (Chapter 11) is introduced by an overview of the Proceeds of Crime Act 2002 and a brief history of the legislative scheme.

As with previous editions the work deserves respect for its presentation of an accurate and realistic account of the doctrine of abuse of process. Advocates are cautioned against potentially hopeless or damaging submissions which is entirely appropriate given the appellate courts' declared anxiety as to the overuse of abuse of process applications.

Foreword

The overriding virtue of the book remains its intensely practical nature. It is designed by practitioners for use by practitioners – both defence and prosecution. It provides practical advice on how best to either present, or respond to, an abuse submission.

I am confident that this third edition will prove as successful as its predecessors. It seems safe to assume that development in the area will continue at such a pace that a new edition will be necessary before too long!

David Ormerod
Professor of Criminal Justice
Queen Mary, University of London

Preface

It has been almost six years since the last edition of this work and few would disagree with the proposition that, in that time, the substantive and procedural legal landscape of criminal law has altered beyond all recognition. To highlight but two obvious examples, the Criminal Procedure Rules have been introduced and the CPIA disclosure regime has been completely restructured.

Applications to stay proceedings on grounds of abuse of process have almost become a part of the Criminal Justice system's home furniture. Indeed, in the 2005 protocol issued by the Lord Chief Justice on the 'Control and Management of Heavy Fraud and other Complex Criminal Cases', the doctrine of 'abuse of process' has its own discreet section. In the protocol, which seeks to improve abuse of process case management, the Lord Chief Justice notes how such applications 'have become a normal feature of heavy and complex cases'.

The second edition of this work provided a snapshot of the common-law abuse 'family' as it existed in 2003. This edition attempts to capture the family as it exists in late 2008. Despite the changing landscape, and despite a direct assault upon them by Parliament, not only are all of the 2003 family members still clearly visible in this 2008 family portrait, and all still in outrageously rude health, but the astute viewer will notice at least two new children born in the intervening years.

It is right to acknowledge that some family members have changed little. Entrapment (chapter 6), for example, in which *R v Looseley* remains the guiding light, has a few more grey hairs, but remains basically recognisable from the 2003 photo. Although it has to be said that her settled demeanour may soon be tested, insofar as private entrapment is concerned, by the Divisional Court's ruling in *Council for the Regulation of Healthcare Professionals v General Medical Council (Re Saluja)* [2007] 1 WLR 3094. Equally, the destruction abuse case law (chapter 3) has benefited from the consistent application of the *R (Ebrahim) v Feltham Magistrates' Court* decision.

By contrast, some members have obviously aged a great deal. Since posing in 2003, delay (chapter 1) has undergone a face lift in light of the House of Lords' ruling in *Attorney-General's Reference (No 2 of 2001)* [2004] 2 AC 72 and her internal conflicts have, to some extent, been resolved by the Privy Council's decision in *Spiers v Ruddy & HM Advocate General* [2008] 2 WLR 608.

A complete newcomer to the brood is confiscation abuse (chapter 11) following the landmark decisions in *R v Mahmood and Shahin* [2006] Cr App R (S) 96, CA, *R v Shabir* [2008] EWCA Crim 1809 and *R v Morgan & Bygrave* [2008] EWCA Crim 1323. Another welcome progeny to the field of executive misconduct (chapter 5) is Laws LJ's ruling in *R v Grant* [2006] 1 QB 60, CA regarding deliberate intrusion upon legal professional privilege.

The 2003 babe-in-arms, extradition abuse (chapter 8), has since grown into a formidable member of the family. The coming of the Extradition Act 2003 proved to be her saviour. The removal of significant traditional procedural safeguards by the 2003 Act meant that the need for an established extradition abuse jurisdiction became an inevitability. Thus it was that her jurisdiction was confirmed in *Bermingham v Director of the Serious Fraud Office* [2007] QB 727, DC, her procedural rubric laid out in *R (Government of the United States of America) v Bow Street Magistrates' Court* [2007] 1 WLR 1157, DC and her substantive limits and policy concerns delineated by the House of Lords in *McKinnon v Government of the United States of America* [2008] 1 WLR 1739, HL. Her presence in the 2008 photo as a healthy family member is significant. She is a microcosm of the entire family. Her jurisdiction having been established, extradition abuse concerns herself with the entire abuse spectrum. From double jeopardy to delay, from breach of promise to executive misconduct, extradition abuse is fashioned by, and herself fashions, the jurisprudence of the rest of the family.

It is now over 15 years since *ex parte Bennett* catapulted the abuse family into the limelight. Initial judicial restraint in scrutinising alleged state impropriety and misconduct has largely dissipated. *R v Grant* is a timely reminder of this; that the ability and willingness of those engaged in the criminal justice system to abuse it, is matched only by the determination of this elder member to stand as a bulwark against such executive misconduct. This matriarch has provided the core strength and stability to the family. Under her watch, other family members, who would perhaps have been unable to establish themselves in their own right, have been able to flourish. The authors commend this family to you again. At their heart lies the rule of law.

We have endeavoured to state the law as at 1 January 2009.

David Young
9 Bedford Row
www.9bedfordrow.co.uk

Mark Summers
Matrix
www.matrixlaw.co.uk

David Corker
Corker Binning
www.corkerbinning.co.uk

Acknowledgements

We gratefully acknowledge the assistance of the following in our efforts to complete the third edition of this book. We are particularly indebted to Craig Harris of Furnival Chambers for his boundless knowledge and assistance on chapters 1, 5 and 6.

We are indebted to Tom Wainwright of Garden Court Chambers for the considerable assistance he provided in the drafting of amendments to the revised Double Jeopardy chapter.

We would especially like to thank Martin Evans, of Andrew Mitchell QC's Chambers, our new contributing author, who was responsible for chapter 11, on Confiscation Abuse, which was introduced in response to recent developments in the law.

We are obliged to Max Hardy and Harry Bentley, of 9 Bedford Row, for their diligent and comprehensive research work in the preparation of this new edition.

We are particularly grateful to Professor David Ormerod, who is a regular commentator on abuse of process case law, for his Foreword to the new edition.

Finally, we owe a considerable debt to the unfailing support, encouragement and professionalism of the publishing team at Tottel Publications and in particular Heather Saward and Sarah Thomas.

Contents

Contents

Contents

Contents

Table of Cases

B

G

H

L

Table of Statutes

International Statutes

Table of Statutory Instruments

[All references are to paragraph number]

Table of European and International Conventions and Agreements

Chapter 1

Delay

INTRODUCTION

1.01   In any system of criminal justice in modern society, delay is an endemic and unalterable characteristic. That there will always be an elapse of time, often substantial, between date of charge and eventual trial is, at least in part, a natural consequence of procedures and processes which are otherwise regarded as hallmarks of fairness. The requirement, for example, of prosecution disclosure of evidence and unused material to the defence pre-trial will, in a complex case, be onerous and protracted in its fulfilment. The availability of a court to host the trial and the availability of trial lawyers are other features which, in practice absent a perfect world, will operate to create delay.

1.02   Delay ultimately is in no one's interest and is inimical to fairness; it fades the memory of prosecution and defence witnesses alike, it causes the inadvertent destruction of relevant documents, it tolerates lengthy periods of pre-trial imprisonment and it contributes to anxiety and expense. That its longevity should be minimised and its effects ameliorated are clear priorities for any system wishing to dispense justice and to instil public confidence in its processes.

1.03   In broad terms two remedies have been favoured to combat the evil of delay: first, the imposition of time limits, and second, an overarching requirement of reasonableness as determined by judicial discretion. To a large extent these remedies are mutually inconsistent; whereas time limits impose objective and measurable demands upon the progress of any criminal case passing through pre-defined points, reasonableness prefers a case-sensitive approach eschewing the imposition of universal formulae, and preferring as yardsticks open-ended concepts such as the appropriate time in the circumstances of the case and whether there is an adequate explanation for the delay. As Sopinka J said in the Canadian case of *R v Smith*,[1] '... it is axiomatic that some delay is inevitable. The question is, at what point does the delay become unreasonable?'

1   [1992] 2 SCR 1120 at 1131.

1.04   Our system, via the abuse jurisdiction, has in serious cases lent heavily in favour of the remedy of judicial discretion. This preference is perhaps the result of two factors; history and a mistrust of time limits. History in that the abuse jurisdiction is of course entirely judge-made and thus developed incrementally over decades. It is a creature, like the law on prosecution disclosure was until the advent of the Criminal Procedure and Investigations

1

Act 1996, of the common law. As such, resort to a sudden bold initiative such as the use of across-the-board time limits or the imposition of administrative or mathematical formula is unavailable to judges no matter how pioneering. Such an initiative can emanate only from Parliament or, at least, the Lord Chancellor by means of new rules and instruments creating at a stroke new 'black letter' law. As the executive has hitherto largely preferred to allow the abuse jurisdiction to develop organically, so the use of time limits has been overlooked in favour of judicial discretion.

1.05 A general mistrust of time limits as a means of delivering justice is rooted in the embedded notion in our system that judicial discretion is best. In many ways the arguments here are similar to those underlying the implementation of the Human Rights Act 1998 (HRA 1998); that the courts play a critical role in protecting defendants in criminal proceedings,[1] and that a fact-sensitive approach is best, allowing the trial judge to hold the ring between the interests of the accused and the wider community. HRA 1998, especially in criminal cases, manifests this doctrine of deference leaving the interpretation of rights in a particular case to the judges.

1   As Lord Steyn argued, especially when public opinion and fair adjudication are at odds, in 'The New Legal System' [2000] EHRLR 549.

Structure of this chapter

1.06 Since the last edition of this work, the House of Lords has given judgment in what is now the seminal authority on delay; *Attorney-General's Reference (No 2 of 2001)*,[1] affirming the Court of Appeal decision in that case.[2] The House of Lords ruling was in direct conflict with an earlier ruling of the Privy Council[3] in respect of the law on delay in Scotland. As we shall see,[4] that conflict has now been unequivocally resolved in favour of the approach taken by the House of Lords in *Attorney-General's Reference (No 2 of 2001)*; the Privy Council having now departed from its initial approach in the light of intervening jurisprudence from the European Court of Human Rights.

1   [2004] 2 AC 72, HL. Discussed below at paras **1.109–1.116**.
2   Discussed below at paras **1.95–1.106**.
3   *HM Advocate v R* [2004] 1 AC 462, PC, discussed below at para **1.108**.
4   Below at paras **1.133–1.144**.

1.07 Bearing in mind that the recent domestic authority on this issue is indelibly enmeshed with the fundamental right to a speedy trial enshrined in Art 6 of the European Convention on Human Rights and Fundamental Freedoms (generally referred to simply as 'the Convention' or as the 'ECHR'), the practitioner cannot approach this subject without some appreciation of the jurisprudence of the Strasbourg Court. Therefore, this chapter retains its initial examination of how the Strasbourg court made this right practical and effective, with a survey of its jurisprudence concerning delay in criminal proceedings prior to the seminal domestic rulings. Following this ECHR survey, the domestic common law is considered. The chapter concludes with reference back to Strasbourg and recent rulings of the European Court that have affirmed the approach of the House of Lords in *Attorney-General's Reference (No 2 of 2001)*.

ECHR JURISPRUDENCE PRIOR TO ATTORNEY-GENERAL'S REFERENCE (NO 2 OF 2001)

Article 6(1): Right to be tried within a reasonable time

The status of this Art 6 right

1.08 The terms of Art 6 are well–known. Article 6(1) deals with the right to a fair trial. It provides that:

> 'In the determination of his civil rights and obligations or of any criminal charge against him, everyone is entitled to a fair and public hearing *within a reasonable time* by an independent and impartial tribunal established by law'. [1] [Emphasis added]

1 Article 5(3) similarly provides for the right to a 'trial within a reasonable time or to release pending trial'.

1.09 Trial within a reasonable time is thus an explicit guarantee of fairness laid down in Art 6(1). Moreover it is an independent or freestanding right separate from the others established by the article. This was confirmed by Lord Hope of Craighead in *Porter v Magill*:[1]

> 'The protections which article 6(1) lays down are that, in the determination of his civil rights and obligations, everyone is entitled to a fair and public hearing within a reasonable time by an independent and impartial tribunal established by law. As I shall explain later when dealing with delay, I consider that this sentence creates a number of rights which, although closely related, can and should be considered separately. The rights to a fair hearing, to a public hearing and to a hearing within a reasonable time are separate and distinct rights from the right to a hearing before an independent and impartial tribunal established by law. This means that a complaint that one of these rights was breached cannot be answered by showing that the other rights were not breached'.

1 [2002] 2 AC 357, HL at para 87.

1.10 Lord Hope added in *Montgomery v HM Advocate*,[1] as regards the status of Art 6 rights:

> 'Article 6, unlike articles 8 to 11 of the Convention, is not subject to any words of limitation. It does not require, nor indeed does it permit, a balance to be struck between the rights which it sets out and other considerations such as the public interest'.

1 [2003] 1 AC 641, PC.

Proportionality and public interest

1.11 The issue of whether the 'public interest' plays a countervailing role to an express Art 6 right, so that the right can be subject to an implied limitation, is one which has frequently bedevilled the jurisprudence of the European Court and more recently, following the advent of the HRA 1998, domestically. Domestically, perhaps the most notable decision hitherto concerned with this tension is that of the Privy Council in *Brown v Stott*.[1] Here it was held that the right to silence was not an absolute right and thus it was legitimate to '... balance the general interests of the community against the interests of the individual ...'. Having performed such a balancing exercise, the Board held that it was not a breach of Art 6 to compel car drivers to, in effect, incriminate themselves. The interests of society in assuring road safety justified this statutory power given to the police.

1   [2003] 1 AC 681, PC.

1.12   The Court itself has, however, displayed a less accommodating attitude to public interest arguments of this kind. In *Heaney and McGuinness v Ireland*,[1] the Court dismissed as a matter of principle the argument that the fight against terrorism justified compelling a suspect to speak.

1   (2001) 33 EHRR 12. See para 58.

1.13   In relation to this particular Art 6 right on the one hand, and public interest and proportionality on the other, the issues are essentially twofold:

(a)   Is it a separate guarantee, as suggested above by Lord Hope in *Magill*?[1] Alternatively, is it only part of a more general right to a fair trial; fairness here as a concept encompassing fairness to the accused as well as to society? The latter approach can be seen in the advice of the Board in *Flowers v R*[2] where Lord Hutton held that in determining whether there had been a breach of the relevant constitutional right[3] concerned with unreasonable delay, relevant factors included the strength of the Crown's case against the accused and that whether the offence for which he had been convicted, murder in the course of a robbery, was prevalent in Jamaica posing a serious risk to innocent citizens; and

(b)   To what extent should reasonableness of the length of proceedings be judged in the light of extrinsic features such as ensuring that rigorous and full investigations are not sacrificed in an obsession for speed and that guilty defendants cannot use the right as a weapon seeking to benefit from a violation?

1   Above, para **1.09**.
2   [2000] 1 WLR 2396, PC.
3   Section 20(1) of the Jamaican Constitution.

1.14   The Court has often stated that an individual does not enjoy his rights in a vacuum. Other members of society also have interests deserving of respect. In numerous cases, the Court has referred to the striking of a fair balance between the demands of the general interest of the community and the requirements of the protection of the individual's fundamental rights, the search for which balance was said to be inherent in the whole of the Convention.[1]

1   See for example *Soering v United Kingdom* (1989) 11 EHRR 439 at 465, para 89; *B v France* (1992) 16 EHRR 1 at 34, para 63. It was again recognised in *Doorson v Netherlands* (1996) 22 EHRR 330 at 358, para 70.

The purpose of the right

1.15   In *Dyer v Watson*[1] Lord Rodger of Earlsferry described the purpose as follows:

'In the case of article 6(1) its principal purpose at least is to prevent an accused being left too long in a state of uncertainty about his fate. Such a protection is, of course, of very real interest to an innocent person who has been charged with an offence or even to a person who has in fact committed an offence but whose guilt the prosecution cannot establish. The accused's whole life, both private and professional, may be thrown into turmoil, doubt and confusion until he is acquitted. Especially for the innocent and for their families the time spent awaiting trial must indeed be 'exquisite agony' (*R v Askov* [1990] 2 SCR 1199, 1219 per Cory J)'.

1   [2004] 1 AC 379, PC, at para 156.

1.16   However he added:

'That is not, however, the whole story. The reality is that, especially when they are on bail, many accused who are in fact guilty may prefer to dwell in the interim state of uncertainty rather than to march steadily to the end of their case where that state of uncertainty may well be replaced with a considerably more agonising state of prolonged imprisonment. Delay may indeed bring positive advantages to such persons: prosecution witnesses may die, leave the country, lose interest or forget. The right conferred by article 6 is therefore somewhat unusual. Not infrequently, accused persons may appear to have an interest in invoking it not in order to benefit from its fulfilment but rather in the hope of benefiting from its breach'.[1]

1   At para 157.

1.17   It is this latter concern which has animated debate around what should be the remedy where there is a breach of this particular aspect of Art 6. Should the type of public interest factors identified by Lord Hutton in *Flowers v R*, considered above,[1] mean that convictions should not be quashed? Moreover, it is a concern that those who are guilty may escape justice, which has led to a particular focus in this jurisdiction with the issue of whether prejudice is an essential element. These concerns are considered further below.

1   Above para **1.13**.

The Strasbourg case law—criteria for determining reasonableness

1.18   Many challenges to the length of proceedings have been brought before the court and it is fair to say that there are now a vast number of judgments concerned with this topic. Accordingly, an exhaustive survey of this jurisprudence is beyond the scope of this work. There are, in addition, a large number of what may be termed 'leading decisions', a survey of which, owing to their number, is also beyond this work. The specialist reader is referred to the speech of Lord Bingham of Cornhill in *Dyer v Watson*[1] for a comprehensive review.

1   Above para **1.15**, at paras 30–55.

1.19 However, in the relevant cases the Court has confined itself to repeatedly confirming and applying a small number of core principles, however voluminous the case law. Having espoused these principles they have then been applied in case after case with the Court sometimes finding a violation and sometimes not. In other words, the outcome is highly dependent on the facts of the case. Lord Rodger of Earlsferry, in *Dyer v Watson*, expressed this point a little more firmly: '... The vast number of cases which come before the court does not mean, unfortunately, that there is a correspondingly large body of increasingly refined guidance on this aspect of article 6...'.[1] This characteristic can, for present purposes, be demonstrated by the judgments of three leading Strasbourg authorities decided over the last 25 years.

1   Above para **1.15**, at para 146.

1.20 In *König v Germany*[1] the European Court gave the following guidance as to the test to be applied on the question of delay:

'The reasonableness of the duration of proceedings covered by article 6(1) of the Convention must be assessed in each case according to its circumstances. When inquiring into the reasonableness of the duration of criminal proceedings, the court has had regard, inter alia, to the complexity of the case, to the applicant's conduct and to the manner in which the matter was dealt with by the administrative and judicial authorities. The court, like those appearing before it, considers that the same criteria must serve in the present case as the basis for its examination of the question whether the duration of the proceedings before the administrative courts exceeded the reasonable time stipulated by article 6(1)'.

1   (1978) 2 EHHR 170 at 197, para 99.

1.21 In *Eckle v Germany*[1] the court stated:

'The reasonableness of the length of the proceedings must be assessed in each instance according to the particular circumstances. In this exercise, the court has regard to, among other things, the complexity of the case, the conduct of the applicants and the conduct of the judicial authorities'.

1   (1982) 5 EHRR 1, at para 80.

1.22 Finally in *Howarth v United Kingdom*[1] the court employed the same approach:

'According to the court's case-law, the reasonableness of the length of proceedings must be assessed in the light of the particular circumstances of the case and having regard to the criteria laid down in the court's case-law, in particular the complexity of the case and the conduct of the applicant and the authorities dealing with the case'.

1   (2001) 31 EHRR 37 at para 25.

1.23 As summarised by Lord Bingham in *Dyer v Watson*,[1] the Strasbourg Court has thus consistently and firmly rejected any laying down of a tariff or set of minimum periods. The emphasis is always on the word 'reasonable', which the Court has determined can only be understood by reference to the facts.

1   Above para **1.15**, at paras 53–55.

1.24   Three essential criteria are thus propounded:

(1)   Complexity;

(2)   The applicant's conduct; and

(3)   The conduct of the State authorities.

Complexity

1.25   The court will permit greater periods of delay in a complex prosecution allowing for the time and resources required to investigate especially economic crimes. In *Eckle v Germany*[1] the court stated:

> 'The court realises that initially the specific forms of economic crime caused the judicial authorities a variety of problems, notably in relation to the speedy and smooth conduct of criminal proceedings'.

1   Above para **1.21**, at para 80.

1.26   In *IJL, GMR and AKP v United Kingdom*[1] the Court held that a period of 4½ years to complete a complex fraud case was not an unreasonable delay. The Court has also recognised that complexity may arise from the need to obtain foreign evidence,[2] the volume of evidence[3] or because of the need to obtain expert evidence.[4] The Court is simply affirming the realistic or self-evident fact that the more complex a case, the longer the time which must necessarily be taken to properly prepare it for trial.

1   [2001] Crim LR 133.
2   *Neumeister v Austria* (1968) 1 EHRR 91.
3   *Wemhoff v Germany* (1968) 1 EHRR 55.
4   *Wemhoff v Germany* (1968) 1 EHRR 55.

Conduct of the defendant

1.27   The Court will consider whether the applicant is in part responsible for the delay. In *Eckle v Germany* the court described the applicants' conduct as follows:

> 'Far from helping to expedite the proceedings, Mr and Mrs Eckle increasingly resorted to actions—including the systematic recourse to challenge of judges—likely to delay matters; some of these actions could even be interpreted as illustrating a policy of deliberate obstruction'.[1]

1   Above para **1.21**, at para 82.

1.28   In answer to the defence argument that such manoeuvring should not count against the applicants, as they were simply exercising their legal rights, the Court held:

> '… their conduct referred to above constitutes an objective fact, not capable of being attributed to the respondent State which is to be taken into account when determining whether or not the proceedings lasted longer than the reasonable time referred to in article 6, para 1'.

The defendant cannot complain of delay of which he is the author; procedural time-wasting must not be used to assist any complaint of delay.

Whether the authorities can excuse or justify the delay

1.29 Again in *Eckle v Germany*, the Court having examined in detail the various periods of delay and the Respondent State's explanation for them, stated:

'The court, like the Commission, has come to the conclusion that the competent authorities did not act with the necessary diligence and expedition'.[1]

1   Above para **1.21**, at para 92.

1.30 The question here is what is the degree of diligence and expedition that must be shown? In other words, was the delay justifiable or not? In *Dyer v Watson*, Lord Bingham of Cornhill provided the following analysis:

'It is plain that contracting States cannot blame unacceptable delays on a general want of prosecutors or judges or courthouses or on chronic under-funding of the legal system. It is generally incumbent on contracting States to organise their legal systems to ensure that the reasonable time requirement is honoured'.

But he observed:

'... it is not objectionable for a prosecutor to deal with cases according to what he reasonably regards as their priority, so as to achieve an orderly dispatch of business. It must be accepted that a prosecutor cannot ordinarily devote his whole time and attention to a single case'.[1]

1   Above para **1.15**, at para 55.

Evidence of prejudice

1.31 In order to establish a violation of Art 6(1), must the applicant establish a sufficient causal connection between the period of the delay and evidence of prejudice? Alternatively, does the Court's notion or concept of 'unreasonableness' here presuppose the existence of prejudice as a necessary factor?

1.32 The above analysis shows that the Strasbourg Court has not identified this as a specific factor when determining unreasonableness. In the above articulation of the principles which guide its approach, it is clear that the presence or absence of prejudice is not determinative. Thus, it is not necessary when asserting a breach of Art 6(1) here to establish prejudice. In fact, in *Eckle v Germany* the Court stated:

'The word 'victim', in the context of article 25, denotes the person directly affected by the act or omission which is in issue, the existence of a violation being conceivable even in the absence of prejudice; prejudice is relevant only in the context of article 50'.[1]

In *HM Advocate v R*[2] Lord Steyn stated that '... the starting point is that prejudice, although a relevant factor, need not be established. It is not necessary to show that a fair trial is no longer possible The scope of the guarantee is wider'.[3]

1   Above para **1.21**, at para 66.
2   Above para **1.06**.
3   At para 10.

1.33   Having established that prejudice is not essential to the question of violation,[1] the next issue is whether its presence or absence is relevant to a determination; that is to say whether the Court should have regard to this factor at all in its considerations. It is submitted that, whilst proof of prejudice is not an essential or necessary prerequisite to the concept of unreasonable delay, it will often be a highly material factor when assessing reasonableness. Its status as a factor here is analogous to that of, for example, whether the accused was particularly vulnerable (eg a child[2]). Also, whether the accused was held in custody awaiting trial or had some other convincing claim to priority. All or any of these factors militate in favour of delay being as short as possible for it to be reasonable. Accordingly, any rational analysis of a complained of delay will take into account, when determining its reasonableness, evidence of prejudice.

1   See also *Boolell v The State* [2006] UKPC 46, at para 32: 'If a criminal case is not heard and completed within a reasonable time, that will of itself constitute a breach ...whether or not the defendant has been prejudiced by the delay'.
2   See for example the UN Convention on the Rights of the Child 1989, art 40(2)(b) and the UN Standard Minimum Rules for the Administration of Juvenile Justice, r 20. Both norms demand expedition in any case where a child is accused of infringing penal law. And see *Procurator Fiscal (Linlithgow) v Watson & Burrows: HM Advocate v JK* [2002] UKPC D1, where the Privy Council found no violation of Art 6(1) in the case of the adult defendants (Watson & Burrows) on the ground of delay, but a violation in the case of JK, a 13 year old boy, seemingly on the basis that the delay in his case would have had a greater prejudicial effect on him, thus crossing the threshold of Art 6(1).

1.34   The concept of unreasonableness, as the above analysis shows, has not been developed as an abstraction but by reference to pragmatic features, which are likely to be present in every case. In the absence of a tariff, one of the most salient markers here will be a search for the extent of any prejudice suffered by the defendant. As shall be seen,[1] in the context of the abuse of process jurisdiction with which we are concerned, the presence of prejudice has become a determinative factor in deciding whether proceedings should be stayed as an abuse once a violation of Art 6(1) has been established.

1   See below paras **1.98** et seq.

The threshold of inordinate or excessive delay

1.35   Whilst the Court has eschewed any approach laying down minimum periods of delay, it has emphasised that, for it to be even presumptively unreasonable, delay must first cross a threshold of being, in the particular circumstances, inordinate or excessive. For 'inordinate' see *Eckle v Germany*[1] and for 'excessive' see *Stogmuller v Austria*.[2] More recently see *Mansur v Turkey*.[3]

1   Above para **1.21**, at para 80.
2   (1969) 1 EHRR 155, para 5, where it is observed that the purpose of the guarantee is to prevent a person charged remaining too long in a state of uncertainty about his fate. See also *Burns v HM Advocate* [2008] UKPC 63.
3   (1995) 20 EHRR 535, para 68.

1.36   Whilst demonstration of prejudice is not essential, the Court has, in reality, imposed a filter on complaints of delay by setting a relatively high threshold to be satisfied before it will conduct any inquiry into the delay and request the prosecutor to supply a justification. In *Dyer v Watson*, Lord Bingham of Cornhill said:

'In any case in which it is said that the reasonable time requirement (to which I will henceforward confine myself) has been or will be violated, the first step is to consider the period of time which has elapsed. Unless that period is one which, on its face and without more, gives grounds for real concern it is almost certainly unnecessary to go further, since the convention is directed not to departures from the ideal but to infringements of basic human rights. The threshold of proving a breach of the reasonable time requirement is a high one, not easily crossed'[1].

1   Above para **1.15**, at para 52. See also Lord Hope of Craighead at para 85 and Lord Rodger of Earlsferry at para 154.

How is 'reasonable time' to be measured?

1.37   As Lord Hope of Craighead said in *Montgomery v HM Advocate*:[1]

'The requirement that the hearing be 'within a reasonable time' predicates that there has been a charge from the date of which the reasonableness of the time can be measured'.

1   Above para **1.10**.

1.38   In criminal proceedings, the concept of 'charge' has been applied by the European Court as the start-point for the measurement of delay. In *Eckle v Germany*[1] the Court stated:

'In criminal matters, the 'reasonable time' referred to in article 6 para 1 begins to run as soon as a person is 'charged'; this may occur on a date prior to the case coming before the trial court'.

1   Above para **1.21**, at para 73.

1.39   Having identified the concept of charge as the start-point for measurement purposes, the Court in *Eckle v Germany* then sought to explain the meaning of this. Significantly the court held that for this definitional purpose, a person may be charged in either of the two following situations:

' "Charge", for the purposes of article 6 para 1, may be defined as "the *official notification* given to an individual by the competent authority of an allegation that he has committed a criminal offence" a definition that also corresponds to the test whether "the situation of the [suspect] has been *substantially affected*".'[1] [Emphasis added]

1   The 'substantial affectation' test recited here is drawn from an earlier decision, *Deweer v Belgium* (1980) 2 EHRR 439.

1.40   The significance in our jurisdiction of this dual definition of charge, one very different to our domestic understanding, is borne out by the practice of the Court to use its own definitions of legal terms, called 'autonomous meanings', when considering whether there has been a breach of the Convention. Accordingly, what the Court regards as the moment of charge will have primacy over any conflicting domestic definition. In *Porter v Magill*[1] Lord Hope said, in relation to the dichotomy between civil and criminal proceedings and autonomous meanings:

> 'For the purposes of the Convention the category into which the proceedings are placed by domestic law, while relevant, is not the only consideration. The court is required to look at the substance of the matter rather than its form, to look behind the appearances and to investigate the realities of the procedure'.

1   Above para **1.09**, at para 84.

1.41   This emphasis upon the character or reality of the case, 'is it criminal?', is best demonstrated by the Court's findings in *Funke v France*.[1] Whilst the investigation into the applicant's tax affairs was classified under French law as administrative, not criminal, the Court held that as he was suspected of criminal tax offences then a de facto criminal investigation was being undertaken.[2]

1   [1993] 1 CMLR 897, 16 EHRR 297.
2   For a further analysis of how the English courts have determined what is a criminal investigation see *Attorney-General's Reference (No 7 of 2000)* [2001] 1 WLR 1879, CA.

Official notification and substantial affectation

1.42   On the above definition of 'charge', criminal proceedings are deemed to commence when State agents inform the suspect that they contend that he has committed a criminal offence and a criminal trial will ensue. This is precisely the equivalent of our jurisdiction. A distinction, however, may arise in relation to who are State agents for this purpose. Here, pursuant to the PACE Codes of Practice, only a custody officer as defined may prefer a charge[1] and so there is no ambiguity. However, it is submitted that the use of the expression 'official notification' permits a wider category of agent who may give the necessary notification. For example it encompasses, but is not coterminous with, law enforcement officials, i e police officers or prosecutors. It appears that so long as the agent making the allegation is clothed with a sufficient element of relevant authority then even if his function is not primarily concerned with criminal investigation or prosecution, his allegation may be a sufficient trigger. An example here may be a local authority social worker seeking a care order against the parents of a child on the basis of their suspected child abuse. Thereafter criminal proceedings get underway.

1   Code C, para 16.1.

1.43   The second limb of the definition of charge, that of 'substantial affectation', is a much more vague concept than that of official notification. It relates to the degree of interference by State authorities in a suspect's life which is then deemed to be sufficient to constitute a substantial interference. Does this concept of interference entail the existence of either prejudice or damage to the suspect? It seems plain that a person may be charged, criminal proceedings being deemed to have commenced, whilst he is still unaware of any such proceedings, the test being an objective one independent of the accused's knowledge.

1.44   Four European Court authorities can be briefly considered on this point; the first three showing the court's willingness to hold that the suspect was substantially affected prior to the moment when they were formally 'charged' in our domestic sense (ie when they were informed that they would stand trial for the alleged offence); the last by contrast holding that only the formal charge was sufficient.

Howarth v United Kingdom[1]

1.45   In a serious fraud investigation, the applicant was interviewed by the SFO in March 1993, charged in July 1993 and his trial commenced in February 1995. For the purpose of considering whether there had been unreasonable delay, the court held that the proceedings commenced at the interview in March 1993:

'the court finds that the proceedings in the present case began on 17 March 1993 when the applicant was first interviewed'.

1   Above para **1.22**.

Heaney and McGuinness v Ireland[1]

1.46   The applicants had been convicted of an offence owing to their refusal to answer questions when interviewed. The court held that these convictions were in breach of Art 6(1) as their privilege against self-incrimination had been violated. Again, as in *Howarth*, the court held that Art 6 was engaged at a pre-charge stage.

1   Above para **1.12**. A similar decision was reached in *Murray v United Kingdom* (1995) 19 EHRR 193.

Teixeira de Castro v Portugal[1]

1.47   Here the court went even further back. It held that the applicant was substantially affected when first approached by the undercover police officers and asked by them to sell drugs. In determining that his Art 6 rights were violated it stated:

'Right from the outset the applicant was deprived of his right to a fair trial'.

1   (1998) 28 EHRR 101.

IJL, GMR and AKP v United Kingdom[1]

1.48   Part of this case concerns the start-point for the measurement of unreasonable delay. Here the date of charge by the SFO was found to be significantly later than the applicants' DTI interviews. For the purpose of alleging unreasonable delay, the applicants submitted that the start-point was their DTI interview. In support of this contention, attention was drawn to the compulsive nature of these interviews and their length. However the Court dismissed this, holding that as the interviews were only investigative then the criminal proceedings did not commence until charge.

1   Above para **1.26**.

1.49   Other than affirming that the Court's definition of charge may be stretched back to a moment considerably prior to that of official notification, can any further principle be discerned from these authorities? It is submitted that the decision in *IJL, GMR and AKP v United Kingdom*, when compared to the other three above authorities, reveals that the Court is concerned to see whether, at the material point, the relevant State agents were conducting a criminal investigation. Being satisfied on this point is a necessary preliminary step before determining whether there has been a substantial affectation. In *IJL, GMR and AKP v United Kingdom,* the Court held that despite the compulsion and consequent degree of intrusion, the DTI investigation was not a criminal investigation; the focus, it held, being on fact-finding not the possible commission of criminal offences. Contrast this with the findings in each of the other authorities considered above.

Remedies for violation of Art 6(1)

1.50   If there is found to be a breach of the reasonable time requirement, what remedy should a court award to mark this? In the context of our abuse jurisdiction, should a breach here lead to a permanent stay or discontinuance? In other words, does the right to a trial within a reasonable time entail a correlative right not to be tried at all after a reasonable time has elapsed?

1.51   The first point to appreciate here is that the Convention itself does not prescribe what the consequence or effect should be of any breach of this right. This is left to Contracting States to determine. Thus the court is not here concerned with remedies, other than in relation to awards of compensation under Art 41. From this, it follows that a number of remedies may be awarded at domestic level.

1.52   Second, arising out of emphasis by the court on the moment of 'charge' being the start point for the measurement of delay, it can be appreciated that Art 6(1) here is essentially concerned with procedural delays once the criminal proceedings are underway. Accordingly, it does not interfere with limitation periods concerned with criminal liability and thereby impose any cut-off point or deadline after which time an individual cannot be prosecuted. In this sense, there is a marked disparity between the time frames applied by the Court and that by the common law in the abuse jurisdiction; the latter taking as its start point the date of alleged commission of the offence.

1.53　Bearing both such points in mind, what has the Court held as sufficient and appropriate redress for a breach of this right? Three cases can be considered where this point was directly addressed.

X v Federal Republic of Germany[1]

1.54　Here the applicant had already had his sentence reduced owing to delay by the German courts. However he contended that his sentence ought to have been mitigated altogether. The Commission disagreed with this and observed[2] that:

'Insofar as the applicant claims a right to discontinuation of the criminal proceedings in view of the long delays which had occurred, the Commission considers that such a right, if it could at all be deduced from the terms of article 6(1) would only apply in very exceptional circumstances. Such circumstances did not exist in the applicant's case'.

The Commission considered the reduction in the applicant's sentence to be 'appropriate and sufficient' redress for breach of the reasonable time requirement.

1　(1980) 25 DR 142.
2　At para 5.

Eckle v Germany[1]

1.55　The Court held a violation of the reasonable time guarantee but observed that:

'The word 'victim', in the context of article 25, denotes the person directly affected by the act or omission which is in issue, the existence of a violation being conceivable even in the absence of prejudice; prejudice is relevant only in the context of article 50. Consequently, mitigation of sentence and discontinuance of prosecution granted on account of the excessive length of proceedings do not in principle deprive the individual concerned of his status as a victim within the meaning of article 25; they are to be taken into consideration solely for the purpose of assessing the extent of the damage he has allegedly suffered'.[2]

In due course, modest compensation was awarded to Mr Eckle and his wife.

1　Above para **1.21**.
2　At para 66.

Bunkate v Netherlands[1]

1.56　The Court found that there had been unreasonable delay in violation of Art 6(1) and then stated:

'The applicant's claims are based on the assumption that a finding by the court that a criminal charge was not decided within a reasonable time automatically results in the extinction of the right to execute the sentence and

14

that consequently, if the sentence has already been executed when the court gives judgment, such execution becomes unlawful with retroactive effect. That assumption is, however, incorrect. The court is unable to discern any other basis for the claims and will therefore dismiss them'.[2]

1   (1995) 19 EHRR 477.
2   At 484, para 25.

1.57   In surveying this jurisprudence in *Dyer v Watson,* Lord Hope of Craighead observed that:

'The European Court has repeatedly held that unreasonable delay does not automatically render the trial or sentence liable to be set aside because of the delay (assuming that there is no other breach of the accused's Convention rights), provided that the breach is acknowledged and the accused is provided with an adequate remedy for the delay in bringing him to trial (though not for the fact that he was brought to trial), for example by a reduction in the sentence'.[1]

1   Above para **1.15**, at para 129.

THE TEST OF THE COMMON LAW

Introduction

1.58   In contrast to other jurisdictions, neither Parliament nor the common law has sought to confer on an accused any constitutional or absolute right to a speedy trial or to judgment within a specific time. In other words, no overarching limitation period restricting the right of a prosecutor to bring charges against an accused has been imposed.

1.59   A clear illustration of the fact that English criminal law has not imposed any limitation period is the enactment of the War Crimes Act 1991. This legislation was passed principally in order to make it possible to bring to justice in the 1990s persons who were suspected of committing war crimes during the 1939–45 war. In *R v Serafinowitz*[1] and *R v Sawoniuk*,[2] the defendants were indicted for war crimes committed during the early 1940s. Both their submissions for abuse based on delay in 1997 and 1999 respectively failed, the trial judges holding that the trial process could overcome any prejudice thereby caused. Moreover, by passing this Act, there was a clear Parliamentary intention that trials for such crimes should occur despite massive delay.

1   (17 January 1997, unreported).
2   [2000] 2 Cr App R 220, CA. This defendant was convicted and sentenced to life imprisonment.

Statutory measures

Limitation period for summary-only offences

1.60   While there is no overarching principle in English law imposing a limitation period on the bringing of criminal charges, Parliament has nonetheless imposed a limitation period for a specific category of alleged offences. These are invariably confined to summary only offences. For example, the Magistrates' Courts Act 1980, s 127 provides that:

'Limitations of time

(1)   Except as otherwise expressly provided by enactment and subject to subsection (2) below, a magistrates' court shall not try an information or hear a complaint unless the information was laid, or the complaint made, within six months from the time when the offence was committed, or the matter of complaint arose.'

Via the discipline of this six-month rule Parliament has sought to ensure that summary offences are both charged and tried as soon as reasonably possible after their alleged commission.

1.61   In the exercise of its supervisory jurisdiction over the magistrates' court where all summary offences are tried, the Divisional Court has sought to ensure that this intention behind s 127 is respected both in its letter and spirit. This determination can be illustrated by the authority of *R v Brentford Justices, ex p Wong.*[1] In this case, the prosecutor decided to lay an information against an accused for the summary only offence of careless driving. However, this information was laid only one day within the six-month period permitted by s 127 and it transpired that the decision by the prosecutor to lay this information had been taken before any decision had been made as to whether proceedings should, in fact, be continued or not. In other words, the prosecutor had sought to circumvent the six-month limitation period by issuing the information as a holding manoeuvre in order to decide whether to proceed with a prosecution later. The Divisional Court held that such prosecutorial manoeuvring constituted an abuse. Lord Donaldson held that the six-month time limit required prosecuting authorities to act with expedition and to decide within that time limit finally whether to bring proceedings or not and said that:

'The process of laying an information is, I think, assumed by Parliament to be the first stage in a continuous process of bringing a prosecution. [MCA 1980, s 127] is designed to ensure that prosecutions shall be brought within a reasonable time. That purpose is wholly frustrated if it is possible for a prosecutor to obtain summonses and then, in his own good time and at his convenience, serve them ... Here there was a deliberate attempt to gain further time in which to reach a decision. It is perhaps hard on the prosecutor to characterise that as an abuse of the process of the court because I am sure that there was no intention by the prosecutor to abuse the process of the court. He thought he could legitimately do this ... I do not think that he can ... it is a matter which has to be investigated by the justices.'

1   [1981] QB 445, DC.

1.62   *Ex p Wong* is, therefore, authority that deliberate prosecutorial delay in the context of summary offences will not be tolerated by the courts. The prosecution must decide on the institution of criminal proceedings in good time and also decide on which factual basis to proceed.

1.63   The principle in *ex p Wong* has also been held to apply where the prosecution lay an information (and so have decided to bring a prosecution) but are undecided between two factual bases on which the case might proceed. This was the situation in *R v Newcastle-upon-Tyne Justices, ex p Hindle*,[1] the defendant was charged with obstructing a police officer in the execution of his duty but the information did not specify the nature of the obstruction alleged and, in the circumstances of the case, the prosecution might have been alleging two different senses of objectionable behaviour. When the prosecution refused to resolve this ambiguity, the Divisional Court held that the obstruction summons ought not to proceed. Goff LJ said that the situation was:

'... at least as objectionable a course as the laying of an information where no decision has been taken to prosecute, for, if permitted, it would allow a prosecution to postpone until after the expiry of the six-month period, their decision whether to prosecute for a particular offence'.[2]

Prejudice had also been caused to the defence because, without knowing how the prosecution intended to put its case, it was unable to properly deal with the question of whether the obstruction charge should be tried before or after other charges against the defendant which arose out of the same incident.

1   [1984] 1 All ER 770, DC.
2   At 778. See also *R v J* [2005] 1 AC 562, HL (bringing of unsuitable charges because most suitable charges time-barred capable of constituting abuse even in the absence of dishonesty or improper motive) and *R (Wardle) v Crown Court at Leeds* [2002] 1 AC 754, HL (bringing new charges to avoid custody time limits capable of constituting abuse even in the absence of dishonesty or improper motive); both discussed in detail in **Chapter 4**.

Implicit limitation periods

1.64   While s 127 is one of very few statutory examples of an explicit limitation period being created on the bringing of criminal proceedings, there are, however, implicit limitation periods which exist by virtue of the obligation being created by the relevant legislation. For example, regs 5 and 12 of the Money Laundering Regulations 1993 make it an offence for a person who conducts 'relevant financial business' not to preserve records of relevant transactions for a period of five years after those transactions have been completed. If, therefore, a prosecution were to be mounted against a person for an offence under regs 5 and 12 more than five years after the relevant transactions occurred, the accused would have an absolute defence in that he was entitled to destroy the records once the statutory period had elapsed. A more recent statutory example which also contains such implicit limitation periods on the bringing of proceedings is the Companies Act 2006, which requires the keeping of minutes of meetings of the company directors for a period of at least 10 years (s 248) and the keeping of accounting records (s 289), a copy of the contract or memorandum of a contract for an 'off-market

17

purchase' or a contract for a 'market purchase' (s 702) and the directors' statement and auditor's report for inspection (s 720), all for defined minimum periods of time.

1.65   In this context the practitioner should note the decision of the Court of Appeal in *R v J*.[1] In this case, the defendant had consensual sexual intercourse with a girl under 16. Owing to the fact that the complainant did not report the conduct for three years, a prosecution of an offence of unlawful sexual intercourse with a girl under 16, contrary to s 6(1) of the Sexual Offences Act 1956, would have been time barred by virtue of para 10(a) of Sch 2 to the Act (since repealed by the Sexual Offences Act 2003). So a prosecution was instead brought for indecent assault, under s 14(1), which was not time barred, based on the act of sexual intercourse. The Crown acknowledged the decision to have been motivated by an intention to avoid the statutory time limit.

1   [2005] 1 AC 562 HL.

1.66   The House of Lords (Baroness Hale dissenting) ruled that the conduct of the Crown was not easily accommodated within any of the traditional categories of abuse of process; the delay was not the fault of the Crown, the Crown had not sought to prejudice the conduct of the defence in any improper way, the fairness of the trial had not been imperilled, the Crown had acted without malice or dishonesty and not been guilty of any devious, underhand or manipulative conduct, indeed the decision to prosecute was one that the general public would applaud. But, the House of Lords recalled, the categories abuse are not closed and defy exhaustive definition. Even if the rationale for the time bar could be regarded as anachronistic, discredited or unconvincing, it remained a statutory time bar that the courts were under a duty to give effect to. Accordingly, when the only evidence relied upon was of consensual sexual intercourse with a girl under 16, a prosecution for indecent assault in respect of that conduct after the 12-month time limit had expired should be stayed.

Practice directions

1.67   Over recent years, efforts have been made to streamline and spread the passage of cases through the Crown Court. As part of this process, practice directions have been promulgated which set down time limits within which cases should be progressed to a specified point. The best example of this is perhaps the Consolidated Criminal Practice Direction (2002),[1] as amended,[2] which dictates that a plea and case management hearing ('PCMH') should take place at the Crown Court 'within about' 14 weeks of the magistrates *sending* a case for trial where the accused is in custody and 'within about' 17 weeks after sending where he is on bail. For all cases committed to the Crown Court for trial, the PCMH should be held 'within about' seven weeks of committal.[3] The practice direction also provides for preliminary hearings to take place about 14 days after sending and further pre-trial hearings to be held where necessary, with a view to ensuring the case is running efficiently and to allow for the court to give directions to that effect. However, it should also be noted that even a breach of statutory time periods regarding case progression (service of papers under ss 51 and 52 of the Crime and Disorder Act 1998 in this case) will not be a ground for the dismissal of proceedings.[4]

1   [2002] 1 WLR 2870.
2   By Amendment No 11 to the Consolidated Criminal Practice Direction (Case Management) (2005), [2005] 1 WLR 1361.
3   See r IV.41.
4   *Fehily v Governor of Wandsworth Prison* [2002] EWHC 1295.

1.68   While PCMH hearings are non-statutory, the policy underlying the practice direction is reinforced by Part IV of the Criminal Procedure and Investigations Act 1996 (ss 39–43), as amended by the Criminal Justice Act 2003, which gives judges power to hold pre-trial hearings in the hope that such hearings will clarify the issues in dispute and lead to shorter and more efficient trials. The Criminal Procedure Rules 2005,[1] brought into force by s 69 of the Courts Act 2003 (which have been subject to numerous subsequent amendments not relevant for our purposes here), have now laid down extensive rules of court and procedure to be implemented in criminal cases, imposing preparative obligations on the parties as well as bearing upon the substantive progress of a case. As the criminal practitioner will be aware, the rules are comprehensive in their scope and deal with issues from the commencement of proceedings through to sentencing, confiscation, appeals and costs hearings, with a view to achieving the overriding objective of dealing with cases 'justly', which includes 'efficiently and expeditiously'.[2]

1   SI 2005/384.
2   Amongst other factors, outlined at r 1.1.

CPS code of practice

1.69   The Director of Public Prosecutions is enjoined by the Prosecution of Offences Act 1985, s 10, to issue a Code for Crown Prosecutors giving guidance on general principles, inter alia, in determining whether proceedings for an offence should be instituted. In the absence of any limitation period, para 5.10 of the Code is headed 'Some common public interest factors against prosecution'. The relevant part of para 5.10 reads as follows:

'A prosecution is less likely to be needed if:

...

(e)   there has been a long delay between the offence taking place and the date of the trial, unless:
   –   the offence is serious;
   –   the delay has been caused in part by the defendant;
   –   the offence has only recently come to light; or
   –   the complexity of the offence has meant that there has been a long investigation'.

1.70   In relation to serious crime, para 5.9 states that the more serious the offence, the more likely it is that a prosecution will be needed in the public interest. There is, therefore, despite a long delay, a general presumption in favour of prosecution where the offence is serious. The prosecutor must apply paras. 5.9 and 5.10 and decide whether to commence a prosecution or not where there has been a long and, perhaps unjustifiable, delay. There is no provision within our legal system for a prosecutor to seek a preliminary opinion or declaration from a court as to whether proceeding after a long delay would amount to an abuse of process.[1]

1   The Code is, in practice, an invaluable measure against which to judge abuse. In *Sharma v Browne-Antoine* [2007] 1 WLR 780, PC, Baroness Hale, and Lords Carswell and Mance observed that '… The power to stay for abuse of process can and should be understood widely enough to embrace an application challenging a decision to prosecute on the ground that it was arrived at under political pressure or influence or was motivated politically rather than by an objective review of proper prosecutorial considerations (such as, in England, those set out in the Code for Crown Prosecutors issued under the Prosecution of Offences Act 1985)…' (at para 32).

Police and Criminal Evidence Act Code of Practice

1.71   Code C of the PACE Codes of Practice[1] is entitled 'Code of Practice for the Detention, Treatment and Questioning of Persons by Police Officers'. Paragraph 11.6 provides that:

'The interview or further interview of a person about an offence with which that person has not been charged or for which they have not been informed they may be prosecuted, must cease when:

(a)   the officer in charge of the investigation is satisfied all the questions they consider relevant to obtaining accurate and reliable information about the offence have been put to the suspect, this includes allowing the suspect an opportunity to give an innocent explanation and asking questions to test if the explanation is accurate and reliable, e.g. to clear up ambiguities or clarify what the suspect said;

(b)   the officer in charge of the investigation has taken account of any other available evidence; and

(c)   the officer in charge of the investigation, or in the case of a detained suspect, the custody officer, see paragraph 16.1, reasonably believes there is sufficient evidence to provide a realistic prospect of conviction for that offence'.

1   As in force from 31 January 2008.

1.72   This provision is designed to ensure that once the substance of a prosecution case is apparent to a police officer/investigator, he should not continue questioning the suspect for the purpose of trying to turn the case into a stronger and better one. Whilst the avoidance of delay is not the primary aim of this provision, it is designed to ensure that once a case is apparent the suspect should be charged and the proceedings should begin at the soonest opportunity. The decision to charge in this context should not be delayed. This point is made even clearer by para 16.1 which reads:

'When the officer in charge of the investigation reasonably believes there is sufficient evidence to provide a realistic prospect of conviction for the offence, they shall [without delay] inform the custody officer who will be responsible for considering whether the detainee should be charged'.

1.73   It is submitted that several qualifications need to be made to the prescriptions contained in the quoted passages from PACE Code C set out above. First, the custody officer has to know what charge is appropriate, bearing in mind the circumstances of the case. There is in our system no provision for a holding charge to enable a suspect to be charged with an offence merely for the purpose of firstly complying with the Code and second for enabling the prosecution to be given a breathing space for the purpose of formulating more specific and appropriate charges. It may therefore be entirely understandable for the police to delay charging in order for their understanding of the case to improve, leading to the decision to charge an appropriate offence. Secondly, it is understandable to defer charging for the purpose of carrying out certain investigations which may have been instigated by the suspect himself in answers he gave during his interview.

1.74   While the wording of the relevant paragraphs of the Code encourages charges to be levelled as soon as the police believe there is sufficient evidence to merit such charges, the courts have been reluctant to adopt this strict approach. Instead, they have preferred a flexible approach allowing investigators not to charge until all relevant evidence is gathered so long as this is achieved within a reasonable period. An example of such judicial tolerance is the judgment of the Lord Chief Justice in *R v Cardiff Magistrates' Court, ex p Hole*.[1] In answer to a specific defence submission that there had been a breach of paras 11.4 (now 11.6) and 16.1 of the Code, Lord Bingham CJ observed that the decision of the police officer to defer charging was reasonable, bearing in mind the complexity of the case and the need to conduct additional enquiries based on what the defendants had said during their respective interviews.

1   [1997] COD 84.

1.75   Other than the discrete provisions referred to above, the common law – via the abuse jurisdiction – has been left to confront and resolve the issue of delay causing unfairness to an accused in the criminal process. Unsurprisingly, it is an established tenet of this jurisdiction that delay is inimical to a fair trial and the efficient working of our criminal justice system. However, despite their adherence to this tenet the courts have, it is submitted, been reluctant to embrace a further principle flowing from the first: that failure to ensure a trial within a reasonable time constitutes infringement of the accused's right to a fair trial.

Pre-HRA 1998 common law authorities

1.76   However, inflexible limitation periods can lead to arbitrary results and, as a result, Parliament rightly has been hesitant about introducing such mechanisms in cases that concern serious criminal conduct. Therefore, in cases that fall outside these statutory attempts to ensure speedy justice, that is to say in almost all allegations of serious crime, the bulwark against injustice to a defendant is the common law abuse of process doctrine. In January 1992, in *R v*

Bow Street Stipendiary Magistrates, ex p DPP[1] (the 'Guildford Four' case), Neill LJ summarised the law as it then stood in relation to delay:

'The authorities establish that an abuse of process may exist in the following circumstances:

(a) if the prosecution have manipulated or misused the process of the court so as to deprive the defendant of a protection provided by the law or to take advantage of a technicality;

(b) if on the balance of probability the defendant has been, or will be, prejudiced in the preparation or conduct of his defence by delay on the part of the prosecution which is unjustifiable; or

(c) if, even though the prosecution are in no way responsible for the delay, the delay has produced genuine prejudice and unfairness for the defendant;

(d) in a case involving delay, the court will consider the reasons for the delay and the responsibility, if any, of either the prosecution or the defence for the delay. The court will also consider the issues which are likely to arise at the hearing and the nature of the evidence which is likely to be relevant. Thus a case which depends largely on documentary evidence may be regarded very differently from one where witnesses will have to try to recollect some swiftly moving event which passed before their eyes years ago;

(e) the purpose and existence of this discretionary power is to ensure that there should be a fair trial according to law'.

1   [1992] Crim LR 790, CA.

1.77   In seeking to apply these general principles, Neill LJ upheld the prosecution's submissions that the Magistrate had been wrong to hold that the proceedings against the defendants should be stayed on the ground of delay. Neill LJ held that the Magistrate had fallen into error because he had agreed with the defence submission that the delay had been sufficiently extreme so as to raise a general inference of prejudice. This was the wrong approach to adopt. Neill LJ held the Magistrate ought to have focused his attention on the critical issue: what specific prejudice would be suffered by the defence as a result of delay at the eventual trial? Neill LJ held, in answer to this question that while inevitably the defence would suffer some prejudice, a fair trial was still nonetheless possible. He rejected the view first, that the accused's right to a fair trial meant that he should not suffer any prejudice at all and secondly, that prejudice could simply be inferred from mere delay even when, as in this case, the delay was enormous.

1.78   *R v Bow Street Stipendiary Magistrates, ex p DPP* was shortly followed by *Attorney-General's Reference (No 1 of 1990)*.[1] The decision by the Attorney-General to seek the authoritative guidance of the Court of Appeal regarding delay demonstrated the degree of official concern regarding the then willingness of courts to stay prosecutions. In allowing the Criminal Division of the Court of Appeal a full opportunity to consider delay in the context of abuse it was obviously hoped, by those responsible for criminal prosecutions, that the court would issue clear guidance which would dramatically restrict the extent of trial courts' jurisdiction to stay cases on the ground of delay. In this respect, prosecutors were not to be disappointed. As Lord Lane CJ commented at the end of his judgment:

'... This judgment will, we hope, result in a significant reduction in the number of applications to stay proceedings on the ground of delay ...'.[2]

1   [1992] QB 630, CA.
2   At 644.

1.79   The facts which gave rise to *Attorney-General's Reference* (*No 1 of 1990*) concerned a police officer who attended an incident in August 1987, giving rise to subsequent complaint. He was summonsed for an offence in March 1989. At the commencement of his Crown Court trial in December 1989, the trial judge accepted a submission that, because of the August 1987 to March 1989 delay in prosecuting him, this alone constituted an abuse and his trial should accordingly be stayed. The Attorney-General viewed this approach as flawed and pursuant to the Criminal Justice Act 1972, s 36, sought a ruling from the Court of Appeal in relation to the following two questions:

(1)   Whether proceedings on indictment may be stayed on the grounds of prejudice resulting from delay in the institution of those proceedings even though the delay had not been occasioned by any fault of the prosecution.

(2)   If the answer to (1) is in the affirmative, what is the degree of:

   (a)   likelihood; and

   (b)   the seriousness of any prejudice which is required to justify a stay of such proceedings.

1.80   During the hearing of *Attorney-General's Reference* (*No 1 of 1990*), the Attorney-General argued that the trial judge had been wrong to hold that the period of delay in the case before him could properly be said to amount to an abuse. Two arguments in support of this were canvassed. First, the delay which did occur was reasonable and justifiable in the circumstances. Secondly, there was no evidence of any specific prejudice to the accused in the preparation of his defence caused by the delay. In reply, the defence submitted that the delay amounted to a breach of Chapter 29 of Magna Carta;[1] the word 'defer' meaning any period which was longer than that required for proper preparation for the trial.

1   Chapter 29: '... will not deny or defer any man justice or right'.

1.81   Lord Lane CJ unhesitatingly rejected this defence submission, holding that the 'deferment' meant wrongful deferment or delay, about which Chapter 29 of Magna Carta could not even begin to offer any guidance. Lord Lane CJ answered the first question as follows:

'On the basis of the decision in *R v Telford Justices, ex p Badhan* ... the Attorney-General, constrained to concede that the answer to the Attorney-General's first question is a qualified "yes". As it is not possible to anticipate in advance all the infinitely variable circumstances which may arise in the future, we feel ourselves, albeit reluctantly, forced to agree to a limited extent with that concession. However, we remind ourselves of the principles outlined earlier in this judgment and the observation of Lord Morris in *Connolly*, 48 Cr App Rep 183, [1964] AC 1254 at page 211 and page 1304 that: "… Generally speaking a prosecutor has as much right as a defendant to demand a verdict of a jury on an outstanding indictment, and where either demands a verdict a judge has no jurisdiction to stand in the way of it". Stays granted on the grounds of delay or for any other reason should only be employed in exceptional circumstances … In principle … even where the delay can be said to have been unjustifiable, the imposition of a permanent stay should be the exception rather than the rule. Still more rare would be cases where a stay can properly be imposed in the absence of any fault on the part of the complainant or prosecution. Delay due merely to the complexity of the case or contributed to by the action of the defendant himself should never be the foundation for a stay'.

1.82   In answer to the second question, Lord Lane CJ said:

'… no stay should be imposed unless the defendant shows on the balance of probabilities that owing to the delay he will suffer serious prejudice to the extent that no fair trial can be held … In asserting whether there is likely to be prejudice and if so whether it can properly be described as serious, the following matters should be borne in mind: first, the power of the judge at common law and under (PACE) to regulate the admissibility of evidence; secondly, the trial process itself should ensure that all relevant factual issues arising from delay will be placed before the jury as part of the evidence for their consideration, together with the powers of the judge to give appropriate directions to the jury before they consider their verdict'.

1.83   Turning to the facts of the case as set out above, Lord Lane CJ held that the trial judge had been in error in agreeing to stay the proceedings:

'The delay, such as it was, was not unjustifiable; the chances of prejudice were remote; the degree of potential prejudice was small; the powers of the judge and the trial process itself would have provided ample protection for the respondent; there was no danger of the trial being unfair; in any event the case was in no sense exceptional so as to justify the ruling'.[1]

1   It is notable, and perhaps regrettable, that this is all Lord Lane CJ said by way of judgment on the facts of the case before him and the erroneous ruling of the trial judge. He did not, for instance, provide any guidance on exactly what material facts in the case led him to his conclusions; why for example the degree of prejudice was 'small' and what the trial judge should have done during the trial to have prevented it from being unfair.

1.84   In *R v Cardiff Magistrates' Court, ex p Hole*[1] Lord Bingham CJ summarised the judgment of Lord Lane CJ thus:

'The clear upshot of that decision therefore is that there must be exceptional circumstances before a stay should be granted; and even where there is unjustified delay a stay should be the exception of the rule; that a stay should be more exceptional in the absence of fault; and that complexity itself should not be the ground for a stay. Furthermore, the decision indicates that there should be no stay unless the defendant can show on a balance of probabilities that, owing to the delay, he has suffered serious prejudice to the extent that no fair trial can be held so as to render the prosecution a misuse of process'.

1   Above para **1.74**, at 92.

1.85   The judgment of Lord Lane CJ was quoted with approval by the Privy Council in *Tan v Cameron*.[1] Furthermore, Lord Mustill sought to remove the confusion which had arisen in relation to burdens of proof to be satisfied when a submission of delay causing prejudice and unfairness was made. There were some authorities to the effect that burdens of proof differed depending on whether the delay was excusable or inexcusable. Lord Mustill sought to eliminate this dichotomy in favour of a more straightforward and unified approach:

'Naturally, the longer the delay the more likely it will be that the prosecution is at fault, and that the delay has caused prejudice to the defendant; and the less that the prosecution has to offer by explanation, the more easily can fault be inferred. But the establishment of these facts is only one step on the way to a consideration of whether, in all the circumstances, the situation created by the delay is such as to make it an unfair employment of the powers of the court any longer to hold the defendant to account. This is a question to be considered in the round, and nothing is gained by the introduction of shifting burdens of proof, which serves only to break down into formal steps what is in reality a single appreciation of what is or is not unfair'.

1   [1992] 2 AC 205, PC.

1.86   Lord Mustill was, therefore, exhorting judges not to over-complicate the application of principles on delay to their abuse jurisdiction. Little was to be gained in his view by having separate rules and standards depending on whether the delay was characterised by adjectives such as inadvertent, inordinate or inexcusable. Furthermore, by focusing attention on the question of what prejudice was really suffered by the accused occasioned by delay and the real importance of it to issues of dispute in a particular case, Lord Mustill was, in common with Lord Lane CJ, seeking to diminish the importance of issues such as the actual length of the delay complained of and whether the prosecution could satisfactorily explain or justify their delay.

1.87   A similar approach is to be found in the seminal House of Lords case of *R v Horseferry Road Magistrates' Court, ex p Bennett*[1] where Lord Lowry said:

'I consider that a court has the discretion to stay any criminal proceedings on the ground that to try those proceedings will amount to an abuse of its own process either (1) because it will be impossible (usually by reason of delay) to give the accused a fair trial or (2) because it offends the court's sense of justice and propriety to be asked to try the accused in the circumstances of a particular case. I agree that prima facie it is the duty of a court to try a person who is charged before it with an offence which the court has power to try and therefore that the jurisdiction to stay must be exercised carefully and sparingly and only for very compelling reasons. The discretion to stay is not a disciplinary jurisdiction and ought not to be exercised in order to express the court's disapproval of official conduct. Accordingly, if the prosecuting authorities have been guilty of culpable delay but the prospect of a fair trial has not been prejudiced the court ought not to stay the proceedings merely for "pour encourager les autres" '.

1   [1994] 1 AC 42, HL.

Analysis of Lord Lane CJ's judgment

1.88   Bearing in mind that Lord Lane CJ's judgment has remained the cornerstone of the law on delay, it is necessary to consider it in some detail. It is submitted that the following points are pertinent:

(1)   *Some prejudice must be tolerated by the defence.* The hurdle to be surmounted by defendants seeking a stay is a high one. The prejudice must be serious to the extent that no fair trial can be held. A defendant must therefore tolerate some prejudice or unfairness to his case caused by delay even if this is no fault of his own. This unfortunate predicament, Lord Lane CJ contended, can however be largely eliminated, as faith can be placed in the flexibility of the trial process to eliminate residual unfairness caused by delay.

(2)   *The remedial effects of the trial process.* Lord Lane CJ urged trial judges to recognise the existence of their other powers to ensure a fair trial as alternatives to the exercise of a stay, ie excluding evidence and ensuring that the jury are made aware of the facts concerning delay. In Lord Lane CJ's view, the exercise of such powers would, in most cases where there had been significant delay, be a sufficient remedy and so would ensure that the proceedings were fair.

However, against this it is difficult to see how the use of such powers and protections will be effective in many delay cases. How, for example, is a jury, when it retires to consider its verdict, to deal with the issue presumably raised by the defence and echoed by the judge as to what the evidence might have been but for the delay? It would appear that this is an open-ended issue which can only be resolved by speculation rather than by fact. How, in a concrete case, can a tribunal of fact seek to resolve this issue based only on the evidence presented to it?

(3)   *The culpability of the prosecution.* In his answer to the first question, Lord Lane CJ suggests that judges should be more reluctant to stay proceedings on account of delay if there has been no fault on the part of the prosecution than if there has been such fault. It is submitted, however, that this distinction creates an immediate uncertainty because in answer to the second question, Lord Lane CJ held that the criterion to be followed is always to be the same, that of serious prejudice to the accused. What then is the relevance of considering the extent of the prosecution's culpability for the delay? Unless Lord Lane CJ meant to suggest that if the prosecution has been culpable then the threshold for imposing a stay should be lower than if it has not, this consideration has no legitimate role. But as Lord Lane CJ did not suggest this, it is submitted that there is

an inconsistency between his answers to the two questions vis-à-vis the relevance of prosecution fault. Despite Lord Lane CJ's insistence that there is only one criterion, he appears to concede that the issue of any fault on the part of the prosecution for delay is to be included in the equation, although unfortunately does not explain how. It would appear that Lord Lane CJ accepts that the courts have a role in disciplining the prosecution in this regard.

(4) *Causes of delay to be excluded from consideration.* In his answer to the first question, Lord Lane CJ makes plain that two factors should never militate in favour of the exercise of a stay:

(i) *Complexity*: where delay is due to the complexity of the prosecution's allegations or genuine difficulty in investigating the alleged crime. Delay may be inevitable in complicated cases especially in those involving allegations of fraud. Lord Lane CJ's view here was reflected earlier in *Holyoake*[1] where the defendant was tried in 1990 for offences alleged to have occurred between 1983 and 1986. It was submitted on appeal that this prolonged delay was prejudicial to the defendant. The defence submitted that a material witness had died and an important part of the prosecution case related to a conversation between defendant and victim which had occurred four years previously and where there was a conflict of recollection. Farquharson LJ, however, did not agree either that the delay had caused an unfair trial or that the prosecution delay had been unjustifiable:

'These are matters which might give rise to some degree of prejudice it is true ...It must be perfectly obviously to everybody concerned that it was a case which required consideration and investigation in depth. Everybody is aware that these company fraud cases (a) take a long time to prepare, (b) generally arrive at the Crown Court at a late date because of the commitments of the people concerned in the case.'

(ii) *The culpability of the defendant.* Unsurprisingly Lord Lane CJ held that when the accused is responsible for the delay he cannot then complain about possible prejudice arising therefrom. Accordingly, a defendant who flees the jurisdiction in order to avoid criminal proceedings against him is in effect estopped from arguing that he cannot receive a fair trial on the grounds of delay.[2] This principle, easy to explain and apply in straightforward situations, has called for qualification when, in the light of a defence complaint about delay, the prosecution riposte that the delay was caused by the defendant's conduct, which itself is to be an issue of dispute in the trial. For example, where the defence complain about delay and deny guilt and the prosecution contend that the accused committed subsequent offences to conceal his principal offence and such attempted concealment caused delay in discovery of the principal offence. In *A-G of Hong Kong v Wai-bun*[3] the question arose as to the accused's responsibility for the delay. The prosecution argued

27

that the defendant was primarily responsible for the delay because he had sought to hinder and delay the investigation by falsifying accounts, the subject of the charge against him. On behalf of the Privy Council, Lord Woolf rejected this argument (upholding the trial judge's decision to stay proceedings). It presupposed the defendant's guilt for the offence alleged against him, which was of course a matter of fact to be decided by a jury necessarily subsequent to any application to stay. Lord Woolf held that prosecutors could not argue, on the strength of Lord Lane CJ's judgment, that in this sense the defendant had contributed to delay. Lord Woolf held that what Lord Lane CJ was referring to in *Attorney-General's Reference* (*No 1 of 1990*) were acts of the defendant outside the subject of the trial, for example absconding.

(5)   *Oral versus documentary evidence cases.* Lord Lane CJ emphasised that a distinction must be drawn between cases which turn largely on contemporaneous documentary evidence and those which do not. Lord Lane CJ perhaps had in mind *R v Buzalek and Schiffer*[4] where the Court of Appeal held that a distinction should be drawn between cases where the prosecution is dependent on available documents, as in most fraud cases, and where it is dependent on a late complaint and oral testimony, as in many sexual offence cases. The court held that generally speaking only in the latter may it be inferred from a long delay that a fair trial would not be possible. This approach was followed by Watkins LJ in *R v Central Criminal Court, ex p Randall and Pottle*[5] where the defendants were in 1990 to be tried for offences that they had allegedly committed in 1963. Watkins LJ rejected the defence submission that the delay between the offence and the trial was sufficiently extreme to warrant a stay on the ground of abuse. Watkins LJ held that, as the defendants had virtually admitted their offence in a book which they had written in 1989, which the prosecution sought to rely on as part of its case, the trial should proceed; fading memory could not realistically be suggested.

1   (24 August 1990, unreported), CA.
2   See, to similar effect, albeit in a different context, *Kakis v The Republic of Cyprus* [1978] 1 WLR 779, HL, discussed in Chapter 8 at paras. **8.13–8.16**.
3   [1994] AC 1, PC.
4   [1991] Crim LR 115, CA. See *R v Telford Justices, ex parte Badhan* [1991] 2 QB 78, DC and *R v Bow Street Magistrates' Court, ex parte DPP* (above para **1.76**) to similar effect
5   [1992] 1 All ER 370, CA.

1.89   It can be seen from this analysis of Lord Lane CJ's judgment in *Attorney-General's Reference* (*No. 1 of 1990*) that the overriding and determinative issue of whether an application to stay on the ground of delay is successful or not should be prejudice to an accused. Furthermore, in seeking to establish a common judicial approach in evaluating such prejudice, Lord Lane CJ emphasised two interrelated and overlapping principles. First, before a stay should be exercised, the prejudice complained of must be adjudged to be so serious that as a result the defendant can no longer receive a fair trial. Secondly, the flexibility of the trial process is such that prejudice can often either be eradicated or largely ameliorated, therefore allowing a fair trial to be held. For illuminating recent examples of the application of Lord Lane CJ's judgment, on either side of the line, see *R v B*,[1] in which the trial judge's refusal to grant a stay of proceedings was overturned by the Court of Appeal on the basis that the defendant could not receive a fair trial, due to him being unable to call witnesses in his defence because of the 30-year lapse in time since the date of the alleged offence, and *R v S*,[2] where the Court of Appeal refused to interfere with the trial judge's exercise of his discretion not to grant a stay of proceedings where the prosecution related to offences committed throughout the 1970s.

1   [2003] EWCA Crim 319.
2   [2006] EWCA Crim 756.

Post-HRA 1998 common law authorities

1.90   The arrival of ECHR jurisprudence into domestic law, courtesy of the scheduling of the Convention to the HRA 1998, obviously prompted a reconsideration of the principles laid down in *Attorney-General's Reference (No 1 of 1990)* and whether, in particular, this extant law required change pursuant to the obligation cast upon the courts by the HRA 1998, s 6. This opportunity was, in due course, taken up by the Court of Appeal and, later, the House of Lords, in another reference case. Before considering this authority, it is helpful to briefly consider three authorities decided in the period between implementation of the HRA 1998 in late 2000 and the decision of the Court of Appeal in July 2001.

1.91   Two Privy Council cases can briefly be considered where, in both, the Board was concerned with similar constitutional rights to Art 6(1), guaranteeing a fair trial within a reasonable time. In *Darmalingum v State*[1] the Board was concerned with the constitution of Mauritius and, in *Flowers v R*,[2] with that of Jamaica. Judgment in *Darmalingum v The State* was delivered in July 2000 and *Flowers* in September 2000. The timings here are significant as, despite the proximity, different and conflicting views were expressed.

1   [2000] 1 WLR 2303, PC.
2   Above para **1.13**.

1.92   In *Darmalingum v The State,* Lord Steyn emphasised three points: First, that the right here was of itself a freestanding constitutional guarantee. Secondly, that proof of prejudice to the accused in consequence of the delay was not essential so long as it has been 'inordinate and expensive' (there, approximately 15 years between arrest and conclusion of appellate proceedings). Finally, that the importance of the right being a constitutional guarantee was such that when violated, the remedy should be the quashing of the accused's conviction.

1.93   In *Flowers v R,* Lord Hutton saw the matter rather differently. First, he held that the relevant constitutional right was not freestanding but only a constituent of an embracing right to a fair trial. Second, that even this more general right was subject to a proportionality test whereby the seriousness of the crime and the public interest in prosecution could be balanced against a violation arising from delay. Accordingly a conviction should only be quashed where there has been prejudice.

1.94 Both of these cases are concerned with the appropriate remedy that should be awarded to an accused where there has been a breach of a constitutional guarantee of a right to be tried within a reasonable time. Another case concerned with the concept of unreasonableness pursuant to Art 6(1) is *King v Walden (Inspector of Taxes),*[1] and the following excerpt from the judgment of Jacob J provides a very helpful exposition of this concept:

'But mere avoidable delay is not of itself enough to make the time to the hearing 'unreasonable'. It is obviously a factor but no more. The word 'unreasonable' clearly implies that one must consider all the circumstances of the case. At least the following factors seem to be material: (i) the complexity of the case – the more complex the longer the period that is reasonable. (ii) In a criminal case, the nature of the potential punishment – particularly whether or not there is a possibility of a custodial sentence. There is a very big difference between holding a threat of punishment over an accused from a mere threat of a fine. And all the more so when the amount of that fine (or its maximum amount) is defined in advance ...(iii) The extent to which the accused has contributed to the delay, e.g. by obfuscation, procedural manoeuvres or some other matters'.[2]

1   *The Times* 12 June 2001, DC.
2   At para 91.

A-G's Reference (No 2 of 2001)[1]

Brief facts of the case

1.95 The facts as narrated by Lord Woolf CJ were as follows:

'A serious disturbance took place in a prison on 26 April 1998. As a result, a large number of the inmates were interviewed in connection with the disturbance on 9 June and 1 July 1998. Subsequently paperwork was submitted to the Crown Prosecution Service on 27 July 1998. Informations were laid against the seven prisoners on 11 February 2000. Of those who were interviewed on the dates to which we have referred, some were the subject of no action of any sort. Others were subject to disciplinary proceedings within the prison. The seven defendants to whom we have referred were singled out as being appropriate persons to be prosecuted. The matter came before the trial judge on 31 January 2001. He came to the conclusion that the delay, which he calculated from the time that the defendants were interviewed in July 1998 until 11 February 2000 when they were summonsed, was a period of unreasonable delay. He concluded that it was appropriate to stay the charges against the seven defendants.'

1   [2001] 1 WLR 1869 (CA); [2004] 2 AC 72 (HL).

Issues of principle

1.96   Arising from these facts, Lord Woolf CJ identified two questions of principle:

'(i)   Whether criminal proceedings may be stayed on the ground that there has been a violation of the reasonable time requirement in article 6(1) of the European Convention for the Protection of Fundamental Rights and Freedoms ("the Convention") in circumstances where the accused cannot demonstrate any prejudice arising from the delay.

(ii)   In the determination of whether, for the purposes of article 6(1) of the Convention, a criminal charge has been heard within a reasonable time, when does the relevant time period commence?'

1.97   Lord Woolf CJ added:

'The first question deals with the remedy where there has been a violation, and the second question deals with the commencement date for the computation of the time which has lapsed so as to ascertain whether or not a reasonable time has passed'.

The Court of Appeal ruling

The commencement date

1.98   Dealing with the second question first, Lord Woolf CJ provided the following answer:

'... in the great majority of situations the date that a defendant is charged (in the sense we use that term in our domestic jurisprudence) will provide the answer. Ordinarily therefore the commencement of the computation in determining whether a reasonable time has elapsed will start with either a defendant being charged or being served with a summons as a result'.

Accordingly when called upon to examine the length of any complained of delay, absent some exceptional circumstance the court should measure it from the date of charge or issuance of summons.

1.99   Lord Woolf CJ accepted, however, that in an exceptional case, the test of substantial affectation as established in *Eckle v Germany*[1] and *Deweer v Belgium*[2] might lead to the moment of charge occurring at an earlier point:

'There will, however, be situations where a broader approach is required to be adopted in order to give full effect to the rights preserved by article 6(1) of the Convention ... For the purposes of that article there could be a period prior to a person formally being charged under English law *if the situation was one where the accused has been substantially affected by the actions of a state so as a matter of substance to be in no different position from a person who has been charged.* The importance of the approach that Mr Perry concedes the court has to adopt is that it takes account of the fact that there may be some stage prior to an accused being formally charged in accordance

31

with our domestic law where, *as a result of the actions of a state linked to an investigation, when he has been materially prejudiced in his position'*. [Emphasis added]

1   Above para **1.21**.
2   Above para **1.39**.

1.100   As can be seen from the second highlighted passage above, Lord Woolf CJ sought to redefine the concept of substantial affectation as akin to that of material prejudice. Unless this existed at the antecedent date, then the date of commencement would be date of charge. Unfortunately, in stipulating this new concept, Lord Woolf CJ offered no elucidation of its meaning and no illustrative examples were provided.

1.101   The efficacy or helpfulness of 'material prejudice' can be considered in relation to an obvious practical issue; whether the actions of the State in conducting a caution interview of a suspect subsequently prosecuted would constitute such prejudice? In our domestic system, 'charge' has a very distinct meaning and it is a clearly defined moment marking the transition from investigation to prosecution. However, especially in complex cases, interviews of suspects can precede by many months their being charged. In *Attorney-General's Reference (No 2 of 2001)* the trial judge had held that the interview stage did mark the commencement of the proceedings and thus concluded that there had been unreasonable delay. But Lord Woolf CJ disagreed:

> 'In the ordinary way an interrogation or an interview of a suspect by itself does not amount to a charging of that suspect for the purpose of the reasonable time requirement in article 6(1)'.

In reaching this conclusion, Lord Woolf CJ made no reference to any of the recent Strasbourg cases cited above[1] especially *Howarth*[2] where, in relation to a serious fraud investigation, the European Court reached the opposite conclusion. If, it is submitted, Lord Woolf CJ, via the articulation of a new concept of material prejudice, was seeking to distinguish this from the European Court concept of substantial affectation, this required at least some analysis of the purported difference(s) and a justification of why the decision in *Howarth* can be distinguished. As it is there seems no substance to a claim of difference here.

1   Above paras **1.44–1.49**.
2   Above para **1.22**.

The appropriate remedy

1.102   Lord Woolf CJ described the approach of the trial judge as follows:

> '... if there has been unreasonable delay, to go on and proceed to try a defendant results in the court acting in a way which is incompatible with that defendant's rights. There is no discretion about the matter. Once the court has come to the conclusion that the reasonable time requirement in article 6(1) has been contravened, the court has to stay the proceedings'.

In other words, the view of the trial judge was that the right to trial within a reasonable time conferred a correlative right not to be tried after the expiry of a reasonable time.

1.103   Lord Woolf CJ, however, expressed strong disagreement with this approach, holding it to be nonsensical. In his view there was no such correlative right and it was erroneous to hold that the Art 6(1) right was a right not to be tried after a reasonable time:

'If a person complains of a contravention of the reasonable time requirement in article 6, and if the court comes to the conclusion that there has been a contravention, then at the request of the complainant the court is required to provide the appropriate remedy. If the court is willing and able to provide the appropriate remedy, then the court is not compelled to take the course of staying the proceedings. That is a remedy which the court can grant, but it is certainly not a remedy which it is required to grant'.

1.104   Alternative remedies to a stay would include reduction of sentence or an award of compensation. Commenting upon the impact of the HRA 1998, Lord Woolf CJ said:

'The difference which the Human Rights Act 1998 makes is that the remedies available to a court can be greater than they were hitherto. In particular, it is now in appropriate circumstances open to the courts to make awards of compensation'.

1.105   Having thus held that a trial could proceed even after an unreasonable delay and that a stay was only the last resort, Lord Woolf CJ went on to consider when this remedy should be applied. Here Lord Woolf CJ sought to provide fresh impetus to the judgment of Lord Lane CJ in the *Attorney-General's Reference (No 1 of 1990)*.[1] He held that the remedy of a stay should only be granted in the circumstances as outlined by Lord Lane CJ. Lord Woolf CJ held:

'As we have already indicated, if there has been prejudice caused to a defendant which interferes with his right to a fair trial in a way which cannot otherwise be remedied, then of course a stay is the appropriate remedy. But in the absence of prejudice of that sort, there is normally no justification for granting a stay. It seems to us in general that the approach that previously existed as to the provision of the remedy of staying the proceedings should be confined, as it was prior to the Convention becoming part of our domestic law, to situations which in general terms can be described as amounting to an abuse of the process of the courts'.

1   Above paras **1.78–1.89**.

Analysis of Woolf CJ's judgment

1.106   Lord Woolf CJ wished to ensure that the advent of the HRA 1998 did not cause (as had happened in that case) the staying of prosecutions which under Lord Lane CJ's test in *Attorney-General's Reference (No 1 of 1990)* would not have been stayed. Consequently he confirmed that rigorous adherence to Lord Lane CJ's judgment should remain. In other words, that only where the test of serious prejudice was satisfied should the remedy of a stay be applied. The cornerstone of prejudice being an essential prerequisite for a stay was not to be disturbed. To Lord Woolf CJ, the principal significance of the advent of the HRA 1998 was that it increased the range of remedies available to a trial judge who was satisfied that there had been an unreasonable delay in breach of Art 6(1): the use of a declaration, of awarding compensation etc. All of these remedies were available as appropriate except a stay whose use was governed by Lord Lane CJ's judgment. Lord Woolf CJ sidestepped the issue of whether an English court has jurisdiction to try a defendant in circumstances where it has already acknowledged that his right to a fair trial under Art 6(1) has been violated. Can a court preside over a trial which axiomatically it has already declared unfair?

Intervening Privy Council decisions

1.107   In the Privy Council case of *Mills v HM Advocate*[1] a four-year delay occurred between the application for and the hearing of the applicant's appeal which was then dismissed. He then appealed again arguing that the delay constituted a breach of his Art 6 rights. The Scottish Court agreed that the excessive delay constituted a breach of Art 6 and considered what remedy ought to be awarded. It reduced the applicant's eight-year sentence by six months. The disappointed applicant appealed to the Privy Council, submitting that his conviction ought to have been quashed altogether. The Board disagreed holding that the six-month reduction was appropriate redress for the breach.

1   [2004] 1 AC 441, PC. For other Court of Appeal authorities reaching a similar conclusion see *Maronier v Larmer* [2003] QB 620, CA and *R v Ashton* [2002] EWCA Crim 2782.

1.108   However, in *HM Advocate v R*[1] the Privy Council, when considering the appropriate remedy in the context of the Scotland Act 1998, held that a prosecution should not occur at all as it would violate a defendant's right to a hearing within a reasonable time. For the majority (3:2), Lord Hope of Craighead held that the Lord Advocate has no power to do anything which is incompatible with an accused's Convention rights.[2] Accordingly the Board expressly declined to follow Lord Woolf CJ's judgment in *Attorney-General's Reference (No 2 of 2001)*, leaving the issue open to the determination of the House of Lords. *Haggart v Spiers*[3] provides another example of a prosecution being stayed on appeal by the High Court of Justiciary, on the ground of unreasonable delay in violation of the Art 6(1) guarantee, albeit in summary proceedings.

1   Above para **1.06**.
2   At para 66.
3   2003 SLT 991.

The House of Lords ruling

1.109   The Court of Appeal referred the same two questions as it had been required to consider to the nine-judge constitution of the House of Lords. In argument there, counsel for the acquitted person did not maintain the argument advanced below, and accepted by the trial judge, that breach of the reasonable time requirement must necessarily lead to a stay of proceedings. Instead, counsel contended for a more flexible approach on the following terms; where the effect of delay or the conduct of the executive is such as to render continuation of the proceedings an abuse of the process of the court, then a stay of the proceedings must be ordered. Otherwise, the court must grant such remedy as is proportionate to the demonstrated breach of the reasonable time requirement. In some cases a stay may be the proportionate remedy, in others it will not.[1]

1   At para 4.

1.110   The House of Lords upheld the ruling of the Court of Appeal on both issues of principle. The House unanimously approved the Court of Appeal on the issue of the commencement date, and, by a 7:2 majority[1] on the question of remedy for violation of the reasonable time requirement of Art 6(1).

1   Lords Bingham, Nicholls, Steyn, Hoffmann, Hobhouse, Millett and Scott (Lords Hope and Rodger dissenting).

Commencement point

1.111   The House of Lords unanimously affirmed the Court of Appeal's decision on this point that the point of interview does not necessarily commence time for the purposes of Art 6, rather time commences at the point of charge;

'In the determination of whether, for the purposes of Art.6(1) of the Convention, a criminal charge has been heard within a reasonable time, the relevant time period commences at the earliest time at which a defendant is officially alerted to the likelihood of criminal proceedings against him, which in England and Wales will ordinarily be when he is charged or served with a summons'.[1]

1   At para 29 (per Lord Bingham). But see *Burns v HM Advocate* [2008] UKPC 63 (defendant 'substantially affected' – see above paras **1.37–1.49** – such that time commenced when, following interview in England, defendant bailed pending decision as to whether he should be charged in England or Scotland).

Violation and the appropriate remedy

1.112   Giving the leading judgment of the majority of the House of Lords, Lord Bingham of Cornhill recalled that, whilst the rights in the Convention were singled out for protection because they were recognised to be of overriding importance:

'the Convention also recognised, implicitly and often explicitly, that "No man is an Island". In the exercise of individual human rights due regard must be paid to the rights of others, and the society of which each individual forms part itself has interests deserving of respect. As pointed out in *Brown v Stott'*.[1]

In making further general observations in respect of Art 6, Lord Bingham also considered that 'the focus of the article is on achieving a result which is, *and is seen to be*, fair'.

He observed that in a criminal case 'the issue usually arises between a prosecutor, who might be taken to represent the public interest, on one side and an individual defendant on the other', before drawing a comparison with the application of the Convention in the civil field, where it '[cannot] be so interpreted and applied as to protect the Convention right of any one party while violating the Convention right of another'.[2]

1   At para 9.
2   At para 11.

1.113   Lord Bingham went on to observe that it is:

'a powerful argument that, if a public authority causes or permits such delay to occur that a criminal charge cannot be heard against a defendant within a reasonable time, so breaching his Convention right guaranteed by Art.6(1), any further prosecution or trial of the charge must be unlawful within the meaning of s.6(1) of the 1998 Act.'

He appreciated that it was not surprising that such an argument has been accepted by respected courts around the world.[1] However, he took the view that there were four reasons which, cumulatively, compelled its rejection:

(1)   It would be anomalous if breach of the reasonable time requirement had an effect more far-reaching than breach of the defendant's other Art 6(1) rights (for example, if a hearing took place before a tribunal which lacked independence or a judgment was not given publicly, a conviction would be quashed and a retrial ordered if a fair hearing could still take place) when (as must be assumed) the breach does not taint the basic fairness of the hearing at all, and even more anomalous that the right to a hearing should be vindicated by ordering that there be no trial at all.[2]

(2)   As the Court of Appeal recognised, at para 19 of its judgment, a rule of automatic termination of proceedings on breach of the reasonable time requirement cannot sensibly be applied in civil proceedings. An unmeritorious defendant might no doubt be very happy to seize on such a breach to escape his liability, but termination of the proceedings would defeat the claimant's right to a hearing altogether and seeking to make good his loss in compensation from the state could well prove a very unsatisfactory alternative.[3]

(3)   A rule of automatic termination on proof of a breach of the reasonable time requirement has been shown to have the effect in practice of emasculating the right which the guarantee is designed to protect. There is a very real risk that if proof of a breach is held to require automatic termination of the proceedings the judicial response will be to set the threshold unacceptably high since, as La Forest J put it in *Rahey v R* (1987) 39 DLR 481, 516: 'Few judges relish the prospect of unleashing dangerous criminals on the public'.[4]

(4)   The Strasbourg jurisprudence gives no support to the contention that there should be no hearing of a criminal charge once a reasonable time

has passed. In its interpretation and application of the Convention it has never treated the holding of a hearing as a violation or a proper subject of compensation.[5]

1   At para 20.
2   At para 20.
3   At para 21.
4   At para 22.
5   At para 23.

1.114   The first reason given by Lord Bingham in rejecting the argument that a delayed trial would automatically lead to a stay of proceedings was supported by Lord Millett, who considered the reasonable time guarantee to be different from the other rights contained in Art 6(1), in that a failure to hold a hearing within a reasonable time does not automatically cast doubt on the verdict:

> 'The defendant cannot and does not challenge the propriety of the verdict on this ground. He can only say in effect: "you were right to convict me, but you should have done so sooner." The vice lies in the delay itself, with all its harmful consequences to the defendant. This is what Art.6 prohibits and for which a remedy must be found. The vice does not lie in the holding of the trial itself.'[1]

Lord Millett observed that the authorities *ought* to hold the trial within a reasonable time, but they remain *entitled* to do so after the reasonable time has expired, subject to making adequate reparation for the failure to hold it sooner.[2]

1   At para 135.
2   At para 138.

1.115   Lord Nicholls formulated the issue to be decided in the case with regard to violation of Art 6 as follows: 'Does the breach lie in the holding of a trial after the lapse of a reasonable time? Or does it lie solely in the state's failure to hold the trial within a reasonable time?'[1] By the first hypothesis, holding a trial would itself amount to a violation of Art 6 once the reasonable time period had passed. In the second of Lord Nicholls's hypotheses, a breach in those terms would not be continuing so as to render the holding of a trial, following the lapse of reasonable time, a breach of Art 6 in and of itself. Lord Nicholls preferred the latter interpretation of the Art 6(1) right. Therefore, whilst he accepted that the holding of the trial would itself amount to a violation in circumstances where the pre-trial delay became so protracted that a fair trial could no longer be held (thus necessitating a stay), Lord Nicholls concluded that under any other circumstances:

> 'Just recompense is needed in respect of the pre-trial delay, which resulted in the defendant being exposed for longer than he should have been to the undesirable consequences of pending proceedings. Recompense is not needed in respect of the holding of the trial itself.'[2]

1   At para 39.
2   At para 40.

The settled law on delay

1.116   In agreement with Lord Bingham, the majority came to the following conclusions in respect of the effect that delay will have on criminal proceedings. These principles can now be taken as the definitive statement of the law on the question of remedy for a violation of the reasonable time requirement under Art 6:

(a)   If a criminal charge is not determined at a hearing within a reasonable time, there is necessarily a breach of the defendant's Convention right under Art 6(1). For such breach there must be afforded such remedy as may be just and appropriate or (in Convention terms) effective, just and proportionate. The appropriate remedy will depend on the nature of the breach and all the circumstances.

(b)   It will not be appropriate to stay or dismiss the proceedings unless:

  (i)   there can no longer be a fair hearing: or

  (ii)   it would otherwise be unfair to try the defendant.

The public interest in the final determination of criminal charges requires that such a charge should not be stayed or dismissed if any lesser remedy will be just and proportionate in all the circumstances. In any case where neither of conditions (i) or (ii) applies, the prosecutor and the court do not act incompatibly with the defendant's convention right in prosecuting or entertaining the proceedings but only by failing to procure a hearing within a reasonable time.

(c)   The category of cases in which it may be unfair to try a defendant of course includes cases of bad faith, unlawfulness and executive manipulation of the kind classically illustrated by *R v Horseferry Road Magistrates' Court, ex p Bennett*.[1]

(d)   There may well be cases (of which *Darmalingum v The State*[2] is an example) where the delay is of such an order, or where a prosecutor's breach of professional duty is such as to make it unfair that the proceedings against a defendant should continue[3]. It would be unwise to attempt to describe such cases in advance. They will be recognisable when they appear. Such cases will however be very exceptional, and a stay will never be an appropriate remedy if any lesser remedy would adequately vindicate the defendant's Convention right.[4]

1   Above para **1.87**.
2   Above para **1.91**.
3   *Martin v Tauranga District Court* [1995] 2 NZLR 419 may be an example of such a case.
4   At paras 24–25.

Illustrations of the settled principles

1.117   For recent examples of general application of these now-settled general principles see: *R v Wheeler (Darielle)*[1] (unjustifiable and undesirable delay was not such that it was unfair for the prosecution to proceed); *Miller v DPP*[2] (unreasonable delay could count as 'exceptional hardship' under s 35(4) of the Road Traffic Offenders Act 1988 for the purposes of reducing a driving disqualification, so as to remedy·violation of the right); *Amis v Commissioner of Police of the Metropolis*[3] (a civil application for damages arising out of a protracted police investigation following which the claimant was informed that no charges would be brought against him); *R (Gibson) v General Medical Council*[4] (delay in the determination of complaints of professional conduct); *R v Allen*[5] (it was fair for the defendant to be tried for murder 30 years after the alleged offence took place); *DWP v Courts*[6] (Magistrates had erred in granting a stay of proceedings relating to benefit fraud on the ground of delay); *Re Blackspur Group Plc*[7] (directors' disqualification hearing to be held after the ECtHR had ruled that the appellant's reasonable time guarantee under Art 6(1) had been violated); *Ali v Crown Prosecution Service*[8] (destruction of evidence in a rape case during the period of delay); *R v Murray*[9] (a Northern Irish case emphasising the exceptional category of circumstances in which a stay will be appropriate); and *R (Johnson) v Professional Conduct Committee of the Nursing and Midwifery Council*[10] (confirming that a stay of proceedings is an exceptional remedy only to be used where a fair trial, relating to charges of professional misconduct in this case, was impossible).

1   [2004] EWCA Crim 572.
2   [2004] EWHC 595.
3   [2004] EWHC 683.
4   [2004] EWHC 2781.
5   [2005] EWCA Crim 911.
6   [2006] EWHC 1156.
7   [2007] EWCA Civ 425; [2007] UKHRR 739.
8   [2007] EWCA Crim 691.
9   [2007] N.I. 49.
10   [2008] EWHC 885.

1.118   In *R v S*,[1] the Court of Appeal, having referred to the earlier authorities, observed that the determination of whether a stay should be granted on the ground of delay is a discretionary decision and sought to further refine the correct approach for a judge to whom such application is made is to consider, laying down the following principles:

(a)   Even where delay is unjustifiable, a permanent stay should be the exception rather than the rule.

(b)   Where there is no fault on the part of the complainant or the prosecution, it will be very rare for a stay to be granted.

(c)   No stay should be granted in the absence of serious prejudice to the defence so that no fair trial can be held.

(d)   When assessing possible serious prejudice, the judge should bear in mind his or her power to regulate the admissibility of evidence and that the trial process itself should ensure that all relevant factual issues arising from delay will be placed before the jury for their consideration in accordance with appropriate direction from the judge.

(e)   If, having considered all these factors, a judge's assessment is that a fair trial will be possible, a stay should not be granted.

1   [2006] EWCA Crim 756, per Rose LJ at para 21.

1.119   As to delay brought about by, and prejudice claimed upon, a change in prosecutorial attitude and public perception in relation to an offence (terrorism in this case) during a period of delay see *R v Abu Hamza*,[1] where the Court of Appeal, citing *Montgomery v HM Advocate*,[2] accepted that adverse publicity could have risked prejudicing a fair trial, but held that that was no reason for not proceeding if the judge had concluded that his powers of trial management were sufficient to enable him to conclude that it is possible to have a fair trial.

1   [2007] QB 659, CA.
2   Above para **1.10**.

Historic sex allegations

1.120   Numerous defendants in cases involving historical allegations of sexual offences have contended for a stay of proceedings as an abuse of process on the ground of delay. That might not be surprising, given the clear potential for prejudice against the defendant who is accused of engaging in sexual misconduct years prior to the allegations being made against him and the inherent potential for lack of forensic evidence, one way or the other, in historic cases. But equally, the justification for delayed complaint in such cases is generally more readily understandable. Such cases are, therefore, invariably concerned more with the question of whether a defendant could be safely convicted on the evidence at his trial, given the effects that the delay (which lies in the making of the allegation itself) will have had upon that evidence, rather than the question of whether the authorities have violated a defendant's rights by failing to bring him to trial within a reasonable time and how that should be remedied. Hence, in *R v Smolinski,*[1] Lord Woolf CJ ruled[2] that an application to stay proceedings as an abuse in such a case should be made and entertained only at the end of a complainants' evidence (and reiterated the need for a case to be 'exceptional' before it will be subject to a successful pre-trial application to stay).[3]

1   [2004] 2 Cr App R 40, CA.
2   At 663–664.
3   In *R v B* (*Anthony*) [2005] EWCA Crim 29, the Court of Appeal, applying *Smolinski*, confirmed that the appropriate time for the judge to hear an application to stay was, in most cases, at the conclusion of the evidence.

1.121   Notable cases that fall into this, in reality distinct,[1] category, include *R v B* (*Brian*),[2] in which the Court of Appeal allowed an appeal against a refusal to stay proceedings where a 30-year delay in allegations of indecent assault had the effect that the defendant could not properly defend himself due to his inability to obtain witnesses; *R v Sheikh*[3] where proceedings were stayed by the Court of Appeal owing principally, to a finding that, in the cradle of events, critical documentary materials had been destroyed, and *R v GG*,[4] where the Court of Appeal reached the 'clear view' that an application on the ground of abuse of process would have failed considering, amongst other authorities, *Attorney-General's Reference* (*No 1 of 1990*).[5]

1   The Courts have always, however, been at pains to state that sexual offences do not constitute a separate category in law; see, for example, *R v Telford Justices, ex p Badhan* (above para **1.88**).
2   [2003] 2 Cr App R.13, CA.

3   [2006] EWCA Crim 2625.
4   [2005] EWCA Crim 1792.
5   For further consideration of these authorities see: *R v A (Paul)* [2005] EWCA Crim 2941, *R v Jensen (Colin)* [2005] EWCA Crim 1984, and *R v S (Stephen Paul)* [2006] 2 Cr App R 23, CA.

1.122   *R v B*[1] in particular is an interesting decision in that it suggests[2] that, in historic sex cases, there may exist a 'residual' appellate power to stay proceedings in circumstances where, notwithstanding that the Appellate Court upholds the decision of the trial judge to permit the case to proceed before a jury and the trial process cannot be faulted, it concludes that it would be, presumably with hindsight, 'unsafe or unfair to allow it to stand'. The factors that will prompt the exercise of such a power remain shrouded in mystery. In *R v B*, the Court of Appeal (Lord Woolf CJ) focussed upon the fact that, it:

> 'has to be recognised that because of the delay that occurred, in our judgment the appellant was put in an impossible position to defend himself. He was not ... able to conduct any proper cross-examination of the complainant. There was no material he could put to the complainant to establish that she had said that something had happened on one occasion which could be established to be incorrect. There was no material in the form of notes ... which showed that she had changed her account. All that the appellant could do was to say that he had not committed the acts alleged against him. [Counsel] says that to say to a jury, when faced with allegations of the sort that were made here, "I have not done it" is virtually no defence at all'

It is likely that the 'residual discretion' will be, in practice, reserved for historic sex cases concerning huge pre-complaint delay, involving a single complainant, and where the nature of the complaint is unspecific as to date or place, and where, because of the delay, there exists no supporting evidence whatsoever.[3] In *Woodcock v Government of New Zealand*,[4] Simon Brown LJ observed[5] that:

> 'R -v- B was a decision on its own particular facts and cannot stand as authority for some broad proposition that, without supporting scientific or documentary evidence, no-one can be fairly tried for sexual offences after a long period of time.'

1   Above para **1.121**.
2   At paras. 27–29.
3   The facts of *R v Smolinski* (above para **1.120**) are, perhaps, a further application of this exceptional residual discretion. Despite finding that the case had properly been left by the trial judge to the jury, the conviction was quashed having particular regard to the nature of the delayed complaints (one prompted by the other) and apparently mutually inconsistent verdicts. Note, however, the note of caution sounded by the Court of Appeal in *R v E* [2004] 2 Cr App R 26, CA as to the operation of this 'residual discretion'.
4   [2004] 1 WLR 1979, DC.
5   At para 15.

1.123   The particular need for urgency in progressing with criminal proceedings in cases involving historical sexual offences was noted by the European Court of Human Rights in *Massey v UK*,[1] where the applicant was awarded €4,000 for non-pecuniary damage on account of the fact that the domestic proceedings against him had not progressed with the necessary expedition, in violation of Art 6(1).

1   Application No 14399/02, Fourth Section; 16 November 2004.

Applicable to all stages of the criminal process

1.124   It now seems reasonably clear that the reasonable time guarantee under Art 6(1) will apply at all stages of the criminal process. A case decided after the decision of the Court of Appeal, but before the decision of the House of Lords, in *Attorney-General's Reference (No 2 of 2001)*, the Divisional Court in *R (Lloyd) v Bow Street Magistrates Court*[1] found a violation of that right and, distinguishing the Court of Appeal ruling in *Attorney-General's Reference (No 2 of 2001)*, stayed proceedings to commit a defendant to prison in default of payment of a confiscation order.

1   [2003] EWHC Admin 2294.

Dissenting judgments of Lords Hope and Rodger

1.125   At the commencement of his lengthy dissent, Lord Hope of Craighead[1] observed that:

> '[The conclusion of the majority] on the first point empties the reasonable time guarantee almost entirely of content, that it runs counter to the principle that the reasonable time requirement is a separate and independent guarantee which is not to be seen simply as part of the overriding right to a fair trial (see *Porter v Magill* [2002] 2 A.C. 357, 497A-B, para [109]), that it overlooks the fact that it is the act of the prosecutor and not the court which is under scrutiny in this case, that it places an unnecessarily strict construction on the word 'unlawful' in s.6(1) of the Human Rights Act 1998 and that it risks creating a divergence of view between two separate and entirely independent criminal jurisdictions in the United Kingdom about the meaning of this guarantee.'[2]

1   Who had given the leading judgment of the Privy Council in *R v HM Advocate* (above para **1.06**), expressly declining to follow Woolf CJ's judgment in the Court of Appeal.
2   At para, 46.

1.126   In a decision that contrasted sharply with that of the majority, Lord Hope considered that the right of the criminal defendant is to a determination of the charge against him at a hearing which had all the characteristics which are set out in Art 6; one of which is that the hearing be within a reasonable time. In reliance upon the fact that Art 6 does not say that the defendant has a right to a hearing, which can be asserted against him come what may and however long it takes,[1] Lord Hope went so far as to make the following observation on the decision of the majority:

> 'One of the great evils which the framers of the Convention may be thought to have had in mind is the holding of the threat of criminal proceedings over the head of the victim indefinitely to his severe prejudice without ever bringing him to trial. Let us hope that this evil, familiar in totalitarian regimes, never raises its ugly head in our country. But its absence from our culture should not blind us to the effect of the decision of the majority. It is to deprive the victim of the protection of being able to establish that the time has come for him to be released from the charge, irrespective of whether or not he can show that he cannot have a fair trial.'[2]

1   At para 46.
2   At para 93.

1.127   Lord Hope agreed that proceedings should be stayed on the ground of delay if either branch of the two-limbed criteria set out in Lord Bingham's speech were met. However, he concluded that the answer to the first question in the appeal was that proceedings *may* also be stayed where there has been a violation of the reasonable time requirement in circumstances where the accused cannot demonstrate that he will suffer any prejudice arising from the delay at his trial, if the court considers a stay to be the 'appropriate remedy'.[1] He accepted that s 8(1) of the Human Rights Act 1998 allowed the court to make such order within its powers as it considers just and appropriate to remedy a breach and, for that reason, would not go so far as to say that a stay was the inevitable remedy in delay cases.[2] Nonetheless, his view was that the two-limbed approach set out by Lord Bingham concentrated on the fair trial guarantee as the test for whether proceedings should be stayed, which referred to a different consideration than their Lordships were being asked to consider in the instant case; namely, the guarantee that one's trial will take place within a reasonable time.[3]

1   At para 110.
2   At para 110.
3   At para 109.

1.128   Lord Rodger of Earlsferry also dissented from the majority's view in respect of the consequence of a violation of Art 6(1), opining that Lord Bingham's reasoning was open to 'profound objection' on the basis that he had wrongly used the 'inevitable but unacceptable' effects of a stay as a basis for concluding that there would not be a violation of the Convention in the instant case. Nevertheless, he agreed with Lord Bingham[1] as to the course to be adopted when a trial cannot be held within a reasonable time. Lord Rodger said this:

'Whether or not there is a violation depends ... on how Art.6(1) should be interpreted and applied to the particular situation. The meaning of an article of the Convention is autonomous. It cannot vary, depending on the nature of the remedies that any individual legal system, such as English law, has chosen to provide for a violation. Parliament's purpose in enacting the 1998 Act so as to 'bring rights home' was to provide remedies in the British courts for the violations of people's Convention rights which could have been dealt with previously only by the Strasbourg authorities. The Convention rights themselves were not to be altered as they passed through customs at Dover and entered our domestic law with its particular system of remedies.'[2]

'Consistently with saying that past trial proceedings need not be set aside, the European Court [referring particularly to its judgment in *Bunkate v The Netherlands*[3] and the approach of the New Zealand courts in *Martin v Tauranga District Court*[4]] has never held that, to comply with the Convention, prospective trial proceedings must automatically be stopped. It accepts that other remedies for the violation, whether by declaration, reduction in sentence or damages, may be effective and so fulfil the requirements of Art.13.'[5]

43

'On that approach the supposed problems which Lord Bingham envisages (in paras 20–22) as resulting from an automatic stay simply do not arise. By contrast, on their interpretation, the majority assume that, by making future violations of Art.6(1) unlawful, Parliament intended that our courts should not have power to choose the appropriate remedy for such violations. They were always to grant a stay in such cases, even though there is nothing in the Convention or in the jurisprudence of the European Court to require this and even though it would be unjust and inappropriate for the court to grant the stay. Neither the mischief prompting the 1998 Act, nor its legislative history, nor its wording, nor any comparative material suggests, far less compels, that perverse conclusion.'[6]

1   Per Lord Bingham, at para 25.
2   At para 162.
3   Above para **1.56**, at 484.
4   [1995] 2 NZLR 419: '… the right to trial without delay … is not a right not to be tried after undue delay.'
5   At para 165.
6   At para 176.

1.129   Similarly to Lord Hope, Lord Rodger was of the opinion that an applicant did not need to show prejudice as a prerequisite to having proceedings stayed, however rare a stay might be, Lord Rodger concluded:

'I would therefore hold that, when a court is faced with a situation where going on with a prosecution and holding a trial would lead to a hearing after the lapse of a reasonable time, it should not hesitate to say that these steps would violate Art.6(1) and, hence, would be unlawful in terms of s.6(1) of the 1998 Act. Then, in terms of s.8(1), the court should go on to consider what relief or remedy would be "just and appropriate" for this unlawful act of violating the reasonable time guarantee. For the reasons given by Lord Bingham, in most cases the court would conclude that a declaration or a reduction in sentence or an award of damages, as the case might be, would be the just and appropriate remedy for this unlawful act. Unless the court had assessed the position incorrectly, that remedy would also constitute an effective remedy for the violation of Art.6(1) in terms of Art.13 and, by granting it, the court would fulfil the United Kingdom's international obligation under the Convention. In these circumstances nothing in the Convention or elsewhere compels the court to go further and grant a stay. Indeed it would be contrary to s.8(1) for the court to grant a stay where a stay would not be the just and appropriate remedy. And, as Lord Bingham suggests, it will only be in rare cases that the just and appropriate remedy for an unreasonable delay will be a stay. Only in those rare cases need, or indeed should, the court grant such a stay under s.8(1). In other cases the trial can proceed and the defendant will get the appropriate remedy at the proper time.'[1]

1   At para 177.

Conflict in domestic case law

1.130   In response to the opinions of the dissenting minority, Lord Hobhouse (on behalf of the majority) concluded that:

> 'The appellants fail on the first element in the main question. The construction of Art.6(1) for which they contend, and which my noble and learned friends Lord Hope and Lord Rodger support and *HM Lord Advocate v R* upheld, is in my respectful opinion clearly wrong. Further the distinction it is sought to make between the law of Scotland and English law regarding the second element is in my respectful opinion clearly unsustainable as a matter of English law ...'[1]

1   At para 127. Lord Millett too found it 'impossible to accept the reasoning of my noble and learned friends Lord Hope of Craighead and Lord Rodger of Earlsferry' (at para 129).

1.131   It was, therefore, clear that the settled law in the area of delay in England and Wales was now in direct conflict with the decision in *HM Advocate v R*[1] in so far as the Convention right would be applied in Scotland. This was confirmed in the speeches of Lord Nicholls, who concluded that *HM Advocate v R* was 'wrongly decided',[2] and Lord Bingham, who commented that *Attorney-General's Reference (No 1 of 2001)*:

> '...[cannot] be reconciled with the decision of the majority in *HM Advocate v R* [2003] 2 W.L.R. 317. While, therefore, the House may not overrule that decision of the Privy Council, I should make clear my preference for the opinion there expressed by the dissenting minority, which I take to be consistent with my own opinion in the present case.'[3]

1   Above para **1.06**.
2   At para 41.
3   At para 30.

1.132   Clearly dismayed at the decision of the majority, Lord Hope was anxious to proclaim that:

> 'A declaration by your Lordships that *HM Advocate v R* should not be followed in this jurisdiction may be thought to be inevitable in view of the conclusion reached by the majority. But a declaration that that case was wrongly decided, as Lord Nicholls would have it, is undesirable. Section 103 of the Scotland Act 1998 provides that any decision of the Judicial Committee shall be binding in all legal proceedings (other than proceedings before the Committee). And there is no appeal to this House from decisions of the High Court of Justiciary in cases decided by that court under the Human Rights Act 1998. So it is open to the Scottish courts to go their own way on this issue.'[1]

> 'The law of Scotland is not directly under review in this case. Moreover, questions arose in *HM Advocate v R* [2003] 2 W.L.R. 317 about the interpretation of the Scotland Act 1998 and aspects of Scottish criminal practice which are not common to the two countries. I would have much preferred it if your Lordships had felt able to arrive at a decision in this English appeal which could be reconciled with that of the Judicial

Committee in R's case. But it does not follow from the fact that this has not been possible that R should not be followed in Scotland.'[2]

'A divergence of view between the two jurisdictions about the meaning of the reasonable time guarantee, as there is at present, is unfortunate but it may have to be accepted as inevitable. The last word as to its meaning must, of course, lie with Strasbourg.'[3]

1   At para 105.
2   At para 107.
3   At para 108.

THE LAST WORD: RECENT ECHR JURISPRUDENCE AND SPIERS V RUDDY & HM ADVOCATE

1.133   On 12 December 2007, the Privy Council gave judgment in *David Spiers, Prosecutor Fiscal v Kevin Ruddy & HM Advocate General*.[1] The Board was asked to consider two questions:

(1)   Whether there had been unreasonable delay in determining the charges against the appellant Ruddy, in breach of his rights under Art 6(1).[2]

(2)   Whether it would be incompatible with Mr Ruddy's right to a determination of the criminal charges against him within a reasonable time for the Lord Advocate to continue to prosecute him on those charges following the lapse of a reasonable time, in circumstances where a fair trial remains possible and there is no other compelling reason why it would be unfair to try Mr Ruddy.

1   [2008] 2 WLR 608, PC.
2   The facts of the case do not require mention as the Board considered that it would be inappropriate for it to make a decision on the first question and refused to do so, it having not yet been decided on the facts by the Scottish courts.

1.134   The second question required the Board to choose between two irreconcilable authorities; the decision of the House of Lords in *Attorney-General's Reference (No 2 of 2001)* on the one hand and the Privy Council Judgment in *HM Advocate v R* on the other. The Board was constituted of Lord Bingham, who had given the leading judgment in *Attorney-General's Reference (No 2 of 2001)* and Lords Hope and Rodger, who had dissented in that case and had been part of the majority in the conflicting ruling in *HM Advocate v R*, in addition to Lords Mance and Neuberger.

1.135   The outcome of the case was a foregone conclusion. As Lord Bingham commented:

'Happily, there is a body of Strasbourg authority, mostly decided after both of these cases and not referred to in either of them, which eases our choice.'[1]

1   At para 6.

1.136   In *Kudla v Poland*[1] the ECtHR upheld the applicant's complaint that a period of one year and eight months between the quashing of his conviction at first instance on appeal and his retrial violated the reasonable time guarantee.

The Court considered that an appropriate remedy for this breach would either prevent the alleged violation or its continuation, or provide adequate redress for the violation that had already taken place. In that case there was no domestic remedy by which the applicant could enforce his right to a hearing within a reasonable time. Nonetheless, the judgment is clear that a violation of the reasonable time requirement will not render all proceedings that follow a continuing breach.

1   (2002) 35 EHRR 11.

1.137   *Kudla* was repeated and applied *in Mifsud v France*,[1] an application concerning civil proceedings that was ruled inadmissible, where the court found that the applicant could yet take advantage of compensatory remedies provided for in domestic law.

1   Application No 57220/00, Grand Chamber, 11 September 2002.

1.138   The Grand Chamber of the ECtHR had given judgment on the issue of the remedy for violations of the reasonable time requirements in *Cocchiarella v Italy*[1] and *Scordino v Italy (No 1)*[2] both on the same day. Both related to civil proceedings. The Court in *Cocchiarella* considered the best solution for problems of delay is indisputably prevention and that a remedy designed to expedite the proceedings in order to prevent them from becoming excessively lengthy has the advantage over a remedy affording only compensation, 'since it also prevents a finding of successive violations in respect of the same set of proceedings and does not merely repair the breach *a posteriori*, as does a compensatory remedy of the type provided for under Italian law for example'[3] On the facts of the case before it, the Court found that the reasonable time guarantee had been breached in *Cocchiarella*, but the sum of damages awarded by the domestic court to be an adequate remedy for the violation, noting that various types of remedy might redress a violation of the guarantee including, in criminal cases, an express reduction in sentence to take into account the length of proceedings.[4] The same principles were applied in *Scordino*, with the result that compensation was found to be an inadequate remedy in that case.

1   Application No 64886/01, Grand Chamber, 29 March 2006.
2   (2007) 45 EHRR 7.
3   At para 74.
4   At para 77.

1.139   In *Zarb v Malta*,[1] a criminal case, the court found the length of domestic proceedings in the applicant's case to be excessive, in violation of Art 6(1). Referring to its earlier authority, the court found[2] the compensation awarded to the applicant to be manifestly inadequate in meeting the requirement for an effective domestic remedy to be provided where a breach occurs.

1   Application No. 16631/04, Fourth Section; 4 July 2006.
2   At para 60.

1.140   Furthermore, in *Massey v United Kingdom*,[1] which was not cited in *Spiers*, the European Court had awarded non-pecuniary damages of €4,000 where the applicants' right under Art 6(1) had been violated by, in particular, a delay of two years and eight months between arrest and trial and a delay of more than two years before an application for leave to appeal against conviction and sentence was refused by the Court of Appeal, such that the proceedings had not progressed with necessary expedition in breach of the Convention.

1   Above para **1.124**.

1.141   In *Henworth v UK*,[1] the European Court held that whether a case had progressed with necessary expedition was to be determined by looking at the case as a whole, such that taking the various delays together there was a breach of Art 6 notwithstanding the fact that some of them were attributable to the applicant.

1   Application No 515/02, Fourth Section; 2 November 2004.

1.142   Having had his ruling in *Attorney-General's Reference* (*No 2 of 2001*) effectively affirmed by this subsequent Strasbourg jurisprudence,[1] Lord Bingham noted in *Spiers* that:

> 'None of these cases concerned the situation where delay jeopardises the fairness of a forthcoming trial or where, for any compelling reason, it is not fair to try an accused at all. It is axiomatic that if an accused cannot be tried fairly he should not be tried at all, and where either of these conditions is held to apply the proceedings must be brought to an end.'[2]

> 'The cases concerned a situation where there has (or may have been) such delay in the conduct of proceedings as to breach a party's right to trial within a reasonable time but where the fairness of the trial has not been or will not be compromised. The authorities relied on and considered above make clear, in my opinion, that such delay does not give rise to a continuing breach which cannot be cured save by a discontinuation of proceedings. It gives rise to a breach which can be cured, even where it cannot be prevented, by expedition, reduction of sentence or compensation, provided always that the breach, where it occurs, is publicly acknowledged and addressed.'[3]

1   And the Privy Council in *Boolell v The State* (above para **1.33**), in which a finding of a violation of the reasonable time guarantee of the Mauritian Constitution did not necessarily lead to a stay; in that case a fine was substituted for the sentence of imprisonment as sufficient recognition of the violation.
2   At para 16.
3   At para 16.

1.143   It was clear, Lord Bingham ruled in departing from the decision in *HM Advocate v R*,[1] that the decision of the House of Lords in *Attorney-General's Reference* (*No 2 of 2001*) gave better effect to the Strasbourg jurisprudence:

> 'Once it is accepted that a breach of the reasonable time requirement does not give rise to a continuing breach, it ineluctably follows that the Lord Advocate does not act incompatibly with a person's Convention right by continuing to prosecute him after such a breach has occurred.'[2]

1   At para 18.
2   At para 17.

1.144   The other members of the Board concurred with Lord Bingham's judgment. Lord Hope, departing from his earlier ruling, confirmed that:

'Under the reasonable time guarantee prejudice, although relevant, need not be established. It is not necessary to show that a fair trial is no longer possible or that for any other reason the proceedings would be unfair ... where the legislature has left it to the courts to decide what that remedy shall be, as is the case under the Human Rights Act 1998, the court has a discretion to choose the remedy for the unlawful act which it considers just and appropriate.'[1]

1   At para 21. See also *Burns v HM Advocate* [2008] UKPC 63 at para 28.

1.145   Such alternative remedies, falling short of an absolute stay, can include, for example, admission to bail, expedition of the trial date, exclusion of evidence or, in post-conviction cases, reduction of sentence[1] or compensation.[2] It will only be in that exceptional category of cases where no other alternative is sufficient to remedy a continuing breach, that a permanent stay will be granted.

1   As in *Boolell v The State* (above para **1.33**).
2   As in *Zarb v Malta* (above para **1.139**), *Massey v United Kingdom* (above para **1.140**).

CONCLUSION

1.146   Whilst the ECtHR cases[1] primarily concerned the issue of appropriate remedy for breach rather than the nature of the violation of the reasonable time guarantee itself, they clearly point, as Lord Rodger accepted in *Spiers,*[2] in favour of the conclusion reached by the majority of the House of Lords in *Attorney-General's Reference (No 2 of 2001)*.

1   As noted above at para **1.18**, the practitioner should appreciate that there exists a voluminous amount of ECtHR jurisprudence on the issue of delay beyond the formative rulings that have been cited above.
2   At para 26.

1.147   If a criminal case is not heard and completed within a reasonable time, that will constitute a breach of a defendant's Art 6(1) rights, whether or not a defendant has been prejudiced by the delay.[1] That breach will need to be declared and remedied but will not, unless the defendant suffers prejudice or the delay would bring matters into disrepute on a *Bennett*-style basis, give rise to a stay of the proceedings.

1   Above para **1.33**.

1.148   The defendant who applies to have the proceedings against him permanently stayed as an abuse of process on this ground, therefore, faces the difficult task of meeting the stringent criteria set out by Lord Bingham in that case, namely that he can no longer receive a fair trial or it would be otherwise unfair to try him, if he is to succeed in having the proceedings discontinued. Nonetheless, the applicant who fails in having the proceedings against him stayed might gain redress by other means, such as compensation or a reduction in sentence, so long as he is able to at least establish that his right to a hearing within a reasonable time has been violated.

Chapter 2

Breach of promise

2.01   If in a criminal case the prosecution reneges on a promise it has given to an accused not to prosecute, does a breach of this promise ipso facto give rise to unfairness and an abuse of process? The law concerned with breach of promise would be easy to state if the answer to this question was an unequivocal yes. However, the Court of Appeal has held that the answer is equivocal. Breach of promise not to prosecute does not necessarily give rise to abuse. It depends on the circumstances and each case should be judged on its merits. All that the Court of Appeal has held is that where a defendant has been induced to believe that he will not be prosecuted, this is capable of founding a stay for abuse.

2.02   The authorities concerned with this head of abuse will necessarily touch on a number of issues which must be resolved in order that the parameters of this head are determined. Furthermore, the parties should know when it is permissible for a prosecution to proceed despite a defendant contending that he received a promise that this would not occur. The issues to be resolved are outlined in paras **2.03–2.05**.

The promise

2.03   Must a promise not to prosecute be an explicit unequivocal undertaking by the prosecutor? Alternatively can a 'promise' be inferred from something lesser, for example, an indication or statement of intent? Also, to be binding, must the promise come only from the prosecutor direct or can it instead emanate from someone who is simply a member of the prosecution team or from what a prosecutor has said to a third party which is known about or overheard by the defendant?

Prejudice

2.04   If a promise has been made, can it nonetheless be withdrawn? For a court to hold the prosecution to its word, is the uttering of a promise enough or must there in addition be some prejudice which would be caused to the defence were the prosecution to be allowed to renege? In other words, using the terminology of the law of contract, must there be an offer, an acceptance and consideration? By 'consideration' is meant prejudice to the defence; the defendant has relied on the promise and as a direct consequence, has done some act or abstained from doing some act, which has prejudiced or been detrimental to his defence.

2.05   The heart of the issue here is the difference of approach between the judgment of Lord Lane CJ in *A-G's Reference (No 1 of 1990)*[1] where he emphasised the need to prove prejudice before an abuse submission can be sustained, versus the approach of the House of Lords in *R v Horseferry Road Magistrates' Court, ex p Bennett*[2] which emphasised prosecution impropriety over prejudice – quoting Lord Lowry in *Bennett*, whether to try the case in a circumstance of breach of promise would 'offend the court's sense of justice and propriety to be asked to try the accused'.[3]

1   [1992] QB 630.
2   [1994] AC 42.
3   [1994] AC 42 at 74.

2.06   The Court of Appeal decision of *R v Abu Hamza*[1] has highlighted the competing, but not mutually inconsistent, approaches in *Bennett* and the *A-G's Reference*, as it attempted to lay down guideline criteria. It has, arguably however, created some further ambiguity over the correct test to apply in a breach of promise situation, which test the courts have struggled to define. While the Bennett type of abuse of process (categorised as a Beckford limb two abuse) appears alive and well in a string of cases, such as *Bloomfield*[2] and in the 2006 House of Lords decision in *Jones v Whalley*,[3] *Hamza* could be interpreted as marking a significant narrowing of the principles established in the earlier case law, with its emphasis on proof of prejudice through detrimental reliance on a promise. The overall significance of this judgement is considered below at paras **2.39–2.44**.

1   [2007] 1 Cr App R 27.
2   [1997] 1 Cr App R 135.
3   [2007] 1 Cr App R 2.

2.07   How the courts have resolved these difficult issues is the subject of this chapter. The categories of breach of promise are considered in the following sections, namely:

(1)   promises not to prosecute;

(2)   promises to offer no evidence;

(3)   promises on acceptable pleas; and

(4)   other promises.

PROMISES NOT TO PROSECUTE

2.08   In England the cornerstone of the law on breach of promise remains the authority *R v Croydon Justices, ex p Dean*.[1] Before analysing the significance of *Dean*, a brief review of some of the earlier authorities may help to place it in a better context.

1   (1993) 98 Cr App Rep 76.

Pre-Dean authorities

2.09   While some of the most relevant authorities emanate from the Privy Council, and from Hong Kong, it is interesting that the English authority of *Lund v Thompson*[1] was not apparently cited in *Dean*.

1   [1959] 1 QB 283.

2.10   In *Lund* Diplock J, giving the judgment of the High Court, said, albeit with some reluctance, that a statement by police that they had no intention to prosecute did not nullify a prior notice of intended prosecution which had been issued in relation to a road traffic offence. The court acknowledged that in certain cases, where the police indicate an intention not to prosecute and subsequently change their mind (as occurred in *Lund*), this may lead to considerable injustice to the person prosecuted. However, strict statutory construction was said to militate against *Lund*. The fact that a citizen was entitled to mount a private prosecution and permitted to act on the basis of the original notice, whatever subsequent representations were made by the police, was deemed to be an overriding factor. For that reason, the suggested concept of some loose form of 'estoppel' binding a police officer to keep another person's promise not to prosecute was dismissed by the court.

2.11   In *Chu Piu-Wing*[1] the appellant had been subpoenaed to attend a police disciplinary tribunal to give evidence of certain payments of 'protection money' he had made to police officers in respect of gambling establishments. The appellant had refused to do so because of the conditions on which he had given the information in the first place. These conditions were first, that he would give the information only once, second, that he would only provide information and not give evidence against the policeman in court, and third, that the information would not be used against him. In due course, he was assured by the interrogating International Commission Against Corruption officers that, if any information which he gave verified the material which they already had (which it apparently did), he would not be prosecuted. Notwithstanding such promise, he was charged, convicted and sentenced to imprisonment, in respect of the matters on which he had given information. When the appellant was subsequently subpoenaed before the police disciplinary tribunal, he attended but refused to give evidence of the matters concerned. For this refusal he was committed to six months' imprisonment for contempt by the High Court. In the light of the circumstances in which the information had been given to the authorities, the Hong Kong Court of Appeal held that the issuance of the subpoena was an abuse of the process of the court.

1   [1984] HKLR 411.

2.12   McMullin VP giving the judgment of Hong Kong's Court of Appeal stated that there was:

'a clear public interest to be observed in holding officials of the state to promises made by them in the full understanding of what is entailed by the bargain'.

The authorities had reneged on a solemn promise where there was no doubt the appellant must reasonably have believed he had kept his side of the bargain. The theme of holding officials to account for promises or representations runs through the subsequent case law, up to the present day.[1]

1   See *Postermobile plc v Brent London Borough Council*, paras **2.35** and **2.36**.

2.13   In *Bell v DPP*[1] the Privy Council considered what was ostensibly a 'delay' case but which had a bearing on the principles relating to implicit promises or expectations. The case concerned an appellant who had been arrested in Jamaica and charged, inter alia, with firearm offences. Having been convicted in the Crown Court, and successful in an appeal against conviction, a retrial was ordered. On several occasions thereafter the prosecution were not ready on the due trial dates. Finally, after more adjournments he was discharged by a judge, the Crown having offered no evidence against him. However, three months later he was re-arrested and a retrial was ordered.

1   [1985] AC 937, PC; The court's reasoning in the Bell decision, in relation to the issue of delay, has subsequently been disapproved of, and effectively overruled, by the Privy Council in Mills v HM Advocate [2004] 1 AC 441

2.14   The Board allowed his appeal. It held that the Jamaican courts had overlooked the significance of the order of the retrial and of his being discharged, on the basis that further delay would then be unfair to him, his constitutional rights having been infringed (to a fair hearing within a reasonable time). Where the defence submitted that the appellant had been given great hope when no evidence was offered, Templeman LJ said that in a proper case the court could treat the renewal of charges, even after the lapse of a reasonable time, as an abuse of process of the court. For, as the Law Lord noted '... the appellant's complaint is that he was discharged and told to go free ...' before being re-arrested.

2.15   In line with the courts' avowed duty to secure 'fair treatment' for those before them, the Privy Council in *Bell* acknowledged, inter alia, the public interest in minimising the '*anxiety and concern of the accused*',[1] in the context of delays awaiting trial. In practice, while there are no doubt many occasions where defendants ought to be aware of the possibility of re-arrest (having been discharged in criminal proceedings), nevertheless, this case illustrates an instance where a legitimate expectation that there would be no further prosecution was foiled.

1   Per Powell J in *Barker v Wingo* 407 US 514 (1972).

2.16   The decisions of *Bell* and *Chu Pui-Wing* were later considered in the 1990 *Harris* decision of the Hong Kong Court of Appeal[1] which court helpfully reviewed the state of the law in relation to the common law jurisdictions on this topic. Harris was a member of the Attorney-General's Chambers who, while at the time personally responsible for the section dealing with vice prosecutions, was himself later convicted of procuring a girl for unlawful sexual intercourse. The defendant appealed on the basis, inter alia, that, having assured him in May 1989 he would not be prosecuted, the Attorney-General should not be permitted to change his mind in October 1989, following what was said to be increased pressure from the mass media.

1   [1991] 1 HKLR at 389.

2.17 In dismissing the appeal, Faud VP ruled that the Attorney-General was quite entitled to change his mind in the light of the changing public interest, notwithstanding that it may entail a possible erosion of confidence in his individual decisions. While Silke VP found that: 'There was no "promise" made to the appellant other than in the widest of layman's terms', and albeit that it came from a colleague, can one easily ignore the fact that it came from the Attorney-General himself? Indeed, as a recent commentator noted,[1] Harris's counsel[2] posed an interesting question which was left unresolved by the court, counsel perhaps having the facts of *Chu Piu-Wing* in mind, namely, 'Why should the recipient of an unqualified assurance be in a worse position than the recipient of one that is qualified?'

1   Sze Ping-Fat, 'Resiling from Assurances not to Prosecute' [1998] 162 JP 604.
2   Mr Anthony Scrivener QC acting pro bono.

2.18 In *A-G of Trinidad and Tobago v Phillip*[1], the Privy Council held that the prosecution of offenders, after a pardon had been granted and an order of habeas corpus made, would constitute an abuse of process even if the pardon was in fact legally invalid. The Islands' Acting President had granted the 'pardon' to a group of individuals who had participated in an armed insurrection. In attempting to overthrow the lawful government, they had seized certain buildings and had taken hostages. Having released the hostages on the promise of this 'pardon' they themselves surrendered, only to be arrested and charged with, inter alia, treason and murder.

1   [1995] 1 AC 396, PC.

2.19 The court's policy of holding officials to their promises was shown in extremis in *Phillip*, where this promise was upheld, albeit it was obtained by coercion and in circumstances where a trial could be fairly held. Lord Woolf, in identifying this particular form of abuse of process, stated that:

> 'The common law has now developed a formidable safeguard to protect persons from being prosecuted in circumstances where it would be seriously unjust to do so'.

R v Croydon Justices, ex p Dean[1]

2.20 The facts were as follows. The applicant, aged 17, along with two other men, were arrested by police in respect of a murder investigation. He denied taking part in the killing but admitted that after it had taken place he had assisted in destroying the victim's car. At the end of a police interview he was informed by the officers that he was regarded as a prosecution witness and had the protection of the police. Five days after the co-defendants had been charged, the applicant further assisted and co-operated and admitted that the co-defendant had driven him to the scene of the crime, and shown him the victim's body. Later, however, after the CPS had taken charge of the prosecution and reviewed the evidence it decided that Dean should be charged. The CPS decided, after a conference with the police, to charge him with assisting in the destruction of the car.

1   (1993) 98 Cr App Rep 76. See para **2.08**.

2.21 Following the committal, where the justices rejected an application for abuse, Dean sought a judicial review. The Divisional Court held that the prosecution of a person who had received a promise, undertaking or representation from the police that he would not be prosecuted earlier was capable of being an abuse of process. On the undisputed evidence the applicant was given to understand, for a considerable time, that he was to be a prosecution witness, from which it almost certainly followed he was not himself to be prosecuted.

2.22 There was a dispute between the parties concerning the number of occasions when more specific assurances were said to have been given by police that there would be no prosecution, such assurances allegedly given when the tape recorder was switched off. A passage in the CPS representative's affidavit, which contradicted the police position, was accepted by the court as being truthful.

2.23 The CPS argument against the application for judicial review was a constitutional one as the police, in any event, did not have the requisite authority to tell the applicant he would not be prosecuted, therefore such police conduct could not amount to an abuse of process. Staughton LJ however, was not persuaded and held that whether or not the promisor had the power to decide, or whether or not it was a case of bad faith or something akin, these were not essential requirements:

> 'The effect on the applicant, or for that matter his father, of an undertaking or promise or representation by police was likely to have been the same ... whether or not it was authorised by the CPS'.

What was found to be in Dean's mind was adjudged highly significant for, as the court noted, '... the impression created was not dispelled for over five weeks, during which period he gave repeated assistance to the police'. The timing of the police promise to use him as a witness, and rule him out as a defendant, was also a feature given that the promise (which the court accepted) was given at an early stage before he provided the important information. Staughton LJ pointed out that the applicant and his father could have taken legal advice as to the binding effect, or not, of such statements by police, but considered it unreasonable to expect that in the particular circumstances of the case (ie the applicant's young age, the nature of assistance he had provided and the length of time involved).

2.24 While no doubt a combination of factors affected the court's decision, the immense prejudice he inflicted on his own position, which was largely irremediable, must have surely been the greatest consideration before the court in opting to stay proceedings. In answer to the CPS's constitutional argument, Staughton LJ held that the remedy 'must surely be a greater degree of liaison at an early state'.

2.25 It is apparent that this case was decided very much on its own particular facts. One can readily foresee a different outcome in circumstances where, for example, an unrealistic promise is either made or implied, by a young police officer to an experienced criminal, who indeed would have realised as much. Further, it is submitted that in practice certain individuals who provide witness statements to the police, having themselves been arrested and charged, expect and/or agree to testify for the Crown not because they expect an immunity but in the hope (or promise sometimes) of a reduced sentence.

2.26   The central importance of *Dean* is that it explored the interrelationship between the police and the CPS and their respective roles in the prosecution of crime. The CPS argument was that if the Prosecution of Offences Act 1985 is to make any sense, then they ought to be unfettered in decision-making where prior police action is unauthorised. The court, while pronouncing that the CPS succeeded, in that they alone are entitled and bound to decide who shall be prosecuted, granted a somewhat hollow victory, given the police's recognised ability to, in effect, tie their hands. While it follows that the police have no authority to tell a suspect that he will not be prosecuted in connection with an offence (save where the CPS authorise such action), nevertheless the police will have to conduct themselves with restraint, for their conduct, even inadvertent or unintentional may lead to a stay of proceedings.

2.27   Police officers will need to be especially wary of having informal unrecorded discussions with the suspect or his solicitor where an impression is conveyed by the officers that if the suspect co-operates as desired, others but not him will be charged. If in reliance on this vague indication, the suspect confesses and/or implicates the others, he will certainly feel aggrieved, if not betrayed, if charges follow. As this case bears out, informing a suspect that he will be a Crown witness might be construed as an implied promise that no prosecution will take place. Practitioners whose clients complain about being charged, or prosecuted, and who state they genuinely believed they were only to act as witnesses, ought to carefully inquire into the circumstances which led to that belief. Did the client have a legitimate, as opposed to a fanciful, expectation that there would be no prosecution? Was the client justified in holding such a belief or did it simply result from gossip, hearsay or informal observation or comment? Which officer made or implied such a promise not to prosecute? Was the client entitled reasonably to rely on an indication given by an officer only marginally connected to the case, and perhaps of very junior rank? These are perhaps some of the practical questions with which the courts will have to grapple in deciding the bona fides of alleged unfairness. Lessons will hopefully be learnt from *Dean*, which serves well to illustrate that a greater liaison between CPS and police is essential for both branches to function more effectively in the interests of justice.[1]

1   'The Crown Prosecution Service and the Police: A Loveless Marriage?' [1994] LQR 376.

2.28   As Julia Fionda neatly observed, when comparing *Dean* with the earlier decision in *Lund*:

'The only possible means of distinguishing that authority [*Lund*] from the circumstances of the recent case [*Dean*] were that in 1958 the court was seeking to prevent the promises of the police being binding on any citizen as a potential prosecutor (that is, third party), whereas in the present case the promise was merely held to be binding on the CPS, a body acting in its official capacity as public prosecutor to whom the police are obliged to refer cases'.

Post-Dean authorities

2.29   *Dean* has been considered and adopted in a number of subsequent cases, most notably in *R v Horseferry Road Magistrates' Court, ex p Bennett*[1] and in *R v Townsend, Dearsley and Bretscher.*[2]

1   [1994] AC 42.
2   [1997] 2 Cr App Rep 540.

2.30   *Townsend* was a case of a suspect in fraud proceedings being treated as a prosecution witness for a considerable period, before eventually the prosecution decided to abandon him as a witness and prosecute instead. While being treated as a witness Bretscher had made a statement implicating his future co-defendant, Townsend. At the trial, however, an abuse submission was rejected, the judge holding that no prejudice had been suffered.

2.31   At the appeal, the prosecution emphasised that in *Dean,* Staughton LJ had made it plain that the facts in that case were exceptional and therefore *Dean* could easily be distinguished. Here, during the period that Bretscher was treated as a witness, the CPS were unaware of the true extent of his central role in the fraud. Rose LJ held in the Court of Appeal that where a defendant has been induced to believe he would not be prosecuted, this is capable of founding a stay for abuse. But such a breach of promise did not necessarily and ipso facto give rise to abuse. Considering the circumstances of this case, the court held that there had been nothing improper in interviewing the appellant first as a witness and, further, that he had not changed his position in reliance on his treatment as a prosecution witness or volunteered incriminating information. However, the conviction was held to be unsafe given that the appellant had seriously prejudiced his chances of a fair trial. For, while still acting in the capacity qua witness, the CPS had served on the co-defending lawyers the appellant's witness statement (as unused material) which heavily implicated the co-defendant. This led to the co-defendant giving evidence against him at a joint trial, where a severance application had failed, and to a hostile situation which might well have been avoided.

2.32   Situations where witnesses metamorphosise into defendants are obviously fraught with potential problems and the courts no doubt will have to remain on guard as to the bona fides of certain abuse claims. Caution ought to be applied in *Townsend* type scenarios for the reasons astutely noted by a recent commentator[1] as follows:

> 'It is perfectly possible to imagine a case of a dishonest witness who is happy to implicate another; the other may have been content not to implicate the witness as long as the witness did not become involved. But if his attitude were to change on being served with a lying statement made by the witness, it would not only be understandable, but it would be a charter for the dishonest and unscrupulous witness if it were to be held that his "co-operation" had effectively earned him immunity.'

1   See also Professor Birch's commentary at [1997] Crim LR 128.

2.33   The concept of fairness and breach of promise arose in *R v Liverpool Magistrates' Court, ex p Slade*[1]. A dog owner was prosecuted for allowing a pitbull terrier in a public place. Under the relevant legislation this was an offence and if it was proved then the magistrates' court was bound to order the destruction of the dog. The issue in the case was therefore whether the dog was of this breed or not. At the trial the prosecution dog expert failed to appear and the magistrates accordingly dismissed the charge. The next day the dog owner duly went to the police station to retrieve his dog which was released to him by the police. However, it appears that the police still felt aggrieved at the situation and subsequently chose to bring fresh proceedings seeking to re-prove that the dog was a pitbull terrier.

1   [1998] 1 WLR 531, [1998] 1 Cr App Rep 147; see also *R v Haringey Magistrates' Court, ex p Cragg* (1996) 161 JP 61.

2.34   The dog owner argued breach of promise. His argument was that by releasing the dog to him at the police station, the police had not only created a legitimate expectation in his mind that having the dog in a public place was perfectly lawful, they had also connived with him continuing to commit the offence. In the Divisional Court this argument found favour. Pill LJ, in holding that there was an abuse here, categorised it as falling under the second strand as delineated by Neill LJ in *R v Beckford*:[1] '... it was unfair to try the accused for the offence and offensive to the court's sense of justice and propriety'.

1   [1996] 1 Cr App Rep 94.

2.35   In *Postermobile plc v Brent London Borough Council*[1] the Divisional Court also applied the second strand of *Beckford*. In this case, 25 separate informations were laid against the appellants by Brent Council for displaying advertisements without obtaining the necessary planning consent. The appellants did not deny the charges but alleged that at a meeting between a planning consultant employed by the appellants, a director of the appellants and officers of the council, they were told that planning consents would not be required for the advertisements in question. Immediately after the advertisements were erected, the council commenced prosecutions against them.

1   (1997) Times, 8 December; see also *R v Aylesbury Justices, ex p Kitching* [1997] Env LR D16; and see also *R v DPP, ex p Duckenfield* [1999] 2 All ER 873.

2.36   Schiemann LJ held that the prosecutions were an abuse of process, on the basis that it would be unfair for the defendants ever to be tried. He emphasised the importance of citizens being able to rely on the statements of public officials and commented, with wry humour, that it was not as if they requested 'planning advice from one of the council's gardeners'.

2.37   Equally, in the decision of *R v D*[1] the Court of Appeal found that a prosecution should have been stayed as an abuse when the police 'went back on their word' and re-instituted proceedings which had been dropped in 1986. In 1986 a Chief Inspector of Police wrote to the defendant, in relation to a police investigation against him alleging gross indecency towards a child, thus:

'Police enquiries have now been completed and having regard to the circumstances and insufficient evidence, I have decided that no further police action will be taken in this matter'.

In 1997 the prosecution told the defendant's solicitors (now dealing with a second complainant making a similar allegation) that the original decision in 1986 had been taken in view of the then rule of evidence which required corroboration of a child's unsworn testimony. The Court of Appeal did not consider the prosecution's stated reason for reviving proceedings to be an 'adequate explanation or justification'. The court was satisfied that the police had 'misused their powers' by reneging on an unequivocal statement that the prosecution was at an end. In addition, by virtue of the antiquity of proceedings, the defence had been deprived of vital documentation (destroyed in the passage of time) which was found to have caused obvious and substantial prejudice to the preparation of the case.

1   (2000) 1 Archbold News 1, CA: 9 July 1999.

2.38   In the decision of *R v Sevenoaks Magistrates Court*[1] the Divisional Court reviewed a number of the earlier 'promises not to prosecute' cases. In quashing a decision of the justices to stay proceedings for abuse in relation to a Planning Act prosecution, the court easily distinguished the case on the facts from the 'very special circumstances' present in the *Dean* and *Bloomfield* decisions. Sullivan J, however, clearly stated:

> 'that, in principle, an implicit promise may be sufficient to found a submission that there has been an abuse of process, but as a matter of common sense the less explicit the promise, the less likely it will be that the court's sense of propriety and justice will be offended by the prosecution'.

1   *R (on the application of Tunbridge Wells Borough Council) v Sevenoaks Magistrates' Court* [2001] EWHC Admin 897.

R V ABU HAMZA[1]

2.39   Hamza was the imam of a mosque, who had been convicted of various counts of solicitation to murder, using threatening, abusive or insulting words or behaviour with intent to stir up racial hatred, and counts relating to his possession of various sound recordings and documents. The counts related to public speeches made by him at the mosque, and in other places between 1997 and 2000. In March 1999 Hamza was arrested on suspicion of involvement in a terrorist incident which occurred in the Yemen in 1998. Upon his arrest, the police seized from his home a large number of audio and video cassettes, as well as 10 volumes of an Afghani Jihad Encyclopaedia. The police kept this material for some nine months, before returning it to him in December 1999. He was informed that no further action would be taken against him.

1   [2007] 1 Cr App R 27.

2.40   A number of grounds of appeal were argued in the Court of Appeal; however, one such ground related to the trial judge's rejection of an application for a stay on this discreet aspect of abuse of process. The defence contended that the actions of the police, in returning the material after scrutiny naturally and reasonably created in the appellant the clear impression that the contents of the returned videos and the Encyclopaedia were not criminal. The police were said to have given the appellant a legitimate expectation that he would not be prosecuted for possession of these items. Against that background, it was contended to be an abuse of process five years later to prosecute him for possession of the same. The Court of Appeal disagreed, and, in dismissing the appeal, found the specific facts relied on to fall a long way short of satisfying the 'criteria' required to succeed.

2.41   Lord Phillips, the then Lord Chief Justice, reviewed the earlier authorities of *ex p Dean*, *Townsend* and *Bloomfield*, and held;

> 'These authorities suggest that it is not likely to constitute an abuse of process to proceed with a prosecution unless (1) there has been an unequivocal representation by those with the conduct of the investigation or prosecution of a case that the defendant will not be prosecuted and (2) that the defendant has acted on that representation to his detriment. Even then, if facts come to light which were not known when the representation was made, these may justify proceeding with the prosecution despite the representation.'

While the Court was rightly critical of the delay in taking the decision to prosecute, it held that the fact the police had not done so for five years, could not be 'taken as an assurance, let alone an unequivocal assurance, that they would not do so in the future'. It was deemed to be significant that the context of the seizing of the materials related much more to the specific allegations of alleged involvement in the Yemen, as opposed to some general investigation into his criminality. The court noted that the appellant had been aware of this distinction, and held that:

> 'There is no reason to conclude that the appellant placed any reliance on the reaction, or lack of reaction, of the police to the cassettes and the Encyclopedia when deciding to retain them in his possession. He was simply continuing a course of conduct that had commenced before the police had intervened.'

1   See para 57 of the judgment.

2.42   The *Hamza* judgment, which in fairness to the court dealt with a whole host of different grounds of appeal, has attracted criticism, in relation to this single discreet topic, from respected academic commentators. Professor Ormerod has raised a number of issues in relation to the judgment.[1] First, the point is made that, whereas the court found no assurance to have been given, there would appear to have been an explicit assurance that no further action would be taken against him. Secondly, that it would be too fine a distinction to make, to suggest that any assurances given could only have been relevant to the Yemen incident. Thirdly, that, given that Hamza was being prosecuted for possession of materials subjected to police scrutiny for some nine months, which were then returned to him, with an assurance of no further action, and no arrest for five years, the appellant's expectation that he could continue to lawfully possess the items was reasonable. Fourthly, there would not appear to have been any material change in the circumstances surrounding his possession between 1999 and the date of his arrest.

1   See [2007] Crim LR 320 at 324.

2.43   Professor Choo, in his work on this doctrine,[1] additionally warns of the dangers of courts misinterpreting the second criteria in *Hamza*, in relation to detrimental reliance:

'What, then, does the requirement of "detriment" entail? In *Dean* the defendant clearly acted on the representation to his detriment, as "he gave repeated assistance to the police". Equally, a defendant may have acted to his detriment by providing, as a potential prosecution witness, a witness statement implicating someone else.[2] In *Bloomfield*, however, it does not seem possible to isolate from the decision any hint of what tangible "detriment" the defendant may have been considered to have suffered. Perhaps the best approach may be to treat the "detriment" requirement as superfluous and to remove it altogether, since otherwise there is a danger that in time it may come to be misinterpreted as a requirement for a showing of forensic prejudice or disadvantage.'

The authors see force in the critical commentaries of the *Hamza* decision on this one aspect, and suggest that, in spite of the apparent ambiguity, it is inconceivable that the court actually meant to take away a defendant's right to argue abuse of process on the basis of a breach of promise in a *Bloomfield* situation, for example, where there was no forensic prejudice to the defendant. Indeed, in a number of the cases considered in this chapter, there was no detrimental reliance on a representation, nor any forensic prejudice, albeit that the cases merited stays of the proceedings. This is because these cases were stayed on the basis of considerations immersed, not in prejudice, but in the protection of the integrity of the courts' process, and the avoidance of the administration of justice being brought into disrepute.

1   Andrew L-T Choo, *Abuse of Process and Judicial Stays of Criminal Proceedings* (2nd Edn) (Oxford University Press, 2008).
2   *R v Townsend* [1997] 2 Cr App R 540.

2.44   Indeed, the Lord Chief Justice, in a preceding paragraph in the *Hamza* judgment,[1] acknowledged the difficulties in formulating a proper test, as follows:

'As the judge held, circumstances can arise where it will be an abuse of process to prosecute a man for conduct in respect of which he has been given an assurance that no prosecution will be brought. It is by no means easy to define a test for those circumstances, other than to say that they must be such as to render the proposed prosecution an affront to justice. The judge expressed reservations as to the extent to which one can apply the common law principle of "legitimate expectation" in this field, and we share those reservations. That principle usually applies to the expectation generated in respect of the exercise of an administrative discretion by or on behalf of the person whose duty it is to exercise that discretion. The duty to prosecute offenders cannot be treated as an administrative discretion, for it is usually in the public interest that those who are reasonably suspected of criminal conduct should be brought to trial. Only in rare circumstances will it be offensive to justice to give effect to this public interest.'

In reality, the Court was simply reiterating, and re-emphasising, the exceptional nature of the application of the circumstances which would lead to a *Beckford* limb two strand of abuse of process. In any event, any concerns which there may have been as to whether this late 2006 judgment may have led to a narrowing of the principles, appear to be ill-founded, given that the court's criteria do not appear to have been followed in subsequent cases, at least to date. Whilst there is no doubt a judicial trend towards 'requiring proof of detrimental reliance,'[2] courts must be wary not to see this as a prerequisite for a stay. There will be cases in the future where there is no obvious, tangible, or discernible prejudice, which nevertheless strike at the core of justice and the heart of unfairness. In these instances, the Judiciary will have the ever-continuing challenge of exercising their judgment as to whether the 'exceptional' threshold has been breached.

1   See para 50 of the judgment.
2   See Professor Ormerod's commentary on the *Hamza* decision, [2007] Crim LR 324.

PROMISES TO OFFER NO EVIDENCE

2.45   In a handful of decisions, the courts have found abuse to apply where, post-charge, the Crown have reneged on promises to offer no evidence.

2.46   *Bloomfield*[1] was an example of a volte face by the prosecution. At a plea and directions hearing in the Crown Court, the prosecution counsel indicated to defence counsel that the Crown wished to offer no evidence. It was accepted that the defendant had been the victim of a set-up. Prosecution counsel confirmed this intention in the trial judge's room. However, it was said that it would be embarrassing to the police and prosecution if no evidence were offered that day, and so the judge was invited, in open court, to adjourn the case and re-list it 'for mention'. The judge duly obliged with the agreement of the defence. However, in the intervening period the CPS arranged a conference with a new prosecution counsel who advised differently and then declared its intention to proceed with the prosecution.

1   [1997] 1 Cr App Rep 135, CA.

2.47   In the Court of Appeal the prosecution counsel, save for stating that the first prosecuting counsel's indication was unauthorised, did not attempt to demonstrate that the original decision was wrong. It would appear that the only hint as to CPS thinking was reference being made first to the fact that the CPS representative was not present in court when the original action was taken and second, that the first prosecutor was 'inexperienced'.

2.48   Staughton LJ, in allowing the appeal on an abuse submission, held:

'... whether or not there was prejudice to the defendant, it would bring the administration of justice into disrepute to allow the Crown to revoke its original decision without any reason being given as to what was wrong with it, particularly as it was made coram judice ... [and] ... That neither the court nor defendant could be expected to enquire whether prosecution counsel had authority to conduct a case in court in any particular way and they were therefore entitled to assume in ordinary circumstances that counsel did have such authority'.

2.49   It is clear that what particularly offended the court's sense of propriety in *Bloomfield*, was the stark manner in which the CPS appeared to treat the court. Staughton LJ emphasised that the statement by the first prosecution counsel was not merely a statement to the defendant or to his legal representative, it was also made in the presence of the judge. This point, in Staughton LJ's opinion, was so significant that considerations of prejudice became immaterial:

> 'it seems to us that whether or not there was prejudice it would bring the administration of justice into disrepute if the Crown Prosecution Service were able to treat the courts as if it were at its beck and call, free to tell it one day that it was not going to prosecute and another day that it was'.

2.50   *Bloomfield* was applied by Auld LJ in *R v Wyatt*[1] where prosecuting counsel informed the judge that, 'depending on the results of the DNA evidence the Crown may be in a position to take a different view which would be in the defendant's favour'. In other words, prosecuting counsel had made plain that if the DNA evidence was found not to incriminate the defendant, the case would be dropped. Eventually, the DNA analyses was forthcoming which was not incriminatory. However, the CPS decided that rather than discontinue the proceedings against the defendant, a new but less serious count to the indictment should be added. The trial judge held that the proceedings should not be stayed because there was no evidence that the defendant could not have a fair trial in relation to the new lesser charge.

1   (1997) 3 Archbold News 2, CA.

2.51   In his judgment, Auld LJ emphasised that an abuse of process may arise, 'even though it may not affect the fairness of the trial, but is so unfair or wrong that the court should mark it by not allowing the prosecution to proceed'. Applying the facts of the case to this principle, Auld LJ held:

> 'it seems to us in the circumstances that the prosecution's very late change of tack when the matter came before the court was very unfair to the defence ... we take the view that the intervention by the CPS at that late stage, prevailing over counsel for the prosecution's better judgment, was unfortunate'.

2.52   In *Mahdi*[1] a stay was deemed appropriate where a change of judge on the adjourned hearing of a trial left a defendant to face a trial, which he should not have had to do, because of some confusion as to certain indications previously given to counsel. The assistant recorder, before whom the trial was re-listed, was not fully and properly informed as to the case history. Two senior judges had previously made plain their firm views as to whether the trial should proceed. Lord Taylor CJ in quashing the conviction, found that '... an injustice was inadvertently done to this appellant by reason of the lack of accurate information placed before the assistant recorder'. It should be added that the Court of Appeal stated, per curiam, that the case did not fall within the scope of the well-known authorities on abuse of process.

1   [1993] Crim LR 793.

2.53   In contrast to the principles embodied in *Bloomfield* it is, at first blush, difficult to reconcile the Divisional Court judgment in *R v DPP, ex p Burke*[1], where an applicant was refused an application for judicial review of the DPP's decision to reinstate a prosecution, the CPS having expressly discontinued proceedings. In *Burke* the applicant had been charged with indecent assault on a 13-year old child. After the Senior Crown Prosecutor, the Principal Crown Prosecutor and a further prosecutor reviewed the case and agreed that there should be no prosecution, the CPS informed the applicant's solicitor that they had decided to discontinue the prosecution, albeit that the formalities of preparing a notice of discontinuance would take a little while. This information was passed on to the applicant, on or about March 1996.

1   [1997] COD 169, DC.

2.54   In April 1996 the Senior Crown Prosecutor received a complaint from the complainant's mother, about the decision to discontinue. While the Branch Crown Prosecutor, to whom the matter had been referred, concluded that the Senior Crown Prosecutor had made the wrong decision, nevertheless it was decided to issue a notice of discontinuance, given that the applicant had already been so informed. The standard form discontinuance letter included the words: 'Exceptionally, if further significant evidence were to become available at a later date this decision may be reconsidered'. While no further significant evidence apparently came to light, significant further discussions took place. The complainant's mother complained to the Prime Minister and her complaints were passed on to the Attorney-General and then the Director of Public Prosecutions. The outcome was that the DPP decided to reinstate the prosecution, the applicant was informed, and a fresh summons issued. While no submissions as to abuse of process were made, the applicant sought judicial review of the DPP's decision, inter alia, on the grounds that he had a legitimate expectation that the prosecution would not be reinstated unless fresh evidence emerged (which it had not).

2.55   While Phillips LJ acknowledged that 'legitimate expectation' was an aspect of fairness, he concluded that the terms of the discontinuance letter were not designed to lead the applicant to believe that he was free of jeopardy. A simple question arises however. What would any ordinary person conclude on receipt of such a letter? Leaving aside a new evidence situation, would one not reasonably conclude that that was the end of the case? Should one be expected to anticipate that the CPS may well, as occurred here, take a different decision at a later date? It is a moot point whether the same decision would have been reached had unfairness been considered in the context of the abuse of process authorities, as opposed to the administrative law ones which were apparently argued before the court. One suspects that the applicant may have been more successful had he argued the public interest in holding the CPS to account for, in effect, a broken promise, where they failed to keep their side of the bargain. It was not an ill-considered notice of discontinuance, served by some administrative error. It resulted from a conscious decision by a high ranking prosecutor.

2.56   The important case of *R v Horseferry Road Magistrates' Court, ex p DPP*[1] serves to highlight the fact that not all broken promises will be sufficient to justify a stay. In that case, a 'relatively junior' police officer told a representative of the defendant's solicitors (so the magistrate found) that he would not be charged in relation to an alleged fraudulent conspiracy. A year later, he was told he would be charged. The magistrate stayed the proceedings as an abuse of process, in apparent reliance on the principles of *Dean*. However, the Divisional Court subsequently concluded that she had been wrong so to do. The court held that it was not possible to say that a breach of an assurance not to prosecute necessarily justified a stay. Earlier cases were distinguished on the facts by reason of their special features, such as the youth of the defendant, and the assistance he had given to police in *Dean* and in *Bloomfield,* the fact that the assurance had been given in the presence of a judge.

1   (1999) 7 Archbold News, 8 March 1999.

2.57   In the course of their respective judgments in *ex p DPP* Kennedy LJ and Blofeld J emphasised the exceptional nature of the abuse jurisdiction. Blofeld J quoted Lord Lowry's judgment in *Bennett* where he said:

> 'the jurisdiction to stay must be exercised carefully and sparingly and only for very compelling reasons. The discretion to stay is not a disciplinary jurisdiction and ought not to be exercised in order to express the court's disapproval of official conduct'[1].

1   *R v Horseferry Road Magistrates' Court, ex p Bennett* [1994] AC 42 at 74.

2.58   In the course of his judgment, Kennedy LJ clearly implied that, for a breach of assurance type abuse submission to succeed, the defence must pass the high hurdle of 'special circumstances' or 'special features', which were found to be lacking in that particular case.

2.59   In the case of *R*[1] the Court of Appeal were required to consider the unusual circumstances of an appellant who, having been convicted of offences of conspiracy to rob and kidnapping, received a letter from the CPS expressing the opinion that the convictions were unsafe. The case was duly listed on the understanding that the Crown would not contest the appeal. However, shortly before the date of hearing, the Crown withdrew the concession in the light of advice from counsel. Whilst recognising this highly unsatisfactory position, the court rejected the appellant's argument that the withdrawal constituted an abuse of process. The court distinguished the *Bloomfield*-type authorities on the basis that, whereas they concerned the control of the Crown's power to pursue a criminal prosecution, this case concerned the Court of Appeal's own duty to determine the safety of convictions. It appears that the appellant, having learnt of the CPS's earlier stance, was specifically advised that the final decision over the quashing of the convictions, remained with the Court of Appeal itself.

1   *R* (2000) 4 Archbold News, 12 November 1999, CA.

2.60   A further example of a revised or re-visited prosecution opinion is apparent in the decision of *R v Murphy*(*Graham*),[1] where the defence sought to argue *Bloomfield/Dean* on appeal. On the facts, it was an argument with little merit, which does not even appear to have been made at trial. In the Magistrates Court the appellant had faced two charges alleging sexual assaults, one on a boy, the other on a girl. At the Magistrates stage, the prosecution decided to proceed solely on the charge relating to the girl. However, when the case reached the Crown Court, Counsel added a second count reinstating the charge on the boy. This was done at a plea and directions hearing without any objection from the defence. Subsequently, the appellant was acquitted of the charge in relation to the girl, but convicted on the count re the boy. The court held that there could not be a rule which meant that an early decision in the Magistrates Court not to proceed on one charge, absent further evidence, could never be re-visited by Prosecution Counsel in the Crown Court, even in circumstances where there was no fresh evidence. This was not a situation where no evidence was offered, but instead one where a charge was withdrawn. The court pointed out that the withdrawal of a summons or charge was not a bar to the issue of a further summons in the same matter.

1   [2003] Crim LR 471.

2.61   In the 2004 decision of *R v Mulla*[1] one has an example of a case which is easily distinguishable on the facts of *Bloomfield*. In this matter, the appellant's case was listed for trial on a charge of causing death by dangerous driving. However, on the morning of trial, prosecuting counsel indicated that they were prepared to accept a plea to the lesser offence of careless driving. When the prosecution counsel told the Judge of his intention to accept the plea to careless driving, the Judge required him to refer the matter back for reconsideration by a senior member of the Crown Prosecution Service. By 2.15pm the same day, prosecution Counsel, having acted as requested, indicated he proposed to proceed with the original more serious charge. The Court of Appeal subsequently dismissed the appeal which followed, with little difficulty. First, the appellant had been aware from the outset that the Judge had not been content with the position, which was clearly some way from being determined or resolved. Secondly, the period of time over which it took prosecution counsel to change his position was very short. Thirdly, there had been no apparent prejudice to the appellant by reason of the change of course.

1   [2004] 1 Cr App R 6, at p 72.

2.62   In the course of his judgment, Rose LJ (Vice President)[1] held that the fact the prosecution had indicated to the Court what its view was, was only one of the factors to be considered, and then helpfully added:

> 'Other factors include what view is expressed by the judge when the prosecution gives its indication, the period of time over which the prosecution reconsiders the matter, before they change their mind, whether or not the defendant's hopes have been inappropriately raised, and whether there has been, by reason of the change of course by the prosecution, any prejudice to the defence.'

1   See p 77 of the CAR report.

2.63   The importance of the principle that an accused should, as a general rule, be able to rely on a prosecutorial decision was further underlined in the 2004 decision of *Taylor*.[1] This case involved a prosecution appeal by case stated against a Magistrates Court's decision to stay an information for careless driving. The case concerned a tragic motor accident, involving Taylor, a bus driver, and another driver who was killed, where both drivers were apparently at fault. On 12 June 2003 Taylor was notified in writing that he would not be prosecuted. However, on 18 July 2003, he was told that he would be so prosecuted. Mitting J, in ruling in favour of the defence on appeal, took the view that the original decision to prosecute, which had been reviewed by three prosecutors, must have been based, at least in part, on public interest grounds. The court found that the Magistrates were entitled to stay the proceedings on the basis of *Bloomfield*, which was accepted to be an authority for the proposition that no prejudice was required to be shown for a case to be abusive. This was not a case where there was found to be a mistaken prosecution approach to the review of their evidential test, which would have justified a change of decision under the CPS Code. The change of decision appears to have followed representations from the family of the deceased driver, which is akin to the situation in the *Burke* case cited previously.

1   *Director of Public Prosecutions v Taylor* [2004] EWHC 1554 (Admin).

2.64   Finally, the 2008 decision of *R (on the application of H) v Guildford Youth Court* is reviewed.[1] H's appeal, against the Youth Court's decision to refuse to stay a prosecution against him for an offence of assault,[2] was not contested. Before his police interview, the 15 year old, H, was told that it was possible to resolve the matter, which concerned a fellow school pupil, by way of a final warning. During the interview itself, H went on to admit the offence, and put forward his account of events, whereupon the officer explained he would seek to have the matter resolved that day, and that, on the date he was due to return on bail, the matter would be dealt with by way of a final warning. Some three months later, he was formally charged with the offence, the police having indicated, in the intervening period, that a final warning might not be appropriate. In allowing the appeal, Silber J, taking account of the principles set down in *Chu Piu-Wing* and *Bloomfield*, considered that there was a clear public interest in upholding the promise made by an officer of the state. Significant factors were no doubt the fact that the officer who made the promise was, at that key stage, in charge of deciding whether or not to prosecute, and also the young age of the appellant.

1   [2008] EWHC 506 (Admin).
2   Offences Against the Persons Act 1861, s 20.

PROMISES ON ACCEPTABLE PLEAS

2.65   While formal American style plea-bargaining is not part of our system, it is an everyday licit practice by the prosecution and defence to broker pleas in order to 'carve the indictment' and so avoid a trial. A considerable amount of time and money is no doubt saved as pragmatic considerations impact on the criminal justice system. Judges are routinely asked to provide sentence indications for specific guilty pleas. It is a practical balancing task, carried out in the public interest, where consideration is keenly given to sentencing levels in respect of various different offences. In the 2005 decision of *R v Goodyear*,[1] a five-Judge Court of Appeal provided detailed guidance in relation to the giving of advance indications of sentence. The procedure should take place in public in open court, where both prosecution and defence are represented, with full recording of proceedings. Prosecutors should now be well versed in the Attorney General's Guidelines on the Acceptance of Pleas, which were updated in 2005, and in the 2004 Code for Crown Prosecutors.

1   [2005] 2 Cr App R 20.

2.66   For any system of plea negotiations to work, of course, it is expected that the prosecution will keep their side of the bargain, particularly where they agree on acceptable pleas. *R v Thomas*[1] is one such case where the Crown failed to keep their side of a bargain. In *Thomas* at a pleas hearing, the defendant pleaded not guilty to offences of s 18 wounding, ABH and affray, but pleaded guilty on a qualified basis to the alternative s 20 charge. Prior to such a hearing the CPS had indicated in unequivocal terms, in response to a letter from defence solicitors, that such a proposed plea was acceptable to the Crown. At the Crown Court hearing, the plea having been so entered, the counsel for the Crown then told the court that the plea was not acceptable to him and that he sought a trial.

1   [1995] Crim LR 938.

2.67   In this first instance decision the court, in holding that there was an abuse, re-emphasised the principle of holding officials of the State to promises made. Whether or not the CPS indication was justifiable, the fact was that the defendant had seriously prejudiced his position by tendering a guilty plea to the s 20 offence. The defendant, of course, may not have tendered a guilty plea at all had it not been for the CPS correspondence.

2.68   This principle was re-affirmed by the Divisional Court in the recent decision of *DPP v Edgar*[1]. In that case the defendant was charged with three road traffic offences, namely, excess alcohol, failing to stop and failing to report. When she pleaded guilty to the latter two offences, the prosecution applied to withdraw the excess alcohol charge. Having retired to consider sentence, the justices returned into court, at the invitation of the prosecutor, who now wished to reinstate the alcohol charge! Whilst the charge was reinstated, the defence subsequently succeeded on an abuse submission, and the prosecutor duly appealed by way of case stated.

1   *DPP v Edgar* (2000) 164 JP 471, DC: see also the critical commentary at [2000] 31 CLW, 14 August.

2.69   In dismissing the prosecutor's appeal, Schiemann LJ stated that:

'For my part, the consideration that is uppermost in my mind, and one suspects was uppermost in the justices' minds, is that compromises of this kind between prosecution and defence, where the defence agrees to plead to some charges in return for the prosecution dropping others, are a commonplace of our criminal proceedings and they occur in magistrates' courts and Crown Courts. It is important in principle that such compromises should generally be stuck to and the integrity of the criminal process requires that they should be'.

OTHER PROMISES

2.70   In addition to the three above-mentioned areas where this category of abuse has been deemed applicable, there are a number of other areas worthy of attention:

(1)   Prosecution promises not to call a witness;

(2)   The prosecution code for 're-starting a prosecution';

(3)   Police cautions;

(4)   Crown divisibility;

(5)   Implied promises.

Prosecution promises not to call a witness

2.71   In the decision of *R v Drury, Clark*[1] the defence made a bold, albeit unsurprisingly unsuccessful, attempt to extend this abuse jurisdiction to include a failure by the Crown to keep its promise to call a particular witness at trial. The case concerned police officers who were indicted for offences of conspiracy to supply Class B drugs and perverting the course of public justice. One of the key witnesses against them was a co-accused, 'F', who had pleaded guilty, and was due to give evidence for the Crown prior to her sentence, the witness being a registered police informant. Upon the discharge of the jury at trial (due to difficulties with F giving evidence), the prosecutor made an unequivocal promise in court that the witness would not be called, at the re-trial, 'under any circumstances'. Upon the re-trial, however, the Crown called the witness (who, by then, was willing to give evidence) and the defendants were convicted.

1   *R v Drury, Clark* [2001] EWCA Crim 975, [2001] Crim LR 847.

2.72   In dismissing the appeals, the Court of Appeal highlighted the fundamental difference between calling a witness in support of a count, as against proceeding on the count in the first place. Whilst the Crown had stated that F was not to be called, nevertheless there was seemingly no suggestion that it would be improper to proceed even if she were content to give evidence. Indeed, there was no real detriment caused to the defendants on account of the witness's altered position. Accordingly, the authors agree with David Ormerod's commentary that:

> 'It would have been a significant extension of existing case law to hold that reneging on such a limited promise renders it unfair to try the accused or that a fair trial was impossible'[1].

1   [2001] EWCA Crim 975, [2001] Crim LR 847.

The prosecution code for 're-starting a prosecution'

2.73   The latest 2004 edition of the code for Crown Prosecutors,which was originally produced pursuant to the Prosecution of Offences Act 1985, s 10(1) is a public document and available on the CPS website.[1] The code, as was pointed out by Staughton LJ in *Bloomfield,* is not law, nor is it delegated legislation. It is simply a code which gives guidance on general principles for Crown Prosecutors, issued by the DPP. Part 12 is entitled 'Re-starting a prosecution' and reads as follows:

'12.1 People should be able to rely on decisions taken by the Crown Prosecution Service. Normally if the Crown Prosecution Service tells a suspect or defendant that there will not be a prosecution, or that the prosecution has been stopped, that is the end of the matter and the case will not start again. But occasionally there are special reasons why the Crown Prosecution Service will re-start the prosecution, particularly if the case is serious.

12.2 These reasons include:

(a)   rare cases where a new look at the original decision shows that it was clearly wrong and should not be allowed to stand;

(b)   cases which are stopped so that more evidence which is likely to become available in the fairly near future can be collected and prepared. In these cases the Crown Prosecutor will tell the defendant that the prosecution may well start again;

(c)   cases which are stopped because of a lack of evidence but where more significant evidence is discovered later.

12.3 There may also be exceptional cases in which, following an acquittal of a serious offence, the Crown Prosecutor may, with the written consent of the Director of Public Prosecutions, apply to the Court of Appeal for an order quashing the acquittal and requiring the defendant to be retried, in accordance with Part 10 of the Criminal Justice Act 2003.'

1   See www.cps.gov.uk; it is also found at Appendix A of this work.

The Crown Prosecution Service Legal Guidance on the 'Re-institution of Proceedings'

2.74   On the CPS website, further guidance is given as to the approach prosecutors should adopt when considering cases which may require the re-institution of proceedings. This is a useful piece of guidance which is set out in full at Appendix B of this book. The section on 'Fundamental principles' reads as follows:

'There is a presumption that once a suspect is informed of a decision not to prosecute, s/he is entitled to rely on that decision. Therefore, such a decision should not ordinarily be revoked. A decision to reinstitute proceedings can only be justified in those exceptional cases that fall into one of the following categories:

i.   Where the decision not to prosecute was taken, and expressed to be taken, on the ground that there was insufficient evidence and **further significant evidence** comes to light (see section 23(9) of the

Prosecution of Offences Act 1985 for the residual power to re-institute proceedings in this category); or

ii. Where **special circumstances** exist that require the re-institution of proceedings to maintain public confidence in the criminal justice system.

The accused should be informed promptly of any decision to reinstitute proceedings.'

During the course of the 'Legal Guidance', the purpose of the guidance is explained, as are the situations which are not covered. What is meant by 'fresh or further evidence ' is dealt with, and the phrase 'special circumstances' is defined. The guidance also goes into 'procedure', and as to how decisions to terminate proceedings should be explained at the different stages; namely, at the (1) Charging/reporting stage, (2) the Pre-Court stage and (3) the Court stage. It also makes clear that one of the factors prosecutors should consider when deciding whether to re-institute proceedings, in addition to taking the views of the victim, and witnesses, and considering any issue over delay, is the question of potential abuse of process arguments. Prosecutors therefore will be expected to be fully au fait with the latest abuse of process case law.

2.75 The tenor of the code and guidance appears to indicate that a decision to re-start proceedings will most likely only occur in rare and exceptional cases, of some gravity. For a defence lawyer who is considering whether an abuse point arises, and who seeks to challenge the reinstitution of proceedings, the first step must be to consider the circumstances in which the case came to a halt, albeit temporarily. Were proceedings discontinued in court, or in writing, or in both? Was the client discharged in the magistrates' court after a contested hearing where evidence had been called, or submissions had been made and argued, or after a review hearing where committal or transfer papers were not prepared in time? The CPS's legal guidance on re-institution expressly excludes from the Attorney General's undertaking decisions to offer no evidence at committal proceedings, and decisions to withdraw transfer proceedings where the court has refused an adjournment. If there was a formal notice of discontinuance in writing from the CPS, it is submitted that the terms of it are crucial to the consideration of an abuse point.

2.76 Where the CPS discontinue on the basis of a particular stated reason, and then on some occasion thereafter seek to restart proceedings on the basis of a different reason altogether, an abuse question may well arise. If, for example, a defendant is told that proceedings are being discontinued due to lack of evidence (with a warning that they may reinstate if more evidence emerges later) and then, after several months, he is told they have no additional evidence but they have decided the first decision was in error, a feeling of injustice may well lead to a successful abuse submission.

2.77 While the terms of the discontinuance letter did not assist the applicant in *Burke*, nevertheless Phillips LJ, in the Divisional Court, expressed his own view that it would be more satisfactory if the CPS standard letter of discontinuance annexed the relevant part of the prosecutor's code 'by way of explanation of the circumstances in which the prosecution might be reinstated'. While this suggestion has much to commend it, and might reduce the number of potential abuse cases, it is submitted that such quasi 'exemption clauses' cannot necessarily prevent unfairness to an accused. Indeed, it is submitted that if the CPS are discontinuing for a particular reason they should say so whenever possible. It may well be argued that to allow the CPS the use of a standard discontinuance letter, which warns of every eventuality (whereby proceedings may be resurrected) is a carte blanche to encourage them to restart in circumstances where it would be unjust.

2.78   Practitioners may also need to consider the operation of the Prosecution of Offences Act 1985, ss 22A and 22B, which were inserted into the Act by virtue of the Crime and Disorder Act 1998, ss 44 and 45. Whereas the declared objective of the legislation is to expedite the trials of offenders under the age of 18, s 22B confers the power on Chief Crown Prosecutors to institute fresh proceedings in circumstances where the original proceedings have been stayed under s 22A(5), as a result of the expiry of the initial stage time limit. Section 22B(5) has been amended by the Criminal Justice Act 2003, s 331.

2.79   In *R (on the application of the DPP) v Croydon Youth Court*[1] a prosecution against a young person had been stayed in the light of an expired 99-day time limit [now revoked], in circumstances where an extension had been refused because the Crown had failed to act with 'all due diligence and expedition'. The Crown re-instituted proceedings under s 22B and the justices duly stayed them as an abuse of process. The Divisional Court, in quashing the justices' decision to stay, did so in spite of the fact that the trial date was listed 300 days after the first court appearance, thus holding that a fair trial was still possible. One curious omission from Poole J's judgment in this decision is the lack of any reference to the alternative basis for a stay, namely the second limb, whereby in spite of the fact a fair trial was possible, it was unfair to try him. As James Richardson noted, in his commentary on the case:

> 'Where proceedings have been stayed on the expiry of a time limit, there must be some scope for some such argument, otherwise the time-limit provisions will be rendered completely pointless. To take an extreme example, if the facts justified the inference that the prosecution had made no effort to comply with the time-limit provisions in the knowledge that, in the event of a stay, the prosecution could be re-instituted, there would surely be the basis of an argument that this constituted such a manipulation of the processes of the court as to warrant a stay'.[2]

1   (2001) 165 JP 181, DC.
2   See [2001] 4 CLW, 29 January.

Police cautions

2.80   In the two decisions discussed below, the Courts have been required to consider cases where private prosecutions were brought against individuals who had previously accepted police cautions in relation to the same charges.

Firstly, we consider the *Hayter* decision.[1] In *Hayter* the police took the view that two 16-year-old defendants, who had been arrested for threatening unlawful violence and assault, could properly be cautioned for the offences, as a means of disposing of the prosecution. Each defendant received legal advice, admitted his involvement in the offences, signed a form indicating that a caution did not preclude the commencement of proceedings against him by an aggrieved party, and was then duly cautioned. The victim's father proceeded to bring a private prosecution against the defendants in the Youth Court. In due course, the Youth Court ordered that the proceedings be stayed as an abuse of process and dismissed the informations. The prosecutor appealed by way of case stated to the Divisional Court. It was held, allowing the appeal, 'that it was not an abuse of process to prosecute a defendant after he had been cautioned by the police unless the particular circumstances of a case disclosed an abuse'.

1   *Hayter v L* [1998] 1 WLR 854, QBD.

2.81   In *Hayter* the defendants were apparently well aware that further criminal proceedings were not precluded, and the court found no unfairness to result from the private prosecution. Indeed, Poole J pointed out that the trial process contained sufficient 'common law and statutory mechanisms to ensure fairness' in reference to the defence's opportunity to apply for exclusion of the evidence of the caution, in the event of the Crown seeking to admit it as evidence of an admission. This was a reference to the court's discretion, at common law, and under PACE, s 78, to exclude evidence.

2.82   In the 2006 House of Lords decision of *Jones v Whalley*[1] the appellant, Whalley, had assaulted and injured Jones. Having admitted the offence of assault in interview, the police officer decided that he should be formally cautioned rather than prosecuted. He was informed that the effect of a caution was that he would not have to go before a Criminal Court in connection with the matter. However, some time later, Jones brought a private prosecution against him in respect of the assault. The CPS declined to take over the prosecution of the case. In due course, the Justices, on hearing of the circumstances, stayed the proceedings as an abuse of process. Jones's appeal by case stated to the Divisional Court succeeded, but, in turn, Whalley's appeal to the House of Lords was allowed, thus reversing the Divisional Court's decision.

1   [2007] 1 Cr App R 2.

2.83   In the House of Lords, Lord Bingham agreed with the justices' conclusion, and held:

'The abuse complained of is not abuse impairing the fairness of the trial, since evidence of the admission and caution should be excluded. The abuse complained of goes, as in ... *Ex parte Bennett* ... to the fairness of trying Mr. Whalley at all in the circumstances.'

2.84   The appeal was decided on what was termed, the 'narrower issue,' namely as to whether a private prosecution may or should be regarded as an abuse of process of the Magistrates' Court where the defendant has agreed to be formally cautioned by the police on the assurance that, if he agrees, he will not have to go before a criminal court. The 'broader issue', which was not decided upon, related to an arguable challenge to the *Hayter* decision, and was put forward by Counsel for Whalley.

2.85   Whalley's Counsel questioned whether, irrespective of what may be said to, or stated in a form given to, a person who is cautioned, conditionally cautioned, reprimanded or warned, it can ever be other than an abuse of process for a court thereafter to entertain a private prosecution against him. Lord Brown and Lord Mance were of the view that, until this broader issue was finally resolved, either by litigation or legislation, some form of modified *Hayter* warning would be helpful, to the effect that the police told an individual receiving a caution, that: 'the caution may not preclude a private prosecution and will not preclude a civil action'. Lord Mance added that the individual should further be advised of the court's power to stay a private prosecution in the event that it finds, despite the warning, it would be abusive for them to continue. Finally, both Lord Bingham and Lord Rodger went on to question the surviving right of private prosecution. Lord Rodger held that:

> ' ... it seems to me that allowing private prosecutions to proceed, despite an assurance that the offender would not have to go to court, would tend to undermine not only the non-statutory system of cautions, but also the schemes for cautioning young offenders and adult offenders which Parliament has endorsed in the Crime and Disorder Act 1998 and the Criminal Justice Act 2003. A court is entitled to ensure that its process is not misused in this way.'[1]

1   See ss 22 and 23, CJA 2003; See the Code of Practice on Conditional Cautioning, and the Home Office Circular 30/2005 on the Cautioning of Adult Offenders.

2.86   While one can understand why the appellants failed in the *Hayter* case on the facts, nevertheless one can equally envisage a different outcome where there was no legal advice prior to the acceptance of the caution, where an unrepresented defendant was not advised by police that a prosecution (be it private or instituted by the CPS or one of the other prosecution agencies) could still take place, or where a defendant did not sign or read a form which explained the correct position, that is, that they may still be in jeopardy of prosecution. Given the large number of individuals who are routinely cautioned in the criminal justice system, there is likely to be further litigation on this topic.

Crown divisibility

2.87   The concept of 'the Crown' or of 'the prosecution' has been in a state of evolution. The ambit of the concept became important in the area of criminal law in connection with the prosecution's common law duty of disclosure. Here the courts were concerned in particular cases to expand the concept so that, for example, forensic scientists were covered. In *R v Liverpool Crown Court, ex p Roberts*[1] Glidewell LJ referred to the 'total apparatus of prosecution'. In *Blackledge,*[2] Taylor CJ referred to the Crown as an 'indivisible unity.'

1   [1986] Crim LR 622.
2   [1996] 1 Cr App Rep 326.

2.88   The concept of an indivisible Crown or, in reality, an indivisible State has not taken root in criminal law, perhaps recognising that the State is composed not only of separate government departments with their separate and possibly conflicting aims and policies, but also composed of an increasing variety of semi-autonomous bodies and agencies. These bodies are the Crown Prosecution Service, the HMRC, the Health and Safety Executive and so on, all of which carry out the public function of criminal investigation and prosecution. Even within these bodies, however, there may be a disparity of function: for example the Inland Revenue is not primarily a prosecutorial agency and the investigation and prosecution of tax fraud is not one of its highest priorities.

2.89   In *R v W*[1] the two applicants were facing trial for conspiracy to defraud. At a preparatory hearing the defence submitted that the Crown was not empowered to prosecute and, further, that the proceedings were an abuse of process. The applicants appealed to the Court of Appeal to challenge the trial judge's first preparatory ruling that the Crown was so empowered. The prosecution case alleged a time-share fraud whereby large amounts of corporation and income tax were said to have been evaded. While the criminal proceedings commenced in 1996, in 1997 the Inland Revenue agreed to accept a large settlement in relation to the company's tax liability.

1   [1998] STC 550, CA.

2.90   The defence argued that if the Crown, through the Inland Revenue, had elected not to prosecute for tax evasion but instead to accept tax, penalties and interest, then it followed that the Crown through the CPS were not empowered or entitled to ignore that election. The defence sought to stress the apparent fact that the Inland Revenue, in deciding not to prosecute, had liaised with the DTI, the Police Commercial Fraud Squad and the CPS. At some stage, however, whereas the Inland Revenue took the view that a £3.5m transfer on bogus invoices could be regarded as a loan, the CPS took the view that the transfers gave rise to theft!

2.91   The question posed was whether, given that two linked government departments took different views, a criminal prosecution could proceed. Rose LJ, while dismissing the appeal for jurisdictional reasons, gave a ruling on Crown divisibility, albeit obiter. The court held that the Crown was divisible, in essence, because both branches were pursuing separate agendas and policies.

2.92   While this was not an abuse case on the facts, Rose LJ commented:

'Of course, Crown indivisibility may well be pertinent to a claim for abuse of process if, for example, the CPS were to prosecute when the Revenue, in accepting settlement from a taxpayer, had told him with the concurrence of the CPS, that he would not be prosecuted by anyone.'

2.93   In so commenting, Rose LJ was rightly acknowledging that, in certain cases, one can readily contemplate the Revenue binding the CPS, in the same way that police officers bound the CPS in *Dean*: see paras **2.20–2.28**. On the facts, it is submitted that the court adopted a realistic approach, given that the applicants had not been misled. Grey areas will no doubt continue to flourish, however, particularly in relation to cases of suspected serious tax fraud where the Inland Revenue's 'Hansard' policy comes into play.[1] For, as was recently said:

> 'Although the statement makes it clear that the Board reserves to itself full discretion as to which course of action it takes, and the statement does not guarantee immunity from prosecution, in practice, once the Hansard statement is given, prosecutions are rare'.[2]

1   The Hansard policy is the system whereby where serious fraud is suspected, the Board may in certain circumstances accept a money settlement instead of instituting legal proceedings in respect of fraud alleged to have been committed by a taxpayer.
2   See Elwes and Clutterbuck 'Tax and Criminal Prosecutions' [1999] Crim LR 139.

2.94   Where taxpayers have co-operated with the Revenue, perhaps having made confessions or declarations against their interest, only to find themselves being prosecuted, practitioners ought to carefully consider whether any express or implied assurances are evidenced, or even legitimate expectations breached. Where no argument lies as to abuse of process, consideration ought to be given to an application for judicial review in the rare circumstances where the decision of the CPS, to bring criminal proceedings, may be attacked on the basis that it was both unfair and contrary to the legitimate expectations of the taxpayer.[1]

1   See in particular the decisions of *R v IRC, ex p Mead* [1993] 1 All ER 772, and *R v IRC, ex p Allen* [1997] STC 1141; see also *R v IRC, ex p MKF Underwriters Agents Ltd* [1990] 1 WLR 1545. See also *R v Board of Inland Revenue, ex p Unilever* [1994] STC 841 and the *Postermobile* case in paras **2.35** and **2.36**.

Implied promises

2.95   In *Hinchliffe*[1] the defendant had faced CDDA proceedings launched against him by the DTI prior to his prosecution by the SFO. In the course of agreeing a settlement with the DTI he signed an agreed statement of facts. However, the admissions made by him in this court document were expressed as being made only for the purpose of the CDDA proceedings. Whilst the fact of his admissions did not play any part in the SFO's case, one of the co-accused nonetheless sought to introduce them and cross-examine him on them. Objection to this was made on the basis that H had only made the admissions on the basis of an implied promise that they would only be relevant as regards the CDDA proceedings. However both the trial judge and Court of Appeal allowed the admissions, dismissing this objection.

1   [2002] EWCA Civ 837.

CONCLUDING REMARKS

2.96   For the practitioner, who is considering the question as to whether or not a breach of promise point arises, there are a number of practical steps to follow. The first, logically, is to determine whether there is, or is not, a 'promise'. It need not simply be a promise in the strict sense, for an 'undertaking' or 'representation' will also suffice. The promise may either be a clear, unequivocal, express promise or one which is implied and inferred from the particular circumstances of a case.

2.97   The second step is to identify whether there is any evidence of a breach of the said promise. Needless to say, where there is no breach, there is no abuse.

2.98   Third, the practitioner may wish to determine whether any significant prejudice has been suffered by the accused. If such prejudice has been sustained that may well go to the fourth question, which relates to 'fairness'. In certain abuse cases, however, the absence of prejudice will not be fatal to a successful submission. Evidence of prejudice to the individual has been declared unnecessary in cases involving unfairness, in the sense of the prosecution process bringing the administration of justice into disrepute[1].

1   Per Staughton LJ in *Bloomfield* [1997] 1 Cr App Rep 135, CA.

2.99   The fourth step is to identify whether or not significant 'unfairness' has resulted. Indeed, by no means every breach of an assurance or promise will satisfy the test of unfairness. In order to attain the threshold of unfairness, practitioners will have to demonstrate that the circumstances are sufficiently special or particular to justify a stay. In drawing together the strands identified in the case law, it is submitted that the courts have defined 'unfairness' from three particular perspectives, albeit there is a degree of overlap.

Unfairness to the accused

2.100   Was the act (or breach) manifestly unfair to the particular defendant or party to litigation? Was his position seriously prejudiced? These questions relate directly to whether or not a fair trial is possible.

Unfairness in the public perception

2.101   Would the act (or breach) bring the administration of justice into disrepute amongst right-thinking people? Is doubt cast on the bona fides of the prosecution? Lord Oliver, in the House of Lords decision in *Bennett*, considered this an important point when considering the *Dean*[1] authority (at p 132).

1   See the judgment of Lord Oliver in *R v Horseferry Road Magistrates' Court, ex p Bennett* [1993] 3 WLR 90 at 112F–H.

Unfairness from the judicial perspective

2.102   Does the act complained of offend the court's own sense of propriety and injustice? This view of unfairness is directly connected to the second strand of abuse identified by Neil LJ in *Beckford*. For in that second strand an abuse of process was said to relate to occasions where it would be unfair to try an accused, albeit a fair trial was yet possible.

2.103   Where the promise, breach, prejudice and unfairness come together, so comes about the makings of a submission with moral integrity. Promises are meant to be kept.

Chapter 3

The loss or destruction of evidence

BACKGROUND

3.01   At the cornerstone of our adversarial system is a belief that 'the search for the truth' in any criminal trial is best procured by combat between the two sides. The role of the criminal justice system through the provision of the various Codes of Practice, and availability of public funding for example, is to ensure that such combat is fair to both sides. If, therefore, the police enjoy a virtual monopoly over the investigation stage of a criminal offence, this advantage is to be ameliorated by an onerous obligation of disclosure to the defence post-charge. The 2005 Criminal Procedure rules state clearly that the overriding objective is that criminal cases be dealt with justly, and that the prosecution and defence should be dealt with fairly.[1] In ECHR jurisprudence the need to ensure a level playing-field, is summed up by the 'equality of arms' principle: despite unequal resources, no party should be allowed an unfair advantage over the other.

1   See r 1.1 of the Criminal Procedure Rules 2005

3.02   In the English system we strive to achieve the right balance between the opposing sides in order that the wrongly accused are acquitted and the guilty are convicted. This elusive balance and optimum state is ultimately the responsibility of judges who, in a concrete case, are obliged to do justice and serve fairness. An awareness of the recent celebrated miscarriage of justice cases, however, reveals that often judges are prevented from securing such noble objectives, prior to the trial, because evidence has been suppressed, lost, destroyed or perverted. This has the inevitable consequence that a trial which in all appearances is scrupulously fair and dignified is reduced to a charade where the search for the truth is an unachievable goal.

3.03   This chapter analyses the circumstances whereby the prosecution's failure to obtain and/or retain material evidence has led to applications to stay proceedings. This particular strand of the abuse of process jurisdiction has developed rapidly over the last few years, having regard both to the defining case law and the increased importance of the revised CPIA Codes in the light of the 2005 Attorney-General's guidelines. In this chapter we first consider the current state of the common law (with emphasis on the guideline decision in *R (on the application of Ebrahim) v Feltham Magistrates*[1]); second, trace back briefly over the historical development of the case law, and finally review the important CPIA Codes of Practice and the Attorney-General's guidelines on disclosure.

1   [2001] EWHC Admin 130, [2001] 1 All ER 831.

3.04   It will be within the experience of many practitioners, when preparing a case for trial, that they discover something is 'missing' from the case. Whether it is a witness who becomes untraceable, an exhibit which disappears, or an item of unused material one discovers has been destroyed, all manner of things can, and do, go wrong within the system. The simple question then arises, as to what to do? More often than not a solution will be at hand, or at least a feasible damage limitation exercise will arise, which will not compromise a fair trial.

3.05   If the problem is remediable, that is the end of the matter. If it is not, the practitioner logically should go on to question what damage, if any, it will necessarily cause to the client's case. If, for example, the damage related to the prosecution's accidental destruction of a prosecution exhibit (of vital importance to the defence case), the question then arises as to the extent of any prejudice this may result to the defence:

(1)   Does it seriously prejudice the preparation and conduct of the defence?

(2)   Is the problem remediable within the trial process? For example, by suitable judicial directions or by the regulation of admissibility of evidence.

(3)   Or is the dilemma so exceptional that the practitioner considers an abuse of process has been identified?

3.06   The above questions are relevant in determining whether the defence has sustained such serious prejudice that a fair trial is no longer possible. This is now described as a 'Category 1 case' in *Ebrahim*, the reference being derived from the first limb of Neil LJ's test in *Beckford*.[1] In the light of the *Ebrahim* decision the courts will have a further consideration to take into account when considering certain prosecution failures to obtain and/or retain material evidence. They may also have to consider whether the defence have proved 'either an element of bad faith or at the very least some serious fault on the part of the police or the prosecution authorities'. These issues will be relevant to the courts' determination as to whether a 'Category 2 case' arises, namely a circumstance where it would be unfair for a defendant to be tried, irrespective of whether a fair trial was possible. Again, from the above, it will be clear this description is taken from the second limb of Neil LJ's definition. Such consideration will relate to the more rare occasions where the integrity of the disclosure system is questioned and where the administration of justice is arguably being brought into disrepute.

1   [1996] 1 Cr App Rep 94.

CONTEXT

3.07   One concomitant of the prosecutions' duty of disclosure of both evidence and unused material is an obligation to preserve such material so that in due course it can be served or disclosed to the defence. An obligation of disclosure which did not also presuppose an obligation to retain material would be rendered otiose. This obligation to retain material also arises as a matter of practical necessity. It is the police who invariably conduct the first investigation into the circumstances of the alleged offence, gathering witness statements and collecting forensic samples and so on.

3.08 Our criminal justice system has not adopted the European model of an independent judge or magistrate supervising and directing a police investigation in an inquisitorial and even-handed manner. Accordingly, in most criminal cases, by the time the defendant has instructed lawyers and such lawyers have become familiar with the issues in the case, the evidential trail has gone cold. This virtual monopoly enjoyed by the police over the gathering and retention of material, however, also carries with it a problem when the question of the obligation to retain material is considered. Clearly, bearing in mind for example the rights of third parties to retain their property, the police cannot be expected to seize and retain everything that might possibly be of relevance and therefore judgements of relevance in the field during the course of an inquiry are inescapable. The practical problem, therefore, is always to determine on the basis of limited information what ought to be preserved, even seized, and what need not. A legal obligation of preserving relevant material is easy to accept and understand in the abstract but relevance in a concrete case may be very hard to determine.

3.09 Inevitably, from time to time, instances have occurred whereby the police/prosecution have lost or failed to preserve material which could have had a bearing on a defendant's case at trial. It can easily be understood how this lapse can lead to prejudice being caused to the defence. The line of cases, to be considered below, traces how the common law has grasped this problem in an abuse context. Increasingly, over the last 20 years both the Court of Appeal and the Divisional Court have had to consider a number of cases where the defence has, at first instance, made a failed abuse application relating to the destruction or loss by the prosecution of allegedly material evidence. On appeal, it has been contended that the trial judge wrongly refused the application and because of the loss of potentially exculpatory material, the defendant did not receive a fair trial. Unsurprisingly, however, these courts of review have been concerned to ensure that unscrupulous and opportunist defendants are prevented from either successfully making false claims concerning the purported prejudice suffered because of the loss by the prosecution or constructing false defences ex post facto based on knowledge of the unfortunate loss. This attitude of scepticism towards defence complaints of prejudice in these circumstances is consistent with that concerning defence complaints arising out of prosecutorial delay. In Chapter 1 the approach of Bingham CJ in *R v Cardiff Magistrates' Court, ex p Hole* was considered.[1] There Bingham CJ insisted that the defence, in arguing abuse, would have to establish precisely how in relation to the defence(s) to be advanced at trial prejudice was suffered, '... it is necessary to look at the charges and see exactly what defence it is that they are impeded from advancing'.

1   See para **1.83**.

3.10 In the light of *Ebrahim*'s focusing of initial attention on the question of investigating authorities' and prosecutor's 'duties', this chapter closes with a scrutiny of the true nature and extent of such 'duties'. We end by considering the more proactive disclosure duties and pose the question as to whether a failure to investigate a case properly can lead to an application to stay proceedings. Let us first consider the state of the common law as it now stands.

THE CURRENT STATE OF THE COMMON LAW

3.11   In *R (on the application of Ebrahim) v Feltham Magistrates*, and the linked case of *Mouat v DPP* (hereinafter called simply *Ebrahim*), the Divisional Court delivered the first clear and authoritative guideline judgment on the circumstances where lost or destroyed video material may lead to an abuse of process application. This important decision was partly motivated by the courts' ever increasing workload of cases based on defence complaints of lost or unavailable CCTV footage. The authors suggest, however, that the principles contained in Brooke LJ's judgment in *Ebrahim* will not simply be limited to video cases. We suggest that, by analogy, they will have a far more general application to all manner of lost or destroyed material, whether it be used or unused.

3.12   Ebrahim's case involved his application for judicial review of a magistrate's decision to stay, on grounds of abuse of process, a prosecution against him for assault. Mouat's was an appeal by way of case stated from a Crown Court judge's decision to dismiss his appeal from his conviction in the magistrates for driving in excess of the speed limit. The facts of the respective cases can be stated briefly.

Mouat

3.13   Mouat had been stopped by police officers whilst driving his car, informed that he had been exceeding the speed limit, and given a fixed penalty ticket. The officers, who had been following him on the dual carriageway, took him into their vehicle and showed him a video recording of the incident. During his magistrates' court trial he contended that, having initially not exceeded the speed limit, there came a time when, by reason of duress, he felt compelled so to do. At trial, the officers said that if Mouat had done or said anything to dispute the video evidence it would have been retained (for, in this case, the recording was destroyed).

3.14   The Divisional Court held that the videotape contained material which might have been relevant to the police investigation, and should have been retained at least until the end of the suspended enforcement period. As it was the police acted in breach of their duty both under the Criminal Procedure and Investigations Act 1996 to preserve relevant material, and also by virtue of local police policy. The appeal was allowed.

Ebrahim

3.15   Ebrahim was charged with assaulting another customer in a Tesco superstore. At trial, he contended that he had only grabbed the man in self-defence, believing that he himself was about to be struck, having regard to an earlier incident when he first entered the store. At a preliminary hearing, the defence requested the CPS' help in obtaining any videotapes which may have shown the earlier incident. When it became apparent the police did not possess the tape in question, the defence applied successfully for a witness summons against Tesco for its production. When it transpired that the superstore had destroyed the tape some weeks after service of the summons, the defence complained that no effort appeared to have been made to preserve the tape or to comply with the summons.

3.16   At trial, the police officer in the case explained, however, that before arresting Ebrahim, he had gone to the CCTV room, and discovered that the location of the alleged assault had not been recorded on film. In those circumstances he did not seize any of the large number of available videotapes. The Divisional Court found that, on the evidence, the officer had made a reasonable investigation in the circumstances, hence there was no breach of the previous CPIA Code, paras 3.4 or 3.5 (now paras. 3.5 and 3.6 in the revised code), pursuant to the Criminal Procedure and Investigations Act 1996. Even if the police could have done more to ensure the retention of material, the court was persuaded by the district judge's statement that it was still possible, on the facts of this case, for the accused to receive a fair trial. Ebrahim's application was dismissed.

Analysis of Brooke LJ's judgment

3.17   In the course of his judgment, Brooke LJ reviewed the development of the common law in this area, restated the principles underlying the abuse of process jurisdiction, and highlighted the salient features of the then 1997 version of the CPIA Code of Practice and the Attorney-General's guidelines. The end product was a commendably clear and succinct statement as to how a court 'should structure its inquiries' when facing a defence submission on abuse of process in the light of lost or destroyed videotape evidence, namely:

> 'We would suggest that in similar cases in future, a court should structure its inquiries in the following way. (1) In the circumstances of the particular case, what was the nature and extent of the investigating authorities' and the prosecutors' duty, if any, to obtain and/or retain the [videotape] evidence in question? Recourse should be had in this context to the contents of the 1997 Code and the Attorney-General's guidelines. (2) If in all the circumstances there was no duty to obtain and/or retain that [videotape] evidence before the defence first sought its retention, then there can be no question of the subsequent trial being unfair on this ground. (3) If such evidence is not obtained and/or retained in breach of the obligations set out in the 1997 Code and/or the guidelines, then the principles set out in paras 25 and 28 of this judgment should generally be applied. (4) If the behaviour of the prosecution has been so very bad that it is not fair that the defendant should be tried, then the proceedings should be stayed on that ground. The test in para 23 of this judgment is a useful one'. [The above square brackets are inserted by the authors.]

3.18   By simply removing the bracketed words 'videotape' from the above passage, we are left with an approach worthy of general application to lost or destroyed evidence cases. Whether the case involves a lost videotape, a lost carpet (as in *Gajree*[1]), or a lost car (as in *Beckford*[1]), surely the principle must remain the same? We suggest that the courts will apply the same or a similar test, irrespective of the factual matrix of a given case, for the simple reason that issues of fairness and prejudice are of universal application, and are clearly not uniquely limited to videotapes. Indeed, the same point applies to investigators' and prosecutors' duties generally in relation to the retention and preservation of material evidence, whatever it may be.

1   (20 September 1994, unreported).
2   [1996] 1 Cr App Rep 94.

3.19   Brooke LJ suggests an approach therefore which may be broken down into three distinct stages.

The first stage

3.20   What was the nature and extent of the investigating authorities' and prosecutors' duty, if any, to obtain and/or retain the evidence? In determining that question the court states that regard should be paid to their duties, both under the CPIA Code and under the Attorney-General's guidelines on disclosure. Thus, in a given case, a court must first decide whether or not a particular videotape, for example, should have been retained. If the court decides there was no such duty, then any argument that a fair trial cannot be held will fail.

3.21   The key question for a court, when determining whether material should have been retained, depends upon the court's view as to whether the videotape, for example, was or may have been 'relevant to the investigation'.[1] The Code defines material which may be relevant in wide terms,[2] thus imposing an onerous obligation on investigators or prosecutors to retain material. Under the CPIA Code of Practice, para 2.1 the following definition is given:

> 'material may be relevant to the investigation if it appears to an investigator, or to the officer in charge of an investigation, or to the disclosure officer, that it has some bearing on any offence under investigation or any person being investigated, or on the surrounding circumstances of the case, unless it is incapable of having any impact on the case'.

1   See CPIA Code, para 5.1.
2   See CPIA Code, para 2.1.

3.22   This broad approach to retention decisions is in line with the Attorney-General guidelines to investigators[1] whereby they: 'should always err on the side of recording and retaining material where they have any doubt as to whether it may be relevant'. It is submitted that the definition of 'relevance' is effectively the same as the *Keane*[2] disclosure test. The Code and guidelines are considered in more detail at paras **3.78–3.92**, however it is important to remember that the investigating authorities' and prosecutors' duty is not simply to retain; it is also, in certain circumstances, to obtain. The question then arises as to when it is appropriate to expect them to be proactive and seek out, for example, a given videotape? Each case will, of course, depend on its own particular facts, however guidance is provided by the CPIA Code of Practice, para 3.5, namely:

'In conducting an investigation, the investigator should pursue all reasonable lines of inquiry, whether these point towards or away from the particular suspect. What is reasonable in each case will depend on the particular circumstances'.

1 See Guidelines, para 24.
2 [1994] 2 All ER 478, 99 Cr App Rep 1.

3.23 If a police officer, for example, palpably failed to make any attempt to acquire a known and highly material videotape which was subsequently destroyed, the first stage of Brooke LJ's test may well be met. The duty to investigate, however, is clearly proportionate to the issues involved[1], relevant considerations being factors such as disclosure requests made and information supplied by a suspect[2]. The importance of the statutory duty, which disclosure officers and investigators have, to gather and record unused material, was underlined by its inclusion in para 16 of the 2006 Protocol on Unused Material.[3] The context for the CPIA code, para 3.5's duty was said, in the Protocol, 'to ensure that justice is not delayed, denied or frustrated'.

1 See *R v Sahdev* [2002] EWCA Crim 1064, [2002] 166 JP 19.
2 See the commentary generally on *Ebrahim* [2001] Crim LR 741 at 743.
3 See the Protocol issued by the Court of Appeal in 2006, on the 'Control and Management of Unused Material in the Crown Court,' which is found at Appendix E to this work.

The second stage

3.24 If the material evidence is not obtained and/or retained, in breach of the CPIA Code obligations and/or the Attorney-General's guidelines, the court must go on to consider whether the defendant could nevertheless receive a fair trial, or whether this was a 'Category 1' abuse of process case.

3.25 The above statement is drawn from Brooke LJ's invitation to apply generally the principles set out in paras 25 and 28 of his judgment. Whilst the first of these paragraphs highlights the principle that the trial process itself is equipped to deal with the bulk of abuse complaints, the second restates Lane CJ's important dictum in *A-G's Reference (No 1 of 1990)*[1] that no stay should be imposed:

'unless the defendant shows on the balance of probabilities that owing to delay he will suffer serious prejudice to the extent that no fair trial can be held, in other words that the continuance of the prosecution amounts to a misuse of the process of the court'.

1 [1992] 3 All ER 169.

3.26 In this context, the simple test for a defendant will be whether or not he has proved, more likely than not, that, owing to the 'serious prejudice' caused by the lost or destroyed material, he cannot receive a fair trial. The 'serious prejudice' test in *Ebrahim* has since been followed by the Court of Appeal in the recent case of *R v Dobson*.[1] It follows therefore that an element of prejudice will not suffice and must be tolerated. Only where the defence can successfully demonstrate a sufficient level of seriousness to the prejudice will a stay be considered, and this will depend on the facts of the particular case.

1   [2001] EWCA Crim 1606, [2001] All ER (D) 109 (Jul).

The third stage

3.27   If the behaviour of the prosecution has been so very bad that it is not fair that the defendant should be tried, then proceedings should be stayed under Category 2 of the abuse of process doctrine. In order to succeed the defence must prove that there was either an element of bad faith or at the very least some serious fault on the part of the police or the prosecution authorities in their failing to obtain and/or retain the relevant material.

3.28   This third stage serves as a clear warning to the police and prosecuting authorities that certain levels of bad conduct on their part may well lead to a stay of proceedings. As a recent commentator on the *Medway* decision noted:[1]

'where a videotape is not available at trial, a key issue will be the degree of likelihood that it actually recorded anything of any consequence. The greater the likelihood that it did, the more significant will be the inquiry as to what happened to it'.

1   See commentary at [2000] 20 Cr LW, 29 May.

3.29   In the light of the extended disclosure obligations on the police, by virtue of the CPIA Code, the Protocol on Unused Material, and the Attorney-General's guidelines, significantly greater scrutiny may be placed on their actions and inactions. Findings by individual officers that videotapes contained 'nothing relevant' (which were then returned to third parties), instances of persistent non-disclosure and examples of the deliberate destruction of material evidence may well fall within this category. Even where police officers disregard or dispose of material in perfectly good faith they may well have to justify their decisions. In deciding whether 'serious fault' has been proven, the courts will presumably have 'to assess how likely it is that the particular evidence would have made a difference'.[1]

1   See Professor Smith's commentary also on the *Medway* decision, at [2000] Cr LRev 415.

Post-Ebrahim case law

3.30   The guidelines laid down in *Ebrahim* appear to have been generally followed in the subsequent case law. In *R v Dobson*[1] the Court of Appeal had to consider an abuse of process appeal mounted on the basis of police officers' admitted failings in their duty to obtain and retain certain closed circuit television footage. The court adopted the *Ebrahim* approach of separately considering both 'Category 1' considerations of 'serious prejudice' and also 'Category 2' considerations of 'serious fault'. On the facts in Dobson's case the appeal was dismissed, for the court held that:

'Whilst there was plainly a degree of prejudice in *Dobson* being deprived of the opportunity of checking the footage in the hope it supported his case, that prejudice was not "serious prejudice", given the uncertainty of the likelihood that it would assist'.

A secondary factor which the court considered relevant to their finding of insufficient prejudice, related to the fact that Dobson's solicitors had not requested that the tapes be preserved. Further, the court drew the obvious distinction between 'malice or intentional omission, as opposed to oversight' and consequently found no element of bad faith.

1   [2001] EWCA Crim 1606, [2001] All ER (D) 109 (Jul).

3.31   We now turn to the Court of Appeal decisions in *R v Howell*[1] and *R v Elliot*.[2] These decisions suggest, as contended above, that the principles in *Ebrahim* are generally applicable to any kind of lost or destroyed evidence argument, not simply to those relating directly to lost videotapes. In *Howell*'s case, which involved a motor vehicle destruction argument, the court, in dismissing the appeal, found insufficient prejudice and only 'minimal' fault on the part of the Crown. In *Elliot*'s, relating to the loss of various drugs exhibits, again the court found no evidence of undue prejudice or bad faith, nor reason to suspect that the loss of the exhibits 'had been due to anything other than an accident or as a result of incompetence'. The authors foresee the courts, in future cases, having to make difficult decisions in their attempts to distinguish between 'incompetence' and 'serious fault'. When does a 'fault' become a 'serious fault'? This will no doubt be answered by margins of fact and degree in individual cases, where paramount considerations relate to both the alleged materiality of the missing evidence and the conduct of the police or prosecuting authority. While the courts can expect difficult cases to come their way, the post-*Ebrahim* decision of *R v Sadler*[3] was not one of them. Keene LJ's judgment in *Sadler* (at paras 15–27), which adopts the test of Brooke LJ in *Ebrahim*, highlights the rarity of the circumstances required before the courts will stay cases on grounds of the 'serious misbehaviour' of the police or prosecution. Whilst the Court of Appeal in *Sadler* thus acknowledged the 'thoroughly reprehensible' negligent failings of the police (in relation to disclosure, and the retention of material exhibits), nevertheless, it held that these 'fell far short of making it unfair to try' the appellant.

1   [2001] EWCA Crim 3009, [2001] All ER (D) 250 (Dec).
2   [2002] 166 JP 18.
3   [2002] EWCA Crim 1722, [2002] All ER (D) 151 (Jun).

3.32   In the decision of *Boyd*[1] the Court of appeal touched on some of the differences between the CCTV, and the non-CCTV, destruction abuse cases. On the facts, a blood sample taken from the defendant, and later analysed by the prosecution, had been allowed to decompose, for it had not been properly preserved in a refrigerator or freezer. The court found that, if a sample had been examined by the defence, it may have established that there was no heroin materially affecting the appellant at the time she drove. Accordingly, the prosecution had deprived the defence of the opportunity of establishing a defence which might have been open to them. The case should have been stayed. Rose LJ held that: 'The situation where the scientific examination of samples is concerned, although subject to the same sort of principles as those enunciated ...in *Ebrahim*, is very different from that where, as in that case, a videotape is not available but other lay witnesses may be able to speak of the events which occurred'.

1   *R v Boyd* [2004] RTR 2.

3.33   The 2007 case of *Ali v Crown Prosecution Service*[1] is an example of a recent decision where the Court had to consider the effect of missing evidence. The two appellants had been convicted at trial of false imprisonment, rape, and aiding and abetting rape. As a result of a seven-year delay, a number of documents were missing, including a copy of one of the victim's applications to the Criminal Compensation Authority, the credibility of which had been questioned, for the other victim admitted to having lied in her application. In addition, a police notebook which contained details of a police interview with the two complainants was missing, as was the evidence of the victims' first accounts of the incident. Moses LJ found that the prejudice flowing from the loss of the evidence was not capable of being cured by any Judicial directions at trial, and allowed the appeals:[2]

'The mere fact that missing evidence might have assisted the defence will not necessarily lead to a stay. But in considering such powers to alleviate prejudice, Brooke LJ [referring to para 23 of the *Ebrahim* judgment] emphasised the need for sufficiently credible evidence, apart from the missing evidence, leaving the defence to exploit the gaps left by the missing evidence. The rationale for refusing a stay is the existence of credible evidence, itself untainted by what has gone missing. In the instant appeals, the missing evidence and the evidence which the jury had to believe cannot be distinguished in that way. That which was missing, T's application to the CICA, was part of the material by which her credibility could be assessed.'

1   [2007] EWCA Crim 691.
2   See paras 29–31 of the judgment.

3.34   By way of contrast to the *Boyd* decision above, we now consider the case of *DPP v Cooper*[1] where the Administrative Court allowed a prosecution appeal by case stated against a stay for abuse of process. The defendant was charged with possession of both diamorphine and criminal property, having been said to possess bank notes, which a prosecution forensic scientist said were overly contaminated with heroin. The Magistrates stayed the case in the light of two principal defence complaints: first, the fact that the scientist's treatment of the notes with the Ninhydrin spray rendered them useless for further testing, and secondly, due to the loss of a video tape which showed the various tests carried out by the scientist on the notes. Silber J., whilst acknowledging the defence were impeded to a certain extent by the missing evidence, nevertheless held that there were adequate alternate means to challenge the prosecution case, for example, by a cross-examination of the scientist's methodology . The Court may well have been of the view that this was a defence argument based upon, what Brooks LJ in *Ebrahim* described as a reliance on 'holes' in the prosecution case,[2] where there was sufficient other credible evidence with which the case could be tried.

1   [2008] EWHC 507 Admin.
2   See para 27 of the judgment.

THE HISTORICAL DEVELOPMENT OF THE COMMON LAW

3.35   The Divisional Court in *Ebrahim* has now laid down a clear set of guiding principles which courts and practitioners should adopt in future cases. A better understanding of exactly how the court arrived at its conclusions is gleaned by briefly reviewing the somewhat haphazard development of the common law. We do so, in chronological order, by considering on a case by case basis instances of lost or destroyed evidence generally, not confining ourselves to unavailable video/CCTV footage cases.

3.36   By conducting this review we can see how courts have previously scrutinised, and responded to, defence complaints of prejudice. It reveals how and when courts have sought to deal with prejudice within the trial process and, conversely, demonstrates the thresholds required before granting stays or allowing appeals.

3.37   The authors suggest that the year 1997 marked a significant turning point in the common law as a result, first, of the advent of the coming into force of the CPIA Code of Practice and, second, in the light of the important judgment in *Reid*[1] which, ironically, was unreported. Where previously the courts had almost exclusively focused attention on the consequential effect of prejudice on a fair trial, from 1997 the equation entertained additional factors involving concepts of 'fault' and 'duty'. It became almost akin to some sort of quasi-criminal tort of negligence, where a 'duty of care' was owed. The new-found responsibilities on investigators and prosecutors (albeit with little or no statutory sanction for breaches of the Code) soon began to make their mark on the common law.

1   (10 March 1997, unreported).

R v Sadridin

3.38   In *R v Sadridin*[1] the appellant had been convicted of a shoplifting offence and appealed on the basis of a failed abuse submission, having allegedly been deprived of vital evidence at trial, namely certain till rolls (which had been routinely destroyed by the store in question). The day after his arrest for theft he handed certain receipts to his solicitor and claimed he had found them subsequent to his arrest in a shopping bag. The receipts, which were in evidence at trial, were for the correct amount of the goods, but did not indicate either the type of goods or the identity of the purchaser. The defence asserted that in order to establish that these receipts really were for the allegedly stolen goods, the till rolls were required.

1   (11 July 1985, unreported).

3.39   In dismissing the appeal Hirst J held that, on the evidence at trial, it was clear the till rolls were only of limited value and, in effect, could not have authenticated the receipts produced by the appellant, which point the appellant's appeal had depended on. The court also found that there was ample other evidence supporting the prosecution case. However, Hirst J stated that:

> 'If at sometime it had become clear that the absence of the destroyed documents was palpably of such crucial significance that a fair trial could not be conducted without them, it would always have been open to the judge, in the exercise of his discretion, to direct an acquittal'.

3.40   The above dicta is a reminder to practitioners to be ever-vigilant of an abuse submission emerging into a position of significance as proceedings continue. The fact that the submission fails on a pre-trial hearing, or at the outset of trial may not necessarily be the end of the matter for, of course, during a trial the significance of an exhibit can vary as the evidence emerges.

R v Sofaer

3.41   In *R v Uxbridge Justices, ex p Sofaer*[1] the applicants were alleged to have attempted to export parts of aircraft, assembled or dismantled, to South Africa in 1983 at a time when such export was forbidden by the Export of Goods (Control) Order 1981. When interviewed, the applicants had claimed they were not in contravention of the export ban, for they had attempted to export scrap, as opposed to usable or serviceable parts. By the time of the committal proceedings, the customs officers, albeit acting within their powers, had disposed of the seized goods, in what was described by Pain J as 'a somewhat clumsy manoeuvre'.

1   (1987) 85 Cr App Rep 367.

3.42   Having made a failed abuse submission at the committal, the applicants applied for judicial review, alleging a breach of natural justice, stating they had been prejudiced in their defence by the disposal of the parts. The application was refused largely on the basis that there was in existence a full set of detailed photographs of the destroyed parts. Croom-Johnson LJ held that the photographs, as secondary evidence, were sufficiently adequate for the jury to reach a conclusion as to whether the aircraft parts were in fact usable parts, or scrap, as the applicants had asserted. A further difficulty which the applicants faced was that their own defence expert on committal proceedings made a damaging concession under cross-examination. While the expert stated that, in his view the parts did not appear to be serviceable ones, nevertheless he conceded that, given the availability of all the photographs, an actual inspection of the parts would not have taken the matter any further! A considerable doubt was thus cast on the weight which might have attached to any examination, had one been possible.

3.43   On the principle of preserving evidence Croom-Johnson LJ cited with approval the case of *R v Lushington, ex p Otto,*[1] wherein Wright J said:

> '... it is undoubted law that it is within the power of, and is the duty of "constables"—and for "constables" here read "Customs"—to retain for use

in court things which may be evidences of crime, and which have come into the possession of the constables without wrong on their part'.

1   [1894] 1 QB 420.

3.44   In commenting on the above, Croom-Johnson LJ noted:

'That indeed is a general and very desirable standard which should be maintained and almost always is maintained. Unfortunately it is not always possible to apply it. Exhibits which are part of the evidence do go astray. Sometimes they are tested to destruction. In some cases it is only by testing them to destruction that you obtain the evidence in the first place ... but where you cannot produce the original, you rely on secondary evidence ...'.[1]

1   (1987) 85 Cr App Rep 367 at 377.

R v Sunderland Magistrates' Court, ex p Z

3.45   In *R v Sunderland Magistrates' Court, ex p Z*[1] in 1988 the applicant Z was committed for trial on a charge of rape, the allegation being that he raped 'X' in 1979. At the committal hearing Z made an abuse application submitting that first, the delay in proceeding with the charge against him was excessive and second, that this delay had resulted in prejudice to him. Examples of such prejudice were the destruction of various documents, clothing and vaginal swabs which made it impossible for the defence to have them forensically examined. However, the magistrates rejected the submission and indicated their intention to proceed with the committal. In response, the defence sought an order of prohibition to prevent the committal taking place.

1   [1989] Crim LR 56.

3.46   The Divisional Court granted the application, agreeing that in the circumstances a fair trial was no longer possible. The court also held that the delay in bringing proceedings against Z was unacceptable. This was on the grounds first, that the applicant had not contributed to the delay, and second, the police had decided in 1979 not to proceed against Z on the grounds of insufficient evidence.

R v Birmingham

3.47   Following Z came the then most celebrated case on this subject, *R v Birmingham*.[1] The significance of *Birmingham* over, say, Z is that for the first time a successful abuse submission was based solely on the ground of destruction of evidence by the prosecution. It was not, for example, bound up with a submission relating to unconscionable delay in bringing the prosecution. While *Birmingham* has undoubtedly become an often-quoted authority on this subject it is important to bear in mind that it was a first instance decision made by HH Judge Bromley sitting at Wood Green Crown Court.

1   [1992] Crim LR 117.

3.48   The facts in *Birmingham* were briefly as follows: seven defendants were charged with violent disorder at or outside a nightclub and also with various assaults on police officers who were called to the scene. Before the jury was sworn, the judge agreed to a voir dire in order to hear 'evidence from two of the prosecution witnesses on the existence and whereabouts of evidence believed to have been in existence at the time and of relevance to the case and possible use to the defence'. This evidence was a video recording of the locus in quo which had been created by an operational camera within the nightclub. After the incidents in question, the recording had been seized by the police and subsequently viewed by them. However, after having done so the recording was then returned to the nightclub and apparently then lost (thrown into a skip). At the voir dire it was discovered that the recording videotape had been viewed by the officers in the case but that its existence had not been revealed to the defence even after specific requests for unused material. To make matters worse, the officers candidly admitted that they had taken no steps to preserve the recording because they had decided that it would not be helpful to the prosecution's case (although this was later corrected and said to mean not to help either side's case).

3.49   Sensibly, in order to attain a full understanding of the likely relevance of the recording, the judge attended the nightclub and surveyed the locus in quo for himself.

3.50   The reasons given by the judge for staying the prosecution were as follows:

(1)   the prosecution had breached its duty of disclosure in relation to the recording which should have been disclosed to the defence;

(2)   the recordings would have been relevant to the defendants' case. The fact that the police had apparently decided otherwise was not only erroneous but also misguided;

(3)   in relation to the defence of alibi run by some of the defendants, the recording would have been relevant to this issue;

(4)   the recordings could have assisted the defence in tracing potential defence witnesses.

For these reasons the judge concluded that a fair trial was now impossible.

3.51   For its part, the prosecution had contended that the defence submission of abuse was in reality a matter to be determined by a jury and hence the trial should not be stayed. The judge, who was initially attracted to this view, held that the defence had been wrongfully deprived of material which should have been available during the course of defence preparation. Furthermore it did not, in the final analysis, relate to issues of guilt or innocence of the defendants but to whether they could be fairly tried. Accordingly, the trial judge declined to follow *Heston-Francois*[1] as prosecution counsel had suggested.

1   For a full consideration of *Heston-Francois* see paras **10.140** to **10.145**.

R v Gajree

3.52   Following *Birmingham* was the case of *R v Gajree*[1] where the appellant was convicted in 1994 of raping a 14-year-old girl, the offence allegedly having been committed in 1987.

1   (20 September 1994, unreported).

3.53   The appellant and the victim worked together at a shop. The victim alleged that after the shop closed she was taken by the appellant to the rear of the shop and there raped. She alleged that after raping her the appellant ejaculated onto the floor, which was carpeted. The victim did not make any complaint about this assault for a period of three weeks and when she reported the matter to the police, there was a dispute between her and the police as to what exactly she told them. In any event, the police did not carry out any investigation of the locus in quo. There the matter remained undisturbed until 1991 (four years later) when an investigation commenced leading to the trial of the appellant. At the trial an abuse application was made which was rejected.

3.54   The Court of Appeal held that the abuse application should have succeeded in the Crown Court because of the destruction of evidence, in this case the shop premises where the alleged rape occurred. During the intervening period there had been a fire at the shop and there was substantial damage to the premises and the carpet in question had also been destroyed. It was also important that a proper plan of the layout of the shop be taken but owing to the fire and lack of recollection this could not now be done. Sachs J stated 'Was it possible for this appellant, at the time he stood trial, to obtain a fair trial?'

3.55   In quashing the conviction, Sachs J went on to add:

'We are satisfied that because of the passage of time and the inertia of the police officers, this appellant was deprived of evidence that might have otherwise been available to him and that … renders the verdict unsafe and unsatisfactory'.

R v Beckford

3.56   Our attention can now be turned to what was then regarded as the leading case on this subject, the judgment of Neil LJ in the Court of Appeal in *R v Beckford*.[1]

1   [1996] 1 Cr App Rep 94.

3.57   The facts were that the appellant was charged with causing death by careless driving when under the influence of drink or drugs. The appellant, who was driving, crashed his car into a concrete block killing his passenger. In terms of the cause of the accident the principle of res ipsa loquitur seemed to apply, the driver being to blame. Following this fatal accident, police examined the scene and the car, apparently finding no evidence of anything which might have caused the accident. Subsequently, the car was examined by a police forensic expert who also found nothing defective with the car. By a process of elimination therefore, the police reached the conclusion that the driver must be to blame. When questioned about what had happened the appellant refused to provide an explanation. Seven months after the accident the appellant was summonsed. However, during the intervening period the car had been scrapped, the police having given no instructions for it to be preserved.

3.58   At the trial an abuse application was made on the ground that if the car had not been scrapped it might have provided vital evidence for the defence. The defence complained it had had no opportunity to examine the car and to discover whether there was any defect in it which caused the accident. It submitted abuse but the trial judge said this was a matter for the jury and rejected the application.

3.59   During the trial the defence also called an expert whose evidence was to the effect that the cause of the accident was probably due to mechanical failure (steering-wheel lock) and not, as the prosecution contended, that the appellant fell asleep while driving. The appellant again, however, did not give evidence of what he claimed had happened, he being the only witness. In the event the appellant was convicted and appealed. The central issue was whether the proceedings should have been stayed because of the premature destruction of the car. Could the defendant receive a fair trial despite the wrongful deprivation of the opportunity to test the findings of the prosecution as to there being no evidence of mechanical fault?

3.60   When considering the law on abuse Neil LJ analysed it as follows:

'The jurisdiction to stay can be exercised in many different circumstances. Nevertheless two main strands can be detected in the authorities:

(1)   cases where the court concludes that the defendant cannot receive a fair trial;

(2)   cases where the court concludes that it would be unfair for the defendant to be tried'.

3.61   Neil LJ considered *Gajree*, which the defence argued was analogous to this case. Without asserting that *Gajree* was of no use to his consideration, Neil LJ emphasised that 'each case has to be considered on its own facts'. Having stated this, he concluded that the judge was correct to reject the abuse application. According to Neil LJ there was no evidence to support the defence hypothesis as to the cause of the accident and that the trial was fair:

'There had been no evidence of problems of steering the car in the past, no marks on the road that the brakes had been applied, and the prosecution witnesses were of the opinion that the position of the car did not accord with the defence hypothesis of a steering-wheel lock'.

3.62   At the end of his judgment Neil LJ said:

'It is to be hoped that procedures have been put in place to ensure that cars are not scrapped before express permission has been given by the police and that permission will never be given where serious criminal charges are to be brought which may involve the possibility of some mechanical defect in a car'.

3.63   Are the decisions in *Gajree* and *Beckford* reconcilable? In the light of the clear similarities between the cases of *Gajree* and *Beckford*, at first it is difficult to comprehend the court's finding in the *Beckford* case that no unfairness resulted. On the face of it, is this not yet another clear case where the defence were wrongly deprived of the opportunity to either put forward a defence or discredit the Crown's case? The difference and the distinguishing feature between these two cases is that in *Gajree* it was accepted that there had been in existence evidence which was relevant to the defence, ie the carpet. Similarly in *Birmingham*. In both these cases the defence had positively asserted that such evidence, if obtainable, would have assisted their cases. But in *Beckford* the relevance of the scrapped car arose only because of a defence expert advancing a hypothesis at the trial. No positive assertion of mechanical failure could be made because the defendant, who could have provided such evidence, had nonetheless chosen not to provide a version of events specifically. He had declined to answer any questions on arrest and interview detailing exactly how the steering-wheel had locked.

3.64   It is submitted that the Court of Appeal (and probably the trial judge) took great cognisance of the fact that the defendant himself had chosen not to give an explanation and not to allow this to be tested by cross-examination. Almost certainly to the court, such a decision had all the hallmarks of a defence being concocted as a result of the discovery of the failure of the police to preserve the car. In such a circumstance, despite the obvious failure by the police and its obvious prejudicial affect, the court was determined to ensure that the defendant did not unfairly profit from this. It is also to be borne in mind that the burden of proving an abuse lies on the defendant and in the final analysis, the court was not satisfied that this burden had been satisfied by the mere fact of the premature destruction of the car and the advancing of a hypothesis by the defence expert at the trial.

3.65   The paradox of the situation in *Beckford* is, of course, that in satisfying the burden on him, the appellant's job was made more difficult because of the loss of evidence. One might well share the view of an author who commented:

> 'The court [in *Beckford*'s case] declined to draw the inference proposed by the appellant, because he produced little or no evidence in support of it. But was that not precisely what he was telling the courts at the trial and on appeal—that he could produce little or no evidence because he had been deprived of it by police inaction'.[1]

1   See (1995) J Cr L 59. See also the commentary on *Beckford* by John Arnold, in *Building on the Decade of Disclosure in Criminal Procedure* (2001), at p 155.

R v Northard

3.66   In *R v Northard*[1] the Court of Appeal allowed an appeal based on another video destruction abuse submission. A jeweller's employee was robbed of a bag containing a quantity of cash, while en route to the bank in a town's shopping centre. The prosecution case was that the appellant had been the 'getaway driver' of a motor car into which the robber had fled. One prosecution witness had an opportunity to observe the driver of the car for some three minutes or so at close range, and took a note of the registration number, at about 11.30 am. The owner of the vehicle was traced and gave evidence between 10 and 11 am on the same day the appellant borrowed his car. That same evening the car was found abandoned, some three miles away from the scene of the robbery. When the owner looked at it, he found a flat battery, burned wiring and a missing radio. Further, police officers at trial conceded that the state of the car was consistent with it having been stolen. At 2.15 pm that day, some hours after the robbery, the appellant visited the town's police station and reported that the car he had borrowed was stolen. He was duly arrested.

1   (19 February 1996, unreported).

3.67   In police interviews he repeated that he had borrowed the car, and had spent the material time shopping in the town centre (noting the particular shops he had been in or looked in), before visiting a public house between noon and 12.30 pm, which visit several witnesses confirmed at trial in statements which were read. Further, in interview he agreed to stand on an identification parade, gave a detailed account of his movements, and challenged the police to verify his movements by viewing shop video films. At a later stage, he withdrew the offer to stand on an ID parade, but nevertheless invited officers to show photographs to the witnesses who claimed to have seen the robbers.

3.68   On appeal, the appellant argued the failed abuse submissions in the lower court, which consisted of numerous complaints into the police and/or prosecution investigation or conduct of the case. It was claimed that the defence had been led to believe that the police would make every effort to trace and preserve any available video evidence that might have supported the alibi. In reality, the police did obtain and view the videotape evidence but neither the police nor the CPS disclosed its existence to the defence. The officer in the case stated that having viewed the videos of the shopping centre, which showed large crowds of shoppers, it had not been possible to identify any individuals. Twenty-eight days after the incident the videos had been re-used and the recordings lost. A second defence complaint was that the investigating officer failed to adequately instruct other officers to check the appellant's alibi, by visiting two particular shops. Additionally, there were further alleged failures to check security videos, arrange ID parades and failures to conduct expert examination of the vehicle in question.

3.69   Auld LJ held that the trial judge should either have stayed the prosecution as an abuse, or withdrawn it from the jury. The court was concerned by a number of deficiencies and unsatisfactory features and identified 'an accumulation of lost opportunities to the defence to vouch for the alibi, if a true one'. The failure of the prosecution to disclose the existence of the video until it was too late was held to deprive the defence of the opportunity to check the video for themselves, to see if it supported the defence account. Auld LJ wisely noted that the appellant and his solicitor may have examined the video with 'keener eyes' than the police officer. The police were further found to have failed to act on the appellant's initial offer to stand on an ID parade in respect of the only witness who apparently had a good opportunity to observe the robbers. As Auld LJ noted, 'her evidence would have damned or exonerated the appellant'.

R v Reid

3.70   In *R v Reid*[1] Owen J considered some of the above authorities in the context of yet another video destruction case. Reid had faced robbery and assault charges arising out of an incident in a chemist's shop. The dispute at trial was as to whether the appellant had been acting by way of self-defence. While both complainants had knife wounds (from the appellant's knife), the appellant had suffered acid burns, and the simple issue was who had started to use force first. A police officer testified that there had been a recording of the interior of the shop (from an internal security video) but that it had not been preserved. The officer stated that he watched it and nothing on it appeared relevant. By the time of trial the recording, for reasons that are not clear, had been destroyed. The defence apparently requested, and were granted, a voir dire before the jury were empanelled, for evidence to be heard. In such a hearing the judge accepted the officer's account that having scanned the video, nothing of relevance arose.

1   (10 March 1997, unreported).

3.71   In dismissing the appeal, Owen J sought to distinguish the facts in *Reid*'s case from those of *Birmingham* and *Northard*. The Court of Appeal found itself unable to conclude, either that the video had been relevant, or that the circumstances in which it had disappeared were so unfair as to make the conviction unsafe. It is submitted that the case might, of course, have been decided differently if the cameras had been trained on a more relevant part of the premises, or in circumstances where the officer had made concessions as to relevance of the video.

3.72   Taking the opportunity available to him in *Reid* Owen J clearly enunciated the existence of the abuse of process jurisdiction in circumstances where there has been a failure to preserve relevant material in criminal proceedings:

> 'There is now a clear duty to preserve material which might be relevant, and nothing in this judgment is meant in any way to cast a doubt on that duty. However, clearly there must be a judgment of some kind by the investigating officer. He must decide whether material may be relevant, and if he does not preserve material which may be relevant, then for sure in the future he may be required to justify his decision, and he may find that, if the breach of his duty is sufficiently serious, that somebody who is in fact a guilty man has to go free because there has been an abuse of process ... The position is that if there has been a failure to preserve relevant material then it may be found that to proceed with a prosecution in those circumstances would be an abuse of process'.

3.73   It is interesting to note that Owen J's judgment in *Reid* was delivered a few weeks before police officers acquired a statutory duty, pursuant to para 5 of the CPIA Code of Practice, to retain material which may be relevant to a police investigation. The wording of the judgment may not, in these circumstances, have been entirely coincidental. This unreported decision of *Reid*, referred to in *Ebrahim*, appears to be the first occasion where the Court of Appeal has openly acknowledged this discrete category of abuse of process, that is, where there has been a failure to preserve relevant material.

R v McNamara[1]

3.74   In this case police officers had searched the family home and allegedly found quantities of drugs. As the search continued, an officer recorded items of interest and the appellant's comments, some of which amounted to admissions to possession of cannabis. The same were recorded in the pro forma Book 101, being the search record. The appellant later denied making the admissions and, by the time of trial, the Book 101 had been lost, apparently due to 'poor exhibit management'. The defence argued at trial, and on appeal, that the loss of the Book 101 rendered the proceedings an abuse of process. A variety of authorities were relied on, principally *Birmingham*.

1   [1998] Crim LR 278.

3.75   The Court of Appeal unsurprisingly rejected the appellant's argument that the *Birmingham* situation was analogous. First, the court noted that unlike *Birmingham*, the Book 101 was not deliberately destroyed by any officer. Second, the loss of the exhibit would only be of detriment to the Crown and finally, unlike the video film example, the Book 101 was not an item of original evidence.

Miscellaneous cases

3.76   Finally, in the two years or so immediately preceding the *Ebrahim* decision, came a number of mainly unreported video destruction cases, which were possibly responsible for prompting the court in *Ebrahim* itself to conduct such a thorough review of the previous authorities. The first of these, *R v Swingler*,[1] concerned a lost video film in the context of a rape investigation. Whilst the Court of Appeal accepted that the lost evidence had been 'of potentially great significance', it dismissed the appeal on the basis that the defence had been unable to point to any significant fault on the part of the police investigating. What was described as a useful test for deciding 'Category 2' abuse submissions, by Brooke LJ in *Ebrahim*, was the same approach suggested earlier by Rougier J in *Swingler*, albeit there in relation generally to arguments based on the disappearance of evidence. The two subsequent decisions of *R v Chipping*[2] and *R v Medway*[3] add little to the development of principle in this area. What can be noted, however, is in both *Swingler* and *Medway* the Court of Appeal appeared to move away from the classic dual fairness test in *Beckford* and towards a narrower more restrictive interpretation. In *Medway*, the court held that there would need to be something wholly exceptional about the circumstances of a case to justify a stay on the ground that evidence had been lost or destroyed, citing as an example, a malicious interference with evidence.

1   (10 July 1988, unreported), CA.
2   (11 January 1999, unreported), DC.
3   [2000] Crim LR 415, CA.

3.77   In the last pre-*Ebrahim* decision which we consider, *R v Stallard*,[1] the pendulum swung back in favour of the broader dual approach, to be later adopted in *Ebrahim* itself. In *Stallard* the Court of Appeal, in yet another video destruction case, considered both whether a fair trial was possible (a Category 1 decision) and also whether the police were seriously at fault (a Category 2 decision).

1   (13 April 2000, unreported), CA.

CRIMINAL PROCEDURE AND INVESTIGATIONS ACT 1996 CODE OF PRACTICE

3.78   This Code of Practice was promulgated pursuant to the Criminal Procedure and Investigations Act 1996, s 23(1) ('CPIA 1996'). It applies in respect of all criminal investigations conducted by police officers which began on or after 1 April 1997. One highly significant aspect of the Code is that for the first time the way in which police or other investigators conduct a criminal investigation generally is governed by a public Code of Practice. In comparison with the PACE Code of Practice which is concerned only with a narrow area of police operation, mainly the treatment and questioning of suspects post-arrest, this Code is directed at all police conduct, pre- and post-arrest, and is designed to impose clear standards of fairness and accountability.

3.79   In general terms, the Code of Practice sets down detailed regulations in respect of:

(1)   the presentation of material by an 'investigator';

(2)   the revelation of such material by the investigator to the prosecutor.

3.80   In the light of the focusing of attention in *Ebrahim* on the duties of investigators and prosecutors to obtain and/or retain evidence, it becomes essential to understand fully the nature and extent of these important duties. Indeed, CPIA 1996 and its respective Code of Practice have now acquired an arguably greater significance with the introduction of the Attorney-General's guidelines, whose avowed aim is to 'build upon the existing law to help to ensure that the legislation is operated more effectively, consistently and fairly'.[1]

1   Attorney-General's guidelines, 2005, para 4.

3.81   Under the heading 'Responsibilities', in relation to Investigators and Disclosure Officers, the Attorney-General (at para 23 of the guidelines) makes the following emphatic statement:

'Investigators and disclosure officers must be fair and objective and must work together with prosecutors to ensure that disclosure obligations are met. A failure to take action leading to inadequate disclosure may result in a wrongful conviction. It may alternatively lead to a successful abuse of process argument, an acquittal against the weight of the evidence or the appellate courts may find that a conviction is unsafe and quash it'.

3.82   The authors submit that the above description of 'a failure to take action leading to inadequate disclosure' may well encompass a failure to obtain and/or retain material evidence. The Attorney-General is correctly acknowledging that, at common law, the judicial remedy of a stay is a possible sanction in relation to disclosure failures. Proven breaches of the Act, Code or guidelines, for that matter, may form the basis of an abuse of process application, or indeed, an application to exclude evidence under PACE, s 78.

3.83   In contrast to the position under PACE, however, where the most effective remedy lies within the Act itself, there is an almost complete absence of sanctions either within the CPIA 1996 or its Code of Practice. The remedy lies within the common law discretion to stay proceedings as an abuse of process. Whereas a practitioner in a PACE case may apply for exclusion of evidence, very serious breaches of the CPIA Code, which might well prejudice an accused's ability to defend himself, do not attract any built-in statutory sanction. The passage of the Criminal Procedure and Investigations Bill through Parliament did indeed see calls for the provision of specific sanctions for non-compliance with the Code, but these were vehemently resisted by the then government. The government's argument was to the effect that serious breaches could, in any event, trigger possible criminal or disciplinary proceedings against the offending police officers. The few sanctions which do exist are not related to the context of this chapter, having regard to prosecutors' observing of time limits (CPIA 1996, s 10(2)) and inferences against an accused (CPIA, s 11(3)(a) and (b)).

THE DUTY TO OBTAIN AND/OR RETAIN MATERIAL UNDER THE CPIA CODE

3.84   The following are relevant extracts taken from the Code, which is set out in full at Appendix D to this work:

'General Responsibilities

3.4   The officer in charge of an investigation may delegate tasks to another investigator, to civilians employed by the police force, or to other persons participating in the investigation under arrangements for joint investigations, but he remains responsible for ensuring that these have been carried out and for accounting for any general policies followed in the investigation. In particular, it is an essential part of his duties to ensure that all material which may be relevant to an investigation is retained, and either made available to the disclosure officer or (in exceptional circumstances) revealed directly to the prosecutor.

3.5   In conducting an investigation, the investigator should pursue all reasonable lines of inquiry, whether these point towards or away from the suspect. What is reasonable in each case will depend on the particular circumstances. For example, where material is held on computer, it is a matter for the investigator to decide which material on the computer it is reasonable to inquire into, and in what manner.

3.6   If the officer in charge of an investigation believes that other persons may be in possession of material that may be relevant to the investigation, and if this has not been obtained under paragraph 3.4 above, he should ask the disclosure officer to inform them of the existence of the investigation and to invite them to retain the material in case they receive a request for its disclosure. The disclosure officer should inform the prosecutor that they may have such material. However, the officer in charge of an investigation is not required to make speculative enquiries of other persons: there must be some reason to believe that they may have relevant material. That reason may come from information provided to the police by the accused or from other inquiries made or from some other source.

Recording of Information

4.1 If material which may be relevant to the investigation consists of information which is not recorded in any form, the officer in charge of an investigation must ensure that it is recorded in a durable or retrievable form (whether in writing, on video or audio tape, or on computer disk).

4.2 Where it is not practicable to retain the initial record of information because it forms part of a larger record which is to be destroyed, its contents should be transferred as a true record to a durable and more easily-stored form before that happens.

4.3 Negative information is often relevant to an investigation. If it may be relevant it must be recorded. An example might be a number of people present in a particular place at a particular time who state that they saw nothing unusual.

4.4 Where information which may be relevant is obtained, it must be recorded at the time it is obtained or as soon as practicable after that time. This includes, for example, information obtained in house-to-house enquiries, although the requirement to record information promptly does not require an investigator to take a statement from a potential witness where it would not otherwise be taken.

Retention of material

(a) Duty to retain material

5.1 The investigator must retain material obtained in a criminal investigation which may be relevant to the investigation. Material may be photographed, video-recorded, captured digitally or otherwise retained in the form of a copy rather than the original at any time, if the original is perishable: the original was supplied to the investigator rather than generated by him and is to be returned to its owner; or the retention of a copy rather than the original is reasonable in all the circumstances.

5.3 If the officer in charge of an investigation becomes aware as a result of developments in the case that material previously examined but not retained (because it was not thought to be relevant) may now be relevant to the investigation, he should, wherever practicable, take steps to obtain it or ensure that it is retained for further inspection or for production in court if required.

5.4 The duty to retain material includes in particular the duty to retain material falling into the following categories, where it may be relevant to the investigation:

– crime reports (including crime report forms, relevant parts of incident report books or police officers' notebooks);

– custody records;

– records which are derived from tapes of telephone messages (for example, 999 calls) containing descriptions of an alleged offence or offender;

– final versions of witness statements (and draft versions where their content differs from the final version), including any exhibits mentioned (unless these have been returned to their owner on the understanding that they will be produced in court if required);

– interview records (written records, or audio or video tapes, of interviews with actual or potential witnesses or suspects);

– communications between the police and experts such as forensic scientists, reports of work carried out by experts, and schedules of scientific material prepared by the expert for the investigator, for the purposes of criminal proceedings;

– records of the first description of a suspect by each potential witness who purports to identify or describe the suspect, whether or not the description differs from that of subsequent descriptions by that or other witnesses;

– any material casting doubt on the reliability of a witness.

Relevant material

3.85   Paragraphs 5.7 to 5.10 of the Code proceed to outline the length of time for which material is to be retained in given circumstances. Clearly the list of categories of material to be retained, as set out in para 5.4 above is a non-exhaustive one. The task on the ground for investigators who routinely have to make hard and fast individual decisions as to relevance, for the purposes of deciding whether or not to retain particular material, will no doubt continue to be challenging. The investigators should be only too aware, however, that prosecutors 'cannot do their job properly without satisfactory recording and retention of material',[1] and errors of judgement at critical moments in an investigation may well compromise future prosecutions down the line. No doubt with these considerations well in mind the Attorney-General issued a number of practical guidelines to prosecutors, encouraging them to liaise closely with investigators and disclosure officers.[2] Prosecutors are told they have to be alert, proactive and prepared to do 'all that they can to facilitate proper disclosure'. For an example of a recent decision where the Court of Appeal rejected defence claims over the alleged necessity to retain material (in the course of an arson investigation) see *R v Parker*[3] where the court again adopted the *Ebrahim* approach to determining such abuse applications.

In the recent 2007 decision of *Leatherland v Powys CC*[4] the High Court considered an appeal by case stated, on the basis of a refusal by a Magistrates

Court to stay proceedings, arising out of an argument over the retention of relevant material. The appellants were convicted of charges under the Animal Health legislation, the relevant material being sheep carcasses. In essence, Leatherland, a farmer, discovered that some of his sheep at market had been assessed by a veterinary surgeon and DEFRA inspector, as in such poor condition they had to be slaughtered. In due course, he went on to be prosecuted, in circumstances where he had generally not been made aware of the decision to slaughter the sheep; consequently his own veterinary surgeon never had the opportunity to assess the sheep, whose carcasses were all destroyed, and where only a few inconclusive photographs of the sheep existed. Owen J thoroughly reviewed the Ebrahim principles, and the statutory duty to retain material obtained in a criminal investigation, and found that the destruction of the carcasses had so severely handicapped the appellant, a fair trial had not been possible. The appellant was left in no realistic position to mount a challenge to the prosecution veterinary surgeon's evidence as to the condition of the sheep. The court considered that a representative selection of the sheep should have been preserved for at least a sufficient time to inform the appellant of the position, which had not been remedied by the few photographs taken. There should have been a stay of proceedings. For an example of a case, where there was found to be no duty on the facts to preserve material, see *Focus (DIY) Ltd v Hillingdon LBC.*[5]

1   See the Commentary to the previous AG's Guidelines, p 1.
2   See the AG's Guidelines, paras 32–41.
3   [2002] EWCA Crim 90, [2003] All ER (D) 300 (Jan).
4   [2007] EWHC 148.
5   [2008] EWHC 1152 (Admin).

DUTY TO 'PURSUE ALL REASONABLE LINES OF INQUIRY'

The CPIA Code of Practice 1996

3.86   Paragraph 3.5 of the Code contains arguably the most significant and wide-ranging obligation cast on criminal investigators. The CPIA Code is set out in full at Appendix D of this work. Practitioners are urged to carefully consider this obligation when determining whether or not the prosecution have fulfilled their duty 'to obtain' or 'retain' material evidence. It is submitted that never before has an explicit legal obligation been imposed on a criminal investigator to act in the manner stipulated. Paragraph 3.5 states as follows:

'In conducting an investigation, the investigator should pursue all reasonable lines of inquiry, whether these point towards or away from the suspect. What is reasonable in each case will depend on the particular circumstances'.

Significance of para 3.5

3.87   Previously in our adversarial system of criminal justice, it was a respectable argument for a prosecutor to make that it was the duty of the accused and his legal team to investigate any matter which was inconsistent with the prosecution's case. If the defence failed to do so and the prosecution were not on notice of any defect or undermining factor so far as their case was concerned, then responsibility for pursuing an exculpatory line of enquiry rested squarely on the defence. Such an argument in the light of para 3.5 is, it is submitted, no longer tenable.

3.88   The significance of para 3.5 can further be emphasised by taking into account that it was presumably inserted into the Code as a quid pro quo for the curtailment under CPIA 1996 of the defence's common law rights to prosecution disclosure. If the original object of the statutory disclosure regime created by CPIA 1996 was to place the prosecution squarely in a management role in so far as decision making concerning disclosure was concerned, then this paragraph, acting as a counterweight, created a clear responsibility to act fairly and impartially while exercising that role.

3.89   Paragraph 3.4 of the Code largely reflects the language used in the CPIA 1996, s 23(1)(a) itself. Interestingly, the duty attaches to the 'investigator' as opposed to, for example, the officer in charge of the case. An 'investigator' is defined as 'any police officer involved in the conduct of a criminal investigation'. The 'officer in charge' of an investigation, who is defined as 'the police officer responsible for directing a criminal investigation', takes on an additional investigative duty, by virtue of para 3.6 of the Code, where it is believed that 'other persons' may be in possession of relevant material. The officer in charge is not obliged to make 'speculative' enquiries of the third parties, but is required to make enquiries where information suggests further action is required. The information which causes him to act may come from a variety of sources, be it the accused himself, other police inquiries or 'from some other source'.

3.90   So what exactly does the para 3.5 investigator's duty actually mean? It certainly does not mean that the investigator should pursue every conceivable line of inquiry. Neither does it mean that vast resources have to be applied to the most simple of investigations. We suggest it does mean, however, that the investigator is obliged to investigate all case-theories fairly, not just the one pointing to the guilt of the accused.

3.91   In the context of this chapter, we submit that the following three propositions are fundamental. First, that the investigator should be expected to recognise where there is material that may be relevant to an investigation. Secondly, that, having determined what may be relevant, the investigator must make a reasonable effort to obtain it and/or retain it. Thirdly, that where the material to be obtained or retained is within the knowledge of the accused or his legal advisors, yet unknown to the investigator, and in circumstances where the investigator could not reasonably be expected to know about it, then the defence should put the investigator properly on notice before they may legitimately complain about an alleged failure to investigate. The defence are now specifically encouraged to play their part in the new culture of disclosure which is intended to pervade our system. In para 5 of the 2005 Attorney-General's Guidelines, it states that:

'A critical element to fair and proper disclosure is that the defence play their role to ensure that the prosecution are directed to material which might reasonably be considered capable of undermining the prosecution case or assisting the case for the accused'.

3.92 The above three propositions largely relate to the 'duty' of the investigator to actually make an investigation, which goes to the first stage of the *Ebrahim* test. As to the shape of the investigation or the extent of the duty, para 3.5 states: 'What is reasonable in each case will depend on the particular circumstances'. The case law, which is considered below, suggests that the 'reasonableness' or otherwise of a given investigation will depend on a multitude of factors. The guiding principle, however, is that the investigator's inquiries should be proportionate to, or commensurate with, what is required.

The Attorney-General's Guidelines (2005)

3.93 The Attorney-General states that the new Guidelines were issued in the light of the abolition of the distinction between primary and secondary disclosure, and the introduction of a single test for disclosure of material that 'might reasonably be considered capable of undermining the prosecution case or assisting the case for the accused'. In the foreword to the Guidelines, the reader is informed of the AG's opinion that, if the disclosure regime is made to work properly, then the corresponding benefit will mean that there will be far fewer applications to stay on non-disclosure grounds, and that such applications are only 'likely to succeed in extreme cases and certainly not where the alleged disclosure is in relation to speculative requests for material'.

3.94 The tenor of the Guidelines (which are set out at Appendix C to this work), consistent with the duty to pursue all reasonable lines of inquiry, is to demand a proactive approach by investigators who seek to obtain material evidence. This is perhaps best exemplified by the provisions which relate to material held by third parties which is set out below:

'a) Material held by Government departments or other Crown bodies

47   Where it appears to an investigator, disclosure officer or prosecutor that a Government department or other Crown body has material that may be relevant to an issue in the case, reasonable steps should be taken to identify and consider such material. Although what is reasonable will vary from case to case, the prosecution should inform the department or other body of the nature of its case and of relevant issues in the case in respect of which the department or body might possess material, and ask whether it has any such material.

b) Material held by other agencies

51   There may be cases where the investigator, disclosure officer or prosecutor believes that a third party (for example, a local authority, a social services department, a hospital, a doctor, a school, a provider of forensic services) has material or information which might be relevant to the prosecution case. In such cases, if the material or information might

reasonably be considered capable of undermining the prosecution case or of assisting the case for the accused prosecutors should take what steps they regard as appropriate in the particular case to obtain it.

52   If the investigator, disclosure officer or prosecutor seeks access to the material or information but the third party declines or refuses to allow access to it, the matter should not be left. If despite any reasons offered by the third party it is still believed that it is reasonable to seek production of the material or information, and the requirements of section 2 of the Criminal Procedure (Attendance of Witnesses) Act 1965 or, as appropriate, section 97 of the Magistrates Court Act 1980 are satisfied, then the prosecutor or investigator should apply for a witness summons causing a representative of the third party to produce the material to the court.'

3.95   When judges are called upon to decide whether an investigator has pursued all 'reasonable lines of enquiry' in a given case, they should take into account the guiding principle that investigators 'should always err on the side of recording and retaining material where they have any doubt as to whether it may be relevant'.[1] The Guidelines make it clear, however, that it is not simply the investigators and disclosure officers who should be alive to these important evidential considerations. At para 33 of the Guidelines, it states: 'Prosecutors must review schedules prepared by disclosure officers thoroughly and must be alert to the possibility that relevant material may exist which has not been revealed to them ...'. Further, in para 36 of the Guidelines, prosecutors are required to 'advise the investigator if, in their view, reasonable and relevant lines of further enquiry should be pursued.'

1   See Guidelines, para 24.

The position at common law

3.96   At the time of writing there are few authorities on the para 3.5 duty, albeit the authors predict a significant development in this area. The first important statement of principle, however, emerges from Brooke LJ in *Ebrahim* itself wherein he stated:

'That the extent of the duty of investigation should be proportionate to the seriousness of the matter being investigated is evident from para 3.4 [ie the previous version of 3.5] of the 1997 Code'.

3.97   By these words, we suggest Brooke LJ did not mean the duty should be assessed in terms of the gravity of the allegation, but rather should be proportionate to the relevance of the inquiry in the context of the issues in the case. There is certainly no mention of 'seriousness' playing a part in the actual wording of this paragraph. The following questions are perhaps more significant to the para 3.5 test: Was there a serious lead or inquiry that should have been followed up? Was there a material issue that should have been investigated given its bearing on the case?

3.98   In *Ebrahim* itself, for example, which concerned a lowly charge of common assault, their Lordships did consider it significant that the officer had made a reasonable investigation to see if there was any video evidence of the assault in question. The court found that the officer 'had no reason to believe that his investigations should encompass what had occurred elsewhere in the store an hour earlier', which meant no breach of then para 3.5 of the Code. The reason why the police were unaware of the significance of the earlier video appears to relate to the fact that Ebrahim was never interviewed. The authors suggest that, in a different case, perhaps against a background of a more serious allegation, police officers could attract legitimate criticism under para 3.5 where they fail to interview an accused. It could well be argued that officers have not pursued lines of inquiry pointing 'away from the suspect' where they have chosen not to even interview the suspect or seek a response to the allegation.

DPP v Metten

3.99   In the earlier decision of *DPP v Metten*[1] the defence alleged a breach of para 3.4 (now 3.5) of the Code in a failure by the police to make any effort to ascertain the identities of potential witnesses to a public order incident for which the defendant was being prosecuted. It is submitted that on the facts of this case there appeared a clear breach of what is now para 3.5, the officers having singularly failed at the only possible moment to speak to those who may have assisted or undermined the prosecution's case. Buxton LJ sitting in the Divisional Court was, it is submitted, nonetheless determined to ensure that despite a clear breach of this paragraph, the defence did not profit from it. While the terms of his judgment are beyond the scope of this chapter, Buxton LJ adopted a highly technical approach to the wording of the Code of Practice holding that there was no breach because the police had not conducted any criminal investigation. As the editor of *Criminal Law Week* observed concerning Buxton LJ's judgment, 'the decision does indeed drive a coach and four through the legislation'.[2]

1   (1999) 13 CLW. See also *R v Roberts* [1998] Crim LR 682, and the commentary at 683.
2   (1999) 13 CLW para 5.

3.100   The principles set out in *Ebrahim* have been followed in the two unreported decisions of *R v Eccleston* and *R v Sahdev*. In *R v Eccleston*[1] the Court of Appeal concluded on the facts of the case that there was no para 3.4 (now para 3.5) duty encumbent on the police to retain a motor car for forensic examination based on a mere 'hint in interview' about the presence of blood on the car. In reaching this decision the court had particular regard to the lack of any 'clear request from either the appellant or his legal advisor' to examine the car, and the fact that the presence or absence of blood on the car was not central to the real issue in the case, which was whether or not the appellant acted in self-defence. It was less than clear that even the proven presence of blood on the car would have materially assisted the defence. On the facts of *Eccleston*, the abuse argument fell at the first hurdle of the *Ebrahim* test, in the sense that there was no duty to obtain or retain the material. Had there been such a duty, it is clear that the court found no serious prejudice in any event, which meant that the abuse argument would similarly have been defeated at the second stage. In contrast, we suggest that the pre-CPIA 1996 case of *Beckford*, where the police allowed the motor car to be scrapped, would have passed the first hurdle of *Ebrahim* in the sense that there was a duty to retain, albeit it may not have passed the second stage 'serious prejudice' test.

1   [2001] EWCA Crim 1626, [2001] All ER (D) 118 (Jul).

3.101   In the recent decision of *R v Sahdev*[1] the Court of Appeal similarly endorsed the approach of *Ebrahim* when faced with an appeal based on an abuse of process argument which was said to arise out of an alleged breach of the previous para 3.4 duty. The facts concerned an incident outside a London tube station, whereby the defendant was alleged to have been unlawfully in possession of a knife and committing assaults on police officers. The police retained certain film footage from the scene, which was disclosed to the defence, albeit it did not show the incident. A year later, after a site visit, the defence contended that there were other cameras which may have revealed the incident. The defence arguments unsurprisingly received short shrift from Goldring J, who found that the investigating officer had done 'all he reasonably could have been expected to do'. The officer seized, retained and disclosed the film from one set of cameras, whilst being unaware of any other video cameras. The defence could not produce any cogent evidence that a second set of cameras were present at the material time, or indeed, working. Goldring J emphasised that the extent of the duty to investigate 'must be proportionate to the seriousness of the issues being investigated', and that in this straightforward case the officer had investigated it 'reasonably and proportionately'.

1   See [2002] EWCA Crim 1064, [2002] 166 JP 19.

3.102   In the course of his judgment, Goldring J cited approvingly the cautionary words of Brooke LJ in *Ebrahim*:

'It must be remembered that it is a commonplace in criminal trials for a defendant to rely on "holes" in the prosecution case, for example, a failure to take fingerprints or a failure to submit evidential material to forensic examination. If, in such a case, there is sufficient credible evidence, apart form the missing evidence, which, if believed, would justify a safe conviction, then a trial should proceed, leaving the defendant to seek to persuade the jury or magistrates not to convict because evidence which might otherwise have been available was not before the court through no fault of his. Often the absence of a video film or fingerprints or DNA material is likely to hamper the prosecution as much as the defence'.

Brooke LJ's words will serve as a warning to trial judges and magistrates to scrutinise closely opportunistic defence complaints over alleged failures to investigate.

THE PROTOCOL ON UNUSED MATERIAL (2006)

3.103   This protocol was first issued by the Court of Appeal in 2006, and is set out in full at Appendix E to this work. Its full title is the protocol for 'The Control and Management of Unused Material in the Crown Court'. It exhorts the need for a complete sea-change in the practice and culture of all parties' approaches to the handling of unused material. In para 16 of the protocol, the 3.5 CPIA code duty upon investigators to pursue all reasonable lines of inquiry is set out, as is a detailed set of guidance in relation to Third Party Disclosure obligations (at paras. 52–62 of the protocol).

EUROPEAN COURT OF HUMAN RIGHTS CASE LAW

3.104 Finally, in this chapter, we turn to some ECHR decisions and consider whether any parallels exist between the domestic abuse of process doctrine and the 'Equality of Arms' provisions applicable to Art 6 of ECHR. Article 6(3)(d) of the Convention provides:

> "Everyone charged with a criminal offence has the following minimum rights;
>
> (d)   to examine or have examined witnesses against him and to obtain the attendance and examination of witnesses on his behalf under the same conditions as witnesses against him;"

In *Sofri v Italy*[1] the Court found a complaint under Art 6 inadmissible as manifestly ill-founded, in circumstances where the complaint had been based on the destruction of a certain evidence relating to a murder trial concerning the killing of a public prosecutor. The dead prosecutor's clothing had gone missing, the bullets from the body were destroyed, as was the car used by the killers. Administrative error, on the part of the Italian authorities, was said to be the likely explanation for the lost material. The destruction of the items did not on the particular facts, however, give rise to any inequality of arms which was to the detriment of the defendants. The court found that the defence were at no significant disadvantage by the loss of the car and bullets, for they had access to forensic reports and photographs which had been made shortly after the killing. Furthermore, the defence were wholly unable to explain how the loss of the clothing had been relevant to their case. The prosecution were adjudged to have laboured under the same difficulties as the defence.

1   Application No 37235/97, May 27, 2003; [2004] Crim LR 846.

3.105 In *Papageorgiou v Greece*[1] however, the Court did find a violation of Art 6(3)(d) in circumstances where 'vital items of evidence were not adduced', or made available to the defence, in spite of repeated disclosure requests. The applicant was a bank clerk charged with a fraud, where it was alleged he and others had used false cheques to withdraw significant sums of money from one of the bank's client's account. For reasons that are not immediately apparent, the domestic court of first instance ordered the destruction of the forged cheques, which were fundamental items of evidence in the proceedings against the applicant. Indeed, the applicant's conviction for fraud was, to a large extent, based on photocopies of the cheques allegedly forged, which cheques the defence claimed had been altered. The court found that it was essential to the applicant's defence for the cheques to have been produced, for they would have enabled him to show that the persons who gave the instructions to make the payments were bank employees and not himself. He had lost the opportunity to use evidence which was potentially exculpatory.

1   (2004) 38 EHRR 30.

3.106   As Professor Ashworth noted in his commentary on *Sofri*, the Strasbourg Court 'is not concerned with the detailed rules of evidence and procedure in domestic law, but rather with the overall fairness of the proceedings'. The different decisions reached by the ECHR in both *Sofri* and *Papageorgiou* are readily understandable on the facts. Had the Court been using the language of abuse of process, the authors suggest that, in *Sofri*'s case, it would have found that a fair trial was possible, in the absence of the lost material, whereas in *Papageorgiou* the conclusion would have been reached that a fair trial was no longer a possibility. In conclusion, the authors agree with the analysis of Professor Choo,[1] that: 'The approach of the courts in England and Wales seems consistent with what appears to be the approach of the European Court of Human Rights'. In both jurisdictions the Courts are looking to analyse the impact of the lost or destroyed evidence upon the overall fairness of the trial proceedings.

1   See Andrew L-T Choo, *Abuse of Process and Judicial Stays of Criminal Proceedings* (2nd Edn, Oxford University Press) p 101.

Chapter 4

Miscellaneous abuse

4.01   In *R v Derby Crown Court, ex p Brooks*[1] Sir Roger Ormrod defined the jurisdiction of abuse of process as follows:

'The power to stop a prosecution arises only when it is an abuse of the process of the court. It may be an abuse of process if either (a) *the prosecution have manipulated or misused the process of the court so as to deprive the defendant of a protection provided by the law or to take unfair advantage of a technicality,* or (b) on the balance of probability the defendant has been or will be, prejudiced in the preparation or conduct of his defence by delay on the part of the prosecution …' (Emphasis added)

1   (1985) 80 Cr App Rep 164 at 169.

4.02   There are an infinite number of situations in which an allegation of prosecutorial manipulation or misuse of the process of the court can be made. This chapter considers only a number of miscellaneous instances of where the abuse jurisdiction has been invoked. It is emphasised that the situations considered below are but mere examples of this head of abuse and the situations in which this can arise cannot be fully predicted. Fairness is obviously a concept whose parameters cannot be fixed or discerned.

PROOF OF PREJUDICE NOT REQUIRED

4.03   A characteristic of the law on abuse concerned with manipulation on misuse of process is that the court does not require any evidence of actual prejudice caused to the defendant. Manipulation or misuse, if established, tends to be regarded so gravely that the courts will stay the proceedings without further consideration. This approach differs from that in relation to delay where there is an insistence by the courts of the need to establish prejudice even when there has been massive delay.[1]

1   See **Chapter 1**.

STATUTORY TIME LIMITS

4.04   The cases under this heading can be conveniently divided into two parts: first, those concerned with the Magistrates' Court Act 1980, s 127(1), which states that summonses must be issued within six months of the commission of the alleged offence, and second, those concerned with alleged circumvention of custody time limits.

Magistrates' Court Act 1980, s 127

4.05   The leading case is *R v Brentford Justices, ex p Wong*.[1] Here the defendant was summonsed for driving without due care and attention. The summons was applied for and issued two days before the expiry of the six-month time limit. The defence solicitor, whose suspicions were aroused by the timing of this manoeuvre, made inquiries. Ultimately the prosecution disclosed that the information (the prerequisite for the issuance of the summons) was laid in order that more time be obtained pending a decision as to whether the defendant should be prosecuted with this offence or not. The prosecution admitted therefore that the information was laid before any decision had been made in relation to prosecution. The magistrates held that they had no jurisdiction to consider an abuse application based on an allegation of misuse of process and the case went to the Divisional Court. The court held that it would be an abuse for the prosecutor to lay an information when he has not reached a decision to prosecute. This judgment in this case is considered in paras **1.59–1.64**.

1   [1981] 1 All ER 884.

4.06   The courts are nonetheless prepared to endorse prosecutions launched just before the expiry of a time limit if one then ensues. In *Wei Hai Restaurant v Kingston City Council*[1] a prosecution was brought just before the expiry of a one-year limit under the Food Safety Act 1990. The court held that this was permissible.

1   [2001] EWHC Admin 490, (2001) 166 JP 185.

Expiry of limitation period

4.07   In *R v Jones (Michael)*[1] the appellant was convicted on three counts of indecent assault in circumstances where the conduct charged was essentially that of unlawful sexual intercourse with a girl under the age of 16, which was then an offence under s 6 of the Sexual Offences Act 1956. The defence sought to mount abuse of process arguments at trial and on appeal, on the basis that the prosecution did not begin until after the expiry of the 12-month statutory limitation period, which applied to s 6 offences. It was contended the prosecution used the indecent assault charges as an improper means of circumventing a time bar imposed by Parliament. Potter LJ rejected the defence arguments, holding that there was no misuse of the court's process on the particular facts. The prosecution had acted promptly once the complaints had been brought to their attention, in relation to circumstances where the sexual conduct took place over several years, where the appellant had exploited the relationship of a family friend and employer. The authors would agree with the commentary of Professor J C Smith:[2]

> '... it is not surprising that the court was unwilling to rule that every charge of indecent assault after the expiry of 12 months from an event that would have justified a charge under s.6 must be an abuse of process. The "public conscience" is a somewhat vague concept but it is difficult to imagine that it would be affronted by the bringing of a prosecution in the circumstances of

111

the present case. Indeed it is more likely that the public would be outraged to learn that a prosecution was not possible.'

1   [2003] 2 Cr App R 8.
2   See [2003] Crim LR 393.

Custody time limits

4.08   Pursuant to the Prosecution of Offences Act 1985, s 22 the Home Secretary may impose by regulation time limits in relation to completion by the prosecution of a particular stage of the proceedings. This section has been amended, most notably in relation to cases sent for trial under s 51 or 51A (3)(d) of the Crime and Disorder Act 1998. Subject to the prosecution completing that stage within the relevant time limit, the accused may be held in custody. Under s 22(3) a court may extend such limits provided that it is satisfied that the prosecution 'has acted with all due diligence and expedition'. The maximum periods of incarceration will depend upon the nature of the offence (ie whether it is a summary offence, triable either way, or indictable only, for example) and whether the case involves a committal or a sending for trial. The various time limits may be found in the amended SI 1987/299. If the prosecution fail to satisfy the respective limit or fail to persuade the court to grant an extension then the accused must be granted bail.

4.09   Clearly the underlying policy of custody time limits is to minimise the period spent by the accused in custody awaiting trial, to oblige the prosecution to prepare cases diligently and to allow the court power to determine whether there should be any extension to the maximum period.

4.10   On occasions an accused held in custody is originally charged with one offence but subsequently another is substituted. The Regulations state that time begins to run when an accused is charged and is thus relevant to a particular offence. Accordingly the charging of a new offence causes a fresh time limit to start, thus enabling overall an accused to be held in custody for a period exceeding the particular set number of days, without the prosecution having to seek the permission of the court to grant an extension.

4.11   Immediately this situation can give rise to a complaint of prosecution manipulation and abuse; by allowing such latitude to the prosecution to substitute and/or charge additional offences it can ensure not only that an accused be kept in custody far longer than intended but also that the requirement to show due diligence can be avoided altogether. Taking this possibility into account it may be alleged that the prosecution have improperly exploited it for the above reasons; that fresh charges have later been added for the purpose of retaining an accused in custody, for example, in excess of the 70 days.

4.12   This situation was considered by the House in *R (Wardle) v Crown Court at Leeds*[1] where a complaint of abuse of process was made. Here the appellant was originally charged with murder and remanded in custody. On the day his limit was to expire, the prosecution substituted a charge of manslaughter and the magistrate ruled a fresh limit of 70 days started that day in respect of the new charge.

1   [2001] UKHL 12, [2002] 1 AC 754.

4.13   Lord Slynn considered the complaint of abuse and held:

'27. It is accepted that where to add or substitute a new charge amounts to an abuse of process, a new custody time limit does not begin. It has been said that where the new charge is brought in bad faith or dishonestly, that would amount to an abuse of process. In my view the ambit of "abuse of process" is not so limited. If a new charge is brought simply to keep the accused in custody for a longer period, that is clearly contrary to the intention of the legislation and constitutes an abuse of process. As Professor Smith said in his commentary to *R v Great Yarmouth Magistrates', ex p Thomas, Davis and Darlington* [1992] Crim LR 116, at p 117:

"Perhaps the more specific question to be asked is whether the charges of possession with intent were brought solely for the purpose of retaining the applicants in custody".

28. Equally if the court is satisfied that the way in which and the time at which the new charge is added or substituted, indicates that it is not done for the genuine purpose of introducing a new charge on a revised assessment of the case, but is done primarily to keep the accused in custody on the initial charge, then this will constitute an abuse of process. Of course on the other hand if the purpose is genuinely to introduce a new charge on such a revised assessment the fact that the accused begins a new custody period does not in itself constitute an abuse of process.'

On the facts Lord Slynn held no abuse. The new charge was brought on the basis of a substantial body of evidence which had been disclosed prior to the charge of manslaughter being laid. He also held that the appellant's art 5 right to liberty had similarly not been violated.

Youth court

4.14   There are now no overall time limits for the youth court, since the regulations were revoked: see Prosecution of Offences (Youth Court Time Limits) (Revocation and Transitional Provisions) Regulations 2003 (SI 2003/917). Previously, the Prosecution of Offences Act 1985, s 22B entitled a prosecutor to re-institute proceedings that have been stayed for a failure to meet that limit.

4.15   In *R on the application of the DPP v Croydon Youth Court*[1] this situation occurred and abuse of process was alleged. Here, as a result of re-instituted proceedings, the trial date was 300 days, ie some 200 days in excess of the old limit. The youth court held an abuse and stayed the case but this was quashed on appeal. Poole J held the prosecutor's conduct permissible under s 22B and there was no other ground of abuse.

1   (2001)165 JP 181 DC

PRE-INTERVIEW DISCLOSURE

4.16 Generally there is no right to such disclosure and ordinarily a failure to effect such disclosure would not enable a suspect to refuse to answer questions in interview and be sure that no adverse inference could be draw from this pursuant to the Criminal Justice and Public Order Act 1994, s 34, as amended. This would all depend on the circumstances.

4.17 In *DPP v Ara*[1] the Administrative Court was, however, willing to lay down a general principle. Here the applicant had been offered a caution prior to interview, on condition that he admitted the offence during it. Perhaps fearing a trap, the applicant's solicitor sought disclosure of the transcript of the applicant's previous caution interview so that he could provide adequate and informed legal advice on what to do in the forthcoming interview. This request was refused. The court held that advice to a person whether to accept a caution was linked to their right to legal advice. Thus it was an abuse to refuse disclosure of the transcript. Rose LJ said:

> 'the justices were fully entitled to conclude that the proceedings should be stayed as an abuse of process, the police having refused to disclose the terms of the interview, without which informed advice and informed consent to a caution could not properly be given'.

1   [2001] EWHC Admin 493, [2001] 4 All ER 559.

4.18 Rose LJ was anxious to avoid attempts to extrapolate his reasoning into a general right to pre-interview or charge disclosure, and added:

> 'I make it clear that this does not mean that there is a general obligation on the police to disclose material prior to charge. That would, in many cases, be impracticable and, in some cases, (for example where there is an ongoing investigation) highly undesirable, as well as being outwith the contemplation of the legislation, the Code or anything to be implied therefrom. But, in the present case, the failure to disclose the terms of the interview followed by the institution and pursuit of a criminal trial in the circumstances described amply justified the justices in reaching the conclusion which they did.'[1]

1   [2001] EWHC Admin 493, [2001] 4 All ER 559, para 24.

PROSECUTOR'S IMPROPER MOTIVE

4.19 Allegations of improper motive normally arise in relation to the bringing of private prosecutions where the defendant alleges that the underlying motive of the prosecutor is either revenge, obsession or some wholly collateral motive to cause embarrassment to the defendant. The attitude of the Divisional Court to such allegations is a permissive one, generally permitting the bringing of private prosecutions unless there is very clear evidence of improper motive. There are perhaps three reasons explaining this reluctance to intervene: first, the court does not wish to bear the burden of inquiring into the detail of the facts of a case including the alleged underlying motive of the prosecutor; secondly, the court knows that where there is a flagrant abuse then the Crown Prosecution

Service has the statutory power to take over and discontinue the proceedings; thirdly, it appears that the policy of the courts has generally been to facilitate the bringing of private prosecutions. Whether the long-term future for the right of private prosecution remains a healthy one, however, has now been called into question as a result of the concerns expressed by Lord Bingham in *Jones v Whalley*.[1]

1   [2007] 1 AC 63.

R v Bow Street Metropolitan Stipendiary Magistrates, ex p South Coast Shipping[1]

4.20   The defendant alleged that the bringing of this private prosecution was an abuse because it was being used as a means of drawing publicity to the 'Marchioness' shipping disaster and as a means of creating political pressure in favour of a public inquiry. The prosecution was alleged to be a mere device to achieve a collateral purpose. The Divisional Court held that even if this attribution of motive to the prosecutor was true, the prosecution would not be an abuse unless this was the prosecutor's sole or dominant motive. That the prosecutor has an ulterior motive other than to bring criminals to justice is not therefore necessarily fatal or open to objection on the grounds of abuse or oppression.

1   [1993] Crim LR 221.

R v Durham Magistrates, ex p Davies[1]

4.21   A similar approach was also taken in this case. Here, the private prosecutor was alleged to be obsessed with achieving the successful prosecution of the defendant. Accordingly his motives were improper, they tainted the prosecution and it should be stayed as an abuse. The Divisional Court disagreed, holding that the motivation of a prosecutor was irrelevant to consideration of the abuse claim. It is submitted that the decision in this case is consistent with the cautionary words expressed by Lord Salmon in *DPP v Humphrys*:[2]

'I respectfully agree that a judge has not and should not appear to have any responsibility for the institution of prosecutions; nor has he any power to refuse to allow the prosecution to proceed merely because he considers that, as a matter of policy, it ought not to have been brought. It is only if the prosecution amounts to an abuse of the process of the court and is oppressive or frivolous that the judge has the power to intervene'.

Lord Edmund-Davies said: 'Judges should pause long before staying proceedings which on their face are perfectly regular'.[3]

Accordingly this decision holds that the fact that a prosecutor/complainant may be unreliable as a witness and obsessive about his cause does not of itself justify a decision to stay.

1   (1993) Times, 25 May.

2   [1977] AC 1 at 46.
3   [1977] AC 1 at 55

R v Gloucester Crown Court, ex p Jackman[1]

4.22   This was another private prosecution, where the criminal prosecution and a civil claim were being run in tandem by the same person against the same defendant. The solicitors acting for the prosecutor/claimant offered to settle both proceedings with the defendant provided that the defendant paid compensation to the prosecutor/claimant. When settlement negotiations broke down, the defendant asserted that the prosecution was oppressive because it was being used as a means of pressuring the defendant to accept settlement terms in relation to the civil proceedings. The court held that the evidence to support this claim was insufficient although it expressed its disapproval of the proposed terms of settlement which included an offer to discontinue the prosecution.

1   [1993] COD 100. See also *R v Horseferry Magistrates' Court, ex p Stephenson* [1989] COD 470.

R v Milton Keynes Magistrates, ex p Roberts[1]

4.23   This was a prosecution brought by the Trading Standards Department of Buckinghamshire County Council for breach of the Trade Descriptions Act 1968. It was alleged that the defendant was dealing in counterfeit parts for Ford cars. The defendant alleged abuse on the ground that the prosecutor was a mere puppet of the Ford motor company who had provided the resources for the investigation. The prosecutor had allegedly not exercised independent judgment and Ford were the real prosecutors. The Divisional Court held that the Trading Standards Department had exercised independent judgment. A stay would only be imposed 'if a prosecutor did indeed make himself the creature of a private interest in exercising his powers, then that conduct would at least be prima facie abusive'. Furthermore a prosecution would only be stopped if to allow it to continue would be 'tantamount to endorsing behaviour which undermines or degrades the rule of law' or 'is an affront to justice'.

1   [1995] Crim LR 224.

R v Adaway[1]

4.24   This case involved a local authority instituted proceedings, which also related to the Trade Descriptions Act 1968. The local authority had a policy whereby, for a prosecution to be justified, there had to be evidence of fraudulent activity or deliberate or persistent breaches of the proposed defendant's legal obligations. In the Court of Appeal it became clear that the defence contentions at trial, and on appeal, were well founded, for there was no material to suggest that the local authority's criteria had been met. The trial judge ought to have allowed the defence application to stay proceedings as an abuse of process, on the grounds that the prosecution was oppressive.

[2004] EWCA Crim 2831; Times, 22 November, 2004,CA

R (Dacre and Associated Newspapers) v City of Westminster Magistrates Court[2]

4.25   These Administrative Court proceedings involved Dacre, the editor of a newspaper, and Associated Newspapers, the publishers, who sought judicial review of a District Judge's refusal to stay a prosecution for an alleged breach of the Children Act 1989 (s 97(6)). The Court held that, when determining whether a private prosecution was an abuse of process on *ex parte Bennett* type grounds, the motive and conduct of the prosecutor could be relevant. In considering the issue of 'motive', proceedings tainted by mala fides or spite, or some other oblique motive could amount to an abuse.[2] The mere presence of an indirect or improper motive, however, did not necessarily vitiate a private prosecution. The court further held it would be slow to halt a prosecution where there were mixed motives, unless the prosecution's conduct was genuinely oppressive.[3]

1   [2008] EWHC 1667 (Admin); 16 July 2008.
2   See *Raymond v Attorney General* [1982] 1 QB 839; see also *R v Baines* [1909] 1 KB 258.
3   See *R v Bow Street Metropolitan Stipendiary Magistrate and another, ex p South Coast Shipping Company Ltd* [1993] QB 645.

4.26   The court held that the correct approach was to decide whether there was a primary motive, and one which was so removed from the proceedings that it rendered the prosecution a misuse or an abuse of process.[1] The court held, on the facts of the case, that the District Judge was permitted to conclude the mixed motives of the prosecutor were unobjectionable (given that they were partly concerned with protecting her child's identity in the context of a newspaper in apparent breach of the law). However, he ought to have found that her willingness to disclose information about her affairs to the newspaper's journalist, which would have led to the child's identification, rendered the prosecution an abuse of process.

1   See also *R v Leeds Magistrates Court, ex p Serif Systems Ltd*, unreported, October 9, 1997.

REMOVAL OF RIGHT TO A PARTICULAR TYPE OF TRIAL

R v Rotherham Justices, ex p Brough[1]

4.27   The defendant was alleged to have committed the offence when aged 16. Pursuant to the Magistrates' Court Act 1980, s 24 if, when the issue of mode of trial was dealt with by the magistrate, the defendant was under 17, then the case could only be remitted to the magistrates for trial. However, the charge was indictable only if the defendant was aged 17. In the event, the return date of the applicant's summons was fixed for the day after his 17th birthday. His suspicious defence solicitor inquired with both the court and the CPS why this should be so and after initial denials from the CPS, ascertained that the timing of the defendant's hearing was not a matter of chance but because the CPS felt that the case should only dealt with by the Crown Court. The applicant alleged misuse of process. The Divisional Court held that manipulation of the date in this way by the CPS was an unacceptable way of advancing the interests of justice. However, the court declined to attribute any element of misconduct or mala fides to anyone within the CPS. The court held that this was not a case where there was 'some element of bad faith or sharp practice or oppressive or overreaching behaviour or, to use a colloquialism some form of dirty trick'. Furthermore, the court held that the defendant was not prejudiced.

1   [1991] Crim LR 522.

R v Redbridge Justices and Fox, ex p Whitehouse[1]

4.28   The defendant was charged with an either way offence and expressed a preference for summary trial. This was opposed by the prosecution, who wished for a Crown Court trial. Subsequently, an additional more serious charge was laid, making the case indictable only. The defendant alleged that this additional charge was motivated by a desire to deprive the defendant of his right to elect for summary trial. The Divisional Court held that such a motive by a prosecutor was permissible provided that the additional more serious charge was justified on the evidence.

1   [1992] COD 234.

R v Martin[1]

4.29   The appellant was charged with murder and convicted. The conviction was awarded by a court-martial which had been convened in Germany. What was exceptional about this case was that the appellant had been brought from England, where he was eligible to trial by jury, to stand trial by a court-martial in Germany. The reason for this was because when the alleged murder occurred, the appellant was subject to military law. The appellant argued that the court-martial procedure was unfair principally for two reasons: first, the trial of a young civilian by court-martial was inherently unfair and oppressive; secondly, the decision to try the appellant by court-martial in Germany rather than allow him to be tried in England constituted an abuse.

1   [1998] 1 All ER 193.

4.30   The House of Lords dismissed this appeal. It construed the relevant provisions of the Army Act 1955 to hold that Parliament had approved trial by court-martial as an appropriate mode of trial for young civilians in certain circumstances. Furthermore, the decision not to allow a trial in England on the grounds of forum conveniens was not inherently unfair or an abuse.

REMOVAL OF A POTENTIAL DEFENCE

4.31   In *R v Asfaw*[1] the Court of Appeal noted its concern over the apparently standard prosecutorial practice, when an asylum seeker seeks to leave the country for another place of refuge using false documents, to combine a charge of infringement of the Forgery and Counterfeiting Act with a charge of attempting to obtain air services by deception. On the facts, Asfaw was acquitted of the forgery count (count 1), but pleaded guilty to the deception count (count 2), there being no statutory defence (under s 31 of the Immigration and Asylum Act 1999) to the new count 2, which was added to the indictment. The court considered the different policy considerations. The prosecution suggested that the second count may have been added out of concern for the financial position of the airlines. However, the sentencing judge hinted other factors were at play. The Court of Appeal held that, if the second count had been added in the interests of immigration control, in order to prevent the asylum seeker from relying on the s 31 defence, there would be strong grounds for contending that the practice amounted to an abuse of process. The decision suggests that there may well be occasions where the defence can call into question prosecutorial policy which leads to unfairness. The Appeal Court substituted the sentence of nine months imprisonment with an absolute discharge.

1   [2006] Crim LR 906; [2006] EWCA Crim 707.

PROSECUTION OVERCHARGING

4.32   This allegation was made in *Hui Chi-Ming v R.*[1] The defendant was alleged to have been an accomplice to murder and was tried for this offence. Prior to his trial, the alleged killer had been acquitted of murder. The prosecution had also offered a plea bargain; the murder count would be dropped in return for a plea of guilty to manslaughter. This was rejected but ultimately the defendant was convicted of murder. He submitted that his trial for murder was an abuse. Bearing in mind the previous acquittal of the alleged principal for murder it was unfair for this trial to proceed. Furthermore, the prosecution should only have charged manslaughter. The Privy Counsel held that there was no evidence of deliberate overcharging by the prosecution and that on the evidence, the prosecution were entitled to bring a charge of murder despite the earlier acquittal of the alleged principal offender. In Lowry LJ's view there was nothing which could credibly be described as an abuse of process:

> 'that is, something so unfair and wrong that the courts should not allow a prosecutor to proceed with what is in all respects a regular proceeding. There can be no suggestion that the appellant was the victim of a plea bargaining situation ... there was no sign of fraud or deceit as between the Crown and the appellant'.[2]

1   (1991) 94 Cr App Rep 236.
2   At 251.

4.33   In *R v Harlow Magistrates' Court, ex p O'Farrell*[1] the prosecution sought to add an additional and more serious charge based on the same facts after the bench had retired to consider its verdict on the original charge. The bench accepted this addition. The Administrative Court held that it was an abuse to add a charge at this stage in the proceedings as it would prejudice the defence case which had already been pleaded in relation to the original charge. This case is thus authority for a prosecutor deciding upon and having to stick with his case despite a late change of mind.

1   [2000] Crim LR 589.

DISPARITY OF TREATMENT ARGUMENTS

4.34 In two recent decisions the Court of Appeal have had to consider appeals based on alleged disparity of treatment type arguments. In the first case, that of *R v Petch and Coleman*[1] a somewhat anomalous situation arose whereby the appellants' murder convictions were upheld, albeit that two co-defendants, who had previously also been charged on a joint enterprise murder, had their pleas to manslaughter and other offences accepted. This left the co-defendants, who had previously fled the jurisdiction, with substantially reduced sentences, and the appellants with a significant sense of grievance. The appellants contended that the resulting unfairness amounted to an abuse of process.

1   [2005] 2 Cr App R. 40.

4.35   Pill LJ held:[1]

'The prosecution's alleged lack of consistency, resulting from pragmatic considerations, which has resulted in an anomaly different from, but in its way as striking as, that in *Hui Chi-ming*, does not open the door to a finding that the verdicts upon the appellants were unsafe. The law does not permit the court to take an overall view of the situation retrospectively and, in the interest of even-handedness, to declare the convictions of the appellants unsafe.'

1   Para 47 judgment.

4.36   The court, however, went on to acknowledge that a review may be called for:

'Subsequent developments in the law may, with respect, encourage a review of the approach in *Hui Chi-ming* to how prosecutions in second trials based upon the same events as earlier trials are to be conducted. The prosecution were consistent in that case but to proceed against a secondary party for murder when the principal offender has already been convicted only of manslaughter creates a particular sense of grievance absent in the present situation.'[1]

1   Para 49 judgment.

4.37   In *R v L*[1] the appellant had been charged with his baby's murder, which led to concerns for the family's other child. In the ensuing proceedings under the Children Act 1989, the judge held that the cause of the baby's death had not been established, and that he was unable to decide whether one parent was more likely to have caused the injuries suffered by the baby than the other. The appellant sought to stay the subsequent murder trial proceedings as an abuse of process, on the basis that the judge's decision and findings in the Children Act proceedings were conclusive of the criminal proceedings. The Court of Appeal dismissed the appeal, holding that the decision in the care proceedings, in which the prosecution took no part, was not, and could not be, a final determination of the criminal proceedings.

1   [2007] 1 Cr App R. 1.

TRIAL IN ABSENCE OF A CO-ACCUSED

4.38   In *R v Forsyth*[1] the defendant was charged with handling stolen goods. Her prosecution arose out of allegations concerning the fugitive Asil Nadir. Her prosecution was exceptional in the sense that, following the absconding of Nadir, the prosecution (Serious Fraud Office) had conceded that the trial of the second defendant should not proceed because, in Nadir's absence, it could not be fair to that defendant. However, in relation to Forsyth the SFO pressed ahead despite accepting that she was a peripheral defendant on the fringe of an immense fraud allegedly committed by Nadir and the second defendant. Beldam LJ held that the decision of the SFO to prosecute Forsyth in the circumstances 'seems a strange decision' but nonetheless:

> 'the decision to do so is the prerogative of the SFO and does not in our judgement itself amount to an abuse of process. It is not for us to say whether such a choice accords with ordinary notions of even handedness, or is likely to enhance the public perception of the fairness of a prosecuting authority'.[2]

1   (1997) 2 Cr App Rep 299.
2   (1997) 2 Cr App Rep 299 at 311.

REPEATED COMMITTAL PROCEEDINGS

4.39   In *R v Manchester City Stipendiary Magistrate, ex p Snelson*[1] Widgery CJ held that a criminal prosecution could be restarted against a defendant by way of fresh committal proceedings or voluntary bill of indictment even where the original proceedings against the defendant at committal had been dismissed. Lord Widgery, however, considered the danger which his judgment might create as vexatious repeated committal proceedings for the same offence against the same defendant. He said:

> '... the only aspect of the whole case which has troubled me is the feeling that if the prosecution are right in their argument there seems to me to be a risk that a defendant might be prejudiced by repeated committal proceedings all failing, resulting in a committal being repeated time after time ... I am satisfied that this particular difficulty is overcome ... by saying that this court has a discretionary power to see that the use of repeated committal proceedings is not allowed to become vexatious or an abuse of the process of the court'.[2]

1   [1977] 1 WLR 911.
2   At 913.

4.40   This issue arose in *R v Horsham Justices, ex p Reeves*[1] where Ackner LJ held that the repeated committal in that case was an abuse. He said:

> 'should the prosecution be entitled as they see it, to treat the first committal proceedings for all practicable purposes as a dummy run and, having concluded that they over-complicated them, from virtually the same proceedings but in a form which they should have been brought if proper thought had been given by the prosecution to them in the first place? In my judgment, to allow such a course in the particular circumstances of this case

would be vexatious to the applicant, and for that reason it would, in my judgment, be an abuse'.

Ackner LJ held that the second set of proceedings, although simplified and shortened compared to the first, were vexatious and an abuse.

1   [1981] Crim LR 566.

4.41   However, in *R v Grays Justices, ex p Graham*[1] the Divisional Court held that the proceedings were not vexatious, the defendant having been discharged in the original proceedings on the grounds of delay.

1   (1982) 75 Cr App Rep 229.

THE RULE IN HUNTER

4.42   In *Hunter v Chief Constable of the West Midlands*[1] the Birmingham Six, following their conviction for terrorist offences, initiated a civil action against the police for assault. Their statement of claim alleged that during their interviews with individual police officers, in which they made alleged confessions, they were beaten and sustained physical injuries. At their criminal trial, the circumstances under which their confessions were obtained was a central issue. A major plank of each of the defendants' cases was the assertion that the confessions were untrue, unreliable and were coerced. The jury however must have disbelieved this because they convicted all six. At the hearing of this civil action, the defendant police officers contended that the initiation of the civil action was an abuse of process as in effect the action sought to refute or throw into doubt the finding of both the trial judge and the jury at the criminal trial that the Birmingham Six had not been assaulted by the police. In holding that this action constituted an abuse of process Lord Diplock articulated a rule which has subsequently come to be known as 'The rule in *Hunter*':

> 'The abuse of process which the instant case exemplifies is the initiation of proceedings in a court of justice for the purpose of mounting a collateral attack on a final decision against the intending plaintiff which has been made by another court of competent jurisdiction in previous proceedings in which the intending plaintiff had a full opportunity of contesting the decision in the court by which it was made'.[2]

1   [1982] AC 529.
2   At 541.

4.43   The rule in *Hunter* was exclusively applied in a criminal context in *R v Belmarsh Magistrates' Court, ex p Watts*.[1] The facts of this case are recounted in **Chapter 10** and are not repeated here. One of the matters to be decided in *Watts* was whether the rule in *Hunter* extended to criminal rather than simply civil proceedings. In his judgment Buxton LJ held that the rule in *Hunter* did apply to criminal proceedings. However, he was careful to restrict its application to where the second proceedings 'must in fact and in effect, and not merely in intention, be a challenge to the finding in the first proceedings'. In other words if the second proceedings were successful, this would contradict the judgment in the earlier proceedings. Buxton LJ also relied on the judgment of Bingham MR in *Smith v Linskills*[2]:

'The main considerations of public policy which underlie the existing rule are, as we understand, threefold; (i) the affront to any coherent system of justice which must necessarily arise if there subsist two final but inconsistent decisions of courts of competent jurisdiction … (ii) the virtual impossibility of fairly retrying at a later date the issue which was before the court on the earlier occasion … (iii) the importance of finality in litigation'.

1   [1999] 2 Cr App Rep 188.
2   [1996] 1 WLR 763 at 773.

4.44   Turning to the merits of the case before him Buxton LJ held that the intention of the prosecutor was to undermine his earlier conviction. However, he should have followed the route of appeal rather than initiate collateral criminal proceedings for the same purpose.

4.45   As to the jurisdiction of the Divisional Court to rule that the rule in *Hunter* applied to exclusively criminal proceedings, Buxton LJ cited Lord Lowry in *Bennett*[1] that it should offend the courts' sense of justice and propriety to be asked to try the accused in the circumstances of this case.[2] Buxton LJ held that this prosecution fell within that category and could therefore be stayed. This, it is submitted, is a novel application to domestic proceedings of *Bennett* which hitherto had been regarded as applying only with regard to international executive lawlessness.

1   [1994] AC 42.
2   [1994] AC 42 at 74.

FAILURE TO CONDUCT A FAIR INTERVIEW

4.46   Interviews under caution are governed by PACE Code of Practice C. Most abuse or s 78 applications relating to interviews are in connection with some allegation of unfairness or oppression which was said to have occurred during the defendant's interview. However, recently the courts have recognised that an abuse can arise where the police/investigators failed to interview the defendant at all or failed to interview him fairly.

4.47   In *R v Trustham*[1] the accused stood trial for drug-money laundering. Following his arrest he was never interviewed but simply charged. The trial judge held that this had prejudiced the defendant in the following way: 'A defendant who does not give evidence having answered questions in interview is nevertheless entitled to have that explanation considered by the jury'. The trial judge also found that the defendant was further prejudiced as follows:

'To deprive a suspect of the right to give an explanation at the earliest opportunity, despite him having been cautioned, that anything he did say would be written down and may be given in evidence, must be a breach of a person's human rights and is clearly an abuse'.

1   (27 November 1997, unreported), Southwark Crown Court.

4.48 In the circumstances of *Trustham*, the trial judge held that the defendant had a right to be interviewed and had a right during such interview to provide an explanation as to his state of mind. Depriving the defendant of an interview deprived him from setting out at the earliest opportunity his defence/innocence which the judge held was unfair because this meant that at his subsequent trial, the defendant could not point to what he said immediately after his arrest.

RETRIALS

4.49 Submissions of abuse have occurred in two situations in this context. First, as in *R v Mercer*[1] where the prosecution case as regards the alleged role played by the defendant in the robbery had changed between his trial and retrial. Second, as in *Bowe v R*,[2] where it was proposed to try the defendant a third time after two juries had been unable to agree.

1   [2001] EWCA Crim 638, [2001] All ER (D) 187 (Mar).
2   [2001] UKPC 19, [2001] 4 LRC 372.

4.50 In *Mercer* the essence of the complaint was that the prosecution should not be permitted to present one set of alleged facts to a court on one occasion and then alter this on a subsequent occasion, almost a claim that an estoppel arose once the prosecution had set out its case in front of one court. This submission was dismissed by the Court of Appeal. There was no principle of law or fairness which prevented the prosecution from calling new evidence at a retrial and so altering its case. If unfairness had resulted this would have to be based on another complaint arising out of the fact of there being a retrial.

4.51 In *R v Swaine*[1] at the commencement of the retrial, the judge permitted the prosecution to add an additional count to the indictment and it was thus amended. The Court of Appeal held that as a matter of law it was permissible to amend an indictment at the stage of a retrial provided no injustice was done to the defendant.

1   [2001] Crim LR 166.

4.52 Whilst not a retrial, the situation in *DPP v Jimale*[1] is relevant. Here the prosecution opened its case before the justices and the court adjourned before it was completed. At the adjourned hearing the prosecution sought to call a witness whom previously it had not intended to call. A complaint of unfair advantage arising out of the adjournment was made; the prosecution should not be permitted to call a witness whose existence was known about when its case was opened. The justices agreed and stayed the case. The Administrative Court disagreed and held that the obtaining of new witnesses between hearings was both proper and in many cases, desirable. In any event if some unfair advantage had been taken in relation to a particular witness this could be dealt with by exclusion under s 78 rather than a stay.

1   [2001] Crim LR 138.

4.53 In *Bowe* a submission was made before the Privy Council that a second retrial in these circumstances amounted to an abuse as it was an established practice that a prosecution should not seek a conviction after two failed attempts to persuade a jury of the defendant's guilt. The Board however declined to agree and held that ipso facto a second retrial did not amount to an abuse. However it made plain its view that in this situation it was incumbent on a prosecutor to consider very carefully whether either the interests of justice or the public interest would be served by a third attempt. Clearly here the Board was sending a message that repeated attempts to convict an accused might well amount to oppression and so an abuse.

4.54   A similar judgment was given in *R v Henworth (Frank)*,[1] where it was held that the practice against a second retrial was only a convention not proposition of law. However any prosecutor contemplating this was duty-bound to assess carefully the interests of justice, this to include the defendant's interests taking into account the effect of delay and prejudice. Whilst the retrial did not amount to an abuse of process, nevertheless the length of the proceedings overall, was adjudged to violate the ECHR Art 6 reasonable time requirements.[2]

1   [2001] 2 Cr App Rep 4.
2   *Henworth v UK* (2005) 40 EHRR 33.

CONTACT WITH WITNESSES

4.55   Within our system there are sensitivities attached to dealings with potential witnesses; for example it is regarded as unprofessional to coach or rehearse them as to what they should say in evidence, something US lawyers regard as remarkable. In *R v Evans*[1] an allegation was made by the defence, of police impropriety in relation to their approach to and meetings with potential defence witnesses. The police in the course of such meetings said that what the witnesses had stated could not be correct. Consequently some of the witnesses retracted their statements, which they had made previously to the defence solicitors. An allegation that undue pressure had been made upon them by the police was made at the trial, this being the explanation for why the witnesses had suddenly withdrawn their evidence. In essence it was claimed that the abuse was the police contacting the witnesses with the intention of persuading them to withdraw their evidence.

1   [2001] EWCA Crim 730, [2001] All ER (D) 289 (Mar).

4.56   The Court of Appeal held that it was proper for either the defence or prosecution to meet with witnesses who were intended to give evidence for the opposite side. Moreover arranging such a meeting for the purpose of seeking the witness to change their evidence was also permissible so long as no 'undue pressure' was applied which, if this happened, would amount to a contempt of court as well as an abuse. Here there was no evidence that the police had sought to apply such pressure and so the complaint of abuse was dismissed. Waller LJ held:

> 'There was nothing improper in the police revisiting the witnesses. It would be quite improper for the police to put inaccurately the evidence in order to obtain a statement or a change in a statement from a witness. However, in

this case it must be remembered it is not the statement which is important, it is the evidence which is ultimately given at the trial. In the circumstances of this case original statements had been obtained, the police had revisited and possibly obtained changes in those statements, but, the defence solicitors were in a position to visit those witnesses themselves and put to those witnesses any aspect on which they had been misled by the police'.

In this regard it would obviously be an abuse for a potential witness to be threatened or offered any inducement in return for them changing their evidence. In *R v Schlesinger*[1] machinations to prevent potential witnesses from giving evidence were held to be an abuse.

1   [1995] Crim LR 137. This case is considered further at para **5.76**.

SELECTIVE PROSECUTION

4.57   Prosecutors are always permitted to exercise a choice over who to prosecute. There is no obligation to treat all suspects equally, in the sense that where the evidence is the same against all it follows that all must be similarly prosecuted. There is no policy or rule of law which requires the prosecution of an individual simply because he/she is guilty of an offence. However, in deciding who to prosecute and, perhaps more importantly, who not to prosecute when the evidence is largely similar, the prosecutor must act fairly. Clearly any form of unjustified discrimination or favouritism would be unlawful or ultra vires. This might constitute an offence under anti-discrimination legislation and would almost certainly be an unlawful act by a public authority under the Human Rights Act 1998.

4.58   The prosecuting agency which perhaps has the most developed policy and practice concerned with selective prosecution is the Inland Revenue, who choose only to prosecute a small proportion of those against whom there is sufficient material to prosecute for tax fraud. For the majority of such recalcitrant taxpayers the priority is to reach a settlement whereby the tax plus interest and penalties is paid over. The Revenue has moreover since 1999 published its selective prosecution policy.

4.59   In criminal trials it is sometimes alleged that a prosecution witness has fabricated or embroidered his evidence as a means of escaping prosecution himself. Accordingly his evidence should be disregarded. In most cases the credibility of this accusation is a matter for the jury and no abuse arises. An abuse may arise, however, where it is alleged that there has been collusion between the suspect-turned-witness and the investigators; the suspect was in effect offered an inducement to give false evidence by the investigators, this being a promise of immunity for him/her or a friend or relative. It is alleged that the prosecution is therefore tainted by this impropriety and is unfair.

4.60   This situation arose in *R v Bigley*[1] where several individuals where arrested for drugs offences. Each was interviewed under caution and some, during their interviews, incriminated the defendant. Having done so, those individuals were then offered immunity in return for agreeing to become prosecution witnesses against the defendant. This offer was taken up. The defendant alleged abuse of power and unfairness. The Court of Appeal held that as a matter of principle it was acceptable for a prosecutor to decide not to prosecute those guilty of less serious offences in order to prosecute those guilty of more serious offences. In itself the means here justified the end. What the court attached great importance to in dismissing the claim of improper inducement was that before there was any consideration of whether anyone should be charged or not, each suspect had been formally interviewed and their version of events obtained. Accordingly the versions were given without any promise of reward held out by the investigators. Only after this stage was there any discussion about inducements, i e assistance in return for immunity.

1   [2001] EWCA Crim 3012, [2001] All ER (D) 253 (Dec).

4.61   Keene LJ stated:

'If the more significant criminals are to be prosecuted, it may be necessary to get lesser offenders to come to court and give evidence against them and that may require the prosecuting authorities, in some instances, to agree not to prosecute. There may be situations where the continuing pressure or inducement on a witness or witnesses to give evidence against the defendant is so strong, even by the stage of trial, that the judge forms the view that it would be wrong for a jury to place any reliance on such evidence. He would then exclude the evidence and might, in appropriate cases, stay the proceedings. There will be other cases where the situation is less extreme, and where the jury can properly hear the evidence of such a witness, and hear evidence also about the circumstances in which that witness came to make a witness statement, and then make up their minds about the honesty of the witness.

In the present case we are not persuaded that the police abused their powers. The procedure generally adopted was one where the person arrested was interviewed on tape, before a caution was discussed. That, in our judgment, is an important safeguard and one which accords with the national guidance on this matter. Once that situation has been reached, there is no reason why the willingness of a suspect to co-operate with the police should not be taken into account by the police, when deciding whether to caution or not'.

4.62   Investigators and prosecutors will need always to be mindful of allegations of collusion and improper inducement in a trial where an important prosecution witness against whom there was sufficient evidence of criminality to mount a prosecution has nonetheless never been prosecuted.

NON-DISCLOSURE ABUSE

Non disclosure and unfairness

4.63   It is trite law that an accused's right to fair disclosure is regarded as inseparable from his right to a fair trial. An accused must be in a position to fairly advance his arguments by way of fair disclosure of material in the Crown's possession. In *R v Togher*[1] the Court of Appeal held that where an accused's right to a fair trial was vitiated, for example because of non-disclosure, this would almost invariably result in the quashing of the conviction. Woolf CJ held 'If they could establish an abuse, then this court would give very serious consideration to whether justice required the conviction to be set aside'.[2]

1   [2001] 1 Cr App Rep 457.
2   At 468.

4.64   Recent developments have underlined that the right to disclosure is regarded as a fundamental condition or hallmark of fairness. The 2005 Attorney-General's Guidelines on the disclosure of unused material in criminal proceedings were issued in the light of the abolition of the distinction between primary and secondary disclosure, and the introduction of a single test for disclosure of material that 'might reasonably be considered capable of undermining the prosecution case or assisting the case for the accused'. The opening paragraph declares:

'Every accused person has a right to a fair trial, a right long embodied in our law and guarantee under article 6 of the European Convention on Human Rights. A fair trial is the proper object and expectation of all participants in the trial process. Fair disclosure to an accused is an inseparable part of a fair trial'.

4.65   These laudable words are followed up, in para 23 of the guidelines, with an unequivocal warning to investigators and disclosure officers, namely:

'Investigators and disclosure officers must be fair and objective and must work together with prosecutors to ensure that disclosure obligations are met. A failure to take action leading to inadequate disclosure may result in a wrongful conviction. It may alternatively lead to a successful abuse of process argument, an acquittal against the weight of the evidence or the appellate courts may find that a conviction is unsafe and quash it.'

4.66   In the foreword to the new Guidelines, the Attorney-General explains the reasons for their introduction, which came about as a result of the new disclosure test, the new code of practice on disclosure, and developments in the other new provisions and in case law. The Attorney-General had also taken note of the concerns, which had previously been expressed by judges, prosecutors and defence practitioners, over the operation of the old disclosure provisions. Practitioners and judges alike are all encouraged to 'make a concerted effort to comply with the CPIA disclosure regime robustly in a consistent way in order to regain the trust and confidence of all those involved in the criminal justice system'.

The CPIA 1996; prosecution failures to comply with their disclosure obligations

4.67   Parts I and II of the Criminal Procedure and Investigations Act 1996, as amended by the Criminal Justice Act 2003, now govern the duties and responsibilities of parties in relation to disclosure, so far as offences where the investigation was begun on or after 4 April 2005. Part I (ss 1–21) has developed a staged approach, which entails initial prosecution disclosure, disclosure by the defence, with a continual review by the prosecution. Part II (ss 22–27) sets out a detailed code of practice in relation to the police's recording and retaining of material which has been obtained during a criminal investigation, and in relation to the provision of material to prosecutors, who are required to make decisions on disclosure. In order to fully understand prosecution disclosure obligations, practitioners will also need to scrutinise the revised Code of Practice, the new Attorney-General's Guidelines, and the 2006 Protocol for the control and management of unused material in the Crown Court, all of which are set out in the Appendices to this work.

4.68   In this new world of disclosure, the defence practitioners are being encouraged to play their own active role. It would appear that those accused who set out their defences in interview, serve full defence case statements (with annexed specific requests for disclosure and/or for various lines of inquiry to be pursued), followed up by chasing letters to the prosecution in correspondence, are likely to be in the best position to maximise their disclosure opportunities. Where a judge finds, however, that the defence have been deprived of material which might reasonably be considered capable of undermining the prosecution case or of assisting the defence case, the next stage would be to determine how this may impact on the fairness of the proceedings.

4.69   Before even contemplating an abuse of process application, defence practitioners should first exhaust all the CPIA 1996 disclosure routes, and, in particular, the opportunity to make s 8 applications. The applications are founded upon the basis that there is reasonable cause to believe there is prosecution material which, under s 7A of the Act, has not been disclosed to the defence. Adverse findings against the prosecution, on such a s 8 application, may also become a factor for a judge to take into account on a subsequent abuse application. For example, the judge may conclude that the prosecution's non-sensitive disclosure schedule was incomplete in material respects.

The problems encountered

4.70   Unfairness can, of course, result in many ways. Examples of disclosure-related problems have included:

(a)   failures by the prosecution to comply with their obligations to provide proper disclosure;

(b)   exceptionally late disclosure of material;

(c)   failures by investigators and/or disclosure officers to properly advise prosecuting solicitors and/or prosecution advocates as to the proper state of disclosure;

(d)   the inadvertent or deliberate misleading of prosecuting solicitors and/or prosecution advocates, in relation to non-sensitive, sensitive or public interest immunity material;

(e)   the consequent inadvertent misleading of judges tasked to determine the disclosure to which the defence may be entitled.

4.71   In practice, most of the above defects are capable of cure within the trial process, without resort to a stay of proceedings. Some complaints of non-disclosure will be met with disclosure, others by the granting of adjournments to the defence when faced with very late disclosure, or by the exclusion of evidence or suitable judicial directions. Non-disclosure and abuse will generally only be intertwined where there is a complaint of deliberate violation of the accused's right to disclosure.

Examples of non-disclosure giving rise to abuse

4.72   In *R v Blackledge*,[1] following pleas of guilty to breach of export controls concerning arms to Iraq, it transpired via the Scott Inquiry that exculpatory material had been withheld from the defence. This material, whilst not affording a defence to the offence charged, would have enabled the accused to mount a probably unassailable abuse application; that the exports of weapons had been secretly approved or deliberately overlooked by the DTI. The Court of Appeal promptly quashed the convictions of all accused on the ground of non-disclosure.

1   [1996] 1 Cr App Rep 326.

4.73   In *R v Osei-Bonsu*[1] the Court of Appeal considered an appeal based on non-disclosure, following a conviction for a minor assault offence. At trial, the defence unsuccessfully contended there had been an abuse of process following non-disclosure of police officers' notebooks and various computer-aided dispatch messages. The Court of Appeal, with the benefit of further information on the 'deplorable' conduct of the police and CPS in relation to disclosure, concluded that the case disclosed an abuse of process and quashed the conviction. The abuse arose from the non-disclosure of material that may have assisted the defence, clear breaches of the CPIA Codes of Practice and a breach of the trial judge's order in relation to disclosure.

1   (22 June 2000, unreported), CA.

4.74   In *R v Humphreys*[1] eight defendants, including a Detective Sergeant in the National Crime Squad, stood trial for conspiracy to supply cannabis resin. After some 10 weeks of preliminary argument HHJ Crush stayed the indictment as an abuse of process on both limbs of the *Beckford* test. The judge based his decision principally on numerous breaches by the prosecution in relation to their disclosure obligations under the CPIA 1996 and its Code of Practice, particularly in relation to material evidence regarding a co-conspirator who was to give evidence on behalf of the Crown. The court branded the prosecution with a 'culture of non-disclosure', which entailed substantial failures to retain and record relevant material, repeatedly late disclosure, 'selective' disclosure and the flouting of judicial orders in relation to disclosure. The cumulative effect was found to undermine the confidence in, and respect for, the rule of law.

1   (14 February 2000, unreported), Maidstone CC.

4.75 In *R v Docker*[1] a stay was granted following a ruling by the trial judge that 'the police had been significantly at fault in the disclosure process'. Disapproval of police misconduct, amongst allegations of fabricating evidence, coupled with non-disclosure by the police acted as the apparent basis for the stay. Finally, in 2005, there were two prime examples of substantial fraud cases which were stayed for abuse of process on disclosure grounds. Both involved prosecutions by HM Customs and Excise in relation to Missing Trader Intra-Community (MTIC) VAT frauds. In the first proceedings, which concerned Operation Vitric,[2] His Honour Judge Pontius stayed the indictment following a complete loss of confidence in the prosecution's disclosure system, which had a history of significantly late disclosure of material to the defence. In the second proceedings, Crane J stayed an indictment under Operation Venison,[3] where the alleged fraud to the Revenue amounted to over £100 million. Crane J was critical of the flawed disclosure exercise, taking the view that certain Customs Officers had misled prosecuting Counsel, which, in turn, had affected the material provided to the defence and the Court. Faced with defence submissions based on *Early* type arguments, the court concluded it would be unfair to try the defendants.

1   (28 September 1993, unreported), Judge Gibbs QC at Wolverhampton CC, referred to in *Darker v Chief Constable of the West Midlands Police* [2001] 1 AC 435, HL.
2   *R v Lindsay & others*, Blackfriars CC, 18 May 2005.
3   *R v Uddin & others*, Southwark CC, 25 May 2005.

Prosecution disclosure

4.76 Section 10(2) of CPIA 1996, as amended by the Criminal Justice Act 2003, relates to failures by a prosecutor to make primary or secondary disclosure within the prescribed time limits. Where the prosecution have consistently failed to adhere to time limits, perhaps finally serving material of crucial significance at trial itself, this s 10 concession or qualification may be yet another contributing factor relevant to the judicial discretion to stay on, for example, a principally non-disclosure abuse application.

RELEVANT ECHR JURISPRUDENCE

4.77 The practitioner submitting on abuse of process may also seek to draw upon the arguably wider duties of disclosure imposed upon the prosecution by the European Convention on Human Rights, art 6 rather than those under the CPIA 1996. Indeed, the making of parallel abuse and art 6 submissions is now commonplace, given the inevitable overlap in the arguments.

4.78 In addition to the fair trial guarantee under the ECHR, art 6(1), the specific art 6(3)(b) guarantee is frequently relied upon, for it states the right 'to have adequate time and facilities for the preparation of his defence'. In *Kaufman v Belgium*[1] the Commission stated that:

'everyone who is a party to ... proceedings should have a reasonable opportunity of presenting his case to the court under conditions which do not place him at a substantial disadvantage vis-à-vis his opponent ...'

1   (1986) 50 DR 98.

4.79   In *Jespers v Belgium*[1] the Commission stated that the now enshrined 'equality of arms' principle imposes on prosecution and investigating authorities an obligation to disclose any material in their possession. The obligation is applicable to any material to which they could gain access which may assist the accused in exonerating himself.[2] The duty is said to be necessary to remedy the inequality of resources between the prosecution and defence, and the principle applies equally to material which might undermine the credibility of a prosecution witness.

1   (1981) 27 DR 61.
2   An important principle which finds some reflection in the amended CPIA 1996 Code para 3.5 duty on police to follow up all reasonable lines of inquiry.

4.80   The European Court has also been prepared to condemn lack of defence access to prosecution papers in the most inferior courts, notably in the decision of *Foucher v France.*[1] In *Foucher* the applicant and his father were prosecuted for insulting behaviour towards public service employees, the case being tried in the local police court where they chose to represent themselves. Against a background of the prosecutor refusing them access to their files (on the basis it could only be supplied to a lawyer not a private individual), the court found a violation of art 6(1) and 6(3)(b).

1   (1997) 25 EHRR 234.

4.81   Whilst the ECtHR has made it clear in the *Edwards v United Kingdom* decision,[1] and in a string of subsequent cases, that art 6 generally requires the prosecution to disclose to the defence all material evidence for or against an accused, nevertheless, it is also clear that the entitlement to disclosure of relevant evidence is not an absolute right. This principle was further emphasised by the Court in the 2008 decision of *Botmeh and Alami v United Kingdom.*[2] In *Van Mechelen v Netherlands*[3] the court adopted a principle of 'strict necessity' in this regard; one which permits on necessity grounds some non-disclosure of otherwise disclosable material. Justifications which have been accepted as falling within this include national security, the protection of vulnerable witnesses and the keeping secret of police methods of investigation.[4] Clearly this principle is analogous to our domestic doctrine of public interest immunity. So far as the ECtHR is concerned, in *Fitt v United Kingdom*[5] the court held that the ex parte system did not contravene the defendant's right to a fair trial.

1   (1992) 15 EHRR 417.
2   (2008) 46 EHRR 31.
2   (1997) 25 EHRR 647.
3   See *PG and JH v United Kingdom* [2002] Crim LR 308; and *Rowe and Davis v United Kingdom* (2000) 30 EHRR 1.
4   (2000) 30 EHRR 480. See also *Jasper v United Kingdom* at 441.

4.82   Finally, it is worthy of note that the duty of disclosure under art 6 of the Convention is not reliant upon service of a defence case statement, which, by contrast, is so required under the CPIA in order to seek to trigger prosecution disclosure.

PUBLIC INTEREST IMMUNITY

4.83   The general principles underlying public interest immunity are well-known. Where the prosecution contend that it would be detrimental to the public interest for certain otherwise disclosable material to be disclosed to the accused, they may seek judicial permission for such non-disclosure. The circumstances where prosecutors should consider the necessity of seeing the judge ex parte, however, have now become heavily proscribed as a result of the leading House of Lords judgment in *R v H and C*, which has had a significant impact on disclosure regimes up and down the country.[1] The forum for such an application for non-disclosure is known as a public interest immunity hearing where, as a general rule, only the prosecution are represented and make submissions. In exceptional cases, a 'Special Counsel' may be instructed to make submissions on the material, which is said to fall into the 'sensitive' category.

1   [2004] 2 Cr App R 10.

4.84   In order that the prosecution do not abuse their right to seek a public interest immunity/non-disclosure order concerning material it is obviously vital that true and full representations concerning the material's relevance and sensitivity are made to the judge. The motivation for such a hearing should never be to withhold material from the defence which might embarrass the prosecution or strengthen a defence application or worse still, to prevent the accused from receiving a fair trial. In essence, if the sole or dominant motive for the making of such an application is to gain a forensic advantage then it should never be made. Without doubt if any or similar motivation influences the prosecution and leads it to seek non-disclosure this will amount to a serious abuse of power falling squarely within the abuse doctrine.

4.85   The procedure for PII applications is set out in rr 25.1 and 25.2 of the Criminal Procedure Rules 2005.[1] The Court of Appeal's dicta in *R v Davis, Johnson and Rowe* remain applicable to prosecution ex parte applications for orders for non-disclosure, under the rules and the legislation. In this decision, the court set out the correct procedure to be followed, where the prosecution attempt to withhold material on the basis of public interest immunity. There may be occasions where, on the basis of the *Davis* decision, a judge will require a prosecutor to provide the defence with notice of an intended PII application, and/or the nature of the material, so as to allow the defence to make the most informed submissions inter partes. Following the House of Lords decision in *R v H*, there is now no obligation upon the prosecution to disclose material which might not reasonably be viewed as capable of undermining the prosecution's case, or of assisting the case for the defence. Further, neutral material or material damaging to the accused is not required to be disclosed, and should not therefore be brought to the court's attention. On the decision of *H*, it will only be in truly borderline cases that the prosecution should seek a ruling from the judge on the disclosability of material in their possession.

1   SI 2005/384.

4.86   An ex parte or one-sided application in an adversarial regime confers a heavy responsibility upon the prosecution to ensure that the judge hearing it is furnished only with accurate information and all points of relevance are clearly made. Inevitably a judge, who may not be the trial judge, in such a hearing is heavily dependent upon the prosecutor's submissions and if they are inaccurate, either accidentally or deliberately, then an injustice results. As one commentator noted:

> 'It is well established that the judge's role in overseeing disclosure of such material is vital in guaranteeing a fair trial, and this depends on there being scrupulously accurate information provided to the judge ... The effect of the trial judge being denied the true picture is to render meaningless any assessment of whether that material should be disclosed to the defence'.[1]

1   See *R v Patel* [2002] Crim LR 304.

4.87   The duty on the Crown to ensure that only accurate information is presented to the judge during an ex parte application, was underlined in *R v Jackson.*[1] In that case, prosecuting counsel, relying on inaccurate information supplied by the officer in the case, misled the trial judge in an ex parte public interest immunity hearing. The extreme danger of this was demonstrated in *Jackson* because it was purely fortuitous that the error was uncovered when, post conviction, the error came to the attention of the prosecuting counsel in the course of a different case.

1   [2000] Crim LR 377; see commentary to the report.

4.88   *Jackson* illustrates that the inherent danger of the, generally speaking, one-sided public interest immunity hearings is that if wrong information is conveyed to the court during one, there is a substantial danger that it will never be identified as such. The defence are excluded and the trial judge is ill-equipped to probe what is said to him/her. It is obviously a matter of concern that absent the appointment of an amicus acting in the interests of the defence, there are inadequate safeguards to either prevent or identify mistakes of the kind which happened in *Jackson* from recurring. The only practical remedy is for the courts to constantly remind the prosecution of their onerous duties of fairness and accuracy and that if the court is misled, this will be treated very seriously via the abuse jurisdiction.

Patel and Early; misleading the judiciary and prosecution bad faith

4.89   In the cases of *R v Patel*[1] and *R v Early,*[2] the Court of Appeal was faced with a situation where it appeared that a number of Crown Court judges had been consistently misled during different public interest immunity hearings by officers of Customs and Excise. Both of these cases involved allegations of massive alcohol diversion against the two groups of appellants concerning the same bonded warehouse, London City Bond. At their individual trials some of the appellants had pleaded guilty whereas others had been convicted by juries. In all of these appeals the complaint of non-disclosure and misleading of judges was the same; that Customs had misled the court as to their relationship with and the status of participating informants who were, in addition, prosecution witnesses.

1   [2001] EWCA 2505.
2   [2002] EWCA Crim 1904, [2002] All ER (D) 419 (Jul).

4.90   In *Patel,* Customs largely conceded that the above complaints were valid. That prosecution counsel when appearing for Customs at the public interest immunity hearings had, because they had been misled themselves, misled the court. Further that when giving evidence in support of the public interest immunity applications, various Customs officers had also given false information. Moreover in view of their having been misled, when presenting their case to the jury, prosecution counsel had also put forward a false case. Faced with such an appalling situation Longmore LJ concluded:

'This failure was so far reaching in nature as to have led, not to those uncomfortable and arguably disturbing omissions that may be the inevitable consequence of considered and proper applications and decisions in relation to non-disclosure but, to both counsel and judge presenting the case to the jury in significant respects on a false basis'.

4.91   The court held there was a serious failure on the part of the prosecution, not simply to disclose the true status of the two individuals in question, but also 'the extent of their participation in the offences with Customs' encouragement'.

4.92   Whilst admitting the catalogue of misconduct by officers, Customs nonetheless submitted that the convictions of the appellants should not be quashed as they were clearly guilty of the offences they had either pleaded to or been convicted of. Thus they had not had an unfair trial and the convictions were safe. Accordingly the court ought not to quash the convictions on the ground of abuse of process. The court was unpersuaded by this submission, holding on the ground of public policy that the misleading of the judges below was an unconscionable act for which the censure of quashed convictions was appropriate. In quashing the convictions in *Patel* the court was influenced by that fundamental consideration for the courts, namely maintaining the integrity of the criminal process itself. On that theme, Longmore LJ cited the words of Roch LJ in *R v Hickey*[1]:

'... the integrity of the criminal process is the most important consideration for courts which have to hear appeals against conviction. Both the innocent and the guilty are entitled to fair trials. If the trial process is not fair: if it is distracted by deceit or by material breaches of the rules of evidence or procedure, then the liberties of all are threatened'.

1   (30 July 1997, unreported) p 371 of the transcript.

4.93   In *Early* eight appellants successfully appealed against their convictions on the ground that they had pleaded guilty, first, on the false assumption that full and proper disclosure had been made to them by the prosecution and, second, in the light of the non-disclosure of the existence and/or roles of the informants. In two of their cases it was further argued that the lying evidence of the prosecution witnesses had precluded them from making an effective application to stay proceedings as an abuse of process.

4.94 The eight appellants' conjoined appeals arose from three different, albeit related, sets of Crown Court proceedings (in Wood Green, Southwark and Kingston-upon-Thames). The Kingston proceedings revealed, first, that lies had been told to the trial judge by prosecution witnesses, both in the course of public interest immunity hearings and on a 'voir dire' and, secondly, that the lies were part of a deliberate concealment policy operated on the part of Customs and Excise officers. The court noted that the trial judge may have acceded to the defence abuse argument had he not been so misled on disclosure. Similar conclusions were drawn in relation to the two other proceedings. Consistent with the Court of Appeal's approach in *R v Mullen,*[1] as approved in *R v Togher*[2] Rose LJ found that the guilty pleas were no bar to preventing the quashing of the convictions.

1   [1999] 2 Cr App Rep 143.
2   [2001] 1 Cr App Rep 33.

4.95 The lessons to be learned from *Early* and *Patel* should be clear, for Rose LJ made it plain the courts will not tolerate such injustice. He held:

'Judges can only make decisions and counsel can only act and advise on the basis of the information with which they are provided. The integrity of our system of criminal trial depends on judges being able to rely on what they are told by counsel and on counsel being able to rely on what they are told by each other. This is particularly crucial in relation to disclosure and public interest immunity hearings … Furthermore, in our judgment, if, in the course of a public interest immunity hearing or an abuse argument, whether on the voir dire or otherwise, prosecution witnesses lie in evidence to the judge, it is to be expected that, if the judge knows of this, or this court subsequently learns of it, an extremely serious view will be taken. It is likely that the prosecution case will be regarded as tainted beyond redemption, however strong the evidence against the defendant may otherwise be'.[1]

'It is a matter of crucial importance to the administration of justice that prosecuting authorities make full relevant disclosure prior to the trial and that prosecuting authorities should not be encouraged to make inadequate disclosure with a view to defendants pleading guilty'.[2]

Taking a number of considerations into account, the court in *Early* did not consider it in the interests of justice to order retrials for any of the eight appellants.

1   [2002] EWCA Crim 1904, para 10.
2   [2002] EWCA Crim 1904, para 18.

4.96 The consequences of the decision in *Early* have reverberated. A retrial was abandoned in December 2001 at Liverpool and in *R v Gell*[1] the court quashed a further seven convictions of all those accused in another Customs operation called Stockade. Here it was conceded by Customs that the Crown Court judge in that case had been misled by prosecution counsel in the context of a defence abuse application.

1   [2003] EWCA Crim 123, [2003] All ER (D) 221 (Feb).

Chapter 5

Abuse of power by the executive

DISGUISED EXTRADITION

5.01 Herein lies the beating heart of the modern law of abuse of process: *R v Horseferry Road Magistrates' Court, ex p Bennett.*[1] An indicator, perhaps, of how healthy that heart is, is that Parliamentary attempts to stop it beating in 2007,[2] and to preclude the Court of Appeal from overturning a conviction if there was no reason to doubt the defendant's guilt, were met with such universal outrage that they were quietly abandoned.

1   [1994] AC 42, HL.
2   Clause 42 of the Immigration and Justice Bill, inserted following a joint review in 2006 by the Home Secretary, the Lord Chancellor and the Attorney-General expressing concern in particular about the implications of the decision in *R v Mullen* [2000] QB 520, CA, discussed below at paras **5.45–5.50**, which was perceived to have been decided on 'purely procedural grounds'.

The issues raised

5.02 The formal process of extradition of a fugitive from another state can be time-consuming and inconvenient, if available at all. The motive for circumvention of extradition procedures may be the absence of extradition arrangements between the foreign State and the UK.[1] Alternatively, it may be that such extradition arrangements exist but are unavailable for the particular offence in question, would fail,[2] perhaps because of a technicality, or are simply deemed too lengthy or 'bogged down'.[3] It may be that the UK officials were aware that the evidence would be insufficient to obtain extradition from any State.[4] It may even be simple expedience[5] or 'an excess of enthusiasm'[6]. But, whatever the motivation, the problem of state-endorsed 'disguised extradition' has been a long-standing one.

1   *R v Horseferry Road Magistrates' Court, ex p Bennett* (above para **5.01**); *R v Plymouth Justices, ex p Driver* [1986] QB 95, DC; *Sinclair v HM Advocate* (1890) 17 R (J) 38; *In re Schmidt* [1995] 1 AC 339, HL.
2   *R v Mullen* (above para **5.01**); *Bozano v France* (1986) 9 EHRR 297.
3   *R v Mullen* (above para **5.01**) at 146–147.
4   *R v Plymouth Justices, ex p Driver* [1986] QB 95, DC at 107.
5   *R v Hartley* [1978] 2 NZLR 199 per Woodhouse J at 216–217.
6   *R v Bow Street Magistrates' Court, ex p Mackeson* (1981) 75 Cr App Rep 24, DC per Lane LCJ at 33.

5.03 The circumstances in which disguised extradition may arise are as varied as the motives that can prompt it. A defendant may have been unlawfully arrested abroad by UK officials.[1] He or she may have been unlawfully arrested abroad by foreign officials and handed over to the UK outwith applicable extradition arrangements.[2] He or she may be the subject of a bogus deportation order made at the behest of UK authorities and in breach of local laws and procedures.[3] He or she may have been lured or tricked from a State with whom the UK has no extradition arrangements into a third State with whom it has for the purposes of onward extradition to the UK.[4] He or she may have been lured from the sanctuary of the foreign State by deceit or trick operative upon him,[5] by deceit or trick operative upon the foreign State,[6] or worse still, by forcible abduction.[7]

1   *Ex parte Susannah Scott* (1829) 9 B & C 446, CA; *R v Officer Commanding Depot Battalion RASC Colchester, ex p Elliot* [1949] 1 All ER 373, DC.
2   *Sinclair v HM Advocate* (above para **5.02**); *R v Hartley* (above para **5.02**).
3   *R v Bow Street Magistrates' Court, ex p Mackeson* (above para **5.02**) per Lord Lane CJ at 30; *R v Plymouth Justices, ex p Driver* (above para **5.02**); *R v Mullen* (above para **5.01**) per Rose LJ; *Bozano v France* (above para **5.02**).
4   *Somchai Liangsirisprasert v Government of the United States of America* [1991] 1 AC 225, PC; *In re Schmidt* (above para **5.02**).
5   *Somchai Liangsirisprasert v Government of the United States of America* [1991] 1 AC 225, PC; *In re Schmidt* (above para **5.02**); *R v Latif & Shazad* [1996] 1 WLR 104, HL and alleged in *R v Gokal* (11 March 1999, unreported), CA transcript 10–15.
6   Also alleged in *R v Gokal* (11 March 1999, unreported), CA transcript 10–15.
7   *R v Horseferry Road Magistrates' Court, ex p Bennett* (above para **5.01**); *Ker v Illinois* 119 US 436 (1986); *Frisbie v Collins* 342 US 519 (1952); *United States of America v Sobell* 142 F Supp 515 (1956); *United States v Toscanino* 500 F 2d 267 (1974); *South Africa v Ebrahim* 1991 (2) SA 553; *United States v Alvarez-Machain* 504 US 655 (1992); *Bozano v France* (above para **5.02**).

5.04   Where a defendant is returned to the UK from a foreign State for trial, should the jurisdiction of the courts extend to either or both of the following situations:

(i)   where there has been bad faith on the part of the relevant UK authorities in that they have colluded in obtaining the defendant's return other than through regular extradition procedures? or

(ii)   extradition was obtained in violation of the domestic law or the requested State, or in violation of international law?

If either of the above apply, then should the trial court have power to stay the proceedings against the defendant as an abuse of process?

Pre-Bennett decisions regarding jurisdiction

5.05   Prior to the House of Lords decision in *R v Horseferry Magistrates' Court, ex p Bennett*[1] there existed two conflicting lines of authority on the issue of whether[2] or not[3] the trial court possessed any power to inquire into the circumstances in which a person, lawfully before the court, had come to be within the jurisdiction. The conflict of authority was brought to a head in *R v Plymouth Justices, ex p Driver*[4] where it was held that the trial court had no power to inquire, and that prior decisions to the contrary[5] were decided *per incuriam*.

1   Above para **5.01**.
2   To the effect that such a power existed; see *R v Hartley* (above para **5.02**); *R v Bow Street*

Magistrates' Court, ex parte Mackeson (above para **5.02**); *R v Guildford Magistrates' Court, ex p Healy* [1983] 1 WLR 108, DC.
3   To the effect that such a power did not exist; see *Ex parte Susannah Scott* (above para **5.03**) per Lord Tenterden CJ at 448; *Sinclair v HM Advocate* (above para **5.02**) per Lord Justice-Clerk MacDonald at 41–42, Lord Adam at 42–43, Lord M'laren at 43–44; *R v Officer Commanding Deport battalion RASC Colchester, ex p Elliot* (above para **5.03**) per Lord Godard CJ at 376–378. This continues to be the approach of the US courts; see *United States v Alvarez-Machain* (above para **5.03**).
4   Above para **5.02**.
5   Above fn 2.

Ex parte Bennett

5.06   Bennett, a New Zealand citizen, was charged in England with offences of dishonesty relating to his purchase of a helicopter. After the charges were laid, he had entered South Africa (via Australia) on a false passport, along with his helicopter. He was detained by the South African authorities as an illegal immigrant and a South African court ordered his deportation (to New Zealand). However, there was at that time no direct flight from South Africa to New Zealand and, despite the obvious geographical factors, it was decided to fly him to New Zealand via London. He was placed on a flight to Heathrow, handcuffed to the seat, and on arrival there was immediately arrested by the English police (who had received advance notice of the route from the South African authorities).

5.07   When he appeared before the Magistrates' Court, Bennett applied for a stay on the grounds of abuse of process. He argued that the facts disclosed that, having taken the decision not to employ the extradition process, the English police colluded with the South African police to have him arrested in South Africa and forcibly deported against his will. The application was refused by the Magistrates' Court and he sought judicial review. The Divisional Court,[1] following *R v Plymouth Justices, ex p Driver*,[2] held that, even if there was evidence of collusion between the two police forces in kidnapping Bennett and securing his enforced illegal removal to England from South Africa, the criminal courts had no jurisdiction to inquire into the circumstances by which he came to be within the jurisdiction. Accordingly, it dismissed his application for review. The Divisional Court held that the role of the judge is confined to the forensic process, to see that the accused has a fair trial and that the process of the court is not manipulated to his disadvantage so that the trial itself is unfair. It held that the wider issues of the rule of law and the behaviour of those charged with its enforcement, be they police or prosecution authority, are not the concern of the judiciary unless such issues impinge directly on the trial process.

1   [1993] 2 All ER 474, DC.
2   Above para **5.02**.

5.08   In support of this view, the Divisional Court relied on the House of Lords case of *R v Sang*,[1] where Lords Diplock and Scarman emphasised that it is no part of the judge's function to exercise disciplinary powers over the police or the prosecution. Lord Diplock had said that:

'the function of the judge at a criminal trial as respects the admission of evidence is to ensure that the accused has a fair trial according to law. It is no part of a judge's function to exercise disciplinary powers over the police or prosecution as respects the way in which evidence to be used at the trial is obtained by them.'

1   [1980] AC 402, HL, at 436.

5.09   Bennett appealed to the House of Lords who, by a majority of four to one,[1] held that, in a situation of illegal extradition (as the House was obliged to assume on the facts of the case before it; there having been no factual determinations), the courts did have a power to stay domestic criminal proceedings for abuse.

1   Lords Griffiths, Bridge, Lowry and Slynn (Lord Oliver dissenting).

5.10   Lord Griffiths perceived the issues posed before the House to be as follows:

'In the present case there is no suggestion that the appellant cannot have a fair trial, nor could it be suggested that it would be unfair to try him if he had been returned to this country through extradition procedures. If the court is to have the power to interfere with the prosecution in the present circumstances it must be because the judiciary accept a responsibility for the maintenance of the rule of law that embraces a willingness to oversee executive action and to refuse to countenance behaviour that threatens either basic human rights or the rule of law.'[1]

1   Above para **5.01**, at 61H.

5.11   Having clearly set out the significance of the issues to be confronted, Lord Griffiths was in no doubt that the courts should widen their abuse jurisdiction:

'I have no doubt that the judiciary should accept this responsibility in the field of criminal law … If it comes to the attention of the court that there has been a serious abuse of power it should, in my view, express its disapproval by refusing to act on it.'[1]

1   Above para **5.01**, at 62B.

5.12   In conclusion Lord Griffiths said that:

'In my view your Lordships should now declare that where process of law is available to return an accused to this country through extradition procedures our courts will refuse to try him if he has been forcibly brought within our jurisdiction in disregard of those procedures by a process to which our own police, prosecuting or other executive authorities have been a knowing party.'[1]

1   Above para **5.01**, at 62G.

5.13   Lord Bridge observed that:

'When it is shown that the law enforcement agency responsible for bringing a prosecution has only been able to do so by participating in violations of international law and laws of another State in order to secure the presence of the accused within the territorial jurisdiction of the court, I think that respect for the rule of law demands that the court take cognisance of that circumstance. To hold that the court may turn a blind eye to executive lawlessness beyond the frontiers of its own jurisdiction is, to my mind, an insular and unacceptable view. Having then taken cognisance of the lawlessness it would again appear to me to be a wholly inadequate response for the court to hold that the only remedy lies in the civil proceedings at the suit of the defendant or in disciplinary or criminal proceedings against the individual officers of the law enforcement agency who were concerned in the illegal action taken. Since the prosecution could never have been brought if the defendant had not been illegally abducted, the whole proceeding is tainted.'[1]

1   Above para **5.01**, at 67G.

5.14   Lord Lowry said:

'I consider that a court has a discretion to stay any criminal proceedings on the ground that to try at those proceedings would amount to an abuse of its own process; either (1) because it would be impossible (usually by reason of delay) to give the accused a fair trial or (ii) because it offends the court's sense of justice and propriety to be asked to try the accused in the circumstances of a particular case ... So far as existing authority is concerned ... the court, in order to protect its own process from being degraded and misused, must have the power to stay proceedings which have come before it and have only been possible by acts which offend the court's conscience as being contrary to the rule of law. Those acts by providing a morally unacceptable foundation for the exercise of jurisdiction over the suspect taint the proposed trial and, if tolerated, would mean that the court's process has been abused.[1]

1   Above para **5.01**, at 74F and 76C.

5.15   In answer to the counter-suggestion that the seriousness of an offence alleged against a defendant, or even incontrovertible evidence of guilt, meant that there was an overriding public interest in trying him no matter under what circumstances he had been brought before a court, Lord Lowry was unpersuaded. He said:

'It may be that a guilty accused finding himself in the circumstances predicated is not deserving of much sympathy, but the principle involved goes beyond the scope of such a pragmatic observation and even beyond the rights of those victims who are or may be innocent. It affects the proper administration of justice according to the rule of law and with respect to international law ...'. [1]

1   Above para **5.01**, at 76G.

5.16   Lord Lowry in his speech was also concerned to deal with two other connected issues; first, whether, via its abuse jurisdiction, the court should exercise disciplinary powers over the police, and secondly, whether, by its preparedness to penalise unworthy conduct on the part of investigators, the House was encouraging a flood of abuse applications. In common with Lords Diplock and Scarman in *R v Sang,*[1] Lords Lowry and Bridge both emphasised that the abuse jurisdiction was not a disciplinary one. Lord Lowry said:

'… the discretion to stay is not a disciplinary jurisdiction and ought not to be exercised in order to express the court's disapproval of official conduct … The court ought not to stay the proceedings merely "pour encourager les autres".'[2]

The significance of this disavowal of any disciplinary jurisdiction should be understood. Were such a jurisdiction to be asserted it would represent a shift towards an automatic or mandatory exclusionary approach when there is police impropriety. As this chapter will show, the courts are determined not to eschew their traditional discretionary or 'public interest' approach.

1   Above para **5.08**.
2.   Above para **5.01**, at 74H.

5.17   In answer to the 'floodgates' argument, Lord Lowry observed that:

'… if proceedings are stayed when wrongful conduct is proved, the result will not only be a sign of judicial disapproval but will discourage similar conduct in future and thus would tend to maintain the purity of a source of justice. No "floodgates" argument applies because the executive can stop the flood at source by refraining from impropriety.'[1]

1   Above para **5.01**, at 77A.

5.18   In relation to complaints of basic unfairness, *Bennett* therefore established that courts have a wider supervisory jurisdiction – to protect persons from being prosecuted in circumstances where it would be seriously unjust to do so. However, as the judgments of Lords Griffiths, Bridge and Lowry make plain, the House in *Bennett* was concerned with a particular instance of illegality and abuse of power, namely breach of extradition procedures. The presence of that fact was crucial, as Lord Griffiths said: '… If extradition is not available various considerations will arise on which I express no opinion'[1]. Moreover, for a court to stay criminal proceedings as an abuse under *Bennett*, it must be satisfied that there was collusion between the foreign and English authorities to avoid the defendant being extradited. In the absence of such evidence, the burden being on the defence, an application for a stay could not succeed.

1   Above para **5.01**, at 62G.

5.19   A reading of the speeches of the majority of the House of Lords in *Bennett* reveals a clear determination that courts should not countenance 'executive lawlessness' (per Lord Bridge). To fail to do so would result in a '… degradation of the court's criminal process' and be an 'affront to the public conscience'. When, therefore, a court is confronted by executive lawlessness it is entitled to stay the trial for abuse of process.

5.20   While the attitude of the House in *Bennett* to executive lawlessness is unambiguous, the speeches do not clarify whether a rule or merely a principle was being pronounced. Did the House in *Bennett* support an absolutist or mandatory stance whereby any prosecution based on illegal extradition should always be stayed? Or, alternatively, should a court in such a situation exercise a discretion in deciding whether or not such lawlessness should result in a stay? The only speech which dealt with this subject directly was that of Lord Lowry who said:

'... it is not jurisdiction which is in issue but the exercise of a discretion to stay proceedings, whilst speaking of "unworthy conduct", I would not expect a court to stay the proceedings of every trial which has been preceded by a venial irregularity. If it be objected that my preferred solution replaces certainty by uncertainty, the latter quality is inseparable from judicial discretion.'[1]

1   Above para **5.01**, at 77A-C.

5.21   In *R v Latif and Shahzad*[1] the House, three years on from its decision in *Bennett,* took the opportunity to reconsider its stance. The sole speech in that case was delivered by Lord Steyn, who held that the House had concluded in *ex p Bennett* that, in a proven situation of executive lawlessness, the trial judge had a discretion to decide whether there had been an abuse of process. Lord Steyn thereby made plain that executive lawlessness should not automatically result in a stay; the court had to exercise a more flexible and pragmatic case-by-case approach:

'... weigh[ing] in the balance the public interest in ensuring those that are charged with grave crimes should be tried and the competing public interest in not conveying the impression that the court will adopt the approach that the end justifies any means ... Weighing countervail considerations of policy and justice, it is for the judge in the exercise of his discretion to decide whether there has been an abuse of process, which amounts to an affront to the public conscience and requires the criminal proceedings to be stayed.'[2]

1   Above para **5.03**.
2   At 112–113.

APPLICATION OF THE BENNETT ABUSE JURISDICTION IN CASES OF DISGUISED EXTRADITION

Pre-Bennett authorities

5.22   As noted above,[1] the pre-*Bennett* authorities were by no means consistent as to the issue of jurisdiction. Consequently, a number of pre-*Bennett* authorities were considered on their merits on the assumption that such a jurisdiction existed, and therefore remain instructive as to the circumstances in which the jurisdiction, which *Bennett* confirmed to exist, would be exercised.

1   Above para **5.05**.

R v Hartley

5.23   In *R v Hartley,*[1] following a retaliatory murder carried out by members of a motorcycle gang, one of the gang (Bennett) fled to Australia. The police had not obtained a warrant for Bennett's extradition and had merely asked the Melbourne police by telephone to put Bennett on the next plane to New Zealand; a request with which they had complied. Bennett appealed against his conviction for manslaughter on the ground that the court had no jurisdiction to try him because he had been illegally brought back to New Zealand. The New

Zealand Court of Appeal ruled that the New Zealand court had jurisdiction to try Bennett on the indictment but also had a discretion to discharge the accused under its inherent jurisdiction to prevent abuse of its own process. On the facts of that case, Woodhouse J found that the New Zealand police had deliberately ignored the requirements of the extradition statute and observed that;

> 'Some may say that in the present case a New Zealand citizen attempted to avoid a criminal responsibility by leaving the country: that his subsequent conviction has demonstrated the utility of the short cut adopted by the police to have him brought back. But this must never become an area where it will be sufficient to consider that the end has justified the means. The issues raised by this affair are basic to the whole concept of freedom in society. On the basis of reciprocity for similar favours earlier received are police officers here in New Zealand to feel free, or even obliged, at the request of their counterparts overseas to spirit New Zealand or other citizens out of the country on the basis of mere suspicion, conveyed perhaps by telephone, that some crime has been committed elsewhere? ... we are ... satisfied that the means which were adopted to make that trial possible are so much at variance with the statute, and so much in conflict with one of the most important principles of the rule of law, that if application had been made at the trial on this ground and the facts had been established by the evidence on the voir dire, the judge would probably have been justified in exercising his discretion.'[2]

1 Above para **5.02**.
2 At 217.

Ex parte Mackeson

5.24 In *R v Bow Street Magistrates' Court, ex p Mackeson*,[1] the applicant, Sir Rupert Mackeson, a British citizen, was resident in Rhodesia (later renamed Zimbabwe), when allegations of fraud were levelled against him in the UK. The Metropolitan Police did not then ask the Rhodesian authorities to extradite him because at that time the de facto government of Rhodesia was in rebellion against the Crown and considered illegal. Subsequently, the Metropolitan Police informed the Rhodesian authorities that the applicant was wanted in England. He was thereupon arrested in Rhodesia as a prohibited immigrant. That determination was accepted to have been based principally upon the existence of the UK fraud charges. A deportation order was thus made against him. His passport was returned to the Metropolitan Police and sent back to the applicant with authorisation for one journey only, to return to the UK. He brought proceedings in Rhodesia for the deportation order to be set aside, which succeeded at first instance (Gubbay J finding that the true purpose of the deportation order was an ulterior one, namely his disguised extradition to the UK). But that decision was set aside on appeal (on a point of law which left the factual findings of the first instance court intact).

1 Above para **5.02**.

5.25 The applicant was escorted back to the UK under the deportation order and handed over to the Metropolitan Police. He applied for judicial review by way of an order of prohibition to prevent the hearing of committal proceedings against him in the Magistrates' Court in respect of those other charges. The Divisional Court (Lord Lane CJ) found that the applicant had been brought back to this country because of the Metropolitan Police persuading the authorities in Rhodesia to deport him for no reason other than that he was wanted for trial in this country. The Court thus found that the applicant had been removed from Rhodesia with ulterior motive. Lord Lane CJ concluded that:

> '... the object of this exercise was simply to achieve extradition by the back door. It seems equally plain to me that the English police authorities were, to say the least, concurring in that exercise[1] ... the Metropolitan Police, no doubt due to an excess of enthusiasm, certainly not due to any conscious intent to do wrong, have in fact transgressed the line.'[2]

1   At 30.
2   At 33.

5.26   Thus, the Divisional Court, in its discretion, having regard to *R v Hartley*,[1] granted the application for prohibition and discharged the applicant. The factors that principally affected this finding were:[2]

(a)   the finding of the Rhodesian court to that effect;

(b)   the fact that it was to be inferred that the Metropolitan police were clearly in communication with the South African authorities at the material time;

(c)   the fact that the Metropolitan police were well aware that extradition was not lawfully possible. Whilst the Metropolitan police did not initiate the proceedings, they adopted the procedure willingly and quickly;

(d)   no attempt was made to extradite the applicant after Zimbabwe-Rhodesia had returned to direct rule under the Crown in December 1979;

(e)   the act of returning the applicant's passport to the Metropolitan police was one which was indicative of the UK authorities having positively requested the applicant's return to the UK, notwithstanding their denial that they had; and

(f)   the circumstances of the applicant's flight to the UK. At Gatwick, when the purpose of the Rhodesian authorities had been accomplished, they maintained their arrest of the applicant until the arrival of the Metropolitan police; if it had genuinely been deportation '... it would have been sufficient, if deportation was the principal object of the exercise, simply to ask him to walk down the steps'.

1   Above para **5.02**.
2   At 29–30.

Ex parte Healy

5.27   On the other side of 'the line' is *R v Guildford Magistrates Court, ex p Healy*.[1] Mr Healy was arrested in the UK on a number of serious charges. He was released on bail on condition that he surrender his passport. He subsequently fled the UK and unlawfully entered the US on a false passport.

Two British police officers went to New York to pursue their inquiries in respect of the applicant. The applicant flew from New York to Los Angeles and was arrested in Los Angeles by the US authorities and charged with being an illegal immigrant. At a bail hearing, which took place before the Immigration Tribunal in Los Angeles, the two British officers gave evidence and told the judge the nature of the crimes with which the applicant had been charged in the UK. They also gave him an estimate of the likely sentence if the applicant were to be convicted. The applicant told the immigration judge 'a pack of lies' at that hearing. The two police officers then returned to the UK. There were a number of further hearings of the tribunal in Los Angeles after which the judge made a deportation order against the applicant. The applicant was deported to the UK and arrested on his arrival.

1   Above para **5.05**.

5.28   The defence raised before the Magistrates' Court, as a preliminary point, the question whether the method by which the applicant had been brought from the US to the UK had involved improper co-operation between the authorities of those two countries, in order to circumvent the need for extradition proceedings. After hearing the evidence of a number of witnesses, the magistrate found that the British police had not attempted to interfere or collude in any improper manner to secure the deportation of the applicant. That ruling was upheld by the Divisional Court, Griffiths LJ (who, ten years later, was to give the leading judgment in the House of Lords in *Bennett*[1]) holding that the facts did not disclose an abuse of process. There was:

'... no ground whatever for supposing the police have tried to persuade the United States' authorities to deport this applicant so that they could arrest him in this country and thus circumvent the provisions of the extradition treaty between the two countries. The facts of the matter are that this man entered the United States on a false passport having allegedly left a trail of crime behind in this country. In those circumstances it was perfectly reasonable that the police should leave this country to try to trace him in America. So far as the United States were concerned, it was perfectly proper for the British police, if they did, to inform the United States of their fears that this man had entered their territory on a false passport. We do not know if his arrest in Los Angeles was as a result of any information given by the British police that they knew he was leaving from New York for Los Angeles, but even if they did give that information to the United States' authorities, we can see nothing improper in that at all. Thereafter, once the man was arrested by the United States' authorities ... [n]aturally enough, the court inquiring into the status of an alleged illegal immigrant would want as much information about the man as they could get. The British police were there in the United States, they apparently knew a great deal about this man and what more natural than that the immigration authorities there should call them before the judge to tell the judge what they knew of him. That is what was done and it would have been improper for them to have refused to give the evidence they did. Thereafter there were prolonged inquiries by the judge into the status of the applicant in America and there is nothing whatever to show that the British police in any way influenced the course of those inquiries. Indeed, they were not in the country during the time that many of the hearings took place ...It is quite clear to this court that the decision of the United States' authorities to deport this man was not prompted by the British police, although no doubt the information given at the request of the United States' authorities must have played a part in Judge Indelicato's final decision.'[2]

1   Above para **5.01**.
2   At 112.

5.29   Griffiths LJ further observed that the evidence did not warrant the inference that the British Government paid for the flight, and that in the absence of such evidence, the court was unable to draw the 'inference that this was truly a concealed extradition'. Finally, as to the submission that, because the applicant was brought back under escort and under restraint, that provided further material from which the inference should be drawn that he was being deported at the request of the British police to avoid extradition proceedings, Griffiths LJ held that:

'The reason he was in handcuffs [was because he had escaped on a number of occasions and his guard was expressly requested by the captain of the aircraft] ... and if a criminal wanted in this country is being deported by the United States' authorities of their own motion and for their own purposes, there is no reason whatever why the authorities in the United States should not report to the authorities in this country that they are deporting him and inform this country of the aircraft upon which he will be arriving so that he can be arrested as soon as he arrives here and brought to justice in this country. It is in the interest of the law abiding community that there should be international co-operation to bring wanted criminals to justice: there is no reason whatever to assume because that is done that there is a collusive agreement between the two countries to use the deportation process as a short cut to extradition.'[1]

1   At 113.

Ex parte Driver

5.30   In *R v Plymouth Justices, ex p Driver*,[1] as noted above,[2] the Divisional Court held there to be no power to inquire into the circumstances in which a person, lawfully before the court, had come to be within the jurisdiction. But, for present purposes, the judgment remains of interest because the Divisional Court also determined how such a power would have been exercised on the facts of the case before it, had it existed.

1   Above para **5.02**.
2   Above para **5.05**.

5.31   Mr. Driver, an Australian citizen, came to England on holiday. During his stay, an elderly woman was killed, and on the following day, before her body was discovered, he left England for France, having made arrangements for the journey some time previously. The police, suspecting him of the woman's murder, made inquiries as to his whereabouts through Interpol. Independently of this, the Turkish authorities subsequently arrested Driver in Turkey on the strength of a newspaper report relating to the murder. The English police were informed and, while not requesting his detention or continued detention, sought, and received, the co-operation of the Turkish authorities by confirming the applicant's identity and assisting in establishing his connection with the killing. There was no extradition treaty between the UK and Turkey and the police told the Turkish authorities that they had no authority to request the applicant's extradition or deportation from Turkey, but that *if it was within their power* to deport him to the UK it would assist the police to interview him. The Turkish authorities replied that they would expel the applicant in the 'United Kingdom direction' but that he would not be accompanied by a police officer on the journey and his arrival could not be guaranteed. They also asked the English police to pay for his fare, which they did. The Turkish authorities told the applicant, untruthfully, that the English police were no longer interested in him and that he was to be released, but they required him to leave Turkey and put him, unaccompanied, on a non-stop flight to London (purportedly the first available flight out of Turkey). The action of the Turkish authorities in returning the applicant to England was unlawful in Turkish law (amounting to an offence of 'a public official using the powers of his office in bad faith'). Upon his arrival in London, the applicant was arrested and charged with murder.

5.32 Stephen Brown LJ held[1] that, even if the court had a discretion to prohibit committal proceedings against a person where there had been an abuse of process within the jurisdiction which had procured his presence there:

> 'The evidence before this court does not establish any impropriety, illegality or collusion on the part of the Devon and Cornwall police in relation to any unlawful act which the Turkish authorities may have committed in requiring the applicant to leave Turkey ... the only action taken ... was to notify the Turkish police that the applicant was suspected of a crime committed in this country and that they desired to interview him. They agreed to pay his fare. However, they did not at any time seek his detention or continued detention in Turkey. They sought and received the co-operation of the Turkish police to establish the applicant's identity. They told the Turkish authorities that the police in this country had no authority to request the applicant's extradition or deportation from Turkey. It is true that they notified the Turkish authorities that the applicant was wanted in the United Kingdom on suspicion of having committed the murder of Mrs. Hopkins and said that if it was within their power to deport him to the United Kingdom it would assist the police to interview him. I stress that both the affidavits make it clear that this request was subject to the important condition that any action taken should be within their power. There was no request by the British police to encourage the Turkish authorities to act illegally in any way, although they agreed to pay his fare. In these circumstances, it is not established that the authorities in this country were guilty of any improper dealing.'

1 At 114.

State v Ebrahim

5.33   Finally, abuse of process was found by the Supreme Court of South Africa in *State v Ebrahim*.[1] The appellant, a South African citizen, was a member of the military wing of the African National Congress (ANC) and had fled South Africa to Swaziland whilst under a restriction order (imposed following conviction for offences of sabotage). He had been forcibly abducted from his home in Swaziland by persons claiming to be members of the South African State. Although the State denied involvement, the Supreme Court found that the abduction was carried out by agents of the State (other than the South African police). He had been bound, blindfolded, gagged and taken back across the border into Pretoria, South Africa, where he had been handed over first to the security services, and then to the police, and detained under the terms of security legislation. He was subsequently charged with treason in a Circuit Local Division. The appellant applied for an order to the effect that the court lacked jurisdiction to try the case as a result of his abduction in breach of international law. The application was dismissed and the trial continued. He was convicted and sentenced to 20 years' imprisonment. There was no evidence that the government of Swaziland protested over the abduction.

1   1991 (2) SA 553.

5.34   On appeal against the dismissal of the above application, Steyn JA, on behalf of the Supreme Court, held that the removal of a person from an area of jurisdiction in which he had been illegally arrested to another area was tantamount to abduction and thus constituted a serious injustice. A court before which such a person was brought lacked jurisdiction to try him, even where such a person had been abducted by agents of the authority governing the area of jurisdiction of the said court.

> 'The individual must be protected against unlawful detention and abduction, the bounds of jurisdiction must not be exceeded, sovereignty must be respected, the legal process must be fair to those affected and abuse of law must be avoided in order to protect and promote the integrity of the administration of justice. This applies equally to the State. When the State is a party to a dispute, as for example in criminal cases, it must come to court with 'clean hands'. When the State itself is involved in an abduction across international borders, as in the present case, its hands are not clean. Principles of this kind testify to a healthy legal system of a high standard.'

Ex parte Bennett

5.35   Having decided the issue of principle in *ex parte Bennett*,[1] the House of Lords remitted the matter to the Divisional Court to determine the facts; *R v Horseferry Road Magistrates' Court, ex p Bennett (No 3)*.[2] Based upon the facts outlined above,[3] Bennett argued that his case disclosed that, having taken the decision not to employ the extradition process, the English police colluded with the South African police to have him arrested in South Africa and forcibly deported against his will. Mann LJ observed that:

'... the inquiry involved the liberty of a subject and we have to be satisfied on a high balance of probabilities that the applicant was properly available for arrest at Heathrow.'[4]

1   Above para **5.01**.
2   [1995] 1 Cr App R.147, DC.
3   At para **5.06**.
4   At 149.

5.36   The English police gave evidence that they did not know that Bennett was being dispatched via England until the night before. However, against this 'well intentioned' evidence there existed an internal CPS memo showing that they had known about the deportation more than two weeks earlier. Mann LJ concluded that:

'... the desire to bring him to trial is understandable but a propriety of procedure in regard to the liberty of any who are brought within our jurisdiction is transcendent.'[1]

1   At 149.

5.37   The termination of the English proceedings was, however, not the end of Bennett's problems. Bennett also faced a warrant for his arrest issued by the Sheriff of Grampian, Highland and Islands, at Aberdeen in respect of offences of dishonesty relating to his purchase of a different helicopter and a Lamborghini motor car. Upon his release, he was brought before the Scottish courts. He argued that the factual findings in *R v Horseferry Road Magistrates' Court, ex p Bennett (No 3)*,[1] namely that his presence within the UK had been procured by abuse, applied to render the Scottish proceedings also abusive, the Lord Advocate not being entitled to take advantage of that impropriety.

1   Above para **5.35**.

5.38   The matter came before the High Court of Justiciary in *Bennett v HM Advocate*.[1] It was accepted that the Scottish authorities had played no part in the affair. It was also ultimately accepted by the Court that the Scottish authorities would not be permitted to turn a blind eye to, and take advantage of, English illegality or impropriety.

1   (1995) SLT 510.

5.39   But the Scottish authorities had conducted further factual enquiries and, as a result, argued that there had not, in fact, been any illegality or collusion on the part of the English authorities. That new evidence indicated that the English authorities understood the South African intention to be repatriation to New Zealand via Australia and the English intention was to seek extradition from either New Zealand or Australia. The English police then fortuitously learned that the South African plan involved transit via London (a route dictated by international travel difficulties in respect of South Africa in 1991 owing to international sanctions in operation against that country) and determined to take advantage of that fortuity. Hence, the CPS memo. But, because of the cost, the South African plan changed and Bennett was instead flown to Taiwan for transfer (via Hong Kong) to New Zealand. Of itself, as the Lord Justice General (Lord Hope) observed, this confirmed that the English authorities could not have been 'in collusion' in respect of the initial transit route.[1] But, en route to

Taiwan, Bennett had destroyed his passport, with the result that the Taiwanese authorities refused him permission to disembark and returned him to South Africa. It was only then that the South African authorities reverted to their initial proposed route via London, and advised the English authorities – hence the evidence given to the High court in *R v Horseferry Road Magistrates' Court, ex p Bennett (No 3)*[2] by the English police that they did not know that Bennett was being dispatched via England until the night before. On the evidence now available, Lord Hope concluded that:

> '... the Lord Advocate was entitled to conclude that what occurred in this case is different from what had been assumed in the decision taken in England by the House of Lords and by the Divisional Court ... there was, so far as the English authorities were concerned, no illegality ... In our opinion it would be unreasonable, where there has been no collusion, to insist that the police must refrain from arresting a person who is wanted for offences committed in this country when he arrives here simply because he is in transit to another country.'[3]

1   At 518 '... if there was already a collusive agreement for him to be sent to London in order that he might be arrested there, it would have been a breach of it to send him instead to Taipei as by that route he would never reach London. Read in its context, the memorandum appears to us to do no more than report on a decision which had been taken by the South African police and which the English police saw as being to their advantage. It does not, in any way, reveal that the English authorities were in collusion with the South African police on this matter. All the information ... indicates that the South African authorities were taking their own decisions about the method of deportation.'

2   Above para **5.35**.

3   At 518.

Post-Bennett authorities

Ex parte Westfallen

5.40   In *R v Staines Magistrates' Court, ex p Westfallen & others*,[1] the applicants Westfallen and Soper were wanted for offences in England. Both flew to Norway on forged passports where they were immediately detained by Norwegian immigration. Their identities and criminal records were confirmed by Interpol, but not the fact that they were wanted. The Norwegian authorities determined to deport them (on the ground that they were believed to be going to commit offences in Norway) to the UK from where they had come. Upon arrival in England they were arrested.

1   [1998] 1 WLR 652, DC.

5.41   The applicant Nangle appeared before Swindon Crown Court on charges of burglary and escape from lawful custody. Sentence was deferred. Prior to the deferred date, he fled to Canada. In Canada, he was convicted of 48 other offences and received a term of six years' imprisonment and was recommended for deportation. During his imprisonment, a deportation order was duly made and served on him. During his imprisonment, the London Police, via Interpol, made their Canadian counterparts aware of the fact that Nangle was wanted in the UK and stated that '... should the subject be deported to the UK please inform us prior to any deportation in order that we can arrange for him to be met.' At the end of his sentence, Nangle was informed that he was to be deported to Ireland where he had been granted citizenship. There were no direct flights to Dublin and so he was flown via Glasgow, this being, on the evidence, the most expedient route. When the flight arrived in Glasgow, Nangle was arrested.

5.42   All three applicants contended that the UK authorities had improperly procured their presence in the UK by means other than extradition which, in their submission, was the only way of properly procuring their presence in the UK. They contended that what had happened was disguised extradition, which the House of Lords in *ex parte Bennett*[1] had condemned as an abuse. For their part the authorities denied this; there was no taint of impropriety and what had happened was not disguised extradition but simply undisguised deportation. In all three cases, the UK police and CPS denied having attempted to influence the foreign authorities in any way. Bingham CJ perceived the test for the court to be as follows:

> 'The question in each of these cases is whether it appears that the police or the prosecuting authorities have acted illegally or procured or connived at unlawful procedures or violated international law or the domestic law of foreign States or abused their powers in a way that should lead this court to stay the proceedings against the applicants.'[2]

1   Above para **5.01**.
2   At 665B-C.

5.43   In respect of Westfallen and Soper, Lord Bingham CJ held that;

> '... the answer to that question is in my judgment plainly in the negative. The Norwegians were entitled under their own law to deport these applicants. The propriety of the deportations is acknowledged and indeed could not be challenged. It is difficult to see why the Kingdom of Norway should be obliged to keep the applicants whilst the British applied for extradition if they wished to deport them. It was indeed a natural step for Norway to send the applicants back to where they had come from. There is in the material before us nothing to suggest that the British authorities procured or influenced that decision. It is true that they did not in any way resist it, and there is no reason why they should have resisted it. It is very probable that they welcomed the decision, but in my judgment they would have been failing in their duty as law enforcement agencies if they had not welcomed it. In my judgment there is nothing to suggest any impropriety'[1]

1   At 665C-E.

5.44   In respect of Nangle, Lord Bingham CJ held that:

> 'The decision was taken to deport him to Ireland, which is where the applicant wished to go, and the Canadian authorities bought him a ticket to that destination. They chose an obvious route in the absence of a direct flight from Canada to Ireland ... [I]t is not suggested ... that the flight via Glasgow was in any way contrived or sinister or other than an ordinary route to choose in order to reach that destination. There is nothing whatever to suggest that

the British authorities influenced the Canadian authorities to deport or procured the choice of route. Again, they did not resist it and probably welcomed the outcome. But again, there is no reason why they should have resisted that decision and no reason why they should not have welcomed it. There was in my judgment no illegality, no violation of international law, no violation of the domestic law of Canada, and no abuse of power.'[1]

1   At 665F-H.

R v Mullen

5.45   In *R v Mullen,*[1] in contrast to *ex parte Westfallen*, the court found that there had been collusion and illegal behaviour on the part of the UK authorities. Shortly before his proposed arrest for terrorist offences in England, Mullen fled to Zimbabwe. Whilst there, during early 1989, the British and Zimbabwean intelligence agencies secretly agreed a process whereby Mullen would be arrested and deported to England from Zimbabwe in a manner which would prevent him from exercising legal rights available to him under Zimbabwean law which could have frustrated this plan. From MI6 files disclosed at the appeal, it was clear that MI6 had informed their Zimbabwean counterparts that Mullen should not be permitted to become involved in protracted extradition proceedings. In the event, Mullen was swiftly deported in breach of Zimbabwean law.

1   Above para **5.01**.

5.46   Before considering the judgment of the Court of Appeal, it is important to appreciate that Mullen accepted that he had received a fair trial and was properly convicted of extremely serious offences. Furthermore, with the law on abuse as it stood in 1990,[1] the year of his trial, it is unlikely that, had the circumstances concerning his deportation from Zimbabwe been disclosed by the prosecution, a stay would then have been granted, or that the Court of Appeal would have intervened. At the hearing of Mullen's appeal 10 years later, when the circumstances in which he was deported to England came to light, the Crown's argument, having conceded the fact of improper collusion between the two authorities, was that the grounds for his deportation under Zimbabwean law were so convincing that, even if the proper extradition procedures had been followed, his removal back to England would inevitably have been the same. Discretion should not, therefore, despite the abuse, be exercised in the appellant's favour.

1   Above para **5.05**.

5.47   In deciding whether or not to hold that there had been an abuse, Rose LJ set out the factors considered by the Court of Appeal to be of significance in reaching its decision. The first[1] was the seriousness of the offence: 'As a primary consideration, it is necessary for the courts to take into account the gravity of the offence in question'. Mullen was a member of the IRA and had ultimately been sentenced in England to 30 years' imprisonment for conspiracy to cause explosions. Secondly,[2] whether Mullen constituted a threat to peace and security in Zimbabwe: it was held that he did not. Thirdly:[3] 'It is necessary to consider the nature of the conduct of those involved in the deportation on behalf of the British government'. Having assessed the evidence, Rose LJ concluded that the British authorities had:

'... initiated and subsequently assisted in and procured the deportation of the appellant by unlawful means, in circumstances in which there were specific extradition facilities between this country and Zimbabwe. In so acting they were not only encouraging unlawful conduct in Zimbabwe but they were also acting in breach of public international law.'[4]

1   At 534C-D.
2   At 534E.
3   At 534F.
4   At 534F-535E.

5.48   Having reached this conclusion of bad faith, Rose LJ then considered the various and competing public interests involved – the serious nature of the offences committed by Mullen versus the need to discourage wrongful official conduct on the part of those who are responsible for criminal prosecution. Rose LJ concluded that, in Mullen's case: 'The discretionary balance comes down decisively against the prosecution of this offence'. In arriving at this conclusion, Rose LJ purported to apply the balancing exercise described by Lord Steyn in *R v Latif*.[1] Rose LJ observed that:

'In arriving at this conclusion we strongly emphasise that nothing in this judgment should be taken to suggest that there may not be cases, such as *Latif,* in which the seriousness of the crime is so great relative to the nature of the abuse of process that it would be a proper exercise of judicial discretion to permit a prosecution to proceed ... notwithstanding an abuse of process in relation to the defendant's presence within the jurisdiction. In each case it is a matter of discretionary balance, to be approached with regard to a particular conduct complained of and a particular offence charged.'[2]

1   Above para **5.03**.
2   At 536G-537A.

5.49   Interestingly, in his judgment Rose LJ sought to distinguish the abuse jurisdiction from all other cases where an exercise of judicial discretion is called for:

'It arises not from the relationship between the prosecution and the defendant but from the relationship between the prosecution and the court. It arises from the court's need to exercise control over executive involvement in the whole prosecution process, not limited to the trial itself.'[1]

1   At 537D-G.

5.50   Accordingly, despite the absence of any assertion of innocence from Mullen, Rose LJ held[1] that the abuse was sufficient to merit the quashing of his conviction:

'Having regard to the fact that the defendant, as he now concedes, was properly convicted, this court must approach the exercise of its discretion on a rather different basis from that which would have been appropriate if an application had been made to the trial judge. In particular, there is before this court no question of consideration of the strength of the evidence of the defendant's guilt of the offence charged. However, as appears from the passage already cited from the speech of Lord Lowry in *Reg. v. Horseferry Road Magistrates' Court, Ex parte Bennett* [1994] 1 A.C. 42, 76, certainty of guilt cannot displace the essential feature of this kind of abuse of process, namely the degradation of the lawful administration of justice.'

1   At 534B-C.

Mohamed & Dalvie v The President

5.51   In *Mohamed & Dalvie v The President of the Republic of South Africa & others*,[1] the applicant Mohamed was wanted by the American authorities in respect of the bombing of the US embassies in Nairobi and Dar es Salaam. He entered South Africa under an assumed name and a false passport. The FBI identified Mohamed while searching through asylum-seekers' records in Cape Town. Extradition proceedings between South Africa and America were possible, but, at the invitation of the FBI, the South African immigration authorities arrested Mohamed as a prohibited person. He was questioned and allegedly confessed in circumstances that violated his right not to incriminate himself, and his right to legal representation. He was then handed over to the FBI, whereupon he was questioned again (allegedly repeating his confession). During a subsequent search of Mohamed's address, both the FBI and South African officials untruthfully advised Mohamed's employer that Mohamed was being deported to Tanzania and told him that it would be a waste of money to employ a lawyer for him as he had admitted entering the country on a false passport. They also informed the employer 'disingenuously' that he was not permitted to visit Mohamed. The employer was '... fobbed off to ensure that Mohamed would continue to be denied access to a lawyer and would remain incommunicado ... to facilitate his removal by the FBI agents', which was promptly carried out. Mohamed was flown out of South Africa by the FBI, in the company of the US Prosecuting Attorney. Mohamed was questioned by the FBI and Prosecuting Attorney during the flight. On arrival in New York, the trial judge formally notified Mohamed that he faced the death penalty.

1   2001 (3) SA 893 (CC).

5.52   After Mohamed's arrival in New York, proceedings were brought on his behalf before a nine-judge South African Constitutional Court, challenging the propriety of the removal, alleging that it constituted disguised extradition, which deprived him of, amongst other rights, protection against the imposition of the death penalty. The Supreme Court of South Africa observed that, whilst the facts of the case could have justified the South African authorities in deporting him:

'That, however, is only part of the story, for the crucial events are those that happened after Mohamed had secured his temporary visa. Having been identified by the FBI as a suspect for whom an international arrest warrant had been issued in connection with the bombing of the United States embassy in Tanzania, he was apprehended by the South African immigration authorities in a joint operation undertaken in cooperation with the FBI. Within two days of his arrest and contrary to the provisions of the Act he was handed over to the FBI by the South African authorities for the purpose of being taken to the United States to be put on trial there for the bombing of the embassy. On his arrival in the United States he was immediately charged with various offences relating to that bombing and was informed by the court that the death sentence could be imposed on him if he were convicted. That this was likely to happen must have been apparent to the South African authorities as well as to the FBI when the arrangements were made for Mohamed to be removed from South Africa to the United States …'[1]

1   At para 44.

5.53   Whilst unable to provide tangible relief to Mohamed, the Constitutional Court ruled that it should nonetheless make its following views known to the American trial court:

'For the South African government to cooperate with a foreign government to secure the removal of a fugitive from South Africa to a country of which the fugitive is not a national and with which he has no connection other than that he is to be put on trial for his life there, is contrary to the underlying values of our Constitution. It is inconsistent with the government's obligation to protect the right to life of everyone in South Africa, and it ignores the commitment implicit in the Constitution that South Africa will not be party to the imposition of cruel, inhuman or degrading punishment … The fact that the government claims to have deported and not to have extradited Mohamed is of no relevance. European courts draw no distinction between deportation and extradition in the application of Article 3 of the European Convention on Human Rights … The removal of Mohamed to the United States could not have been effected without the cooperation of the South African immigration authorities. They cooperated well knowing that he would be put on trial in the United States to face capital charges. That he should be arrested and put on trial was clearly a significant and possibly the predominant motive that determined the course that was followed. Otherwise, why instruct the officials at the border to prevent him from leaving South Africa? And why cooperate in the process of sending him to the United States, a country with which he had no connection? They must also have known that there was a real risk that he would be convicted, and that unless an assurance to the contrary were obtained, he would be sentenced to death. In doing so, they infringed Mohamed's rights under the Constitution and acted contrary to their obligations to uphold and promote the rights entrenched in the Bill of Rights.'[1]

1   At paras 59–61.

R v Burns

5.54   In *R v Burns,*[1] the appellant had been arrested in respect of substantial drugs offences and remanded in custody. He escaped and made his way to Venezuela (entering Venezuela unlawfully under a false name, and using a false passport). An arrest warrant was issued and an Interpol Notice asserted that extradition would be requested from any country with which the UK had an extradition treaty or similar arrangement. The appellant was later arrested in Venezuela for an unrelated drugs offence committed there. The arrest was a purely domestic matter within Venezuela, and the British authorities were neither involved in nor connected with it. The UK authorities were advised of the appellant's presence in Venezuela. There existed no bilateral extradition treaty between the UK and Venezuela, and accordingly, any extradition request would have to have been ad hoc (pursuant to s 15 of the Extradition Act 1989).

1   [2002] EWCA Crim 1324.

5.55   The UK authorities were further advised that the appellant would probably be deported. The UK authorities were then asked to, and did, provide the Venezuelan investigatory judge with the appellant's details, including the fact that he was wanted in England. The Judge ordered the appellant's deportation to England since this was his country of origin. The UK authorities paid for the flight and accompanied him back to London where he was arrested. The trial judge rejected the contention that the British authorities had connived at, or colluded with, any impropriety by the Venezuelan authorities. That conclusion was upheld on its facts by the Court of Appeal, Judge LJ observing that the UK authorities:

> '... were not involved in the initial arrest. They provided the Judge, or investigating magistrate, with facts with which she wished to be provided. They did not exaggerate or falsify. They understood that the process in Venezuela, if not subject to judicial supervision, certainly involved a judicial element. They understood that, on the known facts, the appellant would be likely to be deported to this country. It is of course true that the British authorities did not try and discourage the authorities in Venezuela from the process, on which they seemed determined, nor question or challenge its legality. It was not incumbent on them to do so. And given their understanding of the view likely to be taken by the Venezuelan authorities, they sought to co-operate in the process, no doubt in the hope of achieving the appellant's return to the United Kingdom where he could be arrested. In our judgement, the process of this court was not subverted.'[1]

1   At paras 29–30.

5.56   What is perhaps more interesting from the Court of Appeal's ruling, is its treatment of a somewhat ambitious submission mounted on behalf of the appellant that, *whatever the merits, or the circumstances, of his expulsion*, if his client should have been extradited from Venezuela, and the British authorities participated in the process by which extradition proceedings were bypassed, an abuse of process was established. Rejecting that submission of principle, Judge LJ observed[1] that:

'... while [*ex parte Bennett* and *R v Mullen*] and other, cases identify clear principles, and are thus helpful if they might be in any doubt, the decisions on the individual facts are not decisive of subsequent cases, where similar, but not identical issues are raised. While preventing, or more accurately, acting to prevent the prosecution from benefiting from abuses of the process amounting to what Lord Steyn in *R v Latif* (1996) 1 WLR 104 at 112, graphically described as conduct "so unworthy or shameful that it was an affront to the public conscience to allow the prosecution to proceed," the principles are not apt to require that the conduct of the prosecution at every stage of the process should be unblemished and immaculate. Errors will be made and oversights will occur, and combinations of errors and oversights will take place, which do not justify the conclusion that the process has been abused

... As Lord Lane CJ, pointed out in ... *ex parte Mackeson* ... the decision in an individual case is "very largely a question of fact and the inference which one draws from the available facts on affidavits and on documentary evidence which are before us." An indicative, but not determinative line, may be drawn between cases where the prosecuting authorities have acted in bad faith, or with an excess of misguided enthusiasm for what is perceived to be a proper objective, deliberately subverting the defendant's rights not to be forcibly abducted to this country without proper process, and those cases where the prosecuting authorities, acting in good faith, have undermined or contributed to the undermining of the rights of the defendant. In *R v Mullen* ... Rose LJ pointed out further considerations: "In each case it is a matter of discretionary balance, to be approached with regard to the particular conduct complained of and the particular offence charged." In short, when deciding whether to exercise its undoubted powers to prevent an abuse of its process, the exercise of the court's discretion is fact specific.

... We therefore reject the submission that unless the extradition process, or its equivalent, has taken place, the court here is obliged to stop the prosecution. That is not what the House of Lords decided in *Bennett*. The existence of and the need to, exercise a discretion in each case where the issue is raised clearly contradicts the proposition that failures or breaches in the extradition process lead ineluctably to the termination of the trial. Moreover, if the contention were correct, it would apply to cases where the only interference with the extradition process would have been misconduct by the authorities in the foreign country (over which this court has no supervisory control) without any significant contribution by the British authorities (over which it has).'

1   At paras 26–28.

Article 5 ECHR

5.57   Issues of disguised extradition arose in *Bozano v France*.[1] Mr Bozano had been convicted in his absence in Italy and sentenced to life imprisonment in respect of offences relating to a Swiss national. He had taken refuge in France. He was arrested in France on other matters and kept in custody for the purposes of extradition. The French Court of Appeal ruled against extradition (holding that the Italian procedure relating to trial in absence and the absence of recourse to retrial, was contrary to French public policy). Under French law, that ruling was final and binding upon the French government. Upon release from custody, Mr Bozano was forced into a car by three armed plainclothes policemen. He was handcuffed and taken to police headquarters and served with a deportation order (which was later quashed by the French courts as an abuse of power). He was denied access to the courts or to legal representation, or in fact to anybody. Rather than take him to the nearest (Spanish) border, or to a border of his choice, he was driven hundreds of miles to the Swiss border. He was there met by Swiss police officials, handcuffed and conveyed into Swiss custody. From Switzerland, Mr Bozano's extradition to Italy was readily granted under the terms of the European Convention on Extradition 1957. The European Court of Human Rights unanimously found a violation of Art 5, ruling[2] that:

'Viewing the circumstances of the case as a whole ... the applicant's deprivation of liberty was neither lawful within the meaning of Article 5(1)(f) nor compatible with the right to security of person. Depriving Mr Bozano of his liberty in this way amounted in fact to a disguised form of extradition designed to circumvent the negative ruling ... of the Court of Appeal and not detention necessary in the ordinary course of action taken with a view to deportation ...the deportation procedure was abused in the instant case for objects and purposes other than its normal ones.'

1   Above para **5.02**.
2   At paras 60–61.

5.58   In *Stocké v Germany*, the applicant, a German national, was subject to criminal proceedings before the German courts in respect of tax offences. He failed to comply with the provisions of his bail and was ordered to be re-detained. However, he had fled to France (via Switzerland) to avoid arrest. The Court again considered the issues surrounding 'disguised extradition'. The German authorities first unsuccessfully sought to persuade the government of Luxembourg to receive and expel him on 'trumped up charges'. A plan was then devised by a police informer to lure Mr Stocké either directly into Germany or into a country from which he could be extradited, by means of attending a 'meeting' in respect of a fictitious building project. Mr Stocké was thus enticed onto a private charter plane ostensibly headed for Luxembourg but which proceeded to make an unscheduled stop in Germany, whereupon Mr Stocké was arrested. The police informant was later reimbursed for the cost of the charter hire, and provided with a reward, by the German prosecutor.

5.59   Before the European Court of Human Rights,[1] Mr Stocké claimed to be the victim of collusion between the German authorities and the police informer for the purpose of kidnapping him and bringing him back to the Federal Republic of Germany against his will with a view to arresting him in violation of Art 5(1). It was argued that the prosecuting authorities 'considered that it was too uncertain whether an extradition request to France would succeed and had preferred to make use of a police informer to do "the dirty work abroad".' The Court noted[2] that the applicant was induced by a trick to board a plane chartered by the informant, although he had been warned that they were going to fly over a small part of German territory. French inquiries that had been made had shown that the applicant had boarded the plane of his own free will and not under duress. The Commission examined witnesses; all denied having known about the informant's plan to bring Mr Stocké back to Germany against his will or having agreed to such a plan being carried out; the Commission did not consider their evidence to be inconsistent or unreliable. The Court considered, like the Commission, that it had not been established that the cooperation between the German authorities and the informant extended to unlawful activities abroad.[3] The clear implication of this judgment is that, as in *Bozano v France*,[4] had illegitimate cooperation, in fact, been found to have occurred, Art 5 issues would have been engaged.

1   (1991) App No 11755/85, 19 March.
2   At paras 49–50.
3   At paras 51 and 54.
4   Above para **5.02**.

5.60   Although neither *Bozano v France*[1] nor Art 5(1) contributed heavily, if indeed at all, to the formation of the *R v Hartley*[2]/*State v Ebrahim*[3]/*ex parte Bennett*[4] common law abuse of process principles, it appeared that the principles governing each would largely reflect and complement the other. However, recent decisions of the Strasbourg Court since 1996 would appear to herald a significant division between the two lines of principle, such that Art 5 is likely to be of little assistance to the further development of the common law.

1   Above para **5.02**.
2   Above para **5.02**.
3   Above para **5.33**.
4   Above para **5.01**.

5.61   In *Sanchez Ramirez v France*,[1] the applicant, a Venezuelan citizen, was wanted by the French authorities in respect of a fatal car bomb explosion in Paris, for which he had been convicted *in absentia* and sentenced to life imprisonment. Mr Sanchez Ramirez was living in Khartoum, Sudan, under the protection of the Sudanese national security forces. There existed no extradition treaty between France and the Sudan. Mr Sanchez Ramirez alleged that he had been forcibly expelled from the Sudan at the request of the French Interior Ministry. He alleged that he had been attacked by 12 or so men, including members of his own guard, handcuffed, fettered, tranquilised, and hooded. He was transported to the airport where Frenchmen were waiting. Once on the airplane, he alleged that he was placed in a bag and strapped around his feet, knees, and shoulders and flown to a military airbase in France. The French Court of Cassation ruled that French national courts have no jurisdiction to examine the circumstances in which a person is arrested abroad by local authorities acting alone and in the exercise of their sovereign powers. On an application to the European Commission on Human Rights, Mr Sanchez Ramirez argued that his arrest amounted to disguised extradition in violation of Art 5(1).

1   (1996) 86-B DR 155.

5.62 The Commission ruled[1] that the circumstances in which the applicant was deprived of his liberty in Sudan were outwith the jurisdiction of the Convention.[2] The Commission further observed, without reference to *Bozano v France*,[3] that:

'It does not appear to the Commission that any cooperation which occurred in this case between the Sudanese and French authorities involved any factor which could raise problems from the point of view of Article 5 of the Convention particularly in the field of the fight against terrorism, which frequently necessitates cooperation between States ... The Convention contains no provisions either concerning the circumstances in which extradition may be granted, or the procedure to be followed before extradition may be granted. It follows that even assuming that the circumstances in which the applicant arrived in France could be described as a disguised extradition, this could not, as such, constitute a breach of the Convention.'

1 At 160–161.
2 See, to similar effect, *Freda v Italy* (1980) 21 DR 250; *Altmann v France* (1984) 37 DR 225 and *Reinette v France* (1989) 63 DR 189.
3 Above para **5.02**.

5.63 In *Conka v Belgium*[1] it appeared that the Court may have taken a different approach when it found Art 5 violations in a 'disguised expulsion' case involving the tricking of Slovakian Romany asylum seekers by the Belgian authorities into a police station under the false pretence that their attendance was required to enable asylum forms to be completed. When they attended, the applicants were served with orders to leave Belgium and were informed that the orders were final. They were taken to a closed transit centre and thus removed from Belgium to Slovakia by deceit (a 'little ruse'). The European Court of Human Rights found[2] a violation of Art 5(1) by reason of deliberate abuse of power and thus arbitrariness, citing *Bozano v France*.[3]

1 (2002) 34 EHRR 54.
2 At paras. 38–42.
3 Above para **5.02**.

5.64 In May 2005, however, the Grand Chamber gave judgment in *Ocalan v Turkey*.[1] Mr Öcalan was the leader of the Workers' Party of Kurdistan (PKK). The Turkish courts had issued seven warrants for Mr Öcalan's arrest and a wanted notice (Red Notice) had been circulated by Interpol. In each of those documents, the applicant was accused of founding an armed gang in order to destroy the territorial integrity of the Turkish State and of instigating various terrorist acts that had resulted in loss of life. The offences alleged were punishable with death. Mr Öcalan had been living in Syria for many years, but was expelled from there. He travelled to Greece and claimed political asylum which was refused. He was taken by the Greek authorities to Kenya and accommodated at the Ambassador's residence, the Greek authorities ensuring that he was able to enter without declaring his identity or going through passport control. When they learned of his presence, the Kenyan Ministry for Foreign Affairs announced that Kenyan diplomatic missions abroad had been the target of terrorist attacks and that the applicant's presence in Kenya constituted a major security risk.

1 European Court of Human Rights, Grand Chamber, May 12, 2005, paras 83–99.

5.65   Mr Öcalan was informed by the Greek Ambassador, after the latter had returned from a meeting with the Kenyan Minister for Foreign Affairs, that he was free to leave for the destination of his choice and that the Netherlands were prepared to accept him. Kenyan officials went to the Greek embassy to take Mr Öcalan to the airport. The Greek Ambassador said that he wished to accompany the applicant to the airport in person and a discussion between the Ambassador and the Kenyan officials ensued. In the end, the applicant got into a car driven by a Kenyan official. On the way to the airport, this car left the convoy and, taking a route reserved for security personnel in the international transit area of Nairobi Airport, took him to an aircraft in which Turkish officials were waiting for him. The applicant was then arrested after boarding the aircraft. No proceedings had been brought to extradite him from Kenya and the Kenyan authorities had denied all responsibility for his transfer to Turkey. Mr Öcalan was kept blindfolded throughout the flight except when the Turkish officials wore masks. He also alleged that he had been given tranquillisers, probably at the Greek embassy in Nairobi. He was found guilty by the National Security Court and sentenced to death. That conviction was upheld by the Turkish Court of Cassation, but his death sentence was later commuted to one of life imprisonment.

5.66   Mr Öcalan brought proceedings before the European Court of Human Rights alleging, inter alia, that he had been deprived of his liberty unlawfully, without the applicable extradition procedure being followed, in violation of Art 5(1). He maintained that his interception by Kenyan officials and transfer to the Turkish aircraft where Turkish officials were waiting for him was prima facie evidence that he had been abducted by the Turkish authorities operating abroad, beyond their jurisdiction.

5.67   The Grand Chamber found no violation of Art 5. As regards issues of principle, the Grand Chamber observed that an arrest made by the authorities of one State on the territory of another State, without the consent of the latter, affects the person's individual rights to security under Art 5.[1] The Convention does not prevent cooperation between States, within the framework of extradition treaties or in matters of deportation, for the purpose of bringing fugitive offenders to justice, provided that it does not interfere with any specific rights recognised in the Convention.[2] The fact that a fugitive has been handed over as a result of cooperation between States does not in itself make the arrest unlawful and does not therefore give rise to any problem under Art 5.[3] The Convention contains no provisions concerning the circumstances in which extradition may be granted, or the procedure to be followed before extradition may be granted. Subject to it being the result of cooperation between the States concerned and provided that the legal basis for the order for the fugitive's arrest is an arrest warrant issued by the authorities of the fugitive's State of origin, *even an atypical extradition cannot as such be regarded as being contrary to the Convention.*[4] Irrespective of whether the arrest amounts to a violation of the law of the State in which the fugitive has taken refuge – a question that only falls to be examined by the Court if the host State is a party to the Convention – the Court requires proof in the form of concordant inferences that the authorities of the State to which the applicant has been transferred have acted extra-territorially in a manner that is inconsistent with the sovereignty of the host

State and therefore contrary to international law. Only then will the burden of
proving that the sovereignty of the host State and international law have been
complied with shift to the respondent Government.[5]

1   At para 85.
2   At para 86.
3   At para 87.
4   At para 89.
5   At para 90.

5.68   Applying those principles to the facts before it, the Grand Chamber
noted that the applicant was arrested by members of the Turkish security forces
inside an aircraft registered in Turkey in the international zone of Nairobi
Airport. After being handed over to the Turkish officials by the Kenyan
officials, the applicant was effectively under Turkish authority and therefore
within the 'jurisdiction' of that State. Insofar as the applicant's interception in
Kenya immediately before he was handed over to Turkish officials on board the
aircraft at Nairobi Airport was concerned, the Court sought to determine
whether it was 'the result of [illegitimate] acts by Turkish officials that violated
Kenyan sovereignty and international law ..., or of [legitimate] cooperation
between the Turkish and Kenyan authorities in the absence of any extradition
treaty between Turkey and Kenya laying down a formal procedure'.[1] Having
regard to the facts that: (a) the applicant entered Kenya without declaring his
identity to the immigration officers, (b) the Kenyan authorities invited the
Greek Ambassador to arrange for the applicant to leave Kenyan territory, (c) as
he was being transferred from the Greek embassy to the airport, Kenyan
officials intervened and separated the applicant from the Greek Ambassador,
(d) the car in which the applicant was travelling was driven by a Kenyan official
who took him to the aircraft in which Turkish officials were waiting to arrest
him, (e) the Kenyan authorities did not perceive the applicant's arrest by the
Turkish officials on board an aircraft at Nairobi Airport as being in any way a
violation of Kenyan sovereignty, and (f) the Kenyan authorities did, however,
issue a formal protest to the Greek government, the Court concluded[2] that,
contrary to the statement by the Kenyan Minister for Foreign Affairs, the
Kenyan authorities were involved in the applicant's transfer:

> '... at the material time the Kenyan authorities had decided either to hand the
> applicant over to the Turkish authorities or to facilitate such a handover. The
> applicant has not adduced evidence enabling concordant inferences ... to be
> drawn that Turkey failed to respect Kenyan sovereignty or to comply with
> international law in the present case.'

1   At para 93.
2   At paras 97–98.

5.69   It may be that *Sanchez Ramirez v France* and *Öcalan v Turkey* will be
confined in practice to cases where the host State is not a party to the
Convention and with whom the Convention State has no extradition treaty. But
the width of the observations of the Commission and Grand Chamber are stark
and appear to travel more generally. If so, they undoubtedly run counter to the
pre-1996 Strasbourg case law and flatly conflict with the principles espoused by
the House of Lords in *ex parte Bennett*,[1] the South African Supreme Court in

State v Ebrahim,[2] the South African Constitutional Court in *Mohamed v The President,*[3] and the New Zealand Court of Appeal in *R v Hartley.*[4] Constituting, at their core, instances of state cooperation, cases such as *ex parte Mackeson*[5] and *R v Mullen*[6] would likely suffer a different fate if decided under the principles articulated by the Grand Chamber. Conversely, the facts of *Sanchez Ramirez v France* and *Öcalan v Turkey* would almost certainly suffer a different fate if decided under the common law abuse of process principles. It is surely inconceivable that *ex parte Bennett* would be reconsidered. It is, therefore, likely that Art 5 and the common law doctrine of abuse of principle will remain but distant cousins, each effectively offering little to the jurisprudential development of the latter.

1   Above para **5.01**.
2   Above para **5.33**.
3   Above para **5.51**.
4   Above para **5.02**.
5   Above para **5.02**.
6   Above para **5.01**.

UNLAWFUL ACTS COMMITTED BY UK STATE AGENTS OVERSEAS

5.70   The decision of the House of Lords in *ex parte Bennett*[1] establishes that, where a complaint is made of unlawfulness of State agents in foreign jurisdictions and/or breaches of foreign law by State agents resulting in the arrival of the accused into this jurisdiction, then an English court is competent to hear this complaint pursuant to its abuse jurisdiction.

1   Above para **5.01**.

5.71   The issue next to be considered is whether similar principles apply where similar complaints of illegality are made outside the context of an alleged illegal extradition:

(a)   where it is alleged that the way in which evidence was obtained against the accused by UK agents operating overseas was unlawful under the law of the jurisdiction in which they operated; and

(b)   whether those agents in the course of their investigation assisted or procured breaches of foreign law committed by agents or officials of that foreign jurisdiction.

5.72   Crime, as it is always said in the context of mutual assistance, is increasingly international. From paedophiles to fraudsters and especially via the internet, the notion of national frontiers demarcating one crime from another is regarded as increasingly anachronistic. Hence the convergence of law enforcement agencies within the EU and beyond where international operations, previously largely reserved for anti-drug trafficking, have become almost routine. Heightened fears concerning international terrorism have galvanised this acceptance of international co-operation to combat organised crime.

5.73   The courts, at least in England and Wales, have yet to recognise this endemic change in the nature of law enforcement. This is surely because our legal framework concerning mutual assistance remains rooted in two concepts which are antipathetic to the developments outlined in para **5.72**: first, that of the sovereign nation-state, and secondly, an emphasis on mutual assistance being connected to extant or antecedent court proceedings. Traditional use of mutual assistance relates to the obtaining of evidence by one State on behalf of another for use in proceedings. 'Proceedings' here mean court or judicial proceedings. This approach underlies the European Convention on Mutual Assistance. Essentially the Convention is concerned with the foreign State gathering or obtaining evidence on behalf of the Requesting State.

5.74   The scenario to be considered in this section is, however, not addressed or contemplated by the Convention; where there are no court proceedings in existence and UK State agents are operating on foreign soil in a law enforcement capacity.[1] In this scenario, the agents are investigating crimes which are in the course of being committed in the foreign State. This was the situation in *R v McDonald*.[2]

1   This in contradistinction to an intelligence-gathering capacity, the traditional function of MI6.
2   (April 2002, unreported), Woolwich Crown Court.

R v McDonald

5.75   The accused were all alleged to be participating members of 'The Real IRA', a proscribed terrorist organisation. Further, pursuant to offences under the Terrorism Act 2000, they were alleged to have solicited funds and weapons and conspired to cause explosions. The significance of these offences was that the UK courts have jurisdiction to try such offences irrespective of where they are alleged to have been committed. The evidence adduced by the prosecution related to two recorded conversations between the accused and undercover MI5 agents which had occurred in Slovakia. This evidence was the culmination of contacts between the accused and MI5 agents over several months, which had taken place in several other countries including Ireland, Austria and Hungary. Two novel features of the investigation were apparent. First that 'Operation Samnite' was an investigation conducted and led by MI5 almost entirely overseas. Secondly, and in consequence, the police were only brought in at a very late stage when MI5 was minded to curtail its operation, their role being to advise on evidence and apply for an international arrest warrant.

5.76   In relation to their abuse applications, the accused alleged abuse and bad faith as follows:

(a)   the extradition of the accused from Slovakia at the request of the British authorities was unlawful in that due process requirements under Slovakian law were not observed by the Slovakian authorities and Art 8 of the European Convention on Human Rights was, in any event, violated;

(b)   Slovakia was chosen by MI5 as the preferred country of arrest and extradition and thus the accused were lured into this jurisdiction from another (Ireland) where their extradition would have been more difficult; and

(c)   the surveillance methods used by MI5 were unlawful in several of the countries in which that activity occurred.

Accordingly in relation to such complaints, full disclosure of all relevant material was sought.

5.77   In relation to Operation Samnite, it is interesting to note that, at least during its lifetime, no treaty existed between the UK and another State in relation to the conduct of UK agents working abroad. It must therefore inevitably follow that, at least in relation to this operation, either it was conducted without the consent of the host-State and was thus a flagrant violation of its sovereignty or, and much more likely, there were secret diplomatic agreements or protocols between the UK and the relevant countries permitting MI5 activity in those countries. In fact in *McDonald*, the prosecution admitted that agreements had been reached in relation to the permitting of MI5 activity. It was, however, anxious that there should be no disclosure of these.

5.78   Parliament has already contemplated the overseas use of UK agents. The Regulation of Investigatory Powers Act 2000, s 27(3) and the Intelligence Services Act 1994, s 5 are both concerned with the authorisation within the UK of covert operations conducted on foreign soil. In *McDonald,* the prosecution contended that Operation Samnite was validly authorised pursuant to those sections.

The issues raised

5.79   Put at its simplest, the issue raised by this subject is whether, as in the instance of illegal extradition as in *ex parte Bennett*, the courts here are willing to supervise, via their abuse jurisdiction, executive conduct in relation to the overseas gathering of evidence and deployment of agents during a criminal investigation. As a matter of policy, should the courts eschew any willingness to supervise such conduct or should they hold that their constitutional duty to ensure the fairness of criminal trials requires that no area of executive conduct is beyond their jurisdiction?

5.80   Clearly, there are valid arguments against the courts assuming a jurisdiction. International relations or 'international comity' suggest that a court in one jurisdiction should not determine whether a foreign government agency has acted in breach of its own domestic law in another jurisdiction. There is plenty of authority to the effect that territorial sovereignty requires that an English court should not pronounce upon the validity of a law of a foreign State within its own territory.[1] In addition to reasons of comity, the courts have also imposed self-restraint in relation to sensitive areas of diplomacy between States.[2]

1   See for example *Buck v A-G* [1965] Ch 745; *British Airways v Laker* [1985] AC 58 and *Kuwait Airways v Iraqi Airways* [2002] 2 AC 883, HL.
2   See for example the judgment of the Court of Appeal *R (Abbassi) v Secretary of State for*

Foreign Affairs [2002] EWCA Civ 1598, where, although the Court regarded as objectionable the fact that the British citizen was subject to indefinite detention in territory over which the US had exclusive control with no opportunity to challenge the legitimacy of his detention before any court or tribunal, it was held that there was no direct remedy in the English court.

5.81 Moreover, from a pragmatic perspective, the courts here may rightly be reluctant to consider themselves competent to decide whether, for example, the criminal law of another EU State complies with the European Convention on Human Rights or whether the UK agent active in that State acted in breach of relevant domestic law. Such considerations may quickly embroil an English court in a clash of experts concerning foreign law with the attendant risk of that court interpreting such law in a way inconsistent with its interpretation by the national State courts.

5.82 There are, however, countervailing arguments. The principle firmly established in *ex parte Bennett* is that the rule of law requires any area of executive misconduct to fall within the purview of the courts. An assertion that there are some activities of State affecting the fairness of a criminal trial, which, as a class, should not be subject to judicial accountability, is one which no longer finds any support in English law.

5.83 Furthermore, if Parliament is to assume extraterritorial criminal jurisdiction in relation, for example, to terrorism under the Terrorism Act 2000, such that an individual can be tried for offences under that statute wherever they occurred, then questions of comity lose much of their attraction. Moreover, Parliament has also created a legislative framework in relation to overseas actions of executive agents as outlined above. Against this backdrop it is difficult to comprehend why the safeguard of judicial accountability should nonetheless be excluded.

5.84 For themselves, the courts have expressed a willingness to consider whether the obtaining of evidence for admission into a trial here was in breach of foreign law. Three recent authorities[1] can briefly be considered:

(a) In *R v Khan*[2] Lord Nolan said: 'I am prepared to accept that if evidence has been obtained in circumstances which involve a breach of Article 8, or for that matter an apparent breach of the law of a foreign country, that is a matter which may be relevant to the exercise of the section 78 power'.[3]

(b) In *R v P, C and S,*[4] Potter LJ accepted that an English court could hear evidence relating to the legality of obtaining foreign intercepts under foreign law.

(c) *HM Advocate v Al Megrahi (No 3):*[5] in the Lockerbie trial, the Scottish court considered whether Maltese officials had breached Maltese law in their dealings with Scottish police officers.

1   For a Commonwealth authority on this point, the decision of the Supreme Court of Canada in *R v Cook* [1998] 2 SCR 597 is instructive
2   [1997] AC 558, HL.
3   [1997] AC 558, HL at 582.
4   (Unreported, 16 May 2000).
5   2000 SLT 1401.

5.85   In *R v Hardy (Donovan Anthony)*,[1] the four appellants were convicted of conspiracy to evade the prohibition on the importation of cocaine. At trial, the appellant Hardy had objected to the admission of evidence of the finding of cocaine in his Dutch hotel room. The British authorities had acted wholly appropriately in making a formal application for assistance from the Dutch, who had taken the investigation up from there. On appeal, Hardy and his co-accused Annal argued that the trial judge was wrong to allow that evidence to go before the jury on the basis that it was inadmissible and/or because the judge should have exercised his powers to exclude that evidence under PACE, s 78, on the basis that there had been breaches of the Dutch Criminal Code during the search of the hotel. The appellants complained that the Dutch Criminal Code had been violated in that, firstly, rules relating to the search were not complied with and, secondly, there had been no application to a court for permission to hand over the drugs to the English authorities. On the latter point, the Court of Appeal concluded that, 'no doubt ... there was a breach of the code'.[2]

1   [2003] EWCA Crim 3092.
2   At para 28.

5.86   The Court has thereby once again shown a willingness to consider whether the law of a foreign country has been breached (albeit here not by UK agents), finding that it had been so in Hardy's case[1] and then going on to consider whether the search of the hotel room amounted to a violation of ECHR, Art 8. Ultimately, the Court found that Art 8 was not engaged and noted that, according to *R v Khan*,[2] an apparent breach of the law of a foreign country was only a matter that 'may' be relevant to the exercise of a judge's power under s 78. The Court of Appeal concluded that any breach did not affect the fairness of the appellants' trial in England, nor did it deprive Hardy of his ability to deal properly with the evidence in his case.

1   At para 43.
2   Above para **5.84**.

UNLAWFULLY OBTAINED EVIDENCE

5.87   Both the ECtHR and the common law have held that the fact that evidence has been unlawfully obtained does not lead to automatic exclusion. In *Khan v United Kingdom*,[1] the European Court held that the fact the sole evidence obtained against the accused had been obtained unlawfully in breach of Art 8, did not necessarily require its exclusion pursuant to Art 6. This approach was then adopted and followed by the House of Lords in *Attorney-General's Reference (No 3 of 1999)*[2] and in *R v P*,[3] and has since been applied at the European level in *Chalkley v United Kingdom*[4] *and Hewitson v United Kingdom*[5] (both cases relating to the use of evidence obtained from covert listening devices installed in violation of Art 8).

1   (2000) 8 BHRC 310.
2   [2001] 2 AC 91, HL.
3   [2002] 1 AC 146, HL.
4   (2003) 37 EHRR 30.
5   (2003) 37 EHRR 31.

5.88   The exception to the principle that unlawfully obtained evidence will not be automatically excluded concerns evidence obtained by torture.[1] In *A & Others v Secretary of State for the Home Department*,[2] the House of Lords made clear that both the common law of England, European Convention on Human Rights, and international law (as embodied in the International Convention against Torture and other Cruel, Inhuman or Degrading Treatment 1984 and as a principle of *jus cogens*) prohibited in absolute terms the admissibility of evidence (confessions) obtained by torture. Where a court is persuaded on the balance of probabilities[3] that evidence was obtained by torture, it will refuse to admit that evidence.

1   *Jalloh v Germany* (2007) 44 EHRR 32 at para 105
2   [2006] 2 AC 221, HL.
3   Whilst their Lordships were unanimous on the principle that evidence obtained by torture will be excluded, they were divided on the test by which that principle should be applied. Lord Bingham criticised the conclusion of the majority, that it must be established on the balance of probabilities that evidence was obtained by torture before it will be excluded, taking the view that such a test could never be satisfied in the real world, as the torturer (a foreign party in that case) 'does not boast of his trade' and 'the [domestic] security services ... do not wish to imperil their relations with regimes where torture is practised' by disclosing such information. The detainee, he said, was 'in the dark' and 'it is inconsistent with the most rudimentary notions of fairness to blindfold a man and then impose a standard which only the sighted could hope to meet'.

5.89   Short of torture, the subject of unlawfully obtained evidence raises important questions of ends justifying means and the extent to which courts should uphold the principle of legality. Superficially at least, it might seem surprising that a court would agree to receive such evidence, since a court, above all else, is responsible for upholding the rule of law, and evidence obtained in violation of legal safeguard must tend to undermine that value. In *R v Sang*,[1] Lord Diplock regarded a complaint of unlawfully obtained evidence as not one to be properly considered by a criminal court at all. In his view any disciplining of the police or violation of a legal remedy was the exclusive province of a civil court to which an unhappy defendant should direct his complaint.

1   Above para **5.08**.

5.90   Since the landmark decision in *ex parte Bennett*[1] and the acceptance by the courts of a responsibility to oversee executive conduct, the view of Lord Diplock now appears antique. Moreover his view has been overtaken by the PACE, s 78 power which vested in every trial judge a power to exclude evidence in order to preserve the fairness of a trial. This combination of the common law abuse power in relation to executive misconduct and s 78 in relation to trial fairness must mean that the legal position concerning unlawfully obtained evidence has become more complicated. But before the common law and statutory position are considered, the jurisprudence of the European Court can be reviewed.

1   Above para **5.01**.

The ECtHR jurisprudence

5.91   Perhaps the best explanation for the decision of the court in *Khan v United Kingdom*[1] lies in its established principle that the matter of legal conditions governing the admission of evidence is best left to national courts to determine.[2] In other words, in the field of exclusion of evidence obtained in breach of Art 8, the court affords a substantial margin of appreciation to Member States. This policy in relation to this subject was first applied in *Schenk v Switzerland*.[3] In *Khan,* the UK respondent did not dispute that the evidence presented at the applicant's trial had all been obtained in breach of his Art 8 right and that accordingly his conviction rested entirely upon such tainted evidence. The applicant submitted that the admission of such evidence vitiated the fairness of his trial in breach of Art 6.

1   Above para **5.87**.
2   This self-denying principle however is disregarded in certain cases. For example, the court interfered in *Saunders v United Kingdom* (1996) 23 EHRR 313 to hold that evidence obtained by compulsive questioning violated Art 6. In *Teixeira v Portugal* (1998) 28 EHRR 101, the same view was taken as regards evidence obtained through police incitement.
3   (1988) 13 EHRR 242.

5.92   In its judgment, the European Court held[1] that:

'The central question in the present case is whether the proceedings as a whole were fair. With specific reference to the admission of the contested tape recording, the court notes that, as in the *Schenk* case, the applicant had ample opportunity to challenge both the authenticity and the use of the recording. He did not challenge its authenticity, but challenged its use at the 'voir dire' and again before the Court of Appeal and the House of Lords. The court notes that at each level of jurisdiction the domestic courts assessed the effect of admission of the evidence on the fairness of the trial by reference to s 78 of PACE, and the courts discussed, amongst other matters, the non-statutory basis for the surveillance. The fact that the applicant was at each step unsuccessful makes no difference (see the above-mentioned *Schenk* judgment, paragraph 47).

The court would add that it is clear that, had the domestic courts been of the view that the admission of the evidence would have given rise to substantive unfairness, they would have had a discretion to exclude it under s 78 of PACE.

In these circumstances, the court finds that the use at the applicant's trial of the secretly taped material did not conflict with the requirements of fairness guaranteed by article 6(1) of the Convention.'

1   At paras 38–40.

5.93   Commenting upon the ratio in this case, Lord Hobhouse, in *R v P,*[1] later said:

'It should be noted that the ECtHR again emphasised that the defendant is not entitled to have the unlawfully obtained evidence excluded simply because it has been so obtained. What he is entitled to is an opportunity to challenge its use and admission in evidence and a judicial assessment of the effect of its admission upon the fairness of the trial as is provided for by s 78.'

1   Above para **5.87**.

5.94   In essence, therefore, the Court held that the applicant's ability to test and object to the admission of unlawfully obtained evidence via a s 78 application was a sufficient measure of legal protection in domestic law against arbitrary interferences by public authorities with the rights safeguarded by the Convention.

5.95   Unfortunately, the judgment in *Khan v United Kingdom*[1] did not resolve an important issue concerning the fairness of a criminal trial. As the above analysis reflects, the Court was concerned with whether UK procedures were sufficient to consider whether evidence obtained in breach of Art 8 should be excluded or not. It did not also consider the separate issue of the impact of such an Art 8 breach upon the fairness of the trial,– specifically, why an applicant can have a fair trial when all the evidence against him has been obtained in violation of his Art 8 rights. This issue will be revisited when the relevant abuse jurisprudence is considered below. The Court's decision in *Khan* was followed by a similar decision in *PG and JH v United Kingdom*[2] and has been considered in a host of other cases at the European level.[3] Interestingly, in *Jalloh v Germany*,[4] the Strasbourg court determined that, whilst dependent upon the facts of the particular case, the admission of evidence obtained in breach of Art 3 violated the defendant's Art 6 rights (there, the forcible administration of drugs to expel drugs previously swallowed).

1   Above para **5.87**.
2   [2002] Crim LR 308.
3   See *Taylor-Sabori v United Kingdom* (2003) 36 EHRR 17; *Allan v United Kingdom* (2003) 36 EHRR 12; *Armstrong v United Kingdom* (2003) 36 EHRR 30; and *Lewis v United Kingdom* (2004) 39 EHRR 9.
4   Above para **5.88**.

The common law

The vital role accorded to PACE, s 78

5.96   In *Attorney-General's Reference (No 3 of 1999)*,[1] the House of Lords considered the decision of the trial judge, subsequently supported by the Court of Appeal, that evidence against an accused should be excluded pursuant to s 78 on the ground that it had been obtained in express breach of a statutory provision of PACE.[2] The House of Lords took the view, however, that the courts below had been unnecessarily restrictive about the admissibility of evidence. Whilst Lord Steyn held, as a matter of statutory construction, that the provisions of the section had been misconstrued and thus the evidence had not been unlawfully obtained, he added that in any event the courts should be prepared to accept such evidence. There were, in his view,[3] a triangulation of interests to be considered and given equal respect:

'The purpose of the criminal law is to permit everyone to go about their daily lives without fear of harm to person or property. And it is in the interests of everyone that serious crime should be effectively investigated and prosecuted. There must be fairness to all sides. In a criminal case this requires the court to consider a triangulation of interests. It involves taking into account the position of the accused, the victim and his or her family, and the public. In my view the austere interpretation which the Court of Appeal adopted is not only in conflict with the plain words of the statute but also produces results which are contrary to good sense. A consideration of the public interest reinforces the interpretation which I have adopted.'

1   Above para **5.87**.
2   A DNA sample which proved crucial evidence against the accused which, because of his previous acquittal on another charge, ought, pursuant to s 63 PACE, to have then been destroyed.
3   At 118.

5.97   Applying this framework, Lord Steyn held that a rule, which required the exclusion of unlawfully obtained evidence, would give the accused an unfair preference or trump over the public interest and was thus on his utilitarian basis, unjustifiable.

5.98   In *R v P*,[1] the House of Lords delivered a similar view. Here, as in *R v Khan*,[2] evidence against the accused had been obtained in breach of their Art 8 rights. The issue was to what extent should a proven breach of this right affect or impair the fairness of a trial. Lord Hobhouse commenting upon *Khan* said:[3]

'The importance of the ECtHR decision is that it confirms that the direct operation of articles 8 and 6 does not invalidate their Lordships' conclusion or alter the vital role of s 78 as the means by which questions of the use of evidence obtained in breach of article 8 are to be resolved at a criminal trial. The criterion to be applied is the criterion of fairness in article 6 which is likewise the criterion to be applied by the judge under s 78. Similarly, the ECtHR decision that any remedy for a breach of article 8 lies outside the scope of the criminal trial and that article 13 does not require a remedy for a breach of article 8 to be given within that trial shows that their Lordships were right to say that a breach of article 8 did not require the exclusion of evidence. Such an exclusion, if any, would have to come about because of the application of article 6 and s 78.'

1   Above para **5.87**.
2   Above para **5.84**.
3   At 475.

5.99   The effect of Lord Hobhouse's speech is to emphasise the primary role of s 78 as a remedy and so to marginalise the significance in a criminal case of any breach of Art 8. What really matters in this context is a procedural consideration centred on s 78 – did the accused have a fair hearing of his/her application to apply for exclusion under s 78?[1] Accordingly, the only important article to consider in this context is Art 6, which contains the same test of fairness as s 78. Lord Hobhouse was not suggesting that Art 8 rights are unimportant, rather that, if a judge is satisfied that the consequence of such a breach has no impact upon the accused's right to a fair trial under Art 6 or s 78, then the evidence so obtained from the breach ought to be admitted. In a view reminiscent of that of Lord Diplock in *R v Sang*[2] mentioned above,[3] Lord Hobhouse's view is that absent trial unfairness, breaches of Art 8 are best left to the civil courts.

1   This issue in relation to disclosure is considered in **Chapter 4**.
2   Above para **5.08**.
3   Above para **5.89**.

5.100   Similar views as to the vital role of s 78 were expressed by Lord Hope in the subsequent case of *R v Sargent*:[1]

> '... the scope of this discretionary power [s 78] is plainly wide enough to enable the trial judge to take into account any disadvantage that may result from the rules about the non-disclosure of intercepts.'

1   [2003] 1 AC 347, HL, at para 17.

5.101   The application of this approach established by the House of Lords can be contrasted with the decision of the trial judge in *R v Veneroso*.[1] Here, the trial judge found that the evidence adduced by the prosecution had been obtained by an unlawful search. Consequently the accused's Art 8 rights had also been violated. The judge ruled that, in this circumstance, the evidence ought to be excluded under s 78, holding that there was no justification, before it commenced, for the police conducting their search and only a small quantity of drugs had been found. It is submitted that on the strength of *R v P*, this case is wrongly decided. Assuming that the evidence was probative of the offence charged and that the accused had an opportunity to challenge it at trial, Lord Hobhouse would have admitted it.

1   [2002] Crim LR 306.

5.102   Overall, the unstructured and open-ended discretionary exclusionary approach engendered by the wording of s 78 has been unaltered by the Human Rights Act 1998 challenges, even when there have been blatant violations of Article 8.[1] Recently, in *R v Button*,[2] the Court of Appeal dismissed submissions that the admission of evidence obtained in breach of Art 8 constituted a continuing or repeating violation of that article in a way that was incompatible with the Convention. In applying the principle established in the *Attorney-General's Reference (No 3 of 1999)*,[3] the Court recalled that relevant evidence obtained unlawfully was admissible, subject to the discretion to exclude that evidence provided by s 78 of PACE.

1   See, for example, *R v Mason* [2002] Crim LR 891. Here the court accepted that, despite their violations, the police had acted in good faith.
2   [2005] EWCA Crim 516.
3   Above para **5.87**.

Abuse of process

5.103   The common law abuse jurisdiction has no equivalent in the jurisprudence of the ECtHR and so this domestic right is not addressed there. Section 11 of the HRA 1998, however, makes plain that such a domestic right is preserved despite incorporation and the House of Lords held in *R (Daly) v*

Secretary of State for the Home Department[1] that incorporation did not lessen a legal protection already enjoyed by an accused under domestic law. Thus attention must instead focus on the interrelationship between abuse and s 78.

1   [2001] 2 AC 532, HL, see paras 30–31.

5.104   It is submitted that the second limb of abuse as established by the House in *ex parte Bennett*,[1] that where a court is aware of a serious abuse of power by the executive, it may refuse to allow the police or prosecuting authority to take advantage of such by regarding it as an abuse of process, goes further than the test of fairness as established by s 78. Section 78 discretion is exercised inside, and presupposes, a trial. It is solely concerned with admissibility whereas abuse seeks to consider whether a trial should be held at all. Where, in particular, there is an allegation of bad faith or oppression, there is no symmetry between the test of fairness of proceedings in s 78 and abuse.

1   Above para **5.01**.

5.105   This point is perhaps best illuminated by the submissions made in *R v Stapleton*.[1] Here, the accused were charged with VAT fraud following a very lengthy and intrusive surveillance operation mounted by the police. The defence argued abuse on the ground of bad faith and abuse of power, that the authorities were determined to apprehend one of the accused for some crime and that, in reality, the real motive for the surveillance was not suspicion of ongoing criminal activity but an arbitrary and wholesale investigation of the accused. As such, this *ad hominem* investigation was impermissible and in any event in this particular case was wholly disproportionate. It also constituted a violation of Art 8. Thus, the trial ought to be stayed for *Bennett*-type abuse.

1   [2002] Crim LR 584.

5.106   Such a complaint of abuse, that the evidence was unlawfully obtained because of the investigator's bad faith and/or that the means adopted were disproportionate to the aim pursued, brings back into importance Art 8 issues. As *Bennett*-type abuse is not concerned with forensic fairness but with the motives and conduct of law enforcement, deliberate or unjustified breaches of Art 8 are here highly relevant to supporting a complaint of such abuse. Such complaints of unlawfulness are outside the scope of s 78, but have a bearing on unfairness. Accordingly, it is unfortunate that the Court in *Khan v United Kingdom*[1] and the subsequent House of Lords' authorities considered above do not deal with the interrelationship either between Arts 8 and 6 or between Art 8 and *Bennett*-type abuse. It is submitted that, at least in the context of alleged bad faith, Lord Hobhouse is mistaken in holding that absent trial unfairness under s 78, Art 8 is of little importance to criminal trials. In *R v Stapleton*,[2] for example, whether it had been breached or not was a vital factor.

1   Above para **5.87**.
2   Above para **5.105**.

5.107   This is, perhaps, demonstrated by reference to *R v Khachik*.[1] There was, in that case, no challenge to the integrity of the evidence produced by a covert probe, which formed a fundamental part of the prosecution case against the applicant for conspiring to supply class A drugs. There was, however, a 'root and branch attack' upon the credibility and behaviour of the police officers, who gave evidence against the defendants at their trial, in relation to the covert surveillance aspect of the case.[2] The applicant argued that the proceedings should have been stayed as an abuse of process on the basis that the police had dishonestly created the application form under Pt II of the Regulation of Investigatory Powers Act 2000 for the authorisation of the probe and intentionally flouted the rules relating to its use. The applicant contended that the police had thereby manipulated the process of justice such that the prosecution should have been stayed.

1   [2006] EWCA Crim 1272.
2   See judgment paras 36 et seq.

5.108   The trial judge concluded that whilst the police officers had behaved improperly, they had not been dishonest (in the way in which the application form under RIPA had been completed) and had not set out deliberately to deceive. The Court of Appeal found that it could not go behind the trial judge's findings in that regard and, on the basis of the finding that they had not been dishonest, the police were entitled to the authorisation they had sought in respect of the covert surveillance. As a result, the proceedings were rightly not stayed as an abuse. Nonetheless, the Court observed that if the judge had found that the authorisation had been obtained by deception, 'that would have been a proper basis for staying the proceedings as an abuse of process',[1] notwithstanding the fact that no issue was taken with the integrity of the evidence obtained in itself.

1   At para 39.

COMMISSION OF CRIMINAL OFFENCES OR UNLAWFUL CONDUCT BY INVESTIGATORS

5.109   To what extent is it permissible for law enforcement agents to break the law in order that evidence may thereby be obtained against the accused? Is the law, especially the criminal law, to be obeyed by all no matter how noble their objective, or rather is the commission of criminal offences by State agents acceptable in the pursuit of those guilty of serious crime? In *R v Looseley*,[1] Lord Hoffmann put the issue as follows:

'Drug dealers can be expected to show some wariness about dealing with a stranger who might be a policeman or informer and therefore some protective colour in dress or manner as well as a certain degree of persistence may be necessary to achieve the objective. And it has been said that undercover officers who infiltrate conspiracies to murder, rob or commit terrorist offences could hardly remain concealed unless they showed some enthusiasm for the enterprise. A good deal of active behaviour in the course of an authorised operation may therefore be acceptable.'[2]

1   [2001] 1 WLR 2060, HL (discussed in detail in **Chapter 6**).
2   At para 69.

5.110   He continued:

'No doubt a test purchaser who asks someone to sell him a drug is counselling and procuring, perhaps inciting, the commission of an offence. Furthermore, he has no statutory defence to a prosecution. But the fact that his actions are technically unlawful is not regarded in English law as a ground for treating them as an abuse of power.'[1]

1   At para 70.

5.111   As Lord Hoffmann opines in the above passages, police undercover operations into especially organised crime cannot be conducted on the basis that the officers involved must never contravene the criminal law. The committing of illegal acts may be essential for those officers to gain the necessary credibility and win the trust of those they are seeking to apprehend. To take another case as an example, the facts in *R v Latif*[1] can be considered. Here, Customs officers wanted to apprehend L, a suspected organiser of large importations of heroin into the UK from Pakistan. Based in Pakistan, a country with no extradition treaty with the UK, L could act with impunity insofar as UK law was concerned. Accordingly, an agent H was recruited to approach L on the basis that H had a network of heroin distributors set up in England which could be placed at L's disposal. So that L could be beguiled by H, Customs arranged for an actual shipment of heroin to be imported via Heathrow from Pakistan. In so doing, the officers breached s 3 of the Misuse of Drugs Act 1971 prohibiting drug importations in any circumstances. Clearly, therefore, the importation amounted to a serious offence committed by Customs. Ultimately the ruse worked, as L was then lured into the UK to meet H whereupon he was arrested and charged with conspiracy to import heroin. The question for the courts in *Latif* was thus whether the means adopted by Customs justified the end of capturing L.

1   Above para **5.03**.

5.112   To demonstrate the difficult issues of public policy involved, another case can be briefly considered. In *R (Pretty) v DPP (Secretary of State for the Home Department intervening)*[1] the dying applicant wished her partner to assist her in committing suicide. However, if the partner did so, an offence would be committed under the Suicide Act 1961. The applicant sought a declaration from the Director of Public Prosecutions that, in her extreme circumstances, the partner would not run the risk of prosecution if he so assisted. The DPP refused to oblige and the applicant sought judicial review. In his letter to the applicant, the DPP wrote:

'Successive Directors—and Attorneys General—have explained that they will not grant immunities that condone, require, or purport to authorise or permit the future commission of any criminal offence, no matter how exceptional the circumstances. I must therefore advise you that the Director cannot provide the undertaking that you seek.'

1   [2002] 1 AC 800, HL at para 115.

5.113   The House of Lords endorsed this letter as a correct statement of the DPP's position. Expressing the role of the DPP in constitutional terms, Lord Hobhouse said:

'The power to dispense with and suspend laws and the execution of laws without the consent of Parliament was denied to the Crown and its servants by the Bill of Rights 1688.'[1]

1   At para 117.

5.114   Whilst *Pretty* was concerned with the power of the DPP in advance to immunise a proposed breach of the criminal law, in undercover operations there is an obvious, albeit unspoken, presumption that agents who commit offences in the course of such operations will not subsequently face prosecution by, for example, the CPS. In *R v Latif*[1] no Customs officer ever faced prosecution despite their having committed the actus reus of the offence for which L was prosecuted. De facto, therefore, the DPP does grant immunities despite the impression conveyed in the speeches in *Pretty*.

1   Above para **5.03**.

5.115   State illegality is an obvious subject for the abuse doctrine in determining the extent to which the courts will uphold the principle of the rule of law. As Dr Johnson put it:

'Laws are not made for particular cases but for men in general ... To permit a law to be modified at discretion is to leave the community without law. It is to withdraw the direction of that public wisdom by which the deficiencies of private understanding are to be supplied.'[1]

1   Boswell *Life of Johnson* (3rd Edn, 1970) at pp 735, 496.

Pre-Latif cases

5.116   The scathing judgment of Goddard CJ in *Brannan v Peek*[1] is often recited:

'The court observes with concern and with strong disapproval that the police authority ... apparently thought it right in this case to send a police officer into a public house for the purpose of committing an offence ... I hope that the day is far distant when it will become common practice in this country for police officers, who are sent into premises for the purpose of detecting crime, to be told to commit an offence themselves for the purpose of getting evidence against another person ... I think, this conviction must be set aside.'[2]

1   [1948] 1 KB 68, DC.
2   At 72.

5.117   In *Yip Chiu-Cheung v R*,[1] the Privy Council considered a case where, on the facts, the undercover officer had committed an offence under Hong Kong anti-drugs trafficking law. Giving judgment on behalf of the Board, Lord Griffiths clearly regarded with distaste a submission that the undercover officer had not committed a criminal offence. He said:

'Neither the police, nor customs, nor any other member of the executive have any power to alter the terms of the Ordinance frustrating the export of heroin and the fact that they may turn a blind eye when the heroin is exported does not prevent it from being a criminal offence.'

1   [1994] 1 AC 111, PC.

5.118   Lord Griffiths quoted with approval the ruling of the High Court of Australia in *A v Hayden* (*No 2*).[1] There it declared emphatically that there was no place in Australian criminal law for a general defence of superior orders or of Crown or executive authority. Gibbs CJ said:

'It is fundamental to our legal system that the executive has no power to authorise a breach of the law and that it is no excuse for an offender to say that he acted under the orders of a superior officer.'[2]

Having quoted this passage, Lord Griffiths observed:

'This statement of the law applies with the same force in England and Hong Kong as it does in Australia.'[3]

1   (1984) 156 CLR 532.
2   (1984) 156 CLR 532 at 540.
3   Above para **5.117** at 118.

5.119   *R v Schlesinger*[1] is an example of investigative impropriety and mala fides, which the Court of Appeal described as 'disgraceful'. In 1985, the appellants were convicted of illegally exporting arms to Iraq. Before their trial, the defence became aware of various embassy officials in London who were prepared to state that the arms had not in fact gone to Iraq. However, before witness statements could be taken, the officials announced they could no longer assist, their permission to do so from their embassies having been withdrawn. In the event the defendants pleaded guilty.

1   [1995] Crim LR 137, CA.

5.120   In 1993, the Scott Inquiry discovered why this volte-face had occurred. The Foreign Office at the behest of Customs (the prosecutorial agency) had urged the embassies not to allow their officials to assist the defence. When this information was published, the defendants appealed against their convictions. The Court of Appeal readily quashed the convictions. It held that the prosecution had, in the first instance, improperly interfered with the course of justice and secondly, had concealed this from the defence and trial judge. In holding abuse, the Court held that a defendant does not receive a fair trial if he is prevented by the prosecution from calling witnesses who are believed will be helpful to the defence.

R v Latif

5.121   *R v Latif,*[1] the facts of which are recounted above,2 provided the House of Lords with an opportunity two years on to survey its momentous decision in *ex parte Bennett*. In the case before it, one of alleged entrapment, the House had to consider whether the principles in *ex parte Bennett,* formulated in response to illegal extradition, be applied to this subject. Clearly, the House of Lords in *R v Latif* could have chosen to withdraw from the sentiments expressed in *ex parte Bennett* and so confine the wider abuse jurisdiction to the rare situation of alleged unlawful extradition. However, instead the House opted to confirm its *ex parte Bennett* stance. Giving the only speech, Lord Steyn held that the court had jurisdiction in a case of entrapment to stay the prosecution on the ground that the integrity of the criminal justice system would be compromised by allowing the State to punish someone whom the State itself had caused to transgress.

1   Above para **5.03**.
2   Above para **5.08**.

5.122   Lord Steyn first confirmed the earlier decision of the House in *R v Sang*[1] that entrapment did not afford a substantive defence. But he then held that entrapment raised important issues concerned with abuse of power. There was a dilemma, which he described as follows:

'If the court always refuses to stay such proceedings, the perception will be that the court condones criminal conduct and malpractice by law enforcement agencies. That would undermine public confidence in the criminal justice system and bring it into disrepute. On the other hand, if the court were always to stay proceedings in such cases, it would incur the reproach that it is failing to protect the public from serious crime'[2]

1   Above para **5.08.**
2   At 112.

5.123   Lord Steyn then held that this dilemma could only be resolved as follows:

'The weakness of both extreme positions leaves only one principled solution. The court has a discretion; it has to perform a balancing exercise ... the judge must weigh in the balance the public interest in ensuring those that are charged with grave crimes should be tried and the competing public interest in not conveying the impression that the court will adopt the approach that the end justifies any means.[1]

... In this case the issue is whether, despite the fact that a fair trial was possible, the judge ought to have stayed the criminal proceedings on broader considerations of the integrity of the criminal justice system. The law is settled. Weighing countervail considerations of policy and justice, it is for the judge in the exercise of his discretion to decide whether there has been an abuse of process, which amounts to an affront to the public conscience and requires the criminal proceedings to be stayed.'[2]

1   Above para **5.03**, at 112, 113.
2   At 113.

5.124   On the facts of this case, including the illegal acts committed by the Customs officers, Lord Steyn said:

'The conduct of the customs officer was not so unworthy or shameful that it was an affront to the public conscience to allow the prosecution to proceed. Realistically, any criminal behaviour of the customs officer was venial compared to that of Shahzad. In these circumstances I would reject the submission that the judge erred in refusing to stay the proceedings.'[1]

5.124   *Abuse of power by the executive*

1   Above para **5.03**, at 113.

5.125   What is perhaps most notable about Lord Steyn's speech is that he paid no particular regard to the fact that the prosecution of the accused was in part founded upon deliberate breaches of the criminal law by the officers. The conceptual emphasis was placed elsewhere – did the acts of the officers amount to an affront to the public conscience or were they instead merely venial? This apparent lack of emphasis by Lord Steyn in the issue of whether the executive flouted the law is echoed later by Lord Hoffmann in *R v Looseley*[1] in a passage quoted above:[2]

> 'But the fact that his actions are *technically* unlawful is not regarded in English law as a ground for treating them as an abuse of power.' [Emphasis added]

1   Above para **5.109**.
2   At para 70; discussed above at para **5.110**.

5.126   Moreover, Lord Steyn decided, having set out his two parameters, not to offer any further guidance to judges as to whether unlawful conduct was either an affront or venial, saying: 'general guidance as to how the discretion should be exercised in particular circumstances would rarely be useful.'

5.127   A trial judge following Lord Steyn's speech in *R v Latif* has to conduct a balancing exercise between two competing public interests. First, the imperative for the courts as part of the criminal justice system based fundamentally on the rule of law to preserve their moral integrity by disassociating themselves from investigative impropriety. The fair administration of justice cannot be sacrificed for the sake of expedience. Second, those who are charged and convicted of the serious crimes should not escape justice because such a situation would undermine public confidence in the criminal justice system. As Lord Steyn put it: 'If a court were always to stay proceedings in such cases, it would incur the reproach that it was failing to protect the public from serious crime.'[1]

1   At 112.

5.128   It is submitted that an analysis of Lord Steyn's reasoning reveals the following key principles:

(1)   *That the crime was already in existence.* The appellants had already planned to be involved in the importation of the heroin into England before the customs officer became involved and were therefore already guilty of conspiracy to import heroin into England. Lord Steyn rejected the appellants' assertion that they had been incited.

(2)   *Motive.* Lord Steyn accepted that the officer was acting under the authority of his superiors and was motivated by a courageous desire in his attempt to break a drugs ring and ensure the punishment of those involved.

(3)   *Comparative involvement in the crime.* Lord Steyn compared the degree of criminality of the customs officer ('venial') and that of the appellants who were major drug smugglers.

Post-Latif cases

5.129   Following *R v Latif*,[1] an example of 'venial', but nonetheless unlawful, conduct by investigators is *R v Khan*.[2] In this case, a former Thai diplomat brought with him to Heathrow from Thailand a quantity of heroin in his diplomatic bag. On arrival, the bag was searched and the drugs discovered. At his trial an abuse submission was made on the ground that this search was unlawful as, it was claimed, it was in breach of the Vienna Convention. At the time of the search the defendant was entitled to diplomatic immunity and there was no lawful authority, until this was waived, to search his bag. The trial judge was not impressed by this argument and dismissed the application.

1   Above para **5.03**.
2   (1998, unreported) Crown Court.

R v Carrington[1]

5.130   Here, the defendants were charged with drug trafficking. The prosecution's case rested on the discovery of a cargo of cannabis resin in a boat which was bound for the UK. At the time of the seizure of the boat and discovery of the cannabis, the boat was in international waters off the coast of Portugal. By reason of international maritime law, before the boat could be lawfully intercepted and boarded by agents of HM Customs (in this case British Special Forces), the consent was required of the Attorney-General of Malta. This was because the boat had begun its voyage from there and such consent was required in order to make the interception lawful. This would remain the legal position until the boat entered the territorial waters of another State. However, for some reason, Customs did not wish to track the boat until it entered the territorial waters of the UK and then board it, but wished to do so on the High Seas.

1   (February 1999, unreported), Foley HHJ.

5.131   When the consent of the Maltese Attorney-General was sought, it transpired that he was informed by customs that the location of the boat was 'off the coast of the United Kingdom.'[1] Having made this false representation, consent from the Maltese was forthcoming. At the trial the defence submitted that the prosecution intended to mislead the Maltese and this constituted mala fides, which in turn constituted an abuse. At the 'voir dire' to investigate the matter, Maltese witnesses confirmed that they would not have given consent if they were aware of the true position of the boat. The trial judge held that the behaviour of customs was shameful:

> '... this case has revealed a culture, a climate, of carelessness and recklessness for disregard for the rules of procedures, convention of Maltese law, British law and International law ... this court cannot abdicate its judicial responsibility. It gives me no pleasure, the case for a stay is overwhelming, there was mala fides here.'[2]

1   It appears that when the request was made, the boat was in fact 900 miles from Britain off the coast of Portugal.
2   Page 1051 of the transcript.

R v Doran[1]

5.132 The facts of this case are complex and therefore difficult to summarise. There is also a history of trial, appeal and retrial. It transpired at the retrial that both the judge in the first trial and the defence had been deliberately misled by Customs concerning two factual issues. Firstly, had consent been obtained from the management of various hotels to the bugging of hotel rooms by Customs officers? Contrary to what was claimed, it was established that such consent had not been obtained. Secondly, it transpired that Customs' own internal authorisation procedures, which the investigating officers should have obeyed before placing the defendants under surveillance, had in fact been ignored. Moreover, to conceal this fact, the officers had allegedly created a trail of false paperwork. The trial judge, Turner J held:

'By abuse of executive authority, the prosecution, viewed as a single entity, have, by means which are at least arguably unlawful, deprived the defence of its strategic ability to mount the challenge to the integrity of the prosecution case.'

1   (6 July 1999, unreported) Turner J.

5.133 In assessing the seriousness of the officers' conduct, Turner J held that:

'... the conduct which I have already discussed in some detail cannot fairly be dismissed as 'venial' or as mere 'regrettable error' as the prosecution have invited me to accept ... it is wholly inaccurate to describe what has happened as 'regrettable error.' What has happened has had a significant impact on the ability of the defendants properly to defend themselves and to that extent, as a matter of probability, they have been seriously prejudiced in the conduct of their defence'

In those circumstances, Turner J held that the prosecution were guilty of abuse and that the conduct of the officers struck at the rule of law.

R v Sutherland[1]

5.134 Here, remarkably, members of Lincolnshire Constabulary investigating a brutal murder, decided that privileged conversations between the suspects and their solicitors whilst the suspects were detained at police stations ought to be recorded. Following the prosecution of those suspects for murder, the prosecution unsuccessfully applied to have the fact of the eavesdropping and its product withheld from the defence on public interest immunity grounds. That application having been refused, applications for abuse were made. The trial judge, Newman J, found the police conduct reprehensible and unlawful. He regarded the eavesdropping as amounting to a violation of a fundamental principle of law and human rights, a violation so serious that considerations relating to whether or not any of the accused had been prejudiced were immaterial. The fact that there had been deliberate interference with an accused's right to private legal advice was sufficient in and of itself to prevent a fair trial from taking place. Accordingly, the prosecution of all five accused was stayed.

1   (29 January 2002, unreported) Newman J.

R v Grant[1]

5.135   The immateriality of prejudice to the accused in such circumstances was confirmed by the Court of Appeal in *R v Grant*, a case stemming out of the same activities on the part of Lincolnshire police as had led to the stay of proceedings in *Sutherland*.[2] In this case, the police tape-recorded conversations between the defendant and his solicitor in the police station yard following his arrest (also for conspiracy to murder) and at the same time as the interview process was in motion. None of the material obtained by the police was used for the purposes of the prosecution and, on that basis, the conduct of the police did not impact unfairly upon the accused's trial. In considering that the trial judge ought to have stayed proceedings, Laws LJ said that:

> 'Acts done by the police, in the course of an investigation which leads in due course to the institution of criminal proceedings, with a view to eavesdropping upon communications of suspected persons which are subject to legal professional privilege are categorically unlawful and at the very least capable of infecting the proceedings as abusive of the court's process. So much seems to us to be plain and obvious and no authority is needed to make it good. The only question that requires examination is whether such proceedings ought to be characterised as an abuse of the process, and the prosecution stopped, if the defendant or defendants have suffered no prejudice in consequence of the relevant unlawful acts.'[3]

> 'We are in no doubt but that, in general, unlawful acts of the kind done in this case, amounting to a deliberate violation of a suspected person's right to legal professional privilege, are so great an affront to the integrity of the justice system, and therefore the rule of law, that the associated prosecution is rendered abusive and ought not to be countenanced by the court.'[4]

1   [2006] QB 60, CA.
2   The third case, other than *Sutherland* and *Grant*, to come of the eavesdropping technique employed by Lincolnshire police between November 2000-November 2001 was *R v Sentence* (unreported, Lincoln Crown Court), in which the trial judge, HHJ Heath, also stayed proceedings as an abuse of process.
3   At para 52.
4   At para 54.

5.136   Laws LJ concluded:

> 'Where the court is faced with illegal conduct by police or State prosecutors which is so grave as to threaten or undermine the rule of law itself, the court may readily conclude that it will not tolerate, far less endorse, such a state of affairs and so hold that its duty is to stop the case …We are quite clear that the deliberate interference with a detained suspect's right to the confidence of privileged communications with his solicitor, such as we have found was done here, seriously undermines the rule of law and justifies a stay on grounds of abuse of process, notwithstanding the absence of prejudice consisting in evidence gathered by the Crown as the fruit of police officers' unlawful conduct.'[1]

1   At paras 56–57.

5.137   However, Laws L.J observed that it 'is not in general the function of criminal courts to discipline the police.'[1] That approach concurred with the later judgment of the Court of Appeal in *R v Woolley,*[2] where, in refusing an appeal on the ground of abuse of process (the police being said to have failed to obtain potentially exculpatory CCTV evidence), Hallett LJ observed that:

> '... there is a public interest in having allegations of serious offences such as the present tried and applications to stay on the grounds of abuse of the process of the court should not be granted simply as a way of punishing investigating police officers, even if that is merited [which the Court of Appeal doubted it was in this case in any event].'[3]

1   At para 55.
2   [2006] EWCA Crim 2138.
3   At para 20.

5.138   With that in mind we turn finally to consider unlawful acts committed by the police in the context of entrapment. In *R v Harmes & Crane,*[1] the police engaged in criminal acts as part of undercover drugs operations. The Court of Appeal concluded that 'the officers' conduct [within a drugs conspiracy] was criminal'.[2] However, the Court of Appeal decided that the officers' criminal conduct was 'not to be regarded as so seriously improper as to require the court to intervene to prevent the prosecution for conspiracy.' In coming to this conclusion, the Court noted that officers must show a degree of enthusiasm and persistence to provide protection for their undercover activities and that a good deal of active behaviour – albeit in the context of an entrapment case – may be acceptable.[3] The Court of Appeal's conclusion that the officers' conduct 'did not stray beyond that which was permissible to investigate and prosecute crime'[4] demonstrates the presumption[5] that agents who commit offences in the course of such operations, whether authorised or not, will not subsequently face sanction for their criminal acts.

1   [2006] EWCA Crim 928. Discussed in detail in Chapter 6, para **6.88**.
2   At para 51.
3   At para 51.
4   At para 54.
5   Referred to above at para **5.114**.

Illegitimate funding of the prosecution

5.139   *R v Hounsham & others*[1] concerned allegations against car dealers of working in consort to defraud motor insurers by making false insurance claims in respect of 'staged' traffic accidents. Towards the end of the proceedings, it was disclosed to the defendants that the insurance companies in question had funded the police investigations that had resulted in their arrest. The defendants applied for the proceedings to be stayed as they were an abuse of the process of the court. On appeal, the prosecution conceded that, in seeking and accepting payments from the insurance companies, the police were acting *ultra vires* their statutory powers. The Court of Appeal having rejected bad faith on the part of the police, it was argued that the conduct of the police was unlawful and so contrary to public policy that the court should not allow the prosecution to proceed, whether or not the police had acted in good faith.

1   (2005) Times June 16, CA.

5.140   Gage LJ rejected that contention, ruling[1] that:

'… soliciting by the police of funds from potential victims of fraud, or any other crime, quite apart from being *ultra vires* police powers, is a practice which is fraught with danger. It may compromise the essential independence and objectivity of the police when carrying out a criminal investigation. It might lead to police officers being selective as to which crimes to investigate and which not to investigate. It might lead to victims persuading a police investigating team to act partially. It might also lead to investigating officers carrying out a more thorough preparation of the evidence in a case of a 'paying' victim; or a less careful preparation of the evidence in the case of a non-contributing victim. In short, it is a practice which, in our judgment, would soon lead to a loss of confidence in a police force's ability to investigate crime objectively and impartially … However, in this case, the judge found that PS Wade acted in good faith. He consulted his superior officer, who in turn sought advice. Apart from the issue of disclosure, to which we turn next, none of the appellants' counsel has been able to point to any prejudice caused by the acceptance of the total sum of £4,500 from three insurance companies. The conduct of the police complained of in this case, falls far short of the conduct which led the proceedings in *ex parte Bennett* to be stayed; and the court in *Mullen* to quash the conviction. On its own we are not persuaded that this conduct was such that the judge was wrong to refuse a stay.'

1   At paras 31–33.

DEPRIVATION OF FOREIGN RIGHTS

5.141   One situation, not considered by Lord Steyn in *R v Latif*,[1] is where a defendant is lured by investigators into this country for the purposes of arrest, the consequence of this being that he is thereby denied legal rights and privileges which would have been available to him in the foreign jurisdiction had the investigators instead sought his extradition.

1   Above para **5.03**.

5.142   A defendant so lured has been deprived of the right to resist extradition, to insist upon compliance with extradition time limits, to test a prima facie case, to obtain bail based upon local community ties, and to be present during searching of premises in the state from which he was lured. The legal rights and privileges denied to the defendant may be significant and are discussed in detail in **Chapter 8**. In some cases, notably those involving the US, the extradition process will also immunise a defendant against the possibility of the imposition of the death penalty. In any extradition case, the extradition process will clothe a defendant with the principle of 'specialty' discussed at para **8.104**. Following extradition, a Requesting State may only prosecute for the conduct in respect of which extradition has been granted; the rule of 'specialty'. The rule, and the various exceptions to it, is reflected in every international extradition treaty, and under the Criminal Justice Act 2003 is reflected in ss 17 and 95. A defendant lured or tricked into the jurisdiction of the Requesting State is deprived of this fundamental protection. Therefore, to the State that wants a particular individual returned, deportation is more advantageous. There are no restrictions in terms of what the person, once lured into that State, can be prosecuted for.

5.143 High authority exists in respect of defendants lured into one country for the purpose of onward extradition to another: see *Somchai Liangsiriprasert v Government of the United States of America*[1] and *In re: Schmidt*;[2] both of which were applied in *R v Gokal*.[3] In the latter case, Mr Gokal was sought by the Serious Fraud Office in respect of the collapse of BCCI. He was resident in Pakistan, with whom the UK had no extradition treaty. The US authorities wished to interview him (on the understanding that he would not be arrested by them). The US authorities assured Mr Gokal that they had been assured by the SFO that he was free to travel to New York and return home without fear of arrest or detention. He was thus encouraged to leave the sanctuary of Pakistan and travel (via Frankfurt) to New York. Upon arrival in Frankfurt, he was arrested and extradited to the UK. Mr Gokal appealed against his subsequent conviction for fraud on the basis, amongst others, that the circumstances of his arrest constituted an abuse of process, that the facts gave rise to an inference of collusion between the SFO and the US authorities, whereby the appellant was tricked into believing he had a free passage or that, alternatively, the prosecution had deceived the US authorities, giving rise to executive lawlessness requiring a stay.

1   Above para **5.03**; discussed in detail at Chapter 8 para **8.120**.
2   Above para **5.02**; discussed in detail at Chapter 8 para **8.79**.
3   Above para. **5.03**.

5.144 The Court of Appeal found, on the facts, that the SFO had neither colluded with, nor deceived, the US authorities into tricking the appellant into believing he had a free passage. They had, in fact, made it clear to the US authorities and the appellant that he would be arrested. The UK had taken advantage of the US authorities 'letting slip' the existence of the meeting in New York. But even if the position were otherwise, Rose LJ upheld[1] the trial judge's ruling that no abuse would arise:

'... if correct, this amounted to tricking the appellant into leaving Pakistan. But, in the light of *Schmidt* and *Liangsiriprasert*, there was no abuse of power by the SFO because they had none in Pakistan, the defendant left voluntarily, and there was no threat to basic rights or the rule of law. The circumstances were akin to the enticement in *Liangsiriprasert*, not the forcible abduction in *Bennett* ... Although *Liangsiriprasert* was an extradition case, the principles enunciated applied to abuse. The judge went on, in a balancing exercise by reference to *Latif*, to say he had no doubt that it was of the first importance that conspiracy to undermine the international banking system should be tried. The conduct of the prosecution, even if a trick were proved, was not an affront to the public conscience; on the contrary, it would be an affront if the proceedings were stayed ... there was no unlawful or criminal behaviour by the prosecution; on the authorities, luring was permissible.'

1   At transcript 13–15.

5.145   The Courts have, thus far, treated such conduct as far-enough removed from *Bennett*-type abduction scenarios so as not to be abusive. The current case law of the European Court of Human Rights is no more sympathetic.[1]

1   Discussed above at paras. **5.57–5.69**.

Chapter 6

Entrapment

INTRODUCTION

6.01   Entrapment is a legal term which carries a strong connotation but whose definition has proved problematic and often elusive. In the watershed case of *R v Looseley*[1] Lord Hoffmann offered this definition:

'Entrapment occurs when an agent of the State—usually a law enforcement officer or a controlled informer—causes someone to commit an offence in order that he should be prosecuted.'

But then promptly added, 'I shall in due course have to refine this description but for the moment it will do.'

1   [2001] 1 WLR 2060, HL, at para 36. This appeal was joined with that of *Attorney-General's Reference (No 3 of 2000)* but for convenience, this case will simply be referred to as *Looseley*.

6.02   Writing about entrapment, Professor Ashworth defined it as 'the use of deceptive techniques to test whether a person is willing to commit an offence.'[1] Generally, when dealing with this subject, the courts have eschewed attempts at comprehensive definitions and shown a marked unwillingness even to articulate general principles. The favoured approach has been a pragmatic one always emphasising that in cases of encouraged or induced crime, whether this constitutes the label of entrapment or not is highly fact-dependent. Each case, it has been repeatedly said, turns on its own facts.

1   'Redefining the boundaries of entrapment' [2002] Crim LR 161.

6.03   Ultimately such an approach came under intolerable strain. The 'war on drugs' recently supplemented by the 'war on terrorism' has fundamentally and permanently altered how the police and other law enforcement agencies operate in response to serious or organised crime. The massive growth of intelligence-led policing with its resort to undercover techniques has meant that complaints of entrapment by the accused in relation to their pre-arrest dealings with undercover officers have been made with ever growing frequency. The shortcomings of this cautious and subjective approach were becoming evident. Furthermore, the ECtHR case of *Teixeira de Castro v Portugal*[1] made proper domestic consideration of this subject inevitable. When finally, in *R v Looseley,* the House of Lords gave leave to hear an appeal centrally concerned with entrapment and consequently to enunciate applicable principles, the subject was in urgent need of rationalisation.

1   (1998) 28 EHRR 101.

6.04   *R v Looseley* remains the seminal case in relation to entrapment, having eclipsed the earlier authorities. In the last edition of this work it was suggested that it would nevertheless be erroneous to comfortably believe that all the attendant issues of ambiguity had been clarified. Since the last edition, no domestic court has attempted to redefine, alter or displace the general principles of entrapment as set out by the House of Lords in *R v Looseley*. Nonetheless, the continued application of those principles, in predominantly unsuccessful appeals, has helped to crystallise the parameters within which a defendant will have a meritorious claim to have been entrapped. Whilst the notoriously fact-specific nature of the issues raised in cases of alleged entrapment contributes to a continuing lack of ease in providing an exhaustive statement of the law in this area, the developments since the last edition display, from a defendant or appellant's point of view, a restrictive approach in the courts' application of the *Looseley* principles.

6.05   There has only been one successful appeal against conviction[1] on the ground of entrapment since the successful defendant in *Attorney-General's Reference (No 3 of 2000)* (decided at the same time as *Looseley*). The case law since *R v Looseley*, and the developments in the law relating to the difficulty of private or commercial entrapment in the context of criminal proceedings, serve to firmly illustrate the difficulties that face the defendant who aims to have proceedings stayed as an abuse of process on the ground of entrapment.

1   *R v Moon* [2004] EWCA Crim 2872, discussed below at para **6.80**.

6.06   As *R v Looseley* remains the authoritative ruling, an understanding of the various speeches in that case still requires a prior grasp of preceding judicial attempts to inject consistency and fairness into this subject.

THE RIGHT REMEDY; S 78 OR ABUSE OF PROCESS?

Entrapment not a substantive defence

6.07   Traditionally, the courts have disapproved of the use of entrapment by the police. See, for example, the terse comments of Lord Goddard in *Brannan v Peek*[1], in a case involving undercover officers attempting to buy alcohol in pubs shortly after closing time.

1   [1948] 1 KB 68, DC.

6.08   This admonition, however, was uttered in the context of a civil case and thus the issue of whether, like the defences of insanity or duress or automatism, entrapment in a criminal case was to be afforded such a status remained unresolved. In some jurisdictions, including the US, entrapment is a substantive defence[1] where it is held that, when entrapped, the accused lacks the necessary guilty intent or *mens rea*.

1   *Sherman v United States* 356 US 369 (1957).

6.09   The House of Lords in *R v Sang*,[1] rejected any suggestion that entrapment should be added to the list of substantive defences. Essentially, the House of Lords rejected the notion that where the accused has been induced to commit the *actus reus* of the offence, he thereby lacks the *mens rea*. In the view of the House of Lords, an entrapped accused was as guilty as any other who would have committed the offence without the entrapment. Accordingly in *R v Sang*, it was held that the only appropriate judicial reactions to a proven case of entrapment were either reduction in sentence or public criticism of police conduct.

1   [1980] AC 402, HL.

6.10   The speeches in *Sang*, however, travelled wider than simply being concerned with the legal status of entrapment. This case can be regarded as the high watermark of a judicial policy which sought to disclaim any responsibility for trying and convicting an accused whose presence before the court was only a consequence of State misconduct or abuse of power[1]; that the criminal courts should not be concerned as to how evidence was obtained. In this way, *R v Sang* was a profound move away from what Lord Devlin had famously said earlier in *Connelly v DPP* about the courts' 'inescapable responsibility'[2].

1   See for example Lord Scarman at 451 and 455.
2   See para **7.79**.

6.11   Wishing to avoid an historical narrative of the development of the criminal law post-*Sang*, it is sufficient to note that this steer away from the sentiments of Lord Devlin proved short-lived. Parliament in part reversed *R v Sang* in PACE, s 78, which permitted a judge to exclude evidence on the ground that it had been obtained unfairly. The common law also moved away notably in the landmark decision of the House of Lords in *R v Horseferry Road Magistrates' Court, ex p Bennett*.[1]

1   [1994] 1 AC 42, HL.

ABUSE OF EXECUTIVE POWER

6.12   The decision in *Bennett* is considered in detail in **Chapter 5.**[1] For present purposes, it is sufficient to recall the leading speech of Lord Griffiths, who held that the courts possessed a discretionary power to stay proceedings where anterior executive action amounted to a threat to human rights or the rule of law. In essence, Lord Griffiths described this jurisdiction as one to prevent abuse of executive power.

1   See paras **5.06–5.19**.

6.13   Whilst *Bennett* was not concerned with entrapment, the House of Lords in *R v Latif*[1] was later to hold on the same underlying principles that a stay could be granted on the ground of entrapment if (and only if) the prosecution founded on this amounted to 'an affront to the public conscience'.[2]

1   [1996] 1 WLR 104, HL.
2   For further discussion of this case see paras **5.20–5.21** and **5.121–5.128**.

6.14   In *R v Looseley*, similar language was used. Lord Nicholls described the abuse jurisdiction as follows:

'Every court has an inherent power and duty to prevent abuse of its process. This is a fundamental principle of the rule of law. By recourse to this principle courts ensure that executive agents of the State do not misuse the coercive, law enforcement functions of the courts and thereby oppress citizens of the State. Entrapment, with which these two appeals are concerned, is an instance where such misuse may occur. It is simply not acceptable that the State through its agents should lure its citizens into committing acts forbidden by the law and then seek to prosecute them for doing so. That would be entrapment. That would be a misuse of State power, and an abuse of the process of the courts. The unattractive consequences, frightening and sinister in extreme cases, which State conduct of this nature could have are obvious. The role of the courts is to stand between the State and its citizens and make sure this does not happen.'[1]

1   Above para **6.01**, at para 1.

6.15   Turning his particular attention to issues of unfairness thrown up by entrapment, Lord Nicholls considered what he termed 'State-created crime' as a type of State conduct which ought to result in a stay:

'Entrapment goes to the propriety of there being a prosecution at all for the relevant offence, having regard to the State's involvement in the circumstance in which it was committed[1]... Police conduct which brings about, to use the catch-phrase, State-created crime is unacceptable and improper. To prosecute in such circumstances would be an affront to the public conscience, to borrow the language of Lord Steyn in *R v Latif* [1996] 1 WLR 104, 112. In a very broad sense of the word, such a prosecution would not be fair.'[2]

1   At para 17.
2   At para 19.

6.16   Lords Nicholls and Hoffmann in *R v Looseley* both considered whether this jurisdiction to stay was best understood as emanating from the statutory jurisdiction created by PACE, s 78 or alternatively from the common law abuse of process doctrine. In both speeches their Lordships preferred the latter, holding that when a complaint of entrapment is made by an accused, almost invariably it is directed at a stay of the entire proceedings rather than the exclusion of evidence. Lord Hoffmann said:

'The section 78 discretion enables the judge to safeguard the fairness of the trial. But the entrapped defendant is not ordinarily complaining that the admission of certain evidence would prejudice the fairness of his trial. He is saying that whatever the evidence, he should not be tried at all. The appropriate remedy, if any, is therefore not the exclusion of evidence but a stay of the proceedings.'[1]

1   At para 78.

6.17   Clearly, once the rationale for a stay is recognised as an integrity principle for the courts; that prosecutions founded on entrapment must not be countenanced in order that the integrity of the criminal justice system be preserved, then the abuse jurisdiction will be preferred over s 78. The issue here is clearly not seen as one akin to procedural fairness within the context of a trial; the accused's complaint is not particularly concerned with the reliability of evidence to be adduced by an undercover officer or their credibility. Essentially, the accused is not disputing that their trial will be fair but that for a matter of policy or law, they have been treated unfairly and thus ought not be tried at all. In *R v Latif*, Lord Steyn analysed this issue as follows:

> 'If the court concludes that a fair trial is not possible, it will stay the proceedings. That is not what the present case is concerned with. It is plain that a fair trial was possible and that such a trial took place. In this case the issue is whether, despite the fact that a fair trial was possible, the judge ought to have stayed the criminal proceedings on broader considerations of the integrity of the criminal justice system.'[1]

1   Above para **6.13**, at 112.

6.18   In relation to the complaint of having been treated unfairly, the test was succinctly described by Lord Steyn as being whether:

> '… the State through its agents had lured the accused into committing an act or acts forbidden by law for which the State is now seeking to prosecute.'[1]

1   At para 34.

European Jurisprudence

6.19   Finally, the jurisprudence of the ECtHR on this point should be considered. The principal case on entrapment is *Teixeira de Castro v Portugal.*[1] The *R v Looseley* preference for the abuse jurisdiction is consistent with the Strasbourg approach found in *Teixeira*. In *Teixeira*, the applicant complained that he had not had a fair trial, in violation of art 6(1), because he had been incited to commit the offence by the police. Having considered the facts of the complaint and upheld it the court stated[2]:

> 'In the light of all these considerations, the court concludes that the two police officers' actions went beyond those of undercover agents because they instigated the offence and there is nothing to suggest that without their intervention it would have been committed. *That intervention and its use in the impugned criminal proceedings meant that, right from the outset, the applicant was definitively deprived of a fair trial.* Consequently, there has been a violation of article 6(1).' (Emphasis added)

This passage from *Teixeira* establishes that the English courts' preference for conceptualising entrapment as an abuse rather than an admissibility issue is mirrored by the approach adopted by the Strasbourg Court.

1   Above para **6.03**.
2   At para 39.

6.20   The ECtHR has since affirmed its approach in *Teixeira* in *Vanyan v Russia.*[1] In *Vanyan*, the police had instructed 'OZ' to affect a test purchase of drugs from the applicant by asking him to obtain drugs for her. Like in *Teixeira*, the police had no reason to suspect Vanyan of being a drug dealer before their involvement and 'there was nothing to suggest that the offence would have been committed had it not been for the ... intervention of OZ'. In holding that the police had incited the offence, such that the use of the evidence obtained as a result of their intervention against the applicant 'irremediably undermined the fairness of his trial', the Court said that:

> 'Where the activity of undercover agents appears to have instigated the offence and there is nothing to suggest that it would have been committed without their intervention, it goes beyond that of an undercover agent and may be described as incitement. Such intervention and its use in criminal proceedings may result in the fairness of the trial being irremediably undermined.'[2]

1   Application No 53203/99, First Section (15 December 2005). See also *Khudobin v Russia* Application No 59696/00, Third Section (26 October 2006).
2   At para 47.

6.21   The test laid down in *Teixeira* was applied again in *Eurofinacom v France*[1] with the opposite result. The Court there rejected the applicant's complaint under Art 6(1) on the basis that, whilst an undercover police operation had, to a certain extent, provoked the offers of prostitution that resulted in Eurofinacom's conviction for assisting and profiting from prostitution, there was evidence from prostitutes that the company was engaged in such activity prior to police involvement.

1   Application No 58753/00, Second Section (7 September 2004).

6.22   The most recent consideration of the issue of entrapment at the European level came in the Grand Chamber decision in *Ramanauskas v Lithuania*.[1] The Court found that the actions of the police went beyond 'investigating criminal activity in an essentially passive manner', considering that:

> 'Firstly, there is no evidence that the applicant had committed any offences beforehand, in particular corruption-related offences. Secondly ...all the meetings between the applicant and [the police agent] took place on the latter's initiative, a fact that appears to contradict the [Lithuanian] Government's argument that the authorities did not subject the applicant to any pressure or threats. On the contrary, through the contact established on the initiative of [the police], the applicant seems to have been subject to blatant prompting on their part to perform criminal acts, although there was no objective evidence – other than rumours – to suggest that he had been intending to engage in any such activity.'[2]

1   Application No 74420/01, Grand Chamber (5 February 2008).
2   At para 67.

6.23   In *Ramanaskaus,* the Lithuanian government argued that the police officers concerned had, prior to their authorisation, acted on their 'private initiative without having first informed the authorities.'[1] The Court dismissed this argument, ruling that national authorities cannot abrogate their responsibility for the actions of police officers simply by arguing that the officers had acted in a 'private capacity', whilst still carrying out police duties.[2]

1   At para 62.
2   At para 63.

6.24   As we will see,[1] the active/passive distinction is one from which the English courts have also steered away in determining the issue of entrapment.

1   Below paras **6.29–6.34**.

WHAT COUNTS AS ENTRAPMENT?

The intellectual conundrum

6.25   Derived at least in part from the Strasbourg jurisprudence, the preceding paragraphs have established the following principle as to how the English courts deal with entrapment. Where there has been an abuse of executive power amounting to an affront to the public conscience then a stay will be exercised. But, of course, this abstract proposition begs an enormous question—what constitutes, in relation to entrapment, such an abuse? Alternatively, if the law is to state that undercover officers should not act as *agents provocateurs* or entice people to commit offences, what do these expressions mean? How are the unacceptable actions of such an agent to be distinguished from acceptable or fair state participation in criminal conduct? What are the standards or thresholds to be employed here allowing a court seized of a particular case to determine on a principled basis, what is fair and unfair?

6.26   The inherent problem with any definition of entrapment is that it presupposes the meaning of terms used in the definition. The problem is one of circularity. Accordingly, the search for a definition is in a practical context a search for a chimera. In this sense, when seeking to marginalise entrapment to a subject merely relevant to mitigation of sentence, Lord Diplock in *R v Sang* had a good point:

> '... [w]hat is unfair, what is trickery in the context of the detection and prevention of crime, are questions which are liable to attract highly subjective answers.'[1]

1   Above para **6.09**, at 431.

6.27   Appreciating this difficulty, one has to look at how the courts have attempted to discern principles and identify the factors where emphasis has been placed. The speeches in *R v Looseley* were not, and did not purport to be, a redefinition of entrapment or the imposition of a new set of principles. Instead they were at best an attempt to make more explicit the core of the entrapment doctrine and, in a human rights era, to formulate some fresh and more helpful guidelines.

REJECTED RATIONALES FOR ENTRAPMENT

6.28   In considering complaints of entrapment made by the accused, what doctrine of entrapment have the courts preferred? What has been their approach?

The active/passive distinction

6.29   In *R v Smurthwaite and Gill*[1], Lord Taylor CJ sought to provide some guidelines to assist the courts below in determining whether or not on the facts before them a finding of entrapment against undercover officers should be made. One of these directed attention to whether the officer's conduct had been active or passive:

> 'Was the officer acting as an agent provocateur in the sense that he was enticing the defendant to commit an offence he would not otherwise have committed? How passive or active was the officer's role in obtaining the evidence?'[2]

If the latter than this would, in Lord Taylor CJ's view, point towards entrapment; only passive conduct being permissible.

1   (1994) 98 Cr App R 437, CA.
2   At 440.

6.30   The coherence of this dichotomy of active and passive rests upon a presupposition concerning causality: that an active undercover officer is likely to have enticed the accused into committing the offence whereas a passive one would not. Accordingly, but for this enticement or encouragement, the offender would not have committed the crime. Thus once this causality is established as viewed through the lens of whether the officer was active or not, a finding of entrapment is likely to follow.

6.31   Unfortunately the presupposition upon which this analysis is founded is fallacious. Moreover the whole supposed dichotomy is flawed. First, in practice how is one to distinguish passivity from activity? Is an officer's acquiescence with another's criminal enterprise always to be deemed a passive act even if this may in fact serve to encourage the other? Passivity and activity may not always correspond with omission and commission respectively. In the context of a retail test-purchase case, is the officer being active in attempting to buy? Surely so, but does this attempt amount to entrapment with the consequence that to avoid this allegation, the officer must somehow linger in the store waiting for a member of staff to approach and offer to sell? Is an officer being 'active' where in an operation to deter kerb-crawling by means of identifying male offenders, she disguises herself as a prostitute? At the other extreme of criminality, how can a passive officer expect to ingratiate him/herself into a criminal gang without some cover story and sign of credibility?

6.32   In practice, it is submitted, this supposed dichotomy quickly breaks down. Accordingly it is of little use in helping to find an answer to the underlying or basic issue of whether the officer's conduct was unacceptable or unfair. Nonetheless the supposed distinction has attracted support. In *Teixeira,* the ECtHR relied upon it in part when determining a violation of Art 6 on the ground of entrapment:

> 'The two police officers did not confine themselves to investigating Mr Teixeira de Castro's criminal activity in an essentially passive manner, but exercised an influence such as to incite the commission of the offence.'[1]

1   Above para **6.19**. See also *Ramanauskas v Lithuania*, above at para **6.22**.

6.33   Taken literally, this would treat as entrapment any offer to buy controlled drugs. It is submitted that this cannot be correct. In any event, the court here adds an unfortunate gloss and in effect, a new level of uncertainty. Now it adds the concept of 'essentially passive', presumably to be distinguished from passive.

6.34   In *Nottingham City Council v Amin*[1] this extract was relied upon in argument to the effect that, in flagging down the unlicensed taxi, the officers had entrapped Amin into committing the relevant offence. This interpretation was rejected by Lord Bingham CJ.[2] In *R v Looseley* this concept was abandoned altogether. Lord Hutton[3] endorsed the view of Lord Bingham in *Amin* and Lord Hoffmann[4] expressed no enthusiasm for the concept.

1   [2000] 1 WLR 1071, DC.
2   At 1080.
3   Above para **6.01**, at para 110.
4   At para 69.

Providing an opportunity

Strict causation, the test in *Amin*

6.35   This test relies upon a supposed dichotomy of policing methods: one concerned with crime detection and the other with crime creation. The former is essentially where the undercover officers merely provide someone with an opportunity to commit a specific offence and no more. The latter is enticement. The coherence of the providing an opportunity test, however, rests upon a presupposition about the individual who is so provided and subsequently commits the relevant offence; that that individual would have committed it with someone else, an ordinary member of the public.

6.36   The classic case here is *Nottingham City Council v Amin*[1]. The officers were testing whether taxi drivers were complying with the restrictions imposed on their permits concerning where in Nottingham they could not ply for hire. Amin was duly hailed in an area where he should not stop and accept a fare. He did and was consequently prosecuted. The question was whether Amin had been entrapped. Lord Bingham CJ formulated the following test:

> 'On the one hand it has been recognised as deeply offensive to ordinary notions of fairness if a defendant were to be convicted and punished for committing a crime which he only committed because he had been incited, instigated, persuaded, pressurised or wheedled into committing it by a law enforcement officer. On the other hand it has been recognised that law

enforcement agencies have a general duty to the public to enforce the law and it has been regarded as unobjectionable if a law enforcement officer gives a defendant an opportunity to break the law, of which the defendant freely takes advantage, in circumstances where it appears that the defendant would have behaved in the same way if the opportunity had been offered by anyone else.'[2]

1   Above para **6.34**.
2   At 1076.

6.37   In effect, this test adopts too narrow a conception of causality; if the officers incited, etc then they can be taken to have caused or created the crime, whereas if they only acted like ordinary members of the public and thus merely provided an opportunity etc, they are deemed not to have caused it. However, *Amin* creates a highly strict test of causality in relation to entrapment; a finding of incitement etc should only be made if the accused *only* committed the crime because of it.

6.38   There is, it is submitted, a fundamental difficulty with this test: its notion of causality. In *Amin,* Lord Bingham CJ was seeking to restrict causality to where the offence is committed only as a consequence of the incitement etc. By so restricting it, Lord Bingham CJ could then distinguish such incitement, which in effect he defined as entrapment, from the supposedly non-causal situation of providing an opportunity. But surely causality plays an equal role in both the incitement and providing an opportunity instances. But for the hailing of the taxi in *Amin* in a planned operation by the officers, the offence charged would not have been committed.

6.39   An attempt to distinguish incitement from providing an opportunity on the basis that only the former causes the commission of the offence is, it is submitted, unsustainable. In both paradigms it could fairly be argued that officers are acting as *agents provocateurs*. The means by which acceptable law enforcement stratagems for apprehending offenders can be distinguished from unacceptable is unlikely to be a reliance on a simply causal analysis as suggested by Lord Bingham CJ in *Amin*.

6.40   Moreover, what can be inferred from Lord Bingham CJ's emphasis on entrapment only being held if the 'only' cause or reason for the accused committing the offence was the instigation? Criminal cases are rarely so straightforward. On the facts of *Amin*, was the only cause of the offence the driver being hailed in the prohibited area? Or was it also that he chose to be there in the first place? Alternatively, in a drugs case where a suspected dealer is approached in a nightclub by undercover officers and agrees upon their request to sell drugs, can it be said that the only cause of his prosecution was this approach? Or is the simple fact that the accused had already situated himself in the club also relevant to causation?[1] An endless debate can open up on what facts should count as causes. To resolve this, one would first have to propound a defensible concept of what counted as a cause and what did not, but such an exercise is unlikely to be fruitful. In consequence, it is probably unhelpful and unduly simplistic to speak in terms of single or only causes. If causation is to be the key criterion, it would perhaps be more realistic to speak of predominant rather than only causes.

1   See *R v Mayeri* [1999] 1 Cr App R (S) 304, CA.

6.41   In *R v Looseley,* the House of Lords preferred a wider approach. The view of Lord Hoffmann, for instance, was that whilst causation is certainly relevant, it is unlikely to be an adequate test of entrapment in itself:

> 'Many cases place emphasis upon the question of whether the policeman can be said to have caused the commission of the offence, rather than merely providing an opportunity for the accused to commit it with a policeman rather than in secrecy with someone else. There is no doubt that this will usually be a most important factor deciding whether or not the police have overstepped the line between legitimate crime detection and unacceptable crime creation. But a note of caution must be sounded. First, as Lord Steyn said in *Latif's* case [1996] 1 WLR 104, 111, it is important but not necessarily decisive. Other factors, some of which I shall mention in a moment, may have to be taken into account as well. Secondly, a good deal will depend upon what is accepted as evidence that the accused would have committed the offence with someone else.'[1]

1   Above para **6.01**, at para 50.

Test purchases

6.42   Whilst this test models the ordinary member of the public concept, asking the same question of whether the officer merely provided an opportunity, it does not rely upon strict causation. It omits it by simply posing the issue of whether or not the officer's conduct was consistent with an everyday purchase made by an ordinary person. If this condition is satisfied, then causation and even enticement become peripheral. The emphasis is on whether the accused freely took advantage of an opportunity presented to him by the officer, this opportunity being the same as that as would have been presented by a normal customer.

6.43   In many senses, the test disregards concerns connected with causation and incitement, considering that a simple test purchase is in a special category because it is unobjectionable, almost a sort of occupational hazard that is foreseeable and ought to be expected by regulated sellers and therefore legitimate. A case of 'seller beware'.

6.44   Some support for this test was evident in the speeches in *R v Looseley.* Lord Hutton said:

> 'In my opinion if a person freely takes advantage of an opportunity to break the law given to him by a police officer, the police officer is not to be regarded as inciting or instigating the crime in the context of the prohibition of entrapment. The conduct of the police officer should not be viewed as constituting incitement or instigation where, as McHugh J states in *Ridgeway v Queen* (1995) 184 CLR 19, 92, that conduct is "consistent with the ordinary temptations and stratagems that are likely to be encountered in the course of criminal activity".'[1]

1   Above para **6.01**, at para 112.

6.45   Lord Hoffmann said:

'The test of whether the law enforcement officer behaved like an ordinary member of the public works well and is likely be decisive in many cases of regulatory offences committed with ordinary members of the public, such as selling liquor in unlicensed quantities (*DPP v Marshall* [1988] 3 All ER 683) selling videos to children under age (*Ealing London Borough Council v Woolworths plc* [1995] Crim LR 58, DC), and operating a private hire vehicle without a licence (*Taunton Deane Borough Council v Brice* (DC unreported 10 July 1997)).'[1]

1   Above para **6.01**, at para 55.

6.46   It is submitted that underlying the acceptability of test purchases is the view that unless they were a permissible method of law enforcement, the types of trivial offences concerned could never be detected. Practically, it would be near impossible for local authority trading standards officers to mount surveillance operations in Woolworths etc. Accordingly, subject to the limitation of the ordinary person paradigm, overlooking concerns about enticement is fair *quid pro quo* for the offence under investigation being relatively trivial.

6.47   Furthermore, this triviality sits easily with a stereotype concerning an ordinary person. It is everyday experience to buy videos, liquor and hire taxis etc. We all know what ordinary purchasers do in these situations. It can be safely assumed, because of the ordinariness of the transaction, how an ordinary person would behave. Such an assumption can then easily be compared to how the officers behaved to see if their conduct roughly corresponded. Generally this comparison will not be controversial, the facts being so familiar and simple.

6.48   Lord Hoffmann however identified the severe limitations of this test that become apparent when serious crime is involved:

'But ordinary members of the public do not become involved in large scale drug dealing, conspiracy to rob (*R v Mealey and Sheridan* (1974) 60 Cr App Rep 59) or hiring assassins (*R v Gill* [1989] Crim LR 358; *R v Smurthwaite* [1994] 1 All ER 898). The appropriate standards of behaviour are in such cases rather more problematic.'[1]

1   Above para **6.01**, at para 55.

6.49   In such cases, reliance upon supposed norms of behaviour becomes far less credible and accordingly, concerns about enticement and acceptable State behaviour return to the fore. In other words, in relation, for example, to drug trafficking or terrorism, the question of 'whether the defendant was given an opportunity to commit the offence of which he freely availed himself' or whether he/she was entrapped cannot be answered by a simplistic appeal to how an ordinary person would have behaved. In reality, these 'serious crime' cases can only be addressed by a different approach based on enticement. Was there any inducement, encouragement etc by the officers?

Random virtue-testing

6.50 This is another variant of the 'providing an opportunity' test. Whereas test purchases are aimed at regulated traders, this form of deceptive crime-detection is aimed at the public at large. In conducting an operation of this kind, law-abiding as well as dishonest citizens are equally targeted. The public are subject to some extraordinary temptation as in *Williams and O'Hare v DPP*.[1] Here Essex Police devised an operation to apprehend people who were stealing from cars. A white van was parked up and left with its rear doors open with cartons of cigarettes on view. Eventually, two passing men were successfully baited and arrested red-handed. At their trial and appeal they argued entrapment but this was rejected on the ground that there had not been any police persuasion or encouragement.

1   (1994) 98 Cr App R 209, CA.

6.51 In *R v Looseley* Lord Hoffmann held that this police operation was legitimate, not because virtue-testing provided a workable test, but because it was validly authorised:

'It was justified because it was an authorised investigation into actual crime and the fact that the defendants may not have previously been suspected or even thought of offending was their hard luck.'[1]

1   Above para **6.01**, at para 65.

6.52 The difficulty with virtue-test cases, like *Williams,* is that whilst it is fair to say that the accused freely took advantage of an opportunity offered to him/her, it would be wrong to hold that the opportunity was unexceptional. Deserted van doors open with cigarettes on view or open wallets left full of money are not ordinary events or temptations. This is precisely why such temptations are laid.

6.53 Furthermore, on the facts of *Williams,* it is clear that neither defendant already had the intent to commit the crime prior to being tempted. The police did far more than merely provide an opportunity: they implanted the necessary intent. It is submitted that this is a clear example of State-created crime and a misuse of State power.

6.54 In *Looseley,* Lord Hoffmann stated:

'... normally it is not considered a legitimate use of police power to provide people not suspected of being engaged in any criminal activity with the opportunity to commit crimes. The only proper purpose of police participation is to obtain evidence of criminal acts which they suspect someone is about to commit or in which he is already engaged. It is not to tempt people to commit crimes in order to expose their bad characters and punish them.'[1]

1   Above para **6.01**, at para 56.

6.55 It is submitted that Lord Hoffmann's analysis is entirely correct. His observation[1] that the operation was licit merely because it was validly authorised and accordingly the accused cannot complain as to their misfortune, is inconsistent with this observation. Clearly Lord Hoffmann did not intend to make authorisation the sole criterion of police conduct, otherwise the bulk of his speech in *R v Looseley* would be otiose. He was in the above passage, it is submitted, making a narrower point concerning what can constitute reasonable suspicion, of which more below.

1 Above para **6.51**.

6.56 As Lord Nicholls stated:

'If the defendant was already presently disposed to commit such a crime, should opportunity arise, that is not entrapment. That is not State-created crime. The matter stands differently if the defendant lacked such a predisposition, and the police were responsible for implanting the necessary intent.'[1]

1 Above para **6.01**, at para 21.

Predisposition

6.57 As the foregoing section has demonstrated, the courts attach great importance, when considering a claim of entrapment, to whether the undercover officer simply gave the accused an opportunity to break the law. If so, then the courts feel entitled to presume that the accused would have behaved in the same way if someone else had offered the same opportunity. Accordingly, having taken such free advantage, the courts reject the complaint.

6.58 But how to safely differentiate the objectionable luring or tempting from the acceptable taking free advantage? How to distinguish, for example, a bona fide police operation into ongoing crime from a vendetta against an individual? As the House of Lords observed in *R v Looseley*, in finding a violation in *Teixeira*, the ECtHR attached importance to the lack of good reason to suspect that the applicant was engaged in crime:

'It does not appear either that the competent authorities had good reason to suspect that Mr Teixeira de Castro was a drug-trafficker; on the contrary, he had no criminal record and no preliminary investigation concerning him had been opened. Indeed, he was not known to the police officers, who only came into contact with him through the intermediaries[1] ... the two police officers' actions went beyond those of undercover agents because they instigated the offence *and there was nothing to suggest that without their intervention it would have been committed.* That intervention and its use in the impugned criminal proceedings meant that, right from the outset, the applicant was definitively deprived of a fair trial.'[2] (Emphasis added)

1 At para 38.
2 At para 39.

6.59 An obvious method of determining whether the approach made to the accused was acceptable, whether they were 'fair game', is to consider how predisposed they were to have committed the offence in any event. In *R v Edwards*[1] the Court held that 'from the way E behaved, including his reaction to the request for drugs, his familiarity with the drugs scene ... and his agreement to discount future supplies, it is manifestly plain that, at the time of the approach [by the officer], he was already an established drugs dealer'. Similarly, in *R v Shannon*,[2] Potter LJ said:

'As the judge has found, by reason of the appellant's obvious familiarity with the current price of cocaine and his ready advice as to obtaining it … he displayed a familiarity with the dealing scene which itself suggested a predisposition to be part of it.'[3]

1   [1991] Crim LR 45, CA.
2   [2001] 1 WLR 51, CA.
3   At para 49.

6.60   It can be observed that, in both the cases, the courts were justifying the operation with the benefit of hindsight. Such reasoning, with respect, does not justify the principle of predisposition. Surely to avoid arbitrariness and for there to be some objective criterion, there must be a basis for suspicion beforehand. The means must justify the end, not vice versa.

6.61   The need to adduce prior grounds of predisposition has normally led to a reliance upon a target's previous convictions or current lifestyle.[1] However, the difficulty with this approach is that, first, it inevitably exposes some individuals to police attention on inherently speculative grounds; the fact that an individual has previous drugs convictions or is an addict does not provide a sound basis for inferring that they are currently engaged in crime. Second, such a view is objectionable as it will inevitably lead to stereotyping, particularly in relation to drugs, of a racial kind, and it condones wholesale police intrusions against a class of people who become fair game simply because of their background. In turn, this must raise considerable concerns in connection with the Art 8 right to privacy and the need for proportionality.

1   For example, that they are a drug addict.

6.62   It is submitted that, in common with virtue-testing, predisposition fails altogether to address the required justification for mounting an undercover operation; that there are adequate grounds to suggest that the target is either presently engaged in, or at least presently disposed to commit, the crime under investigation. His/her personal history and current lifestyle may be relevant to this issue but they can be neither sufficient nor necessary factors in establishing a current predisposition. Both Lords Nicholls and Hoffmann in *R v Looseley* enunciated disdain for this test. For example, in relation to why previous convictions are an insufficient guide to predisposition, Lord Hoffmann said:

'Suspicion may attach to a person who has previously escaped conviction and, contrariwise, the fact that a person has been previously convicted may provide no ground for suspecting a current course of criminality which would justify the use of covert operations.'[1]

1   Above para **6.01**, at para 68.

6.63   More generally, Lord Nicholls expressed disquiet about whether, even if the accused had been predisposed, this would be acceptable police conduct. He observed that:

'Predisposition does not make acceptable what would otherwise be unacceptable conduct on the part of the police or other law enforcement agencies. Predisposition does not negative misuse of State power.'[1]

1   Above para **6.01**, at para 22.

THE ACCEPTED RATIONALE; REASONABLE SUSPICION

6.64   In essence, this is a test of police good faith; that there were reasonable grounds for suspecting an individual, or a group, of ongoing involvement in a particular crime. The need to satisfy this requirement is an adequate guard against ill thought out and unjustified police intrusive operations. Arbitrary investigations of citizens selected at random would thus be regarded as unacceptable police conduct amounting to entrapment.

6.65   Unfortunately, confusion and disagreement will inevitably arise when identifying what counts as reasonable suspicion. How in practice does this requirement operate to prevent arbitrary or unjustified investigations? This issue is demonstrated by the approach of Lord Hoffmann in *R v Looseley*, who held that:

> 'The requirement of reasonable suspicion does not necessarily mean that there must have been suspicion of the particular person who happens to have committed the offence.'[1]

On the example of the facts in *Williams v DPP*,[2] Lord Hoffmann opined that such an operation could satisfy the requirement of reasonable suspicion if the operation had been conducted in an area where the crime in question was prevalent. Accordingly, the requirement may be satisfied not in relation to an individual at all; reasonable suspicion may be directed at an area and by implication, to premises or an organisation. Lord Nicholls adopted a similar approach: '... having grounds for suspicion of a particular individual is not always essential. Sometimes suspicion may be centred on a particular place, such as a particular public house.'[3]

1   Above para **6.01**, at para 65.
2   Above para **6.50**.
3   Above para **6.01**, at para 27.

6.66   The difficulty with this diluted concept of reasonable suspicion, which need not be individual-related, is that it justifies, as in *Williams,* the tempting of individuals merely because they happen to be in the wrong place at the wrong moment. Subject only to an undefined requirement of the relevant crime being prevalent in the area, random virtue-testing becomes acceptable. In the context of a nightclub where drug dealing is suspected, this means that it is acceptable for anyone inside it to be approached by undercover officers and asked to supply them with drugs; there, on this example, being no need to first identify likely dealers on the basis of prior surveillance.

6.67   It is submitted that this requirement in its diluted form is difficult to reconcile with the policy in *R v Looseley*, that arbitrary investigation is an unworthy form of State conduct.[1] Nonetheless, in the conjoined appeal with

Looseley, Attorney-General's Reference (No 3 of 2000), a lack of reasonable suspicion proved determinative to a finding by the House that the accused had been entrapped. Here, it was held that there were not any grounds to suspect that the accused, who was dealing in contraband cigarettes, also dealt in heroin. Accordingly, the offer to buy heroin from him by the undercover officers, was held as an example of State-created crime.

1   See, for example, per Lord Hoffmann at para 56.

THE LOOSELEY FACTORS FOR ENTRAPMENT

6.68   Lords Hoffmann and Nicholls emphasised that the boundary between acceptable and unacceptable State participation in criminal conduct depends upon a comprehensive review of the operation as a whole. The following extract from Lord Hoffmann's speech fairly describes this approach:

'... the principles of English law on which a stay of proceedings may be granted on grounds of entrapment involve the consideration of a number of aspects of the behaviour of the law enforcement authorities, some of which I have examined in detail, and deciding whether the involvement of the court in the conviction of a defendant who had been subjected to such behaviour would compromise the integrity of the judicial system.'[1]

The relevant factors identified were as follows.

1   Above para **6.01**, at para 71.

Reasonable suspicion

6.69   Arbitrary investigations into citizens selected at random is considered an unworthy form of State abuse. Lord Hoffmann said:

'... normally it is not considered a legitimate use of police power to provide people not suspected of being engaged in any criminal activity with the opportunity to commit crimes. The only proper purpose of police participation is to obtain evidence of criminal acts which they suspect someone is about to commit or in which he is already engaged. It is not to tempt people to commit crimes in order to expose their bad characters and punish them.'[1]

1   Above para **6.01**, at para 56.

6.70   The preference in *R v Looseley* for this factor is considered in detail above[1]. It is evident that the House of Lords did not require that suspicion has to be directed at a particular individual; it was sufficient that it attached to an area or an organisation. So, in the example of an alleged terrorist organisation, it is sufficient justification to target any member or representative.

1   Above paras **6.28–6.67**.

Supervision

6.71 This was considered a critical factor, one necessary for the operation to be considered acceptable at all. Lord Hoffmann said:

> 'Although the United Kingdom technique for authorising and supervising such operations (as described in the Code of Practice) is very different from the judicial supervision in continental countries, the purpose is the same, namely to remove the risk of extortion, corruption or abuse of power by policemen operating without proper supervision.'[1]

1   Above para **6.01**, at para 72.

6.72 The necessary elements of proper supervision are as follows:

(i)   Were the appropriate authorities obtained under the relevant statutory framework?[1] Seriousness of the alleged offence will not justify an ignoring of such provisions.

(ii) Was the conduct of the undercover officers monitored during the currency of the operation? For example, were the meetings between the officers and the target(s) recorded?

1   For example the various codes of practice concerned with undercover operations and the authorisation requirements under RIPA.

6.73 The ECtHR certainly regards proper authorisation as fundamental. In *Teixeira*, it was said that:

> 'The use of undercover agents must be restricted and safeguards put in place even in cases concerning the fight against drug-trafficking. While the rise in organised crime undoubtedly requires that appropriate measures be taken, the right to a fair administration of justice nevertheless holds such a prominent place that it cannot be sacrificed for the sake of expedience.'[1]

1   Above para **6.19**, at para 36. Similar sentiments were expressed in *Kopp v Switzerland* (1998) 27 EHRR 91, see especially para 64, where the court held that 'because of the lack of public scrutiny and the risk of misuse of power, the domestic law must provide some protection to the individual against arbitrary interference with article 8 rights'.

The nature and extent of State participation in the crime[1]

6.74 This is the most imprecise factor. It begins in *R v Looseley* with a clear denunciation of what Lord Nicholls described as 'State-created crime'.[2] Beyond this, the following were considered as relevant factors:

(i)   Proactive conduct by officers may be acceptable in relation to consensual crimes which otherwise will be difficult to prosecute. Trafficking in drugs would be an example here where victims rarely report the crime and there are unlikely to be available witnesses[3]. In other words, such is the nature of the offence that evidence will only be obtained if undercover methods are used.

(ii)   The greater the degree of intrusiveness, the more demanding will be the justification for resort to this method. The test of proportionality applies here[4]. Essentially this factor is based on the seriousness of the suspected offence under investigation. Does it present a danger to society, such that accordingly the State has a duty to seek to thwart it? In relation to an alleged terrorist organisation or criminal gang, intrusiveness may be justified at least partly on the basis of past crimes and the overall threat posed to the public.

(iii)   Did the State do no more than give the accused an unexceptional opportunity to break the law of which he/she freely took advantage in circumstances in which it appears that if the opportunity had been presented by someone who was not an agent, the accused would have acted similarly?[5] If so, then such conduct is unlikely to be regarded as inciting or instigating crime. Lord Nicholls quoted with approval McHugh J in *Ridgway v R*:[6]

'The State can justify the use of entrapment techniques to induce the commission of an offence only when the inducement is consistent with the ordinary temptations and stratagems that are likely to be encountered in the course of criminal activity. That may mean that some degree of deception, importunity and even threats on the part of the authorities may be acceptable. But once the State goes beyond the ordinary, it is likely to increase the incidence of crime by artificial means.'

1   The issue of whether illegality by the officer/agent should found an abuse is considered in **Chapter 5**.
2   Above para **6.01**, at para 19.
3   At paras 2 and 4.
4   At para 24.
5   At paras 53 to 55.
6   At para 23.

6.75   An issue here will be the nature of any inducement made to the accused. If, for example, a suspected terrorist in meeting with an undercover officer, asks for money and weapons for his/her organisation and in response, encouraging noises are made, is that an improper inducement? It is submitted that the answer is probably not as the request was made by the accused and the agent/officer had acted in a way consistent with his/her expectations.

6.76   Second, in relation to persuasion, if the accused was approached several times before agreeing to commit the offence, the State will need to justify why such persistence or persuasion was necessary and was not tantamount to incitement. On this point, Lord Hoffmann observed:

'Drug dealers can be expected to show some wariness about dealing with a stranger who might be a policeman or informer and therefore some protective colour in dress or manner as well as a certain degree of persistence may be necessary to achieve the objective. And it has been said that undercover officers who infiltrate conspiracies to murder, rob or commit terrorist offences could hardly remain concealed unless they showed some enthusiasm for the enterprise. A good deal of active behaviour in the course of an authorised operation may therefore be acceptable without crossing the boundary between causing the offence to be committed and providing an opportunity for the defendant to commit it.'[1]

1   Above para **6.01**, at paras 69 and 102.

6.77   On the basis of these factors or criteria, the House of Lords in *R v Looseley* recommended the approach for assessing complaints of entrapment. In other words, in determining whether the conduct of the State was so unworthy or shameful such that a prosecution based upon it would be an affront to the public conscience.

Post-Looseley case law

6.78   If the post-*Looseley* case law is notable for anything, it is the restrictive manner in which the courts have applied the principles laid down by the House of Lords. What follows is a practical summary of cases that have been decided since *Looseley* to guide the practitioner who attempts to have proceedings against his client stayed on this unusually fact-specific ground.

6.79   The principle clearly still stands that 'entrapment of itself does not necessarily give rise to such an abuse of process as would require a stay of proceedings'.[1] The mere fact that an offence would not have been committed *but for* the actions of the police will not warrant a stay of proceedings.

1   *R v Lewis* [2005] EWCA Crim 859.

6.80   There has only been one successful appeal to the Court of Appeal on the ground of entrapment since *Looseley* was decided; in *R v Moon*.[1] Moon was a vulnerable drug addict, with no predisposition to dealing, who was targeted and approached by police and asked (persistently) to supply an undercover officer with a small quantity of heroin, which she was to obtain from her dealer. Upon so doing, she told the undercover officer that she [the officer] was never to approach her again and that she would never help her again. Moon was charged and successfully prosecuted for possession with intent to supply the drug, the judge at first instance having refused to stay proceedings as an abuse of process on the ground of entrapment following a *voir dire*. The Court of Appeal held that Moon had been entrapped, taking into account the fact that she had only ever held the status of a drug addict, against whom there was no evidence of any previous dealing in or supply of heroin,[2] and that she had taken some persuading to commit the offence after taking sympathy on the undercover officer – who pretended to be an addict displaying the unhappy physical consequences of drug withdrawal[3] – such that she had been lured[4] into committing the offence.

1   Above para **6.05**.
2   At para 44.
3   See para 9.
4   At para 51.

6.81   Whilst *Looseley* established that a defendant's predisposition to commit an offence of the type concerned would not negative or preclude any claim made by him to have been entrapped ('predisposition does not negative misuse of State power'), the Court in *R v Moon* confirmed that:

'Nothing said there [in *Looseley*] by Lord Nicholls, however, would support a view that the *absence* of predisposition of a defendant to commit the crime in question is not relevant to the judge's consideration.[1]

Whilst that observation is of benefit to the defendant of good character (or at least no previous convictions for offences of the same type as those for which he is to be tried) who makes claim to an entrapment, *R v Moon* displays the gravity of circumstances that must otherwise fall in a defendant's favour before a claim of entrapment is likely to succeed.

1   Above para **6.05**.

6.82   In *R v Holt*,[1] an extensive undercover police operation resulted in officers infiltrating a loose organisation which imported large quantities of cannabis into the UK. Holt was not initially in contact with the officers but, during their efforts to obtain evidence against the head of the organisation, he was introduced to them, as being part of the operation, and evidence was consequently obtained against him as well. The Court of Appeal found that there was no reason for going behind the trial judge's conclusion – that Holt had not been entrapped – on that ground[2] and, more notably, affirmed that the Court '… is and should be slow to interfere with the judge who has clearly had regard to the correct principles of law and formed his own judgment as to what is and what is not fair in the trial of which he has the conduct.'[3]

1   [2003] EWCA Crim 1891.
2   At para 19.
3   At para 15.

6.83   In *R v Winter*,[1] the appellant told his friend (M) of his intention to kill his wife and M informed the police. The police authorised M to covertly record conversations between himself and the appellant in order to gather evidence in relation to the intended murder. The appellant was eventually convicted of two offences of soliciting murder and a third of attempting to pervert the course of justice. As well as recording conversations, the police had M introduce an undercover police officer (T) to the appellant on the pretence that T was an acquaintance of M's and would drive the appellant's car in the view of CCTV cameras on the day of the murder so as to provide the appellant with an alibi. The Court of Appeal held that there had been no entrapment. It is submitted that the claim of entrapment in that case was inherently weak in any event, as the offences for which the appellant had been convicted were by no means 'state-created crime'; the appellant's plan to murder his wife had been in place and was discussed with M before the police were contacted[2] (just as the appellant in *R v Holt* had been introduced to the undercover police officer through pre-existing drugs deals relating to intended drugs supply, seemingly with criminal intent in mind, rather than having been sought out or targeted by the police). The police in *Winter*'s case merely allowed the plan to continue (albeit facilitating the plan by the offer of an alibi) giving him only the opportunity that he had wished for to commit the offence of his own volition,[3] in such a way that it could be evidenced for the purposes of prosecution. The

Court so held in dismissing the appeal: 'It is quite clear from the transcript that whether or not the appellant had a driver to provide an alibi he was going to commit the offence.'[4]

1 [2007] EWCA Crim 3493.
2 Note, at para 15, that even the appellant accepted that he could have been arrested and the plan stopped when M first contacted the police, suggesting that his real complaint was at the fact that the police had allowed the plan to continue and thus strengthened the case against him by the gathering of covert evidence.
3 At paras 28 and 33.
4 At para 30.

6.84 Interestingly, in *Jenkins v Government of the United States of America*,[1] the Administrative Court displayed its pre-*Looseley* willingness[2] to allow the courts to gauge whether the police had behaved as would an ordinary customer of trade being carried on by the defendant, even in cases concerning the highest level of criminal enterprise.[3] It might have been thought that only those involved in the sale of decommissioned radioactive metals could know how an ordinary customer of the trade would behave, the type of offending concerned being far removed from 'common place' crimes in which the typical actions of the perpetrators could easily be envisaged by the courts.

1 [2005] EWHC 1051 (Admin).
2 See above paras **6.42–6.49**.
3 See Sedley LJ para 20. This was an extradition case involving undercover police officers offering to supply the requested persons with drugs as payment for approximately £220m worth of radioactive material.

Non-compliance with procedural requirements

6.85 The facts in *R v Chandler*[1] were similar to those in *R v Moon*[2] – an undercover police officer posed as a drug addict suffering a state of withdrawal and purchased class A drugs from the appellant, who was convicted of four counts of supplying the drugs. Unlike *R v Moon* however, the appellant in *Chandler* had displayed signs of being a drug dealer and was seemingly not lured into committing the offence. Applying the *Looseley* principles, the Court of Appeal found that there had been no entrapment and on the facts of the case there was nothing notable about the ruling to that extent.

1 [2002] EWCA Crim 3167.
2 Above para **6.05**.

6.86 However, in *R v Chandler* there was an absence of an unassailable record of the undercover officer's conversations with the appellant. The relevance of the absence of an unassailable record was not addressed in *Looseley* and the position therefore stood as it was decided in *R v Smurthwaite and Gill*,[1] that a record was desirable rather than an absolute requirement. It was argued that recordings enable the Court to assess the degree of pressure imposed on the suspect and his willingness to offend. It was submitted that the Courts should be loathe to admit evidence without recordings, even if the absence is explained as being to prevent an officer's cover being blown. However, the Court of Appeal concluded that:

'It seems to us that the position with regard to the absence of an unassailable record is and should continue to be regarded as it was stated in *Smurthwaite*; that is to say that the absence of an unassailable record is but one relevant factor to be taken into account in deciding whether or not to admit evidence from officers of what was said by defendants in the course of crimes committed in the context of undercover activity … The weight to be given to the absence of an unassailable record will vary from case to case. Where the conversation of which there is no unassailable record is substantially the whole of the evidence against a defendant, then the absence of an unassailable record will be a matter of greater importance than in a case where the conversation does not lie at the heart of the prosecution case and where there is substantial other evidence of what took place between the defendant and the officers … Another factor which is highly material to the question of what weight should be given to the absence of an unassailable record is the extent to which the oral evidence given by the officer of what took place during the conversation is contested. In a case where there is a stark and fundamental conflict of evidence between the police officer or officers on the one hand and the defendant on the other as to what was said, then the absence of an unassailable record will plainly be a more important factor than in a case where there is little or no such dispute.'[2]

1   Above para **6.29**.
2   At paras 44–46.

Non-authorisation

6.87   It will be recalled that the House of Lords in *R v Looseley* regarded proper authorisation as a condition precedent, a critical factor.[1] One of the factors that caused the Court of Appeal to allow the appeal against conviction in *R v Moon*[2] was that the police operation had not been authorised.[3]

1   Above paras **6.71–6.73**.
2   Discussed above at para **6.80**.
3   See paras 50–51: 'Thus whether the matter is looked through the lens of the proper safeguards of authorisation, or through the lens of the appellant's absence of predisposition or antecedents, or through the lens of the actual nature of the police activities in relation to this appellant, the conclusion to which we are driven is that this appellant was lured into crime or was entrapped, and that it was a case of causing crime rather than merely providing an opportunity for it, and ultimately that it would be unfair for the State to prosecute her for this offending.'

6.88   *R v Harmes and Crane*[1] concerned procedural non-compliance of the police in conducting proactive investigatory techniques, upon which the appellant relied heavily in arguing that his prosecution should have been stayed as an abuse of process on the basis of entrapment in an appeal that it is submitted might otherwise have been on weak ground.[2] The police actions had offended against the provisions of the Regulation of Investigatory Powers Act 2000 ('RIPA') and the Covert Human Intelligence Sources Codes of Practice ('the Codes of Practice'), made under RIPA, s 71. In respect of the extent of the violations of those provisions, the Court observed that:

'In our judgment there were serious breaches of the Act and the Code in the process of authorisation [of the undercover operation]. The importance of compliance with the Act and Code in the procedure to be adopted for authorisation should not be underestimated. Absent careful compliance with the requirements of the Act and of the Code, the purpose of the Act is frustrated. Without a careful record of that which is proposed and approved, a court is deprived of the opportunity of assessing whether the undercover actions of officers are necessary and proportionate ... The suggestion, which admittedly came from the officers, that they should be supplied with cocaine in exchange for the soft drinks, was a crime. It was not authorised. That it was merely a small part in infiltrating what was suspected to be a gang of drug smugglers may be relevant to the question of the proportionality of the operation viewed as a whole. But the judge misdirected herself as to the criminal nature of the officers' activities at this point in her ruling ... We conclude that, for the reasons we have given, there were substantial defects in the process of authorisation in the instant case. There is no evidence that it was impracticable to obtain authorisation for what was done in advance. Such authorisation was not obtained.'[3]

1   [2006] EWCA Crim 928.
2   The police had infiltrated a racket which was involved in the importation of drugs and the appellant Harmes had himself revealed to the undercover officers a system of drugs importation by which the major importation of cocaine (200 kilos) was to take place; although the police had played a role in the initial deal that instigated trade between themselves and the appellants (Harmes had been supplied with soft drinks, which he needed to facilitate his criminal enterprise, in exchange for a small amount of drugs). Counsel for Harmes contended that he had been entrapped because, even though the initial deal with the soft drinks did not trap the appellants into the major conspiracy, it had been the trigger for the revelation of the system by which the major drugs importation would take place.
3   At paras 42 and 45–46.

6.89   In determining what the Court of Appeal regarded as the 'essential issue in [the] case ... [of] whether the undercover officers' declared willingness to deal in drugs and the officers' own criminal conduct was such that the prosecution for conspiracy should have been stayed', the Court of Appeal ruled that: 'The breach of the Code is an important factor but not dispositive,'[1] Ultimately, the Court of Appeal ruled that the trial judge had correctly concluded that it was the 'hope of big returns for himself' that caused Harmes to partake in the offences for which he was convicted and, for that reason, there was no entrapment to which non-authorisation could attach as a factor militating in favour of a stay. In dismissing the appeal the Court held that:

'We have already concluded that the officers' conduct was criminal and it was not properly authorised. Nonetheless, we take the view that it should not be regarded as so seriously improper as to require the court to intervene to prevent the prosecution for conspiracy. It was conduct which merely exposed, for the purposes of the undercover operation, the undercover officers' interest in drugs and eagerness to receive a small quantity. That was, in our judgment, no more than might be expected of any criminal willing to engage in illicit dealing in drugs ... Undercover officers, seeking to expose drug dealers, must show enthusiasm and a degree of persistence to provide protection for their undercover activities. As Lord Hoffmann accepts [in *R v*

Looseley], a good deal of active behaviour may be acceptable (see paragraph 69) ... In our judgment the conduct of the police officers was not exceptional and did not go beyond that which was necessary to show their willingness to deal in drugs. An exchange of a small amount of cocaine triggered the revelation that these defendants were not only happy to import very substantial quantities of cocaine but had the ability to do so. The officers' activities pale into insignificance in comparison to the offers made by Harmes to import, on their behalf, large amounts of cocaine of a high value ... But in our judgment, the trial judge, whilst underestimating the breaches of the Code, correctly concluded that the prosecution for conspiracy should not be stayed. The officers' conduct, viewed as a whole, did not stray beyond that which was permissible to investigate and prosecute crime. In the instant case, that which had originally been suspected, namely, that the appellants were members of a gang engaged in the distribution of large amounts of cocaine, proved to be only too true.'[2]

1   At para 47.
2   At paras 51–52 and 54.

6.90   Whilst the Court's approach to the issues in *R v Chandler* and *R v Harmes* is in keeping with the fact-dependent nature of almost all issues that arise in entrapment cases, the intrusive nature of the policing technique employed in such cases might engender an intuitive desire to ensure that unassailable records are kept and the Codes of Practice are complied with in all such cases. It is difficult to envisage an undercover operation in which the Codes might be violated to a greater extent than they were in *Harmes*, notwithstanding the fact that no issue can be taken with the Court's findings in respect of the outcome of the investigation and the level of drugs importation with which the appellants had been involved.

6.91   Nevertheless, in *R v Brett*[1] the Court of Appeal reiterated the significance of adherence to RIPA and the Codes of Practice, saying that:

'... if the requirements of section 29 [of RIPA] and indeed the [Code of Practice] were shown to have been flouted or ignored by the police, that circumstance might very well give rise to an inference that the conduct of the police or prosecution was indeed seriously improper within the approach given by [*R v Looseley*]'.

In that case, the Court found that it was not seriously improper, unnecessary or disproportionate for the police to have directed their undercover operation against the appellant, whose conviction was upheld.

1   [2005] EWCA Crim 983.

6.92   The Court of Appeal has, therefore, refused to erect a strict hurdle over which the prosecuting authorities must jump (by compliance with the Codes of Practice, for example) to ensure that a case is not automatically stayed as an abuse on the ground of entrapment, even where the statutory safeguards in place for the benefit of a defendant have been flagrantly ignored and violated. Non-authorisation and procedural non-compliance, remain but two of the myriad factors that feed into entrapment abuse judgments, none being determinative at the absolute discretion of the trial court.

6.93   Finally, by way of example of the post-*Looseley* developments in this area, we consider *R v Jones*.[1] The appellant in that case had left graffiti messages on toilets and trains asking girls of eight to thirteen years of age for sex, offering payment in return and leaving his contact number. A journalist instigated contact with the appellant before informing the police, who struck up a 'relationship' with the appellant through an officer posing as a girl of 12 years of age and arrested him at an arranged meeting place. Much of the case regarded the interpretation of s 8 of the Sexual Offences Act 2003, the appellant arguing (unsuccessfully) that the offence was not made out because he was in fact not in contact with a 12-year-old girl and only believed that he was because the police had, arbitrarily by his contention, chosen that age when in contact with the appellant so as to make out a charge under s 8 of the Act. The appellant argued that he had been entrapped by the conduct of the police generally and that the offence amounted to state-created crime because no offence under s 8 would have been committed had the police not pretended to be a girl of 12 years of age.

1   [2008] 1 QB 460, CA.

6.94   With regard to the choice of the fictitious girl's age, the court found that, as 'the essence of the criminality is in the incitement ... the crime does not need an identifiable person as the object of the incitement.'[1] The offence could not, therefore, amount to state-created crime by virtue of the police choosing the age of 12 when making contact with the appellant, not least because he had offered sex to girls between eight and thirteen in his graffiti.

1   At paras 16 and 22.

6.95   Of significance in more general terms was the Court's finding that the actions of the police on the whole did not amount to entrapment, notwithstanding the protracted contact they engaged with the defendant. In finding that the police did no more than offer the appellant an opportunity to commit the offence, and that given the nature of the offence[1] the investigative technique used was necessary to gather evidence to bring the prosecution at all,[2] the Court placed weight on the fact that the police officer's conduct in relation to the appellant followed on from the actions as between the appellant and the journalist who instigated the contact:

'... It is also relevant to take into account the actions of the journalist in answering the [graffiti] message as a further measure by which the acceptability of the conduct of the police can be judged ...'[3]

1   At para 21.
2   At para 28.
3   At para 32.

6.96   Whilst the court, in making that observation, was clearly using the journalist's conduct as a yardstick by which to judge whether the police officer's actions were no more than might have been expected of any ordinary member of the public, this consideration suggests that where, as with *R v Winter*,[1] the police simply facilitate the continuance of a course of conduct in which the defendant is already engaged so as to found a prosecution, that is a factor that will weigh strongly against a finding that there has been an entrapment.

1   Discussed above at para **6.83**.

6.97   Such a conclusion also appears to legitimise the actions of the journalist in the first place, as something of a private entrapper (or at least suggests that the defendant could not have proper complaint at having been entrapped by the journalist to begin with), which raises the question of the extent to which a defendant might claim to have been the victim of entrapment committed by a private party. Does the defendant have any recourse in such circumstances? If so, to what extent do the courts offer protection against 'private entrapment'? It is to those questions that we now turn.

PRIVATE ENTRAPMENT

6.98   Journalism based on deception and entrapment of celebrities or those in high society by undercover newspaper reporters remains feverishly popular in an increasingly celebrity-interested society. The legendary 'sting' inflicted on the Countess of Wessex by the *News of the World*'s 'fake sheikh' illustrates the degree of planning and sophistication to which parts of the media will resort in an effort to expose a celebrity's bad character.

6.99   This private form of entrapment is, by its nature, not carried out by State agents and, primarily at least, is not for law enforcement purposes. Seeing the celebrity ultimately prosecuted based on evidence obtained by undercover journalists may constitute a public interest purpose but the rationale for the 'sting' is to increase circulation and to entertain the readership.

6.100   In *Morley and Hutton*[1] in 1994, the Court of Appeal observed that:

'Although one might dislike the activities of certain informants or journalists, the criterion for admissibility did not depend on this or the motive of a newspaper to sell a story or make money. It was clear that there was no defence in English law of entrapment, and it made no difference whether an undercover officer or a journalist was involved ... [The appellants] were not making admissions which might be unreliable but actually committing offences in front of the camera. They were not enticed or provoked by the reporter to commit offences.'

1   [1994] Crim LR 919, CA. That the identity and motives of the entrapper were not primarily concerned with law enforcement but for a private commercial purpose, was also held to be immaterial in *R v Tonnessen* [1998] 2 Cr App R (S) 328, CA.

6.101   At both domestic and European level, the courts have now made clear that the principles laid down in *R v Looseley* and *Teixeira* do not apply to cases concerning private entrapment, where the fundamental need for state participation in a course of conduct that can be said to amount to an abuse of process is absent. However, in the most recent case in this area, *Re Saluja*, Goldring J left the door open for proceedings to be stayed on the basis of private entrapment. As shall be seen, the issue of private entrapment remains shrouded in uncertainty.

1   [2007] 1 WLR 3094, DC

Early authorities

6.102 In *R v Shannon*[1] an actor from the then popular television show *London's Burning* was steered into supplying drugs for a party by a *News of the World* journalist. The newspaper shortly after published a front-page article under the headline 'London's Burning Star is Cocaine Dealer', based on the evidence of drug offences procured by the sting. The actor was later prosecuted for offences involving drugs supply and the Crown relied primarily upon evidence collected by the newspaper. Shannon was subsequently convicted, having failed in his attempt to have the evidence excluded under s 78 of PACE on the basis of entrapment, and appealed against the decision to admit that evidence

1   Above para **6.59**.

6.103 In dismissing the appeal, Potter LJ rejected an argument that commercial entrapment was unworthy and that, in such cases, the incitement or encouragement of journalists to commit the offence should found a stay. In Potter LJ's view, the principles to be considered were the same as those in proactive policing cases. Citizens do not enjoy any right not to be tempted by either law enforcement or private agents. Potter LJ endorsed the trial judge's observations that:

'In so far as abuse of process considerations might be relevant, there was no suggestion of criticism of the part played by the police or Crown prosecution Service, the organs of the state responsible for gathering and presenting the evidence and of instituting proceedings …, [If the unfairness complained of by the defendant was no more than] … a visceral reaction that it is in principle unfair as a matter of policy, or wrong as a matter of law, for a person to be prosecuted for a crime which he would not have committed without the incitement or encouragement of others, then it is not itself sufficient, unless the behaviour of the police (or someone acting on behalf of or in league with the police) and/or the prosecuting authority has been such as to justify a stay on the grounds of abuse of process.'

6.104 These passages suggest that the subsequent conduct of the police and/or the prosecuting authority is a determinative factor of an application for a stay of proceedings on the grounds of abuse of process in cases involving private entrapment.

6.105 This was further demonstrated in the case of *R v Hardwicke and Thwaites*.[1] In this case the Earl of Hardwicke and his co-defendant had been plied with alcohol at the Savoy Hotel by undercover journalists, including the same journalist who had conducted the sting in *Shannon*. They posed as 'wealthy Arabs' interested in doing business in the sale of motor scooters for export to the Middle East. The journalists steered the alcohol-induced conversations towards drug use and the appellants eventually arranged for the group to be supplied with heroin. They were subsequently prosecuted and convicted for that supply on the evidence obtained by the undercover journalists.

1   (2000) Times, November 16, CA.

6.106   When returning their guilty verdicts the jury added this rider:

> 'The jury would like to say that the circumstances surrounding this case have made it very difficult for us to reach a decision. Had we been allowed to take the extreme provocation into account we would undoubtedly have reached a different verdict.'[1]

1   At para 10.

6.107   The rider plainly demonstrated the sense of discomfort that the jury held at the thought of a criminal prosecution being founded upon private entrapment. The appellant Hardwicke understandably took the point, on the strength of the rider, that his conviction amounted to an affront to the public conscience.[1] The Court of Appeal nevertheless stressed the difference between the extent to which an appellant might rely upon their prosecution bringing the system into disrepute when there has been malpractice by the State as compared with the extent to which it can be relied upon in cases of private entrapment;

> 'It is of some importance to note that what [*R v Latif*[2]] seeks not to condone is "malpractice by law enforcement agencies" which "would undermine public confidence in the criminal justice system and bring it into disrepute". Obviously that is not a consideration which applies with anything like the same force when the investigator allegedly guilty of malpractice is outside the criminal justice system altogether.'[3]

1   At para 34.
2   Above para **6.13**.
3   At para 22.

Problems in the application of Looseley to private entrapment

6.108   *R v Shannon* and *R v Hardwicke and Thwaites* caused an obvious divergence in the paths down which the courts would explore whether there has been an entrapment based upon the actions of private parties, operating independently of the State and the justice system.

6.109   The *R v Looseley* principles cannot be applied to cases involving private entrapment with any degree of satisfaction. The reasons for this are twofold: First, central to the factors to be taken into account under *R v Looseley* are the nature of the crime that is to be detected and the means by which the police might gain evidence of such for the purposes of prosecution. In cases of private entrapment, there may be no pre-existing crime of the type that is to be captured by the 'sting' in mind and the entrapper is not operating towards an aim of obtaining evidence of that crime for the purposes of prosecution. Consequently, there is no consideration of what might be a more appropriate means by which the 'evidence' could be obtained. No assessment can therefore be made of the undercover journalist's actions by reference to an acceptable common standard of behaviour that might apply to the actions of a police officer.

6.110   Secondly, and more fundamentally, the abuse of process jurisdiction is limited, by its very definition, to sanctioning those who abuse a process over which they assert some form of control. In the case of the criminal justice system that is the State and its agents. The courts' ability to stay proceedings emanate from their inherent 'responsibility'[1] to prevent and sanction the abuse of *state* power. Where entrapment is concerned, a stay of proceedings will reflect the outrage that would be caused to society's conscience if those who have the power to commence a prosecution, incite or create a crime and then proceed to utilise that power to hold the perpetrator responsible and punish him for it – thereby *abusing the system*, rather than merely causing harm to the individual concerned. Journalists exert no power to prosecute those who they encourage to commit crime, nor do they aim to have those people prosecuted (ie abuse the *system*) when operating the 'sting', even if they later publish self-acclaiming articles documenting the successful prosecutions that have been brought about by their actions.

1   *R v Horseferry Road Magistrates' Court, ex p Bennett,* above para **6.11**.

6.111   Whilst some would see injustice in a defendant being prosecuted following a journalistic sting, others would no doubt see the police and the state as failing in their duty to investigate crime and prosecute offenders if those 'caught' by the press were not brought to justice in the usual way. Where the latter is true, the rationale for the *R v Looseley* principles are not transferrable and do not apply to cases of private entrapment.

Recent case law

6.112   The apparent need for a defendant to be entrapped at the hands of *the State* before the subsequent prosecution will be considered one that should be stayed was demonstrated upon Shannon's application for leave to appeal to the European Court of Human Rights,[1] which rejected the application as 'manifestly ill-founded'. It should be recalled that the appeal was based upon the refusal of the trial judge to exclude the evidence obtained by the *News of the World* under s 78 of PACE,[2] rather than to have the proceedings stayed as an abuse of process. Nonetheless, considering its earlier ruling in *Teixeira de Castro*[3] on entrapment, the ECtHR observed that:

'... [I]n the first place that, in concluding that the applicant was from the outset deprived of a fair trial, the Court in its *Teixeira* judgment was addressing the facts and circumstances of the case before it. The Court recalls that, as emphasised by the national courts, the *Teixeira* case was concerned with an entrapment operation undertaken by police officers and that the Court's judgment did not address the question of entrapment by individuals other than agents of the State. The operation which was there being examined constituted a misuse of State power, the police officers having gone beyond their legitimate role as undercover agents obtaining evidence against a suspected offender to incite the commission of the offence itself. The Court considers that the principles set out in the *Teixeira* judgment are to be viewed in this context and to be seen as principally directed to the use in a criminal trial of evidence gained by means of an entrapment operation carried out by or on behalf of the State or its agents.'

1   *Shannon v the United Kingdom* (Application No 67537/01, Fourth Section, 6 April 2004).
2   The ECtHR found that there was no reason to question the assessment of the domestic courts in deciding to admit the evidence concerned, and that it could not reach a different conclusion as to the admission of that evidence on its own examination of the material before it.
3   Above para **6.19**.

6.113   Whilst the ECtHR held against Shannon, the fact that *Teixeira* addressed only entrapment by state parties, as the domestic courts would later observe in their application of *R v Looseley*, it must be observed that neither *Teixeira* nor *R v Looseley* involved any consideration of the extent to which the principles laid down in respect of police entrapment would apply to cases of private entrapment. One might question whether the courts in *Teixeira* and *R v Looseley* failed to mention private entrapment merely because it was not an issue in the matters before them, rather than because the principles were not to apply to private entrapment.

6.114   However, reflection upon the rationale behind the abuse of process jurisdiction in entrapment cases[1] and the approach of the domestic courts seems to confirm that the *Teixeira* and *R v Looseley* principles for determining whether proceedings should be stayed as an abuse of process are not to be confused with and applied to the issues at stake in cases of private entrapment.

1   Discussed above at paras **6.109–6.111**.

6.115   In *R v Marriner,*[1] the defendants (members of a group of organised football hooligans convicted of committing a series of violent offences as part of that group upon evidence obtained by undercover journalists reporting for the programme *MacIntyre Undercover*) were subjected to a level of flattery on the journalists' part that arguably surpasses any such technique seen in the police entrapment cases. The journalists themselves committed illegal acts and employed 'undoubted flattery, wheedling, falsehoods and the making of apparent offers of legitimate and illegitimate business' as part of a 'journalistic operation'[2] through which the evidence was procured.

1   [2002] EWCA Crim 2855.
2   At para 39.

6.116   Despite the 'elaborate trick' that had been played by the journalists, the Court of Appeal held that the trial judge properly left the evidence obtained by them to the jury and dismissed the appeal brought on the ground that the prosecution should have been stayed as an abuse of process,[1] noting that:

'The present case is not concerned with conduct of the police or prosecuting authorities. The inducements to talk were applied in quite different circumstances and were of a quite different order. The judge was in the best position to evaluate whether it was fair to allow the proceedings to go before the jury on their basis, and we consider that his decision to do so cannot be faulted.'[2]

1   Considered in the context of the appellant's submission that his privacy had been infringed, as the ECtHR had held in *Allan v United Kingdom* (Application No 48539/99, Fourth Section, 5 November 2002).

2   At para 39.

6.117   In *R v Paulssen,*[1] the defendant was held in custody on remand awaiting trial for conspiracy to defraud. He had sought the help of a fellow inmate (MG) to murder a co-defendant in the conspiracy case. MG informed the police and, via a plan devised by the police, introduced an undercover police officer (David) to the defendant on the pretence that David would offer his services as a hit-man to carry out the killing. The defendant applied for permission to appeal against his convictions for soliciting both MG and the undercover officer to murder on the ground of entrapment. Much of the Court of Appeal's ruling deals with the issue of whether a conviction stemming out of a guilty plea might be 'unsafe',[2] with the result that the submissions focused on the concept of convictions in such circumstances being 'affront to justice' rather than considering the wider definition and remedies available in cases of private entrapment.

1   [2003] EWCA Crim 3109.
2   For specific consideration of this issue see *R v Togher* [2001] 3 All ER 463, CA and *R v Rajcoomar* [1999] Crim LR 728, CA.

6.118   Nonetheless, in dismissing the application the Court of Appeal noted that any entrapment that might have occurred, in so far as the defendant was entrapped to solicit MG to murder, took place without the authorisation of the police (ie before they were informed of the plan by MG), who duly authorised the continuance of the operation when they became involved.[1] This highlights the role of the state as being a fundamental factor in deciding whether proceedings should be stayed as an abuse of process, although it is difficult to see how there could have been entrapment at any point in this case when its similarity with the facts[2] in the (albeit later) case of *Winter*[3] is considered.

1   At para 48.
2   In particular, see paras 9, 10, 11 and 18, relating to the trial judge's ruling that the offence of soliciting MG to murder was complete before MG left the prison, again noting that anything that MG did to 'entrap' the appellant was done without the authority of the State and therefore did not amount to a basis upon which to stay proceedings.
3   Above para **6.83**.

Re Saluja

6.119   *Council for the Regulation of Healthcare Professionals v General Medical Council (Re Saluja)*[1] was a quasi-criminal case in which a doctor (S) was charged before the GMC with serious professional misconduct for providing a sickness certificate to an undercover journalist, posing as a patient, who had asked for the certificate to enable her to take time off work and have a holiday, S knowing that she was not sick at all. The tribunal at first instance, the Fitness to Practice Panel of the GMC, found that S had been entrapped and the proceedings against him were stayed. The Council for the Regulation of Healthcare Professionals appealed to the Administrative Court.

1   Above para **6.101**.

6.120   The Council argued that on a proper analysis, abuse of process was essentially about deliberate misuse of executive power, but accepted that there might be exceptional cases where conduct by non-state agents might found a basis for a stay of proceedings. The Council submitted that the panel had therefore fallen into error[1] in failing to draw the distinction between journalists and agents of the state in merely substituting journalists for policemen in the test set out in *Looseley*.

1   Paras 97–98.

6.121   Goldring J reviewed the earlier authorities and derived from them the following nine points of law to be applied to a private entrapment case:[1]

'[79]. First, to impose a stay is exceptional.

[80]. Second, the principle behind it is the court's repugnance in permitting its process to be used in the face of the executive's misuse of state power by its agents. To involve the court in convicting a defendant who has been the victim of such misuse of state power would compromise the integrity of the judicial system.

[81]. Third, as both domestic and European authority make plain, the position as far as misconduct of non-state agents is concerned, is wholly different. By definition no question arises in such a case of the state seeking to rely upon evidence which by its own misuse of power it has effectively created. The rationale of the doctrine of abuse of process is therefore absent. *However, the authorities leave open the possibility of a successful application of a stay on the basis of entrapment by non-state agents. The reasoning I take to be this: given sufficiently gross misconduct by the non-state agent, it would be an abuse of the court's process (and a breach of article 6) for the state to seek to rely on the resulting evidence. In other words, so serious would the conduct of the non-state agent have to be that reliance upon it in the court's proceedings would compromise the court's integrity.* There has been no reported case of the higher courts, domestic or European, in which such 'commercial lawlessness' has founded a successful application for a stay. That is not surprising. The situations in which that might arise must be very rare indeed. [emphasis added]

[82]. As will become apparent, I do not accept that for a journalist to go into a doctor's surgery and pretend to be a patient in circumstances such as the present is similar to abuse of power by an agent of the state.

[83]. Fourth, in the present disciplinary hearing there is no state involvement in the proceedings being brought. These are proceedings *3111 brought against a doctor by his regulator in order to protect the public, uphold professional standards and maintain confidence in the profession. These are to a significant degree different considerations from those that apply to a criminal prosecution and misuse of executive powers by the state's agents.

[84]. Fifth, it would be an error of law in considering any application for abuse of process for the tribunal not to have well in mind the differences to which I have referred. It would not be appropriate for an FPP to approach the conduct of journalists as though they were agents of the state.

[85]. Sixth, "commercial lawlessness" can be a factor in an application to exclude evidence under section 78, although again different considerations apply as between state and non-state agents.

[86]. Seventh, when deciding in any given case whether there has been an abuse of process, the tribunal, here the FPP, is exercising a discretion. In doing so, it must consider all the facts of the case as well as the factors to which I have already referred. While guidance can be obtained from such aspects as were referred to in *R v Looseley* [2001] 1 WLR 2060, no one aspect is determinative and the aspects there set out are not exhaustive.

[87]. Eighth, if the defendant's article 8 rights have been infringed that is merely a matter to be taken into account when deciding whether there has been an abuse of process or, (and it amounts to the same thing), his article 6 rights have been infringed: see for example *R v P* [2002] 1 AC 146 and *Jones v University of Warwick* [2003] 1 WLR 954.

[88]. Ninth, section 78 is concerned with the admissibility of evidence. As Lord Nicholls said in *R v Looseley* [2001] 1 WLR 2060, para 12, it is directed primarily at matters going to the fairness of the conduct of the trial; the reliability of the evidence, how the defendant might test it and so on. Entrapment does not mean the evidence must be excluded. It is a factor to take into account. In considering broader matters going to fairness it is necessary to bear in mind the features referred to above (among others)'.

1   At paras 79–88.

6.122   In ruling for the Council, Goldring J thus made clear that the position as far as misconduct of non-state agents was concerned was wholly different from misconduct of state agents,[1] but left open the possibility of a successful application for a stay on the basis of entrapment by non-state agents in exceptional cases. He found that, had the panel applied the law properly in that regard, it would not have stayed proceedings as an abuse of process. For a journalist to go into a doctor's surgery and pretend to be a patient in circumstances similar to those in this case would seemingly be no more than to offer the doctor an unexceptional opportunity to commit the offence in any event, such that it is unlikely that the facts of this case, if undertaken with state authority, would ever have amounted to an entrapment even on the *Looseley* guidelines.[1]

1   At para 125.
2   See paras 3, 10, 129 and, by way of comparison, para 73 of the judgment.

6.123   *Re Saluja* is the latest, and might therefore be seen as the leading, authority on private entrapment, consolidating the ruling in *Looseley*. Whilst no authority has laid down a practical benchmark as to the extent of conduct that would be required to have proceedings stayed in a case of entrapment by a non-state agent, it is clear that that benchmark will very rarely be crossed.

6.124   Goldring J's judgment does beggar the question of what amounts to 'gross misconduct', or conduct of a non-state agent 'so serious', as to merit a stay of proceedings for these purposes? Bearing in mind the preceding authorities, both in relation to commercial and state entrapment,[1] the authors venture to suggest that 'gross misconduct' and conduct 'so serious' as to warrant a stay might mean conduct which (i) preys upon the vulnerability of a defendant whose capacity to resist the course of action being encouraged by the entrapper is seriously impaired,[2] (ii) amounts to a violation of the defendant's human rights by the non-state agent or (iii) is driven by a real degree of bad faith on their part – with malicious intent towards the victim of the entrapment in mind, rather than the mere pursuance of an ulterior motive (ie the sale of newspapers) in disregard of the detrimental effects that would obviously be caused to them. Although this list is by no means intended to be exhaustive, it seems that, in reality, only considerations such as these would be likely to render the state's subsequent reliance on evidence obtained by non-state agents an abuse of process in and of itself.

1   Recalling the case of *R v Moon* (discussed above para **6.80**), Goldring J's ruling in *Re Saluja*, that a different threshold needs to be met for a stay to be granted in cases of private entrapment as compared with cases of entrapment by state agents, one wonders whether the proceedings against the defendant in *Moon* would have been stayed as an entrapment had she been persuaded to sell drugs to an undercover journalist reporting, say, on the prevalence of street drug dealing in the UK or in a particular area of the country, rather than by a police officer. In those circumstances, Moon would surely still have been on strong ground in arguing that her conviction would affront the public conscience, given that the basis upon which the Court of Appeal ruled that she had been entrapped related in the main part to her state of mind as a drug addict, who supplied drugs out of sympathy to another 'addict' who was displaying the symptoms of withdrawal, ie even if the police did not positively act in bad faith in persuading Moon to supply drugs, the effect of that persuasion on a person in her vulnerable position rendered a stay of proceedings appropriate. Surely that moral principle would remain regardless of whether the entrapper was an agent of the state or an undercover journalist.
2   See the discussion of *R v Moon* at para **6.80** above.

Conclusions on private entrapment

6.125   Even if *Re Saluja* has resurrected an abuse of process doctrine in cases of private entrapment, pending further definition of the concepts of 'gross misconduct' and conduct 'so serious' as to warrant a stay, a defendant who has been the victim of a private entrapment is, in reality, likely to have better potential recourse by way of an application to exclude the evidence under section 78 of PACE rather than an application to stay as an abuse.

Entrapment as mitigation

6.126   As most defendants who lay claim to having been entrapped will have little remedy other than recourse to this point in mitigation, this chapter is worthy of conclusion by brief mention of the effect of entrapment on sentence.

6.127   The general position, set out in *R v Underhill*,[1] is that a court may, in principle, mitigate the penalty imposed upon an offender if it takes the view that he would not have committed the offence of which he has been convicted but for the actions of the entrapper (although that is obviously not to say the crime is 'state-created' in any broader sense than that the entrapper is an undercover police officer).

1   1 Cr App R (S) 270. The defendant's sentence was not reduced in this case, on account of the

Court of Appeal's conclusion that, on the evidence, the appellant had regularly been engaged in drug trafficking in any event so that there was no justification for reducing his sentence.

6.128   In *R v Beaumont,*[1] entrapment was held to be a substantial mitigating factor (*Underhill* was not cited in that ruling). That approach was applied in *R v Chapman and Denton*[2] and *R v Mackey and Shaw,*[3] where the appellant's sentences were reduced on account of 'entrapment'. However, more recently, the Court of Appeal in *R v Springer*[4] held that where undercover police officers purchased drugs from established dealers, that would not afford mitigation in sentence, following the approach actually applied to the facts in *R v Underhill* itself.

1   9 Cr App R (S) 342, CA.
2   11 Cr App R (S) 222, CA.
3   14 Cr App R (S) 53, CA.
4   [1999] 1 Cr App R (S) 217, CA.

Chapter 7

Double jeopardy

7.01 The prohibition of a defendant in criminal proceedings being tried more than once is as follows; 'a defendant should not be tried twice on the same general allegation'. Alternatively, a defendant should not be put in peril of conviction more than once for the same or substantially the same offence. Closely associated with the legal concept of res judicata, this prohibition is intended to prevent relitigation of similar factual issues and, in the context of crime, to prevent over-zealous prosecutors seeking to retry the same defendant against whom a previous prosecution has been dismissed by a court. It also prevents a prosecutor where proceedings have resulted 'successfully' with a conviction but one that is perceived as only being a precursor or dummy-run to subsequent more grave allegations.

7.02 The rationale of why double jeopardy has been regarded as repugnant to justice is explained by Professor Choo:

'to put a person in double jeopardy may increase the chances of his or her being convicted even though innocent, and will also undermine the moral integrity of the criminal process. The accused may, as a result of having revealed his complete defence at the first trial, be at a greater disadvantage at the second trial and thus less able to defend him or herself effectively. Irrespective of this, it is in any event morally objectionable to subject someone to the embarrassment, expense and anxiety of a second prosecution, with the possibility that a verdict might be returned which is inconsistent with that reached the first time. Considerations such as these ought to be borne in mind when considering stays of proceedings in the double jeopardy context'.[1]

1   A L-T Choo 'Halting Criminal Prosecutions' [1995] Crim LR at 866.

7.03 In *Green v United States*[1] Black J explained the principle in the following terms:

'The underlying idea, one that is deeply ingrained in at least the Anglo-American system of jurisprudence, is that the State with all its resources and power should not be allowed to make repeated attempts to convict an individual for an alleged offence, thereby subjecting him to embarrassment, expense and ordeal and compelling him to live in a continuing state of anxiety and insecurity, as well as enhancing the possibility that even though innocent he may be found guilty.'

1   (1957) 355 US 184.

7.04   The origin of the rule against double jeopardy lies in the ancient remedies of autrefois acquit ('AA') and autrefois convict ('AC'). These remedies are known as 'pleas in bar'. They constitute an alternative plea to guilty or not guilty. A defendant who pleads either AA or AC challenges the validity of the indictment, whereas a plea of guilty or not guilty presupposes its validity. Regarding AC, Blackburn J in *Wemyss v Hopkins*[1] said it is:

> 'a well established common law principle that where a person has been convicted and punished for an offence by a court of competent jurisdiction ... the conviction shall be a bar to all further proceedings for the same offence, and he shall not be punished again for the same matter'.

1   (1875) LR 10 QB 378 at 381.

7.05   The scope of AA and AC and their relationship with the rule against double jeopardy was considered by the House of Lords in *Connelly v DPP.*[1]

1   [1964] AC 1254.

7.06   The speeches of all five Law Lords in *Connelly* evidence a debate as to whether the rule against double jeopardy was only a modern reformulation of AA and AC and was thus co-terminus with their scope or instead whether the rule against double jeopardy was founded in a wider and discretionary power to halt a prosecution because it was for some reason, unfair.

7.07   In *Connelly* the House resolved in favour of the latter. Since *Connelly* all the leading authorities on double jeopardy have adopted the same approach. In *Humphrys* Lord Salmon recognised the existence of judicial power to intervene: 'if the prosecution amounts to an abuse of the process of the court and is oppressive and vexatious'.[1] Lord Edmund-Davies took a similar view: '... in my judgment, *Connelly* ... established that they [Judges] are vested with the power to do what the justice of the case clearly demands'.[2] More recently, in *R v Beedie*[3] the Court of Appeal confirmed that the rule against double jeopardy should not be regarded as within the doctrine of AA or AC, but should instead be conceived as part of the court's wider discretionary power to stay proceedings which constitute an abuse of process. In *Beedie* Lord Rose held that in *Connelly* the House had 'identified a narrow principle of autrefois, applicable only where the same offence was alleged in the second indictment'.[4]

1   [1977] AC 1 at 46.
2   [1977] AC 1 at 55.
3   [1998] QB 356.
4   [1998] QB 356 at 360.

7.08   Whilst *Connelly* did not go so far as to hold that AA and AC were otiose legal concepts the House obviously intended to relegate them and the concept of pleas in bar to a subsidiary role. Where a situation of double jeopardy was alleged unless the situation came clearly within AA and AC the abuse of process jurisdiction, one based on discretion, was always to be preferred.

7.09   This chapter can conveniently be divided into two parts: the first relates to the scope and availability of the pleas in bar, AA and AC, and the second to the scope and availability of the abuse of process jurisdiction in relation to double jeopardy.

AUTREFOIS ACQUIT AND CONVICT

The scope of the pleas as determined in Connelly

The factual situation

7.10   The factual situation in *Connelly* was briefly as follows. An armed robbery took place at a dairy in south London during which an employee of the dairy was shot and killed by the robbers. Subsequently Connelly was arrested and charged with the murder. The prosecution did not contend that he was the killer but contended that as he was part of the gang that had committed the murder, he had the requisite criminal intent to be legally responsible for it. At his trial before Roskill J, Connelly's defence was essentially two-fold. First, he claimed alibi—that he had not been involved in any way with the robbery and had not been present at the scene of the crime. Second, and alternatively, that in any event the prosecution had not proved that he had the requisite intent even if he had been a member of the gang and had been present. Connelly was tried only for murder, not for robbery in the alternative. This was because of a then practice rule laid down by the House of Lords in *R v Jones*[1] which stated that an indictment containing a count for murder should not be combined with any other count alleging a different offence.

1   [1918] 1 KB 416.

7.11   When it retired to consider its verdict, the jury at Connelly's trial had three options available to it: guilty or not guilty of murder but if not guilty of murder, then guilty of manslaughter. In the event, the jury convicted Connelly of murder. His subsequent appeal to the Court of Appeal was grounded on important misdirections committed by Roskill J during his summing up. Albeit with great reluctance, the Court of Appeal agreed and accordingly quashed Connelly's conviction for murder. In law therefore, at this point, Connelly stood acquitted of murder.

7.12   However, immediately after this appeal hearing, the prosecution then proceeded with the leave of the Court of Appeal, to lay a second indictment against Connelly, only alleging that he had committed a robbery at the dairy.

7.13   At the opening of his second trial Connelly pleaded AA, a plea which was rejected by the trial judge. Indisputably this rejection was legally correct. AA could not avail as Connelly was not being retried for murder, the offence for which he had been acquitted. However, while the trial judge rejected Connelly's plea of AA he declared that the prosecution ought not to proceed against Connelly for the count of robbery. This was unjust in his opinion; the factual issue of whether Connelly had taken part in the robbery had already been decided in the previous proceedings in Connelly's favour. The trial judge opined that the quashing of his conviction for murder by the Court of Appeal surely meant that it had been determined by that court that he was not present at the crime. The prosecution, however, disagreed and wished to press ahead with the trial. In this circumstance the judge noted that as AA was not engaged, he had no power to stop the prosecution despite his disapproval of it. Subsequently, Connelly was convicted by the second jury for robbery and sentenced to imprisonment. He appealed alleging that the ruling of the trial judge was erroneous.

7.14 The case duly came before the House of Lords for its consideration. The House was unanimous in the view that the plea of AA had properly been rejected by the trial judge and upheld Connelly's conviction. The House also set aside the practice direction given in *R v Jones* and held that the situation which had occurred in *Connelly* should not recur, ie that in future an indictment could be framed containing counts of both murder and, for example, robbery. What, however, has made *Connelly* a landmark case is the debate which divided the Lords, concerning the scope and availability of the pleas in bar. Lord Morris held that they remained adequate to cover all situations where injustice could be caused by double jeopardy. Lord Connelly disagreed holding that they were no longer adequate and should be replaced. He and the majority in the House preferred a new approach.

The governing principles underlying the availability of AA or AC

7.15 In an exhaustive judgment, Lord Morris considered all the authorities concerning pleas in bar in order to formulate a set of what he termed 'governing principles' which ought to determine in future the availability of either AA or AC. These remain extant and will be briefly considered below.

Same offence

7.16 The first and basic norm underlying both pleas in bar is that a person cannot be tried for an offence in respect of which they have previously been acquitted or convicted. As Lord Devlin in *Connelly* put it, 'it must be the same offence both in fact and in law'.[1] The narrowness of this test means that a person can be tried a second time for the same conduct where the offence charged is different from that charged at the earlier trial.[2] This was the situation in *Connelly*. The effect of this rule is now circumscribed both by the Criminal Procedure and Investigations Act 1996, ss 54–56 dealing with tainted acquittals, and Pts 9 and 10 of the Criminal Justice Act 2003, dealing with prosecution appeals and retrial for serious offences: see paras **7.62–7.63** and **7.67–69**.

1   [1998] QB 356 at 449.
2   See also Reid LJ's speech at 419.

7.17 As the test for either AA or AC is offence-based, it is immaterial that the facts under examination or the witnesses being called in the subsequent proceedings are the same as those in the earlier proceedings. Instead, what matters is whether the offence charged in the later indictment is the same as that offence charged in the earlier indictment.

7.18   This test can be illustrated by the facts in *Connelly* and *DPP v Humphrys.*[1] In *Connelly,* the facts of which have already been outlined in paras **7.10** and **7.14**, the evidence called and the facts relied on by the prosecution at the trial for robbery were the same as they had relied on in the earlier trial for murder, an offence for which the defendant had been acquitted. However, the House of Lords were unanimous in holding that the coincidence of factual evidence at the two trials did not form the basis of a successful plea for AA.[2]

1   [1977] AC 1.
2   See also *Thomas* [1950] 1 KB 26, where a plea of AC failed in circumstances where the defendant had been convicted of wounding and was subsequently following the death of the victim charged with murder.

7.19   In *Humphrys*, (the first occasion after *Connelly* when the House of Lords considered issues relating to double jeopardy) a plea of AA was similarly rejected. In that case the defendant had been charged with driving a motor vehicle while disqualified. He pleaded not guilty and in his defence gave evidence asserting that not only had he not driven on the date in question but that he had also not driven for a period of one year prior to that date. The jury acquitted Humphrys, obviously believing his testimony. Subsequently fresh evidence concerning the veracity of Humphrys' evidence came to light suggesting that he had driven at times during that preceding year and he was charged with perjury in relation to his evidence given at the first trial. He pleaded AA partly on the basis that the main witness against him, a police officer at the first trial who claimed to have observed Humphrys driving, would be giving the same evidence at the proposed second trial – evidence which the jury at the first trial must have rejected. The House rejected the plea of AA holding that the offence of driving while disqualified and of perjury were different and separable. What mattered was not that similar facts would be under scrutiny in both trials but whether similar crimes or offences would be under scrutiny. The plea of AA related only to offences not also facts and was therefore unavailable[1].

1   It should not be overlooked that H had pleaded guilty to forging an MOT certificate in relation to the car he had denied driving. This admission may have jaundiced the view of H's protestation of innocence.

7.20   The House in *Humphrys* also approved the Scottish case of *HM Advocate v Cairns.*[1] Here the defendant had been acquitted of murder and then subsequently confessed to a newspaper that he was guilty. On the strength of this confession he was subsequently tried for perjury despite the fact that the evidence would in effect be that he had committed the murder for which he had been acquitted. Lord Grant held that this did not bar a second trial, 'identity of the charges and not of the evidence is the crucial factor'.

1   1967 JC 37.

Prosecution of an alternative offence

7.21   The second principle enunciated by Lord Morris is that, a person cannot be tried for an offence in respect of which they could in previous proceedings have been lawfully convicted; where the offence tried in the earlier proceedings, in which the defendant was either convicted or acquitted, constituted an alternative to the offence now proposed to be tried.

7.22   This principle is not concerned with similarity of evidence across the two sets of proceedings but a purely legal question of whether the person's acquittal in the first proceedings necessarily in law involves an acquittal in the second. An 'implied acquittal' would be where the jury could lawfully have convicted the defendant on an alternative charge to the one being tried but have returned no verdict on it. An express acquittal arises when there are alternative charges, for example, theft and handling which are expressly averred in the indictment but are alternative to each other. Where a jury returned a verdict on one charge this would allow a defendant to plead autrefois to the other.

7.23   This principle can be explained by two examples. First, an implied acquittal: In *Connelly* the defendant could in his first trial have been convicted by the jury of murder or manslaughter. Accordingly, once he was acquitted of murder by the Court of Appeal this also constituted in law an acquittal of manslaughter. This was an implied acquittal. The defence argument in *Connelly* was that there was also an implied acquittal in relation to a charge of robbery. The House disagreed. It held that the evidence relied on by the prosecution to charge robbery would not have been sufficient to procure a conviction for manslaughter. His acquittal for murder and implied acquittal for manslaughter therefore did not bar a subsequent trial for robbery.

7.24   Second an express committal: In the more recent case of *R v Velasquez*[1] the defendant was tried for two offences, rape and attempted rape in relation to the same victim. In delivering its verdicts, the jury acquitted Velasquez of attempted rape but then went on to convict him of rape. With perhaps a degree of resourcefulness, he appealed his conviction for rape arguing that he was entitled to a plea of AA and his conviction for rape should be quashed. As he was acquitted of the attempt, the prosecution should then have been barred from seeking his conviction for the substantive offence. The Court of Appeal rejected this argument, holding that the defendant had not in law been acquitted of the substantive offence in relation to the attempt. It held that it did not offend the autrefois principles for a defendant where the facts were exactly the same to be not guilty of the attempt but guilty of the substantive offence. The charges were logical alternatives.

1   [1996] 1 Cr App Rep 155.

Substantially the same offence

7.25   The third principle is if the offence in respect of which a person is to be tried, is the same or substantially the same as that in respect of which they were in previous proceedings acquitted or convicted (or could have been convicted by way of alternative verdict). This rule is subject to one proviso: the offence charged in the second indictment must have been committed at the same time as the first alleged offence.

7.26   In Lord Morris's view the best test of whether the second charge is the same or substantially the same as the earlier is whether the evidence which is necessary to support the second charge would have been sufficient to prove a legal conviction on the first.[1] An example of this would be where it is shown that the offence for which the accused was convicted is a necessary step towards proving the offence now charged; as Lord Hodson put it in *Connelly*, whether the acquittal of the first charge necessarily involved an acquittal on the second'.[2] This principle can be illustrated by the following three cases:

(1) In *R v Dabhade*[3] the defendant was first charged with obtaining property by deception contrary to the Theft Act 1978, s 15(1). He pleaded not guilty and the prosecution decided to offer no evidence, leading to the charge being dismissed. A new charge based on the same facts, theft contrary to s 1 of the Theft Act 1968 was then preferred. Dabhade pleaded AA in relation to the theft charge, submitting that the two charges were, in the circumstances of his case, the same or substantially the same (even though theft is not an alternative verdict on a charge of obtaining by deception). The Court of Appeal rejected the plea of AA, holding that it did not come within the requirement that the evidence supporting the theft charge would have sufficed to secure a conviction of the obtaining by deception charge. It held that, although in some cases because of the evidence theft is an alternative verdict to obtaining by deception, the evidence in this case to support a charge of theft would not suffice alone to support a charge of obtaining by deception.

(2) In *R v Valasquez*[4] the Court of Appeal was minded to apply Lord Hodson's proposition quoted above and hold that an acquittal on an attempt should bar a conviction for the full offence on a later indictment. The two crimes charged, rape and attempted rape, were arguably substantially the same. However, it held on the facts before it that there was no necessary inconsistency between the verdicts delivered in that case. In its discretion, therefore, the court, it is submitted, declined to follow this principle. In *Velasquez* the Court of Appeal was in fact applying its discretion to refuse relief believing that no injustice was done to the defendant by the verdicts.

(3) In *Salvi*[5] the defendant, after being acquitted of a charge of wounding with intent to murder was, after the victim's death, indicted for murder and convicted. His plea of AA failed in the Court of Appeal. It held that a person can be convicted in law for murder without an intention to murder being proven. Therefore the evidence on the indictment for murder would not necessarily have supported a conviction on the first, wounding with intent to murder.

1   [1964] AC 1254 at 1310–1311.
2   [1964] AC 1254 at 1332.
3   (1992) 96 Cr App Rep 146.
4   See para **7.24**.
5   (1857) 10 Cox CC 481n.

7.27   The judgment of the Court of Appeal in *Valasquez* is, it is submitted, an endorsement of the view of Lord Devlin who, in *Connelly*, disagreed with Lord Morris that this third principle should properly form part of the autrefois doctrine. Lord Devlin's view was that this principle belonged more to courts' inherent discretionary power pursuant to an abuse of process rather than to autrefois:

> 'I have no difficulty about the idea that one set of facts may be substantially, but not exactly the same as another. I have more difficulty with the idea that an offence may be substantially the same as another in its legal characteristics; legal characteristics are precise things and are either the same or not. If I had felt that the doctrine of autrefois was the only form of relief available to the defendant I should be tempted to stretch the doctrine as far as it would go. But as that is not my view I am inclined to favour keeping it within limits that are precise'.[1]

1   [1964] AC 1254 at 1340.

7.28   In *R v Beedie*[1] the Court of Appeal opined that this principle should not be viewed as part of the doctrine of autrefois at all, but should instead, in the absence of special circumstances, lead to the exercise of the wider discretionary power to stay proceedings on the grounds of abuse. In the light of *Beedie* it may be that the decision in *Dabhade* should be reclassified as falling under the abuse jurisdiction rather than that of autrefois.

1   See para **7.100**.

'In peril' of conviction

7.29   Lord Morris' fourth principle is that for the previous set of criminal proceedings to be able to form the basis for a plea of AA or AC, they must have borne the following two features:

(a)   that the defendant's guilt must have been decided upon; and

(b)   was 'adjudicated', i e made by a court of competent jurisdiction.

7.30   The meaning of 'adjudication' was strictly defined in *DPP v Nasralla*[1] as the occurrence of any of the following events: a jury's express verdict, a plea of guilty being entered and accepted or a verdict of not guilty having been directed pursuant to the Criminal Justice Act 1967, s 17.[2]

1   [1967] 2 AC 238.
2   In reciting this list, the court perhaps should have included Magistrates' Court Act 1980, s 27; a magistrates' dismissal of a prosecutor's information under s 15 constitutes an acquittal.

7.31   An example of the narrow interpretation of adjudication is where a court has acted *ultra vires* and the accused could never have been legally convicted. It has been held that the accused was never therefore technically in peril or in jeopardy. See for example *R v West*[1] where magistrates purported to acquit the accused of the offence which was triable only on indictment. Having realised this error the prosecution then recharged the accused who then pleaded AA in order to resist his committal for trial. This was rejected: as the summary proceedings were a nullity, the subsequent committal and trial were unobjectionable.

1   [1964] 1 QB 15.

Situations that do not form a basis for a plea of AA or AC

7.32   The cases considered below are mostly concerned with proceedings in the magistrates' court. As a matter of legal form, the pleas of AA and AC are not available in those proceedings as they are pleas in bar to an indictment. However, in practice they are recognised as valid defences in the lower court on the basis that it is bound by the rule against double jeopardy. See *Williams v DPP*.[1]

1   [1991] 3 All ER 651 at 654.

Discharge of an accused at committal proceedings following a ruling of no case to answer

7.33   In *R v Manchester City Stipendiary Magistrate, ex p Snelson*[1] the accused was discharged at his committal following the offering of no evidence by the prosecution. Subsequently, the prosecution initiated fresh proceedings in relation to which the accused asserted AA. His plea was that as the magistrates had already discharged him for the offence in question, they were unable to reconsider it. The magistrate disagreed and committed the accused at trial. The accused sought judicial review of this finding. Lord Widgery CJ upheld the magistrate's decision, holding that a plea of AA was not available to a defendant by reason of his earlier discharge in committal proceedings.[2]

1   [1978] 2 All ER 62.
2   But see also limits imposed as a matter of discretion on the prosecution's right to pursue charges basically the same as those already dismissed, *R v Horsham Justices, ex p Reeves* (1980) 75 Cr App R 236n considered at para **7.87** below.

Withdrawal of a summons by the prosecution in the magistrates' court prior to the accused having pleaded to it

7.34   In *R v Grays Justices, ex p Low*[1] the prosecution issued a summons for actual bodily harm against the accused which was subsequently withdrawn once the accused accepted a bind over. Subsequently, the alleged victim of the assault (who felt aggrieved at the prosecution's decision to accept a bind over) launched a private prosecution and a second summons was issued. The accused pleaded AA in relation to this second summons. The magistrates disagreed and the accused sought judicial review. Lord Nolan upheld the magistrates' refusal to recognise a plea of AA. He held that the withdrawal of a summons did not operate as a bar to the issuance of a further summons for the same charge because there had been no adjudication by the court on the merits of the allegation contained in the first summons and the defendant had not been put in peril of conviction on it.[2]

1   [1990] 1 QB 54.
2   However, on the ground of abuse of process the court set aside the summons—the alleged victim had not told the court, as he should have done, when he applied for the issuance of the second summons about there being a first trial and what had happened then.

7.35   The same point was also made in *R v Liverpool Magistrates' Court, ex p Slade*.[1] If a summons is withdrawn before a trial and therefore as a result the case is dismissed, a plea of AA cannot be made in relation to a subsequent summons for the same offence because there has been no earlier trial on the merits. See also *Brookes,*[2] where acceptance by the prosecution of a plea of not guilty to grievous bodily harm (Offences Against the Person Act 1861, s 20) did not establish a plea of AA to bar a subsequent charge of GBH with intent (s 18).

1   [1998] 1 All ER 60.
2   [1995] Crim LR 630.

Notices of discontinuance

7.36   In the same vein, a plea of AA cannot arise in relation to proceedings which are begun for the same offence charged in earlier proceedings but which are terminated by the prosecution pursuant to it serving a notice of discontinuance under the Prosecution of Offences Act 1985, s 23. A plea in bar will not thwart a prosecution proceedings against the same defendant in respect of whom they were earlier discontinued.

Where 'the accused was, as a matter of fact, never in peril or in jeopardy because the earlier proceedings against him were irregular and/or without jurisdiction'

7.37   This rule can be broken down into three sub-categories as follows:

(1)   Where the summons or charge against the accused has been dismissed before he has pleaded to it: this concerns what was conceptualised by Roujier J in *Williams v DPP*[1] as a 'temporal question'. In *Williams*, a motorist was charged with driving with excess alcohol in his breath. When he was called on to plead at court but before he did so, his advocate took a legal objection to the charge, which because of an error in procedure committed by the police was bound to succeed. The prosecution realising their mistake applied for an adjournment to enable the bringing of an amended summons but this was refused by the court who then dismissed the summons. However, subsequently the prosecution having corrected the legal error brought a fresh summons which was now legally unanswerable by the defendant. The defendant pleaded AA contending that because the earlier summons had been dismissed he could not be tried again on a charge based on the same facts. The prosecution conceded that the offence charged in the second proceedings was the same or substantially the same offence as that charged in the first, ie driving on a road after ingesting an excess of alcohol. The issue, however, was whether the defendant had been in jeopardy at the time when the justices dismissed the original charge. Roujier J concluded, pursuant to his 'temporal question', that the first set of proceedings had not reached such a stage that the defendant had been in danger of conviction. He held that this would only have arisen once he had actually pleaded, and only then would he have been in jeopardy or in peril. To support this view, Roujier J quoted with approval the remarks of Lush J in *Haynes v Davis*[2] who held in relation to the expression

'acquittal on the merits' that 'in my view the expression is used by way of antithesis to a dismissal of the charge upon some technical ground which had been a bar to the adjudicating upon it'.

(2)   Dismissal of proceedings against an accused following the withdrawal of a charge by the prosecution on the grounds of its legal defectiveness; the case of *Dabhade* has already been considered in para **7.26**. The accused was originally charged with obtaining property by deception but the prosecution offered no evidence and the charge was dismissed. A new charge of theft was subsequently preferred. The accused claimed AA and sought judicial review. The court held that because of the manifest defects in the original charge the accused had in fact never been in danger of conviction in relation to it. The court established as a principle of law that if the summary dismissal of a charge is because it is apparent that it is defective for any reason then the defendant has never been in danger of conviction and so cannot claim AA. There was *'no real sense'* in which it could be said that the defendant was in jeopardy on the first charge. To support this view, the court stated that it would be absurd to prescribe a situation whereby the prosecution keep alive a charge it has no intention of pursuing, merely to defeat a feared attempt of a plea of AA *'in circumstances which are both technical and without merit.'*

If a new charge, which was more appropriate to the facts, was substituted, then a consensual dismissal of the original charge and the substitution of a new one does not give rise to AA.

(3)   Where the proceedings are a legal nullity, a plea of AA or AC arising from them cannot be pleaded in relation to subsequent proceedings. Thus, in *R v Kent Justices, ex p Machin*[3] it was stated that the prosecution would be entitled to bring fresh proceedings where the magistrates had acted ultra vires in convicting and committing the defendant for sentence, without having followed the correct procedure for determining mode of trial. In *R v West*[4] the defendant was not entitled to rely on AA where the magistrates had acted ultra vires in acquitting him of an indictable only offence.

1   [1991] 1 WLR 1160.
2   [1915] 1 KB 332 at 340.
3   [1952] 2 QB 355.
4   (1964) 1 QB 15.

7.38   In less clear-cut cases the application of this rule can appear harsh on the defendant. In both *R v Pressick*[1] and *R v Dorking Justices, ex p Harrington*[2] the prosecution, at a hearing which was listed for a trial sought an adjournment of it, but this application was refused by the magistrates who also dismissed the charges. Subsequently, the prosecution initiated fresh proceedings in respect of which the accused pleaded AA. In *Pressick* the Divisional Court held that the magistrates had acted within their jurisdiction to refuse the adjournment and to dismiss the charge and therefore a plea of AA was properly founded. However, Lord Roskill in *ex p Harrington* held that the magistrates had acted in a grossly unfair way towards the prosecution, so that their dismissal of the prosecution's summonses was without jurisdiction and was a legal nullity. A remedy of mandamus was therefore granted to the prosecution with the effect that the case would be remitted to the magistrates for re-hearing. A third permutation is illustrated by *Holmes v Campbell*[3] where the prosecutor did not appear at the trial following a mistake over dates and the summonses were dismissed. The Divisional Court held that although the magistrates were entitled to dismiss the charges against the defendant, the first hearing was not therefore a nullity as per *Harrington*. Nonetheless, because for legal reasons he could not have been convicted, there was no acquittal on the merits.

1   [1978] Crim LR 377.
2   [1994] 2 All ER 474.
3   (1998) 162 JP 655, QBD.

7.39   For a defendant who could not be held responsible for the magistrates' decision to dismiss and who, presumably, had arrived in court in the expectation (and possibly apprehension) of a trial then to face a complete retrial because of magistrates' misbehaviour seems a prospect which the rules relating to AA and AC were intended to prevent. These rules are defendant-orientated. Furthermore, in *Harrington*, the court cut the link between a defendant's sense of ordeal of being subject to trial and successive legal proceedings against him, the former appearing to have no relevance to the latter.

A finding of contempt of court in relation to similar facts in respect of which the accused was subsequently convicted

7.40   In *R v Sherry*[1] the defendant was convicted of an offence of conspiracy to abduct a child. However, prior to his trial he had been committed to prison for contempt for a violation of a civil court injunction banning him from removing the child from its mother. The defendant claimed that the finding that he was in contempt constituted a valid plea of AC in relation to his subsequent trial for conspiracy. However, the Court of Appeal disagreed on two grounds:

(a)   AC did not arise because the defendant had never previously been charged with the offence of conspiracy and there were no previous proceedings where he could possibly have been convicted of this offence;

(b)   in any event, the proceedings for contempt were civil not criminal proceedings and therefore AC could not arise. In *R v Green*[2] it was held that although a plea of double jeopardy is available in civil as in criminal proceedings, such a plea cannot jump the boundary between those different types of proceedings.

1   [1993] Crim LR 536.
2   [1993] Crim LR 46.

7.41   The same view was taken in *DPP v Tweddle*[1] where the applicant had breached a non-molestation injunction and in consequence received a sentence of 10 weeks' imprisonment for contempt. Subsequently he was prosecuted for assault arising out of the same incident. He submitted AC which was rejected on the ground that the contempt jurisdiction was civil and not to criminal and in any event, his criminal prosecution was not vexatious. Section 1 of the Domestic Violence, Crime and Victims Act 2004 which came into force on

1 July 2007 provides that breach of a non-molestation order will be punishable as a criminal offence. It is specifically provided that a person convicted of this offence cannot also be punished for contempt in relation to the same conduct, and vice versa.

1   (1 March 2001, unreported).

A finding of a foreign court of competent jurisdiction that the accused is guilty of the same offence for which he has been tried by an English court but where there is no prospect of the accused being punished by the foreign court in relation to the conviction awarded

7.42   In *Treacy v DPP*[1] Lord Diplock held that AA and AC was 'a doctrine which has always applied whether the previous conviction or acquittal based on the same facts was by an English court or by a foreign court'. This view was expressed obiter and it is submitted there is a lack of authority determining this issue. In its 2001 report on double jeopardy, the Law Commission[2] was unable to unearth any case (see para **6.34**). The only case is *R v Aughet*[3], a First World War case where the English court upheld a claim of AC on the basis that the accused had already been convicted of the same offence by a court-martial in Belgium. *Treacy* was not however followed in *R v Thomas*.[4] Thomas was tried in England for the same conduct for which he had already been convicted in absentia by a court in Italy. He pleaded AC in relation to the English trial. The court rejected this plea holding that the mere fact of a foreign conviction is not, of itself, sufficient to found a plea of AC unless the accused had genuinely been in jeopardy, which in this case meant being in jeopardy of punishment post-conviction. On the facts, Thomas had fled to England and could not be extradited to Italy. In view of this, the Court of Appeal held that he was in no real risk of danger of punishment in Italy and therefore had not, in relation to the Italian proceedings, ever been in peril or in jeopardy. The court also took into account the fact that the defendant had been convicted in Italy in absence and had taken no part in his trial there.

1   [1971] AC 537 at 562.
2   Cmnd 5048, March 2001.
3   (1918) 13 Cr App R 101.
4   [1985] QB 604.

7.43   The principle enunciated in *Thomas* concerning the necessary connection between jeopardy or peril and punishment was followed by the Privy Council in *Richards v R*.[1] The Board held that a finding of guilt alone is not a sufficient condition for a plea of AC, that finding has to be accompanied by the infliction of an actual penalty in order for the plea to succeed. Lord Bridge held that the underlying rationale of AC was to prevent double punishment and could therefore only be based on a complete adjudication against the accused which as a matter of definition must include the final disposal of the case by the passing of a sentence.

1   [1993] AC 217.

The taking of an offence into consideration when passing sentence for other offences of which the offender has been convicted

7.44 In *R v Nicholson*[1] the accused was convicted and at his sentencing asked for the other offences to be taken into consideration. This occurred. Subsequently his conviction was quashed and the prosecution decided to proceed on those offences. The accused pleaded AC but this was rejected on the ground that he had not been 'convicted' in respect of them. The Court of Appeal, however held that the practice of trying a person for offences previously only taken into consideration was generally undesirable.

1   (1947) 32 Cr App R 98.

The issuing of a police caution

7.45 In Jones v Whalley[1] a police caution was issued for an offence of assault occasioning actual bodily harm. The victim of the offence then began a private prosecution. The Administrative Court held that a police caution could not found the basis for a plea of AC as it did not have the status of a conviction. The decision was overturned on appeal to the House of Lords[2] on the narrow grounds that the defendant was assured in taking the caution that he would not subsequently be prosecuted and therefore had a legitimate expectation.[3]

1   [2005] EWHC 931 (Admin).
2   [2006] UKHL 41, [2007] 1 AC 63.
3   The broader question as to whether it would ever be other than an abuse of process to bring a private prosecution following the issuing of a caution was unfortunately not decided and therefore it seems that the issue will depend upon the wording of the caution issued.

A finding of guilt in disciplinary proceedings, even where that finding is followed by the imposition of a penalty

7.46 In *R v Hogan*[1], prison escapees were punished by justices with loss of remission pursuant to the Prison Rules. Subsequently, they stood trial for an offence of escaping by force and pleaded AC. This was rejected.

1   [1960] 2 QB 513.

7.47 This issue also arose in *Secretary of State for Trade and Industry v Baker*[1]. Baker was a director of a bank which became insolvent. The Secretary of State decided to seek his disqualification as a director pursuant to the Company Directors Disqualification Act 1986. Baker pleaded AC because he actually had already faced disciplinary proceedings brought against him by his regulator, the Securities and Futures Authority (SFA). Those proceedings had been based substantially on the same conduct as that on which the disqualification proceedings were founded. This claim was rejected, the Court of Appeal finding that the SFA proceedings were concerned with whether Baker had professional competence (and was therefore a fit and proper person to run a bank) whereas the CDDA action was concerned with whether acting as a director of a company, he was unfit to be concerned with its management.

1   (1998) Times, 6 July.

7.48   In *R (Redgrave) v Metropolitan Police Comr*[1] a police officer faced a disciplinary charge arising out of conduct which had given rise to a criminal charge. In respect of the criminal charge, he had been discharged at committal. He submitted AA, as the factual allegation was the same in both sets of proceedings. The Administrative Court disagreed; a discharge at committal is not equivalent to an acquittal. Secondly as a matter of principle AC applied only to courts of competent jurisdiction, not a disciplinary tribunal.

1   [2003] EWCA Civ 4, (2003) 1 WLR 1136.

A finding of fact in care proceedings

7.49   In *R v L*[1] the defendant's three month old son, E, died. In the course of care proceedings for the defendant's partner's other son, the Family Court concluded that E had died of non-accidental injuries but it could not be ascertained whether these had been inflicted by the defendant or E's mother. In the defendant's subsequent trial for the murder of E, an application to stay proceedings was rejected and the refusal upheld by the Court of Appeal. The family proceedings had been concerned with different issues and the defendant had never been at risk of conviction.

1   [2007] 1 Cr App R 1.

Proceedings before the Special Immigration Appeals Commission ('SIAC').

7.50   In R v IK, R v AB, R v KA[1] a certificate was issued by the Secretary of State for the Home Department against IK under s 21(1) of the Anti-Terrorism, Crime and Security Act 2001 on the basis that IK was believed to have links with Al-Qaeda. As a result IK was detained for 16 months. The decision was appealed to SIAC and the certificate was cancelled. Criminal proceedings were then launched under the Terrorism Act 2000. The proceedings were stayed as an abuse of process on the basis that although SIAC was not a criminal court, the consequences for the defendant were so similar that the proceedings should be stayed. The Court of Appeal allowed the prosecutor's appeal, following R v L above and maintaining the strict rule that, whatever the practical consequences, as the SIAC proceedings were not criminal IK was never at risk of conviction and they could not bar a subsequent criminal prosecution. In addition the criminal proceedings involved different issues and different evidence than the SIAC proceedings.

1   [2007] 2 Cr App R 15.

Civil proceedings following acquittal in criminal proceedings.

7.51   In Raja v Van Hoogstraaten[1] an acquittal in criminal proceedings for murder and manslaughter was held not to be a bar to civil proceedings pursued by the estate of the murder victim. In particular the High Court had regard to the lower standard of proof in civil proceedings and the different rules relating to the admissibility of evidence.[2] In Y v Norway,[3] the European Court of Human Rights supported such an approach so long as the decision on compensation did not contain a statement imputing the criminal liability of the defendant. The issue is likely to be relevant to criminal practitioners in the context of Anti-Social Behaviour Orders ('ASBOs'). Although classified as civil proceedings and without the criminal rules of evidence, the applicable standard of proof is the criminal standard. Two questions have arisen in relation to ASBOs and unfortunately no answer has been given in relation to either of them.

1   [2005] All ER (D) 264 (Dec).
2   *Raja v Van Hoogstraten* was followed in *Ashley and another v Ch Const Sussex Police* [2008] 3 All ER 573, HL.
3   (2005) 41 EHRR 87.

7.52   In *Daar v Ch Const of Merseyside Police*[1] the appellant brought civil proceedings against the police for false imprisonment, assault and malicious prosecution arising out of matters for which he had been charged and acquitted. The local authority, at the police's request, then brought proceedings for an ASBO relying, in part, upon the incidents of which the defendant had been acquitted. The ASBO was granted, the District Judge finding that the allegations for which the defendant had been acquitted were proved. All three proceedings were based on essentially the same evidence. The question the court decided was that, on the facts of that case, the civil proceedings were not an abuse of process by calling into question the determination made against the appellant in the ASBO proceedings.

1 [2005] EWCA Civ 1774.

7.53   In relation to the ambit of the case, it was 'not fruitful to consider' whether the ASBO application may have been stayed as an abuse. It is submitted that each ASBO application will turn on its own facts. If the evidence submitted is the same as that which was used in proceedings which led to an acquittal, then it would be an abuse of process for those matters to be re-litigated. However, in many cases there will be hearsay evidence, inadmissible in the criminal proceedings, which would justify the court coming to the conclusion that the criminal standard of proof was reached.

7.54   In *R(W) v DPP*,[1] one of the questions before the court was whether, where an ASBO specifically prohibited conduct which would be an offence in any event, a defendant would be entitled to plead AA or AC to breach of the order where he has already been convicted of the specific offence in criminal proceedings. Due to the judgment on a preceding question, it was not necessary to give an answer to this question but it is submitted that in such circumstances, the offence of which the accused has already been convicted or acquitted is a necessary step towards proving the offence now charged and a defendant should be entitled to plead AA or AC in such a case. Alternatively, it is submitted that such proceedings would be a clear abuse of process, involving sequential prosecutions arising out of the same activity.

1   [2005] EWCA Civ 1333, (2005) Times, 20 June.

Procedure on autrefois pleas

7.55   The most obvious moment for pleading autrefois is at arraignment but before the indictment is put to the accused. If the accused is legally represented the conventional procedure is for the plea to be entered in writing and signed by counsel using the following form of words:

> '[*Name of accused*] says that the Queen ought not further to prosecute the indictment against him/her because he has been lawfully acquitted/convicted of the offence charged therein'.

Having made the plea the prosecution must either admit it is good or join issue. Pursuant to s 122 of the Criminal Justice Act 1988 it is then the role of the trial judge sitting without a jury to determine whether the plea is correctly made or not.

7.56   In *Coughlan*[1] the Court of Appeal held that if a person enters a plea of AA/AC they must establish their plea on a balance of probabilities. Evidence can be called in support of contentions made by either side as if the hearing were a voir dire. The court can also consider the validity of the earlier court's jurisdiction: see *West*.[2] If the plea succeeds it bars any further proceedings in relation to the indictment. If it fails, the indictment must then be put and the accused can then plead guilty or not guilty in the normal way.

1   (1976) 63 Cr App R 33.
2   See para **7.37**.

7.57   In seeking to prove the validity of either AA or AC, a defendant is not confined to a comparison between the latter and the earlier indictment or to the records of the court. Evidence can be called from other sources in relation to the identity of the persons, dates and facts as is required. In other words the test is one of substance not form. In *West* this principle was interpreted as entitling a later court to inquire into the validity of an earlier court's jurisdiction and hold that the initial proceedings were a nullity.

7.58   A plea can be made at any time during the currency of the criminal proceedings even after the accused has pleaded guilty. In *Cooper v New Forest District Council*[1] the accused pleaded guilty to various breaches of planning enforcement notices and was sentenced by the magistrates. Subsequently, the accused was advised that a plea of autrefois was available and he appealed to the Crown Court acting in its appellant capacity. The Crown Court refused the appeal because of the previous unequivocal plea of guilty before the magistrates. The accused sought judicial review of this refusal and the Divisional Court held that despite the plea of guilty, a plea in bar was so fundamental to the fairness of the proceedings and was a special plea that the Crown Court should accept the plea and consider it.

1   [1992] Crim LR 877.

STATUTORY EXCEPTIONS TO THE AUTREFOIS RULE

Case stated

7.59   Pursuant to the Magistrates' Courts Act 1980, s 111 the prosecution may appeal to the Divisional Court in the case of a summary acquittal on the ground that the acquittal 'is wrong in law or is an excess of jurisdiction'. If the prosecution appeal succeeds, the Divisional Court can substitute its own finding or order a rehearing.

Appeal to the House of Lords

7.60   Pursuant to the Administration of Justice Act 1960, ss 1 and 2 when the Court of Appeal quashes a conviction, the prosecution can appeal to the House of Lords.

Retrial following successful appeal against conviction

7.61   Pursuant to the Criminal Appeal Act 1968, s 1, the Court of Appeal has the power to order retrial whenever it allows an appeal against conviction if this is in the interests of justice.

Tainted acquittals

7.62   Pursuant to the Criminal Procedure and Investigations Act 1996, ss 54–56, a procedure has been created whereby a person can be retried for an offence for which he or she has already been acquitted so long as that acquittal is judged to be 'tainted'.

7.63   These sections were inserted into the CPIA 1996 as a result of fears concerning the practice of 'jury nobbling'. Such was the concern that major criminals were evading justice by corrupting or intimidating jurors that Parliament created an unprecedented procedure whereby a valid acquittal could be quashed by the High Court if it was satisfied that four conditions set out in s 55 were satisfied. The first condition, the most significant for present purposes, is as follows: 'that it appears to the High Court likely that, but for the interference or intimidation [of a juror or witness], the acquitted person would not have been acquitted.' The relevant procedure to be followed is set out at Pt 40 of the Criminal Procedure Rules. No application has yet been made to quash an acquittal.

Army Act 1955, s 33

7.64 A person tried by a court-martial shall not subsequently retried by a civil court.

Magistrates' Courts Act 1980, s 27

7.65 'Where on the summary trial of an information for an offence triable either way the court dismissed the information, the dismissal shall have the same effect as an acquittal on an indictment.'

Extradition

7.66 See **Chapter 8** of this work for consideration of this topic.

Criminal Justice Act 2003

7.67 Part 9 of the Criminal Justice Act 2003 (CJA) is entitled 'Prosecution Appeals'. First, since 4 April 2005, the prosecution is able to apply for leave to appeal against any 'terminating' ruling other than a ruling discharging the jury, or a ruling which may be challenged under any other procedure. Secondly, when brought into force, the prosecution will be allowed to apply for leave to appeal against any ruling or rulings as to the admissibility or inadmissibility of prosecution evidence in relation to cases involving certain sexual, violent or drug offences, made prior to the opening of the defence case. Leave will only be given if the ruling or rulings significantly weaken the prosecution case. The Court of Appeal can only reverse the ruling if it was wrong in law, involved an error of law or principle or was unreasonable.

7.68 Part 10 of the Criminal Justice Act is entitled 'Retrial for Serious Offences' and was brought into force on 4 April 2005. Pursuant to s 76, the DPP may apply to the Court of Appeal for an order quashing a person's acquittal and directing that the person be retried. The court may only grant such orders if it is satisfied that, first, there is new and compelling evidence, and, secondly, a retrial is in the interests of justice (ss 78 and 79).

7.69 'New' evidence is defined in s 78(2) of the CJA as evidence which was not adduced in the proceedings in which the person was acquitted. This contrasts with an early draft of the Criminal Justice Bill, which defined new evidence as evidence 'not available or known to an officer or prosecutor at the time of the acquittal', may conflict with the UK's obligations under the International Covenant on Civil and Political Rights, Art 14.7[1] as it may allow a retrial on the basis of evidence which was known but not used at the time of the original trial for example, for tactical reasons.[2]

1   See para **7.135** below.
2   See Joint Committee on Human Rights 'Criminal Justice Bill: Further Report' HL Paper 118, HC 724.

7.70 In *R v Dunlop*,[1] the first such application to come before the Court of Appeal under these provisions, the Court of Appeal considered three arguments in relation to whether it was in the interests of justice to order a re-trial. In 1991 D had been tried and acquitted of a murder which took place in 1989. During 1999 he confessed to the murder on a number of occasions and subsequently pleaded guilty to perjury for lying at the original trial.

1   [2007] 1 WLR 1657.

7.71   Arguments in relation to prejudicial pre-trial publicity and delay received short shrift from the Court but more consideration was given to an argument that the defendant had only confessed to the murder on the basis that he could not be re-tried for it. This was not held to be a sufficient reason to prevent a re-trial taking place. The Court of Appeal may, however, have been influenced by two factors specific to that case. First, the defendant did not seek to resile from his previous confessions and therefore the overwhelming likelihood was that he would not contest any future trial. In *R v Miell*,[1] the second application under these provisions, similar facts arose except that the defendant had retracted his confession and in the course of argument before the Court of Appeal, significant doubts were raised as to its reliability. In those circumstances the application for a re-trial was refused.

1   [2008] 1 Cr App R 23.

7.72   Secondly in *R v Dunlop*, the assertion that the defendant would not have confessed if he knew he could be re-tried for murder was undermined by an interview in which he demonstrated his awareness of the Consultation Paper on the exception taking place at that time. Therefore, although it may not be surprising that the Court of Appeal quashed the acquittal in that case there may be scope for the arguments succeeding with more favourable facts. When proposing the new law, the Law Commission recognised that there may be circumstances in which it would be unjust to reopen acquittals which had taken place before the Act came into force in circumstances in which the defendant had acted to his prejudice in the belief that he could not be prosecuted.

7.73   The DPP must be satisfied, when applying for such an order that it would not be inconsistent with the UK's obligations under Arts 31 or 34 of the European Union Treaty relating to the principle of '*ne bis in idem*'. The Court of Appeal does not specifically have to be satisfied that these obligations are not interfered with, but it may be able to consider this factor in deciding whether a retrial is in the interests of justice. These provisions apply to any offence listed in the Criminal Justice Act 2003, Sch 5, Pt 1 of the Act, for which the defendant has previously been acquitted in the UK (other than Scotland), or elsewhere in the world if that acquittal would otherwise act as a bar to proceedings in the UK. They obviously constitute a rupture with the tradition of the English common law concerned with AA and the supremacy of trial by jury.

ABUSE OF PROCESS

7.74   The starting point for any consideration of the law of abuse of process in relation to double jeopardy is the House of Lords decision in *Connelly*.[1]

1   See para **7.05**.

7.75   In *Connelly*, one of the grounds of appeal was that the trial judge in the second trial was wrong to hold that he had no discretion to stay the proceedings even if he held that they were unfair. Before the House, Connelly contended that a court possessed an inherent power to protect an accused against abuses of criminal procedure. Notwithstanding the narrowness of the availability of the pleas in bar, the court could, pursuant to this power, stay the proceedings if it felt the trial would be unfair. The issues of whether a criminal court possessed such power beyond the scope of the pleas in bar and whether a court had any overall responsibility to ensure the fairness of the proceedings before it, preoccupied the speeches of all five Law Lords.

7.76   Lord Morris contended that a court did not have the power to stay a prosecution because it judged it to be unfair unless this unfairness came within the scope of a plea in bar. His view can be encapsulated from the following short extracts from his speech:

'... that generally speaking a prosecutor has as much right as a defendant to demand a verdict of a jury on an outstanding indictment, and where either demands a verdict a judge has no jurisdiction to stand in the way of it ... It would in my judgment, be an unfortunate innovation if it were held that the power of a court to prevent any abuse of its process or to ensure compliance with correct procedure enabled a judge to suppress a prosecution merely because he regretted that it was taking place. There is no abuse of process if to a charge which is properly brought before the court and which is framed in an indictment to which no objection can in any way be taken there is no plea such as that of autrefois acquit or convict which can successfully be made'.[1]

1   [1964] AC 1254 at 1304.

7.77   However, Lord Morris did concede that:

'There is inherent in our criminal administration a policy and a tradition that even in the case of wrongdoers, there must be an avoidance of anything that savours of oppression ... The power to prevent abuses of its own process and to control its own procedure must in the criminal court, include a power to safeguard an accused from oppression or prejudice'.[1]

1   [1964] AC 1254 at 1301.

7.78   Lord Devlin expressing the majority view held that the courts did possess an inherent jurisdiction to enforce rules in order to ensure that the court's process was used fairly. He stated:

'... a general power, taking various specific forms, to prevent unfairness to the accused has always been a part of the English criminal law, and I shall illustrate this with special reference to the framing of the indictments. Secondly, if the power of the prosecutor to spread his case over any number of indictments was unrestrained there could be grave injustice to defendants. Thirdly, a controlling power of this character is well established in the civil law'.[1]

1   [1964] AC 1254 at 1347.

7.79 Later Lord Devlin added, in a passage which has now become famous for both its statement of principle and its prescience:

'The fact that the Crown has, as is to be expected, and that private prosecutors have (as is also to be expected, for they are usually public authorities) generally behaved with great propriety in the conduct of prosecutions, up till now avoided the need for any consideration of this point. Now that it emerges, it is seen to be one of great constitutional importance. Are the courts to rely on the Executive to protect their process from abuse? Have they not themselves an inescapable duty to secure fair treatment for those who come or are brought before them? To questions of this sort there is only one possible answer. The courts cannot contemplate for a moment the transference to the Executive of the responsibility for seeing that the process of law is not abused'.[1]

1   [1964] AC 1254 at 1354.

7.80 Lord Devlin argued that the courts have always possessed a general power to prevent any unfairness to an accused, this after all was the basis for the development of the judge's rules and the common law duty of prosecution disclosure.[1]

1   Rules were formulated in various cases concerned with the questioning of suspects in police detention. They were superseded by the codes of practice created by PACE.

7.81 With particular regard to the possibility of sequential trials, ie where a defendant faces separate proceedings arising out of the same events albeit that different offences are alleged, Lord Devlin held that these were normally to be regarded as oppressive:

'a second trial on the same or similar facts is not always and necessarily oppressive and there may be in a particular case special circumstances which make it just and convenient in that case'.

Once special circumstances are absented, then the rule is that sequential prosecutions or trials are to be stayed.

7.82 Lord Pearce agreed with Lord Devlin, that a court must possess an inherent power to ensure the fairness of its proceedings. Furthermore, he observed that this power could not be constrained within the limits of extant pleas in bar. He concluded:

'It is clear that the formal pleas [in bar] which a defendant can claim as of right will not cover all such cases. Instead of attempting to enlarge the pleas beyond their proper scope, it is better that the courts should apply to such cases and avowed judicial discretion based on broader principles which underlie the pleas'.[1]

Lord Reid, in his speech of only one page, agreed with the speeches of Lords Devlin and Pearce, holding that: 'There must always be a residual discretion to prevent anything which savours of abuse of process'.[2]

1   [1964] AC 1254 at 1364.
2   [1964] AC 1254 at 1296.

Issue estoppel

7.83   One of the issues considered by the House of Lords in *Humphrys* was whether the doctrine of issue estoppel applied to criminal cases and whether it was available as a plea in bar to an indictment. The doctrine can be defined as follows: if in the course of deciding a cause of action, one specific issue is determined, then if that issue arises as an essential ingredient in subsequent proceedings between the prosecution and defence, that issue cannot be re-litigated.

7.84   In *Connelly* the defence contended that the doctrine did apply and operated in favour of the accused, which should have prevented his second trial for robbery. On the facts (see para **7.10**) the defence contended that the quashing of the murder conviction must constitute a finding in favour of the defendant on the essential issue of alibi, i e the court must have held that his alibi was correct and therefore vis-à-vis the second trial, the prosecution could not seek to argue that he was present during the robbery. While this submission was rejected, the availability of the doctrine was not decided by the House in *Connelly*, the matter being left to the consideration of the House in *Humphrys*.[1] There the House held that the doctrine had no place in English criminal proceedings. The House held that as it cannot be known how juries arrive at their verdicts, reasons never being given, it would be an exercise fraught with both speculation and uncertainty in a particular case as to what issues a jury had determined in favour of the defence and what in favour of the prosecution.

1   [1977] AC 1.

7.85   It is submitted, however, that the doctrine does still survive, albeit in a rudimentary form. In *R v Hay*[1] the defendant was alleged to have made a statement to the police admitting two offences, burglary and arson. He was tried first on the arson charge the prosecution asserting that he had made a confession and it was true. The defendant said he had never made the confession, it was a police fabrication. He was acquitted. The prosecution then decided to press ahead with a second trial for burglary again relying on the disputed confession. The defendant asserted that this was fabricated and, in support of that claim, to rely on his previous acquittal. The trial judge refused to admit evidence of the acquittal in the first trial. The Court of Appeal disagreed with this refusal holding that the jury's acquittal was conclusive evidence that the defendant was not guilty of arson and that his confession to that offence was untrue. They should, therefore, have been made aware of this and directed that in deciding the issue in relation to the burglary they should bear in mind that the admission in relation to the arson made at the same time as that appertaining to the burglary, had to be regarded as untrue. As the editors of *Archbold* state, 'there is a fine distinction between the principle in this case and the principle that issue estoppel has no place in criminal proceedings'.[2]

1   (1983) 77 Cr App Rep 70. See also *R v B* (3 December 1999, unreported).
2   2003 edn, para 4–331.

7.86   This distinction was somewhat exploded by Lane CJ in *H*[1], where he stated that fairness, rather than any abstruse legal principle, was the basis upon which a judge's reasoning should be based. Lord Lane clearly believed that issue estoppel was unnecessary in view of the availability of the abuse of process discretion in a double jeopardy context.

1   (1989) 90 Cr App R 440.

7.87   The effect of this rejection of issue estoppel from our jurisprudence on abuse of process can also be illustrated by *R v Horsham Justices, ex p Reeves*.[1] Here, the accused's submission of no case to answer in respect of various charges against him was upheld by the magistrates at the committal and he was discharged in respect of them. Subsequently, the prosecution restarted its case and recharged the same offences. The accused pleaded both AA and issue estoppel and the case went to the Divisional Court. Ackner LJ dismissed both pleas: AA did not arise because, as had been held in *Snelson*,[2] AA does not lie in respect of a discharge at committal proceedings. In relation to issue estoppel, despite the fact that the magistrates had already explicitly and directly considered and dismissed the charges against him, it could not be asserted, because of the decision in *Humphrys* which rejected the applicability of the doctrine. Ackner LJ, however, held that the court was not powerless to stymie repeated attempts by the prosecution to have the accused committed for trial. If, following scrutiny of all the circumstances, such attempts were vexatious and/or oppressive and therefore constituted an abuse of process, the case could be stayed.

1   See para **7.104**.
2   See para **7.104**.

7.88   Bearing in mind this wholesale rejection of issue estoppel, a doctrine which is regarded as a fundamental part of US jurisprudence concerned with double jeopardy, three observations can be made:

(1)   In accepting that abuse of process should be the principal remedy against situations of double jeopardy, the House in *Humphrys* in effect decided that the court's approach would be based on discretion and fairness and not on legal concepts of estoppel.

(2)   In determining whether proceedings were fair or unfair, a court of review should avoid being drawn into an assessment of how for example the jury arrived at its verdict. To avoid any temptation of creating a notional but fictional rational jury in order to then decide how such a jury would have arrived at its verdict upon a particular issue which the defence would seek to foreclose from consideration in subsequent proceedings.

(3)   In considering pursuant to its abuse jurisdiction whether a second trial for the defendant would be unfair or oppressive, a court can certainly consider what issues were aired in the first trial and whether they were resolved in favour of the defence. If so, then this is highly relevant to a consideration of whether in relation to the same general allegations or issues, a defendant should be in danger of being tried twice. See para **7.110** for consideration of the ruling of Buckley J in *R v Maxwell*.[1]

1   (September 1996, unreported).

Authorities post-Connelly

7.89   The House in *Connelly* held that courts had an inherent jurisdiction to stay prosecutions on the grounds of unfairness created by double jeopardy. It was then left to the courts to apply it whenever necessary. The first post-*Connelly* authority was *Riebold.*[1] In *Riebold* the two accused were indicted on 29 counts, the first two being counts of conspiracy. The remaining 27 related to overt acts which were relied on by the prosecution as acts in furtherance of the conspiracy and therefore probative of the conspiracy counts. At the first trial the prosecution proceeded only on the second count of conspiracy. The defendants were acquitted. The prosecution then sought leave to proceed on all the remaining counts. Barry J refused leave on the ground that the prosecution was effectively seeking to secure a retrial of the whole case. He held that the subject matter of counts 3 to 29:

'… did in fact constitute the whole of the overt acts of conspiracy on which the prosecution relied, and there were no additional facts or evidence on which the prosecution relied in order to secure a conviction on the conspiracy charge'.[2]

1   [1965] 1 All ER 653.
2   At 656.

7.90   It is submitted that *Riebold*[1] is an important authority. It establishes that it is not permissible for prosecutors to enjoy a free licence to have, using a colloquialism, a 'second bite of the cherry'. In *Riebold*, the defendants having been acquitted in circumstances where the prosecution had carefully chosen which count to proceed on in the first trial, were entitled to expect that a second trial would not commence against them based on the same evidence given in the first trial. The prosecution's desire to maximise the chances of a conviction needed to be constrained by the values of both fairness and avoidance of oppression.

1   [1965] 1 All ER 653.

7.91   Post-*Riebold,* double jeopardy was reconsidered by the House in *Humphrys*. It is apparent from reading the speeches delivered in that case that the Lords were concerned that their decision in *Connelly* would be interpreted by lower courts as tantamount to a near unbridled discretion to stop prosecutions if the tribunal felt that they were unfair or oppressive. The Lords sought to correct this perceived error and make plain that a judge should only intervene where there is, on the clearest grounds, an abuse. For example, Salmon LJ said:

'… a judge [has no] power to refuse to allow a prosecution to proceed merely because he considers that, as a matter of policy, it ought not to have been brought. It is only if the prosecution amounts to an abuse of process of the court and is oppressive and vexatious that the judge has the power to intervene'.[1]

1   [1977] AC 1 at 46.

7.92   Viscount Dilhorne echoed similar sentiments, warning that the power to stop a prosecution should only be used 'in the most exceptional circumstances'. He continued, 'a judge has no power to quash a properly preferred indictment because he thinks that the prosecution of the defendant for the defence should not have been instituted'.[1] Further, 'the judge must not appear to have any responsibility for the institution of a prosecution'.[2]

1   At 509.
2   At 511.

7.93   Courts have, since *Humphrys*, intermittently felt it necessary to restate similar principles, perhaps perceiving that various tribunals have shown an undue willingness to stay prosecutions. An example would be the judgment of Lord Bingham CJ in *Enviroment Agency v Stanford*[1] who, in that case, felt that a magistrate had improperly refused to commit a defendant for trial in view of a perceived abuse. Lord Bingham stated that even if on reasonable grounds a court considers that a prosecution should never have been brought, such views are only to be reflected in mitigation of the sentence imposed. Furthermore, it was of no benefit to the defendant if a stay was granted by the magistrate if this were only to be reversed on appeal. Post-*Humphrys*, the main authorities concerning double jeopardy can be considered.

1   [1998] COD 373.

'Same activity' cases

7.94   Cases concerned with this theme are largely road traffic cases. In *R v Moxon-Tritsch*[1] the defendant was convicted of driving without due care and attention and driving with excess alcohol. Subsequently, a private prosecution was instituted for causing death by reckless driving. The defendant applied for a stay which was successful. It was clear that the proposed prosecution arose from the same facts as those on which the defendant had already been convicted. In essence the case was concerned with whether the court should countenance a situation where one conviction is followed by a prosecution for a greater and encompassing offence, where the defendant's careless driving necessarily being subsumed into the question of whether such driving was also reckless. Faulks J was satisfied that it would be an abuse to allow the private prosecution to continue. It would be oppressive for the defendant to be tried twice for a more aggravated form of the same offence to which she had already pleaded guilty and she had suffered enough.

1   [1988] Crim LR 46.

7.95   A similar situation arose in *R v Forest of Dean Justices, ex p Farley*[1] where there was a clear overlap of fact between two charges of driving with excess alcohol and causing death by reckless driving. The defendant was charged with both offences but was brought before the justices first only for the offence of driving with excess alcohol. His application for an adjournment of this charge until after the determination of the graver charge, causing death by reckless driving, was resisted by the prosecution. The prosecution submitted that the summary offence should be dealt with as it was important to ascertain in relation to the graver offence whether the defendant had driven with excess alcohol. Furthermore, so the prosecution contended, a conviction for this

249

offence would then mean that at the trial of the graver offence, the defendant would have the burden of proof establishing that his driving was not reckless. In other words, the prosecution were making plain that their wish was to have a trial in the magistrates' court for the purpose of obtaining evidence to use against the defendant at a later trial in the Crown Court for a more serious offence.

1   [1990] RTR 228.

7.96   The defence argued that this was unfair and was an abuse, particularly because the defendant would be forced to give evidence at two separate trials and would be open to cross-examination at the second trial on any discrepancy between these two sets of evidence. The prosecution riposte to this submission was that the prosecution enjoyed a discretion of how to proceed with cases, and in any event, the unfairness could be dealt with by the trial judge under PACE, s 78. The Divisional Court held that the prosecution's attempt to reverse the burden of proof constituted an abuse. Neil J relied on the general 'rule' that after trial on a lesser charge, a person should not be tried again on the same facts for a more serious offence. There are, however, two special features of *Farley* which should not be overlooked. Firstly, it related to subsequent trials and not two charges brought on the same occasion to be tried together. Secondly, in *Farley* the only basis for alleging reckless driving was the evidence of excess alcohol. Where there is additional evidence of a dangerous manoeuvre for example, the outcome may be different. *R v Farley* was distinguished in *R v LSA*[1], *R v Prigmore*[2] and *R v Hartnett*[3] on the basis of these special features. It was however followed in *R v Phipps*[4] where a prosecution for dangerous driving was stayed as an abuse as it appeared to have arisen from an injured party's dissatisfaction with the sentence for the original offence of driving with excess alcohol.

1   [2008] RTR 25.
2   [2005] EWCA Crim 2476.
3   [2003] EWCA Crim 345.
4   [2005] EWCA Crim 33.

7.97   In R v K, B and A[1] an application to stay the prosecution was made on the grounds that material available to the Crown in the course of prior forgery proceedings should have been sufficient to alert the Crown to the defendants' alleged terrorist activities. It was argued successfully in the Crown Court that the Crown's failure to charge the defendants at that earlier stage should bar subsequent proceedings under the Terrorism Act 2000. The stay was however overturned in the Court of Appeal as the mere existence of evidence was insufficient to put the defendants in jeopardy of conviction and, in any event, the facts of the two offences were held to be too different.

1   See **7.50** above.

7.98   These cases can also be contrasted with the situation in *R v Thomson Holidays Ltd.*[1] Here, the defendants pleaded guilty to an offence under the Trade Descriptions Act 1968 in relation to the making of false statements in a travel brochure. The statements related to a particular hotel in Greece and its amenities. One year later they were charged with the same provision in relation to the same statement. Both prosecutions had arisen from separate complaints made by people who had booked separate holidays at the hotel. The defendants submitted that the second proceedings constituted an abuse. The Court of Appeal however, disagreed holding that the Trade Descriptions Act contemplated that more than one prosecution could be brought in respect of the same course of conduct, the Act was designed to protect the public as individuals.

1   [1974] QB 592.

7.99   *Thomson Holidays* was followed in *North Yorkshire Trading Standards v Coleman*[1] where the defendant was being prosecuted for the same offences under the Trade Descriptions Act as it had been previously before a different court. However it had been acquitted in that earlier trial and so argued abuse in relation to the second trial bearing in mind that the facts in both were closely similar. This complaint of abuse was rejected.

1   [2001] EWHC 818, (2001) 166 JP 76.

Separate prosecutions by different prosecution agencies: Sequential trials and special circumstances

7.100   The diversity of statutes creating criminal offences had led to a diversity of separate and independent prosecutors. An important example of lack of co-ordination leading to the finding of an abuse was *R v Beedie*[1]. In *Beedie* a tenant died of carbon monoxide poisoning caused by defects in a gas fire in premises owned by the defendant landlord. The death was investigated by a variety of agencies including the Health and Safety Executive (HSE) and the police. Before the police reported to the Crown Prosecution Service concerning a prosecution by it, the landlord had already been charged and convicted at the behest of the HSE in relation to offences against the Health and Safety at Work etc Act 1974. Furthermore, the local authority had also prosecuted him in relation to dangerous gas fires. Only after these two convictions and an inquest was the landlord charged with manslaughter by the police and the case taken up by the CPS.

1   [1998] QB 356.

7.101   At the trial the landlord pleaded both AC and argued for a stay. The judge rejected both grounds. The defendant's appeal was principally based on whether the judge should have stayed the prosecution because of the rule established in *Connelly* that apart from special circumstances, there should be no sequential trials on an ascending scale of gravity. In recognising this rule and applying it in this case, the Court of Appeal held that the rule is not part of the doctrine of autrefois but it should, in the absence of exceptional circumstances, give rise to the exercise of the wider discretionary power to stay proceedings as an abuse. Here, the charge of manslaughter should have been stayed because of the previous sets of proceedings and, in the court's view, there were no special circumstances which should have persuaded the judge not to have done this. Rose LJ opined that, for example, the rule might be overruled where a charge of murder or manslaughter was brought where the victim has died after proceedings for assault. The additional fact of the death means that exceptional circumstances would exist. This was indeed the decision of the Court of Appeal in *R v Young*.[1]

1   (2005) EWCA Crim 2963.

7.102   Another illustration of 'special circumstances' is the decision of the Court of Appeal for Gibraltar in *A-G for Gibraltar v Leoni*.[1] In that case the court held that the discovery of new evidence may amount to a special circumstance. It should also be noted that in both *Beedie* and in *Phipps*[2] it was held that, unlike other cases of abuse of process, the burden is not on the defence to show that there cannot be a fair trial. Instead, the burden is on the Prosecution to show that there are special circumstances justifying a second trial.

1   Criminal Appeal No 4 (1998).
2   See **7.96** above.

7.103   An instance of the rule against sequential trials not being applied was in *R v South Hampshire Magistrates' Court, ex p Crown Prosecution Service*[1] where the defendant was tried in December 1995 and acquitted. In January 1996 along with others he was re-arrested and charged with a series of connected but different offences. He argued that the failure of the prosecution to consolidate all their charges against him in one indictment and in one trial was an abuse. At committal the magistrates agreed but the Divisional Court, on a judicial review application brought by the DPP, disagreed. A second trial on the same or similar facts was, in the view of the court, not necessarily oppressive and in this case there were special circumstances which made it just and convenient for there to be two trials: for example the lack of a significant evidential overlap between the two proceedings and the delay to the first trial which would have occurred had it not proceeded but been consolidated with the second.

1   [1998] Crim LR 422.

Repeated committal proceedings cases

7.104   In *R v Manchester City Stipendiary Magistrate, ex p Snelson*[1] it was held that a discharge at committal proceedings did not prohibit fresh committal proceedings for the same offence. The doctrine of AA did not apply neither was it an abuse. However, in *R v Horsham Justices, ex p Reeves*[2] it was held that the second set of committal proceedings should be stayed as an abuse. The court held in this case that the prosecution had treated the first set of proceedings as a 'dummy run' and having learned lessons had brought the same proceedings albeit in a simplified form. Ackner LJ began his judgment stating that the case provided a cautionary tale 'the moral of which is do not overload a prosecution with unnecessary charges'[3]. He held that to allow the prosecution to proceed would be wrong:

'to grant such an indulgence would in my judgment, encourage poor preparation with a resultant waste of time and money … the prosecution must direct its energies to the simplification of cases they desire to proceed'.[4]

In a call for such simplification Ackner LJ said:

'All too often juries, and to a lesser extent magistrates, are treated like computers into whom superfluous and ill-digested material is fed in the over-optimistic hope that somehow or another they will produce the right result'.[4]

1   (1977) 66 Cr App R 44.
2   (1980) 75 Cr App R 236n.
3   (1980) 75 Cr App R 236n.
4   (1980) 75 Cr App R 236n at 240.

7.105   *Reeves* was, however, distinguished in *R v Willesden Justices, ex p Clemmings*[1]. Here the first set of committal proceedings had been dismissed by the magistrates for failure to serve the advance information on time. A fortnight later the defendant had been recharged and the advance information properly served. The defendant, relying on *Reeves*, argued that this was an abuse. Bingham LJ disagreed. In refusing a stay Bingham LJ said:

'The ultimate objective of this discretionary power is to ensure that there shall be a fair trial according to law which involves fairness both to the defendant and the prosecution, for as Lord Diplock said in *Sang* "The fairness of the trial ... is not all one sided".'

In his view, the decision to recharge the defendant was not manifestly unreasonable, there was no evidence that the second proceedings would unfairly prejudice the defendant and finally there was no evidence of a prosecution desire to deprive the defendant of any lawful protection.

1   (1987) 87 Cr App R 280.

Sequential trials in complex trials arising out of severance of the indictment

7.106   Particularly in the area of serious or complex fraud, the courts have repeatedly emphasised the need for severance of an indictment so as to ensure manageable and not unduly long trials.[1] The best example of a prosecutor's failure to heed this exhortation was the *Blue Arrow* case – the Serious Fraud Office's (SFO) prosecution of *R v Cohen*[2] where the Court of Appeal criticised both the trial judge and the SFO for failing to exercise the power of severance to ensure a fair and manageable trial. The consequence of severance, however, must be more than one trial.

1   See for example *R v Novac* (1977) 65 Cr App Rep 107 and *R v Kellard* [1995] 2 Cr App Rep 134.
2   [1992] NLJR 1267, CA.

7.107   In the context of double jeopardy, the interplay between severance and abuse arose in the proposed second trial of Kevin Maxwell following his acquittal in the first. Prior to the first trial, with the consent of all concerned, the SFO had severed the indictment accepting that not all counts could be tried together. At the first trial, Kevin Maxwell and the other defendants were tried on only two counts (counts 4 and 10) of the original ten-count indictment on which they were arraigned. Following the acquittal on these counts the prosecution proposed a second trial of counts 1, 2 and 9. The prosecution contended that these counts were in a separate category from 4 and 10 and factual issues in the first trial would not need to be relitigated in the second.

7.108 In answer to the defence contention that it would be oppressive for Kevin Maxwell to be tried again, the prosecution contended that the second trial was a result of the earlier severance of the indictment which the defence had agreed to. Furthermore, the prosecution had agreed to this, respecting the courts' entreaties to avoid long trials. Were a second trial to be stayed it would mean that mere complexity of the issues would result in the prosecution being unfairly and permanently deprived of presenting a significant part of its case to a jury. How then could it be unfair and an abuse of the court's process for it to proceed with the second trial?

7.109 The defence fundamentally disagreed, arguing that all along the prosecution's case had been presented as one continuing offence of fraud and that in any event, it would be impossible to separate the factual issues raised in the first trial from those to be raised in the second. For example Kevin Maxwell's honesty or dishonesty was a central feature in the first trial and it would again be in the second trial.

7.110 Buckley J ruled that a second trial would constitute an abuse. He held that a central theme in the first trial was Kevin Maxwell's alleged dishonesty and that there would be a significant overlap of factual issues between the first and the proposed second trial. Furthermore, he held that the counts, 4 and 10, tried at the first trial:

> 'constituted a fair presentation of the real dishonesty or fraud alleged by the prosecution … I have no doubt that those were clearly the most serious examples the prosecution had of the fraudulent course of conduct alleged doubtless that is why they were put forward as a basis for the first trial'.[1]

1   At p 22.

7.111 Buckley J also took cognisance of the fact that he had:

> 'not been referred to any long fraud case in which after an acquittal a further trial has proceeded. Mr Lissack drew my attention to several instances of retrials following abortive first trials or appeals. I do not consider those analogous. In such cases there have been either no acquittal on the merits or determination at all'.[1]

1   At p 23.

7.112 In the most significant passage of his judgment dealing with both the prosecution and the defence submissions Buckley J said:

> 'I wish to make it plain, I am not suggesting that an acquittal even after a long trial necessarily means that severed counts cannot be tried. Each case will turn on its own particular circumstances; there are many factors to be considered as I have already observed. I am suggesting that if all parties have played their part and the essential criminality alleged has been placed before a jury who have acquitted, it should be unusual for a second trial to take place. The reason is that it would be very likely to appear to the public that the authorities were not prepared to accept the verdict of a jury and were

determined to pursue the defendant at whatever cost to the public purse, or time, or disruption of the defendant's personal life, business or professional career. But that must not happen'.[1]

1   At p 23.

SIMILAR FACT

7.113   The interrelationship between double jeopardy and the common law similar fact rule of admissibility (now replaced by the Criminal Justice Act 2003) was the issue for consideration for the House of Lords in *R v Z*.[1] Here a man was tried for rape where his defence was consent. To rebut this defence the prosecution sought and obtained the leave of the trial judge to admit evidence of three previous allegations of rape against the accused where he had similarly denied this on the basis of purported consent. In particular the prosecution wished to call the alleged victims of these attacks. By admitting such evidence, the relevance of which was accepted by all as sufficient to fall within the similar fact rule, the prosecution wished to undermine or discredit the accused's defence of consent. The issue of double jeopardy arose because the accused had previously been tried and acquitted of each of these rape allegations.

1   [2000] 2 AC 483.

7.114   Lord Hope set out the issue in *Z* succinctly:

'It is accepted by the defendant that the evidence of the three complainants in respect of whose complaints he was acquitted is relevant to the question whether he is guilty of the offence of rape with which he has been charged in this case. This is because the similar fact evidence of these complainants, if accepted by the jury, has a direct bearing on the allegation which the Crown makes in this case that the defendant's intercourse with C was without consent. Furthermore the issue in the present case is not whether the defendant is guilty of having raped the three other complainants. He is not being put on trial again for those offences. The only issue is whether he is guilty of this fresh allegation of rape. The guiding principle is that prima facie all evidence which is relevant to the question whether the accused is guilty or innocent of the offence charged is admissible. It would seem to follow that the evidence of these three complainants should be held to be admissible in this case, subject to the discretion of the trial judge to exclude unfair evidence under section 78 of the Police and Criminal Evidence Act 1984.

The objection to the admissibility of this evidence is based on LordMacDermott's statement in *Sambasivam v Public Prosecutor, Federation of Malaya*[1] that the effect of a verdict of acquittal pronounced by a competent court after a lawful trial is not restricted to the fact that the person acquitted cannot be tried again for the same offence. He said that it is binding and conclusive in all subsequent proceedings between the parties to the adjudication'.[2]

1   [1950] AC 458 at 479.
2   At p 1.

7.115   In *Sambasivam*, the defendant was charged with possession of a firearm and possession of ammunition (some of which was loaded in the firearm). The defendant was acquitted of possession of the ammunition and a retrial ordered on possession of the firearm. On the retrial the prosecution relied on a statement, which the defendant denied making, in which he allegedly stated that he had been in possession of a firearm and ammunition. The defendant was convicted of possession of a firearm.

The rule in *Sambasivam* had since been used to prevent the prosecution bringing any proceedings or calling any evidence which suggested that the previous acquittal was wrong. However, in *Z*, their Lordships restricted the rule whilst confirming the correctness of the original decision. The defendant in *Sambasivam* should not have been tried again on the basis that a defendant should not be prosecuted again where two offences arose out of one incident and a conviction on one count would be inconsistent with acquittal on the other.

Viewed in this way *Sambasivam* was a simple case of double jeopardy and was in fact one of the cases considered and approved in *Connelly*. However, as a rule of evidence in proceedings for a separate offence the House held that the principle of double jeopardy was not breached by suggesting that the accused was guilty of that offence on the basis of his alleged commission of similar offences for which he had been tried and acquitted. Lord Hutton summed up the position as established in *Z* as follows:

> '(1) The principle of double jeopardy operates to cause a criminal court in the exercise of its discretion, and subject to the qualification as to special circumstances stated by Lord Devlin in *Connelly* at p 1360, to stop a prosecution where the defendant is being prosecuted on the same facts or substantially the same facts as gave rise to an earlier prosecution which resulted in his acquittal (or conviction), as occurred in *R v Riebold* [1967] 1 WLR 674 and the cases cited by Lord Pearce in *Connelly* at pp 1362–1364, and see also *R v Beedie* [1998] QB 356.
>
> (2) Provided that a defendant is not placed in double jeopardy as described in (1) above evidence which is relevant on a subsequent prosecution is not inadmissible because it shows or tends to show that the defendant was, in fact, guilty of an offence of which he had earlier been acquitted.
>
> (3) It follows from (2) above that a distinction should not be drawn between evidence which shows guilt of an earlier offence of which the defendant had been acquitted and evidence which tends to show guilt of such an offence or which appears to relate to one distinct issue rather than to the issue of guilt of such an offence'.

7.116   In *R v Terry*[1] the Court of Appeal held that the principles in *Z* were not simply limited to similar fact evidence and in *R v Nguyen*[2] it was confirmed that *Z* applied not only to previous allegations of which a defendant had been acquitted, but also to allegations which the Crown had chosen not to pursue.

1 (2005) 2 Cr App R 7.
2 [2008] EWCA Crim 585, (2008) The Times, 16 May.

7.117   On the issue of fairness, the House in *Z* relied heavily on the power of the trial judge to exclude evidence pursuant to s 78. Lord Hobhouse said:

'Fairness requires that the jury hear all relevant evidence. It also requires that the defendant shall not without sufficient reason be required more than once to rebut the same factual allegations. In principle a case supported by probative similar fact evidence is a sufficient reason. However, in exercising his discretion under s 78, the judge must take into account the position of both the prosecution and the defendant. If the fairness of the trial will be compromised by the non-exclusion of the similar fact evidence, the evidence should be excluded although otherwise admissible. Trial judges are experienced in exercising their discretion under s 78 and regularly have to balance probative value against prejudice. Any prejudice to the defendant arising from having to deal a second time with evidence proving facts which were in issue at an earlier trial is simply another factor to be put into the balance. The fact that the previous trial ended in an acquittal is a relevant factor in striking this balance but is no more than that.'

DOUBLE JEOPARDY UNDER EUROPEAN HUMAN RIGHTS LAW

7.118   Bearing in mind that the rule or prohibition on double jeopardy has been an elemental principle of the English common law for a long period and that English jurists played a major role in the drafting of the European Convention on Human Rights, it is surprising that the Convention itself does not contain any explicit prohibition on double jeopardy. Recognising this omission in the case of *X v Austria*,[1] the Commission held that such a prohibition may be implicit within the terms of Art 6.[2] However, in *S v Germany*[3] the Commission took a contrary view, holding that the prohibition was 'neither expressly nor by way of implication' included within Art 6 guarantees.

1   (1970) 35 CD 151.
2   On occasions the court has been willing to imply into art 6, guarantees which are not mentioned within its text, e g *Funke v France* (1993) 16 EHRR 297 (protection against self-incrimination).
3   (1983) 39 DR 43.

7.119   The Seventh Protocol to the Convention is generally concerned with additional fair trial guarantees in criminal cases. Article 2 of the Protocol, for example, is concerned with the granting of a right to a review of a criminal conviction or sentence. Article 4 is directly concerned with double jeopardy. Before reciting this article, however, it is important to bear in mind that the Protocol has not yet been formally ratified by the UK and therefore does not form part of the Convention implemented in our domestic law by the Human Rights Act 1998. The government has indicated an intention to ratify this Protocol, in its White Paper 'Rights Brought Home'[1] it stated that, 'in general, the provisions of Protocol 7 reflect principles already inherent in our law'. Pursuant to the 1998 Act, the Protocol can be made enforceable via an order under s 1(4). The Government has been saying since 2001 that the Protocol would be ratified once legislation has been implemented to amend certain family law provisions. However, the family law provisions remain unamended and the Protocol unratified.

1   Cm 3782, p 18.

7.120   Article 4 of Protocol 7 provides:

'(1)   No one shall be liable to be tried or punished again in criminal proceedings under the jurisdiction of the same state for an offence for which he has already been finally acquitted or convicted in accordance with the law and penal procedure of that state;

(2)   The provisions of the preceding paragraph shall not prevent the re-opening of the case in accordance with the law and penal procedure of the state concerned, if there is evidence or new or newly discovered facts, or if there has been a fundamental defect in the previous proceedings, which could affect the outcome of the case;

(3)   No derogation from the Article shall be made under article 15 of the Convention'.

7.121   Article 4(1) speaks of 'final acquittal or conviction' and this being 'in accordance with the law and penal procedure of that State'. The Explanatory Report to Protocol 7 states that an acquittal or conviction is only to be regarded as final:

'if, according to the traditional expression, it has acquired the force of res judicata. This is the case where it is irrevocable, that is to say when no further ordinary remedies are available or when the parties have exhausted such remedies or have permitted the time limit to expire without availing themselves of them.'

This, in other words, means that there is no prohibition on an appeal against acquittal per se, so long as the appeal did not constitute fresh proceedings.

European Court of Human Rights ('ECtHR') authorities

7.122   In *Gradinger v Austria*[1] the applicant was convicted of causing death by negligent driving. Subsequently, an administrative penalty was imposed on the applicant for driving with excess alcohol, evidence of alcohol presumably not being available at the original trial. The applicant asserted that the subsequent penalty was a breach of Art 4(1). The ECtHR agreed, both charges were based on the same conduct although the offences were different. The ECtHR was also persuaded that the administrative authorities who imposed the penalty were 'criminal' for the purposes of this article. (Had the ECtHR been persuaded that the authorities were in fact 'civil', it would not have found a violation.)

1   (1995) Series A/328-C.

7.123   In *Oliveira v Switzerland*[1] the ECtHR held that successive prosecutions were not necessarily in violation of Art 4 if they related to separate offences arising out of the same act. The applicant was originally convicted of a lesser offence of failure to control a motor vehicle and then subsequently for a more serious offence of negligently inflicting personal injury. The applicant complained that she had been prosecuted twice in respect of the same offence but this was rejected. The ECtHR held that Art 4:

'does not preclude separate offences, even if they are all part of single criminal act, being tried by different courts especially where, as in the present case, the penalties were not cumulative, the lesser being absorbed by the greater'.[2]

1   [1998] V 1990.
2   At para 27.

7.124   *Oliveira* therefore suggests that a breach of Art 4(1) occurs only when the offence with which the applicant is charged is, in law, the same offence as that with which he was previously acquitted or convicted. In other words the ambit of Art 4(1) is no further than the autrefois rule considered above.

7.125   It is submitted that there is a conflict between *Gradinger* and *Oliveira*, the former preferring a substantive over a formalistic approach to the principle of double jeopardy whereas the latter preferring the opposite.[1] In a run of subsequent cases, the approach in *Gradinger* has been followed, the court stating in *Franz Fischer v Austria*[2] that:

' ... whilst it is true that the mere fact that a single act constitutes more than one offence is not contrary to [art 4], the Court must not limit itself to finding that an applicant was, on the basis of one act, tried or punished for nominally different offences.'

1   See the dissenting judgment in *Oliveira* of Repik J.
2   37950/97. [2001] ECHR 352, 29 May 2001.

7.126   Article 4(2) allows for the re-opening of a case after a final decision has been made, when a decision is res judicata. Re-opening in this sense can be contrasted to a fresh prosecution; what is envisaged by Art 4(2) is a way of challenging an acquittal by persuading a higher court to re-open it. Article 4(2) allows for this to occur only on two specified grounds; discovery of new evidence or acceptance that there was a fundamental defect in the original proceedings.

7.127   In relation to tainted acquittals which can now be quashed by the High Court pursuant to the Criminal Procedure and Investigations Act 1996, ss 54 and 56 it is submitted that as this is consistent with Art 4(2) it must surely be the case that if jurors or witnesses have been intimidated or interfered with, this must amount to a 'fundamental defect' in the proceedings.

7.128   In relation to prosecution right of appeal under Pt 9 of the Criminal Justice Act 2003, a similar system was considered in *State of Trinidad and Tobago v Boyce*[1]. Article 4(2) was considered and it was held that the ability of an appellate court to correct an error of law which had led to an acquittal was not incompatible with the general principles of fairness. It is therefore submitted that the new provisions are compatible with Art 4(2), as the matter will not be *res judicata* until the appellate court has had the opportunity to consider whether there has been a 'fundamental defect'.

1   [2006] 2 WLR 284, PC.

7.129   It is submitted that based on the above overview of European authorities, the English law on double jeopardy is consistent with ECtHR law.

OTHER RELEVANT INTERNATIONAL OBLIGATIONS

7.130   Following *Criminal Proceedings against Pupino,*[1] courts in the UK are obliged to interpret national law in conformity with Community law, so far as possible. This includes giving effect to preliminary rulings by the European Court of Justice on the interpretation of framework decisions. Furthermore, as noted above, under the Criminal Justice Act 2003 provisions for retrial for serious offences the DPP is required to consider the UK's obligations under the principle of *'ne bis in idem'* before applying for such a retrial. The concept of *'ne bis in idem'* in civil jurisdictions corresponds approximately with the common law concept of double jeopardy and appears in a number of the UK's international obligations. Article 50 of the European Charter of Fundamental Rights states:

> 'No one shall be liable to be tried or punished again in criminal proceedings for an offence for which he or she has already been finally acquitted or convicted within the Union in accordance with the law.'

1   C105/03 (16 June 2005) ECJ.

7.131   The Charter only applies to Member States insofar as they apply Community law. The principle was enshrined in European jurisprudence by the Convention implementing the Schengen Agreement, Art 54 of which reads:

> 'A person whose trial has been finally disposed of in one Contracting Party may not be prosecuted in another Contracting Party for the same acts provided that, if a penalty has been imposed, it has been enforced, is actually in the process of being enforced or can no longer be enforced under the laws of the sentencing Contracting Party.'

7.132   In *Criminal Proceedings concerning van Esbroeck*[1] the European Court of Justice decided that the reference to 'the same acts' meant that the legal classification of the offence was irrelevant in deciding whether a person could be prosecuted in two different Member States. The criterion was whether the two proceedings involved inextricably linked facts. In that case, it was decided that proceedings in one Member State for exporting narcotic drugs, after the defendant had been prosecuted and convicted in another Member State for importing the same drugs, were in principle contrary to Art 54.

1   C-436/04 (9 March 2006), ECJ.

7.133   In *Criminal Proceedings against Hüseyin Gözütok and Klaus Brügge*[1] proceedings in the Netherlands were discontinued after the defendants agreed to pay a sum of money determined by the prosecution. The ECJ held that subsequent proceedings brought by the German authorities were barred. It was relevant to this decision that the payment of the money constituted a definitive bar to further proceedings under Dutch law.

1   C-187/01 and C-385/01 (11 February 2003), ECJ.

7.134   A Green Paper[1] has been produced by the European Commission dealing with the problems of allocation of jurisdiction and ne bis in idem and specifically the problem of what constitutes 'the same facts'. No legislative proposal has yet been produced as a result.

1   COM (2005) 696 Final.

7.135   The International Covenant on Civil and Political Rights, Art 14.7 is also binding on the UK and provides that:

'No one shall be liable to be tried or punished again for an offence for which he has already been finally convicted or acquitted in accordance with the law and penal procedure of each country.'

Chapter 8

Extradition proceedings

8.01   Abuse of process can arise in myriad ways in the context of requests for extradition. The safeguards provided to a criminal defendant (or fugitive) by extradition arrangements are extensive. Historically, they have also been accurately characterised as highly technical and notoriously time-consuming, so much so that the temptation to withhold material or otherwise manipulate proceedings can, especially in politically-sensitive or urgent cases, be great. In more extreme cases, the temptation may be to 'bypass' or circumvent them altogether. This is assuming that the extradition request itself is made in good faith in the first place.

8.02   The practitioner here will be concerned with resisting his client's extradition from the UK. It is crucial at the outset to appreciate that extradition proceedings cannot be equated to domestic criminal proceedings. Not only are they governed by different rules and procedures, they are also fashioned from different public interests.

8.03   The Supreme Court of Canada put it thus in 1991:

'Extradition occupies a unique and important position in the structure of law enforcement ... the investigation, prosecution, and suppression of crime for the protection of the citizen and the maintenance of peace and public order is an important goal of all organized societies. The pursuit of that goal cannot realistically be confined within national boundaries. That has long been the case, but it is increasingly evident today. Extradition is a practice which has deep historical roots in this country ... While the extradition process is an important part of our system of criminal justice, *it would be wrong to equate it to the criminal trial process. It differs from the criminal process in purpose and procedure and, most importantly, in the factors which render it fair. Extradition procedure, unlike the criminal procedure, is founded on the concepts of reciprocity, comity and respect for differences in other jurisdictions.* This unique foundation means that the law of extradition must accommodate many factors foreign to our internal criminal law. While our conceptions of what constitutes a fair criminal law are important to the process of extradition, they are necessarily tempered by other considerations. Most importantly, our extradition process, while premised on our conceptions of what is fundamentally just, must accommodate differences between our system of criminal justice and the systems in place in reciprocating states. The simple fact is that if we were to insist on strict conformity with our own system, there would be virtually no state in the world with which we could reciprocate. Canada, unable to obtain extradition of persons who commit crimes here and flee elsewhere, would be the loser. For this reason, we require a limited but not absolute degree of similarity between our laws and those of the reciprocating state. We will not extradite for acts which are not offences in this country. We sign treaties only with states which can assure us that their systems of criminal justice are fair and offer sufficient procedural protections to accused persons. We permit our Minister to demand assurances relating to penalties where the Minister considers such a demand appropriate. But beyond these basic conditions precedent of reciprocity, much diversity is, of necessity, tolerated.'[1] (emphasis added)

1   *Kindler v Canada (Minister of Justice)* [1991] 2 SCR 779 per McLachlin J at 843–845.

STATUTORY PROTECTIONS AGAINST ABUSE

8.04   In *Knowles v Government of the United States of America & another,*[1] Lord Bingham of Cornhill observed that:

'Laws governing extradition seek to reconcile two objectives, both of concern to states recognising the rule of law. One objective is to give effect to the principle that, in the ordinary way, persons in one state who are credibly accused of committing serious crimes triable in another should be surrendered to that other to answer for their alleged misdeeds. This is a principle which national authorities, including courts, will seek to honour. The second objective is to protect those whose surrender is sought against such surrender in circumstances where they would, putting it very generally, suffer injustice or oppression. States ordinarily seek to provide some safeguards against the surrender of those within their borders in such circumstances.'

1   [2007] 1 WLR 47, PC at para 12.

8.05   Traditionally, extradition legislation has sought to meet this 'second objective', not by providing the courts with an overriding abuse of process jurisdiction, but by providing specific statutory redress for specific injustice or oppression. Thus it is that the Extradition Act 2003 (the '2003 Act') itself provides many significant inherent safeguards, over and above those which exist in domestic criminal proceedings, that indirectly militate against abuse. In respect of all countries except Part 1 territories[1] and specifically designated Part 2 territories,[2] the requesting government must adduce evidence before a district judge, which constitutes a prima facie case in respect of the charges. Additionally, the many technical prohibitions upon extradition, authentication requirements,[3] and strict time limits[4] of the Extradition Act 2003 provide some general safeguards to a defendant against abuse.

1   Presently Austria, Belgium, Bulgaria, Cyprus, Czech Republic, Denmark, Estonia, Finland, France, Germany, Gibraltar, Greece, Hungary, Ireland, Italy, Latvia, Lithuania, Luxembourg, Malta, The Netherlands, Poland, Portugal, Romania, Slovakia, Slovenia, Spain, Sweden.
2   Presently Albania, Andorra, Armenia, Australia, Azerbaijan, Bosnia and Herzegovina, Canada, Croatia, Georgia, Iceland, Israel, Liechtenstein, Macedonia FYR, Moldova, Montenegro, New Zealand, Norway, Russian Federation, Serbia, South Africa, Switzerland, Turkey, Ukraine, United States of America.
3   Section 202.
4   See *Nikonovs v Governor of Brixton Prison & another* [2006] 1 WLR 1518, DC in which

discharge was ordered in a case where the defendant was not brought to court for his first appearance 'as soon as practicable', contrary to s 4(2) of the Extradition Act 2003. In respect of the bringing of appeals, the courts have applied the statutory time limits strictly: *District Court of Vilnius v Barcys* [2007] 1 WLR 3249; *R (on the application of Mendy) v Crown Prosecution Service* [2007] EWHC 1765; *Mucelli v Government of the Republic of Albania* [2007] EWHC 2632 (Admin); *Gercans v The Government of Latvia* [2008] EWHC 884 (Admin) and *Moulai v Deputy Public Prosecutor in Creteil France* [2008] EWHC 1024 (Admin). For example, in *Barcys*, a Requesting State's appeal against discharge was held to be out of time where the Requesting State had been prevented from filing its Notice of Appeal within the applicable seven-day period owing to an electrical blackout in London which had closed the High Court.

8.06   However, some provisions of the 2003 Act are specifically aimed at providing extradition courts with the power to refuse extradition in certain specified circumstances that offend against the rules of natural justice and which inevitably call into question the bona fides of the Requesting State.

Extraneous considerations

8.07   Sections 13 and 81 of the 2003 Act provide that a person's extradition will be barred by reason of extraneous considerations if it appears that the Part 1 warrant, or Part 2 request, issued in respect of him, (a) though purporting to be issued on account of the extradition offence, is, in fact, issued for the purpose of prosecuting or punishing him on account of his race, religion, nationality, gender, sexual orientation or political opinions, or (b) if extradited he might be prejudiced at his trial or punished, detained or restricted in his personal liberty by reason of his race, religion, nationality, gender, sexual orientation or political opinions. Speaking in the context of the more restrictively drafted s 3 of the Extradition Act 1870 in *Schtraks v Israel*,[1] Lord Reid observed that '… it appears to me that the provisions … are clearly intended to give effect to the principle that there should in this country be asylum for political refugees' from the Requesting State[2]. Viscount Radcliffe stated that:

'… in my opinion, the idea that lies behind the phrase 'offence of a political character' is that the fugitive is at odds with the State that applies for his extradition on some issue connected with the political control or government of the country … It does indicate, I think, that the Requesting State is after him for reasons other than the enforcement of the criminal law in its ordinary, what I may call its common or international, aspect'.[3]

1   [1964] AC 556, HL.
2   At 584. See also 582–583. See also Viscount Radcliffe at 591, Lord Evershed at 598. Approved in *Cheng v Governor of Pentonville Prison* [1973] AC 931, HL per Lord Hodson at 942E–H, Lord Diplock at 946F–H, Lord Simon of Glaisdale at 951A, Lord Wilberforce at 951A, 953A–E and 954A, Lord Salmon at 961A–D, G–H and 965B–C. See also *R v Governor of Pentonville Prison, ex p Budlong* [1980] 1 WLR 1110, DC per Widgery LCJ and Griffiths J at 1123G–H.
3   At 591. See also Lord Hodson at 612.

8.08   The burden is on the appellant to make out the bar.[1] He does not have to prove on the balance of probabilities that the events described will take place, but he must show that there is a 'reasonable chance' or 'reasonable grounds for thinking' or a 'serious possibility' that such events will occur (*Fernandez v The*

Government of Singapore[2]). In the same case, LordParker CJ had observed in the High Court[3] that the central question would be 'was the request, as it were, bona fide for the purposes of prosecuting him for the offence or was it for other purposes on account of his political opinions'.[4] The Court in considering these matters is not bound by the ordinary rules of evidence; the appellant may rely on any material in support of a submission based on ss 13 or 81 (*Schtraks v Government of Israel*[5]). However, the fact that the defendant's actions were (or are said to have been) politically motivated is insufficient: '... if the central government stands apart and is concerned only to enforce the criminal law that has been violated ... I see no reason why fugitives should be protected by this country from its jurisdiction on the ground that they are political offenders.' (*R v Home Secretary ex parte Fininvest S.p.A.*[6])

1   *Hilali v The Central Court of Criminal Proceedings No 5 of the National Court, Madrid* [2006] 4 All ER 435, DC per Scott Baker LJ at para 62; *Tamarevichute v The Government of the Russian Federation* [2008] EWHC 534 (Admin) per Swift J at para 12; *Ahsan v the Director of Public Prosecutions & others* [2008] EWHC 666 (Admin) per Richards LJ at para 131.
2   [1971] 1 WLR 987, HL per Lord Diplock at 994; *Tamarevichute* (above) per Swift J at para 12.
3   [1971] 1 WLR 459, DC at 466.
4   In *Ahmad v Government of the United States of America* [2006] EWHC 2927 (Admin), the High Court rejected (per Laws LJ at paras 91–100) a submission that the imposition of Special Administrative Measures were applied in America only to Muslim prisoners (and were thus referable to the defendant's religion). See also *Ahsan* at paras 129–141. In *Jaso & others v Central Criminal Court No 2, Madrid* [2007] EWHC 2983 (Admin), the High Court rejected (Per Dyson LJ at paras 59–61) a submission that incommunicado detention policy and a prison dispersal policy were applied only to Muslim prisoners; '[t]here is no basis for a finding other than that all detainees charged with serious offences of terrorism, whatever their political beliefs, will be subject to the same or similar restrictions ...There is no reasonable ground for thinking that there is a causal link between the restrictions on personal liberty and the appellants' political beliefs'. In *Tamarevichute* (above), the High Court rejected a submission that as a person of Romany origin, the appellant might be prejudiced at her trial in Kaliningrad on account of her race. Swift J observed (at para 99) that suffering general prejudice as a result of ethnic origin is not sufficient to constitute a bar to her extradition under the provisions of s 81; specific prejudice is required.
5   [1964] AC 556, HL, at 582 per Lord Reid. See, under the 2003 Act, *Hilali* (above) per Scott Baker LJ at para 63.
6   [1997] 1 WLR 743, per Simon Brown LJ at 762C-763H. See also *McKinnon v Government of the United States of America* [2007] EWHC 762 (Admin) per Maurice Kay LJ at para 17.

8.09   The risk of exposure to 'extraneous considerations' can be indirect. Whilst a defendant is expressly protected under the 2003 Act from illegitimate onward extradition from the Requesting State,[1] he may nonetheless be at risk of refoulement or executive expulsion to a state in which he risks facing 'extraneous considerations'. Non-refoulement[2] is *jus cogens* and a peremptory norm of international law. Extradition will be refused by reference to Article 3 ECHR if a defendant can demonstrate a real risk of refoulement[3]. The fact that the requesting State is a signatory to the ECHR will not be determinative[4.] Moreover, ss 39 and 121 provides that a person must not be extradited before any asylum claim is determined, save where extradition is to a Part 1 territory and where the person is not a national or a citizen of the Part 1 territory and either (a) the Part 1 territory has accepted responsibility for determining the claim, or (b) the Secretary of State is satisfied that the person's life and liberty will not be threatened in that state and that state will not refoule the person in breach of the Refugee Convention.[5]

1   Sections 56–59 and 130–131 of the 2003 Act.
2   Article 33(1) of the 1951 Refugee Convention
3   *Faraj v The Government of Italy* [2004] EWHC 2950 (Admin) (no real risk of forcible expulsion to Libya by Italy); *Ramda v Secretary of State for the Home Department* [2005] EWHC 2526 (Admin) at para 60 (risk of forcible expulsion to Algeria by France post-sentence speculative); *Boudhiba v Central Examining Court No. 5 of the High Court of Madrid* [2007] 1 WLR 124, DC at paras 56–57 (risk of forcible expulsion to Tunisia by Spain post-sentence speculative); *Dabas v The High Court of Justice, Madrid* [2007] 1 WLR 145, DC at para 39 (no real risk of forcible expulsion to Syria by Spain and no evidence of risk of persecution were he to be expelled to Syria); *Hilali* (above para **8.08**) at paras 96–106 (risk of forcible expulsion to Morocco by Spain post-sentence speculative); *Ahmad* (above para **8.08**) at paras 87–90 (no real risk of extraordinary rendition by America); *Khemiri & others v The Court of Milan* [2008] EWHC 1988 (Admin) (no real risk of forcible expulsion to Tunisia by Italy).
4   *R (Yogathas) v Secretary of State for the Home Department* [2003] 1 AC 920, HL per Lord Bingham of Cornhill at para 9; *Faraj* (above) per Tuckey LJ at para 21.
5   Section 40. Obvious difficulties, and obvious potential for abuse, can arise where the state from whom the defendant has been granted asylum, etc is the state requesting his extradition. The asylum provisions of ss 39–40 and 121 of the 2003 Act do not deal with this. It is submitted that, if the CPS and Requesting State have been informed that the requested person holds refugee status as against the Requesting State, but maintain the extradition request nonetheless, then they are liable to be found, subject to specific factual considerations indicating otherwise, to be attempting to circumvent the requested person's asylum protection/appeal procedures and thereby abusing the Court's process.

8.10   These 'extraneous considerations' would, in reality, amount to instances of abuse of process under domestic law.[1] In *R v Governor of Belmarsh Prison, ex p Gilligan & Ellis*,[2] the House of Lords observed that the existence of this fundamental protection is, of itself, inconsistent with the need for a general extradition abuse jurisdiction:

'It is inconsistent with a general abuse of process jurisdiction ...If an abuse of process jurisdiction existed there would be no need for such a specific protection.'[3]

1   *R (Government of the United States of America) v Bow Street Magistrates' Court* [2007] 1 WLR 1157, DC per Lord Phillips CJ at paras 68 and 80.
2   [2001] 1 AC 84, HL.
3   Per Lord Steyn at 97C-D; with whom Lords Browne-Wilkinson, Cooke and Hope agreed. See also, to similar effect, per Lord Clyde at 101E.

Double jeopardy

8.11   Sections 12 and 80 of the 2003 Act protect against double jeopardy. In *Fofana & Belize v Deputy Prosecutor Thubin, Tribunal de Grande Instance de Meaux, France*,[1] this protection was held to encompass not only the narrow concepts of *autrefois convict/acquit*, but also the wider abuse jurisdiction acknowledged domestically in *Connelly v DPP*,[2] *DPP v Humphrys*[3] and *R v Beedie*[4] (discussed in detail in **Chapter 7**).

1   [2006] EWHC 744 per Auld LJ at paras 17–23. See also *Maxwell-King v The Government of the United States of America* [2006] EWHC 3033 (Admin) per Lloyd-Jones J at paras 24–31; *John v The Government of the United States of America* [2006] EWHC 3512 (Admin), [2006]

Extradition LR 305 per Wilkie J at paras 17–24; *Mitchell v France (from High Court of Boulogne Sur Mer)* [2007] EWHC 2006 (Admin) per Collins J at paras 26–28.
2   [1964] AC 1254, HL per Lord Pearce at 1365.
3   [1977] AC 1 HL per Lord Hailsham of Marylebone at 41D-E.
4   [1998] QB 356, CA per Rose LJ, at 361–366.

8.12   *Fofana* concerned a French extradition warrant which purported to relate to one offence of fraudulent conduct (the 'Serviware' fraud) but which also described wider allegations of fraud (against other companies) by the two defendants. The defendants had previously been the subject of an indictment in England relating to the same Serviware conduct for which extradition was sought. In the UK, the appellant Fofana pleaded guilty to lesser counts and was sentenced. In respect of the appellant Belize, formal not guilty verdicts were entered. Auld LJ noted[1] that the concept of double jeopardy was 'now a broader concept than a plea in bar of autrefois acquit'. Notwithstanding that the English indictment, confined to the Serviware allegation, 'did not reflect the seriousness and general range of conduct referred to in the [French] warrant',[2] which 'was of a much wider and lengthy course of fraud against a number of French companies, of which the June 2005 Serviware transaction was only part',[3] Auld LJ concluded that:

'although the extradition offence specified in the Warrant is not based on exactly, or only partly, the same facts as those charged [in England], there would be such a significant overlap between them as to have required the District Judge to stay the extradition proceedings as an abuse of process.'[4]

1   At para 2.
2   At para 7.
3   At para 11.
4   At para 29.

Passage of time

8.13   Sections 14 and 82 of the 2003 Act protect a defendant against extradition in circumstances where he may be subject to injustice or oppression by reason of the passage of time since the commission of the offence or, in conviction cases, the conviction.[1] In *Kakis v Government of the Republic of Cyprus,*[2] Lord Diplock observed[3] that 'unjust' is directed to 'the risk of prejudice to the accused in the conduct of the trial itself', whereas 'oppression' is directed to 'hardship to the accused resulting from changes in his circumstances that have occurred during the period to be taken into consideration'. Both propositions may overlap and, together, 'cover all cases where to return him would not be fair'. The relevant period (or 'cradle of events') runs from the last date of the offence to the date of the extradition hearing.[4]

1   Previously s 11(3)(b) of the Extradition Act 1989.
2   [1978] 1 WLR 779, HL.
3   At 782H-783A.
4   At 782G per Lord Diplock; at 790D-E per Lord Scarman; *Government of the United States of America v Tollman (No 2)* [2008] 3 All ER 150, DC per Moses LJ at para 79.

8.14   The protection afforded by ss 14 and 82 is, in practice, significantly wider than that afforded to defendants in domestic criminal proceedings by way of abuse of process (discussed in detail in **Chapter 1**). Unlike the test to be applied in domestic proceedings, the District Judge should not confine imposition of the statutory bar to exceptional or rare cases or circumstances.[1] Discharge should not be limited to cases where there is 'evidence' of prejudice; the question in such cases is whether there is a 'risk' of prejudice.[2] If it appears that a return will be unjust or oppressive there is no room for any exercise of a residual discretion by the Court – the applicant must be discharged.[3] Therefore, extradition case law under the statutory bar on extradition was observed in *R v Abu Hamza*,[4] in the context of a complaint about pre-trial publicity resulting from unjustified delay, to be neither a close nor helpful analogy to the test to be applied for staying a trial on the grounds of abuse of process in domestic proceedings. Although the converse is not necessarily true,[5] in *Re: Ashley Riddle*, Sedley J observed[6] that the provision:

> 'it should be remembered, is neither a limitation clause nor a disciplinary measure. Its focus is the person sought and the effect on him or her of whatever delay there has been. Thus, excusable delay, if its effect meets the statutory test, may require discharge; and inexcusable delay, if its impact on the person sought is not within the mischief aimed at, may fail to do so. Whether, in either case, this is the result will depend in part on 'all the circumstances', and these may undoubtedly include any good reasons or want of good reasons for the lapse of time, and whether any bad reasons have been the fault of the person sought or the Requesting State.'

1   *Union of India v Manohar lal Narang* [1978] AC 247, HL per Lord Morris of Borth-y-Gest at 279C-E, per Lord Edmund-Davies at 285F-G, per Lord Keith of Kinkell at 293G–294D; *Tollman (No 2)* (above para **8.13**) per Moses LJ at paras 44–47.
2   *Tollman (No 2)* (above para **8.13**) per Moses LJ at para 47.
3   *Narang* (above) per Viscount Dilhorne at 273A-B, per Lord Edmund-Davies at 283E-284B & 285C-G, per Lord Fraser of Tullybelton at 287F-289B, per Lord Keith of Kinkell at 293C-F
4   [2006] EWCA Crim 2918 per Lord Phillips CJ at paragraph 80.
5   *Tollman (No 2)* (above para **8.13**) per Moses LJ at paras 44–47.
6   [1993] unreported 2 November, DC at transcript p 8. See also *Tollman (No 2)* (above para **8.13**) per Moses LJ at paras 79–80.

8.15   Over 40 per cent of the case law under the 2003 Act concerns passage of time and a detailed examination of the case law is beyond the scope of this work. But, ss 14 and 82 reflect long-standing principles of extradition law and have historically been held to cover situations where, by virtue of delay, the passage of time inhibits, by dimming recollection or otherwise, proper consideration of trial issues or inhibits the tracing of witnesses still able to recollect specific events,[1] or cases where witnesses, materials, or certain lines of defence are no longer available,[2] even in cases of relatively short delay.[3] 'Culpable delay' on the part of the Requesting State, will be a relevant factor in 'borderline' cases[4]. Delay on the part of the applicant, i e by fleeing the country, concealing his whereabouts, or evading arrest, cannot – save in the most exceptional circumstances – count towards making his return 'unjust' or 'oppressive'.[5] 'Oppression' may arise where a defendant has lived openly and established family ties in the UK and to remove him would be oppressive. Oppression can also arise in circumstances where the inaction of the

Requesting State, or its positive conduct, has caused in the defendant a legitimate sense of false security.[6] Oppression can attach to persons for whom the defendant has responsibility.[7] The onus is ultimately on the defendant[8] to demonstrate, on the balance of probabilities, that it would be unjust or oppressive, because of the delay, having regard to all the circumstances, to return him. In seeking to discharge the onus on him, a defendant must produce cogent evidence of injustice or oppression. It is not sufficient to offer mere assertions or speculation.

1   *Kakis* (above para **8.13**). See, for example, *R v Secretary of State, ex parte Patel* (1995) 7 Admin LR 56 at p70F-G.
2   See, for example, *Narang* (above para **8.14**) at 280G per Lord Morris of Borth-y Gest; *Re: Ashley Riddle* (above para **8.14**) per Sedley J at transcript p 3.
3   See, for example, the absence of an alibi witness in the context of 4½ years' delay in *Kakis* (above para **8.13**) and the absence of witnesses of fact in the context of a four-year delay (three of which were culpable) in *Re: Ashley Riddle* (above para **8.14**).
4   *R v Governor of Brixton Prison, ex p Osman (No 4)* [1992] 1 All ER 579 at 587D–H per Woolf LJ.
5   *Kakis* (above para **8.13**) per Lord Diplock at 783A.
6   *Hunt v Court of First Instance, Antwerp* [2006] 2 All ER 735, DC per Newman J at para 25.
7   *Re: Ashley-Riddle* (above para **8.14**); *Cookeson v Government of Australia* [2001] EWHC Admin 149; *Hunt* (above); *Tollman (No. 2)* (above para **8.13**) at para 110.
8   *Union of India v Manohar lal Narang* (above para **8.13**) per Lord Keith of Kinkell at 293H-294A

8.16   The Courts will, however, pay particular regard to any abuse jurisdiction shown to exist in the Requesting State capable of addressing any injustice or oppression alleged. The existence of such a jurisdiction is highly relevant to, but not determinative of, how the UK Courts judge the issues. In *Woodcock v Government of New Zealand*[1], Simon Brown LJ observed[2] that the applicable statutory provisions:

'... [require] this court's decision not upon whether, having regard to the passage of time, it would be unjust to *try* the accused, but rather whether it would be unjust to *return* him (albeit, of course, return him for trial). To my mind that entitles, indeed requires, this court to have regard to whatever safeguards may exist in the domestic law of the Requesting State to ensure that the accused would not be subjected to an unjust trial there. There are, it should be borne in mind, clear advantages in having the question whether or not a fair trial is now possible decided in the domestic court rather than by us. That court will have an altogether clearer picture than we have of precisely what evidence is available and the issues likely to arise. For example, the accused is likely to be interviewed on return ... so that more is likely to be known about his defence. If, of course, we were to conclude that the domestic court in the Requesting State would be *bound* to hold that a fair trial of the accused is now impossible, then plainly we would regard it as unjust (and/or oppressive) to return him. Equally, we would have no alternative but to reach our own conclusion on whether a fair trial would now be possible in the Requesting State if we were not persuaded that the courts of that state have what we would regard as satisfactory procedures of their own akin to our (and the New Zealand courts') abuse of process jurisdiction.'[3]

1   [2004] 1 WLR 1979, DC.

2   At paras 20–21.

3   In *Woodcock*, the court found that extradition was not barred by reason of passage of time because, firstly, the evidence demonstrated that the New Zealand courts have satisfactory procedures for guarding against an unjust trial and, secondly, that, under those procedures, they would certainly not be bound to find a fair trial impossible. The *Woodcock* approach applies under the 2003 Act (*Crean v The Government of Ireland* [2007] EWHC 814 (Admin)). But, where there is no information or evidence as to how the court in the Requesting State would approach an abuse of process argument, it is for this court to consider the risk of hardship or injustice which could arise (*Hunt* (above para **8.15**) per Newman J at para 21). It appears, however, that a different approach will apply in Part 1 cases, where the Requesting State is a signatory to the European Convention on Human Rights. In light of *Lisowski v Regional Court of Bialystok, Poland* [2006] EWHC 3227 (Admin) per Walker J at paras 17–18; *La Torre v The Republic of Italy* [2007] EWHC 1370 (Admin) per Laws LJ at paras 43–45; *Government of Croatia v Spanovic* [2007] EWHC 1770 (Admin) Hughes LJ at para 24; *Krzyzowski v The Circuit Court in Glewice, Poland* [2007] EWHC 2754 (Admin) per Longmore LJ at para,. 24 and Mitting J at para 31; *Harvey v Judicial Authority of Portugal* [2007] EWHC 3282 (Admin) per Maurice Kay LJ at paras 26–30, it appears that, in such cases, the onus is on the defendant to adduce material suggesting deficiencies in the Requesting State's system or justifying a departure from the obligation to give full faith and credence to the legal and judicial system of a fellow European country. In the absence of such a showing, the court is entitled to assume that such procedures exist, and that *Woodcock* applies.

Trials in absence

8.17   Sections 20 and 85 of the 2003 Act provide that, in cases where a person has been tried in their absence and has not deliberately absented themselves from the trial, extradition of a convicted person shall not lie unless the person is guaranteed a retrial or a review amounting to a retrial. In practice, these provisions give mandatory effect to the line of decisions under previous legislation confirming that it would not be 'in the interests of justice' [1] to extradite in such cases in the absence of an unconditional guarantee of a full and unfettered retrial.[2] In cases where a person has been tried in their absence and has not deliberately absented themselves from the trial, but the trial process remains ongoing (because of, say, an extant appeal), the person will be categorised as an 'accused' person, so that s 20 will not apply. But, Art 6 of the ECHR would, in such a case, provide the same result (via ss 21 and 87).[3]

1   Under s 6(2) of the 1989 Act, or as a matter of jurisdiction under s 26 of the Extradition Act 1870 (and para 20 of Sch 1 to the 1989 Act).

2   For cases under previous statutory provisions in which the right to a re-hearing did not exist or was fettered in some way, see *R v Governor of Brixton Prison & Ors, ex p Caborn-Waterfield* [1960] 2 QB 498; *Athanassiadis v Government of Greece (Note)* [1971] AC 282; *Regina v Governor of Pentonville Prison & Anor, ex p Zezza* [1983] AC 46, HL; *In re Avashilom Sarig* [1993] COD 472; *Regina (Guisto) v Governor of Brixton Prison & Anor.* [2004] 1 AC 101, HL; *R v Governor of Brixton Prison, ex p Cavallo* (unreported) (13 March 1997) DC per Simon Brown LJ at transcript p 4; *R v Governor of Brixton Prison, ex p Barone* (unreported) (7 November 1997) DC, per Kennedy LJ. at transcript pp 10–11; *Peci v Governor of Brixton Prison* (unreported) (5 November 1999) DC, per Moses J at transcript pp 2 and 5–9; *R v Government of Bulgaria, ex p Ratchev* (unreported) (17 May 2000) DC per Henry LJ at paras 8 and 24–35; *Government of Italy v Saia* (unreported) (16 November 2001), DC per Pitchford J at paras 4, 13, 15–17; *Farrow v Government of Italy* (unreported) (14 June 2002) DC, per Rose LJ at paras 9–11; *Sadutto v Governor of HMP Brixton & Anor* [2004] EWHC 563 (Admin).

3   *Stoichkov v Bulgaria* [2005] ECHR 24 June at para 56; *Sejdovic v Italy* [2006] ECHR 1 March

at paras 87–88 and 99; *Da An Chen v Government of Romania* [2006] EWHC 1752 (Admin) per Mitting J at para: 10; *Caldarelli v Court of Naples* [2008] 1 WLR 1724, HL.

Physical or mental health

8.18   Sections 25 and 91 protect a defendant against extradition in circumstances where a defendant's physical or mental condition is such that it would be unjust or oppressive to extradite him. Prior to the 2003 Act, issues of physical or mental health fell to be determined pursuant to the overriding discretion afforded to the Secretary of State. It was well-settled law that, in the event that there existed, as between the medical experts instructed by the parties, a live issue to be determined as to fitness to plead/stand trial, that issue should be decided by the courts of the Requesting State.[1] Whereas, if there is no such live issue, because the respective experts agree that the defendant is unfit, extradition should be refused (*In re Davies*[2]). For a case under the 2003 Act in which s 91 was applied, see *Tollman (No 2)*.[3] 'Oppression' would encompass, amongst other issues, risks associated with travel, as to which, see *McCaughey v Government of the United States of America.*[4]

1   *R (Warren) v Secretary of State for the Home Department* [2003] EWHC 1177.
2   [1998] COD 1–83, pp 30–32.
3   Above para **8.13**, per Ouseley J at paras 120 et seq.
4   [2006] EWHC 248 (Admin).

National Security

8.19   Section 208 of the 2003 Act enables the Secretary of State to prevent extradition where the person's extradition in respect of the offence would be against the interests of national security and where the person was either (a) engaging in the conduct constituting (or alleged to constitute) the offence for the purpose of assisting in the exercise of a function conferred or imposed by or under an enactment, or (b) is not liable under the criminal law of any part of the UK for the conduct constituting (or alleged to constitute) the offence, as a result of an authorisation given by the Secretary of State. This would obviously encompass a particular class of entrapment (emanating from the authorities of the UK) that, in a domestic context, would fall to be considered under the principles in *R v Looseley*[1] or *Teixiera de Castro v Portugal,*[2] discussed in detail in **Chapter 6**. For cases where, by contrast, entrapment has been argued to emanate from the authorities of the Requesting State, see below at paragraph **8.120**.

1   [2001] 1 WLR 2060, HL.
2   (1998) 28 EHRR 101.

HUMAN RIGHTS

8.20   The enactment of ss 21 and 87 of the 2003 Act marked a dramatic change in extradition law and practice. For the first time, ECHR rights became an integral part of the extradition machinery. The District Judge is now required in every case to determine whether extradition is Convention compliant.

Articles 2 & 3 of the ECHR

8.21   Articles 2 and 3 of the ECHR contain fundamental protections against prospective abusive treatment in the Requesting State. Whilst overlapping with the 'extraneous considerations' protections of ss 13 and 81, Arts 2 and 3 apply regardless of the motivation for the treatment or its source in the Requesting State. Art 3 has been expressly held to apply to extradition proceedings. In *Soering v United Kingdom*[1] the European Court of Human Rights held that 'the decision by a Contracting State to extradite a fugitive may give rise to an issue under article 3, and hence, engage the responsibility of that State under the Convention.' [2] The basis for liability of the UK court being that it has 'taken action which has, as a direct consequence, caused the exposure of an individual to proscribed ill-treatment'.[3] The test to be applied was outlined in *Soering*, and said to be whether a defendant has 'shown ... substantial grounds ... for believing' that the person concerned faces a 'real risk' of being subjected to treatment contrary to Art 3 (in *Soering*, the 'death row' phenomenon) if extradited.[4] But the threshold for engaging Art 3 in extradition proceedings is, in practice, a high one.[5]

1   (1989) 11 EHRR 439.
2   At para 91. The provisions of Art 3 are absolute. There exists no balancing exercise to be carried out (*Chahal v United Kingdom* (1996) 23 EHRR 413 at paras 79–80; *Saadi v Italy* (Appl No 37201/06) at paras 125–138). In practice, there is no difference between the case law governing asylum/expulsion and that governing extradition. It is irrelevant that the risk is of torture or inhuman or degrading treatment or punishment carried out clandestinely either by the authorities in the Requesting State or by third parties (*HLR v France* (1997) 26 EHRR 29; *D v United Kingdom* (1997) 24 EHRR 423; *R (Bagdanavicius) v Secretary of State for the Home Department* [2005] 2 AC 668, HL; *Mclean v The High Court of Dublin, Ireland* [2008] EWHC 547 (Admin)). It should be noted that Arts 2–4 of Protocol 4 to the European Convention (specific provision for freedom of movement and protection from arbitrary expulsion) have not been ratified by the UK. However, that does not detract from (or limit) the protection provided by other convention rights (*Abdulaziz, Cabales and Balkandali v United Kingdom* (1985) 7 EHRR 471 at para 60).
3   At paras 90–91.
4   At para 91; *R (Ullah) v Special Adjudicator* [2004] 2 AC 352 per Lord Bingham of Cornhill at para 24. See more recently *Saadi v Italy* (above) at paras 125 and 140.
5   See, for example, *N v Secretary of State for the Home Department* [2005] 2 AC 296, HL. The threshold for engaging Art 2 was thought to be higher still and require a showing of 'near certainty', but the High Court has opined that the same threshold applies for Arts 2 and 3; *Mclean* (above) at paras 5–11.

Article 5 ECHR

8.22   Article 5(1)(f) of ECHR expressly provides for lawful detention for the purposes of extradition or deportation;

'Everyone has the right to liberty and security of person. No one shall be deprived of his liberty save in the following cases and in accordance with a procedure prescribed by law:

...

(f)   the lawful arrest or detention of a person ... against whom action is being taken with a view to deportation or extradition ...'

8.23   Article 5(1) of ECHR requires that the detention of the defendant in the requested state pursuant to ECHR, Art 5(1)(f) should not be arbitrary or vitiated by misuse of authority or bad faith:

'... Article 5(1)(f) clearly permits the Commission to decide on the lawfulness ("lawful detention/detention reguliere") of a person against whom action is being taken with a view to extradition (une procedure d'extradition est en cours). The wording of both the French and English texts makes it clear that only the existence of extradition proceedings justifies deprivation of liberty in such a case. It follows that if, for example, the proceedings are not conducted with the requisite diligence, or if the detention results from some misuse of authority, it ceases to be justifiable under Article 5(1)(f)...' (*Lynas v Switzerland*[1]).

1   (1976) 6 DR 141 at 167. Note also ECHR, Art 18 which provides that 'The restrictions permitted under this Convention to the ... rights and freedoms [secured in it] shall not be applied for any purpose other than those for which they have been prescribed ...'. In Quinn v France (1995) 21 EHRR 529, the Court observed that 'the provision (Art. 18) afforded specific protection and could be invoked on its own without reference to other articles of the Convention' (at para 57). There, the Court examined the evidence relating to proceedings in France and found no evidence of 'an abuse of procedure' (para 59).

8.24   In *R v Governor of Brockhill Prison, ex p Evans (No 2)*[1] Lord Hope observed that, under Art 5(1), assuming that the detention is lawful under domestic law, the Court must be satisfied that it is nevertheless not open to criticism on the ground that it is arbitrary because, for example, it was resorted to in bad faith or was not proportionate:...'.[2] Arbitrariness and bad faith are the keystones of most abuses of process. Although the threshold is high,[3] the jurisprudence of the European Court of Human Rights demonstrates that in cases concerning alleged abuse of extradition procedures and/or executive misconduct in the procuring of the defendant's return, ECHR, Art 5 may be engaged. As will be seen later, Art 5 has been the foundation upon which the extradition abuse of process jurisdiction has been built.

1   [2001] 2 AC 19, HL at p 39B-E.
2   This requirement flows from innumerable decisions of the European Court of Human Rights to the effect that: 'The main issue to be determined is whether the disputed detention was "lawful", including whether it was in accordance with "a procedure prescribed by law". The Convention here refers essentially to national law and establishes the need to apply its rules, but it also requires that any measure depriving the individual of his liberty must be compatible with the purpose of Article 5 (art. 5), namely to protect the individual from arbitrariness ... What is at stake here is not only the "right to liberty" but also the "right to security of person"...' (See for example, *Bozano v France* (1986) 9 ECHR 297 at paras 54 and 59).
3   The test is one of 'flagrant breach'; *R (Ullah) v Special Adjudicator* (above para **8.21**) per Lord Bingham of Cornhill at para 24; *Government of Romani v Ceausescu* [2006] EWHC 2615 (Admin) per Maurice Kay LJ at para 12.

8.25   For example, *Bozano v France*,[1] discussed in detail in **Chapter 5** in para **5.57**, concerned facts not dissimilar to *R v Bow Street Magistrates' Court, ex p Mackeson*,[2] *R v Plymouth Justices, ex p Driver*[3] and *R v Mullen*.[4] The European Court unanimously found a violation of Art 5, ruling that:

'... the applicant's deprivation of liberty was neither lawful within the meaning of Article 5(1)(f) nor compatible with the right to security of person. Depriving Mr Bozano of his liberty in this way amounted in fact to a disguised form of extradition designed to circumvent the negative ruling of the Court of Appeal and not detention necessary in the ordinary course of action taken with a view to deportation[5]... the deportation procedure was abused' .[6]

1   Above para **8.24**.
2   (1981) 75 Cr App Rep 24, DC.
3   [1986] QB 95, DC.
4   [2000] 1 QB 520, CA.
5   (1986) 9 EHRR 297 at para 60.
6   At para 61. Compare the facts of *Stocke v Germany* [1991] App No 11755/85 (discussed in detail in Chapter **5**, paras **5.58–5.59**) and the approach of the Court in *Sanchez Ramirez v France* (1996) 86-B DR 155 and *Ocalan v Turkey*, Grand Chamber, 12 May 12 2005, paras 83–99; (both discussed in detail in Chapter **5**, paras **5.61–5.69**) all concerning allegations of disguised extradition.

8.26   Extradition Acts have historically contained express protection against extradition requests made in bad faith. The test for bad faith has always been a broad one. Under s 11(3)(c) of the 1989 Act[1], it was stated by Woolf LJ in *In Re Osman*[2] that:

'the term good faith has to be given a reasonably generous interpretation so that if the proceedings were brought for a collateral purpose, or with an improper motive and not for the purpose of achieving the proper administration of justice, they would not be regarded as complying with this statutory requirement. Likewise, the accusations would not be made in good faith in the interests of justice if the prosecution deliberately manipulates or misuses the process of the court to deprive the defendant of a protection to which he is entitled by law'.

1   'Without prejudice to the jurisdiction of the High Court apart from this section, the court shall order the person's discharge if it appears to the court in relation to the offence, or each of the offences, in respect of which the applicant's return is sought, that ... (c) because the accusation against him is not made in good faith in the interests of justice'. Section 12(2)(a)(iii) gave a like power to the Secretary of State.
2   (25 February 1992, unreported), DC at transcript pp 8–9. Cited by Rose LJ in *R (Saifi) v Governor of Brixton Prison* [2001] 1 WLR 1134 at para 22, Brooke LJ in *Lodhi v Governor of Brixton Prison* [2001] EWHC 178 (Admin) at para 106.

8.27   The 2003 Act contains no 'bad faith' exception. That is because, as was made clear during Parliamentary debate during the passage of the 2003 Act[1], ECHR, Art 5 would be engaged (via ss 21 or 87 of the 2003 Act) in the case of an extradition request made in bad faith. Such a request would amount to 'arbitrary' extradition contrary to Art 5. Therefore, the developed case law under s 11(3)(c) of the 1989 Act remains applicable. Bad faith may attach to anything in the laying of the allegation/charge that would disclose bad faith on the part of the Requesting State. In *R (Saifi) v Governor of Brixton Prison,*[2] bad faith was found on the part of the Indian prosecuting authorities in circumstances which disclosed a failure to disclose a magistrates' recording that pressure had been applied to the sole witness upon whose evidence the case depended, public attempts on the part of the police to prejudice a fair trial, failure to disclose a retraction statement and failure to disclose the fact that the witness' statement had been written by a third person. Moreover, Brooke LJ made plain[3] that bad faith is not confined to the Requesting State or its law-enforcement authorities. It may emanate from a witness or complainant. Other examples of successful reliance upon s 11(3)(c) include *Asliturk v Government of Turkey*[4] and *Sutej v Governor of HMP Holloway & another.*[5] For an example of the difficulties in establishing bad faith in a post-conviction extradition request, see *Mariotti v Government of Italy.*[6]

1   Hansard, House of Commons, 25 March 2003, Second Reading, Vol 402, col 188; Hansard, House of Lords, 27 October 2003, Report stage, Vol 654, cols 114–115: 'Can it seriously be said that the High Court has no power to discharge a fugitive where it is plain that the accusation has been made against him in bad faith? Of course not, such a result would bring the whole extradition process into disrepute', per Baroness Scotland of Asthal.
2   Above para **8.26** per Rose LJ at paras 64–66.
3   At para 63.
4   [2002] EWHC 2326 (Admin); extradition of Mayor of Istanbul sought for political reasons.
5   [2003] EWHC 1940 (Admin); allegations made for purposes of bolstering civil proceedings.
6   [2005] EWHC 2745 (Admin) per Maurice Kay LJ at para 27: 'Whether or not the over-enthusiastic and careless statements of Italian officials are also tainted by bad faith (and we do not consider it necessary to make such a finding), we do not believe that it would be appropriate to discharge the applicant in the interests of justice by reference to them. This is a conviction case and we find no bad faith on the part of the Italian authorities or anyone for whom they are responsible in the processes which resulted in the conviction. In circumstances where a conviction for a very grave offence has been obtained by due process, in my judgment it would be a very rare case in which extradition would be refused simply because officials acting on the extradition request have been shown to have overegged the pudding.'

8.28   It is also clear from *Re Murat Calis*[1] that supervening bad faith on the part of the prosecuting/investigating authority is capable of rendering a charge or complaint, albeit initially honest, one of bad faith within s 11(3)(c). In that case, the complainant had visited Mr Calis's lawyer and offered to withdraw his complaint in return for payment. Sedley J held that:

'it becomes inescapable in my judgement that the accusation … is no longer being made in good faith, assuming it to have been originally an honest complaint. It is being pursued against the … applicant as a means of blackmail … [T]he facts which establish bad faith in the present case also establish that to return the applicant would be both unjust and oppressive.' [2]

1   (19 November 1993, unreported), DC. See also *Castillo v The Kingdom of Spain* [2005] 1 WLR 1043, DC per Thomas LJ at paras 41–44 (deliberate exaggeration by a Requesting State of the description of conduct in an extradition request capable of evidencing bad faith).
2   At transcript p 10.

Article 6 ECHR

8.29   Article 6 does not apply to the Court's examination of an extradition request from a foreign State, even in cases where the Court carries out an assessment of whether there is a case to answer. Extradition proceedings do not involve the determination of guilt or innocence and thus do not amount to the determination of a criminal charge within the meaning of Art 6(1).[1] It is not the function of the Strasbourg authorities to supervise the correct applica-tion of extradition law.[2] Thus Strasbourg has, for example, declined to investigate complaints that extradition proceedings have been vitiated by the length of detention pending extradition in violation of ECHR, Art 6(1),[3] non-service of extradition decisions in violation of ECHR, Art 6(1),[4] non-access to the court file and the inability to advance arguments regarding the characterisation of the offence in violation of ECHR, Art 6(1),[5] inadequate representation and interpretation in violation of ECHR, Arts 6(3)(b) and 6(3)(e),[6] the absence of legal aid in the Requesting State in violation of ECHR, Art 6(3)(c)[7] and the inability to cross-examine in violation of ECHR, Art 6(3)(d).[8] The House of Lords summarised the position in *R (Al-Fawwaz) v Brixton Prison Governor:*[9]

> '... it is clear from the decision of the European Commission of Human Rights in *Kirkwood v United Kingdom* (1984) 37 DR 158 that the provisions of Article 6 do not apply to a committal hearing on an application for extradition, the Commission stating, at p 191, para 9, of its decision: 'Nevertheless, the Commission concludes that these proceedings did not in themselves form part of the determination of the applicant's guilt or innocence, which will be the subject of separate proceedings in the United States which may be expected to conform to standards of fairness equivalent to the requirements of Article 6, including the presumption of innocence, notwithstanding the committal proceedings. In these circumstances, the Commission concludes that the committal proceedings did not form part of or constitute the determination of a criminal charge within the meaning of Article 6 of the Convention.'

1   See *Maaouia v France* (2000) App No 39652/98 at paras 33–41 and *Mamatkulov & Askarov v Turkey* (2005) 18 BHRC 203: 'The Court reiterates that decisions regarding the entry, stay and deportation of aliens do not concern the determination of an applicant's civil rights or obligations or of a criminal charge against him, within the meaning of Article 6 § 1 of the Convention' (at para 82).
2   *Altun v Germany* (1983) 36 DR 209 at 231.
3   *Maaouia v France* (above) at paras 33–41; *Raf v Spain* (2001) (dec) App No 53652/00 at para 1; *Albo v Italy* (2004) (dec) App No 56271/00 at para 3(b); *Farmakopoulos v Greece* (1990) 64 DR 52 and *EGM v Luxembourg* (1994) EHRR 144.
4   *Raidl v Austria* (1995) (dec) App No 25342/94 at para 3(e); *Raf v Spain* (above).
5   *Mamatkulov & Askarov v Turkey* (above) at paras 81–82.
6   *H v Spain* (1983) 37 DR 93 at 94.
7   *Soering v UK* (above para **8.21**) at para 113
8   *Kirkwood v UK* (1984) 37 DR 158 at 191.
9   [2002] 2 WLR 101, HL per Lord Hutton at para 87.

8.30   However, it was stated in *Soering v United Kingdom*[1] that the act of extradition to a country lacking Article 6 fair trial guarantees can have indirect application (through Art 3). That is to say that UK State responsibility may be engaged under Art 3 in circumstances where extradition may be said to have as a direct consequence the exposure of an individual to an Art 6 incompatible trial:

> '... the right to a fair trial in criminal proceedings, as embodied in Article 6, holds a prominent place in a democratic society. The court does not exclude that an issue might exceptionally be raised under Article 6 by an extradition decision in circumstances where the fugitive has suffered or risks suffering a flagrant denial of a fair trial in the Requesting State.'[2]

1   Above para **8.21**, at para 113. This principle was subsequently referred to by the European Court in the following terms in *Drozd and Janousek v France and Spain* (1992) 14 EHRR 745 at para 110: 'As the Convention does not require the Contracting Parties to impose its standards on third States or territories, France was not obliged to verify whether the proceedings which resulted in the conviction were compatible with all the requirements of Article 6 of the Convention ... would also thwart the current trend towards strengthening international cooperation in the administration of justice, a trend which is in principle in the interests of the persons concerned. The Contracting States are, however, obliged to refuse their co-operation if it emerges that the conviction is the result of a flagrant denial of justice'.

2   See also *R (Al-Fawwaz) v Governor of Brixton Prison* (above para **8.29**) per Lord Scott at 136, para 116: 'But alleged malefactors who are present in this country, whether as permanent residents, as refugees or asylum seekers, or as visitors, are entitled, while they are here, to the protection of our laws and our standards of criminal justice. They should not be exported abroad to face trial under a foreign criminal justice system unless, by our standards, there is a case against them that is fit for trial, and unless, by our standards, they will receive a fair trial in accordance with the requirements of Article 6 of the European Convention for the Protection of Human Rights and Fundamental Freedoms. The ... purpose of extradition arrangements is, or should be, to provide the requisite safeguards'.

8.31   The limits of this indirect application are, however, strict[1]. The matter was put as follows in *R (Ullah) v Special Adjudicator.*[2] Lord Bingham of Cornhill (with whom all other Law Lords agreed) reviewed the ECHR authorities at para 17, and concluded that:

'The authority cited in para 17 shows that the court has not excluded the possibility of relying on Article 6, and even Article 5, while fully recognising the great difficulty of doing so and the exceptional nature of such cases ...'[3]

and

'... the Strasbourg jurisprudence ... makes it quite clear that successful reliance demands presentation of a very strong case ... Where reliance is placed on Article 6 it must be shown that a person has suffered or risks suffering a flagrant denial of a fair trial in the Receiving State ... The lack of success of applicants relying on Articles 2, 5 and 6 before the Strasbourg court highlights the difficulty of meeting the stringent test which that court imposes.'[4]

1   In *Soering* (above para **8.21**), the European Court observed (at para 86) that 'the Convention does not govern the actions of States nor Parties to it, nor does it purport to be a means of requiring the Contracting States to impose Convention standards on other States. Article 1 cannot be read as justifying a general principle to the effect that, notwithstanding its extradition obligations, a Contracting State may not surrender an individual unless satisfied that the conditions awaiting him in the country of destination arc in full accord with each of the safeguards of the Convention', and (at para 91) that '... [I]nherent in the whole of the Convention is a search for a fair balance between the demands of the general interest of the community and the requirements of the protection of the individual's fundamental rights. As movement about the world becomes easier and crime takes on a larger international dimension, it is increasingly in the interests of all nations that suspected offenders who flee abroad should be brought to justice. Conversely, the establishment of safe havens for fugitives would not only result in danger for the State obliged to harbour the protected person but also tend to undermine the foundations of extradition.'

2   Above para **8.21**.

3   At para 21.

4   At para 24. See also Lord Steyn (with whom all other Law Lords agreed) at para 50: '... a high threshold test will always have to be satisfied. It will be necessary to establish at least a real risk of a flagrant violation of the very essence of the right before other articles could become engaged', and Lord Carswell (with whom all other Law Lords also agreed) at para 63: '... it

cannot now be said that persons seeking asylum in a member state of the Council of Europe are unable to invoke any of the provisions of the Convention when resisting an expulsion decision. I do regard it as important, however, that member states should not attempt to impose Convention standards on other countries by decisions which have the effect of requiring adherence to those standards in those countries ...', and at para 69: 'The concept of a flagrant breach or violation may not always be easy for domestic courts to apply ... but it seems to me that it was well expressed by ... the criterion that the right in question would be completely denied or nullified in the destination country. This would harmonise with the concept of a fundamental breach, with which courts in this jurisdiction are familiar'. For an early application of those principles under the 2003 Act, see *R (on the application of Bermingham) v Director of the Serious Fraud Office* [2007] QB 727 per Laws LJ at para 111.

8.32 Extradition may, therefore, be granted in circumstances where the system of the Requesting State does not comply with Art 6 standards. Examples include *Altun v Federal Republic of Germany*[1] (military tribunals not independent and impartial); *Mamatkulov & Askarov v Turkey*[2] ('... there may have been reasons for doubting at the time that they would receive a fair trial ...') and *Lodhi v Governor of HMP Brixton & another*[3] ('... features of the judicial system in the UAE which would not be regarded as Convention-compliant ...'). By contrast, the possibility of a prospective flagrant breach of Art 6 was recognised in *Okandeji v The Government of the Commonwealth of Australia*[4] (reverse burdens of proof).

1   Above para **8.29**, at para 6 (232).
2   Above para **8.29**, at para 91.
3   Above para **8.26**, at para 105 per Brooke LJ.
4   [2005] EWHC 2925 (Admin).

Article 7 ECHR

8.33 Extradition does not fall within the ambit of ECHR, Art 7.[1] In the absence of trans-national provisions, extradition legislation has retroactive effect. Extradition legislation is procedural in nature. It involves no determination of guilt or innocence. Therefore, the fact that the offence for which extradition is sought was committed at a time when there were no extradition arrangements in place with the Requesting State, will not affect the application of subsequent extradition arrangements. See, in particular, *Marais v Governor of HMP Brixton.*[2] Indeed, that is the very premise upon which ad hoc extradition arrangements may be entered into under s 194 of the 2003 Act. In fact, entire extradition schemes may have retroactive effect.[3] The position is different, however, in respect of the substantive requirement of dual criminality. In cases where dual criminality is required,[4] the conduct alleged must have been criminal according to the laws of both the Requesting and Requested States at the time it is alleged to have been committed. Thus, if the conduct was, at the time it was committed, not an offence contrary to English law, extradition cannot lie.[5]

1   *X v Netherlands* (1976) 6 DR 184 (Appl 7512/76); *Bakhtiar v Switzerland* (1996) ECHR Appl 27292/95.
2   [2001] EWHC 1051 (Admin).
3   *R v Secretary of State for the Home Department, ex p Hill* [1999] QB 886, per Hooper J at 900–903, per Rose LJ at 918.
4   See ss 63(2) and 64(2) of the 2003 Act for circumstances in which the dual criminality requirement is abrogated in Part 1 cases.

5   *R v Bow Street Metropolitan Stipendiary Magistrate, ex p Pinochet (No 3)* [2000] AC 147, HL
     per Lord Browne-Wilkinson at p 196; *Dabas v High Court of Madrid* [2007] 1 AC 31, HL per
     Lord Hope of Craighead at para 46. In Norris v Government of the United States of America
     [2008] 2 WLR 673, this was described by the House of Lords as 'elementary' (at para 63).

Article 8 ECHR

8.34   In *R (Razgar) v Secretary of State for the Home Department,*[1] the
House of Lords ruled that the rights protected by Art 8 may be engaged by the
foreseeable consequences for health or welfare of removal from the UK
pursuant to an expulsion decision, even where such removal does not violate
Art 3. In Art 8 terms, the act of extradition constitutes a prima facie interference
with the appellant's rights under Art 8(1). Proposed extradition will invariably
be 'in accordance with the law' and is sought in pursuance of a legitimate aim,
namely 'the prevention of … crime'. Thus, for any extradition to be Art 8(2)
(and thus s 87) compliant, it must be shown to be 'necessary in a democratic
society' which, in turn, requires the showing of a pressing social need and
requires that the interference at issue be proportionate to the legitimate aim
pursued[2]. Following *Huang v Secretary of State for the Home Department,*[3] it is
not right to apply 'exceptionality' as a formula for determining proportionality.[4]

1   [2004] 2 AC 368, HL.
2   *Bermingham v Director of Public Prosecutions* (above para **8.31**) per Laws LJ at paras 112
     and 118. Note that, in deciding whether extradition is 'necessary in a democratic society in the
     interests of …public safety …for the prevention of disorder or crime', in *Razgar* (above),
     Lord Bingham of Cornhill observed, at para 19, that: 'Where removal is proposed in
     pursuance of a lawful immigration policy, [this] question will almost always fall to be
     answered affirmatively … In the absence of bad faith, ulterior motive or deliberate abuse of
     power it is hard to imagine an adjudicator answering this question other than affirmatively'.
3   [2007] 2 WLR 581, HL per Lord Bingham of Cornhill at para 20.
4   *Jaso* (above para **8.08**) per Dyson LJ at paras 56–57: 'What is required is that the court should
     decide whether the interference with a person's right to respect for his private or (as the case
     may be) family life which would result from his or her extradition is proportionate to the
     legitimate aim of honouring extradition treaties with other states. It is clear that great weight
     should be accorded to the legitimate aim of honouring extradition treaties made with other
     states. Thus, although it is wrong to apply an exceptionality test, in an extradition case there
     will have to be striking and unusual facts to lead to the conclusion that it is disproportionate to
     interfere with an extraditee's Article 8 rights.'

8.35   Although mostly argued in respect of personal circumstances, in
reality, ECHR, Art 8, and in particular the concept of proportionality, is a
particularly subtle and potentially effective tool that a defendant is able to wield
in most abuse-related scenarios. In certain circumstances, it could, for example,
serve to prevent extradition in a case where, although technically available, a
Requesting State was exercising an exorbitant jurisdiction,[1] in cases where the
UK is the more appropriate trial forum,[2] or in cases of triviality.[3]

1   *R (Al Fawwaz) v Governor of Brixton Prison* (above para **8.29**) per Lord Slynn of Hadley at
     para 39, per Lord Millett at para 102, per Lord Scott at para 121, per Lord Rodger of Earlsferry
     at para 149; Boudhiba (above para 8.09) per Smith LJ at paras 43–44; *Hashmi v Government
     of the United States of America* [2007] EWHC 564 (Admin) per Scott Baker LJ at paras
     24–26.
2   The principles were considered in *Bermingham* (above para **8.31**) per Laws LJ at paras
     112–130. Whilst justiciability in this country might be relevant to the Art 8 issue, its
     application would only be triggered in 'wholly exceptional circumstances' (per Laws LJ at

para 118). Where a proposed extradition is properly constituted according to the domestic law of the UK and the relevant bilateral treaty, and its execution is resisted on Art 8 grounds, a wholly exceptional case would have to be shown to justify a finding that the extradition would on the particular facts be disproportionate to its legitimate aim (per Laws LJ at paras 112–118). The starting point is that the prospective extradition (as well as satisfying all relevant formal requirements) is not tainted by abuse (per Laws LJ at para 124). The fact that the appellant could be prosecuted here (and that there would be consequential advantages and disadvantages from the prosecution and defence perspectives) does not amount to an exceptional circumstance (per Laws. LJ at para 129). The fact that the appellant is a UK national does not render the case exceptional (per Laws LJ at paras 120 and 125–130). For cases in which 'forum' arguments have failed under Pt 2 of the 2003 Act, see *Bentley v Government of the United States of America* [2005] EWHC 1078 (admin) at para 26, *Norris v Government of the United States of America (No 2)* [2007] 1 WLR 1730, DC at paras 157–172. Under Pt 1 of the 2003 Act, see *Hosseini v Head of the Prosecution Department of the Courts of Higher Instance, Paris* [2006] EWHC 1333 (Admin) at paras 49–53. In Scotland, see *Wright v the Scottish Ministers* [2005] SLT 613 at paras 56–70 and *La Torre v Her Majesty's Advocate & another* [2006] HCJAC 56 at paras 78–79, 97–104, and in Strasbourg, see *Raidl v Austria* (above para **8.29**).

3   *Zak v Regional Court of Bydgoszcz, Poland* [2008] EWHC 470 (Admin) at paras 19–24. Previously, s 11(3)(a) of the Extradition Act 1989 provided that a defendant could be discharged in circumstances of triviality. It must be appreciated that the Extradition Act already prohibits extradition in respect of offences which attract maximum terms of imprisonment of less than 12 months (or for which sentences of less than four months have been imposed).

PACE

8.36   Finally, PACE, ss 76 and 78 apply to extradition proceedings.[1] However, the application of s 78 is confined to cases where a prima facie case is required to be established and is, even then, highly restricted:

'… when the section is being applied to committal or extradition proceedings, the question is whether the admission of the evidence would have such an adverse effect on the fairness of *those* proceedings that the court ought not to admit it … the magistrates should ordinarily assume that the powers available to the judge at the trial will ensure that the proceedings are fair. The question is, therefore, whether the admission of the evidence would have an adverse effect on the fairness of the decision to commit or extradite the accused for trial, even if the trial is a fair one. I think that the circumstances would have to be very unusual before magistrates could properly come to such a decision … extradition procedure is founded on concepts of comity and reciprocity. It would undermine the effectiveness of international treaty obligations if the courts were to superimpose discretions based on local notions of fairness upon the ordinary rules of admissibility. I do not wish to exclude the possibility that the discretion may be used in extradition proceedings founded upon evidence which, though technically admissible, has been obtained in a way which outrages civilised values. But such cases are also likely to be very rare '.[2]

1   *R v Governor of Brixton Prison, ex p Levin* [1997] AC 741 per Lord Hoffman at 746F. Although note the doubts expressed in *Wellington v The Governor of Her Majesty's Prison Belmarsh* [2004] EWHC 418 (Admin) per Mitting J at paras 16–17 and *Harkins v Secretary of State for the Home Department* [2007] EWHC 639 (Admin) per Lloyd-Jones J at para 38.

2   Per Lord Hoffmann at 748. Accordingly, committals have been upheld even though based

upon facts that '..would have caused considerable difficulty' to a domestic prosecution under PACE 1984, s 78, but which did not satisfy the higher *Levin* extradition threshold of 'outrag[ing] civilised values' test. See, for example, *R v Bow Street Magistrates' Court, ex p Proulx* [2001] 1 All ER 57, DC per Mance LJ at para 75; *R (Saifi) v Governor of Brixton Prison* (above para **8.26**) per Rose LJ at para 61.

THE ROLE AND POWERS OF THE SECRETARY OF STATE

8.37   These statutory provisions constitute a formidable array of safeguards that protect against most species of abusive conduct on the part of a Requesting State. In some respects (particularly passage of time under ss 14 and 82), an extradition defendant arguably has greater protection than a defendant in domestic proceedings. Where there have been significant gaps in protection, the courts have shown an inclination to close them, notably in the context of double jeopardy. However, this type of statutory framework does not, and cannot, cater for all forms of abuse, especially in the arena of deliberate manipulation of extradition procedures and process. In such cases, prior to the 2003 Act, the sole bulwark against manipulative abuse of process by a Requesting State was in the additional over-arching executive discretionary power vested in the Secretary of State for the Home Department under previous extradition legislation[1] to refuse extradition.

1   Sections 12–13 of, and Sch 1, para 8(2) to the 1989 Act. Sections 12(1) and 12(2) provided for his 'general discretion as to the making of an order for the return'. A similar discretion was to be found in Sch 1, para 8(2).

KNOCKING AT THE DOOR

8.38   Against this background, numerous attempts have been made to read a general common law abuse jurisdiction into the Extradition Acts. Yet, until the very final days of the pre-2003 legislation, the courts remained steadfastly resolute in their reluctance to extend statutory powers by reading a broad abuse of process jurisdiction into extradition legislation. Until very recently, and despite the fact that the district judge has always been expressly afforded 'like powers, as nearly as may be … as if the proceedings were a summary trial',[1] and even where (under the Extradition Act 1870) many of the statutory protections discussed above were absent, the courts had excluded the application of abuse of process in extradition proceedings, always on the basis that the overriding executive discretion of the Secretary of State[2] provides sufficient bulwark against abuse. In fact, fewer areas of law can have witnessed such a sustained but unsuccessful attempt to establish a legal principle. In the 30 years between 1971 and 2001, the House of Lords alone entertained, and rejected, eight attempts to establish an extradition abuse jurisdiction.

1   Extradition Act 1989, s 9(2) and Sch 1, para 6(1); as amended by the Criminal Justice and Public Order Act 1994, s 158.
2   Above para **8.37**.

8.39   In 1971, the House of Lords first ruled that there existed no such jurisdiction in *Atkinson v United States of America*.[1] Atkinson had been charged with armed robbery and attempted murder in Louisiana. Pursuant to a plea agreement, the attempted murder charge was discontinued and the armed robbery charge was reduced to attempted armed robbery (to which the defendant, like his co-defendants, pleaded guilty and was sentenced to 18 years' imprisonment). The defendant escaped from prison and fled to England. His extradition was sought in respect of the charge of attempted armed robbery. Attempted armed robbery was not, at that time, an extradition crime. Nor was prison-breaking. When this was realised, the authorities in Louisiana revived the charges of attempted murder. The defendant argued that the plea-bargain amounted to an undertaking by the prosecutor that if the appellant pleaded guilty to attempted armed robbery no further action would be taken on the charges of attempted murder, such that the resurrection of that charge now was oppressive or contrary to natural justice (constituted an abuse of process).

1   [1971] AC 197, HL.

8.40   The House of Lords ruled that there existed no abuse of process – or natural justice – jurisdiction in extradition proceedings. Lord Reid[1] observed that the magistrates' court in domestic proceedings did not (then) possess jurisdiction to refuse to commit an accused for trial on the ground that it would be unjust or oppressive to require him to be tried. A magistrate in extradition proceedings had no greater powers than those in domestic proceedings.[2] However, Lord Reid went on to state:

'... but that is not the end of the matter. It is now well recognised that the court has power to expand procedure laid down by statute if that is necessary to prevent infringement of natural justice and is not plainly contrary to the intention of Parliament. There can be cases where it would clearly be contrary to natural justice to surrender a man although there is sufficient evidence to justify committal ... It is not unknown for convictions to be obtained in a few foreign countries by improper means, and it would be intolerable if a man so convicted had to be surrendered. Parliament can never have so intended when the 1870 Act was passed'. [3]

1   With whom Lords MacDermot, Upjohn and Guest agreed.
2   Section 9 of the Extradition Act 1870 provided that the magistrate 'shall have the same jurisdiction and powers as near as may be as if the prisoner were brought before him charged with an indictable offence according to the law of England'.
3   At 232E-G.

8.41   In Lord Reid's view, however, that power lay with the Home Secretary:

'But the Act does provide a safeguard. The Secretary of State always has power to refuse to surrender a man committed to prison by the magistrate. It appears to me that Parliament must have intended the Secretary of State to use that power whenever in his view it would be wrong, unjust or oppressive to surrender the man ... If I had thought that Parliament did not intend this safeguard to be used in this way, then I would think it necessary to infer that the magistrate has power to refuse to commit if he finds that it would be contrary to natural justice to surrender the man. But in my judgment Parliament by providing this safeguard has excluded the jurisdiction of the courts'.[1]

1   At 232G-233B. See also Lord Morris of Borth-y-Gest at 238G–239A and Lord Guest at 246B–247C.

8.42   On the same day, the House of Lords also delivered judgment in similar terms in *Royal Government of Greece v Governor of Brixton Prison*.[1] In that case, the defendant argued that his conviction in absence in Greece was a nullity because it was obtained in circumstances contrary to natural justice. Lord Reid[2] adopted his opinion in *Atkinson*. Lord Morris of Borth-y-Gest observed that:

> 'The statutory provisions point with some precision to the functions of the courts and show that those functions are limited. It is for the courts to say whether the statutory conditions have been complied with to the extent that a fugitive criminal could be surrendered: it is for the Secretary of State to decide whether, having regard to all the circumstances, he should be surrendered ... In the exercise of his discretion the Secretary of State (who, in the first place, had a discretion as to whether he would make an order requiring the magistrate to proceed) can consider all the facts and circumstances of a case and it is for him to give consideration to any questions and contentions which invoke the rules of natural justice'.[3]

1   [1971] AC 250, HL, sub nom *R v Governor of Brixton Prison, ex p Kotronis* [1969] 3 All ER 304. The defendant in this case was ultimately to become the only person under the 1870 Act that the Secretary of State declined to surrender in the exercise of his discretion.
2   At 277H-278C.
3   At 281B-D.

8.43   However, in 1986, the House of Lords gave judgment in *In re Rees*[1] in terms that indicated that, at least in cases where executive misconduct in the context of English proceedings deprive a defendant of extradition safeguards, an abuse of process jurisdiction did exist. Mr Rees was the subject of an extradition request made by the Federal Republic of Germany in respect of hostage-taking offences in Bolivia. Evidence was received from Bolivia and the magistrate commenced committal proceedings. During the course of those proceedings, further statements were received from Bolivia. Their admission into evidence was subject to technical difficulties. In order to avoid those difficulties, a second order to proceed was received from the Secretary of State. The first committal proceedings were then terminated and Mr Rees was discharged. He was immediately re-arrested on a warrant issued by the magistrate in accordance with the second order to proceed. Proceedings re-commenced (and the latest Bolivian statements were adduced). The magistrate entertained and rejected a submission that the renewed proceedings constituted an abuse of process. The House of Lords (notwithstanding expressly referring to *Atkinson*[2]) entertained the abuse of process submission. Lord Mackay (with whom all other members of their Lordships' House agreed) accepted[3] that 'the authorities illustrate [that] the initiation of new proceedings may, in some circumstances, amount to an abuse of process ...', but rejected, on the facts, a submission that Mr Rees had been denied the protection of time limits contained within the applicable treaty.[4] Lord Mackay stated that:

> '... so far as abuse of process is concerned ... [it] is, in my opinion, entirely without merit ... I consider it inappropriate in this appeal to deal with

questions (6) and (7) which asked whether the police, magistrate or the High Court has jurisdiction to prevent the abuse of process in respect of proceedings under the 1870 Act since it is not necessary to answer them to dispose of the appeal, and the answer might well depend on the circumstances in which the relevant abuse occurred'. [5]

1   [1986] AC 937, HL.
2   At 962.
3   At 962.
4   Federal Republic of Germany (Extradition) Order 1960 (SI 1960/1375), Sch 2, art XII.
5   At 964.

8.44   That decision[1] spawned a small number of decisions between 1986 and 1990 in which the High Court considered abuse of process submissions on their merits[2], whilst some High Court decisions continued to apply *Atkinson*.[3] But in 1991, in *R v Governor of Pentonville Prison, ex p Sinclair*[4] the House of Lords revisited the issue. Lord Ackner[5] observed[6] that, since the decision in *Atkinson,* and since the commencement of proceedings in *Sinclair*'s case, the Extradition Act 1989 had been enacted and drew specific attention to the provisions of s 11(3). Despite the prior existence of the Fugitive Offenders Act 1881, s 10 and the Fugitive Offenders Act 1967, s 8(3) in like terms, and without reference to *In re Rees*, Lord Ackner observed[7] that:

'By this section a radical alteration has been made by giving to the High Court, in part at least, the same kind of discretion, as to whether or not to discharge an applicant, as the Secretary of State has in deciding whether or not to order a fugitive criminal to be returned to a Requesting State. It is the clearest possible recognition by the legislature that hitherto no such discretion existed in the courts and in particular in the magistrate's court. I therefore conclude that in extradition proceedings the magistrate has no jurisdiction to consider whether such proceedings may be an abuse of the process of the court'.

1   And the fact that, contrary to Lord Reid's opinion in *Atkinson*, it had been established that a magistrates' court in domestic proceedings did have jurisdiction to refuse to commit an accused for trial on the ground that it would be unjust or oppressive to require him to be tried (*R v Secretary of State for the Home Department & another, ex p Rees* (unreported) (7 March 1985), DC per Watkins LJ).
2   See *R v Bow Street Magistrates' Court, ex p Van der Holst* (1986) 83 Cr App R. 114, DC per Lloyd LJ at p 124; *R v Governor of Pentonville Prison, ex p Chinoy* [1992] 1 All ER 317, DC per Nolan J.
3   *R v Governor of Pentonville Prison, ex p Parekh* (1988) Times, 19 May, DC; sub nom *In re Parekh* [1988] Crim LR 832, per Stocker LJ (although note the dissenting judgment of Hutchison J).
4   [1991] 2 AC 64, HL.
5   With whom Lords Bridge, Templeman, Griffiths and Goff agreed.
6   At 75–81.
7   At 80–81.

8.45   The matter came back before the House of Lords for a fourth time in 1992 in *R v Governor of Pentonville Prison, ex p Alves*.[1] Mr Alves' extradition was sought by the Swedish Government under Sch 1 to the Extradition Act 1989, in the face of the sole witness having retracted his evidence on oath before the magistrate in London. This time the House of Lords had been referred to *In re Rees*. However, Lord Goff of Chieveley[2] observed that:

'... [I]t is well established by authority of this House (see *Atkinson* ... and ... *ex p Kotronis* ...) that, until the enactment of s 11(3) of the Act of 1989, no such discretion was vested in the English courts in extradition matters, the relevant discretion being vested in the Secretary of State: see *Ex parte Sinclair* ... at 80–81, per Lord Ackner. It is of course open to the applicant to make such representations as he thinks fit in this regard to the Secretary of State'.[3]

1   [1993] AC 284, HL.
2   With whom Lords Templeman, Roskill, Bridge and Jauncey agreed.
3   At 294.

8.46   There then came the House of Lords' landmark ruling in 1993 in *R v Horseferry Road Magistrates' Court, ex p Bennett*,[1] discussed in detail in **Chapter 5**. It appeared from the various wide-ranging and unqualified judgments[2] that the abuse of process jurisdiction (in its now extended form) was equally applicable to extradition proceedings (albeit vested in the High Court rather than the magistrates' court). Therefore, an understandably confident submission was made to the House of Lords the following year in *In Re Schmidt*,[3] to the effect that the principles of *Bennett* were applicable in extradition proceedings. It was submitted on Mr Schmidt's behalf that he had been brought before the court of committal by an abuse of process, namely the ruse adopted by the police, and that the Divisional Court possessed an inherent and unlimited supervisory jurisdiction to correct such an abuse. Section 11(3) of the Act of 1989 preserved rather than created the jurisdiction of the High Court. It was submitted that *Atkinson* was out of date and should not be followed and that there was in any event an inherent jurisdiction in the High Court to intervene in such proceedings; which jurisdiction is recognised by the opening words of s 11(3).

1   [1994] 1 AC 42, HL.
2   Per Lord Griffiths at 61–62, per Lord Bridge of Harwich at 67–68, per Lord Lowry at 74 and 76–77.
3   [1995] 1 AC 339, HL.

8.47   However, Lord Jauncey of Tullichettle[1] re-affirmed the decisions of *Atkinson* and *Sinclair* and ruled[2] that:

'I am satisfied that *Bennett* has no such general application as the applicant contends. The issue in that case was whether the English courts should decline to try the accused by staying the prosecution. That the power to intervene, which was held to exist in the High Court, was related only to a trial is abundantly clear from the passages in the speeches to which I have referred. Indeed, there was no reason in that case to consider the power in any other context ... In my view the position in relation to a pending trial in England is wholly different to that in relation to pending proceedings for extradition from England. In the former case the High Court in its supervisory jurisdiction is the only bulwark against any abuse of process resulting in injustice or oppression which may have resulted in the accused being brought to trial in England. In the latter case, not only has the Secretary of State power to refuse to surrender the accused in such circumstances, but the courts of the requesting authority are likely to have powers similar to those held to exist in *R v Horseferry Road Magistrates' Court, ex p Bennett*. An accused fugitive is thus likely to have not one but two safeguards against injustice and oppression before being brought to trial in the Requesting State … It must also be remembered that the extradition procedures to which this appeal relates flow from the European Convention on Extradition and are designed to facilitate the return of accused or convicted persons from one contracting state to another. The removal of the requirement that the Requesting State should provide prima facie evidence of the alleged crime demonstrates that extradition proceedings between contracting states were intended to be simple and speedy, each state accepting that it could rely upon the genuineness and bona fides of a request made by another one. The advantages of bringing an accused to trial while evidence on both sides is fresh are obvious. To confer on the High Court power such as the applicant contends for would be to inhibit the carrying out of this intention'.

1   With whom Lords Templeman, Ackner, Slynn and Lloyd agreed.
2   At 377D–378C.

8.48   This line of authority was again referred to with approval by the House of Lords in 1997 in *R v Secretary of State for the Home Department, ex p Launder*[1] and in 2001 in *R (Al-Fawwaz) v Governor of Brixton Prison*.[2] Between those two decisions, the House of Lords had rejected the argument once more, this time in the context of the Backing of Warrants (Republic of Ireland) Act 1965 in *R v Governor of Belmarsh Prison, ex p Gilligan*.[3] In one of the two linked cases heard by their Lordships, the Irish authorities had applied to a stipendiary magistrate for an order that the applicant, who was wanted on 18 arrest warrants issued in Dublin and had also been arrested and charged with offences in England, be handed over to the Garda. The applicant contended that the application was abusive, claiming among other things that he had been improperly arrested in England so as to hold him while the Irish charges were drawn up. Despite reliance by counsel upon the subsequent ruling of Laws J in *R v Lord Chancellor, ex p Witham*,[4] to the effect that the 'fundamental' fair-trial right to challenge proceedings on the grounds of abuse of process cannot be abrogated by the State save by specific provision in an Act of Parliament,[5] a similar conclusion was reached.[6] It was held that the magistrate possessed no abuse jurisdiction. Lord Steyn referred[7] to the ability of the Irish courts to guard against abuse; this was seen as an analogue to the protection in extradition cases under the 1989 Act afforded by the Secretary of State's discretion, which was critical in *Schmidt*.

1   [1997] 1 WLR 839, HL at pp 854–855, per Lord Hope of Craighead (with whom Lords Browne-Wilkinson, Steyn, Clyde and Hutton agreed).
2   Above para **8.29**, per Lord Slynn of Hadley at para 39, per Lord Millett at para 102, per Lord Scott at para 121, per Lord Rodger of Earlsferry at para 149.
3   Above para **8.10**.
4   [1998] QB 575.
5   Per Laws J at 581 and 585–586.
6   Per Lord Steyn (with whom Lords Browne-Wilkinson, Cooke and Hope agreed) at 97–98 and Lord Clyde at 101.
7   At p 97G. During the same period, save for the period 1986–1990, the High Court consistently held that a magistrate conducting extradition proceedings possesses no abuse of process jurisdiction (see, for example, *In re Johnson* (unreported) (14 February 1997), DC per

McCowan LJ) but, on occasion, expressed views upon the likely outcome of abuse submissions had such jurisdiction existed (see, for example, *R v Governor of Brixton Prison, ex p Cuoghi* [1998] 1 WLR 1513, DC per Kennedy LJ at pp 1521G-1522B (in a case concerning submissions as to authentication, where the defence had sought an adjournment and counsel for the Requesting State had indicated that the adjournment would not be used to obtain properly authenticated documents, there was no abuse where the Requesting State, of its own volition, had supplied properly authenticated documents in the interim period).

THE IMPACT OF THE HUMAN RIGHTS ACT 1998 AND KASHAMU

8.49   The exercise of supervisory jurisdiction by the Secretary of State had been a matter of significant disquiet for many years. She was plainly the subject of conflicting duties. Her role as ultimate protector against oppression was in conflict with her obligation on behalf of the State to extradite on the basis of extradition treaties (treaties which invariably make no reference to the Secretary of State exercising any general, or supervisory, discretion). Moreover, she was singularly ill-placed to deal with the complex issues of fact that often arose in connection with abuse of process submissions.

8.50   Extradition proceedings are criminal proceedings 'albeit of a very special kind'.[1] Accordingly, as from October 2000, the Human Rights Act 1998 applied to extradition proceedings. Section 3 of the Human Rights Act 1998 requires that existing legislation 'must be read ... in a way which is compatible so far as it is possible to do so' with the Convention. Section 6 of the Human Rights Act 1998 states that it is 'unlawful' for a public authority (prosecution and/or court) 'to act in a way which is incompatible with any Convention right'.

1   *R (Government of the United States of America) v Bow Street Magistrates' Court* (above para **8.10**) per Lord Phillips CJ at para 76; *R v Governor of Brixton Prison, ex p Levin* [1997] AC 741, HL, per Lord Hoffmann at 746F.

8.51   In the circumstances, in *R (Kashamu) v Governor of Brixton Prison (No 2)*,[1] the *Atkinson/Schmidt* line of authority was argued to be incompatible with the Human Rights Act 1998. Kashamu was detained under Sch 1 to the 1989 Act in response to an extradition request from the US government in respect of serious drugs offences. On application for habeas corpus, the High Court quashed the committal as a result of material non-disclosure.[2] He was detained immediately on a second warrant. At the second committal proceedings the district judge declined to hear a submission that those committal proceedings constituted an abuse of process.

1   [2002] 2 QB 887.
2   [2001] EWHC 980 (Admin).

8.52   Rose LJ held[1] that:

'It is common ground that, whichever is the Requesting State, the Secretary of State is empowered not to order surrender of the fugitive if it would be unjust or oppressive to do so. It is also common ground that, prior to the coming into force of the Human Rights Act 1998 in October 2000, the House of Lords, in *Atkinson, Ex p Sinclair* and *In Re Schmidt*, clearly established that the courts have no discretion to refuse extradition on the ground that the proceedings are an abuse of the court's process ... The question which presently arises is whether, since the coming into force of the Human Rights Act 1998, Article 5 of the Convention requires a different view to be taken'.

1   At paras 8–9.

8.53   It was submitted that, following enactment of the Human Rights Act 1998, it must be the courts, rather than the Secretary of State, who determine the lawfulness of detention under Art 5(1)(f). Rose LJ ruled that:

'... It is, in my judgment, plain that Article 5 expressly requires the lawfulness of the detention of a person detained with a view to extradition under paragraph (1)(f) to be decided speedily by a court. It is equally plain to my mind that, in the extradition context, the Secretary of State lacks the qualities of independence and impartiality required of the court-like body by the Strasbourg jurisprudence ...'[1]

'... it seems to me to be clear that a court and not the Secretary of State is the appropriate forum for a decision as to the lawfulness of a fugitive's detention and, provided the Extradition Act 1989 can be so read, the magistrates' court is to be preferred to the High Court. As I have said, the House of Lords in *Atkinson, Ex p Sinclair* and *In Re Schmidt* held that a magistrate has no power to refuse to commit in extradition proceedings because of an abuse of process. The rationale of each of those authorities, however, is that it is open to the Secretary of State to respond to abuse by refusing to return the fugitive ...'[2]

'... In my judgment, although that is so, it does not now, in the light of the provisions of Article 5(4), provide a rationale for excluding the courts from exercising abuse jurisdiction in relation to the lawfulness of detention ... [not providing] sufficient basis on which to oust the jurisdiction of magistrates which, at first blush, is conferred by the wide language of paragraph 6(1), to consider the lawfulness of a fugitive's detention. Put another way, both section 11(3) and paragraph 6(1) of Schedule 1 can, and in my judgment should, be so read as to enable both the High Court and a committing magistrate to consider the lawfulness of detention under Article 5(4) ...'[3]

'... that determination should be in accordance with Lord Hope's analysis in *R v Governor of Brockhill Prison, ex p Evans (No 2)* [2001] 2 AC 19, that is he must consider whether the detention is lawful by English domestic law, complies with the general requirements of the Convention and is not open to criticism for arbitrariness'.[4]

1   At para 27. See above paras **8.22–8.28**.
2   At para 29.
3   At para 30.
4   At para 32. Rose LJ concluded that the magistrates' court was the appropriate tribunal to hear submissions and finding facts relevant to abuse of process. Note that a third attempt to proceed against Kashamu was subsequently rejected by the magistrates' court.

THE POSITION UNDER THE 2003 ACT

8.54   The 2003 Act removed the supervisory powers of the Secretary of State. In Part 1 cases, the Secretary of State plays no part at all. In Part 2 cases, her role is limited to three confined matters.[1] Moreover, ss 21 and 87 provide that the court of extradition is, in turn, obliged to decide whether the person's extradition would be compatible with the Convention rights within the meaning of the Human Rights Act. In light of these twin developments, it was assumed in early cases that Kashamu applied under the 2003 Act and that the judge who conducts an extradition hearing under the 2003 Act possesses an implied jurisdiction to hold that the prosecutor is abusing the process of the court and to refuse to order extradition for that reason.

1   Sections 94–96 regarding death penalty, specialty and earlier extradition to the UK.

8.55   Therefore, in *Okandeji v The Government of the Commonwealth of Australia*[1] and *Jenkins v Government of the United States of America*,[2] 'entrapment' abuse submissions were considered and rejected by the High Court on their merits without detailed consideration of the issue of jurisdiction.[3] In *Government of the Federal Republic of Germany v Kleinschmidt & another*,[4] the High Court (Beatson J) indicated,[5] obiter, that Kashamu applied under the 2003 Act and, having determined that s 78(4)(c) did not mandate the service by the Requesting State of the extradition papers before the commencement of the extradition hearing, further indicated at para 36 that 'deliberate flouting of the provisions for service may give rise to consideration of whether the proceedings should be stayed as an abuse of process'.

1   Above para 8.32, at paras 28–31.
2   [2005] EWHC 1051 (Admin) at paras 14–23.
3   It was accepted by the US government in *Jenkins* that *Kashamu* 'has resurrected, in the wake of the Human Rights Act 1998, the abuse jurisdiction previously excluded by the decision of the House of Lords in *Schmidt*' but deemed it unnecessary on the facts to determine a submission that 'the inherent power is limited to such things as refusal of a request made in bad faith'; see paras 31–32.
4   [2006] 1 WLR1, DC.
5   At para 27.

8.56   In *Boudhiba*,[1] the appellant was interviewed as a suspect at the request of the Spanish authorities pursuant to the Mutual Legal Assistance arrangements in March 2004, during which he exercised his right to silence. On 1 May 2005, a further request was communicated to the appellant's solicitors by the Metropolitan Police asking that the appellant should be interviewed at the request of the Spanish authorities, but this time as a witness. On 19 May 2005, the Metropolitan Police confirmed in writing that he was to be interviewed as a witness and not as a suspect. The appellant decided that he would not cooperate with the request. He was then arrested pursuant to a European Arrest Warrant that had been issued on 18 May 2005. On appeal, he argued that the extradition machinery was being used to secure the presence of an uncooperative witness or possibly to punish the appellant for not cooperating. The High Court (Smith LJ) assumed the existence of an abuse jurisdiction, but rejected the claim on its merits, holding[2] that:

'As confusion or failure of communication is a real possibility, I would not be prepared to draw the inference that the warrant was issued as a device to secure the appellant's presence or to punish him for his lack of cooperation ... If that confusion or failure of communication had resulted in any prejudice to the appellant, I might well have been prepared to say that the extradition proceedings were an abuse of process. If, for example, the appellant had agreed to be interviewed as a witness and had made potentially damaging admissions at a time when he was unaware of the existence of the Order for Commitment, he might have a real complaint. But, he did not; he declined to cooperate'.

1   Above para **8.09**.
2   At paras 24–25.

Jurisdiction finally established

8.57   The issue of jurisdiction was fully considered by the High Court in *Bermingham v Director of the Serious Fraud Office.*[1] It was argued by the appellants that abuse arose by virtue of (a) the US government's refusal to disclose any of the evidential material it possessed beyond what was contained in the extradition request, including materials alleged to 'fundamentally undermine' the US case, and (b) deliberate delay in seeking the defendants' extradition so as to take advantage of the 2003 Act and thereby denying the appellants' safeguards they would have enjoyed under the 1989 Act, such as the Secretary of State's discretion and the requirement that the Requesting State should demonstrate a case to answer. It was conceded by the Requesting State that the judge who conducts an extradition hearing under the 2003 Act possesses an implied jurisdiction to hold that the prosecutor is abusing the process of the court and to refuse to order extradition for that reason. Nonetheless, Laws LJ examined and approved the basis upon which that concession was made. Having considered *Atkinson*, *Schmidt* and *Gilligan*, Laws LJ observed[2] that:

'In my judgment the reasoning in these cases of high authority has no application in the context of the 2003 Act. Under its provisions the Secretary of State has no statutory discretion to refuse extradition. The safeguard emphasised in *Atkinson* and *Schmidt* is lacking. Moreover in Part I cases, and Part II cases where the category 2 territory has (like the United States) been designated for the purpose of s.84, the prosecutor is not required to establish a *prima facie* case on the evidence. Under the old law that requirement was itself an important discipline. Its absence makes the need for a residual abuse jurisdiction all the plainer ...I should not leave the point without considering the nature of the juridical exercise involved in concluding, as I would, that the judge conducting an extradition hearing under the 2003 Act possesses a jurisdiction to hold that the prosecutor is abusing the process of the court. Lord Reid, in the passage from *Atkinson* which I have cited, would if necessary have *inferred* that the magistrate had power to refuse to commit. Now, it is plain that the judge's functions under the 2003 Act, and those of the magistrate under the predecessor legislation, are and were wholly statutory. He therefore possesses no inherent powers. But that is not to say that he may not enjoy an *implied* power. The implication arises from the express provisions of the statutory regime which it is his responsibility to administer. It is justified by the imperative that the regime's integrity must not be usurped. Where its integrity is protected by other powers, as in *Atkinson, Schmidt* and *Gilligan*, the implication is not justified. But under the 2003 Act that is not the case. The implication of an abuse jurisdiction – Lord Reid's inference – follows'.

1   Above para **8.31**.
2   At paras 96–97.

8.58   In *Knowles v Government of the United States of America & another,*[1] in the context of Bahamian extradition proceedings, the Privy Council ruled[2] that Art 19 of the Bahamian constitution was purposefully drafted in terms that differed from ECHR, Art 5(4), omitting any requirement of speedy decision or of a decision by a court, upon which the decision in *Kashamu* turned. Thus it was held[3] that the Bahamian courts remained bound by 'the *Atkinson* line of authority' as opposed to *Kashamu*. But, in so ruling, it was clearly apparent from Lord Bingham's opinion[4] that *Kashamu* was regarded as correctly decided and applicable in the UK under the 2003 Act.

1   Above para **8.04**.
2   At paras 26–28.
3   At para 28.
4   With whom Lords Hutton, Rodger, Carswell and Baroness Hale agreed.

8.59   The jurisdiction was affirmed by Lord Phillips CJ in the High Court in *R (Government of the United States of America) v Bow Street Magistrates' Court*[1] where it was said that:

'The 2003 Act places a duty on the judge to decide a large number of matters before acceding to a request for extradition. To these should be added the duty to decide whether the process is being abused, if put on enquiry as to the possibility of this. The judge will usually, though not inevitably, be put on enquiry as to the possibility of abuse of process by allegations made by the person whose extradition is sought'.

Lord Phillips CJ 'would go further' than *Bermingham* and apply to extradition proceedings the statement made by Bingham LJ in *R v Liverpool Stipendiary Magistrate, ex p Ellison*[2] in relation to conventional criminal proceedings:

'If any criminal court at any time has cause to suspect that a prosecutor may be manipulating or using the procedures of the court in order to oppress or unfairly to prejudice a defendant before the court, I have not doubt that it is the duty of the court to inquire into the situation and ensure that its procedure is not being so abused. Usually, no doubt, such inquiry will be prompted by a complaint on the part of the defendant. But the duty of the court in my view exists even in the absence of a complaint'.

1   Above para **8.10**, at paras 81–83.
2   [1990] RTR 220 at p 227.

8.60   In *R (Hilali) v Governor of Whitemoor Prison & another,*[1] Lord Hope of Craighead[2] rejected on its merits[3] a submission that an extradition request continued in the face of acquittal of the principal defendant represented an abuse of process; the issue was relevant only to whether there existed a case to answer in Spain.[4] Similarly, in *Norris v Government of the United States of America,*[5] the joint opinion of the Judicial Committee[6] observed[7], obiter, that:

'In R (Government of the United States of America) v Bow Street Magistrates' Court [2007] 1 WLR 1157, the Divisional Court indicated that such a request might be appropriate where the judge considered that an abuse of process might have occurred. But, again, such cases are likely to be exceptional.'

1   [2008] 2 WLR 299, HL.
2   With whom Lord Bingham, Baroness Hale and Lords Brown and Neuberger agreed.
3   At para 24.
4   'But the Framework Decision makes it clear that the admissibility or sufficiency of the evidence is not for determination by a judge in the Requested State. These issues were not within the jurisdiction of the judge at the extradition hearing in this case' (at para 23).
5   Above para **8.33**.
6   Lords Bingham, Rodger, Carswell, Brown and Neuberger.
7   At para 107.

8.61   The issue of jurisdiction was finally settled by the House of Lords in *McKinnon v Government of the United States of America*[1] in which the House of Lords[2] held[3] that:

'The district judge also had jurisdiction to consider whether the extradition proceedings constituted an abuse of process so as to protect the integrity of the statutory regime, the Secretary of State having no general discretion to refuse extradition. So much was stated by Laws LJ in the Divisional Court in R (Bermingham) v Director of the Serious Fraud Office [2007] QB 727, para 97 and by Lord Phillips of Worth Matravers CJ in R (Government of the United States of America) v Bow Street Magistrates' Court [2007] 1 WLR 1157, paras 82—83. What was not expressly stated in these decisions but was necessarily implicit was that the abuse of process for consideration was such as to require the extradition proceedings to be permanently stayed and the accused discharged.'

1   [2008] 1 WLR 1739, HL.
2   Lord Brown of Eaton-under-Heywood, with whom Lords Scott, Phillips, Baroness Hale and Lord Neuberger agreed.
3   At para 8.

Procedure

8.62   In *R (Government of the United States of America) v Bow Street Magistrates' Court,*[1] Lord Phillips CJ ruled[2] that abuse of process submissions fell to be decided inside, and pursuant to, the statutory procedural rubric of the 2003 Act. At para 84, Lord Phillips CJ outlined the procedure to be followed in cases where an abuse issue is raised:

'The judge should be alert to the possibility of allegations of abuse of process being made by way of delaying tactics. No steps should be taken to investigate an alleged abuse of process unless the judge is satisfied that there is reason to believe that an abuse may have taken place. Where an allegation of abuse of process is made, the first step [1] must be to insist on the conduct alleged to constitute the abuse being identified with particularity. The judge must then [2] consider whether the conduct, if established, is capable of amounting to an abuse of process. If it is, he must next [3] consider whether there are reasonable grounds for believing that such conduct may have occurred. If there are, then [4] the judge should not accede to the request for extradition unless he has satisfied himself that such abuse has not occurred.' (numbering added)

1   Above para **8.10**.
2   At para 80: 'Where extradition is challenged on grounds, such as abuse of process, which are not dealt with expressly under the Act, they should nonetheless normally be considered within the extradition hearing. The 2003 Act lays down special rules in relation to extradition that are designed to ensure that extradition proceedings are concluded with expedition. This objective will be torpedoed if allegations of abuse of process are pursued outside the statutory regime'. See also paras 105–109.

STAGE 1: THE CONDUCT ALLEGED TO CONSTITUTE THE ABUSE BEING IDENTIFIED WITH PARTICULARITY

8.63   This requires the defence to set out, usually in writing, exactly what is said to have occurred, and why it is alleged that that constitutes an abuse of the extradition process. Consideration of this issue requires no evidence, merely particulars.

STAGE 2: CONSIDER WHETHER THE CONDUCT, IF ESTABLISHED, IS CAPABLE OF AMOUNTING TO AN ABUSE OF PROCESS

8.64   This requires the court to assume that the conduct identified can be established in evidence, and to determine whether, on that hypothetical assumption, the conduct identified is capable of amounting to an abuse as a matter of law. It is obviously not in the interests of the administration of justice to embark on a lengthy hearing when the application has no chance of success or there is no basis for granting the remedy sought:

> 'The …criterion is self-evident. There is no point in engaging in a lengthy evidentiary inquiry where it cannot in law yield the result sought by the appellant'.[1]

1   *Larosa v Her Majesty the Queen* (2002) 166 CCC (3d) 449, Ont CA, per Doherty JA at para 77. The procedural rubric established by Lord Phillips CJ in 2006 is of relatively recent advent in English extradition proceedings. However, it has been in operation in Canada since at least 2001 and, therefore, the Canadian case law is of particular assistance in its application.

The intrinsic limits of the jurisdiction

8.65   The giving of an answer under stage 2, in any case, requires the practitioner to appreciate the context and limits of the extradition abuse jurisdiction, and the rationale for it being an animal of a different nature to its domestic cousin. Having established the jurisdiction in *Kashamu,*[1] Rose LJ went on[2] to make the following important qualification:

'It does not, however, follow that the district judge can be addressed on all the issues which may arise in the course of a summary trial. Extradition proceedings do not, nor does fairness require that they should, involve resolution of trial issues. Self-evidently, extradition contemplates trial in another jurisdiction according to the law there. It is there that questions of admissibility, adequacy of evidence and fairness of the trial itself will be addressed; and, if the Secretary of State has concerns in relation to these or other matters, it is open to him to refuse to order a fugitive's return ... *What is pertinent here in the present cases is solely whether the detention is unlawful by English domestic law and/or arbitrary, because of bad faith or deliberate abuse of the English courts' procedure.* The scope of the inquiry is, therefore, narrow. In that connection, it by no means follows, merely because second proceedings have been instituted against Kashamu, following failure of the first proceedings in the circumstances earlier set out, that there has been an abuse. I add that it will only be in a very rare extradition case, *provided the statutory procedures have been followed,* that it will be possible to argue that abuse of process has rendered the detention unlawful under Article 5(4).' (Emphasis added)

1   Above para **8.51**.
2   At paras 33–34. Pitchford J ruled in similar terms at paras 37–38.

8.66   This limitation accords with the Canadian case law, from which the English courts have derived much assistance in establishing the boundaries of the fledgling abuse jurisdiction. In *United States of America v Kwok,*[1] Arbour J ruled[2] that the extradition abuse jurisdiction does '... not confer unlimited *Charter* jurisdiction on the extradition judge and therefore do[es] not render obsolete all previous extradition case law. Section 9(3) clearly confers *Charter* jurisdiction upon the extradition judge insofar as the issues are specific to the functions of the extradition hearing ...The added jurisdiction conferred upon the extradition judge must be understood in light of this governing principle'.[3]

1   [2001] 1 SCR 532.
2   At para 54.
3   In *Government of the United States of America v Tollman* [2006] OJ 3672, 14 September (Ont Sup Crt), Malloy J put it this way: 'An extradition judge has the power to stay proceedings for abuse of process both at common law and under the *Charter* ... The extent of that power must be analyzed within the context in which it arises ... It does not expand the limited role of the extradition judge under the *Extradition Act,* but neither is the power so circumscribed that it applies only where the abuse relates directly to the sufficiency of the evidence issue to be determined by the extradition judge. The focus must be on the Canadian judicial process. The abuse power cannot be used to remedy the actions of foreign states outside our borders, nor can it be invoked in respect of any perceived unfairness of the ultimate trial to be held in the foreign state. However, the power applies to any conduct that reaches into this jurisdiction and undermines the integrity of the judicial system here' (at para 18).

8.67   It is crucial to appreciate the significance of this limitation, which fundamentally distinguishes the extradition abuse jurisdiction from the domestic abuse jurisdiction. It is derived from two interlinked factors that are peculiar to extradition proceedings.

8.68 First, there exists a strong international and public interest in the honouring of extradition treaties. In *R (Warren) v Secretary of State for the Home Department,*[1] Hale LJ observed[2] that:

'The object of extradition is to return a person who is properly accused or has been convicted of an extradition crime in a foreign country to face trial or to serve his sentence there ... The extradition process is only available for return to friendly foreign states with whom this country has entered into either a multi or a bilateral treaty obligation involving mutually agreed and reciprocal commitments ... [T]here is a strong public interest in our respecting such treaty obligations. Such international cooperation is all the more important in modern times, when cross-border problems are becoming ever more common, and the need to provide international solutions for them is ever clearer.'

1 Above para **8.18**.
2 At para 40.

8.69 Allied to that is the duty to construe extradition laws, and conduct extradition proceedings, having full and proper regard to the need to accommodate differences, cultural or legal, between the legal systems of those friendly foreign states with whom the UK has entered into mutual reciprocal extradition arrangements. These principles have been acknowledged by the House Lords to govern extradition proceedings for decades. In *Royal Government of Greece v Governor of Brixton Prison,*[1] Lord Morris of Borth-y-Gest observed[2] that:

'Mutual belief and understanding that conditions and undertakings would be honoured and mutual respect for each other's legal systems must be the basis on which extradition treaties are made or are continued in being ... I cannot think that it was open to a magistrate or to the court in habeas corpus proceedings to go behind the conviction and to treat it as no conviction for any such reason as that the law and practice in Greece is not the same as the law and practice elsewhere. It is not for the courts to say that a conviction which by authenticated proof is shown to be a conviction in another country is here to be regarded as a nullity because the law of the other country is thought not to be in line with conceptions widely or generally held ... We are here concerned with a statutory code which becomes operative consequent upon the making of reciprocal arrangements between friendly states'.

1 Above para **8.42**.
2 At 279C. In *In re Rees* (above para **8.43**), Lord Mackay of Clashfern (with whom Lords Bridge, Brandon, Oliver and Goff agreed) observed (at 959C-D) that: 'The ultimate trial will take place according to the provisions of the judicial system of the state requesting the extradition if the prisoner is handed over. As I said, the fact that an extradition arrangement has been made with such a state may be taken as indicating that her Majesty's government is satisfied with the system of justice under which that trial will take place.'

8.70 In *In re: Ismail*[1] Lord Steyn[2] observed[3] that:

'a statute intended to serve the purpose of bringing to justice those accused of serious crimes. There is a transnational interest in the achievement of this aim. Extradition treaties, and extradition statutes, ought, therefore, to be accorded a broad and generous construction so far as the texts permits it in order to facilitate extradition …It follows that it would be wrong to approach the problem of construction solely from the perspective of English criminal procedure … All one can say with confidence is that a purposive interpretation of 'accused' ought to be adopted in order to accommodate the differences between legal systems.'[4]

1   [1999] AC 320, HL.
2   With whom Lords Browne-Wilkinson, Jauncey, Slynn and Hutton agreed.
3   At 327.
4   See, to similar effect, *Government of Belgium v Postlethwaite* [1988] AC 924, HL, per Lord Bridge of Harwich (with whom Lords Templemen, Griffiths, Ackner and Goff agreed) at 947A-D; *R (Al-Fawwaz) v Governor of Brixton Prison* (above para **8.29**) per Lord Millett at para 102(4) and Lord Rodger of Earlsferry at para 148; *Cartwright v Superintendent of Her Majesty's Prison* [2004] 1 WLR 902, PC, per Lord Steyn at para 15. Under the 2003 Act, mutual respect for, and an accommodation of the differences between, the established legal systems of friendly foreign states with whom the UK has seen fit to enter into international extradition arrangements remain the keystones of extradition law and procedure; whether under Part 1 or Part 2 of the Act. See, for example, *Norris v Government of the United States of America* (above para **8.33**) at para 86 and *McKinnon v Government of the United States of America* (above para **8.61**) per Lord Brown of Eaton-under-Heywood at para 37 (with whom Lords Scott and Phillips, Baroness Hale and Lord Neuberger agreed).

8.71   Therefore, in *Bermingham*[1], having established its existence, Laws LJ went on to reiterate the intrinsic limits of the extradition abuse jurisdiction:

'[98] But the question whether abuse is demonstrated has to be asked and answered in light of the specifics of the statutory scheme. Accordingly, subject to an important qualification which I will explain, no finding of abuse can be justified (in a case like the present where the category 2 territory has been designated for the purpose of s.84) by the prosecutor's refusal or failure to disclose evidential material beyond what was contained in the extradition request. The reason is straightforward. In such an instance, as I have shown, the prosecutor does not have to establish a case to answer. Evidence going to whether there is in fact a case to answer is therefore not relevant to the court's task. Mr Jones submitted that while no doubt the prosecutor was not required to produce evidence of merits, if he failed to do so he would or should be at peril of adverse rulings from the court under s 82 or s 87 of the 2003 Act. Here, Mr Jones makes a like mistake to the major flaw in his argument in the judicial review: his submission looks for a statutory regime which Parliament has chosen not to provide. The prosecutor cannot be penalised, under s.82, 87, or by any other route, for limiting the material he places before the court to what is required for the proper execution of the court's function under ss.78 ff.…

[99] Likewise a defendant cannot ordinarily complain of abuse on grounds that if only the prosecutor had acted more promptly the 1989 Act, and not the 2003 Act, would have governed the proceedings, and in that case he (the defendant) would have enjoyed the right to test the prosecutor's case and persuade the court, if he could, that there was no case to answer. We cannot entertain any kind of presumption that where in an extradition case the facts arose in the life of the 1989 Act, the defendant should ordinarily have the benefit of that Act and not be fixed with the effects of the supervening statute. Such a presumption would be unconstitutional: it would imply a value

judgment by this court that the scheme of the earlier legislation was to be preferred to that of the 2003 Act. We have no authority to propound any such judgment …

[100] I have referred to an important qualification. It applies to both of the points I have discussed: the prosecutor's failure to give more disclosure, and his failure to facilitate the defendant's enjoyment of the relative benefits of the 1989 Act. The prosecutor must act in good faith. Thus if he knew he had no real case, but was pressing the extradition request for some collateral motive and accordingly tailored the choice of documents accompanying the request, there might be a good submission of abuse of process. Again, if he knew he could not (or perhaps, could not without great difficulty) make out a *prima facie* case and so deliberately delayed the extradition process until the 1989 Act had been safely superseded by the 2003 Act, that also might be held to be abusive …'

[127]… the court must feel the weight of what Lord Bingham called 'the great desirability of honouring extradition treaties made with other states'. And given the cross-border nature of the accusation here, these observations of Hale LJ as she then was in *R (Warren) v Secretary of State for the Home Department* [2003] EWHC 1177 are especially in point (at paragraph 40)…'

1   Above para **8.31**.

The applicable threshold

8.72   For these interlinked reasons, whatever the position in a domestic context, the courts will require exceptional facts to be made out to warrant a finding of abuse in an extradition context. In *McKinnon v USA*,[1] the House of Lords held[2] that the question to be asked is whether extradition would 'violate those fundamental principles of justice which underlie the community's sense of fair play and decency'? and noted[3] that it would require a 'wholly extreme case' to do so.[4]

1   Above para **8.61**.
2   At para 33 per Lord Brown of Eaton-under-Heywood.
3   At para 41. See also *Hilali v The Central Court of Criminal Proceedings No 5 of the National Court, Madrid* (above para **8.08**) per Scott Baker LJ at para 107: '… such circumstances are likely to be rare and there would have to be bad faith or something of that kind'.
4   In *Aswat & Ahmad v Government of the United States of America* (above para **8.08**), Laws LJ observed (at para 101) that '… the starting-point: Kennedy LJ's observation in *Serbeh* that 'there is (still) a fundamental assumption that the Requesting State is acting in good faith'. This is a premise of effective relations between sovereign States. As I have said the assumption may be contradicted by evidence; and it is the court's plain duty to consider such evidence (where it is presented) on a statutory appeal under the 2003 Act. But where the Requesting State is one in which the UK has for many years reposed the confidence not only of general good relations, but also of successive bilateral treaties consistently honoured, the evidence required to displace good faith must possess special force'.

8.73   That approach mirrors the '..outrag[ing] civilised values' test identified by the House of Lords in applying s 78 of the Police & Criminal Evidence Act 1984 to extradition proceedings.[1] It also correlates to the limited exception to the principle of non-enquiry in the US, enunciated in *Gallina v*

Fraser of 'procedures or punishment so antipathetic to a Federal Court's sense of decency'[2].

1   Above para **8.36**.
2   (1960) 278 F.2d 77 (2nd Cir) at 79.

Not concerned with the prospective trial process

8.74   The first point to note is that extradition abuse is not concerned with the ultimate trial process. Mitting J noted in *Wellington*[1] that: 'The fairness of the use of evidence at trial is a question for the trial court, not for the committing magistrate'.

1   Above para **8.36**, at para 17(3). This too accords with the Canadian position. See *Canada v Schmidt* [1987] 1 SCR 500 per La Forest J at paras 47–49 and 54–55. In *Cobb & Grossman v USA* [2001] 1 SCR 587, the Supreme Court of Canada noted that: 'The issue is not whether the appellants will have a fair trial if extradited, but whether they are having a fair extradition hearing in light of the threats and inducements imposed upon them, by those involved in their extradition, to force them to abandon their right to such a hearing.' (Arbour J at para 33). For an illustration of this principle in operation in Canada, see *United States of America v Kinsella (2006) NBQB 435* concerning allegations of attempts by the US prosecutor to oppress and intimidate the defendant during pre-trial hearings in the US.

8.75   For an example of a recent case, albeit decided under the 1989 Act, of this principle in operation, see *R (Harkins) v Secretary of State for the Home Department*.[1] In 1999, Harkins was arrested in Florida on suspicion of the murder and attempted robbery of Joshua Hayes. He was interviewed and he informed the police that he had spent the night at home with his fiancé, having been dropped there by an acquaintance by the name of Glover. Glover was arrested and interviewed. In the third different version of events provided by Glover, he alleged that Harkins had, in fact, carried out the murder. As a result of further enquiries, the case was dropped against Harkins and he was notified that the District Attorney was not going to prosecute him for any involvement in the killing of Hayes. A formal notice was entered on the record as to the discontinuance of the prosecution. In 2000, a different Assistant State Attorney revisited the case. Glover was re-interviewed, following which a written agreement was produced in which Glover agreed to co-operate fully with the prosecution against Harkins and on terms that Glover's co-operation could not be used against himself, in return for Glover's plea to offences of robbery with a weapon and being an accessory after the fact to first degree murder (punishable with up to 15 years in a Florida State prison). Harkins was charged again with capital murder and attempted robbery. It was alleged that the Assistant State Attorney had offered a witness (exculpating Harkins) the discontinuance of unrelated charges, and immunity in respect of the index offence, in return for falsely implicating Harkins. Harkins left America and was arrested in Scotland as a result of the provisional arrest warrant issued by the Bow Street Magistrates' Court pursuant to the Extradition Act 1989. Harkins alleged that the manner in which the evidence of Glover was obtained was an abuse of process by the prosecution.

1   Above para **8.36**.

8.76 In refusing to stay the proceedings, the High Court (Lloyd-Jones J) held[1] that:

'... questions as to the admissibility or fairness of evidence at trial are, in general, matters for the court of the trial, in this case Florida ... Furthermore, there is evidence before this court that it would be open to the claimant to file a motion before the Florida court challenging the admissibility of this evidence ... In these circumstances I consider that it was open to the Secretary of State to conclude that arguments in relation to the admissibility of the evidence of Glover should more appropriately be left for consideration by the courts of Florida. Moreover, for these reasons I consider that the Secretary of State was entitled to conclude that this was not a case in which the claimant's extradition is barred because the application of his return is not made in good faith in the interests of justice'. [2]

1   At paras 4–43.
2   See also *Jaso* (above para **8.08**) in which it was submitted that material showed that there was a real possibility that, at least in part, the evidence on which the prosecution against the appellants was based was obtained by torture, and therefore an abuse of process. The High Court ruled (per Dyson LJ at paras 34 and 39) that 'the relevant question in the present context is not whether there is a real possibility that evidence implicating all or any of the appellants was obtained from Mr Cillero by torture. Rather it is whether there is a real possibility that, if such evidence was obtained by torture, the Spanish court will admit it. Unless there is a real possibility that the evidence will be deployed against the appellants in the Spanish courts, it cannot be an abuse of process to extradite them to Spain. That is why this abuse of process argument is closely linked to the question whether there is a risk that the appellants' Article 6 rights will be violated if they are extradited. In my judgment, the decision in *A v Secretary of State for the Home Department (No 2)* [2006] 2 AC 221 is not relevant ... There is jurisdiction under Spanish law to exclude unlawfully obtained evidence ... The correct forum for determining whether the evidence was in fact so obtained is the Spanish courts. The district judge was not required to investigate the allegation of torture herself'. See also *Mustafa (aka Hamza) v Government of the United States of America & another* [2008] EWHC 1357 (Admin) at paras 8 and 37–41.

Pre-2004 case law

8.77 Because of the absence of jurisdiction until 2004, examples of pre-2004 abuse allegations considered on their merits are few and far between, but do exist.

8.78 In *In re Rees*[1], the defendant was the subject of an extradition request made by the Federal Republic of Germany in respect of hostage-taking offences in Bolivia. Evidence was received from Bolivia and the magistrate commenced committal proceedings. During the course of those proceedings, further statements were received from Bolivia. Their admission into evidence was subject to technical difficulties. To avoid those difficulties, on the day of the extradition hearing, and outside the applicable time limit for receipt of evidence, a second order to proceed was procured from the Secretary of State in respect of the same offences (no further request having been received from Germany). The first committal proceedings were then terminated and the defendant was discharged. On leaving the dock, he was immediately re-arrested on a warrant issued by the magistrate in accordance with the second order to proceed. Proceedings re-commenced (and the latest Bolivian statements were adduced without hindrance). The magistrate entertained and rejected a submission that the renewed proceedings constituted an abuse of process. The House of Lords declined to decide whether an abuse jurisdiction existed,[2] holding that, on the facts, even if the extradition court did possess an abuse jurisdiction, the tactics employed were 'perfectly proper'[3] and that such an application was 'without merit'.[4]

1   Above para **8.43**.
2   Certified questions 6 and 7 listed at p 941G-H.
3   At 963G-H per Lord Mackay of Clashfern, with whom Lords Bridge, Brandon, Oliver and Goff agreed.
4   At 964C-D.

8.79   *In re Schmidt*[1] concerned a German national living in the Republic of Ireland. Tentative German requests to Ireland to issue a provisional arrest warrant had failed. In 1992, an officer of the extradition squad of the International and Organised Crime Branch of the Metropolitan Police telephoned Schmidt and his solicitor in Ireland and (wrongly) said that he was investigating a cheque fraud and was anxious to exclude Schmidt from his inquiries. He invited Schmidt to come to England to be interviewed and went so far as to tell Schmidt's solicitor that, if Schmidt did not come, his name would probably be circulated as that of a suspect, a warrant would be issued for his arrest and he would be liable to be arrested when he next came to the UK. This was all repeated to Schmidt's Irish solicitor. It was all a lie. There was no allegation of cheque fraud. It was simply a device to persuade Schmidt to enter the UK. In fact, the UK had received an extradition request from Germany in respect of 58 charges of supplying and possessing over 386kg of cannabis between 1987 and 1991. Germany had no extradition treaty with the Republic of Ireland and, therefore, needed to get Schmidt into the UK (with whom it did). In November 1992, Schmidt and his Irish solicitor met the police officer in London. Schmidt accompanied the officer to a police station where he was arrested on a provisional warrant under the Extradition Act 1989 issued that morning. Lord Jauncey of Tullichettle[2] ruled[3] that, even if the court did have jurisdiction to entertain an application for abuse of process, it would be rejected on the merits:

'At the very worst, he was tricked into coming to England but not coerced ... The 58 German charges outstanding against the applicant suggest that he may be a substantial international dealer in drugs. As such, his frequent visits to England are unlikely to be in the public interest. To bring such a person to justice the police and other drug enforcement agencies may from time to time have to tempt him to enter their fief. In my view, what was done by D.S. Jones was far more akin to the enticement of the drug enforcement agent in *Liangsiriprasert* than to the forceable abduction in *Reg. v. Horseferry Road Magistrates' Court, Ex parte Bennett* [1994] 1 A.C. 42. I agree with Roch LJ that the detective sergeant's conduct was not so grave or serious as would have warranted the intervention of the High Court had it possessed such a power'.

1   Above para **8.46**.
2   With whom Lords Templeman, Ackner, Slynn and Lloyd agreed.
3   At pp 379–380.

8.80   In *R v Bow Street Magistrates' Court, ex p Van der Holst,*[1] failure, categorised as 'stupid' and 'irregular' but falling short of bad faith, to bring a defendant before the court as soon as possible following arrest pursuant to an extradition request; so as to frustrate statutory and treaty time limits, was held not to constitute a deliberate manipulation of the court's process. In *R v Governor of Pentonville Prison, ex parte Chinoy,*[2] it was held that reliance by the US upon telephone intercept evidence obtained in France in breach of French law and sovereignty was not an abuse where the unlawful conduct had occurred prior to the matter coming within the jurisdiction of the English Court. *R v Governor of Brixton Prison, ex p Cuoghi*[3] was a case in which submissions were advanced as to authentication. The defence had sought an adjournment, and counsel for the Requesting State had indicated that the adjournment would not be used to obtain properly authenticated documents. The High Court held[4] no abuse to have occurred where the Requesting State, of its own volition, had supplied properly authenticated documents in the interim period.

1   Above para **8.44**, per Lloyd LJ at 124.
2   Above para **8.44**, per Nolan J (with whom Farquharson LJ agreed) at 327A-330J.
3   [1998] 1 WLR 1513, DC.
4   Per Kennedy LJ at 1521G-1522B,

8.81   In respect of successive requests for extradition, in *R (Kashamu) v Governor of Brixton Prison (No 2),* [1] the High Court held that immediate detention on a second warrant extradition request following dismissal of the first by the High Court as a result of material non-disclosure did not constitute an abuse.[2] In a decision soon after the fledgling *Kashamu* abuse jurisdiction had been established, the High Court in *Lodhi v Governor of Brixton Prison (No 2)* [3] gave short shrift to the argument based on *R v Horsham Justices, ex p Reeves*[4] that a second extradition request amounted to an abuse of process.[5]

1   Above para **8.51**.
2   Rose LJ at para 34.
3   (9 October 2002), unreported.
4   (1980) 75 Cr App Rep 236.
5   These cases should not, however, be seen as laying down a principle that successive requests will never be abusive. See *Central Examining Court of the National Court of Madrid v City of Westminster Magistrates' Court* discussed below at para **8.91**.

CASE LAW UNDER THE 2003 ACT

8.82   In *R v Horseferry Road Magistrates' Court, ex p Bennett,*[1] the House of Lords postulated two species of abuse of process in a domestic context, which can be summarised as: (i) where the conduct complained of prejudices the defence to such an extent that it is not possible to have a fair trial, or (ii) where, no matter how fair the trial may be, circumstances exist which render it offensive to justice and propriety to try the defendant at all. Neither of these translate directly into an extradition context. Limb (i) does not fall within the scope of the narrow extradition abuse jurisdiction at all; insofar as an extradition defendant seeks to raise issues as to the fairness of his prospective trial in the Requesting State, he must do so under ss 21 or 87 via the medium of ECHR, Art 6 and satisfy the 'flagrant denial of justice' test.[2] Limb (ii) must be modified so as to focus not upon the propriety or manipulation of the prospective trial but rather upon the propriety or manipulation of the extradition process.

1   [1994] 1 AC 42, HL.
2   Above paras **8.29–8.32**.

8.83   Whilst there is clearly overlap, the need to translate the domestic abuse jurisdiction to the extradition context has led the Court of Appeal of Ontario[1] to re-formulate the *Bennett* test:

(i)   Where the conduct complained of prejudices the conduct of the defence to such an extent that it is not possible to have a fair *extradition* hearing, or

(ii)   Where, no matter how fairly an extradition hearing could be conducted, circumstances exist which render it offensive to justice and propriety to proceed at all.

1   *Larosa v Her Majesty The Queen* (above para **8.64**) per Doherty JA at para 52.

Manipulation of the extradition machinery

8.84   Here, the practitioner is concerned with a case in which the extradition request, albeit made in good faith, has been (or has attempted to have been) implemented or enforced in a manner involving deliberate manipulation of the extradition machinery to the advantage of the Requesting State, and the prejudice of the requested person. Here, the conduct complained of prejudices the conduct of the defence to such an extent that it is not possible to have a fair *extradition* hearing. The focus of enquiry will not be upon the underlying foreign process but will be upon the conduct of the Requesting State in the UK proceedings. *In re Rees*[1] and *R v Bow Street Magistrates' Court, ex p Van der Holst*[2] (alleged manipulation of applicable time limits), *In re Schmidt*[3] (luring a defendant by deceit into the UK from which he might be extradited), *R v Governor of Brixton Prison, ex p Cuoghi*[4] (alleged misuse of adjournment/ alleged breach of undertaking), *R (Kashamu) v Governor of Brixton Prison (No 2)*[5] and *Lohdi v Governor of British Prison (No 2)*[6] (repetitive requests) are all examples of allegations of deliberate manipulation of the extradition machinery, all refused on their facts.

1   Discussed above para **8.78**.
2   Discussed above para **8.80**.
3   Discussed above para **8.79**.
4   Discussed above para **8.80**.
5   Discussed above para **8.81**.
6   Discussed above para **8.81**.

8.85   Unless it can be shown that a prosecutor 'knew he could not, or perhaps, could not without great difficulty, make out a *prima facie* case and so deliberately delayed the extradition process until the 1989 Act had been safely superseded by the 2003 Act', it is, in principle, not abusive to delay an extradition request until such time as more favourable extradition laws are in force (*Bermingham*[1]) or even to withdraw an extant request so as to proceed under a different extradition regime. In *R (Government of the United States of*

America) v Bow Street Magistrates' Court,[2] it was argued there had been deliberate delay in seeking the defendants' extradition so as to take advantage of the 2003 Act and thereby denying the appellants safeguards they would have enjoyed under the 1989 Act (such as the Secretary of State's discretion and the requirement that the Requesting State should demonstrate a case to answer). Lord Phillips CJ held[3] that:

'We think that it is clear from all of this that the United States Government decided to withdraw the first requests, not because it had decided not to proceed with their attempts to extradite Mr. and Mrs Tollman under the 1989 Act, but because they had concluded that this could be more satisfactorily achieved under the 2003 Act ... We do not consider that these facts, of themselves, constitute an abuse of process. If the present requests could properly have been made had the earlier requests never been made, we cannot see how the fact that the earlier requests were made, but not pursued, materially affects the position. If Mr and Mrs Tollman are to demonstrate an arguable case of abuse of process they need to demonstrate that there are grounds for suspecting that the present proceedings are being pursued for some improper motive, or are otherwise abusive.'[4]

1   Above para **8.31**, per Laws LJ at paras 99–100. See also *R v Bow Street Magistrates' Court, ex p Odoll* (unreported) (26 January 1999), DC per Ralph-Gibson LJ at transcript 16C-D: 'There is, in my judgment, nothing in the point that, if the application had been made on an earlier date, it would have been made under different legal provisions. If Parliament had thought it right to provide that the new provisions should not apply to alleged offences said to have been committed before the coming into force of the new provisions, it could, and would, have so provided'. See, to similar effect, *McKinnon v Government of the United States of America* [2007] EWHC 762 (Admin) per Maurice Kay LJ at para 39.
2   Above at para **8.10**, per Lord Phillips CJ at paras 113–117. It is also not abusive to discontinue extant domestic criminal charges to make way for extradition proceedings, even where both sets of proceedings relate to the same conduct (*Larosa v Her Majesty the Queen* (above para **8.64**) per Doherty JA at para 60). The Ontario Court of Appeal did recognise, however, that an arguable abuse would be made out if there existed some evidential basis for finding that the domestic charges were a ruse or were manipulated to hold the defendant in custody pending the submission of the extradition request (at para 62). Equally, if a person is detained under immigration powers in order to keep him in custody until the US authorities could commence extradition proceedings, that is also improper (*Government of the United States of America v Tollman* (above para **8.66**) per Malloy J at para 128).
3   At paras 116–117.
4   Neither should extradition proceedings be stayed because the evidentiary provisions of the Extradition Act create a different standard for the person sought in tendering evidence from that which the extradition partner must meet (*United States of America v Ferras* [2006] 2 SCR 77 at para 50; *United States of America v Kinsella* (above para **8.72**) at paras 39–44.

8.86   Unless acting without instructions, and so long as the extradition request, or European Arrest warrant, is ultimately approved and issued ('not merely rubber-stamped') by the Requesting State, or Part 1 Issuing Judicial Authority, it is, in principle, not abusive to assist a Requesting State in the drafting of an extradition request so as to ensure compliance with legislative requirements; *Central Examining Court of the National Court of Madrid v City of Westminster Magistrates' Court*[1] per Sedley LJ:[2]

'... the partial drafting of the Spanish court's warrants by the CPS ... represents neither an abdication of its functions by the [Issuing Judicial Authority] nor a usurpation of the IJA's functions by the CPS. It is a practical and, in my judgment, legitimate endeavour on the part of one country to get a suitable form of extradition process before the courts of another country … the material was not capable of founding or generating a rational suspicion of abusive conduct on the part of the IJA or the CPS … The simple provision of drafting assistance to the IJA is not, in law, capable of constituting an abuse. It impacts neither on the principle of equality of arms, nor on the visible independence and impartiality of the Spanish Judicial Authority'.

1   [2007] EWHC 2059 (Admin).
2   At paras 24 and 31–35.

8.87   In *R (Ahsan) v Director of Public Prosecutions & another,*[1] it was argued that failure to consider guidance agreed between the Attorney General of the US and the Attorney General of the UK in respect of handling criminal cases with concurrent jurisdiction (in respect of forum) rendered extradition proceedings abusive. Richards LJ ruled[2] that the guidance did not apply where there had been no investigation initiated in the UK but observed in any event that: 'Even if the guidance had applied and there had been a failure to consider it, the failure would not be capable of rendering the extradition proceedings an abuse of process'.

1   Above para **8.08**.
2   At para 128.

8.88   In *Lopetas v Minister of Justice for Lithuania,*[1] the appellant was arrested in Cornwall on a European Arrest Warrant. Because of a difficulty in transporting him to court, he was not produced at the City of Westminster Magistrates' Court until three days later, and so fell to be discharged under s 4(3) and (5) of the 2003 Act because he had not been brought to court, in the words of the provision, 'as soon as practicable'. That led the Lithuanian authorities to issue a further European Arrest Warrant, certified by the Serious Organised Crime Agency (SOCA) pursuant to s 2(7) of the Act, which was executed immediately upon the appellant's discharge. However, the appellant fell to be discharged for a second time, this time under s 4(2) and (4) of the Act, because he had not been handed a copy of the warrant as soon as practicable after his arrest. However, a member of the SOCA, present at court that day, observing that second error, wrongly took the view that it could be dealt with by issuing a new certificate under s 2(7) of the Act.[2] The result was that the appellant remained in custody awaiting hearing of the extradition proceedings for 14 days on an unlawful basis, until a third warrant was issued and certified. At the extradition hearing, it was argued that the unlawful re-certification of the second warrant had constituted an abuse of process, or alternatively that once it was realised by those representing the Lithuanian authorities that the appellant's continued detention was unlawful, failure to have been listed (instead, the Crown Prosecution Service advised the Lithuanian authorities to re-issue the warrant) was abusive. The District Judge held that 'the course of conduct could have been abusive if known to be unlawful and done to detain the defendant', but found no evidence to suggest that that had been the motivation. The decision plainly envisages that, had there been evidence from which manipulative intent might reasonably have been inferred, then an abuse would have been made out. The High Court reached a similar conclusion. Before the

High Court, the appellant disclaimed any suggestion of bad faith. The High Court proceeded on the basis that (but declined to decide whether) the re-certification of the second warrant had been unlawful. Assuming that it had been, it was held[3] by Auld LJ that:

'... it cannot, given the circumstances, possibly be regarded in itself as an abuse of process so as to taint in any way the reinstitution of proceedings following the issue of the third properly-certified warrant. [In respect of a submission that the High Court should mark what happened ... as an abuse of process by discharging [the Appellant] to condone the unlawfulness] ... Such a submission is totally inappropriate to the circumstances of this case, the facts of which disclose, whether lawful or unlawful, no error in the way in which the proceedings were reinstituted. This does not approach the type of egregious conduct that the court has considered, notably that in Bennett ... there was clearly no basis for suspicion [of some skulduggery] ... Quite plainly that it had been a mistake and one which, as soon as the Crown Prosecution Service appreciated it, they corrected properly by the reissue of proceedings'.

1   [2007] EWHC 2407 (Admin).
2   There should have been a reissue of the warrant, properly certified, not certification of an old warrant that was no longer valid: see s 213.
3   At paras 16–17.

8.89   It would, however, be abusive for those representing a Requesting State deliberately to withhold service of its extradition request until the commencement of the extradition hearing so as to ambush a defendant and deprive him of a proper opportunity to contest them: Government of the Federal Republic of Germany v Kleinschmidt & another.[1]

1   Above para 8.55.

8.90   In Boudhiba,[1] Smith LJ observed[2] that the court would have been prepared to hold extradition proceedings to be an abuse of process if a defendant had been tricked into prejudicing himself by making admissions in an interview in the UK (conducted under the auspices of the mutual legal assistance provisions of the Crime (International Cooperation) Act 2003 whilst under the false impression that he was being interviewed as a witness, even in the absence of bad faith on the part of the Requesting State or interviewing authorities.

1   Above para **8.09**.
2   At paras 24–25.

8.91   As regards repetitive extradition requests, in *Central Examining Court of the National Court of Madrid v City of Westminster Magistrates' Court*,[1] Sedley LJ observed[2] that: 'I do not doubt that a point may come at which an [Issuing Judicial Authority] can be stopped from repeated use of the European arrest warrant process if it is turning into a form of harassment'.

1   [2007] EWHC 2059 (Admin).
2   At para 21.

8.92   In *R (Raissi) v Secretary of State for the Home Department*,[1] in addition to finding abuse by reason of ulterior motive,[2] the Court of Appeal additionally, and separately, held in the same case that, independent of the actions or motive of a Requesting State, extradition proceedings had been abused by the legal representative of the Requesting State in the UK. The Court of Appeal examined the status of the Crown Prosecution Service when acting in its capacity as legal representative of a Requesting State in extradition proceedings and concluded that, even though the CPS was acting as representative of the Requesting State, that did not mean that it did not owe a duty to the UK Court.[3] The CPS's duty to the court might require it not to 'act unquestioningly' on its instructions.[4] In the event of conflict between its instructions from the Requesting State and its duty to the court, the CPS's primary duty was to the court[5]. The duty of the CPS to the court extended also to a duty not to take part in proceedings which it knew or ought to know were an abuse of the process of the court.[6] In this case, the preliminary[7] findings of the Court of Appeal disclosed that the CPS had abused the process of the court. The extradition request related to what can only be described as minor charges, for which the appellant would normally have been entitled to bail. He was remanded in custody because it was said that he was a terrorist involved in the 9/11 atrocities, and that the charges were only 'holding charges'. The material available to CPS did not support such an allegation and/or the CPS were being reckless as to its accuracy. In the circumstances, the Court of Appeal[8] held[9] that:

> 'We also consider that the way in which the extradition proceedings were conducted in this country, with opposition to bail based on allegations which appear unfounded in evidence amounted to an abuse of process ... the opposition to bail, based on unsubstantiated assertions, was also an abuse' (para 146).

1   [2008] EWCA Civ 72.
2   See below paras **8.116–8.117**.
3   At para 135.
4   At para 138.
5   At para 139.
6   At para 141.
7   See below para **8.116**.
8   Sir Anthony Clarke MR, Smith LJ and Hooper LJ.
9   At paras 144 and 146.

8.93   An infamous example of such a category of case is to be found in the Canadian Supreme Court decision of *Cobb & Grossman v USA*.[1] In that case, the appellants, Canadian citizens, allegedly defrauded American residents of some $22 million through a telemarketing scheme executed from Canada concerning illegal sale of gemstones. Canadian police declined to initiate proceedings but instead provided the materials gathered by them to the US authorities. The US requested extradition on charges of fraud and conspiracy to commit fraud. While many of the co-conspirators voluntarily returned to the jurisdiction of Pennsylvania, the appellants contested their extradition on the basis that extraditing them would unjustifiedly violate their rights under the Canadian Charter of Rights and Freedoms in the light of statements made by the American judge and prosecuting attorney with conduct of the matter in the US. First, as he was sentencing a co-conspirator in the scheme, the American judge assigned to their trial had stated that: 'I want you to believe me that as to those people who don't come in and cooperate and if we get them extradited and they're found guilty, as far as I'm concerned they're going to get the absolute maximum jail sentence that the law permits me to give'. Second, the prosecuting attorney subsequently said during a television interview that: 'I have told some of these individuals, "Look, you can come down and you can put this behind you by serving your time in prison and making restitution to the victims, or you can wind up serving a great deal longer sentence under much more stringent conditions", and described those conditions to them [as] '"You're going to be the boyfriend of a very bad man if you wait out your extradition" out of the 89 people we've indicted so far, approximately 55 of them have said '"We give up"'.

1   Above para **8.72**.

8.94   The extradition Judge (Hawkins J) stayed the extradition proceedings as an abuse of process, finding that the Judge's remark was 'nothing short of a bold, undisguised threat intended to intimidate the applicants and others into abandoning their right to resist extradition by lawful means' and, in respect of the comments of the prosecutor, that 'I believe and I hope I can safely say that no right-thinking Canadian would endorse the use of a threat of homosexual rape as a means of persuading Canadian residents to abandon their rights to a full extradition hearing'. Hawkins J concluded that:

> 'In my view, to commit these fugitives for surrender to be tried before a judge who has publicly threatened them with the imposition of a maximum sentence before having commenced their trial and to be prosecuted by a prosecutor who has publicly threatened them with homosexual rape (boasting at the same time how effective the technique has been) "shocks the Canadian conscience" and is "simply not acceptable" '.

8.95   That decision was overturned by the Court of Appeal for Ontario but reinstated by the Canadian Supreme Court. On issues of jurisdiction, the Supreme Court, overturning prior authority,[1] held that the extradition judge is competent to grant *Charter* remedies, including a stay of proceedings, on the basis of a *Charter* violation but only insofar as the *Charter* breach pertains directly to the circumscribed issues relevant at the committal stage of the extradition process.[2] The issue is not whether the appellants will have a fair trial if extradited, but whether they are having a fair extradition hearing in the light of the threats and inducements imposed upon them, by those involved in requesting their extradition, to force them to abandon their right to such a hearing. Conduct by the Requesting State, or by its representatives, agents or officials, which interferes or attempts to interfere with the conduct of judicial proceedings in Canada is a matter that directly concerns the extradition judge.[3] The Requesting State is a party to judicial proceedings before a Canadian court and is subject to the application of rules and remedies that serve to control the conduct of parties who turn to the courts for assistance. Even aside from any claim of *Charter* protection, litigants are protected from unfair, abusive proceedings through the doctrine of abuse of process, which bars litigants – and not only the State – from pursuing frivolous or vexatious proceedings, or otherwise abusing the process of the courts.[4] A stay of proceedings will be entered only in the clearest of cases and is always better dealt with by the court where the abuse occurs.[5]

1   *Argentina v Mellino* [1987] 1 SCR 536.
2   Per Arbour J at para 26.
3   At para 33.
4   At para 35.
5   At para 38.

8.96   But in this case, a stay of proceedings was justified either as a remedy based on s 7 of the Canadian *Charter*[1] or on the basis of the doctrine of abuse of process.[2] The statements made by the American Judge and the US Attorney may properly be visited upon the Requesting State itself, who was a party before the court. One interpretation of the Judge's statement, and any interpretation of the 'sinister' prosecutor's statement, were an attempt to influence the unfolding of Canadian judicial proceedings by putting undue pressure on the appellants to desist from their objections to the extradition request. The pressures were not only inappropriate but also, in the case of the statements made by the prosecutor on the eve of the opening of the judicial hearing in Canada, amounted unequivocally to an abuse of the process of the court. Litigants should not be expected to overcome well-founded fears of violent reprisals in order to be participants in a judicial process. Aside from such intimidation itself, it is plain that a committal order requiring a fugitive to return to face such an ominous climate – which was created by those who would play a large, if not decisive role in determining the fugitive's ultimate fate – would not be consistent with the principles of fundamental justice. The intimidation bore directly upon the very proceedings before the extradition judge. Aside from the intimidation itself, a committal order obtained in the present circumstances would clearly not be consistent with the principles of fundamental justice.[3] Whilst 'foreign' conduct may not attract *Charter* scrutiny, conduct attributable to a litigant before a Canadian court is sufficient to trigger the application of the common law doctrine of abuse of process.[4]

1   The right to life, liberty and security of the person and the right not to be deprived thereof except in accordance with the principles of fundamental justice
2   At para 40.
3   At para 43.
4   At para 49. The Supreme Court further held that the existence of potential remedies at the executive stage does not oust the jurisdiction of the courts to control their own process (at paras 42 and 44).

8.97   The threats from the American authorities did not in fact induce the persons sought to abandon their right to resist extradition. The Supreme Court of Canada found this to be immaterial. It was the attempt to interfere with the due process of the court that mattered, not the success or failure of that attempt.[1] The Supreme Court concluded[2] that:

> 'By placing undue pressure on Canadian citizens to forego due legal process in Canada, the foreign State has disentitled itself from pursuing its recourse before the courts and attempting to show why extradition should legally proceed. The intimidation bore directly upon the very proceedings before the extradition judge, thus engaging the appellants' right to fundamental justice at common law, under the doctrine of abuse of process … this was one of the clearest of cases where to proceed further with the extradition hearing would violate "those fundamental principles of justice which

underlie the community's sense of fair play and decency", since the Requesting State in the proceedings, represented by the Attorney General of Canada, had not repudiated the statements of some of its officials that an unconscionable price would be paid by the appellants for having insisted on exercising their rights under Canadian law.'

1   At para 50.
2   At paras 52–53.

8.98   It should be noted, however, that a partially different result was reached in the linked case of *Shulman v USA*[1] concerning one of Cobb's co-conspirators. Here, by contrast, the appellant received a fair extradition hearing. He was not subjected to undue pressure by American officials before or during his committal hearing because he was not aware of the American Judge's statement and the prosecuting attorney's threat had not yet been uttered. The Supreme Court held[2] that the comments could not in any way have had any impact on the fairness of the committal hearing, and thus the extradition judge was correct in denying the appellant's application for a stay of proceedings. However, by the time Shulman's appeal had been listed, he had become aware of the American Judge's statement and the prosecuting attorney's threat had been uttered. Whilst holding that the extradition appeal court also has an implied, if not inherent, jurisdiction to control its own process, including through the application of the common law doctrine of abuse of process,[3] in light of the fact that the ambiguous statement was made by the American Judge a few months before the appellant's extradition hearing and had gone unnoticed by the appellant until it was raised by others in related proceedings, the Supreme Court was not bound by any factual findings of the extradition judge and was able to come to its own conclusions about the nature of the American Judge's statement. The Supreme Court ruled that:

'It is quite possible that the Judge did not mean that he would impose the maximum sentence regardless of any other relevant factor, but simply that he would discount the maximum sentence by any other legally relevant factor, and then give no additional reduction in light of the absence of cooperation. This is, I would have thought, all that the law permits[3] ... his remarks, made in the course of a sentencing hearing, may not necessarily be construed as a threat of judicial retaliation directed at those who avail themselves of the Canadian judicial system to oppose an extradition request, as is their right. Taken alone, and in their proper context, these comments, in my judgment, would not be sufficient to sustain a claim of abuse of process'.[4]

1   [2001] 1 SCR 616.
2   At para 24.
3   At para 38.
4   At para 50. By contrast, the 'unambiguous' prosecutor's statement was of a different nature and properly characterised as a shocking use of threats by a US official attempting to induce Canadian citizens to renounce the exercise of their lawful access to courts in Canada in order to resist a US extradition request. The statement was made almost two years after Shulman had been committed for surrender by the extradition judge, but before the hearing of his appeal by the Court of Appeal. The statement was properly attributed to the Requesting State, the respondent in the Court of Appeal. The Appeal Court should have received evidence as to its utterance and, having received that evidence, and the respondent having made no efforts to

distance itself from the impugned statements, should have stayed the proceedings as an abuse of the ongoing judicial process.

8.99 In *McKinnon v Government of the United States of America*[1] the House of Lords adopted and applied *Cobb*. The appellant, a British citizen, was alleged to have hacked into US government computers and installed unauthorised software which enabled him to access, alter and delete data on those computers, causing damage. When interviewed under caution, the defendant admitted responsibility although not that he had caused damage. Grand jury indictments were returned against him alleging seven counts of fraud and related activity in connection with computers, and warrants issued for his arrest. But, before making a request for the appellant's extradition, the US prosecutors informed his legal representatives that if he went voluntarily to the US without contesting extradition and if he pleaded guilty to two counts, the prosecution would be prepared to limit its allegations of monetary damage and not pursue allegations of endangering national security, thus enabling them to make a recommendation to the court which was likely to result in the appellant receiving a sentence of 37–46 months' imprisonment, probably at the shorter end of that bracket, and, after serving six to twelve months in the US, the prosecutor would recommend to the Department of Justice that the appellant be repatriated to serve the rest of his sentence in the UK, and that that recommendation was likely to be accepted (the practical effect being that the appellant's release date would then be determined by the UK rules on remission, such that he might serve a total of eighteen months to two years in prison). The appellant was offered a plea agreement on those terms. The appellant alleged that he was also informed through his legal representatives that if he chose not to co-operate and was extradited to the US and convicted by a jury after pleading not guilty, he could expect to receive a sentence of at least eight to ten years' imprisonment (based upon the extant allegations of monetary damage and endangering national security), possibly longer, and would not be repatriated to the UK to serve any part of it, so that he would serve the whole sentence in the US, possibly in a high security prison, with at best some 15 per cent remission. The defendant took advice from an American defence lawyer and refused the 'deal'. Extradition proceedings were commenced.

1   Above para **8.61**.

8.100 The appellant relied on *Cobb*[1] and argued that where the respondent government is seeking the assistance of the English courts to extradite an accused, it must comply with the legal principles of this jurisdiction. That he has in fact resisted the pressure improperly put upon him is no answer to the contention that it constituted an abuse of process; it was calculated to interfere with the extradition proceedings. Lord Brown of Eaton-under-Heywood[2] ruled[3] that:

'The district judge … had jurisdiction to consider whether the extradition proceedings constituted an abuse of process so as to protect the integrity of the statutory regime, the Secretary of State having no general discretion to refuse extradition. So much was stated by Laws LJ in … R (Bermingham) v Director of the Serious Fraud Office … and by Lord Phillips of Worth Matravers CJ in R (Government of the United States of America) v Bow

Street Magistrates' Court ... What was not expressly stated in these decisions but was necessarily implicit was that the abuse of process for consideration was such as to require the extradition proceedings to be permanently stayed and the accused discharged'.

1 Discussed above at paras **8.93–8.97**.
2 With whom Lords Scott and Phillips and Baroness Hale and Lord Neuberger agreed.
3 At para 8.

8.101 Approving[1] (at paras 30–32) the principles laid down in *Cobb*, the House of Lords stated[2] that the 'essential questions underlying' the determination of whether it is an abuse of process in the circumstances of this case were:

'Did the US prosecuting authority here "attempt to interfere with the due process of the court"? Did it place "undue pressure [on the appellant] to forego due legal process" in the UK and so disentitle itself from pursuing extradition proceedings? Would extradition in this case "violate those fundamental principles of justice which underlie the community's sense of fair play and decency"? Would the appellant following extradition be paying "an unconscionable price ... having insisted on exercising [his] rights under [English] law"?.'

1 At paras 30–32.
2 At para 33.

8.102 However, the House of Lords found differences between the alleged conduct in this case, and the conduct in *Cobb*, to be striking. In respect of the disparity between the predicted sentences, the House of Lords observed[1] that the discount would have to be very substantially more generous than anything promised here (as to the way the case would be put and the likely outcome) before it constituted unlawful pressure such as to vitiate the process. So too would the predicted consequences of non-co-operation need to go significantly beyond what could properly be regarded as the defendant's just deserts on conviction for that to constitute unlawful pressure. As regards the allegation that the US authorities had threatened to oppose repatriation, the House of Lords observed that, even were it to be regarded as an unlawful threat, it has now been expressly repudiated by the US prosecutor, again in marked contrast to the position in *Cobb*.[2] Lord Brown concluded[3] that:

'it would only be in a wholly extreme case like *Cobb* itself that the court should properly regard any encouragement to accused persons to surrender for trial and plead guilty, in particular if made by a prosecutor during a regulated process of plea bargaining, as so unconscionable as to constitute an abuse of process justifying the Requested State's refusal to extradite the accused. It is difficult, indeed, to think of anything other than the threat of unlawful action which could fairly be said so to imperil the integrity of the extradition process as to require the accused, notwithstanding his having resisted the undue pressure, to be discharged irrespective of the strength of the case against him.'

1 At para 38.
2 At para 40.
3 At para 41.

Failed disguised extradition

8.103   Before coming to 'ulterior motive' or 'bad faith' category of cases, it is instructive to consider one particular species of conduct of abuse that straddles both categories of abuse; failed disguised extradition.

8.104   Both the Extradition Act and the international treaties which it implements contemplate that a foreign state wishing to have a person returned to it from the UK to face charges must proceed under the Extradition Act. An individual has greater procedural protections in an extradition proceeding than in a deportation proceeding. Deportation and extradition have different underlying objectives. Deportation, which is a discretionary decision of the immigration authorities, is aimed at protecting the public good. Extradition, which is initiated by foreign authorities, is aimed at delivering a person sought for prosecution to the appropriate jurisdiction. Generally, the extradition process engages more rigorous standards in terms of the kind of process that UK authorities are obliged to undertake in order to return the person to a foreign state. Specifically, one significant advantage of extradition over deportation to the person sought is in the long established rule of international law that, following extradition, a Requesting State may only prosecute for the conduct in respect of which extradition has been granted; the rule of 'specialty'. The rule, and the various exceptions to it, is reflected in every international extradition treaty, and under the 2003 Act is reflected in ss 17 and 95. A fugitive returned pursuant to deportation procedures is deprived of this fundamental protection. Therefore, to the state that wants a particular individual returned, deportation is more advantageous. There are no restrictions in terms of what the person, once deported to that state, can be prosecuted for.

8.105   Issues of *successful* disguised extradition arise in the context of domestic criminal proceedings where the practitioner will be concerned with an allegation that his or her client's very presence before the UK courts has been obtained in breach of extradition arrangements between the UK and the State in which he or she was previously situated. These issues are discussed in **Chapter 5**. But, while less common, issues of *failed* disguised extradition can arise in deportation[1] or extradition proceedings. In an extradition context, cases do occur in which a Requesting State has attempted, but failed, to secure illegitimately a person's deportation in circumvention of extradition procedure, and is then forced to resort to an extradition request. In such a case, it is possible to argue that the subsequent extradition proceedings are tainted by the prior attempt to interfere with the due process of the court. This scenario has yet to arise in an extradition case in the UK. Although English case law has established the principle, to ascertain the factors that underlie such a submission, the practitioner must turn to Canadian case law.

1   In immigration proceedings the issue will arise in circumstances where the Requesting State has failed to prove its case in an extradition context, and is therefore seeking to achieve the return of the person through another forum (where the individual receives less procedural protections).

8.106   In practical terms, there is significant overlap between extradition and deportation, which is not, in and of itself, improper. A host State may well have an entirely legitimate basis, irrespective of any prospective prosecution, for deporting an individual in the public interest. There is, in principle, nothing improper or abusive in a host State deporting such an individual, even if the practical effect of that deportation will be removal to a foreign state where he will face prosecution for offences allegedly committed there (and even offences that would be precluded by the rule of specialty). The end result of extradition, namely the return of a person to a place where he or she is wanted for prosecution, may be legitimately achieved through deportation, if the removal of that person from the UK is conducive to the public good:[1]

> 'the fact that the present applicant will serve an existing sentence of imprisonment, if he is sent to the United States, does not mean that an act which otherwise would be deportation and nothing else becomes instead not deportation but the surrender of a fugitive criminal. To hold otherwise would be to give assent to the proposition that the quality of an act is determined by its consequence, which is obviously untrue; otherwise cause would become the same thing as effect. There may, it is true, be no practical difference from the applicant's point of view between a deportation which gives the United States authorities the power to make him serve his sentence, and an illegal surrender having the same effect. But that cannot involve that in law the two things must be regarded as the same. If, therefore, this deportation order is to be regarded as invalid, it must be for some other reason than the consequence to which it will lead.'

1   *R v Governor of Brixton Prison, ex p Soblen* [1963] 2 QB 243, CA per Donovan LJ at p 307. See also Lord Denning MR at 301–302; *Government of the United States of America v Tollman* (above para **8.66**) per Malloy J para 26). See also *Halm v Canada (Minister of Employment and Immigration)* [1996] 1 FC 547 (TD) per Rothstein J at paras 18–23; *Kissell v The Attorney-General of Canada on behalf of the United States of America* [2006] 47314 (Ont. Supr. Crt.) per Beaulieu J at paras 142–143.

8.107   What, by contrast, is not permissible is use of the power of deportation to remove a foreign national to another country *for the purpose of* enabling that foreign state to prosecute him or her for offences allegedly committed. It is an abuse of process to exercise a statutory power for a reason that is unrelated to the purpose for which that power was granted.[1] The guiding principle was clearly stated by Lord Denning in *R v Governor of Brixton Prison, ex p Soblen.*[2] The powers of deportation and extradition must each be exercised for their own distinct purpose. Where a proceeding is undertaken professedly for an authorised purpose, but in fact with an ulterior object, it is unlawful. In appropriate cases, the courts will, therefore, be duty-bound to inquire into this purpose, engaging in a factual inquiry which focuses on the purposes for which immigration procedures were engaged.[3] Lord Denning MR observed[4] that:

> 'So there we have in this case the two principles: on the one hand the principle arising out of the law of extradition under which the officers of the Crown cannot and must not surrender a fugitive criminal to another country at its request except in accordance with the Extradition Acts duly fulfilled; on the other hand the principle arising out of the law of deportation, under which the Secretary of State can deport an alien and put him on board a ship or aircraft bound for his own country if he considers it conducive to the public good that that should be done. How are we to decide between these two principles? It seems to me that it depends on the purpose with which the

act is done. If it was done for an authorised purpose, it was lawful. If it was done professedly for an authorised purpose, but in fact for a different purpose with an ulterior object, it was unlawful. If, therefore, the purpose of the Home Secretary in this case was to surrender the applicant as a fugitive criminal to the United States of America, because they had asked for him, then it would be unlawful; but if his purpose was to deport him to his home country because he considered his presence here to be not conducive to the public good, then his action is lawful. It is open to these courts to inquire whether the purpose of the Home Secretary was a lawful or an unlawful purpose. Was there a misuse of the power or not? The courts can always go behind the face of the deportation order in order to see whether the powers entrusted by Parliament have been exercised lawfully or not.'[5]

1   See *Government of the United States of America v Tollman* (above para **8.66**) per Malloy J at para 26: '… if a foreign state seeks the assistance of Canada to have a fugitive returned there for prosecution, that foreign state must bring the appropriate extradition application through diplomatic channels pursuant to the treaty and the *Extradition Act*. It would be improper for Canadian immigration authorities to apprehend a person and return him to the United States solely because they were requested to do so by the United States, for to do so would be to completely circumvent the *Extradition Act* and the safeguards built into that legislative scheme', and para 121: 'There is clear and binding authority that it is an abuse of process to use the immigration system for the purpose of effecting extradition. We have extradition treaties and extradition legislation for a purpose, just as we have immigration legislation for a purpose.'

2   Above para **8.106**.

3   See, to similar effect, *Moore v Minister of Manpower and Immigration* [1968] SCR 839 in which the Supreme Court of Canada held, at para 12, that: 'To decide that the deportation proceedings are a sham or not bona fide it would be necessary to hold that the Minister did not genuinely consider it in the public interest to expel the appellant', and held on the facts of that case that the applicant had failed to discharge his onus of showing that the deportation proceedings taken were in fact a sham designed to effect the applicant's extradition to Panama rather than for a legitimate purpose under the Immigration Act. In that case, Mr Moore had previously been deported from Canada, was illegally in this country, and had been travelling under a false passport. See also *Kindler v Minister of Employment and Immigration* (1985) 47 CR (3d) 225 (Fed Ct). Mr. Kindler had been convicted of first-degree murder in Pennsylvania and the jury had recommended the death penalty. He escaped the jurisdiction before sentencing and had been living and working illegally in Quebec. Rouleau J concluded that on the facts of that case there was insufficient evidence to prove that the Minister did not genuinely consider it in the public interest to order the deportation. Having made that determination, however, he noted (at p 234) that: 'I should add that, if the petitioner had been able to show that the real purpose of the deportation proceedings was to surrender him to a foreign state because he is a fugitive criminal sought by such foreign state, this would have been an abuse of the power to deport and as such would have been restrained by the court. Parliament has set up, in the Extradition Act, a special procedure for the surrender of foreign criminals and the general discretionary power to deport cannot be utilized to replace this special procedure. *Generalia specialibus non derogant.*'

4   At 302.

5   See also *Caddoux v Bow Street Magistrates' Court* [2004] EWHC 642 (Admin) per Kennedy LJ at paras 11–12, where it is observed that, even in a case where a deportation order may legitimately be made 'once the request for extradition was received I accept that there were powerful reasons of comity for giving it priority. The fact then was that a person wanted by the French authorities was still on English soil. If he were to be deported without notice to the French authorities, and that would we were told be the normal practice, they might well be deprived of the opportunity to require him to stand trial in France, so, as it seems to me, the Secretary of State was right to allow the extradition proceedings to go ahead, leaving the deportation order to be implemented if necessary at the conclusion of these proceedings'.

8.108 The lynchpin of an abuse of process argument based on failed disguised extradition is, therefore, whether the UK authorities had, from the outset, legitimate grounds in seeking to deport the person sought. Where the authorities undertake deportation in order to surrender the person as a fugitive criminal in response to a request from another state, their purpose is unlawful. However, where the authorities seek to deport in order to protect domestic public good, the action is legitimate. The fact that there is a practical overlap between the outcome of these two proceedings therefore does not necessarily suggest that extradition proceedings, rather than deportation, should always be undertaken where a person is wanted by a state. In order to show impropriety, the defendant must bring enough evidence to show, or at least strongly to suggest, that the deportation proceedings were undertaken by UK authorities in bad faith and with an ulterior motive.[1] This is a difficult argument to make. The threshold is high, and a finding of bad faith is reserved only for exceptional cases.[2]

1   *Kissell* (above para **8.106**) at paras 144 and 154.
2   *Soblen* (above para **8.106**) *at* 307–308 per Donovan LJ; *Moore* (above para **8.107**) at para 11; *Halm* (above para **8.106**) at para 21; *Government of the United States of America v Tollman* (Above para **8.66**) at para 22.

8.109 There is nothing improper in a Requesting State making a tactical or strategic choice between deportation and extradition, so long as the immigration authorities of the host State have a legitimate basis to pursue deportation. Put another way, if a host State is proposing legitimately to deport a fugitive, there is nothing abusive in the Requesting State accepting the fugitive on that basis or even facilitating those proceedings.[1]

1   *Kissell* (above para **8.106**) at paras 151 and 160–161: '... there are not sufficient grounds for inferring that the American authorities decided to pursue extradition because they somehow "knew" that the immigration process would not go their way. Yet, even if this was the case, there would not be anything illegitimate about it, to the extent that ... the American authorities are entitled to make any strategic choices that they wish, so long as domestic deportation proceedings were founded on a legitimate basis'. See also *Bembenek v Canada (MEI)* (1991) 69 CCC (3d) 34 (Ont Ct Gen Div). This decision is also authority for the proposition that there is nothing improper about pursuing extradition when deportation proceedings are also pending.

8.110 Equally, there is nothing improper in the Requesting State providing the host State with information and assistance in ongoing legitimate deportation proceedings. Co-operation and communication between state authorities with respect to a certain individual who is sought for prosecution does not, by itself, suggest bad faith or improper motive. Indeed, such communication and cooperation is necessary in order for authorities of the host State successfully to pursue the objectives of immigration law.[1] There is even nothing improper about the Requesting State notifying the host State of the presence of a person wanted for criminal charges, thereby effectively initiating a process of investigation under the host State's immigration law, or co-operating with the host State in locating and arresting that person.[2]

1   *Kissell* (above para **8.106**) para 152, 156. See also *Soblen* (above para **8.106**) per Donovan LJ at pp 309–310; *Bembenek* (above para **8.109**) per Campbell J at pp 11–13: 'there is nothing sinister or improper in assisting the Canadian authorities in their own opposition to the refugee claim, so long as the Canadian authorities are acting in good faith in pursuit of

legitimate Canadian objectives'; *Halm* (above para **8.106**) per Rothstein J at para 25: 'The fact that the United States wanted the applicant back or that there were communications between U.S. and Canadian officials is also not evidence of bad faith or improper motive' and *Attorney General of Canada on behalf of the United States of America v Welsh & Romero* (2007) BCSC 1567 at para 39.

2   *Kissell* (above para **8.106**) at paras 153 and 156.

8.111   The dividing line is, however, crossed when the Requesting State and the host State collude so as to bring about deportation proceedings *for the purpose of* enabling that foreign state to prosecute him or her for offences allegedly committed. Thus, to make good a *Cobb*-type abuse submission in a failed disguised extradition case, it will be necessary for the defendant to show not only that deportation proceedings have been attempted, but that their purpose was to avoid or circumvent extradition. This will require showing not only that this was the purpose of the Requesting State, but also that the UK authorities colluded in such a plan.[1] In *Halm*,[2] Rothstein J adopted[3] the following principles as a guideline for distinguishing between a legitimate deportation and a disguised extradition:

(1)   If the purpose of the exercise is to deport the person because his presence is not conducive to the public good, that is a legitimate exercise of the power of deportation.

(2)   If the purpose is to surrender the person as a fugitive criminal to a state because it asked for him, that is not a legitimate exercise of the power of deportation.

(3)   It is open to the courts to inquire whether the purpose of the government was lawful or otherwise.

(4)   The onus is on the party alleging an unlawful exercise of power. It is a heavy onus.

(5)   To succeed, it would be necessary to hold that the Minister did not genuinely consider it in the public interest to expel the person in question.

1   Kissell (above para **8.106**) at para 136.
2   Above para **8.106**.
3   At para 21.

8.112   *Government of the United States of America v Tollman*[1] is a clear illustration of how the authorities can cross this line by engaging in an extra-legal process that flouts established norms and rules. Mr Tollman, a US citizen, was wanted by the US authorities on allegations of income tax evasion. To the knowledge of the US. authorities, he was permanently resident in London. The US authorities took no steps until they received information that Mr Tollman would be travelling on business to Bermuda via Toronto. The US authorities took no steps to bring extradition proceedings against Mr Tollman in the UK or in Canada. Instead, they contacted Canadian immigration authorities and asked them to detain Mr Tollman as soon as he entered Canada and to deliver him to the US border where US authorities would be waiting to take him into custody to face the charges against him. The sole basis for this request was the outstanding charges against Mr Tollman in the US. This was an attempt to use the Canadian immigration system to effect Mr Tollman's removal to the US to face trial, improperly ignoring the extradition process. Initially, Canadian immigration authorities agreed to assist and Mr Tollman was detained by Canadian immigration authorities. However, despite objection by the Canadian immigration authorities, Mr Tollman's release was ordered on bail by the Immigration Review Board (IRB) pending a full immigration hearing. A Canadian immigration official unilaterally took the position that the IRB order was made without jurisdiction and refused to release Mr Tollman. During the time thus afforded, the US authorities sought and obtained a provisional arrest warrant under the Extradition Act. Although the material filed in support of that application may not have been overtly false, it was characterised by 'strategic omissions'. It was misleading in many respects and many material facts were either not disclosed or were buried in attachments and not referred to in the main affidavit. The Superior Court of Justice of Ontario[2] concluded that the US deliberately set out to thwart the Canadian extradition process and to deny him the protections afforded to him under Canadian legislation and concluded[3] that:

'It would appear that the intention behind all of this was to bring maximum pressure to bear upon Mr. Tollman in the hopes that he would simply agree to deportation and give up his rights under the *Extradition Act*. The fact that none of these efforts was successful is irrelevant. The conduct of the United States constitutes an affront to the processes of this court that cannot be condoned. This case falls squarely within the principles enunciated by the Supreme Court of Canada in *United States of America v. Cobb* ... By attempting to thwart the appropriate legal process in Canada in the hopes of having Mr. Tollman abandon his rights under Canadian law, the foreign state has disentitled itself to any relief from this court. This is conduct that offends this community's sense of fair play and decency and constitutes an abuse of process. The only suitable remedy in these circumstances is a stay of proceedings.'

1 Above para **8.66**.
2 Malloy J.
3 At para 13. The core findings in this case (at paras 120–132) were that there was a discernable overall plan by the US authorities to engineer a situation that avoided a legal process altogether (at paras 120–121), whether extradition (from the UK or Canada) or deportation. The US deliberately tried to pressure Canadian immigration authorities into swiftly detaining Mr Tollman at the airport, and 'delivering' him to the US border without due process. Secondly, the American authorities were found to have actually pressured immigration authorities deliberately to disobey a court order, thereby preventing the lawful release of the applicant from detention (at para 132). Further, it was found by Molloy J that the underlying intent of the American authorities was to pressure the applicant into relinquishing his rights under the extradition process. To this end, the American authorities deliberately chose to seek to apprehend Mr Tollman in Canada, a jurisdiction to which he did not have many ties, instead of at his regular place of residence (the UK) so that he would become more willing to surrender if he became caught up in lengthy proceedings (at para 129). To this end, the American authorities were also found to have deliberately instructed immigration authorities to put him in unjustifiably harsh conditions of detention with the purpose of ensuring that his detention was as unpleasant as possible so as to pressure him into abandoning his rights and surrendering to the US (at paras 129–130). 'The actions taken by the United States against Gavin Tollman in this country speak loudly of a deliberate plan to engineer the return of Mr. Tollman to the United States to face tax fraud charges without having to go through the nuisance of an extradition proceeding. The fall-back plan was that if extradition had to be resorted to at all, it would be pursued in this country where Mr. Tollman had no ties to the community, away from his wife, his children, his friends and his work; a place where he was

more likely to be held in custody or to have his freedom severely curtailed, and therefore more likely to waive his rights and simply surrender to the United States' (at para 120).

8.113 In respect of a specific submission advanced on behalf of the Requesting State, that there can be no prejudice to Mr Tollman once the extradition arrest warrant is issued, that ultimately he got what claims he is entitled to – an extradition hearing rather than a deportation hearing, with all of the rights that that entails – Malloy J observed[1] that :

'First of all, the success or failure of the abusive steps taken is irrelevant: *Cobb*. The US hoped to obtain custody of Mr. Tollman without having to undergo an extradition proceeding; they have not been successful. However, the Canadian judicial system was engaged when the US attempted to achieve extradition through the immigration process. It is not open to a party to excuse previous abusive actions by eventually resorting to the appropriate legal processes'.

1   At para 142. See also para 146. For *Cobb*, see above para **8.97**.

8.114 Malloy J concluded that:

'this is a situation, as recognized by the Ontario Court of Appeal in *Larosa*, where proceeding with the extradition committal hearing would be a breach of fundamental justice, no matter how fairly that hearing might be conducted[1] … In addition to the personal impact on Mr. Tollman, the conduct here must be condemned as contrary to the fundamental principles upon which our justice system is based. The justice system must be fair for all who become enmeshed in it, regardless of intellect, wealth or station in life. Mr. Tollman was able to insist on his rights, albeit at considerable personal and financial cost. However, he was armed with intelligence, stamina, a social position of power and prestige, and enormous personal wealth. Very few people would have been able to do what he has done. If the system went awry for him, what hope is there for the weak, the poor and those less powerful? The answer must be in the vigilance of the justice system itself. Misconduct of this sort cannot ever be tolerated, for to do so is to condone, perhaps even to invite, similar conduct in the future. This is the kind of conduct that offends this community's sense of fair play and decency. Having conducted itself in this manner, the Requesting State is disentitled to any relief from this court. Accordingly, this extradition proceeding is permanently stayed'.[2]

1   At para 145.
2   At para 149. By contrast, facts found to fall on the correct side of the line are to be found in *Kissell* (above at para **8.106**).

Ulterior motive or purpose

8.115 Here, the examination will necessarily focus upon the conduct of the Requesting State and the circumstances giving rise to the underlying criminal allegation. *R v Governor of Pentonville Prison, ex p Chinoy*[1] is an example of such a category of allegation (alleged reliance upon evidence unlawfully obtained in a third state). Moreover, the principles upon which the Court will act pursuant to an abuse of process application are likely to be materially identical to those which previously applied under s 11(3)(c) of the 1989 Act, and the case law outlined above at paragraphs **8.27–8.28** remains of considerable importance in establishing the relevant benchmark.

1   Discussed above at para **8.80**.

8.116   Facts giving rise to a proper inference of ulterior intent are to be found in the provisional[1] findings of the Court of Appeal in *R (Raissi) v Secretary of State for the Home Department*.[2] It was here held[3] that extradition proceedings had been used for an ulterior purpose, namely to secure the defendant's detention in custody on trivial charges to allow time for the US authorities to gather or provide evidence of another more serious offence, or alternatively, to secure the defendant's presence in the US for the purpose of investigating that more serious offence. The initial intention of the US authorities was that the UK police should make some preliminary discreet enquiries about the appellant, without arresting him. However, within a short time, the appellant had been arrested by the UK domestic authorities on suspicion of terrorism, involvement in 9/11. During the seven-day period for which he could lawfully be held without charge, a case for extradition was put together by the US authorities and sent to London. Following questioning by the UK authorities, the appellant was 'de-arrested' and immediately re-arrested on a provisional extradition warrant where the charges (making false statements to obtain a pilot's licence) were of a trivial nature and were only obliquely capable of being related to any act of terrorism. The US government sought a remand in custody on the ground that the appellant would be charged with an offence of terrorism connected with 9/11, the present charges being merely 'holding charges'. The appellant spent over four months in custody until he was discharged in respect of the minor charges (no prima facie case having been established) and no alternative terrorism charges having materialised. In an application for judicial review of a refusal of ex gratia compensation, the appellant contended that the extradition charges which he faced were a device to enable him to be detained in custody whilst the US authorities investigated whether he was involved in 9/11. They were trivial and, of themselves, would never have warranted extradition proceedings or detention in custody. The appellant contended that his detention on trivial extradition charges was a breach of Art 5 of the ECHR and a device to get round the law of this country which prevented him from being held without charge as a suspect for terrorism offences for more than seven days (as the law then stood). As such, it was an abuse of the process of the court. It was finally submitted that the extradition proceedings were also a device to enable the US authorities to bring the appellant back to the US for intelligence-gathering purposes.

1   Provisional because the Court proceeded without receiving counter-evidence from the US government and because the case was decided in the context of an ex gratia compensation application.
2   Above para **8.92**.
3   At paras 139–146.

8.117   The Court of Appeal held[1] that:

'it appears … likely that the extradition proceedings were used for an ulterior purpose, namely to secure the appellant's detention in custody in order to allow time for the US authorities to provide evidence of a terrorist offence. It should be noted that it would have been unlawful for the UK police to detain the appellant any longer [than 7 days] without evidence to justify a charge; such evidence did not exist ... We think it almost inconceivable that the US authorities would have bothered to bring extradition proceedings on the charges alleged. We note as a matter of interest that the charges had not been brought by the grand jury when the extradition proceedings were begun. The grand jury made its decisions on 27 November, the very day on which the extradition case had to be presented in the UK court. It looks very much as though events in London were driving events in Arizona. In addition, if the quotation from the Washington Post be accurate, it would appear that at least part of the motive of the US Government behind the extradition proceedings was not to secure the appellant's attendance at a trial of the non-disclosure offences but to secure his presence in the US for the purposes of questioning about 9/11. We do not for a moment doubt the honesty of the belief of either the US Government or the CPS as to need to investigate the appellant's possible involvement in 9/11 and we fully recognise the heightened emotional atmosphere of late 2001. But having said that, it seems to us that the extradition proceedings themselves were a device to secure the appellant's presence in the US for the purpose of investigating 9/11 rather than for the purpose of putting him on trial for non-disclosure offences ... The proceedings were used as a device to circumvent the rule of English law that a terrorist suspect could (at that time) be held without charge for only 7 days.'

1   At para 144.

8.118   By contrast, in *Knowles v Government of the United States of America*,[1] following the defeat of an extradition request based upon one Grand Jury indictment, the US government deployed a second extradition request based upon an earlier Grand Jury indictment relating to earlier events. It was argued that the US government had deliberately held the second indictment/request back and its conduct constituted an abuse of process. Lord Bingham observed[2] that:

'The appellant faces an uphill task in seeking to dislodge the conclusion of three courts below that the Government's conduct in proceeding on the second extradition request was not abusive. The Board would be very slow to intervene in the absence of a clear legal misdirection, and it finds none ... it is, within broad limits, for a prosecutor to decide what charges he will prefer, and how he will frame his charges. In the absence of unfairness or oppression, this is not a matter for the Requested State and not a matter which calls for explanation. Since the appellant did not know of the first grand jury indictment, he was not misled by the Government's initial decision not to rely on it and it cannot be said that the Government made any implied representation to him'.

1   Above para **8.04**.
2   At para 25.

8.119   In *Tonge & Yarrow v Public Prosecutor's Office of Appeal, Crete*,[1] the appellants contended that their flight from Greece had been the result of ill-treatment having occurred while they were in custody in Crete (about which they complained at the time). The alleged ill-treatment was held not to be sufficient to meet the test of showing that there were material grounds for believing that there was a real risk of ECHR, Art 3 ill-treatment of these two appellants or either of them if they were returned to Greece. Nor did the evidence establish that psychological or psychiatric harm would result in either appellant being extradited to a place where they may have been ill-treated in the past. In those circumstances, in respect of an alternative submission that the alleged ill-treatment in the past rendered their return to Greece an abuse of process, Keene LJ ruled[2] that:

'I cannot see that the extradition of these two appellants would amount to an abuse of process. They have not been identified or arrested because of such ill-treatment. Nor does it seem that their availability now to be returned to Greece to stand trial has been the result of anything that can amount to an abuse of process. However regrettable any such ill- treatment that occurred may have been, I cannot see that it gives rise to any potential breach of their Article 5(4) rights if extradition is now ordered'.

1   [2006] EWHC 3388 (Admin).
2   At para 20.

8.120   As regards entrapment, *Okandeji v The Government of the Commonwealth of Australia,*[1] *Jenkins v Government of the United States of America,*[2] *Stepp v Government of the United States of America*[3] and *R (Ahsan) v Director of Public Prosecutions & another*[4] are all examples of allegations of the underlying criminal allegation being tainted by abusive entrapment; all being considered on their merits, but failing on their merits. In this area, perhaps above all others, the weight of the cross-jurisdictional nature of extradition proceedings is most profoundly felt. In *Somchai Liangsiriprasert v Government of the United States of America,*[5] a drug dealer was persuaded by a US drug enforcement agent to travel from Thailand to Hong Kong in order to receive payment for drugs exported from Thailand to the US. There was no extradition between the two countries for drug offences. On arrival in Hong Kong the applicant was arrested and proceedings for his extradition to the US were commenced. He submitted, inter alia, that it would be oppressive and an abuse of process for a government agency to entice a criminal to a jurisdiction from which extradition was available. In answer to this submission, Lord Griffiths said:[6]

'As to the suggestion that it was oppressive or an abuse of process, the short answer is that international crime has to be fought by international co-operation between law enforcement agencies. It is notoriously difficult to apprehend those at the centre of the drug trade; it is only their couriers who are usually caught. If the courts were to regard the penetration of a drug-dealing organisation by the agents of a law enforcement agency and a plan to tempt the criminals into a jurisdiction from which they could be extradited as an abuse of process it would indeed be a red letter day for the drug barons ... In the present case the applicant and S.C. came to Hong Kong of their own free will to collect, as they thought, the illicit profits of their heroin trade. They were present in Hong Kong not because of any unlawful conduct of the authorities but because of their own criminality and greed. The proper extradition procedures have been observed and their Lordships reject without hesitation that it is in the circumstances of this case oppressive or an abuse of the judicial process for the United States to seek their extradition'.

1   Above para **8.32**.
2   Above para **8.55**.
3   [2006] EWHC 1033 (Admin).
4   Above para **8.08** at paras 109–126.
5   [1991] 1 AC 225, PC.
6   At 242–243.

8.121   Subject to those matters discussed below at paragraphs **8.123–8.124**, and a defendant being able to positively demonstrate that the evidence,[1] or description of conduct,[2] provided by the Requesting State is deliberately false or exaggerated, it is not open to a defendant to argue abuse based upon the strength, or perceived strength, of evidence against him, or co-defendants, in the underlying criminal proceedings in the Requesting State.[3] In *Kashamu (No 2)*,[4] Rose LJ observed[5] that 'extradition contemplates trial in another jurisdiction according to the law there. It is there that questions of admissibility, adequacy of evidence and fairness of the trial itself will be addressed'. In *Jaso*[6] the appellants were arrested upon a European Arrest warrant alleging membership of 'Urederra'; a cell of ETA. It was submitted that a recent comprehensive investigation of *Urederra* membership had been carried out by another investigating magistrate which made no mention of the appellants. It was, therefore, submitted that there existed cause for suspecting that abuse of process may have occurred and the decision to issue the EAWs had been taken in bad faith. The High Court held[7] that:

'The allegation of bad faith against the Spanish authorities is very serious. It amounts to saying that the prosecution is being brought by the authorities knowing that the case against the appellants is without foundation. In my judgment, the appellants have fallen far short of establishing even a *prima facie* case of bad faith … it was no part of the function of the district judge to examine the evidential basis for the issue of the EAWs, still less to reach any conclusion as to whether the prosecutions have any prospect of success. To require her to do this would be to undermine the trust in the integrity and fairness of the judicial institutions of member states to which I have earlier referred. Under the guise of an abuse of process argument, that is precisely what the appellants are seeking to do …In any event, the case against the appellants of membership of ETA does not wholly depend on showing that they were members of the *Urederra* …Thus, even if it were appropriate for the district judge to consider whether the appellants were members of *Urederra* and she decided that there was no evidence of such membership, that would not raise a prima facie case of abuse of process'.

1   *United States of America v Vreeland* (2002) 164 CCC (3d) 266 (Ont SC); there exists jurisdiction to consider whether the State requesting extradition has knowingly presented false or fabricated evidence to the court of the Requested State. In a procedural ruling given in *Government of the United States of America v Tollman* (above para **8.66**) dated 1 June 2006, the matter was put this way per Malloy J at paras 65 & 70: '… the court should be particularly

322

sedulous to ensure that the abuse of process application is not merely being used to obtain disclosure of, or to attack the weight of, the evidence in support of the charges underlying the extradition. Otherwise, there is a risk that extradition proceedings will become mired in procedural motions for disclosure of the evidence in the hands of the foreign authorities, brought in the guise of abuse of process proceedings. This is not to say that the allegations that the evidence against an individual is untrue can never be made in an abuse of process proceeding. However, the allegations must go further than attacking the truth or reliability of the evidence; it will be necessary to show additional evidence of wrongdoing by the foreign authority, over and above an attack on the accuracy of the evidence in the Record of Case. Evidence that the foreign authorities knew the evidence in the Record of Case was untrue at the time of certification is, however, capable of supporting a finding of abuse of process … prosecutorial bad faith in misrepresenting facts to the court. A finding of abuse of process by prosecutorial misconduct will only be made in the clearest of circumstances. Singling out an inaccuracy or exaggeration of one small part of the evidence stated in a case of this nature is not, in my view, sufficient to give rise to a remedy for abuse of process'.

2   *Castillo v The Kingdom of Spain* (above at para **8.28**).
3   *R (Hilali) v Governor of Whitemoor Prison & another* (above para **8.60**) per Lord Hope of Craighead at paras 23–24.
4   Above para **8.51**.
5   At para 33.
6   Above para **8.08**.
7   Dyson LJ at paras 73–74.

8.122   Neither is it, in principle, abusive for a Requesting State to continue with an extradition request in the face of acquittal of the principal defendant.[1]

1   *R (Hilali) v Governor of Whitemoor Prison & another* (above para **8.60**) per Lord Hope of Craighead at paras 23–24.

Non-disclosure as evidence of bad faith

8.123   It is now fairly well established that, although a defendant cannot compel a Requesting State to make disclosure, if he is otherwise able to gain access to materials that demonstrate material non-disclosure on the part of the Requesting State, then that may, depending upon the nature of the non-disclosure, constitute, of itself, evidence of bad faith or abuse. In *R v Governor of Brixton Prison, ex p Kashamu (No 1),*[1] the government of the US conceded that disclosure should have been made in respect of evidence to the effect that the witness upon whom the government's case rested had attended an identification procedure and failed to identify Mr Kashamu from a photograph line-up (in fact he had picked out a volunteer). No reference was made to this fact in any of the material provided by the US government in support of its extradition request. The US government accepted that the effect of the failure had been to vitiate the committal and render it void. Application for habeas corpus was, accordingly, granted. Pill LJ was prepared to categorise the failure to supply the material as:

'… a misjudgement of the extent of the legal requirement of disclosure in an extradition request … the decision of the magistrate had been taken in ignorance of crucial information, and the failure to supply that information to the magistrate might have resulted in injustice to the defendant[2] … It had a fundamental effect on the proceedings before the magistrate … the proceedings before the magistrate were unfair'.[3]

1   Above para **8.51**.

2   At para 23.
3   At para 26.

8.124   In *R (Kashamu) v Governor of Brixton Prison No 2)*,[1] Pitchford J referred[2] to the facts of *ex p Kashamu (No 1)* as an example of the newly established narrow abuse definition:[3] '... the claimant had been deprived of the opportunity of addressing the district judge upon all the material which should have been before him'. In *R (Saifi) v Governor of Brixton Prison*,[4] Rose LJ placed significant reliance upon non-disclosure in the context of a finding of bad faith under s 11(3)(c) of the 1989 Act[5]. In *Bermingham*,[6] it was acknowledged by Laws LJ that a tenable case of abuse might lie if a defendant can show that a prosecutor 'knew he had no real case, but was pressing the extradition request for some collateral motive and accordingly tailored the choice of documents accompanying the request'.[7] Thus it has been repeatedly recognised that a Requesting State has an underlying duty of candour in making requests for extradition.[8] The same principle applies to cases where the obligation to provide a prima facie case is abrogated. If a defendant is able, independently, to show deliberate exaggeration of the description of conduct, that is capable of evidencing bad faith.[9]

1   Above para **8.51**.
2   At para 39.
3   Set out at paras 37–38.
4   Above para **8.26.**
5   '... this non-disclosure [of the circumstances surrounding the confession made by Ali Sheikh] on such a central feature of the case has not been explained. It is to be inferred that it was deliberate and calculated to leave those considering the case with the impression that it was stronger than the true facts merited' at para 64(3).
6   Above para **8.31**.
7   At paras 98 and 100, set out above at para **8.71**.
8   *Wellington v Governor of HMP Belmarsh* (above para **8.36**) per Mitting J at para 26. In *Jenkins v Government of the United States of America* (above para **8.55**), Sedley LJ observed (at para 29) that 'there is a general duty on a Requesting State to be candid about vitiating factors in its case ... If the defence is able independently to establish a case of breach of the accused's Convention rights, the court must of course entertain it'. In *Knowles v Government of the United States of America* (above para **8.04**), Lord Bingham of Cornhill observed (at para 35), that a Requesting State 'does ... owe the court of the Requested State a duty of candour and good faith. While it is for the Requesting State to decide what evidence it will rely on to seek a committal, it must in pursuance of that duty disclose evidence which destroys or very severely undermines the evidence on which it relies. It is for the party seeking to resist an order to establish a breach of duty by the Requesting State. The Board would endorse the general approach laid down by Mitting J (sitting with Lord Woolf CJ in the Divisional Court) in *Wellington* "... In the present case the appellant has failed to discharge the burden lying on him ..."'.
9.   See *Castillo v Kingdom of Spain* (above para **8.28**) per Thomas LJ at para 25 and 37–44: 'a description of the conduct in the request which was deliberately exaggerated would form part of the accusation for the purposes of determining whether or not the accusation had been made in good faith ... given the fact there is no enquiry into evidential sufficiency, it is of the utmost importance that the description of conduct alleged is framed with the greatest care; it is an essential protection to the person whose extradition is sought'.

'STAGE 3': WHETHER THERE ARE REASONABLE GROUNDS FOR BELIEVING THAT SUCH CONDUCT MAY HAVE OCCURRED

8.125 No steps should be taken to investigate an alleged abuse of process unless the judge is satisfied that there is reason to believe that an abuse may have taken place.[1] As regards 'stage 3', Canadian case law makes it clear that this stage requires the court to be satisfied that the appellant's evidence possesses an 'air of reality'.[2] In *Larosa v Her Majesty The Queen*,[3] Doherty JA observed[4] that '... [t]he appellant bears the burden of demonstrating the "air of reality" and may do so by reference to the appeal record or to evidence, normally by way of affidavit, tendered in support ... A bald assertion in the notice of motion will not suffice to trigger the evidentiary inquiry sought by the appellant'. Doherty further observed[5] that:

> 'In order to ask the court to delve into the circumstances surrounding the exercise of the Crown's discretion, or to inquire into the motivation of the Crown officers responsible for advising the Attorney-General, the accused bears the burden of making a tenable allegation of *mala fides* on the part of the Crown. Such an allegation must be supportable by the record before the court, or if the record is lacking or insufficient, by an offer of proof. Without such an allegation, the court is entitled to assume what is inherent in the process, that the Crown exercised its discretion properly, and not for improper or arbitrary motives. [T]he allegation of improper or arbitrary motives cannot be an irresponsible allegation made solely for the purpose of initiating a "fishing expedition" in the hope that something of value will accrue to the defence'.[6]

1   *R (Government of the United States of America) v Bow Street Magistrates' Court* (above para **8.10**) per Lord Phillips CJ at para 84).
2   *Larosa v Her Majesty The Queen* (above para **8.64**) per Doherty JA at paras 76 and 78–81. See also *United States of America v Kwok* (above para **8.66**) at para 88).
3   Above para **8.64**.
4   At paras 81 and 85.
5   At para 795.
6   In the *United States v Freimuth* (2004) 183 CCC (3d) 296 (BCSC) Romilly J said (at para 56) that: 'Allegations of misconduct by foreign authorities should not be given any credence without further proof. In the absence of such evidence, entertaining allegations that foreign officials are misleading our Courts conveys a reflection of the gravest possible kind, not only upon the motives and actions of the responsible government, but also impliedly upon the judicial authorities of a neighbouring and friendly power.'

8.126

'The function of the "air of reality" test is two-fold. First, it provides a mechanism to weed out frivolous applications before incurring the expense and delay of a lengthy evidentiary hearing. Second, it imposes a threshold of plausibility before the applicant will be entitled to relief such as production of documents, particulars, or the compelling of viva voce testimony ... The level of plausibility required to survive the air of reality test is somewhat amorphous. Typically, when cases are dismissed as having no air of reality, the allegations can fairly be described as ludicrous or preposterous. However, in my opinion, the actual test is, and must be, higher than that.

Obviously, at this point, the applicant cannot be expected to reach the standard of proof on a balance of probabilities, as this is the ultimate standard to be applied at the abuse of process hearing itself. However, it is not enough for the applicant to show that his allegations are not ridiculous; he must be able to show some reasonable prospect of success on the application. The Ontario Court of Appeal's decision in *Larosa* contains the best working definition of the test I have found, namely that the applicant must demonstrate "some realistic possibility that the allegations can be substantiated".'[1]

1   *United States of America v Tollman (procedural ruling)* (above para **8.121**) per Malloy J at para 21.

No right to disclosure at stage 3

8.127   It has long been recognised that a significant, and often insurmountable, practical hurdle in the way of mounting abuse submissions in extradition proceedings will be the absence of any disclosure from the Requesting State. Donovan LJ recognised the difficulty of this task in *R v Brixton Prison (Governor), ex parte Soblen*:[1]

'The task of the subject who seeks to establish such an allegation as this is indeed heavy. On the face of it, the [deportation] order which he wished the court to quash will look perfectly valid on its face, and to get behind it and to demonstrate its alleged true character he will need to have revealed to him the communications, oral and written, which have passed between the home and the foreign authorities. But if the appropriate minister here certifies, as he has done in this case, that such disclosure will be contrary to the public interest, then, as a rule, the subject will not obtain it. He will be left to do his best without such assistance, and in the nature of things, therefore, he will seldom be able to raise a prima facie case, or alternatively to sow such substantial and disquieting doubts in the minds of the court as to the bona fides of the order he is challenging that the court will consider that some answer is called for. If that answer is withheld, or being furnished is found unsatisfactory, then in my view, the order challenged ought not to be upheld, for otherwise there would be virtually no protection for the subject against the illegal order which had been clothed with the garments of legality simply for the sake of appearances and where discovery was resisted.'[2]

1   Above para **8.106**, at 307–308.
2   See, to similar effect, *Government of the United States of America v Tollman* (above para **8.66**) at para 22: 'The onus is on [a defendant] to establish his allegations of abuse. The applicable standard is the balance of probabilities, but abuse will only be found in the "clearest of cases" and the case law has repeatedly described this as a "heavy onus", particularly where prosecutorial misconduct is alleged. That said, it is virtually impossible for one person to prove by direct evidence the motive or intent behind the acts of another. In the absence of some direct evidence from the person whose conduct is challenged, the motivation behind that conduct must typically be inferred from the surrounding circumstances. The onus, however, remains on the person alleging the misconduct to prove the improper motivation.'

8.128   There was thus recognised two interlinked principles by the Court of Appeal:

(1)   A person resisting extradition has no right to seek disclosure so as to assist in his establishing a prima facie case of abuse (now stage 3). But,

(2)   If he can raise a prima facie case of abuse notwithstanding this (now stage 4 below), then the Court may expect an answer from the Requesting State and, if none is forthcoming or the answer is not satisfactory, then the order for extradition will not be upheld. With modification, that remains the position today.

The second principle is discussed below at paragraphs **8.136–8.139**. In respect of the first principle, in extradition proceedings, it had been held[1] that the Requesting Government alone is the sole arbiter of such material as it chooses to place before the court. Neither principles of comity nor the express terms of the Act afford the court in this country any right – still less power – to request further material from the Requesting State as a condition precedent to committal.[2]

1   *R v Governor of Pentonville Prison, ex p Lee* [1993] 1 WLR 1294 at 1298 per Ognall J: 'It is important to remember that the conduct of extradition proceedings is entirely the creature of statute. This has a number of consequences ... The Requesting State must be the sole arbiter of such material as it chooses to place before the court in support of its application and in purported compliance with the relevant domestic extradition legislation. It alone will decide what material in support of its allegations it places before the Secretary of State and the court under sections 7 and 9 of the Act of 1989. If it furnishes inadequate evidence, then it takes the risk that its request will be refused, in which event it will be up to the Requesting State to determine whether it starts fresh proceedings or not. Neither principles of comity nor the express terms of the Act afford the court in this country any right – still less power – to request further material from the Requesting State as a condition precedent to committal.'
2   At p 1300 Ognall J further observed that: 'Provided that there has been compliance with the terms of the Extradition Act 1989, fairness is not a criterion relevant to the function of the committing court '. Therefore, an application to adjourn for the purposes of seeking documentation to throw doubt upon the credibility of accomplice evidence was refused.

8.129   *Ex parte Lee* was doubted by Pill LJ In *Kashamu (No 1)*.[1] However the Divisional Court revisited the issue in *Lodhi v Governor of Brixton Prison*.[2] Brooke LJ ruled that *ex parte Lee* is 'clearly right ... still good law'.[3] No duty of disclosure exists. And in *Serbeh v Governor of Brixton Prison*,[4] Kennedy LJ, with whom Pitchford J agreed, reviewed the above authorities[5] and concluded[6] that:

'I can find nothing in the authorities to support [the] proposition that even where, as here, there is not even a suspicion of bad faith the Requesting Country must now, as a result of the implementation of the Human Rights Act, make full disclosure of its prosecution case, and of any relevant unused material or be at risk of having the proceedings struck out as an abuse of process ... In my judgment, as was made clear by Ognall J in *ex p Lee* and by the European Commission in *Kirkwood*, extradition proceedings are not to be equated with criminal proceedings before domestic courts. In extradition proceedings it is still for the Requesting State to decide what material it chooses to place before the Court ... there is a fundamental assumption that the Requesting State is acting in good faith. If there is reason ... to call that assumption into question, then the reason can be examined, and, if appropriate, acted upon, but there was and is no such reason in this case, and accordingly, in my judgment the complaints of non–disclosure and abuse of process are misconceived.'

1   Above para **8.51**, at paras 38–39.
2   Above para **8.26**.
3   At paras 108–115.
4   [2002] EWHC 2356 (Admin).
5   At paras 31–38.
6   At paras 39–40.

8.130   In *Wellington v Governor of Her Majesty's Prison Belmarsh,*[1] Mitting J again reviewed the authorities[2] and summarised their effect[3] as follows: '(1) It is for the Requesting State alone to determine the evidence upon which it relies to seek a committal. (2) The Requesting State is not under any general duty of disclosure similar to that imposed on the prosecution at any stage in domestic criminal proceedings'. Having observed that a provable breach of a Requesting State's duty of candour may constitute an abuse[4], Mitting J observed that: 'it is for the person subject to the extradition process to establish that the Requesting State is abusing the process of the court'.

1   Above para **8.36**.
2   At paras 15(5)(iii) and (7) and 20–25.
3   At para 26.
4   Above para **8.124**.

8.131   Under the 2003 Act, in *Jenkins,*[1] Sedley LJ approved[2] a concession made to the effect that no power to order disclosure exists. In *Bermingham,*[3] Laws LJ observed[4] that: ' The prosecutor cannot be penalised, under s 82, 87, or by any other route, for limiting the material he places before the court to what is required for the proper execution of the court's function under ss 78 ff. The observations of Ognall J in *Lee* … are in point'. In *R (Government of the United States of America) v Bow Street Magistrates' Court*[5], Lord Phillips CJ reiterated[6] that there exists no power to order disclosure in extradition proceedings:

> 'Neither the rules governing disclosure in a civil action, nor those governing disclosure in a criminal trial can be applied to an extradition hearing. Furthermore, those rules form part of an adversarial process which differs from extradition proceedings. Where an order for disclosure is made, it requires one party to disclose documents to the other, not to the court. But where extradition is sought, the court is under a duty to satisfy itself that all the requirements for making the order are satisfied and that none of the bars to making the order exists … There is a further objection to ordering disclosure. The order will be made either against a judicial authority within the European Union or against a foreign Sovereign State that is requesting the Secretary of State to comply with treaty obligations. In neither case would it be appropriate to order discovery.'

1   Above para **8.55**.
2   At para 29.
3   Above para **8.31**.
4   At para 98.
5   Above para **8.10**.
6   At paras 85–86.

8.132 In *Knowles v Government of the United States of America,*[1] Lord Bingham of Cornhill reiterated[2] that it is for the party seeking to resist an order to establish a breach of duty (of candour to disclose evidence which destroys or very severely undermines the evidence on which it relies) by the Requesting State. In *R (Raissi) v Secretary of State for the Home Department,*[3] the Court of Appeal extended *Knowles* to apply to the Crown Prosecution Service (as agent for the Requesting State) 'a duty to disclose evidence about which it knows and which destroys or severely undermines the evidence on which the Requesting State relies', [4] but again recognised[5] that this duty of candour is not enforceable by means of order for disclosure.

1   Above para **8.04**.
2   At para 35.
3   Above para **8.92**.
4   The Court observed that this duty would also apply in the context of contested applications for bail.
5   Per Hooper LJ at paras 139–143.

8.133   In *Norris v Government of the United States of America,*[1] the House of Lords observed[2] that:

> 'The system of extradition under Part 2 of the 2003 Act does not require the Requesting State to provide details of the evidence (witnesses, documents etc) on which the prosecution would rely at trial. Nor does the district judge have any occasion to inquire into it. It is well settled that, consistently with that approach, in extradition proceedings the accused has no right to disclosure of the kind that would be available in domestic proceedings'.[3]

1   Above para **8.33**.
2   At para 107.
3   Approving *Wellington, Jenkins* and *R (Government of the United States of America) v Bow Street Magistrates' Court.*

'STAGE 4': THE JUDGE SHOULD NOT ACCEDE TO THE REQUEST FOR EXTRADITION UNLESS HE HAS SATISFIED HIMSELF THAT SUCH ABUSE HAS NOT OCCURRED

8.134   As regards 'stage 4', it is at this stage that the judge will conduct a full evidential enquiry. The defence will here be obliged to substantiate its allegations by evidence. The defence and Requesting State may call such evidence as they wish. Both sides are entitled to submit written evidence[1] in lieu of live evidence. In extradition proceedings, there exists no right to cross-examine the foreign prosecutor. The foreign state is permitted to file its evidence in the form required by the 2003 Act and cannot be forced to do otherwise. As a matter of reality, there may be cases where the person sought is able to establish an air of reality to his allegations, but where all of the direct evidence is within the knowledge of the foreign state authorities, and unfairness might arise where the person sought testifies under oath as to one version of facts and the Requesting State seeks to contradict that evidence by written evidence untested by cross-examination. The English and Canadian Courts, both recognising this problem, have addressed it in different ways. The Canadian Courts have held that the evidential abuse hearing held at this stage is not part of the extradition hearing and, therefore, carries with it the ability of the judge to order cross-examination of the foreign prosecutor.[2] However, in England, that approach is precluded by the ruling of Lord Phillips CJ in *R (Government of the United States of America) v Bow Street Magistrates' Court* [3] to the effect that a 'stage 4' hearing falls to be determined within the rubric of the extradition hearing. Therefore, in *Tollman (No 2)*,[4] Moses LJ observed[5] that, absent oral evidence, there is always the risk that the judge will credit the complaints made by those whom the opposing party has called live.

1   Properly authenticated under s 202.
2   *United States of America v Tollman (procedural ruling)* (above para **8.121**) per Malloy J at paras 30–35.
3   Above para **8.62**.
4   Above para **8.13**.
5   At para 100.

8.135   When abuse is raised, for the first time in the appellate court (as in *Shulman*[1]), and the appellate court determines that steps 1–3 have been established, then the appropriate course is to remit to the Magistrates' Court.[2]

1   Above para **8.98**.
2   *Larosa v Her Majesty The Queen* (above para **8.64**) per Doherty JA at para 83.

The disclosure position at stage 4

8.136   If a defendant has reached 'stage 4', he will have demonstrated that there is reason to believe that an abuse of process may have occurred. Pursuant to *Government of the United States of America) v Bow Street Magistrates' Court,*[1] it is now open to the District Judge to 'call upon the judicial authority that has issued the arrest warrant, or the State seeking extradition in a Part 2 case, for whatever information or evidence the Judge requires in order to determine whether an abuse of process has occurred or not'.[2] The Magistrate has no authority to invoke the power unless and until he finds that the material already available to him is capable of founding or generating a rational suspicion of abusive conduct on the part of the Issuing Judicial Authority ('IJA') or the CPS (*Central Examining Court of the National Court of Madrid v City of Westminster Magistrates' Court*[3]). And, where triggered, 'the Magistrates' Court has no power to make any coercive order against an IJA. What the magistrate can do is "all upon" the IJA for such information as is needed to decide whether a reasonably suspected or apparent abuse has in fact occurred. What he or she cannot do is to make a speculative request in order to see if any indications of abuse of process can be found'.[4] In *Norris v Government of the United States of America*[5] the House of Lords observed[6] that such requests will be exceptional.

1   Above para **8.10**, per Lord Phillips CJ at paras 85–89. This is an exercise of the powers given to the Requested State by most extradition treaties, including, for example, Art 15(2) of the European Council Framework Decision 2002/584/JHA of 13 June 2002 on the European arrest warrant and the surrender procedures between member states and Art 10 of the 2003 US-UK extradition treaty. The first recognition of this power is to be found in the judgment of Mitting J in *Wellington* (above para **8.36**) at paras 25–26, where it is stated that where 'there was evidence that the process of the court was being abused, the court would have been entitled, in my view, to ask the United Kingdom authorities to request the United

States Government that it provide further evidence relevant to that question under … Article [IX(2)] of the Order in Council'. However, in the same case, Lord Woolf CJ 'remain[ed] to be persuaded that Article IX(2) is intended to give to the judge hearing the extradition proceedings a discretion to require the appropriate authorities to obtain information from the requesting party. If such a power does exist, certainly it should only be exercised in the most exceptional cases. The district judge hearing extradition proceedings should determine them in the ordinary way on the material placed before him and come to the appropriate conclusion on that evidence' (at para 29). In *Jenkins v Government of the United States of America* (above para **8.55**), it was conceded, under the 2003 Act, that the Court may ask the Home Secretary to exercise his power under Art IX(2) and that 'it may be appropriate to use it … where there is before the court of the Requested State sufficient evidence of an abuse of its process to call for more information before a decision is arrived at'.

2   The position is different in Canada where the Canadian Courts exercise a power to order disclosure once a defendant establishes that 'the allegations must be capable of supporting the remedy sought [stage 2 above], there must be an air of reality to the allegations [stage 3 above] and it must be likely that the documents sought and the testimony sought would be relevant to the allegations' (*Larosa v Her Majesty The Queen* (above para **8.64**) per Doherty JA at para 76). Whilst the extent of the power is not settled (see *The Attorney General of Canada on behalf of the Government of the United States of America v Welsh & Romero* (above para **8.110**) at paras 50–51), the power has been exercised to order production of documents outside Canada, on the basis that an abuse hearing is fundamentally different to an extradition hearing and more akin to a trial of an issue to which the Requesting State is a party litigant (*United States of America v Tollman (procedural ruling)* (above para **8.121**) per Malloy J at paras 58–63).

3   Above para **8.86**, per Sedley LJ at para 25.

4   At para 30.

5   Above para **8.33**.

6   At para 107.

8.137   The information and evidence obtained should be made available to the party contesting extradition since equality of arms requires that, in normal circumstances, the party contesting extradition should be aware of, and thus able to comment on, the material upon which the court will be basing its decision.[1] There may be occasions where a judicial authority or Requesting State is content that the court should see evidence but, on reasonable grounds, is not prepared that this should be disclosed to the person whose extradition is sought. The evidence might, for instance, disclose details of ongoing investigations into suspected co-defendants. The judge will be capable of evaluating the material that is provided to him, whether it is favourable or unfavourable to the person resisting extradition. The issue will then be whether, if a decision is reached without allowing that person the chance to comment on the material, the procedure will fail to satisfy the requirement of fairness. That question will be fact-specific and must be left to the judge to decide on the particular facts. If the judge concludes that fairness requires that the material be disclosed, but the Requesting Authority or State is not prepared to agree to this, then the appropriate course will be for the judge to hold that fair process is impossible, that to grant the application for extradition in the circumstances would involve an abuse of process, and to discharge the person whose extradition is sought.[2]

1   *Government of the United States of America v Bow Street Magistrates' Court* (above para **8.10**) per Lord Phillips CJ at para 90.

2   At para 92.

8.138   If, on the other hand, a Requesting State fails or refuses to comply with such a request altogether, 'the overwhelming inference' would be that matters had occurred as alleged by the defence.[1]

1   *Government of the United States of America) v Bow Street Magistrates' Court* (above para **8.10**) per Lord Phillips CJ at para 122. For an example of a case in which such an inference was drawn, see *Government of the United States of America v Tollman* (above para **8.66**) per Malloy J at para 132.

8.139   'Stage 4', as currently formulated[1] might appear to reverse the established burden of proof. Indeed, at least one High Court decision assumes this.[2] But, the burden of establishing an abuse in any criminal proceedings rests on the defendant, on the balance of probabilities. Section 206 of the 2003 Act applies that principle to extradition proceedings.[3] Therefore, the authors respectfully submit that the ultimate test must be that the judge should accede to the request for extradition unless he has satisfied himself, on the balance of probabilities, that such abuse has occurred. Perhaps a true reflection of the reality of the position lies in the statement of Bealieu J in *Kissell v The Attorney General on behalf of the Government of the United States of America*[4] to the effect that a reversal of the burden is only legitimate in a case where a defendant has gone beyond showing an 'air of reality' and has, in fact, shown a 'very strong circumstantial' case:

> 'I take into account the admonition of British and Canadian courts that, while the onus is on the Applicant, he or she may not always be able to bring direct evidence, and therefore may ask the court to draw certain inferences (*Tollman*, at para 22). However, I also agree with the submission of the Respondent that to draw a negative inference based on the responding state's failure to produce further evidence to justify its position can only be done in rare cases, where the Applicant has made a very strong circumstantial case suggesting impropriety. This is not the case here, as, for example, it was in *Tollman*, where Molloy J held not only that there was an 'air of reality' to the Applicant's allegations, but that he made a 'prima facie' case'. [5]

1   Above para 8.62.
2   *Central Examining Court of the National Court of Madrid v City of Westminster Magistrates' Court* (above para **8.86**) per Sedley LJ at para 25: '… where there is reason to suspect departure from these principles – but not otherwise – the examining judicial authority in this country may seek further information with a view to satisfying itself, as in law it must, that there has not been an abuse of process. In other words, the burden shifts'.
3   *Kociukow v District Court of Bialystok III Penal Division* [2006] 1 WLR 3061, DC per Jack J at para 9; *Mitoi v Government of Romania [2006] EWHC 1977 (Admin)* per Mitting J at para 23.
4   Above para **8.106**.
5   At para 155.

POSTSCRIPT

8.140   Authority to date assumes that the abuse of process jurisdiction under the 2003 Act applies in Part 1 cases.[1] But the issue has never been the subject of full argument and it remains at least arguable that the jurisdiction is limited to Part 2 cases. As the House of Lords observed in *Office of The King's Prosecutor, Brussels v Cando Armas:*[2] 'what Part 1 of the 2003 Act provides for, in its simplest form ... is really just a system of backing of warrants'. The position under Part 1 is arguably[3] analogous to the position considered by the House of Lords in *R v Governor of Belmarsh prison, ex parte Gilligan & Ellis*[4] under the Backing of Warrants (Republic of Ireland) Act 1965. There, Gilligan contended that the extradition request was abusive by reason of him having been improperly arrested for domestic proceedings in the UK in an effort to hold him in custody so that an extradition request from Ireland could be perfected. Notwithstanding that there was no discretion afforded to the Secretary of State under the 1965 Act, the House of Lords held[5] that the Act set out precise but limited protections against oppression which, taken with the legislative purpose of a simple and expeditious procedure for rendition to the Republic of Ireland and the fact that the Irish courts are 'well able' to guard against abuses, did not permit recourse to claims of abuse of process before the magistrates' court. The Australian courts apply a similar approach in intra-state extradition proceedings.[6]

1   *Government of the United States of America v Bow Street Magistrates' Court* (above para **8.10**), *Central Examining Court of the National Court of Madrid v City of Westminster Magistrates' Court* (above para **8.86**) and, by implication, *Bermingham* (above para **8.31**).
2   [2006] 2 AC 1, HL, per Lord Hope of Craighead at para 22.
3   See also the case law above at para **8.16**.
4   Above para **8.10**.
5   Per Lord Steyn at p 97C-G; with whom Lords Browne-Wilkinson, Cooke and Hope agreed, and at p 101B-F per Lord Clyde.
6   *Berichon v Chief Commissioner, Victoria Police* [2007] VSC 143: '... the question of abuse of process is a matter for the courts of the Issuing state' per Mandie J at paras 13 and 21.

Chapter 9

Pre-trial publicity

9.01 Judicial anxiety concerning the prejudicial effect of pre-trial publicity on criminal trials is not of a recent vintage. A cursory glance at nineteenth century newspapers suggests that coverage of the same sort of crimes that are newsworthy today, for example hooliganism, sexual violence and homicide, was lurid and sensational then. The earliest reported authority of judicial concern on this subject is the judgment of Lord Ellenborough in *R v Fisher*[1] which concerned a rape trial where a newspaper reported that the defendant was guilty of the offence charged. Lord Ellenborough said:

> 'if anything is more important than another in the administration of justice, it is that jurymen should come to the trial of those persons on whose guilt or innocence they are to decide, with minds pure and unprejudiced. Is it possible that they should do so, after having read for weeks and months before, ex parte statements of the evidence against the accused, which the latter have no opportunity to disprove or to controvert?'

Similar nineteenth century judicial anxiety was expressed in *A-G v Parnell*[2] and by Alverstone CJ in *R v Tibbits*.[3]

1   (1811) 2 Camp 563.
2   (1880) 14 Cox CC 474.
3   [1902] 1 KB 77.

9.02 Traditionally, the responsibility for ensuring that defendants do not suffer 'undue' prejudice from media reported comment is not that of the individual defendant but that of the State itself. A public interest has always been recognised in ensuring that conduct in any form which tends to interfere with the course of justice in particular legal proceedings should be deterred and, if necessary, punished. This has spawned the jurisprudence of criminal contempt of court whereby the State in the personage of the Attorney-General has issued proceedings, especially against newspapers, where it is felt that reportage has interfered with or perverted the course of justice. While a full consideration of the law relating to criminal contempt is beyond the scope of this chapter, it is important to appreciate that this jurisprudence was the forerunner to that relating to abuse of process. Furthermore, the interrelationship is more than just historical. In seeking to understand the court's abuse of process jurisdiction in the context of pre-trial publicity, it is vital to appreciate that the law on criminal contempt has both shaped and promoted the law relating to pre-trial publicity.

9.03 The law on abuse as it relates to pre-trial publicity is relatively new. However, applications on the basis of this type of argument has been recently described as a 'growth area'.[1] Only since the early 1990s have there been decisions on the power and responsibility of the courts, as part of their abuse jurisdiction, to stay criminal proceedings on the ground of prejudicial pre-trial publicity. Previously, in the absence of proceedings brought by the Attorney-General for such contempt, the courts were unwilling to intervene and accept on the basis of submissions made by the defendant alone that even before the criminal proceedings had begun, there was a risk of unfairness arising out of prior publicity. Why this sudden development or willingness? This is perhaps the result of first, an acceptance that modern media is able to create and orchestrate an unprecedented level of hostility towards a particular defendant, media 'abuses' thus becoming more powerful and insidious. Secondly, a perception that the State can no longer be relied on exclusively to deter and punish such abuses via actions for contempt or by other means: this perception perhaps going hand in hand with the development of new remedies by the courts especially in the field of public law, recognising that the State alone cannot any longer be regarded as the sole guardian of individual rights. Thirdly, in view of the high evidential threshold for contempt introduced by the Contempt of Court Act 1981 and in particular the requirement that each allegedly contemptuous item of publicity be judged in isolation from any others, which together have probably created a climate of prejudice, the test for contempt has increasingly been regarded as less relevant or helpful in an abuse context.

1   See the judgment of Lord Phillips of Worth Matravers CJ, para 87, in *R v Abu Hamza* [2007] 1 Cr App R 27.

PUBLICITY AND JURY DECISION-MAKING

9.04   In our jurisdiction all serious criminal cases are decided on by a jury and not by professional judges. Juries are never asked to provide reasons for their verdicts and indeed it is a criminal offence under the Contempt of Court Act 1981 for individual jurors to be interviewed after a verdict has been delivered as to how it was arrived at. This absence of reasons or inscrutability is in stark contrast to jurisdictions where a judge sits as the tribunal of fact, for example under the Diplock Court regime in Northern Ireland where a High Court Judge sits as the tribunal of fact. If a defendant is convicted, the judge always provides reasons which, furthermore, are directly appealable.

9.05   In proceedings against a particular defendant which have attracted substantial, predominantly hostile publicity and where he is convicted, one can readily appreciate why that defendant may feel he did not receive a fair trial or hearing by the jury. The inscrutability of the jury verdict can do nothing to alleviate this grievance. However, against this is the stark fact that public confidence in the criminal justice system would surely be undermined if notorious defendants accused of horrific crimes could escape justice, not even stand trial, because of adverse publicity.

9.06   Confronting this dilemma the courts have tenaciously grasped the axiom that in criminal trials a jury of ordinary and randomly selected people can be empanelled to try the case objectively. Time and again, English judges have vouchsafed the objectivity and robustness of the traditional English jury where the danger of undesirable 'bias' is excluded.[1] This traditional and endemic view of the English jury is so entrenched by our system that attempts in highly publicised trials to exclude potentially biased jurors by means of questionnaires and so on, have almost always been rejected by trial judges holding that the jury system untouched can be relied on to act dispassionately. Nonetheless, since the early 1990s this conventional wisdom has come under direct attack. There have been cases, to be considered later, where proceedings have been halted or convictions been quashed, at least in part, because of a judicial acceptance that pre-trial publicity rendered a fair trial impossible.

1   Interestingly, the original jury system comprised people from the area where the defendant lived who were expected to use their local knowledge, including their knowledge of the defendant, to judge the plausibility of the prosecution and defence cases.

CONTEMPT OF COURT IN THE CONTEXT OF PRE-TRIAL PUBLICITY

9.07   It has long been recognised by the common law in the realm of contempt that adverse pre-trial publicity can inhibit a fair trial. Perhaps the most famous judicial statement of this is the judgment of Lord Diplock in *A-G v Times Newspapers Ltd*[1] which was concerned with pre-trial reportage by the *Sunday Times* of the thalidomide scandal. That newspaper intended to print a full story about the scandal and the consequent litigation between the manufacturers, Distillers, and the affected children. Distillers complained about this to the Attorney-General who then sought an injunction banning publication. Lord Diplock, in granting the Attorney-General's application said:

'the due administration of justice requires ... that all citizens ... should be able to rely upon obtaining in the courts the arbitrament of a tribunal which is free from bias against any party and whose decision be based upon those facts only that have been proved in evidence and deduced before it in accordance with the procedure adopted in courts of law; and ... that, once the dispute has been submitted to a court of law, they should be able to rely upon there being no usurpation by any other person of the function of the court to decide it according to law'.[2]

Lord Diplock was therefore of the view that if the due administration of justice is hindered or usurped then the result must be that the trial will be unfair.

1   [1974] AC 273.
2   [1974] AC 273 at 309.

9.08   In a later case, *A-G v English*, Lord Diplock said:[1]

'trial by newspaper, or as it should be more compendiously expressed today, trial by the media is not to be permitted in this country ... the true course of justice must not at any stage be put at risk'.

1   [1983] 1 AC 116 at 141.

9.09   In the same case, but sitting in the Divisional Court Watkins LJ expressed the issue in more florid language:[1]

'everyone surely agrees that the well of justice must remain clear. Thus, by one means or another the poison of prejudice must be kept away from it. If it is not, then the possibility of a miscarriage of justice inevitably accompanies prejudice. No-one will know what harm is done except the jury whose verdict, whatever it be, will not inform others as to whether or not it is tainted by prejudice.'

1   [1983] 1 AC 116 at 125.

9.10   The courts' power to prevent or punish instances of prejudicial pre-trial publicity is now governed by the Contempt of Court Act 1981. Pursuant to s 4(2) a judge seised of active proceedings is empowered to make an order banning publication for a defined period of those proceedings. Section 4(2) provides:

'in any such proceedings the court may, where it appears to be necessary for avoiding a substantial risk of prejudice to the administration of justice in those proceedings ... order that the publication of any report of the proceedings be postponed for such period as the court think necessary for that purpose'.

9.11   There must therefore be a substantial risk of prejudice, which would be caused by publicity. In relation to the jurors being affected by prejudice, in *R v Horsham Justice, ex p Farquharson*[1] Denning MR held that the risk really must be substantial:

'in considering to make an Order under section 4(2), the sole consideration is the risk of prejudice to be the administration of justice. Whoever has to consider it should remember that at a trial judges are not influenced by what they may have read in the newspapers. Nor are the ordinary folk who sit on juries, they are good sensible people ... the risk of them being influenced is so slight that it can usually be disregarded as insubstantial—and therefore not the subject of an order under s 4(2)'.[2]

1   [1982] QB 762.
2   [1982] QB 762 at 794.

9.12   In cases concerned with the application of a s 4(2) order, and in particular with the meaning of a substantial risk of prejudice, the appellate courts have emphasised the need for judicial restraint. Such restraint has been encouraged first, by emphasising in general terms the competing public interests involved, in particular the desirability of ensuring freedom of expression and open justice. Secondly, as the quote from Denning MR in para **9.11** shows, the courts have also evinced a belief that judges and jurors are able to discard from their thinking, prejudicial publicity. Eleven years after Denning MR's views in *Farquharson,* Lord Taylor in *R v Central Criminal Court ex p Telegraph plc*[1] said in this context:

'In determining whether publication of matter would cause a substantial risk of prejudice to a future trial, a court should credit the jury with the will and ability to provide by the judge's direction to decide the case only on the evidence before them. The court should also bear in mind the staying power and the detail of publicity, even in case of notoriety, are limited and that the

337

nature of the trial is to focus the jury's minds on the evidence before them rather than matters outside the courtroom'[2].

1   [1993] 1 WLR 980.
2   [1993] 1 WLR 980 at 987.

9.13   However, the courts have on occasions accepted that a banning order under s 4(2) is required, otherwise the anticipated publicity would imperil the fairness of future criminal proceedings. For example, in *A-G v Steadman*[1] Bell J granted an injunction against any performances of 'Maxwell; the Musical' a satirical and disparaging play about the life of the late Robert Maxwell on the grounds that it would prejudice the forthcoming trial of his sons, Kevin and Ian.

1   (February 1995, unreported).

9.14   In addition to giving the courts a preventative power pursuant to s 4, the Act also provides a 'strict liability' rule of contempt. An intention to cause prejudice is not an essential element of the contempt. What matters is the effect of the publicity on active proceedings. By s 2(2) this rule, 'applies only to a publication which creates a substantial risk that the course of justice in the proceedings in question will be seriously impeded or prejudiced'. There has been a great deal of jurisprudence on the meaning of the terms 'substantial risk' and 'serious prejudice'.

9.15   In *A-G v Hat Trick Productions Ltd*[1] Auld LJ said:

'Serious prejudice is not capable of useful paraphrase save possibly as something which puts the course of justice at risk, as, in a criminal trial, by affecting its outcome or necessitating the discharge of the jury'.[2]

In that case Auld LJ held that a broadcast from an episode of 'Have I Got News for You' which denigrated Ian and Kevin Maxwell six months before their trial did create a substantial risk of serious prejudice against them. During the programme Angus Deayton had said: 'The BBC are in fact cracking down on references to Ian and Kevin Maxwell just in case programme makers appear biased in their treatment of these two heartless scheming bastards'.

1   [1997] EMLR 76.
2   At 81.

9.16   In *A-G v Associated Newspapers*[1] a contempt was held arising out of prejudicial publicity in the *Evening Standard* against various defendants who were, at the date of publication, on trial for serious offences. The newspaper correctly informed its readers that those defendants currently on trial for prison escape were convicted IRA terrorists. The trial judge held this disclosure was very prejudicial to the defendants and stayed the trial. Subsequently the High Court in effect upheld this view by holding pursuant to s 2(2) that the newspaper had committed a contempt.

1   [1998] EMLR 711.

9.17   These cases demonstrate the existence of a concern which the courts have regarding the prejudicial effects of media coverage. Using the test of s 2(2), the courts have on occasions been satisfied beyond reasonable doubt that pre-trial publicity has created a serious risk of substantial prejudice.

Abuse of process

9.18   The Court of Appeal's judgment in the 2006 case of *R v Abu Hamza*[1] should be the starting point for any lawyer contemplating an abuse of process argument based on adverse publicity. In the course of this judgment, the then Lord Chief Justice, reviewed the history of the case law, from the 1969 *Kray* decision, through to *In re B*.[2] Whilst the court acknowledged that such applications were now a growth area for lawyers, nevertheless, it made it quite clear that few such applications were ever likely to succeed.

The court further emphasised in *Abu Hamza* that there was no different or discreet abuse of process test for arguments based on the effect of adverse publicity. The authors suggest that where a fair trial is no longer possible, on account of adverse publicity, or where it may be adjudged unfair to try a defendant, in the light of the same, the proceedings must be stayed. This is the classic abuse of process test. The Lord Chief Justice in *Abu Hamza* further described the test thus:[3] 'Only where the effect of the publicity has been so extreme that it is not possible to expect the jury to disregard it will it be appropriate to stay a trial on the ground of abuse of process'.

1   *R v Abu Hamza* [2007] 1 Cr App R 27.
2   [2006] EWCA Crim 2692.
3   See para 78 of the judgment.

9.19   In the abuse context, just as in the cases on contempt considered in paras **9.07–9.17**, judicial faith in the will and the ability of jurors to ignore any potential prejudicial effect of publicity has always been expressed. This is hardly surprising in view of it being a fundamental tenet of our system that jury trial provides the fairest and most reliable method of determining guilt or innocence. It must be presupposed that the jury will try the case according to the evidence. Perhaps the most frequently quoted reference of this faith in the jury is the robust judgment of Lawton J in *R v Kray*[1] where the notorious Kray twins were on trial only one month after they had been convicted for murder, that first trial having attracted massive media publicity. In rejecting the Kray twins' application for a stay of the second trial against them arising out of this publicity Lawton J said:

> 'I have enough confidence in my fellow-countryman to think that they have got newspapers sized up just as they have got other public institutions sized up, and they are capable in normal circumstances of looking at a matter fairly and without prejudice even though they have to disregard what they may have read in a newspaper ... it is, however, a matter of human experience, and certainly a matter of the experience of those who practice in the criminal court, first, that the public's recollection is short, and, secondly, that the drama, if I may use that term, of a trial will almost have the effect of excluding from recollection that which went before. A person summoned for the case would not, in my judgment, disqualify himself merely because he had read any of the newspapers containing allegation of the kind I have referred to; but the position would be different if, as a result of reading what he had, his mind had become so clogged with prejudice that he was unable to try the case impartially'.[2]

1   (1969) 53 Cr App Rep 412.
2   (1969) 53 Cr App Rep 412 at 414–415.

9.20   Later as Lawton LJ in *R v Coughlan*[1] he expressed a similar view:

'it is our experience that juries in general understand the responsibility which rests upon them … Juries are capable of disregarding that which is not properly before them. They are expected to disregard what one accused says about another in his absence. If they can do that, which is far from easy, they can disregard what is said in the newspapers.'

1   (1976) 64 Cr App R 11.

9.21   The views of Lawton LJ have, it is submitted, been followed by the courts thereafter. In *Ex p B*[1] for example Scott Baker J held that Lawton J's observations in *Kray* about juries are as true in 1994 as they were 25 years ago. Similar sentiments have been expressed in a contempt of court context by Denning MR and Taylor CJ in the cases reported in paras **9.11–9.12**.

1   (17 February 1994, unreported).

9.22   In *Abu Hamza* the Court of Appeal recognised that, in general:

'the courts have not been prepared to accede to submissions that publicity before a trial has made a fair trial impossible. Rather they have held that directions from the judge coupled with the effect of the trial process itself will result in the jury disregarding such publicity'.[1]

Having noted exceptions to the general rule, in the shape of the *McCann* and *Taylor and Taylor* decisions, the court went on to review the case law, which demonstrated a confidence in the integrity of juries to act fairly.

1   See para 89 of the judgment.

Trust in the jury

9.23   The Court of Appeal in *Abu Hamza* made reference to the *West*, *Kray* and *Young and Coughlan* decisions, before endorsing the statement made by the President of the Queen's Bench Division, Sir Igor Judge, as he then was, in the 2006 case of *In re B*[1] which read as follows:

'There is a feature of our trial system which is sometimes overlooked or taken for granted … that juries up and down the country have a passionate and profound belief in, and a commitment to, the right of the defendant to be given a fair trial. They know that it is integral to their responsibility. It is, when all is said and done, their birthright; it is shared by each one of them with the defendant. They guard it faithfully. The integrity of the jury is an essential feature of our trial process. Juries follow the directions which the judge will give them to focus exclusively on the evidence and to ignore anything they may have heard or read out of court … the directions themselves will appeal directly to their own instinctive and fundamental belief in the need for the trial process to be fair.'

1   [2006] EWCA Crim 2692.

9.24   Further on in the judgment, the Court of Appeal noted the observations of Lord Hope of Craighead in *Montgomery*, who acknowledged the obvious point that:

' ... the entire system of trial by jury is based upon the assumption that the jury will follow the instructions which they receive from the judge and that they will return a true verdict in accordance with the evidence'.[1]

The judiciary naturally must have confidence in the assumption that their faith in juries is well placed. The authors suggest that the challenges the judiciary will face, when confronted with adverse publicity in high-profile cases, will continue to grow, with the advancements in technology which allow public access to all manner of information. The principal threat to the fairness of trials will come from the internet, which will prove to be much more difficult to regulate than media broadcasts on the television or reports in newspapers.

1   *Montgomery v HM Advocate* [2003] 1 AC 641 PC.

9.25   It is within the direct experience of the authors, for example, that, during the course of the Afghan Hijacking trial at the Central Criminal Court,[1] Mr Justice Butterfield was faced with a genuine problem posed by the internet, when it was drawn to the court's, and counsels' attention, that a bundle of a juror's internet reports on an aspect of the case, but not part of the evidence, were found inside the actual jury room. Butterfield J dealt with the problem swiftly, with a strong direction that they ignore such material, and refrain from any further research on the internet. The reality is, however, that jurors now have instant access to a library of material, and in circumstances which are not currently capable of being policed. Jurors who choose not to follow judicial directions, are now perfectly able to research information about a defendant, much of which may be prejudicial, irrelevant, and inadmissible for trial purposes.

1   *R v Safi and others* (2001).

The risk of prejudice

9.26   The *Abu Hamza* decision is of particular interest for the Court of Appeal's guidance to judges in relation to the approach a court should take, in adverse publicity cases, where there is a proven risk of prejudice. In para 92 of the judgment it states:

'The risk that members of a jury may be affected by prejudice is one that cannot wholly be eliminated. Any member may bring personal prejudices to the jury room and equally there will be a risk that a jury may disregard the directions of the judge when they consider that they are contrary to what justice requires. Our legal principles are designed to reduce such risks to the minimum, but they cannot obviate them altogether if those reasonably suspected of criminal conduct are to be brought to trial ... Prejudicial publicity renders more difficult the task of the court, that is of the judge and jury together, in trying the case fairly. Our laws of contempt of court are designed to prevent the media from interfering with the due process of justice by making it more difficult to conduct a fair trial. The fact, however, that adverse publicity may have risked prejudicing a fair trial is no reason for not proceeding with the trial if the judge concludes that, with his assistance, it will be possible to have a fair trial.'

From this statement, the court is making it clear that certain levels of proven prejudice, or risks of prejudice, will have to be tolerated, so long as the trial judge maintains the view that a fair trial is still achievable. It will be for individual judges to make a judgement call, based on their experience, their assessment of the prejudice, and its likely effect on the fairness of the proceedings.

Proximity to trial—the fade factor

9.27 In *A-G v News Group Newspapers*[1] Sir John Donaldson MR said:

'proximity to the trial is clearly a factor of great importance and this trial will not have taken place for another ten months, by which time many wickets will have fallen, not to mention much water having flowed under many bridges, all of which would blunt the impact of publications'.[2]

1 [1987] QB 1.
2 [1987] QB 1 at 16.

9.28 The courts, as this quotation explains, have adopted the belief that a 'fade factor' is an effective diluter of prejudice. Part of this belief is how juries behave especially in longer complex trials: a gradual focusing of the jury's mind on the evidence before it to the exclusion of all information which has been communicated outside the courtroom. Sir John Donaldson MR said:

'the fact is that for one reason or another a trial by its very nature, seems to cause all concerned to be become progressively more inward looking, studying the evidence given and submissions made to the exclusion of all other sources of enlightenment. This is a well known phenomenon'.[1]

A similar view was expressed by Taylor CJ in *Ex p Telegraph plc*[2] quoted in para **9.12**.

1 [1987] QB 1 at 16.
2 [1993] 1 WLR 980.

9.29 Belief in this fade factor was confidently asserted by Scott Baker J in *Ex p B*:[1]

'in most cases, one day's headline news is the next day's fire lighter. Most members of the public do not remember in any detail what they have seen on television, heard on the radio or read in the newspaper except for a very short period of time ... In this country public trust and confidence is placed in juries to decide the facts in all serious criminal cases, and jurors are well able to put out of their minds extraneous material and try the case on the evidence they hear in court.'

1 (17 February 1994, unreported).

9.30   In *Abu Hamza*, the court took note of the Scottish position on pre-trial publicity, set out in the judgment of Lord Hope of Craighead in the Privy Council decision of *Montgomery v HM Advocate*:[1]

> 'Recent research conducted for the New Zealand Law Commission suggests that the impact of pre-trial publicity and of prejudicial media coverage during the trial, even in high profile cases, is minimal: Young, Cameron and Tinsley, Juries in Criminal trials: part Two, vol 1, ch 9, para 287 (New Zealand Law Commission preliminary paper no 37, November 1999).The lapse of time since the last exposure may increasingly be regarded, with each month that passes, in itself as some kind of a safeguard. Nevertheless the risk that the widespread, prolonged and prejudicial publicity that occurred in this case will have a residual effect on the minds of at least some members of the jury cannot be regarded as negligible. The principal safeguards of the objective impartiality of the tribunal lie in the trial process itself and the conduct of the trial by the trial judge. On the one hand there is the discipline to which the jury will be subjected of listening to and thinking about the evidence. The actions of seeing and hearing the witnesses may be expected to have a far greater impact on their minds than such residual recollections as may exist about reports about the case in the media. This impact can be expected to be reinforced on the other hand by such warnings and directions as the trial judge may think it appropriate to give them as the trial proceeds, in particular when he delivers his charge before they retire to consider their verdicts.'

Based on this line of authorities, there is clearly a widespread judicial scepticism in the context of abuse of process as to pre-trial publicity having any lasting or corrupting effect on the fairness of criminal trials. Such scepticism, for reasons described in this chapter already, is unsurprising. Furthermore, until the 1990s it appears that no criminal trial was stayed on this ground. This disbelief in a criminal context as to the effect of publicity after it has occurred, created a disjuncture with the approach of judges in a contempt context. The authorities considered above, in paras **9.11–9.17**, evidence this difference of approach between the older abuse of process decisions, and the contempt cases. It is, however, submitted that since the early 1990s this disbelief has been superseded by a more flexible and pragmatic approach, albeit that the instances where defence arguments will succeed are expected to continue to remain few and far between.

1   [2003] 1 AC 641.

A REVIEW OF THE CASE LAW

9.31   It is submitted that since the early 1990s there has been an increased judicial willingness to recognise that, in criminal trials, pre-trial publicity can cause a risk of substantial prejudice. The earliest case was *R v McCann*[1] where the Court of Appeal quashed the conviction of alleged Irish terrorists because the trial judge failed to discharge the jury following a sudden wave of publicity as it retired to consider its verdict. In *McCann* the alleged target of the terrorist plot, Tom King MP, and also Denning LJ made widely publicised comments suggesting that people who refuse to answer police questions are probably guilty. McCann and others had refused to answer such questions. In his judgment Beldam LJ stated that:

'we are left with a definite impression that the impact which those statements and the television interviews may well have had on the fairness of the trial could not be overcome by any direction to the jury'.[2]

Notice, however, that *McCann* is concerned with publicity from senior or authoritative figures occurring at the crucial moment when the jury was about to retire. *McCann* is therefore easy to distinguish on its facts.

1   (1991) 92 Cr App R 239.
2   (1991) 92 Cr App R 239 at 253.

9.32   A case of far greater significance is the judgment of the Court of Appeal in *R v Taylor and Taylor.*[1] In that case the court took special notice of the adverse publicity which in its view rendered it, 'quite impossible to say that the jury were not influenced in their decision by what they had read in the press'.[2] While the court did not quash the convictions of the defendants simply on the publicity ground alone, it is significant to note that it declined to order a re-trial because, 'by reason of the view taken of the way in which this case was reported, we do not think that a fair trial could now take place'.[3] In his description of the pre-trial publicity itself McCowan LJ said this:

'in giving leave to appeal, the single judge described that coverage as "unremitting, extensive, sensational, inaccurate and misleading". Having had the opportunity of reading a substantial selection of the newspaper reports in question, we see no reason to dissent from that view'.[4]

1   (1993) 98 Cr App R 361.
2   (1993) 98 Cr App R 361 at 368.
3   (1993) 98 Cr App R 361 at 369.
4   (1993) 98 Cr App R 361 at 368.

9.33   The Court of Appeal's judgment in *Taylor* was followed by the ruling of Garland J in *R v Reade.*[1] Garland J stayed the trial of police officers who were accused of extracting false confessions from members of the Birmingham Six in 1974. Again, as with *Taylor,* the judge in part stayed the trial on the grounds of pre-trial publicity. Two aspects of Garland J's judgment are worthy of special note. First, Garland J accepted that the volume intensity and continuing nature of the publicity against the defendant had a 'snowball effect'. This snowball effect was the antithesis of the fade factor because in the view of Garland J, each extra bit of added adverse publicity served to fuel and continue the effect of past adverse publicity. Secondly, because of the enormous publicity concerning the quashing of the convictions of the Birmingham Six, it would be impossible to avoid a jury from having the impression that in quashing those convictions, the Court of Appeal was, as a matter of fact, finding the police officer defendants guilty of conspiracy and perjury.

1   (1993) Independent, 19 October.

9.34   One further aspect of this judgment which deserves mention is the acceptance by Garland J that the prejudice need not be specifically directed at the actual defendants personally. Garland J accepted that the identities of the Birmingham Six police officers was of itself unimportant because the prejudice was generalised and aimed at whichever police officers it was who had allegedly beaten confessions out of the Birmingham Six. Garland J's acceptance of generalised prejudice in this regard can be contrasted with the view of Turner J in *R v Alcindor*[1] which concerned publicity arising out of the capsize of the 'Herald of Free Enterprise'. Here, Turner J held that because the publicity was generalised there was no serious risk of prejudice against the individual defendants.

1   (11 June 1990, unreported).

R v Maxwell

9.35   Perhaps the most elaborate attempt ever made to persuade a judge to stay proceedings on the grounds of pre-trial publicity was that of Kevin and Ian Maxwell in May 1995. In addition to placing before the trial judge, Phillips J, evidence of allegedly prejudicial newspaper reports and videos of television programmes, the defendants also sought to adduce direct evidence of prejudice by means of findings gathered by opinion polls which they had commissioned from a polling organisation. They commissioned three separate polls in an effort to gauge the public's attitude and depth of prejudice. This was the first time in criminal proceedings that evidence of opinion polls was admitted (although in trademark and passing-off cases such evidence is routinely admissible)[1].

1   See for example *Customglass Boats Ltd v Sorthouse Bros Ltd* [1976] RPC 589 and *Lego System A/S v Lego M Lemelstrich* [1983] FSR 155. Phillips J was not persuaded by the evidence of the opinion pollsters: 'I do not believe I would have reached a significantly different conclusion as to the effects of publicity without the assistance of these [opinion polls] and I hope that their use in this case will not be taken as a precedent in future.'

9.36   After an extensive hearing of the abuse application Phillips J rejected it, holding that the Maxwell brothers could receive a fair trial.[1] However, Phillips J took the opportunity to consider the jurisdiction to stay proceedings on the grounds of pre-trial publicity:

'No stay should be imposed unless the defendant shows on the balance of probabilities that owing to the extent and the nature of the pre-trial publicity he will suffer serious prejudice to the extent that no fair trial can be held. I would accept this test, so far as it goes, but it remains necessary to identify the essential aspects of a fair trial for the purpose of the test. If it were enough to render a trial unfair that publicity has created the risk of prejudice against the defendant our system of criminal justice would be seriously flawed. There will inevitably be cases where the facts are so dramatic that almost everyone in the land will know of them. There will be circumstances when arrests are made of defendants whose guilt will, or may, appear likely. Intense media coverage may well take place before a suspect is identified or apprehended. If in the most notorious cases defendants were to claim immunity from trial because of the risk of prejudice public confidence in the criminal justice system would be destroyed'.

1   In the event, Phillips J was proved right because, of course, the brothers were both acquitted.

9.37   The judge continued:

'Our system of criminal justice is founded on the belief that the jury trial provides the fairest and most reliable method of determining whether guilt is established. This belief is based on the premise that the jury will do their best to be true to their oath and to try the case according to the evidence. The ability of the jury to disregard extrinsic material has been repeatedly emphasised by judges of great experience'.

9.38   Phillips J then quoted from *Kray*[1] and concluded:

'It seems to me that the court will only be justified in staying a trial on the ground of adverse pre-trial publicity if satisfied on a balance of probabilities that if the jury return a verdict of guilty the effect of the pre-trial publicity will be such as to render that verdict unsafe and unsatisfactory. In considering this question the court has to consider the likely length of time the jury will be subject to the trial process, the issues that are likely to arise and the evidence that is likely to be called in order to form a view as to whether it is probable that—try as they may to disregard the pre-trial publicity—the jury's verdict will be rendered unsafe on account of it'.

1   See para **9.19** above.

9.39   On a more general point concerning the *Maxwell* case, it would, it is submitted, be overly simplistic to deduce from the acquittal of the Maxwell brothers that the views of, for example, Lawton J considered in paras **9.19–9.20**, have been vindicated; ie that the jury can be trusted to exclude all kinds of prejudice. While refusing the application for a stay in *Maxwell* it is to be recalled that Phillips J did allow the use of an extensive questionnaire, consisting of 40 questions, in order to sift out from the jury panel those persons who evinced any prejudice. The eventual jury was therefore only drawn from the 'survivors' of the much larger panel. How efficacious this highly unusual exercise really was is of course unknown.

9.40   In *R v Andrews*[1] a similar attempt to permit jury questionnaires was made by the defence but rejected by the trial judge. This was upheld by the Court of Appeal, who said that the questioning of jurors 'whether orally or by the use of questionnaires was to be avoided save in the most exceptional circumstances'. The court further held that questionnaires were a flawed instrument as answers were likely to be vague and questions would tend to remind jurors of issues which they would be told to disregard.

1   [1999] Crim LR 156.

Post-Maxwell authorities

9.41   In *R v Knights*[1] HH Judge Sanders granted a stay of proceedings against the defendant. The judge held that:

'the reporting was unlawful, misleading and scandalous ... certain reporters were determined to run a hate campaign against Knights unchecked by their editors and without any regard to the interests of justice. I have absolutely no doubt that the massive media publicity in this case was unfair, outrageous and oppressive'.

Interestingly, following this determination of the criminal proceedings the Attorney-General consequently brought contempt proceedings against five newspapers whose reportage had been denounced by the judge. However, the High Court dismissed all the actions holding that they had not caused a substantial risk of serious prejudice.

1   (1995, unreported), Harrow Crown Court.

9.42   In *R v Hassan and Caldon*[1] HH Judge Colgan stayed the proceedings. This case arose out of a 'sting' operation carried out by the *News of the World*. That newspaper gave wide prominence to its article concerning the defendants in September 1994. It described the defendants as 'veteran villains' with 'long criminal records' etc. At the start of the trial in July 1995 the trial was stayed. The judge held the article was grossly prejudicial, 'especially in attributing criminal records to the accused'. Subsequently, the Attorney-General cited the *News of the World* for contempt which was upheld by the Divisional Court, who imposed a fine of £50,000.[2] To avoid the problem of being held so liable again, the newspaper publishes stories about crime before any proceedings or investigations are undertaken by police. This, therefore, prevents the test of 'active proceedings' in the Contempt of Court Act 1981 being triggered.

1   (July 1995, unreported), Isleworth Crown Court.
2   *A-G v News Group Newspapers* (1997) Independent, 17 July.

9.43   The 'Cromwell Street murders' and the cases against Fred and Rosemary West attracted massive pre-trial and during trial publicity. Following her conviction for 10 murders, Rosemary West appealed partly on the ground of adverse publicity.[1] However Taylor LCJ roundly dismissed this ground, holding that it would be absurd for a defendant to escape a trial on most grave charges on the ground of pre-trial publicity. He held that only adverse and prejudicial publicity during the trial itself could possibly justify a stay. However Taylor LCJ accepted that the incidence of such publicity could be such that a judicial direction to the jury to disregard it may be an inadequate means of removing the effect of it from jurors' minds. This dicta was subsequently applied in the 2001 Leeds footballer prosecution, *R v Woodgate*.[2] Here the judge stayed the trial on the basis of a single article published in the *Sunday Mirror* when the jury had retired.

1   [1996] 2 Cr App Rep 374.
2   (Unreported).

9.44   Taylor LCJ's dichotomy in *West* was adopted by Kay J in *R v Magee*.[1] Kay J stayed proceedings against six defendants arising out of newspaper reports concerning their criminal backgrounds during the trial. He held that there was 'a real difference between pre-trial publicity and publicity which comes to the attention of the jury after they have been selected'. Consistent with his dichotomy Kay J refused applications to stay the proceedings based on publicity which occurred before the trial had, which he accepted was prejudicial because it had publicised the criminal past of the defendants. In this regard he held that the jury could be expected to disregard such publicity. However, when it again occurred during the trial this faith was undermined.

1   (January 1997, unreported), Woolwich Crown Court.

R v Stone[1]

9.45   This case raises a novel issue concerning adverse publicity following a conviction which is then subsequently quashed by the Court of Appeal. However the court went further and also reconsidered whether trials should be stayed on this ground of abuse.

1   [2001] EWCA 297, (2001) 145 Sol Jo LB 68.

9.46   In relation to post-conviction publicity about criminal trials generally it is important to bear in mind that such post-conviction publicity, freed from the constraints of contempt of court and sub judice restrictions, will inevitably tend to communicate information about the accused which would not have occurred pre-conviction. Such restrictions intended to keep a jury in ignorance of various facts normally concerned with an accused's previous bad character, fall away or lose their rationale once he/she has been convicted. Accordingly information which would have been deemed highly prejudicial pre-conviction can be freely published.

9.47   In *Stone* a ghastly double murder of mother and daughter occurred in July 1996. They attracted massive publicity. A year later Stone was charged with the murders and ultimately was convicted in October 1988. In the following days there was extensive publicity about Stone, much of which was related to his alleged antecedence. Much which was detrimental was publicised which had not been known to the trial jury. For example he was described as a childhood depraved psychopath, details of his previous convictions for violent crime were reported and he was said to fantasise about killing. In other words there was clearly publicity post-conviction which was highly adverse to Stone.

9.48   Following the successful appeal on grounds unrelated to abuse, the prosecution applied for leave to have Stone retried. This was resisted on the ground that the post-trial publicity meant that he could not now receive a fair (re)trial. The prosecution, however, submitted that the adverse publicity was restricted to late 1998 and moreover there had been substantial publicity that had been in favour of Stone's appeal. Accordingly its overall likely prejudicial effect due to the elapse of time had been so diluted as to have become insignificant.

9.49   Prior to *Stone* the only other occasion when the court directly considered a retrial in the circumstance of adverse publicity was in *Taylor and Taylor* considered at para **9.32** above. Here the court had declined to order a retrial, although no reasons for this were given. In *Stone* however, Kennedy LJ was critical of this earlier decision, holding that a justification for this decision against a retrial ought to have been given and therefore the case was of little relevance. Instead Kennedy LJ was much more impressed with the approach of Philips J in *Maxwell* (see para **9.35** above) which he regarded as a 'valuable approach'.

9.50   Kennedy LJ also took advantage to emphasise the courts' reluctance to ever stay a trial for a serious offence on the ground of adverse publicity. First, in a section of his judgment marked 'Caveat' he sought to deride the proposition that a right to a fair trial equated with keeping a jury in ignorance of various facts about the accused. He listed examples of how a jury may become properly aware of such information without it ever being alleged that this had caused an unfair trial. Second, he held that in almost all cases, pre-trial adverse publicity could never properly found a stay. Only if it occurred during the actual trial might a stay be granted:

> 'Mr Clegg submits that in the light of decisions such as *McCann, Taylor*, and *Reade* it must now be accepted that there can be situations where an appropriate direction will not suffice. It is unreasonable to expect a jury to put the adverse publicity out of their minds. We agree, but that can only happen rarely, and usually in relation to adverse publicity which occurs during the course of the trial'.[1]

Kennedy LJ quoted with approval the opinion of Schiemann LJ in *A-G v MGN Ltd;*[2] the ability of a jury 'not to accept as true the contents of a publication just because it has been published'. Accordingly a retrial was ordered and duly occurred in late 2001. Stone was convicted again.

1   [2001] EWCA 297, para 58.
2   [1997] 1 All ER 456 at 461.

R v Abu Hamza

9.51   On the facts, the Court of Appeal considered the evidence upon which the defence contended the trial judge should have stayed proceedings against this Imam of a London mosque. There were 600 pages of newspaper reports, and articles spanning a two-year period, which were put before the trial judge, who treated them as samples of a sustained campaign against the defendant, which were almost entirely hostile to him. The Court of Appeal agreed there had been a prolonged barrage of adverse publicity, some of which had characterised the appellant as an ogre, and a public enemy. Indeed, the court agreed with the trial judge's assessment that the publicity had put at risk the fairness of the trial.

The court described the trial judge's position as follows:

> 'The challenge posed to the judge of taking appropriate steps to neutralise the effect of these matters by appropriate directions and guidance in the course of his summing up was considerable. The task was an exacting one'.

Having acknowledged the difficulties, the court went on to find that the judge's detailed, careful and skilful directions on the media coverage had lived up to the task. There had been no requirement to stay the proceedings.

9.52   The Court of Appeal's earlier judgments in *Stone* and *West* can be regarded as an attempt to curtail the nascent, largely 1990s, jurisprudence concerning the right of an accused to avoid trial on the ground of prejudicial publicity. Underlying this approach is a belief concerning the shortness of human memory or strength of the fade factor. Kennedy LJ held in the final paragraph of his judgment: '... people do forget. Even if they do not forget entirely, the passage of time makes it easier for them to set aside that which they are told to disregard'.

9.53 It is submitted that the approach adopted by Taylor LCJ and Kennedy LJ is not without difficulty. First, it assumes that the prejudice engendered by publicity is liable to be grossly exaggerated by defendants. Ultimately, short of the opinion poll evidence adduced by the Maxwells in their case, this subject is largely one of conjecture. However both the traditional approach of the law on contempt considered above and contemporary fears regarding the power of the media are based on the view that adverse publicity can engender bias in the mind of a decision-maker. As Lord Goff said in *R v Gough*[1], 'bias is such an insidious thing that, even though a person may in good faith believe that he was acting impartially, his mind may unconsciously be affected by bias'. Kennedy LJ's lofty dismissal of the proposition concerning prejudice sits uneasily with this.

1   (1993) 97 Cr App Rep 188 at 191.

9.54 Second, this view runs the risk of encouraging the media on the one hand to believe that they enjoy, pre-trial at least, a relatively free licence to publish what they like, and the accused on the other to believe that the courts will not protect their right to a fair trial. Such a loss of faith will create a vacuum which, it is submitted, will quickly be filled with the defence team feeling the need to engage with the media to help obtain a more friendly portrayal. In *R v Andrews*[1] the Court of Appeal criticised the role played by the defence solicitors in holding a press conference with their client which understandably they regarded as unsavoury. Such actions may become more common, even if unattractive and alien to English legal tradition, if the courts refuse to accept a view held by many that prejudice can engender an unfair trial.

1   [1999] Crim LR 156.

9.55 The policy underlying the judgments in *West* and *Stone* is readily understandable. If jury trial is to survive in an age of formidable media power, high-profile and notorious defendants cannot be seen to escape justice. Far from blaming itself, the media outcry in the event of such a stay would be frenzied and with this a substantial danger of public disquiet about the criminal justice system would be caused. Against this backdrop the position, or rather compromise, established in these two cases can be understood.

9.56 But compromises are generally unstable and fragile. Recent reportage of allegations of paedophilia against TV celebrities seems sufficient to destroy their careers even before any charge is laid. Worse still is the branding of unconvicted defendants charged with offences of terrorism as, quite simply, terrorists. They are assumed to be and labelled as that which they are subsequently tried for. Any prospect that the media might have acted with self-restraint in the reporting of police investigations and charges in such cases seems unfounded.

9.57 The perennial problem will thus return to haunt trial judges and the Court of Appeal. Absent rigorous action by the Attorney-General, a politician who by nature will always be reluctant to create enemies in the media camp, any solution will have to come from the courts.

ALTERNATIVE TO A STAY—REMEDIES TO REDUCE THE RISK OF PREJUDICE

9.58   There are remedies available to a trial judge short of exercising a stay which can dilute or remove the risk of prejudice. Such remedies include:

(1)   Moving the trial venue to a different geographical location if the risk of prejudice has predominantly been caused by local publicity. Accordingly in *Stone* the appellant who had originally been tried in Maidstone was retried in Nottingham. Of course if the publicity is national, there is nowhere to go.

(2)   As in *Maxwell*, questioning potential jurors to weed out the most prejudiced. It is submitted that there are two difficulties with this remedy, one principled and the other practical. The principled objection is that questioning a potential jury for the purpose of weeding out members constitutes a derogation from the principle that members of the jury should be selected at random, this to ensure fairness and that the jury is a cross-section of society. Secondly, it creates the insoluble problem of determining how prejudiced a potential juror should be before he is removed from the panel; on what empirical basis is the court to decide that one level of prejudice is acceptable but another not? As Phillips J said in *R v Maxwell*, 'the fact that a juror may have read or heard prejudicial matter about a defendant, and even formed an adverse opinion of him on the basis of it, does not of itself disqualify the juror on the ground of bias'. The view of the Ontario Court of Appeal in *R v Hubbert*[1] is also constructive:

> 'in this era of rapid dissemination of the news by the various media, it would be naïve to think that in the case of a crime involving considerable notoriety, it would be impossible to select 12 jurors who have not heard anything about the case, information about a case, and even the holding of a tentative opinion about it, does make partial juror sworn to render a true verdict according to the evidence'.

The exercise, it is submitted, is entirely speculative. Moreover, the questioning process may of itself create further problems. First, will the prejudice in fact be identified or elicited as a result of the screening process? As Mason CJ and Toohey J in *Murphy v R* put it:

> 'the challenge for cause based on partiality run into an obvious difficulty; it seems unlikely that a prejudiced juror will recognise his own personal prejudice, or, knowing it, would admit it'.[2]

Secondly, the process may be self-defeating in that it brings to the attention of a juror those matters which the parties would wish him to disregard.

(3)   Delaying the start of the trial to allow feelings of prejudice to subside. However, this remedy is only likely to succeed if it can be safely assumed that during the 'cooling-off' period no further prejudicial publicity occurs. In *Stone* the Court of Appeal took into account the date of a possible re-trial holding that the delay would further reduce the risk of prejudice. Hamza's original trial date was postponed given the obvious prejudice of the timing of his trial at the time of the London bombings of 7 July 2005.

This is the most commonly used remedy whereby at any time during the course of the trial, probably more than once, the judge directs the jury to base its verdict on the evidence it hears in court and nothing else. Depending on the nature of the prejudicial publicity and its specificity a judge is also able to comment in detail informing the jury that various allegations made in the media are, for example, totally false and to be disregarded. In *R v Andrews*[3] the trial judge directed prosecution counsel, before opening his case to the jury, to inform it that certain allegations made in newspapers were entirely bogus and formed no part of the Crown's case. While it is unknown as to whether such directions have the desired effect, based on the presupposition that juries do act fairly, it is presumed that they do so.

1   (1975) 29 CCC (2d) 279.
2   (1989) 167 CLR 94 at 103.
3   [1999] Crim LR 156. See para **9.54**.

JURISPRUDENCE OF THE ECHR

9.59   It is submitted that there is only sparse ECHR jurisprudence concerned with this subject. Unsurprisingly as a general principle the Strasbourg Court has held that pre-trial publicity can adversely affect the fairness of criminal proceedings,[1] particularly where such publicity is instigated or encouraged by those in authority. Accordingly, the court has accepted that press freedom may be curtailed in order to ensure a fair trial and protect members of the jury from exposure to prejudicial influences.[2] Furthermore the Commission has accepted that publicity which creates an atmosphere of animosity or a virulent press campaign can prejudice a fair trial.[3] Finally, the court will also assess whether the effect of prejudicial coverage has been appropriately dealt with by judicial directions to a jury to ignore the same.[4]

1   See *X v Austria* [1963] 1476/62.
2   See *Hodgson v United Kingdom* (1987) 10 EHRR 503.
3   See *Berns and Ewart v Luxembourg* (1991) 68 DR 137.
4   See *X v UK* (1978) App No 7542/76, and see *Noye v UK* (2003) 36 EHRRCD 231.

Chapter 10

Procedural considerations

INTRODUCTION

10.01　In this chapter it is proposed to analyse the various options open to practitioners seeking to make submissions on abuse of process, from the magistrates' court level up to the Court of Appeal, and beyond. Procedural opportunities will be considered as much as the constraints on the same, the object being to answer the various issues of when, where and how such applications may be made. In addition, the aim is to assist the practitioner with practical advice on how best to either present, or respond to, an abuse submission.

10.02　The starting point naturally is to satisfy oneself that a proper argument exists on the merits, and that the case meets the stringent criterion required. While this may sound self-evident the courts continue to sound out regular warnings to practitioners as to the need for self-restraint before embarking. Indeed, since *Attorney-General's Reference (No 1 of 1990)*[1] the courts have, in the face of an ever-burgeoning body of abuse case law, sought to encourage practitioners to exercise greater self-restraint, in the light of a history of what some courts clearly consider to be a significant number of palpably unmeritorious applications.

1　[1992] QB 630.

10.03　Lord Bingham CJ in *Environment Agency v Stanford*[1] stated that the courts have repeatedly emphasised how the jurisdiction to stay proceedings as an abuse of process ought to be exercised with the greatest caution. His Lordship commented that the lower courts were too often invited to stay proceedings in inappropriate circumstances, for example where a prosecution was merely ill-advised or unwise, issues which in his view were largely relevant in relation to mitigation.

1　[1998] COD 373, QBD.

10.04　In the *Childs* decision[1] Lord Woolf issued the strongest judicial warning to date to those advocates who advance unwarranted abuse applications:

> 'If they were advanced when they were not warranted, courts should make it clear that that was inappropriate conduct, and would take appropriate steps where, as sometimes happened, a huge amount of court time was wasted in consequence.'

Whilst the Court of Appeal will no doubt continue to dispose swiftly of unmeritorious abuse appeals, trial courts have been generally unsuccessful in holding back the tide of applications. In the light of the ever-expanding nature of the doctrine, the judiciary will further expect that, at the very least, the parties use the correct procedures.

1   *R v Childs* (2002) Times, 30 November.

10.05   Finally, any observer of recent judicial policy in the criminal courts will notice an increased willingness to use wasted costs orders as a means of punishing unmeritorious defence applications and to deter others. Practitioners should bear this possibility closely in mind.

THE MAGISTRATES' COURT: JURISDICTION

The legal context

10.06   Magistrates' courts may encounter defence applications to stay the proceedings on the grounds of abuse in two sets of circumstances. First, in relation to a summary trial to be heard before them and secondly, in relation to when they act as examining justices in the context of committal proceedings. In practice, as summary proceedings rarely give rise to abuse of process issues and they are, in any event, never concerned with serious crime, it is in the context of committal that the issue arises of whether magistrates should have the power to halt a prosecution: in effect, to stigmatise it as an abuse of process at this preliminary stage and prior to any member of the judiciary being able to decide the issue.

10.07   Bearing in mind that the law concerning abuse of process is exclusively derived from the common law and that magistrates are inferior tribunals wholly subject to the supervisory jurisdiction of the High Court, the issue of whether magistrates should enjoy a jurisdiction to rule on abuse applications is ultimately a policy issue to be decided by the High Court. As abuse applications frequently involve complex matrices of fact and law, usually accompanied by defence complaints of prosecution impropriety in the context of serious allegations of criminality against the defendant, it is understandable that the High Court has, in various cases which have come before it, wanted to consider carefully the wisdom of allowing magistrates jurisdiction in this area.

The general position

10.08   In *R v Derby Magistrates' Court, ex p Brooks*[1] Sir Roger Ormrod said:

'The discretionary power of a magistrates' court to stop a prosecution has only recently been recognised by this court, and this development of the law is in a phase of rapid growth. It has no statutory basis ...'

1   (1985) 80 Cr App Rep 164.

10.09   Sir Roger Ormrod then referred to various authorities and held that a magistrates' court did have this discretionary power. He observed:

'the ultimate objective of this discretionary power is to ensure that there should be a fair trial according to law, which involves fairness both to the defendant and the prosecution'.

10.10 Another useful statement of general principal in this regard is the statement of general principle laid down by Mann LJ in *R v Telford Justices, ex p Badhan*.[1] In that case Mann LJ affirmed that magistrates did enjoy an abuse jurisdiction:

'We ... can see no reason why examining justices (even one examining magistrate; see the Act of 1980, s 4(1)) should not be able to decide that an initiation of the process of committal is an abuse of that process. A question of abuse is one which is within the ability of justices to decide, and it is one they admittedly have power to determine on summary trial'.

1   (1991) 93 Cr App Rep 171.

The creation of a split jurisdiction in Bennett

10.11 In *R v Horseferry Road Magistrates' Court, ex p Bennett*[1] the House of Lords followed the principle of the *Telford Justices* case, holding that magistrates enjoy a power to stay proceedings on the grounds of abuse in relation to both summary trials and committal proceedings. However, bearing in mind that in *Bennett* the House of Lords had significantly pushed outwards the boundaries of the abuse jurisdiction generally, the question naturally arose as to whether it was wise to vest in magistrates, in common with the judiciary, a full jurisdiction over abuse matters. In the context of the facts in *Bennett* which are recounted elsewhere in this book,[2] it was understandable that various speeches in that case were concerned in part with whether magistrates really were a competent tribunal to determine complex matters concerned with alleged international lawlessness by the executive and breach of extradition procedures, neither of these matters strictly having an impact on the fairness of the trial. It was one thing for the House, as it did in *Bennett,* to widen the circumstances in which a Crown Court could stay proceedings and another to provide the same ambit of discretion to legally unqualified persons sitting as part-time magistrates in context of a committal.

1   [1994] AC 42.
2   See paras **5.03–5.06**.

10.12 The result of such concerns in *Bennett* led to the creation of a split jurisdiction in relation to abuse matters. Whereas the judiciary would enjoy a full jurisdiction, magistrates would not and their jurisdiction would be made more narrow. In *Bennett* Lord Griffiths held that magistrates' jurisdiction in this context 'should be strictly confined to matters directly affecting the fairness of the trial of the particular accused'.[1] Examples of matters falling within this category were, according to Lord Griffiths, those concerning delay or the unfair manipulation of court procedures.

1   (1994) 98 Cr App Rep 114 at 127.

10.13   According to Lord Griffiths, a line could be drawn between this and a special exclusive category of abuse concerned with upholding the rule of law, which he held should be confined to the jurisdiction of the High Court. Accordingly, when an allegation of abuse akin to that made in *Bennett* arose then magistrates were not competent to decide the matter. The remedy in this situation was for magistrates to exercise their discretion to allow an adjournment of the proceedings before them in order to enable the defence to then immediately make an application to the Divisional Court which would be empowered to rule.

Problems arising from the split jurisdiction

10.14   Before considering the relevant authorities subsequent to *Bennett* it should be appreciated that the creation of this split jurisdiction in the context of abuse and the powers of magistrates creates two practical difficulties. First, is it really possible in practice to draw a line between what Lord Griffiths said were 'matters directly affecting the fairness of the trial of the particular accused' and avowedly more policy-type issues concerned with upholding the rule of law? On what side of the line, for example, does an allegation of prosecution mala fides or oppressive conduct fall? Second, by creating a system whereby in the context of committal proceedings, abuse applications concerned with the rule of law category are to be remitted for consideration to the High Court, a problem is thereby created in relation to the powers of a trial judge sitting in the Crown Court. If a complaint of abuse is referred to the High Court and rejected following which the accused is committed for trial to the Crown Court, what is a trial judge to do when he becomes seised of the case and the defence then makes a similar abuse application? In the context of a prior adverse ruling by magistrates, there is no difficulty in principle as a Crown Court judge can examine the issues afresh and reach a different conclusion. His discretion is unfettered in this respect. The problem, however, arises when the High Court composed of a Lord Justice of Appeal and a High Court judge has ruled against the defendant and the trial judge is then in effect being asked to reconsider the matter.

10.15   To this problem there appears only one principled solution, that the trial judge abide by the ruling of the High Court even though generally speaking the High Court as a court of review is less equipped to give careful consideration to the complex issues of fact and law which generally surround abuse applications than a trial judge before whom, for example, live evidence can be called and be cross-examined. But in a less clear-cut situation, what is a trial judge to do when the defence submit that there have been supervening matters between the ruling of the High Court and the application before him which had they occurred or been known about at the time of the High Court application, could have led that court to have reached an opposite conclusion. If such supervening matters really have arisen, can a trial judge de facto or de jure confine consideration of abuse to only these events posing the theoretical question of what would the High Court have done if it had been aware of such events?

10.16   Bearing in mind that the decision in *Bennett* is relatively recent and
that international lawlessness or *Bennett*-type abuse applications are rare, the
problems in paras **10.14** and **10.15** do not appear in practice to have caused real
difficulty. However, from time to time the High Court is called on to clarify
whether a magistrates' court should have jurisdiction to entertain a particular
abuse application. For example, in *R v Belmarsh Magistrates' Court, ex p Watts*[1]
the defendant made an abuse application at committal on the ground that the
prosecution fell foul of the *Hunter*[2] rule. This rule is discussed fully in
Chapter 4. In *Watts* the magistrate found that he did not as a matter of law have
jurisdiction to entertain this application. In the Divisional Court Buxton LJ
disagreed: 'We are indeed satisfied that the magistrate was wrong to think that
he lacked jurisdiction to act on a finding of abuse of process on *Hunter*
grounds'. The judgment in *Watts* is more fully considered at para **10.19**.

1   [1999] 2 Cr App Rep 188.
2   *Hunter v Chief Constable of West Midlands Police* [1982] AC 529.

Post-Bennett authorities—widening of magistrates' jurisdiction

10.17   Post-*Bennett* the next relevant authority is the judgment of
Lord Bingham CJ in *R v Staines Magistrates' Court, ex p Westfallen*. In his
judgment Lord Bingham considered the 'narrow category' of *Bennett*-type
abuse and concluded that Lord Griffiths was there 'plainly concerned with a
flouting of the rule of law and abuse of power by police and prosecuting
authorities'.

10.18   By the time of the judgment of Rose LJ sitting in the Court of Appeal
in *R v Mullen* the area of abuse jurisdiction beyond that of magistrates had
become characterised or described as a useful shorthand as '*Bennett*-type
abuse'. In *Mullen* Rose LJ described *Bennett*-type abuse as follows:

'it seems to us that *Bennett*-type abuse, where it would be offensive to justice
and propriety to try the defendant at all, is different both from the type of
abuse which renders a fair trial impossible and from all other cases where an
exercise of judicial discretion is called for. It arises not from the relationship
between the prosecution and the defendant but from the relationship
between the prosecution and the court. It arises from the courts' need to
exercise control over executive involvement in the whole prosecution
process, not limited to the trial itself'.[1]

The import of this definition was an attempt to clarify the dividing line between
the abuse categories available to magistrates and those which are not.
Respecting the dichotomy created by the House in *Bennett*, Rose LJ was
perhaps seeking to helpfully explain the parameters in a more clear and useful
way.

1   [1999] 3 WLR 777 at 791C.

10.19   The final authority to consider is *R v Belmarsh Magistrates' Court,
ex p Watts*.[1] The facts of the case were briefly as follows: Watts, an HM Customs

and Excise officer, had been an important prosecution witness in a trial leading to the conviction for drugs trafficking offences of the defendant. Subsequently and presumably as a reaction to later confiscation proceedings initiated against him, the defendant launched a private prosecution of Ms Watts alleging false defamatory libel and misfeasance. Following issuance of the summonses Watts contended that they were an abuse of process and the (private) prosecution should be stayed. The particular abuse alleged was that the defendant was in fact seeking to reopen the safety of his conviction and was therefore in breach of the rule established by the House of Lords in *Hunter v Chief Constable of the West Midlands Police.*[2]

1   [1999] 2 Cr App Rep 188.
2   [1982] AC 529.

10.20   While the magistrate held that the defendant's summonses did amount to a violation of the rule in *Hunter* he also held that because of the dichotomy of jurisdiction created in *Bennett* this meant that he had no jurisdiction to stay the proceedings as an abuse, this being a matter exclusively for the High Court. Accordingly, the magistrate declined to stay the proceedings and Ms Watts then appealed to the High Court in part contending that the magistrate was wrong in law to hold that he lacked the power to stay the proceedings. The ruling of the court was given by Buxton LJ. Buxton LJ concluded:

'Within the general jurisdiction ... there is a limited category of cases, involving infractions of the rule of law outside the narrow confines of the actual trial or court process, where the magistrates do not have jurisdiction, or alternatively as a matter of law should not exercise such jurisdiction as they may have ... Such cases should, as in *Bennett*, be addressed by ... the Divisional Court. That category is however a narrow one. It excludes every complaint that is directed at the fairness or propriety of the trial process itself[1].'

1   [1999] 2 Cr App Rep 188 at 195C.

10.21   Buxton LJ held that in all circumstances in alleged abuse short of *Bennett*-type abuse magistrates did enjoy a jurisdiction. On the facts of the case before him, Buxton LJ held that the magistrate did have jurisdiction to inquire into allegations concerning the bona fides of the prosecution and whether the prosecution had been commenced oppressively or unfairly. This would include an allegation of abuse arising out of a purported breach of the rule in *Hunter* and accordingly, the magistrate had wrongly decided that he lacked the jurisdiction to deal with that complaint. Having established this point of principle, Buxton LJ held that the defendant summonses were an abuse and stayed the proceedings.

Significance of Watts

10.22   In addition to seeking to clarify the dividing line between *Bennett*-type abuse and all other types of abuse with only the former being beyond the jurisdiction of magistrates, Buxton LJ's clear policy was to seek as far as possible to allow magistrates a discretion to determine abuse applications.

Moreover, the High Court does not wish to find itself regularly embroiled in abuse applications arising out of magistrates declining jurisdiction believing that they are unable to rule on an application. Magistrates should therefore accept, except in extreme and hopefully very rare circumstances, the role of dealing with abuse applications while respecting the split jurisdiction created in *Bennett*.

10.23 While holding that magistrates did enjoy a wide jurisdiction in this context Buxton LJ also made two further pronouncements. First, that where there was uncertainty as to which side of the dividing line an abuse application fell, then magistrates should remit the matter to the High Court adjourning the proceedings in the meantime. Secondly, in relation to cases which clearly did not fall into the *Bennett*-type abuse category Buxton LJ made clear that magistrates who still felt themselves unsuited to determining a particularly difficult or convoluted abuse application always possessed the discretion to decline jurisdiction and in effect tell the defendant to refer his complaint to the Divisional Court instead. The court will act as a sort of safety net or last resort for troubled magistrates, for as Buxton LJ stated:

> 'It will however, always be open to magistrates in cases that do not fall within the narrow *Bennett* category to decline jurisdiction, and require the matter to be pursued in the Divisional Court, whether because of the complexity or novelty of the point, or because of the length of investigation that is required. Any such decision by a magistrate, being one taken within the limits of his judgment, will be unlikely to be overturned in this court'.

10.24 One largely pragmatic advantage of allowing magistrates jurisdiction here is the obvious saving of time and legal cost gained by staying a case at the earliest opportunity. If there is an abuse which should result in the proceedings being halted then there is advantage to all concerned in magistrates being able to do so. From a defendant's perspective, it is probably also correct in principle that he should be able to complain about the proceedings being brought at the earliest opportunity.

Conclusions

10.25 On the basis of all the authorities listed above it is submitted that magistrates have jurisdiction to consider abuse applications in almost all circumstances. These circumstances can be categorised as follows:

(1) abuse complaints directed at the propriety or fairness of the trial process or procedure;

(2) abuse complaints concerning mala fides of the prosecution, investigations of the bona fides of the prosecution, or investigations into whether the prosecution had been instituted oppressively or unfairly;

(3) in cases of delay;

(4) in cases of alleged unfair manipulation of court procedures.

10.26 Further examples of instances where jurisdiction would exist, given the above headings, are non-availability of evidence type abuses, non-disclosure abuses and double jeopardy species of abuse. Finally, it is contended that a magistrate does not have jurisdiction in these particular areas:

(1) instances of abuse of process under the narrow category of *ex p Bennett*;

(2) illegality and abuse of power by police, prosecution authorities or government officials pursuant to ulterior motives or wrongful purposes in violation of international law and for fundamental human rights.

SENDING CASES UNDER S 51[1]

10.27 The provisions of s 51 have now substantially curtailed defence opportunities to make abuse of process applications in the magistrates' courts in relation to indictable only offences. The legislation has virtually abolished committal proceedings for these offences. This curtailment was inevitable given that:

> 'The purpose of sending defendants to the Crown Court pursuant to s 51 of the 1998 Act was to reduce delay in dealing with indictable only offences and related either-way offences or serious summary offences, so that the Crown Court was enabled to deal with management and progress of a trial from an early stage'.[2]

1   Crime and Disorder Act 1998, s 51.
2   See *Fehily v Governor of Wandsworth Prison* (2002) Times, 18 July, DC.

10.28 In the decision of *R v Salubi*,[1] however, Auld LJ held that the magistrates still retained a limited jurisdiction to stay cases for abuse even where their s 51(1) duty was to send indictable-only cases 'forthwith' to the Crown Court, albeit that 'such a case would be very rare'. Whilst identifying what may constitute such a rare circumstance, Auld LJ stated:

> 'Even in the rare cases where it might be appropriate to make an abuse of process application to a magistrates' court at the sending stage, it should be remembered that the onus is on the defence to establish bad faith or serious misconduct and that incorrect procedure based on lack of judgment does not suffice; … In most cases the Crown Court is likely to be better equipped to make such value judgments. Instances of possible bad faith might be the addition of an unmeritorious indictable-only charge in the late stages of committal proceedings for either-way offences, solely with the object of overcoming custody time limits or of overcoming evidential difficulties that would otherwise delay or defeat a committal'.[2]

1   *R v Salubi* [2002] EWHC 919 (Admin), [2002] 2 Cr App R 40 at 660.
2   At 670, para 21.

Summary trials

10.29 The timing of the making of any such application obviously depends on a variety of factors, the most important of which is usually the timing of service by the prosecution of its evidence on the defence. Absent a prosecution duty to act with expedition when the defendant is in custody so as to respect custody time limits and a magistrates' overall jurisdiction concerned with case management and delay, there is no timetable for the service of evidence. Furthermore, as practitioners will be aware, the peculiar feature remains in our law that there is no statutory obligation on the prosecution in relation to summary only matters to serve any evidence at all, although curiously there is an obligation to serve unused material. Having noted that, the 2005 Attorney-General's guidelines, which surpass the amended CPIA 1996's legislative requirements, recommend that prosecutors should 'provide to the defence all evidence upon which the Crown proposes to rely in a summary trial'.[1] The Attorney-General commended that the 'spirit of the Guidelines' should be followed equally in the Magistrates Courts.[2] The practitioner should also have regard to the Advance information provisions set out in Pt 21 of the Criminal Procedure Rules 2005.[3]

1   See the 2005 Attorney-General's Guidelines , at para 57.
2   See Guidelines, para 7.
3   SI 2005/384.

10.30   In *R (P)(A) v Leeds Youth Court*[1] the Divisional Court were required to consider the abuse jurisdiction of the magistrates in the context of a failure by the prosecution to serve advance information. The Youth Court had ordered that the prosecution disclose its case by a certain date, stating that the case would be dismissed upon a failure so to do. A differently constituted bench, however, chose to adjourn rather than dismiss the case upon a subsequent failure, whereupon the defence sought judicial review of the decision. The High Court held that the magistrates had no jurisdiction to stay proceedings for abuse of process in these circumstances, and that the only appropriate remedy, provided by the rules, was to adjourn proceedings.[2]

1   (2001) 5 Archbold News 1, DC.
2   See also *King v Kucharz* (1989) 153 JP 336.

10.31   There have been several recent authorities concerned with alleged abuse arising from non-disclosure by the prosecution of unused material and evidence prior to committal. The two important cases are *R v Stratford Magistrates, ex p Imbert*[1] and *R v DPP, ex p Lee*.[2]

1   [1999] 2 Cr App Rep 276, QBD.
2   [1999] 2 All ER 737.

10.32   In *R v DPP, ex p Lee* the fairness of the prosecution's refusal to make disclosure pre-committal to the defence was considered by the High Court. The prosecution contended that the code of practice does not require disclosure of unused material until post-committal when it would be regulated by the provisions of the code and CPIA. The defence contended that their case would be prejudiced if no disclosure was made until a subsequent stage in the proceedings, ie post-committal, because it would delay defence preparation generally and hinder the making of a successful contested bail application.

10.33   Faced with compelling arguments from both sides, Kennedy LJ held that the prosecution did have a residual common law obligation to make pre-committal disclosure. Kennedy LJ provided examples of circumstances where such an obligation would arise. Two relevant examples were first, where the disclosure of unused material could reasonably be expected to assist in making an application for bail and secondly, where such material could assist an application made in the magistrates' court for a stay based on abuse. While Kennedy LJ was concerned to prevent the notion arising that 'full-blown' common law disclosure is required pre-committal, he was also anxious to ensure that the defence were not unfairly prejudiced by the provisions of the CPIA.

10.34   *Ex p Lee* is therefore authority for the proposition that there is a common law duty of disclosure from the prosecution to make disclosure of material which would assist defence preparation at the earliest possible opportunity in the proceedings. Accordingly, a failure to abide by this duty may subsequently found an application for a stay. It is submitted that while in this regard the decision in *Ex p Lee* is undoubtedly correct, it is entirely at odds with the disclosure regime created by the CPIA which specifically postponed in indictable proceedings issues of disclosure until the committal stage had passed. Moreover, via its fundamental carrot-and-stick approach, rewarding defendants who made defence statements with secondary prosecution disclosure and penalising with inferences of guilt those who do not, the CPIA certainly envisages that disclosure of unused material appertaining to a possible abuse application would only occur once a defence statement had been served. *Ex p Lee* has the potential to upset this delicate but fundamental approach to prosecution disclosure created by the CPIA.

Committal proceedings

10.35   With regard to committal proceedings, it is obviously sensible that the abuse application be made and determined before the committal itself commences. A successful application in this circumstance means that the committal stage may never be reached. In *R v Worcester Magistrates' Court, ex p Leavesley*[1] the question arose of whether magistrates who hear and adjudicate on an abuse application were in effect acting as examining justices in a committal hearing. In *ex p Leavesley* the magistrates rejected the defence's abuse application and then adjourned the proceedings. Following the adjournment, a fresh (stipendiary) magistrate was appointed to hear the committal but the defence objected to this substitution. The High Court held that a committal did not commence until either the prosecution opened its case, or called witnesses or took some other step which was pertinent to committal. An abuse application was not pertinent to committal and so a different constitution of magistrates could hear the abuse application on the one hand and the committal on the other.

1   (1993) Times, 14 January; *R v Worcester Magistrates' Court, ex p Bell* (1992) 157 JP 921.

10.36   From a magistrates' court perspective it is usually preferable, bearing in mind the frequent significant factual overlap between the making of an abuse application and the submission of no case to answer, for the same magistrates whenever possible to hear an abuse application and deal with committal. If not, then a problem may arise where the defence having made one unsuccessful abuse application then proceed at the later committal hearing to make another arguing that there has been a significant change of circumstances. As a magistrates' court is not a court of record it would perhaps be difficult to resist such a representation and so refuse to hear the renewed application.

10.37 However, from a defence perspective it is usually preferable for the abuse application and the committal hearing to be heard separately. If the two hearings are disconnected then it follows that there is no reason why abuse applications cannot precede any other application or hearing in a magistrates' court, for example plea before venue and mode of trial. There may be positive advantages to making an abuse application prior to these hearings, for example when the defendant will plead guilty if the abuse application fails. If the application is made before a plea before venue then his/her mitigation is fully preserved.

Transfer for trial cases

10.38 The 'sending' system introduced by the Crime and Disorder Act 1998, s 51 is largely a replica of the transfer system in relation to serious or complex fraud cases contained in the Criminal Justice Act 1987 and sexual and violent offences concerning children contained in the Criminal Justice Act 1988.[1] The issue is whether, under such a regime, magistrates possess the jurisdiction to determine abuse applications if they are made before the transfer takes place? It is submitted that there is no clear authority on this subject but bearing in mind that under all the relevant statutes, a notice of transfer served by a prosecutor in effect extinguishes the jurisdiction of magistrates over the relevant proceedings, save for matters concerning bail and public funding, it would appear that if this notice is served on the court before any abuse application is begun, the magistrates would be prevented from hearing and determining it. Certainly the underlying aim of all of the relevant statutes is to allow a Crown Court judge to be seised of an indictable case as soon as possible and it would therefore seem anomalous and contrary to the transfer scheme if, despite this, magistrates could embark on a complex abuse application.

1   See the 2005 Practice Direction (Crown Court: Classification and Allocation of Business) [2005] 1 WLR 2215.

In the Crown Court can the defence repeat its abuse application previously rejected by magistrates?

10.39 This issue was in part considered by the Divisional Court in, *ex p Hole*[1] and *ex p Malpas*.[2] The Divisional Court held that the defence is not prevented or debarred from advancing the same or indeed even a different abuse application in the Crown Court when one had previously been made before magistrates. The Crown Court can consider the application de novo and in effect therefore the defence is allowed a second attempt. In practice the defence rarely take advantage of these two chances preferring for tactical reasons 'to keep the powder dry' for the Crown Court judge; for example, by virtue of a wish to preserve the weapon of surprise or to minimise the possibility of the prosecution serving notices of further evidence to cure any exposed deficiency in its case.

1   *R v Cardiff Magistrates' Court, ex p Hole* [1997] COD 84.
2   *R v Barry Magistrates' Court, ex p Malpas* [1998] COD 90.

CASE STATED AND JUDICIAL REVIEW OF THE MAGISTRATES' COURT

10.40   Case stated is a remedy of ancient origin. It developed at a time when there was no Court of Appeal in criminal cases. It was a facility whereby the opinion of the High Court could be taken on a difficult area of law by a quarter session. In the Crown Court the procedure is now governed by the Supreme Court Act 1981, s 28(1). No appeal lies by way of case stated on an interlocutory matter from the Crown Court. In *Loade v DPP*[1] the court decided that 'any order, judgment or decision' in s 28(1) meant the final decision.

1   [1990] 1 QB 1052.

Appeal by way of case stated

10.41   Appeals by way of case stated are relatively uncommon in the context of abuse of process. Indeed, authorities on the subject are few, which is unsurprising given the limitations inherent in such an avenue of appeal. Case stated is a procedure whereby the High Court is able to review the decisions of inferior courts in relation to points of law. Unlike judicial review, case stated is not generally concerned with how a decision was reached, but only as to its legal merit. If an appeal was therefore to be based for instance on an alleged breach of natural justice by magistrates, the general rule suggests that judicial review is the appropriate option.

10.42   This right of appeal, under the Magistrates' Courts Act 1980, s 3, states that an aggrieved person may question a magistrate on the ground that:

(1)   he is acting in excess of the jurisdiction; or

(2)   he is wrong in law.

Availability of case stated

10.43   In *Atkinson v United States Government*[1], a case concerned with extradition proceedings, Lord Reid opined that there was no power to state a case unless there had first been some final adjudication.[2] It is, however, submitted that the Magistrates' Court Act 1980, s 111(1) does provide for the possibility of the availability of this remedy. In *Environment Agency v Stanford*[3] it was held that in summary proceedings a decision against the prosecution on grounds of abuse is final and is therefore capable of being the subject of case stated. *Stanford*, however, did not deal with the situation where a decision adverse to the Crown in committal proceedings can similarly be so subject.

1   [1971] AC 197.
2   [1971] AC 197 at 234.
3   [1998] COD 373, QBD.

10.44   The procedure is applicable where there are no factual disputes, for the High Court is bound by the findings of fact as stated by the magistrates' court (except where it is contended there was no evidence on which one could have arrived at a particular finding of fact). The aggrieved party may question 'the conviction, order, determination or other proceeding of the court' and the remedy is available to both prosecution and defence. The majority of appeals by way of case stated are based on attempts to overturn either a summary conviction or a summary acquittal. Indeed, it is only available where there has been a final determination in the proceedings, such as a conviction, sentence, acquittal, or (as in abuse cases) an order to stay proceedings.[1] Given this restriction, where a magistrates' court has ruled against the defence at a pre-trial review or preliminary hearing, it has no jurisdiction to state what is, in essence, an 'interlocutory' case throughout the hearing.[2]

1   See *DPP v Karl Metten* (22 January 1999, unreported); and *Environment Agency v Stanford* [1998] COD 373.
2   See *Streames v Copping* (1985) 149 JP 305; which was followed in *R v Greater Manchester Justices, ex p Aldi GmbH & Co KG* (1994) 159 JP 717.

10.45   For examples of cases where the prosecution have successfully appealed, by way of case stated, against magistrates' decisions to stay proceedings for abuse of process, see *DPP v Jimale*[1] and also *DPP v Chalmers*.[2] In a further decision of the High Court, where an issue arose as to whether case stated or judicial review was the more appropriate remedy for challenging a magistrates' decision to stay, Sullivan J in the *Sevenoaks Magistrates' Court* case[3] stated that:

'In many cases it may well be more convenient to challenge the alleged irregularity by way of case stated, because there will then be no room for doubt as to the facts found by the magistrates and their reasons for allowing the application'.

1   [2001] Crim LR 138.
2   [2000] COD 2.
3   *R (on the application of Tunbridge Wells Borough Council) v Sevenoaks Magistrates' Court* [2001] EWHC Admin 897.

10.46   It is submitted, however, that as the prosecution in practice very rarely accept all the factual assertions made by the defence in abuse applications, so the case stated route is generally inappropriate and the judicial review route is almost always to be preferred. On a purely tactical point, however, if it is felt that the case stated is available the question then arises of whether the route should be pursued in respect of the magistrates' ruling. Alternatively, should the matter be left for the judgment of the trial judge?

10.47   There seems, in principle, only two advantages why the case stated route might be preferred. First, if the magistrate has not provided any reasoning when rejecting an abuse submission or holding it, this remedy can be used to expose the underlying reasoning. Secondly, the case stated procedure does not require leave from any superior court prior to the hearing.

JUDICIAL REVIEW

Applications for judicial review

10.48   An application to the High Court for judicial review may be made by either the defence or the prosecution, in respect of any ruling or decision of the magistrates' court. Judicial review, which is designed to be expeditious, is not an appeal from a decision, but rather a review of the manner in which it was made.[1]

1   See *Chief Constable of North Wales Police v Evans* [1982] 1 WLR 1155; the procedure for judicial review is governed by the Supreme Court Act 1981, ss 29–31 and RSC Ord 53, as amended; note the revised Ord 53 and the new CPR Practice Directions.

10.49   In the context of abuse of process applications, the case law suggests that the two most sought after prerogative orders are prohibition[1] and certiorari.[2] The order of prohibition would have the effect, in essence, of having the proceedings stayed, for such an order would prevent magistrates from starting or continuing with a hearing. The object of the order is to prevent magistrates from acting in a manner which is either inconsistent with or in excess of their jurisdiction. In practice this may be used, for example, to challenge a decision to commence or continue with a summary trial or committal proceedings, the abuse of process arguments having been rejected, possibly at an earlier preliminary hearing. The order of certiorari, by way of contrast, would have the effect of quashing the magistrates' decision to permit the proceedings to continue. Less common remedies in the abuse context would be found in mandamus and in declarations. In the case of *Hindle*[3] one finds an example of a case where an order of mandamus was sought to oblige the magistrate to exercise the abuse of process discretion to stay proceedings.

1   See *R v Brentford Justices, ex p Wong* (1980) 73 Cr App R 67; *R v Horsham Justices, ex p Reeves* (1980) 75 Cr App R 236n; *R v Derby Magistrates' Court, ex p Brooks* (1984) 80 Cr App R 164; *R v Willesden Justices, ex p Clemmings* (1987) 87 Cr App R 280; *R v Telford Justices, ex p Badham* [1991] 2 WLR 866.
2   See *R v Guildford Magistrates' Court, ex p Healy* [1983] 1 WLR 108; *R v Liverpool Stipendiary Magistrate, ex p Ellison* [1990] RTR 220n; *R v Rotherham Justices, ex p Brough* [1991] Crim LR 522; *R v Croydon Justices, ex p Dean* (1993) 98 Cr App R 76.
3   See *R v Newcastle-upon-Tyne Justices, ex p Hindle* [1984] 1 All ER 770.

10.50   Where magistrates have ruled that it is permissible for proceedings to continue, there have also been instances of defendants seeking declarations that such decisions were unlawful.[1] The prosecution, on the other hand, also have an interest in the remedies available through judicial review. Such interest would normally lie in the orders of mandamus and certiorari, in the reverse abuse circumstances. For while they may seek mandamus to oblige a magistrate to allow proceedings to continue,[1] equally they may seek an order of certiorari to quash a magistrate's decision to stay proceedings.[2]

1   See *R v Colwyn Justices, ex p DPP* (1988) 154 JP 989; *R v Bow Street Stipendiary Magistrate, ex p DPP and Cherry* (1989) 91 Cr App R 283; *R v Bow Street Metropolitan Stipendiary Magistrate, ex p DPP* (1992) 95 Cr App R 9.
2   See *Ex p DPP and Cherry*; and *R v Bow Street MSM, ex p DPP*.

The grounds for judicial review

10.51   The grounds on which the High Court may grant relief fall broadly into the following three categories, namely:

(1)   *Illegality* – where the magistrates' court has exceeded or abused its powers, or made an error in law;

(2)   *Procedural impropriety* – where the court has acted in breach of the rules of natural justice;

(3)   *Irrationality* – where the court has reached a decision, which no reasonable tribunal, properly directed and on the evidence, could have reached.

10.52   Defendants seeking a review of a failed abuse application in the magistrates' court will be seeking to argue that the magistrates acted irrationally or were *Wednesbury*[1] unreasonable. In other words, on the merits of the application put forward by the defence, the application ought to have succeeded.

1   *Associated Provincial Picture House Ltd v Wednesbury Corpn* [1948] 1 KB 223.

Approach of the High Court

10.53   On numerous occasions the High Court has shown itself to be unwilling to become a de facto Court of Appeal in relation to failed abuse applications made in the magistrates' court. The overall policy of the High Court in relation to judicial review proceedings arising out of criminal proceedings was set out by Lord Bingham CJ in *R v DPP, ex p Kebilene*:[1]

'Where the grant of leave to move judicial review would delay or obstruct the conduct of criminal proceedings which ought, in the public interest, to be resolved with all appropriate expedition, the court will always scrutinise the application with the greatest care, both to satisfy itself that there are sound reasons for making the application and satisfy itself that there are no discretionary grounds (such as delay or the availability of alternative remedies or vexatious conduct by the applicant) which should lead it to refuse leave. The court would be very slow to intervene where the applicant's complaint is one that can be met by appropriate orders or directions in the criminal proceedings ...'.[2]

1   [1999] 3 WLR 175; see also the House of Lords' judgment *R v DPP, ex p Kebilene* [2000] 2 AC 326.
2   At 183.

10.54   Commenting on this principle, Lord Steyn in *Kebeline* said:

'There is a common law principle ... which provides a strong presumption against the Divisional Court entertaining a judicial review application where the complaint can be raised within the criminal trial and appeal process'.

10.55   It is submitted that the root of this principle can be traced to the judgment of Lord Mustill in *Neill v North Antrim Magistrates' Court*:[1]

'it is, however, one thing to hold that it is for the magistrates to rule on admissibility, if invited to do so, so that a decision on the issue must in principle be reviewable, and quite another to say that the grant of relief should follow as a matter of course. I wholly share the sentiments of those who, over the years, have exclaimed in dismay at the vision of the streams of applications by persons committed for trial seeking to put off the evil day by drawing attention to supposed errors in the application at the committal stage of the high technical rules of criminal evidence. It is only in the case of a really substantial error leading to a demonstrable injustice that the judge in the Divisional Court should contemplate the granting of leave to move'.[2]

1   (1992) 97 Cr App R 121.
2   (1992) 97 Cr App R 121 at 131.

10.56   The principle expressed in this case was reaffirmed by the House of Lords in *R v Bedwellty Justices, ex p Williams*.[1]

1   [1997] AC 225.

10.57   With regard to applications for judicial review based on an alleged abuse of process application which has failed before the magistrates, two authorities make the position plain. First, the judgment of Brook LJ in *R v Liverpool City Justices and Crown Prosecution Service, ex p Price*:[1]

'It still did not seem sufficiently well-known that it is only in a very exceptional case that the High Court will exercise its supervisory jurisdiction to intervene and quash a decision by justices in the exercise of their discretion not to stay criminal proceedings for abuse of process. The test was not whether the court agreed with the decision which the magistrates reached, but whether their decision was so plainly irrational and untenable that no reasonable bench of justices, properly directed, could have reached it'.[2]

1   (1998) 162 JP 766, [1998] COD 453 at 455.
2   See also *R v Willesden Justices, ex p Clemmings* (1987) 87 Cr App R 280; *R v Barry Magistrates' Court, ex p Malpas* [1998] COD 90; *R v Canterbury and St Augustine Justices, ex p Turner* (1983) 147 JP 193.

10.58   The High Court is, therefore, expressing the view that the burden of proof on the defence is high and necessarily higher than the burden which it will face in the Crown Court where, if a Crown Court judge disagrees with a magistrate's decision, he can overrule it.

10.59   In *R v Bow Street Magistrates' Court, ex p Finch and Bossino*[1] an application was made for judicial review of the committal, in part because of the magistrates' rejection of abuse submission, where Auld LJ held:

'the courts have made plain that stays by any court on the ground of abuse of process should only be granted in the most exceptional circumstances and where a defendant is able to demonstrate that he has suffered serious prejudice. This is particularly so in committal proceedings before magistrates where the final airing of the evidence and decision at trial are yet to come'.[2]

1   (9 June 1999, unreported).

2   At p 9 of the transcript. Here a complaint of covert non-disclosure by the prosecution at committal of edited parts of tapes was relied on. Auld LJ held that the court of trial would be best placed to determine the propriety and effect of this alleged non-disclosure.

A procedural note

10.60   In *Ebrahim*[1] Brooke LJ, in the High Court, set out the following procedural guidance for practitioners and magistrates alike, namely:

'If a ruling on a stay application is made in a lower court, the court should give its reasons, however briefly, and it is the professional duty of the advocates for the parties to take a note of these. If the decision is to be challenged on judicial review, this court will expect to see a note of the lower court's reasons before deciding whether to grant permission for the application to proceed. If any relevant oral evidence was given, this court will hope that an agreed note can be prepared, summarising its effect'.

1   *R (Ebrahim) v Feltham Magistrates' Court; Monat v DPP* [2001] EWHC Admin 130, [2001] 1 WLR 1293, DC.

Procedural tactics in summary cases

10.61   An accused in summary proceedings who has made a failed abuse application before magistrates faces a choice of avenues. He can seek judicial review of the refusal in the High Court or instead exercise the right for a retrial in the Crown Court. The existence of an accused having this choice was doubted in *R v Peterborough Magistrates' Court, ex p Dowler*[1] which questioned whether an accused should have a right to apply for judicial review when there was a subsisting right of appeal to the Crown Court. However, in *R v Hereford Magistrates' Court, ex p Rowlands*[2], *Dowler* in this regard was doubted and the existence of a choice affirmed. However, bearing in mind the present largely unwelcoming attitude of the High Court as considered above, in most cases and unless the accused feels very confident as to the strength of his abuse claim, it would seem that the accused should opt for the Crown Court over the High Court.

1   [1996] 2 Cr App R 561.
2   [1998] QB 110.

10.62   There are also other disadvantages which appertain to the High Court practice which favour the Crown Court. Judicial review is not a suitable forum for a re-examination of facts found by justices and a detailed reassessment of how such findings should determine the final determination. The High Court by its nature has a need for expedition in its hearings and it will not be sympathetic to being asked to reconsider complex facts especially when it is probably known that there is a judge in the Crown Court available with greater ability and time to consider such matters. The authors have experienced judges sitting in the High Court stating that while it would seem that the applicant has an arguable abuse case on the merits, it is the trial judge who will be best suited to determining this and accordingly so have refused leave to move for judicial review.

10.63   It should also be appreciated that before a Crown Court judge, the accused has the potential to request a voir dire and therefore the calling of live evidence, a facility unavailable in the High Court which is purely based on statement of truth or affidavit evidence. Perhaps finally it can rarely be in the defendant's interest to embark on a judicial review application which is unlikely to succeed and thereon renew it in the Crown Court. An adverse finding in the High Court, even if it is only at the 'permission'[1] stage, with admittedly there being no detailed consideration of the facts, is still nonetheless unlikely to seem appealing to a Crown Court judge.

1   'Permission' being the new term for 'leave', per the CPR practice directions.

10.64   However, if the judicial review is to be pursued then applications must promptly be made in both courts. Bearing in mind the superiority of the High Court over the Crown Court it would appear necessary that, when lodging an appeal with the Crown Court, that court be asked to adjourn the hearing of that appeal until the outcome of the judicial review application. In relation to this application, it should be made clear that an appeal has been lodged with the Crown Court but it has been asked to be adjourned.

THE CROWN COURT

Appeals to the Crown Court

10.65   A defendant who has been convicted, after summary proceedings before the justices, may appeal to the Crown Court against his conviction.[1] The appeal is by way of rehearing and, consequently, there would be nothing to prevent the defence practitioner from raising the same abuse of process argument as adopted in the lower court, or indeed in amending the same, or trying a new approach altogether. Likewise there is no obligation on the prosecution to put their case forward, on the same basis or in the same manner, as was the case before the justices.[2]

1   See MCA 1980, ss 108–110, Criminal Procedure Rules 2005 (SI 2005/384), rr 63.1–63.4, and
     Supreme Court Act 1981, s 79(3).
2   See *Hingley-Finch v DPP* (1998) 1 Archbold News 2, DC.

10.66   If either or both of the parties seek to call evidence in support of an abuse of process application, it is contended that they must first, if a short voir dire is to be held at the outset of the appeal, seek the court's leave so to do (as with any other such application before a Crown Court judge). It will be within the judge's discretion as to what evidence may be allowed or not, whether or not it was called in the lower court, the criteria for such discretion presumably being one of relevance. As is the case with any appeal against conviction, the practitioner will no doubt want to advise the appellant that the appeal will put the sentence at large together with a possible liability as to costs, in the event of an adverse finding or conviction. No grounds of appeal need actually be provided (so long as the notice states that the appeal is against conviction, as opposed to sentence) within the 21 days of sentence. Nevertheless the better practice is to briefly state the basis of the appeal, in general terms, putting both the court and prosecution on notice.

10.67 In the *Ebrahim* decision Brooke LJ opined that the Crown Court appellant, raising a complaint of abuse of process, should not apply for the proceedings to be stayed. The appropriate course rather was to apply for an order allowing the appeal and quashing the conviction on the grounds that the original trial was unfair, and that the unfairness was of such a nature that it could not be remedied on appeal.

Abuse of process applications in the Crown Court

10.68 Once a case has been committed or transferred for trial in the Crown Court, the first occasion on which it would be appropriate to raise the question of an abuse of process application is normally at a Plea and Case Management Hearing (PCMH) (or a preparatory hearing if a transfer case).[1] At a Plea and Case Management Hearing the defence would be expected to inform the court of 'any point of law anticipated' in addition to a list of other obligations which both parties have in relation to general matters of case management and preparation. A similar situation applies to the preparatory hearings regime whether they be for serious or complex cases under Pt III of the Criminal Procedure and Investigations Act 1996 or serious or complex fraud cases under the Criminal Justice Act 1987, as amended by CJA 2003.

1 See Practice Direction (Criminal Proceedings: Consolidation), para 4.41 (as substituted by Practice Direction (Criminal Proceedings: Further Directions) [2007] 1 WLR 1790); re Preparatory hearings, see CPIA 1996, s 31, as amended by CJA 2003, ss 310(5), 331 and 332, Sch 36, paras 65 and 67, and Sch 37, Pt 3.

10.69 In relation to pre-trial hearings, which are now governed by the CPIA 1996, s 39 (as amended by CJA 2003), the special feature that rulings made in such hearings have, pursuant to s 40 of that Act, is that they are binding until the determination of all the proceedings. Section 40(3)–(5) reads as follows:

'(3) Subject to subsection (4), a ruling made under this section has binding effect from the time it is made until the case against the accused or, if there is more than one, against each of them is disposed of; and the case against an accused is disposed of if—
(a) he is acquitted or convicted, or
(b) the prosecutor decides not to proceed with the case against him.

(4) A judge may discharge or vary (or further vary) a ruling made under this section if it appears to him that it is in the interests of justice to do so; and a judge may act under this subsection—
(a) on an application by a party to the case, or
(b) of the judge's own motion.

(5) No application may be made under subsection (4) unless there has been a material change of circumstances since the ruling was made or if a previous application has been made, since the application (or last application) was made.'

10.70 It is submitted that the effect of this more formalised regime is that while a trial judge always has the discretion to review a pre-trial ruling made by him, it means that the defence, if they wish to renew a previously unsuccessful abuse application, will have to establish pursuant to subs (5) a material change of circumstances. This may not be easy and so it is submitted that an abuse application should not be mounted until the optimum moment when all material evidence has been gathered and arguments refined.

Challenging adverse rulings of the Crown Court

10.71   Whether the High Court has power to entertain an application for judicial review arising out of a ruling made by a Crown Court judge is a matter, not of common law principle, but of statutory construction. Section 29(3) of the Supreme Court Act 1981 provides:

'In relation to the jurisdiction of the Crown Court, other than its jurisdiction in matters relating to trial on indictment, the High Court shall have all such jurisdiction to make orders of mandamus, prohibition or certiorari as the High Court possesses in relation to the jurisdiction of an inferior court [in matters relating to trial on indictment]'.

10.72   Section 29(3) therefore prevents a decision made by the Crown Court from being challenged by an application for judicial review if it was deemed to be relating to a matter relating to trial on indictment. The same rule is applicable to appeals by way of case stated from the Crown Court.[1]

1   Supreme Court Act 1981, s 28.

10.73   The rationale for s 29(3) was explained by Lord Bridge in *Re Smalley*[1] as follows:

'it is not difficult to discern a sensible legislative purpose in excluding appeal or judicial review of any decision affecting the conduct of a trial on indictment, whether given in the course of the trial or by way of pre-trial directions. In any such case to allow an appellate or review process might … seriously delay the trial. If it is the prosecutor who is aggrieved by such a decision, it is no way surprising that he has no remedy, since prosecutors have never enjoyed rights of appeal or review when unsuccessful in trials on indictment. If, on the other hand, the defendant is so aggrieved, he will have his remedy by way of appeal against conviction …'.

1   See *Re Smalley* [1985] AC 622 at 642–643.

10.74   This explanation was approved by Lord Slynn (speaking for a unanimous House) in *Re Ashton*.[1] In *Ashton* the trial judge had refused an application to stay the trial for grounds of abuse and judicial review of this refusal was sought. The decisions of *Re Ashton* and *Re Smalley* were applied in *R (Snelgrove) v Woolwich Crown Court* in the context of a failed attempt to judicially review an unsuccessful dismissal application.[2] While the position which Lord Bridge commented upon above has changed, given that prosecutors do now enjoy the right to appeal a terminating ruling, the authors do not anticipate any movement in the current position. Crown Court Judges' rulings on abuse of process are likely to continue to remain outside the ambit of any application for judicial review.

1   See *Re Ashton* [1994] 1 AC 9.
2   [2005] 1 Cr App R 18.

10.75   In relation to a future application for judicial review where a Crown Court judge is refusing to hold a prosecution to be an abuse of process, by reason of an alleged breach of the European Convention, the House of Lords held in *R v DPP, ex p Kebilene* that s 29(3) would likewise prohibit such an application.[1]

1   See for example the judgment of Lord Steyn at p 9 of transcript (1999) Times, 2 November.

Preparatory hearings and interlocutory appeals

10.76   The preparatory hearing regime introduced by the Criminal Justice Act 1987 was a central part of the new scheme for serious fraud trials. One of the radical concepts introduced by the Act was that of interlocutory appeals allowing the parties to appeal to the Court of Appeal pre-trial any ruling on a point of law which could affect the outcome of a trial. Section 9(11) of the Act granted this right of interlocutory appeal in respect of such rulings made during a preparatory hearing.

10.77   In the recent House of Lords decision of *Regina v H*[1] a significantly new approach was adopted to the scope of these interlocutory appeals. Their Lordships overruled the previous line of authority of *Re Gunarwardena,*[2] which had held abuse of process applications fell outside CJA 1987, s 7(1).

1   Reported at [2007] 2 W.L.R. 364
2   [1990] 91 Cr App R 55.

10.78   In *Regina v H* it was held that the purposes for which a preparatory hearing could be held, pursuant to s 7(1) of the 1987 Act, should be given a broad and generous interpretation, and that the aim of those purposes was the efficient and expeditious disposal of criminal proceedings so as to reduce the amount of time which would otherwise be wasted. In his commentary on this decision, Professor Ormerod[1] discusses this apparently new found right of defence appeal, as follows:

> 'A majority of the House has arguably accepted that a decision to stay or make other terminating rulings may be made at a preparatory hearing, under s.9, and as a consequence, be appealed by the defence if rejected. This might be seen as a useful balance to the Crown's right of appeal under section 58 of the Criminal Justice Act 2003, but arguments will now no doubt arise as to whether an application to stay for abuse should be delayed until a preparatory hearing occurs (and D has been arraigned) in order to secure the chance of a defence appeal if rejected.'

1   [2007] Crim LR 731–735.

Decisions which do not relate to trial on indictment

10.79   Appeal by way of case stated or judicial review are both possible options open to an applicant seeking to question a Crown Court decision in a matter not relating to trial on indictment.[1] A Crown Court decision to allow or dismiss an appeal from a magistrates' court would clearly fall within that category and thus allow the unsuccessful party a further appeal, from the Crown Court to the Divisional Court, by case stated. This also applies to an aggrieved prosecutor who had a summary conviction overturned, or else, to a defendant who was convicted for the second time, on appeal to the Crown Court. An appellant contemplating an appeal by case stated, on the basis of some form of abuse of process submission, must have regard to the fact that an appeal would only lie on the ground that the Crown Court decision was either wrong in law or in excess of jurisdiction. The principles which govern the granting of relief by way of judicial review of a Crown Court decision, are broadly the same as those discussed at para **10.51** in relation to judicial review of magistrates' courts decisions.[2]

1   See the Supreme Court Act 1981, ss 28 and 29(3).
2   See also, in relation to the powers of the High Court, *R v Chelmsford Crown Court, ex p Chief Constable of Essex Police* [1994] 99 Cr App R 59, DC: and *R v Leeds Crown Court, ex p Barlow* [1989] RTR 246, DC.

APPEALS TO THE COURT OF APPEAL AGAINST ADVERSE RULINGS IN THE CROWN COURT

10.80   As a result of the amendment to the Criminal Appeal Act 1968, s 2[1] the single criterion for interference by the Court of Appeal with a conviction reached by a jury is now its unsafety. The amended s 2(1) is as follows:

'Subject to the provisions of this Act, the Court of Appeal—

(a)   shall allow an appeal against conviction if they think that the conviction is unsafe; and

(b)   shall dismiss such an appeal in any other case'.

1   By virtue of the Criminal Appeal Act 1995.

10.81   The court's jurisdiction is entirely statutory and it depends on interpretation of the word 'unsafe'. What does 'unsafe' mean? In the absence of any statutory definition, this crucial word has been the subject of debate by lawyers, academics and judges alike. Sir John Smith, in his prescient 1995 article, predicted that the powers of the Court of Appeal to allow an appeal against conviction were in danger of being severely curtailed (albeit that was never the intention of the Royal Commission, the Home Office or Parliament) on the basis of the simple rules of statutory construction.[1] As it was to transpire, the deletion by the CAA 1995 of the second limb criteria 'or unsatisfactory', 'wrong decision of any question of law' and 'material irregularity' found in the 1968 Act was to cause significant difficulties in the years to come for practitioners seeking to argue abuse of process as a ground of appeal. This was largely because the Court of Appeal in some cases drew a restrictive and narrow definition of 'unsafe' which appeared to rule out certain forms of abuse of process as a route to appeal.

1   See Sir John Smith 'The Criminal Appeal Act 1995' [1995] Crim LR 920, his commentary at 1997 CLR 48 and Professor JR Spencer 'When is a conviction 'unsafe" (1998) 5 Archbold News.

10.82   Against a background of uncertainty and ambiguity in the case law, the lowest point for abuse of process as a ground of appeal, was the decision of *R v Chalkley and Jeffries*[1] which defined 'unsafe' in a most narrow fashion. Recently, however, the pendulum appears to have swung strongly back in favour of a broader interpretation of 'unsafe' as in the case of *R v Mullen*[2] where the Court of Appeal acknowledged the various circumstances in which abuse of process submissions could lead to successful appeals against conviction.

1   (1998) 2 Cr App R 79.
2   [2000] QB 520, CA.

10.83   Before turning to an analysis of the recent case law on the subject, it is proposed to start by briefly looking at the pre-1995 Act practice of the Court of Appeal (which is still of relevance in the light of *R v Mullen*).

Pre-1995 Act practice

10.84   In the 1984 decision in *Heston-Francois,*[1] the Court of Appeal acknowledged abuse of process as a ground of appeal. Lord Justice Watkins stated that:

'Where there has been oppressive conduct savouring of abuse of process, it seems clear that the Court of Appeal ... may quash a conviction on the ground that it is "unsatisfactory" or "unsafe".'

He added that the Court of Appeal was well placed to decide whether or not a particular accused suffered any actual prejudice in the course of a trial. In 1992, the court reaffirmed this doctrine as a ground of appeal in the *Attorney-General's Reference (No 1 of 1990).*[2]

1   *R v Heston-Francois* (1984) 78 Cr App R 209.
2   *A-G's Reference* (1992) 95 Cr App R 296.

10.85   One of the other popular catch phrases of the Court of Appeal pre-1995 was the 'lurking doubt' approach formulated by Widgery LJ in *Cooper.*[1] This was an alternative approach to considering a conviction as being unsafe or unsatisfactory. However, in *Farrow*[2] the court denigrated the continued use of this phrase, arguing that unsafety was a simpler, briefer and therefore a superior concept.

1   *R v Cooper* [1969] 1 QB 267, 53 Cr App R 82.
2   See *R v F* [1999] Crim LR 306.

10.86   The other significant issue which concerned the role of the court was its jurisdiction to hold a conviction unsafe or unsatisfactory when the defendant has unequivocally pleaded guilty. As a plea of guilty is said to be the best evidence of a defendant's guilt, how then could the court seek to upset this? In suitable circumstances this paradox did not trouble the court. For example, in two cases concerned with the cause celebre of the Arms to Iraq affair, *Schlesinger* and *Blackledge,* the appellants had pleaded guilty. The investigation by Sir Richard Scott however, revealed that prior to the respective trials, important evidence which undermined the prosecution's case had not been disclosed and accordingly when the defendants decided to plead guilty they had done so without knowledge of this abuse by the prosecution. In *Schlesinger* and *Blackledge* the court was in no doubt that the appellant's convictions were unsafe and unsatisfactory. Prosecution machinations had deprived the appellants of their right to a fair trial, they had pleaded guilty on a false basis and therefore their convictions could be overturned.

Post-1995 Act but pre-Mullen case law

10.87   A better understanding of the *Mullen* decision will no doubt be reached by a brief review of the earlier authorities, which place it in a proper context. In *R v Graham*[1] the Court of Appeal held that the amended version of s 2(1) pursuant to the 1995 Act, was intended to focus attention on one question only, namely whether the court considered the conviction unsafe. Where the court was satisfied, despite any misdirection or irregularity in the conduct of the trial or any fresh evidence, that the conviction was nonetheless safe the appeal would be dismissed. So arguably if the court felt that the trial judge should have granted an abuse application and stayed the proceedings on the evidence before him but nonetheless the trial was fair then according to this logic, the conviction could still nonetheless be safe.

1   [1997] 1 Cr App R 302.

10.88   In *R v Chalkley* the appellant had pleaded guilty following an adverse s 78 ruling as to the admissibility of certain highly damaging evidence. It was contended that if the ruling of the trial judge was wrong in law then this should lead to the quashing of his conviction. The court found this argument legally erroneous. An irregularity in the trial procedure including an error of law by the judge, which might prior to amendment by the 1995 Act have rendered a conviction unsatisfactory, is not of itself a ground for quashing a conviction. Now it is only a ground if it leads on to the conclusion that the conviction is for some reason unsafe. The Court of Appeal held that, when considering an appeal against conviction the previous tests of 'unsatisfactoriness' and 'material irregularity' were no longer at the disposal of the court, save as aids in determining the safety of a conviction. Accordingly, the court held that it had no power to allow an appeal against conviction which was not considered unsafe, albeit that in some regard the conviction was unsatisfactory.

10.89   In relation to a plea of guilty the court held that a conviction here would only be unsafe where the consequence of an incorrect ruling of law on admitted facts was to leave an accused with no legal escape from a verdict of guilty on those facts. A conviction, however, would not normally be unsafe, per Auld LJ, where an accused was influenced to change his plea to guilty having recognised that, as a result of a ruling to admit damning evidence against him, a defence was hopeless. 'The court has no power under the substituted s 2(1) to allow an appeal if it does not think the conviction unsafe but is dissatisfied in some way with what went on at the trial'. The court did not consider the scenario of whether a conviction may be held to be unsafe where there has been an abuse of process. In other words, can a conviction be regarded as unsafe where the appellant has had a fair trial but it was for some reason unfair to try him? Better in such a circumstance that the accused was never tried at all but the accused was and had a fair trial and was properly convicted. Is such a conviction 'safe'? The approach of the court in *Chalkley* was that even if the court held there was an abuse, the conviction could still be safe.

10.90 In *R v Martin* the House considered obiter the same issue and there was a difference of opinion. Lord Hope in an abuse context, adopted a broader interpretation of 'unsafe':

'I do not think it can be doubted that the Appeal Court ... have power to declare a conviction to be unsafe and to quash a conviction if they find that the course of proceedings leading to what would otherwise have been a fair trial has been such as to threaten either basic human rights or the rule of law'.

10.91 Lord Lloyd, however, felt that it would not be sufficient for the appellant to establish that the proceedings constituted an abuse of process for the conviction to be quashed.

10.92 Two other cases were decided by the court soon after *Chalkley* and *Martin*. In *Simpson* the court pondered whether it could ever quash a conviction as unsafe arising out of a prosecution abuse if no abuse application had ever been made at the trial. In *McDonald* Auld LJ took the opportunity to withdraw from the position which he had adopted in *Chalkley*. Considering what should happen in a *Bennett*-type abuse situation Auld LJ said:

'It may be that a conviction in a trial which should never have taken place is to be regarded as unsafe for that reason. It may be that, despite the statutory basis of the court's jurisdiction, it also has some inherent or ancillary jurisdictional basis for intervening to mark abuse of process by quashing a conviction when it considers that the court below should have stayed the proceeding. Or it may be that the recent amendment to the 1968 Act has removed the supervisory role of this court over abuse of criminal process where the affront to justice, however, outrageous, has not so prejudiced a defendant in his trial as to render his conviction unsafe. All that is for decision by another court in an appropriate case'.

The *Mullen* decision neatly fits the description of that 'appropriate case'. It is proposed, finally therefore, to turn to the *Mullen* case itself.

The decision in Mullen

10.93 Until the Court of Appeal decision in *Mullen*[1] the state of the case law in relation to post-amendment appeals on abuse of process, was highly unsatisfactory. The pre-*Mullen* case law was frequently in a state of ambiguity and uncertainty where certain decisions were, it is submitted, decided on an overly restrictive interpretation of the word 'unsafe', the *Chalkley* case being a prime example. It is submitted that the *Mullen* decision is a landmark case, of fundamental importance to the question of abuse of process in the context of appeals to the Court of Appeal.

1   [2000] QB 520, CA.

10.94   In the judgment of the Vice President, Rose LJ, considerable attention was given to the proper meaning of the amendment to the Criminal Appeal Act, and the correct interpretation of the word 'unsafe'. Rose LJ held that:

> '… for a conviction to be safe it must be lawful; and if it results from a trial which should never have taken place it can hardly be regarded as "safe". Indeed the Oxford Dictionary gives the legal meaning of "unsafe" as "likely to constitute a miscarriage of justice". Sir John Smith's article to which we have referred does not deal with "unsafe" in relation to abuse, though his commentary on *Simpson* … raises directly pertinent questions. But, for the reasons which we have given, we agree with his 1995 conclusion that "unsafe" bears a broad meaning and one which is apt to embrace abuse of process of the *Bennett*–type or any other kind.'

10.95   While Rose LJ stressed, elsewhere in the judgment, that there may be certain circumstances where a finding of abuse of process by the Court of Appeal may not necessarily lead to the quashing of a conviction on appeal, nevertheless this judgment clearly opens up many avenues for arguing abuse of process as a ground of appeal. It is of considerable significance that Rose LJ ended the above passage with reference, not only to the *Bennett*-type abuse (ie where it would be unfair for a defendant to be tried, for example, by reason of procedural unfairness by the prosecution) situation, but also to abuse of 'any other kind'. This must presumably include the first main limb of abuse of process (using the two limb *Beckford* test), where the circumstances are such that it is not possible for a defendant to receive a fair trial.

10.96   A number of points of principle and procedure emerge from this important judgment. First, the Court of Appeal reaffirmed that it has a supervisory discretion to oversee appeals on the ground of abuse of process. Secondly, that it will entertain appeals which cover all species of abuse of process, that is, consider appeals on the basis that the trial was unfair or that it was unfair to try the accused because of some abuse. Thirdly, that not all findings of abuse of process by the court will necessarily lead to a conviction being quashed or a retrial avoided. Rose LJ explained that in this circumstance the court would not exercise its power to quash convictions automatically: 'In each case it is a matter of discretionary balance, to be approached with regard to the particular conduct complained of and the particular offence charged'. Furthermore he added:

> 'In arriving at this conclusion we strongly emphasise that nothing in this judgment should be taken to suggest that there may not be cases, such as *Latif*, in which the seriousness of the crime is so great relative to the nature of the abuse of process that it would be a proper exercise of judicial discretion to permit a prosecution to proceed or to allow a conviction to stand notwithstanding an abuse of process of this kind'.

10.97 The *Latif* case[1] which Rose LJ referred to in the above passage involved strong public policy considerations in relation to the fight against organised crime, in the context of a serious drugs case (where customs officers arranged for the appellant to be lured from Pakistan to the UK by trickery and deception and also committed criminal offences). The 'discretionary balance' mentioned by Rose LJ was in *Latif* described by Lord Steyn in the following terms:

'If the court always refuses to stay such proceedings, the perception will be that the court condones criminal conduct and malpractice by law enforcement agencies. That would undermine public confidence in the criminal justice system and bring it into disrepute. On the other hand, if the court were always to stay proceedings in such cases, it would incur the reproach that it is failing to protect the public from serious crime. The weakness of both extreme positions leaves only one principled solution. The court has a discretion; it has to perform a balancing exercise'.

1   *R v Latif; R v Shahzad* [1996] 1 All ER 353, HL.

10.98 Weighing up the public policy considerations involved, the House held that the officer's conduct was not so unworthy or shameful that it was an affront to the public conscience to allow the prosecution to proceed. Lord Steyn observed 'realistically any criminal behaviour of the customs officer was venial compared to that of *Shahzad*' who was said to have been an organiser in the heroin trade[1].

1   See WG Roser 'Entrapment: have the courts found a solution to this fundamental dilemma to the criminal justice system? [1993] 67 ALJ 722 and Andrew L-T Choo 'Halting criminal prosecutions: The abuse of process doctrine revisited' [1995] Crim LR 864 as referred to in *Latif*.

10.99 It is submitted that *R v Mullen* should be regarded as the authoritative decision on appeals to the Court of Appeal. The judgment of Rose LJ both answers the questions posed by *Chalkley* and rids us of the ambiguities it created.[1] Indeed, not only has *Mullen* given effect, to a large extent, to the intention of the Home Office, the Royal Commission and Parliament (in conferring a broad meaning to 'unsafe') it has also rejuvenated the pre-amendment case law and resurrected, after their temporary demise at the hands of *Chalkley*, the decisions of *Bloomfield*, *Mahdi* and *Blackledge*. The test of whether a conviction is safe no longer simply depends on whether the court is satisfied that the appellant is guilty on the evidence. The court now has a discretion to consider issues such as procedural unfairness by the prosecution, for example, non-disclosure, material irregularities and abuse.

1   Note Professor Smith's commentary on *Mullen* at [1999] Crim LR 562.

The approval of Mullen

10.100 In the decision of *R v Togher*[1] the Court of Appeal resoundingly approved the *Mullen* decision, Lord Woolf CJ, at para 30 of his judgment, stating the following:

'Applying the broader approach identified by Rose LJ, we consider that if a defendant has been denied a fair trial it will almost be inevitable that the conviction will be regarded as unsafe. For this reason we endorse the approach of Rose LJ in *Mullen* and prefer the broader approach to the narrower approach supported by Auld LJ. Certainly, if it would be right to stop a prosecution on the basis that it was an abuse of process, this court would be most unlikely to conclude that if there was a conviction despite this fact, the conviction should not be set aside'.

The authors respectfully agree with the Lord Chief Justice's judgment for, if an appellate court has decided either that it was unfair for an appellant to have been tried, or that a fair trial was not possible, it is difficult to conceive of proper circumstances where the court can nevertheless maintain the safety of the conviction.

1   *R v Togher* [2001] 1 Cr App R 457.

What is the effect of pleading guilty on an appeal to the Court of Appeal?

10.101   In *Mullen* the Court of Appeal made plain that pursuant to its statutory jurisdiction to entertain appeals against conviction pursuant to the Criminal Appeal Act 1995, it was able to entertain such appeals based on the ground that the fairness of the trial was negated by an abuse of process. What, however, is the position where a defendant unsuccessfully argues abuse of process before the trial court, subsequently changes his plea to guilty, before appealing against the conviction on the grounds of the adverse abuse ruling? Does the Court of Appeal have jurisdiction to entertain such an appeal, or is the defendant required to maintain the not guilty plea in order to preserve his subsequent appeal rights? The decisions of *Togher* and *Early*[1] have thrown much light on this subject, albeit that the shadow of *Chalkley* still leaves some questions, on this singular aspect, somewhat unclear.

1   *R v Early* [2002] EWCA Crim 1904, [2002] 39 LS Gaz R 38.

10.102   On the authorities there appear to be two conflicting schools of thought. In *Chalkley*[1] the court held that a conviction following a plea of guilty will not normally be deemed in any circumstances to be unsafe, even if the proceedings had been irregular in some significant way or amounted to an abuse of process. So far as the court was concerned in *Chalkley*, the decisive factor overriding all others was if the defendant had entered a valid plea of guilty.[2] Following *Chalkley* in *Rajcoomar,* which was a post-*Mullen* case, the court ruled that *Mullen* did not affect the court's ruling in *Chalkley*. As it pointed out in *Rajcoomar*, in *Mullen* the defendant had pleaded not guilty and had contested his trial.

1   At [1998] 2 Cr App R 79.
2   See, for example, a plea which is not vitiated by mistake or duress.

10.103   The opposing school of thought based principally on a construction of the court's judgment in *Mullen* is that the court does have a jurisdiction to consider appeals against conviction even after valid guilty pleas. In his commentary on *Rajcoomar*, Professor Smith succinctly sets out the argument:

'... But if, as the court said in *Mullen*, ... for a conviction to be safe, it must be lawful; and, if it results from a trial which should never have taken place, it can hardly be regarded as safe, what does it matter whether the conviction results from a plea of guilty or a verdict of guilty by the jury? In both cases the defendant is in law guilty of the offence charged, but in neither case should the trial have taken place at all. According to the reasoning in *Mullen*, it is safe in both, or it is safe in neither'.[1]

1   [1999] Crim LR 728.

10.104 The authors submit that Professor Smith's reasoning is to be preferred over the view of the court in *Chalkley* and *Rajcoomar*. Moreover Rose LJ in *Mullen* appeared to cover the point when he summarised his judgment in the following terms:

'... by reason of this abuse of process, the prosecution and therefore the conviction of the appellant were unlawful'.[1]

The view of Rose LJ being that if the foundation for the prosecution was itself legally objectionable then it matters little how the defendant came to be convicted. One should also appreciate that both in *Chalkley* and *Rajcoomar*, the court was not directly concerned with appeals based on abuse grounds. In contrast, *Mullen* was entirely focused on this point.

1   [1999] 2 Cr App R 143 at 157G.

10.105 In *Togher* the Court of Appeal held that an appeal against conviction after a plea of guilty could be allowed if the proceedings constituted an abuse of process such that it would be inconsistent with the due administration of justice to allow the guilty plea to stand. The actual appeals were dismissed in *Togher*, however, for the court was thoroughly unimpressed with the argument that there had in fact been an abuse of process in the related trial proceedings. On the facts of that case there was found to be no justification for interfering with the freely-entered pleas of guilty. Whilst the court accepted that the appellants had been deprived of certain prosecution disclosure, the non-disclosure did not amount to an abuse of process, for, as the Lord Chief Justice said:

'They were never ignorant of any evidence which went directly to their innocence or guilt. They were only unaware of material which could, but for their pleas, have been used in order to attack the credibility of the prosecution witnesses. Ignorance of this nature does not justify reopening their pleas of guilty'.[1]

1   At para 59.

10.106 By contrast, the non-disclosure and misconduct in *Early* was so significant that the convictions of all eight appellants (who had pleaded guilty) were quashed in the Court of Appeal. Lord Justice Rose, in *Early*, stated that the Court of Appeal would approach the question of the safety of convictions, following pleas of guilty, in accordance with the *Mullen* and *Togher* decisions. In *Early* the court clearly had no doubt that the non-disclosure impinged upon issues relating to 'innocence or guilt'. Indeed, in relation to two of the appellants, the court declared that, had the trial judge been aware of the true position, he may well have decided not to refuse the abuse of process applications.

10.107 A recent commentator[1] further suggests that the *Early* case introduces a new principle that 'gross misconduct by the prosecution or its witnesses' will vitiate a guilty plea. In *Early* Rose LJ certainly made it clear that prosecution witnesses who perjure themselves in a public interest immunity or abuse voir dire are likely to 'taint beyond redemption' a prosecution case, irrespective of the strength of the case against a particular defendant. This decision suggests therefore that situations 'where it would be inconsistent with the due administration of justice to allow the pleas of guilty to stand'[2] include, first, proven instances of gross misconduct by the prosecution and/or, second, significant prosecution non-disclosure, at the time the pleas were entered.

1   See commentary on 'Guilty pleas and abuse of process', *Blackstone's Criminal Practice*, at D10.41.
2   Per Woolf CJ in *R v Togher* [2001] 1 Cr App R 457 at 468, para 33.

Is Chalkley still relevant to the abuse jurisdiction?

10.108   In the following much-quoted passage, Auld LJ in *Chalkley*[1] held that:

'… a conviction would be unsafe where the effect of an incorrect ruling of law on admitted facts was to leave an accused with no legal escape from a verdict of guilty on those facts. But a conviction would not normally be unsafe where an accused is influenced to change his plea to guilty because he recognises that, as a result of a ruling to admit strong evidence against him, his case on the facts is hopeless. A change of plea to guilty in such circumstances would normally be regarded as an acknowledgement of the truth of the facts constituting the offence charged.

We qualify the above propositions with the word "normally", because there remains the basic rule that the court should quash as unsafe a conviction where the plea was mistaken or without intention to admit the truth of the offence charged'.

1   Page 94D of his judgment.

10.109   Whereas this part of the judgment has been followed subsequently with approval in essentially PACE, s 78 strength of evidence-type cases, does it have any applicability to abuse of process, where a guilty plea is entered after an adverse ruling? Whilst Woolf CJ in *Togher* refused to question this passage in Auld LJ's judgment, he immediately added that, where appellants could establish an abuse at the Court of Appeal stage, in relation to material matters which they had previously been ignorant of at trial, the court would nevertheless: 'give very serious consideration to whether justice required the conviction to be set aside'. Leaving to one side the non-disclosure type scenario however, how should a defence practitioner advise a client where the application to stay is said to fail on the merits? Can one, for the sake of expediency, having received an adverse abuse ruling, safely plead guilty and still hope to appeal against a conviction where there has never been an intention, by the guilty plea, to admit the truth of the offence?

10.110 This remains a difficult and uncertain area of law. In practice, we suggest that the overwhelming majority of accused, faced with an adverse abuse ruling, will continue to contest proceedings given that the effect of an incorrect ruling will not generally deprive an accused of 'legal escape from a verdict of guilty'. If this aspect of the *Chalkley* decision is correctly decided (and as relevant to abuse of process as to s 78), then an appellant, in order to succeed on appeal, would have to demonstrate that the erroneous ruling left him or her with no legal escape from a guilty verdict. In *Llewellyn,*[1] for example, the appeal was dismissed on the grounds that the trial judge's ruling presented no legal impediment to the continuation of the trial and the advancing of the defence. Similarly in the decision of *R v Hardy,*[2] the Court of Appeal, who considered the case exactly in line with the *Chalkley* and *Llewellyn* decisions, found that the defendants were not prevented from advancing their defence at trial, and thus were not entitled to challenge their convictions, having pleaded guilty in circumstances where there was no abuse of process.

1   *R v Llewellyn* [2001] EWCA Crim 1555, [2001] All ER (D) 10 (Jul).
2   [2003] 1Cr App R 30; see also Professor Ormerod's commentary at [2003] Crim LR 396.

10.111 Finally it is relevant to consider the position of the court pre-implementation of the 1995 Act. For example, in *Schlesinger*[1] there was an unequivocal plea of guilty at the trial. Nonetheless, the court unhesitatingly quashed the conviction holding that the entire prosecution of the defendant was an abuse[2]. It is submitted that the decision in *Mullen* is in conformity with the decision in *Schlesinger*.

1   *R v Schlesinger* [1995] Crim LR 137.
2   Here the defendant had entered a guilty plea in ignorance of abusive behaviour committed by the prosecution. See paras **5.119–5.120** for further consideration of this case.

10.112 It is submitted that to deprive an appellant who has pleaded guilty from any avenue of appeal would be wrong in principle and inconsistent with the interests of justice. Moreover, on pragmatic grounds it would mean that a defendant, properly advised, would contest every prosecution no matter how hopeless his defence or how legally inescapable his conviction. A defendant pleading not guilty in such circumstances would result in his trial being almost a farce with defence counsel simply adopting a formalistic role. Nonetheless, bearing in mind the prevailing ambiguity in the authorities, it seems that for the purpose of preserving appeal rights, every defendant must be advised to plead not guilty for fear that otherwise appeal rights may be precluded.

Abuse of process as a novel ground of appeal

10.113 In the Court of Appeal can it be argued that the trial was unfair because of a specific abuse which was known to the defence at the trial but never complained about?

10.114 In *Mullen* the court held that, where no ruling is sought by the defence on a matter within the trial judge's discretion, this will 'usually be fatal to any subsequent attempt to rely on that matter by way of appeal to this court'. In these circumstances practitioners would be well advised to make their abuse of process application at the appropriate time in the Crown Court, in order to avoid being precluded from arguing it on appeal. In *Mullen* itself the court excused the defence's failure to argue abuse at trial for two reasons. First, the prosecution were responsible for non-disclosure of documents which were at the time of trial relevant to the abuse issue and secondly, the state of the law on this species of abuse was not so favourable to the defence at the time, the trial having occurred in 1990 pre-*Bennett*.[1]

1   At that time there were conflicting authorities on the issue of whether a court should ever inquire into circumstances concerning how a defendant had come into the jurisdiction.

Prosecution appeals to the Court of Appeal

10.115   The prosecution now have a right of appeal against a Crown Court judge's ruling to stay a case for abuse of process. This right of appeal was introduced by ss 58–61 of the Criminal Justice Act 2003, whose provisions came into force on 4 April 2005.[1] The appeal procedure is available on the basis that a stay of proceedings amounts to a 'Terminating Ruling.'

1   See Criminal Justice Act 2003 (Commencement No 8 and Transitional and Saving Provisions) Order 2005 (SI 2005/950).

10.116   The limitations upon this recently conferred right, however, were highlighted in the recent decision of *Regina v B*.[1] On the facts of the case, Sir Igor Judge, as he then was, dismissed the prosecution's appeal, and found that there was no possible basis for interfering with the trial judge's decision to stay. The case had involved the alleged attempted abduction of a child, the issue being identification. On appeal, the Court accepted that critical evidence, which had been destroyed, relating to identification, justified the trial judge's 'judgment' that a fair trial was then no longer possible. The only issue taken with the trial judge, by the Court of Appeal, related to his decision to give the prosecution leave to appeal in the first place.

1   See [2008] EWCA Crim 1144, CA, judgment of 1 May 2008.

10.117   The court held that when a judge exercised his discretion or made his judgment in the course of a trial, the 'very fact that he has had carefully to balance conflicting considerations will almost inevitably mean that he might reasonably have reached a different, or the opposite conclusion to the one he did reach'.[1] The mere fact, however, that there were valid opposing arguments does not begin to provide the prosecution with the basis for a successful appeal. The Court held that an application for leave to appeal will not be given unless it is seriously arguable that it had been unreasonable for the judge to have made his decision on the ruling in the manner that he did. Section 67 of the Criminal Justice Act 2003 expressly sets out the Appeal Court's powers to reverse a ruling.

1   See para 19 of Sir Igor Judge's judgment.

10.118   Where the prosecution fail to obtain leave to appeal, or abandon the appeal, then the proper course, pursuant to CJA 2003, s 58(8) will be for the

Appeal Court to order an acquittal in respect of the offence or offences which are the subject of appeal.[1]

1   See *R v R* [2008] 3 Archbold News 2, CA on the 'acquittal agreement'; for other examples of terminating ruling appeals in abuse of process cases, see *R v O* [2007] EWCA Crim 3483, and *R v Arnold* [2008] EWCA Crim 1034, in relation to a Courts-Martial appeal.

RETRIALS

10.119   A less common area where abuse arguments arise is in relation to retrials. They occur either after a first trial has had a 'hung' or discharged jury,[1] or by direction of the Court of Appeal. By the very nature of a retrial, 'delay' will commonly be an issue, particularly where serious and complex proceedings are involved, but are there any additional abuse factors peculiar to retrial situations?

1   See *R v Piggott and Litwin* [1999] 2 Cr App R 320 for an example of a retrial amounting to an abuse of process (where late prosecution amendments to the first trial's indictment significantly affected the fairness of proceeding to a second trial).

10.120   The Privy Council decision of *Charles v State of Trinidad and Tobago*[1] contains important statements of principle in this regard. In *Charles* the Privy Council found an abuse of process where a defendant had to endure a third trial for murder some nine years after the event, in circumstances where he had remained in custody under sentence of death. In the course of his judgment Slynn LJ made it clear that the Board ought to have regard both to the history to the protracted proceedings and, more significantly, to the personal concerns and anxieties that may be left by an accused. Lord Slynn emphasised the importance of the principles enunciated in the decision of *Barker v Wingo*[2] whereby:

'... the United States Supreme Court considered that the right to speedy trial was designed to protect three interests of defendants, namely (i) to prevent oppressive pre-trial incarceration; (ii) to minimise anxiety and concern of the accused; and (iii) to limit the possibility that the defence will be impaired'.

1   [2000] 1 WLR 384.
2   407 US 514 (1972).

10.121   While the facts of *Charles* are clearly in the extreme, nevertheless it is suggested that the general principle, namely that we should have regard to the personal distress of an accused, is of more general application.

10.122   In the subsequent decision of *R v Henworth*[1] however, the Court of Appeal made it clear that there was no principle of law that, where a prosecution had failed twice, it was necessarily an abuse of process to hold a third trial. Having emphasised the clear public interest in juries deciding serious criminal cases, one way or the other, Kennedy LJ in *Henworth*[2] nevertheless stated that:

'... we recognise the possibility that in any given case a time may come when it would be an abuse of process for the prosecution to try again. Whether that situation arises must depend on the facts of the case which include, first, the overall period of delay and the reasons for the delay; second, the results of previous trials; thirdly, the seriousness of the offence or offences under consideration; and, fourthly, possibly, the extent to which the case now to be met has changed from that which was considered in previous trials'.

1   [2001] EWCA Crim 120, [2001] 2 Cr App R 47.
2   [2001] EWCA Crim 120, [2001] 2 Cr App R 47 at 52, para 26.

10.123   The Privy Council adopted a similar stance, to this vexed question of second retrials, in the decision of *Bowe v R*.[1] In *Bowe* it was held that whether a second retrial should be allowed depended on an informed and dispassionate assessment of how the interests of justice, in the broadest sense, could best be served. On the one hand, the court should take into account the defendant's interests, particularly where there has been a long delay or where the defence may be prejudiced in some significant way, whilst on the other hand, however, the court must take account of the public interest in convicting the guilty, deterring violent crime and maintaining confidence in the efficacy of our system of criminal justice.

1   *Bowe v R* [2001] UKPC 19, [2001] 4 LRC 372.

Where the Crown adopt a change of stance at the retrial

10.124   In *R v Mercer*[1] the Court of Appeal held that where fresh evidence becomes available to the prosecution between trial and retrial, it is entirely acceptable for them to take it into account. Where the Crown therefore choose to act on it, and subsequently put their case against an accused on a different basis, this was held not to constitute circumstances giving rise to an abuse of process. On the facts of *Mercer* two males entered and robbed a building society, whilst a third drove the getaway car. At the first trial the Crown's case had been that the appellant entered the building society, whereas on the retrial the suggestion was that he acted as the getaway driver. The change of stance arose as a result of new evidence having come to light, which identified the second robber who entered the premises, the identity of the first having been clear throughout.

1   *R v Mercer* [2001] EWCA Crim 638, [2001] All ER (D) 187 (Mar).

Where the Court of Appeal orders a retrial

10.125   Section 7 of the Criminal Appeal Act 1968 states that the power to order a retrial is as follows:

'(1) Where the Court of Appeal allows an appeal against conviction and it appears to the court that the interests of justice so require, they may order the appellant to be retried'.

The simple question thus arises: does this prevent one from arguing abuse of process on a retrial?

10.126   In *Charles* Lord Slynn noted the potential for overlap between the two freestanding decisions: the decision to order a stay and to order a retrial:

'Whether a stay should be granted raised some questions analogous to those which arise when a decision has to be taken as to whether there should be a retrial. In *Reid v R* ([1980] AC 343, 350) the Board gave general guidance as to the factors which might be relevant in the exercise of the Court of Appeal's function in deciding whether to order a retrial; "The seriousness or otherwise of the offence must always be a relevant factor; so may its prevalence; and where the previous trial was prolonged and complex, the expense and the length of time for which the court and jury would be involved in a fresh hearing may also be relevant considerations".

So too is the consideration that any criminal trial is to some extent an ordeal for the defendant, which the defendant ought not to be condemned to undergo for a second time through no fault of his own unless the interests of justice require that he should do so.'

10.127 The authors suggest that, where the Court of Appeal have fully and properly considered the abuse-type arguments, before making the order for retrial, the defence will have considerable problems in even persuading the trial judge to entertain the abuse argument. Where the Court of Appeal have, for example, rejected a defence delay argument on the order of a retrial, one would not expect a Crown Court judge (where the timetable for the retrial has been followed) to allow the defence to resurrect the self-same argument as to abuse of process. This was the approach adopted by Turner J in the recent case of *R v Doran*[1] in relation to defence submissions which had previously been argued and ruled on:

'Not only has a court of competent jurisdiction ruled on those matters which were at present before it as issues, but that decision is one which is plainly binding this court in respect of matters which were raised in the higher court'.

1   (6 July 1999, unreported), Bristol Crown Court.

10.128 In *Doran* Turner J, however, naturally adopted a contrary position in relation to arguments which had not previously been advanced or ruled on. Indeed, it is further suggested that an abuse of process submission could still be made after an order for retrial where there had been a material change of circumstances, such as a significant unexpected delay in the listing of the retrial, which had not been within the contemplation of the Court of Appeal.

Compensation in miscarriage cases

10.129 On the somewhat exceptional facts of the *Mullen* case, however, the Court of Appeal decision on compensation was reversed by the House of Lords.[1] Lord Bingham opined that, as the Secretary of State was only bound by s 133 of the Criminal Justice Act 1988 and Art 14.6 of the International Covenant on Civil and Political Rights 1966 to pay compensation for failures of the trial process, Mullen was not entitled to compensation. Practitioners considering the arguably grey and complex issue of compensation, following a successful abuse argument, should also take note of the differing views expressed by Lord Steyn.

1   See *R v Secretary of State for the Home Department, ex p Mullen* [2004] UKHL 18.

THE ABUSE OF PROCESS HEARING

Rules of procedure

10.130 On 23 May 2000, Lord Bingham CJ issued a practice direction outlining the procedural requirements for making an application to stay an indictment on the grounds of abuse of process, which is now part of a Consolidated Practice Direction, and further, a part of the 2005 Criminal Procedure Rules:[1]

1   The following arrangements will take effect immediately.

2   In all cases where a defendant in the Crown Court proposes to make an application to stay an indictment on the grounds of abuse of process, written notice of such application must be given to the prosecuting authority and to any co-defendant no later than 14 days before the date fixed or warned for trial ('the relevant date'). Such notice must:

   (a)   give the name of the case and the indictment number;

   (b)   state the fixed date or the warned date as appropriate;

   (c)   specify the nature of the application;

   (d)   set out in numbered sub-paragraphs the grounds upon which the application is to be made;

   (e)   be copied to the Chief Listing Officer at the Court Centre where the case is due to be heard.

3   Any co-defendant who wishes to make a like application must give a like notice not later than seven days before the relevant date, setting out any additional grounds relied upon.

4   In relation to such applications, the following automatic directions shall apply:

   (a)   the advocate for the applicant(s) must lodge with the court and serve on all other parties a skeleton argument in support of the application at least five clear working days before the relevant date. If reference is to be made to any document not in the existing trial documents, a paginated and indexed bundle of such documents is to be provided with the skeleton argument;

   (b)   the advocate for the prosecution must lodge with the court and serve on all other parties a responsive skeleton argument at least two clear working days before the relevant date, together with a supplementary bundle if appropriate.

5   All skeleton arguments must specify any propositions of law to be advanced (together with the authorities relied upon in support, with page references to passages relied upon), and where appropriate include a chronology of events and a list of dramatis personae. In all instances where reference is made to a document, the reference in the trial documents or supplementary bundle is to be given.

6   The above time limits are minimum time limits. In appropriate cases the court will order longer lead times. To this end in all cases where defence advocates are, at the time of the plea and directions hearing, considering the possibility of an abuse of process application, this must be raised with the judge dealing with the matter who will order a different timetable if appropriate, and may wish in any event to give additional directions about the conduct of the application.

1   See Practice Direction (Criminal Proceedings: Consolidation) [2002] 1 WLR 2870, at para 4.36.

10.131   The new obligation upon defence advocates, who are 'considering the possibility' of an abuse application, to raise the matter with a judge at a pleas and directions hearing, is consistent with the Crown Court rules requirement to give advance notice of a question of law which would attract a binding ruling (see CPIA 1996, s 40). A similar requirement is found in the standard pleas and directions questionnaire. The above practice direction should significantly assist with efficient case management in the Crown Court, however there are no similar rules for the magistrates' courts. The practitioner in the magistrates' court would, nevertheless, be well advised, as is commonly the practice, to give the court advance notice if only for listing purposes.

The Protocol for the Control and Management of Heavy Fraud and other Complex Criminal Cases

10.132   On 22 March 2005 Lord Woolf CJ issued this protocol with the avowed aim of promoting good practice and efficient case management, with a view to the reduction in the length of court hearings. One particular section of the protocol directly focuses on abuse of process. The protocol, which supplements the Criminal Procedure Rules, is primarily directed towards cases which are estimated to last eight weeks or longer, but should also be followed in all cases estimated to last more than four weeks. The abuse of process section states as follows:

'5. Abuse of process

i   Applications to stay or dismiss for abuse of process have become a normal feature of heavy and complex cases. Such applications may be based on delay and the health of defendants.

ii   Applications in relation to absent special circumstances[sic] tend to be unsuccessful and not to be pursued on appeal. For this reason there is comparatively little Court of Appeal guidance: but see Harris and Howells [2003] EWCA Crim 486. It should be noted that abuse of process is not there to discipline the prosecution or the police.

iii   The arguments on both sides must be reduced to writing. Oral evidence is seldom relevant.

iv   The Judge should direct full written submissions (rather than "skeleton arguments") on any abuse application in accordance with a

389

timetable set by him; these should identify any element of prejudice the defendant is alleged to have suffered.

v   The judge should normally aim to conclude the hearing within an absolute maximum of one day, if necessary in accordance with a timetable. The parties should therefore prepare their papers on this basis and not expect the judge to allow the oral hearing to be anything more than an occasion to highlight concisely their arguments and answer any questions the court may have of them; applications will not be allowed to drag on.'

10.133   In the introduction to the above, a flexibility of application of the protocol according to the needs of each case was deemed to be essential, given that it was 'designed to inform but not to proscribe'. Having taken account of that, however, the protocol serves as a clear warning to practitioners who are involved in abuse applications relating to trials of more than four weeks in length, to set out their detailed written arguments in full, for there will generally be a strictly limited time allowed by judges for oral submissions. This is consistent with the general cultural trend towards much tighter control over advocates' opportunities to address the court.

10.134   The application is normally instigated by the defence. However, it would appear there is some authority to suggest that where the court itself has some reason to suspect there is a ground for staying proceedings, it has a duty to raise it of its own motion, irrespective of the lack of any defence application[1].

1   See *R v City of Liverpool Stipendiary Magistrate, ex p Ellison* [1990] RTR 220n, 227 per Bingham LJ; and *Gillick v West Norfolk and Wisbech Area Health Authority* [1986] AC 112.

Timing of application

10.135   An application to stay proceedings is obviously a preliminary issue which should be raised either pre-trial or at the outset of the trial. Self-evidently, as a successful abuse application may bring an end to the entire proceedings (although this is not necessarily so, for a successful abuse application may only relate to a stay of part of the prosecution's case), it ought to be heard at the earliest opportunity. In *R v Aldershot Youth Court, ex p A*[1] the Divisional Court held that by its nature an application to stay proceedings as an abuse is a plea in bar and as with a plea of autrefois acquit or convict, the plea was to be taken and determined before the accused pleaded to the indictment/charge.

1   (1997) 3 Archbold News 2, QBD.

10.136   In *R v Smolinski*[1] the Court of Appeal provided guidance as to whether and when an application should be made to have cases stayed on the basis of abuse of process where there has been delay. The guidance given amounts to a significant departure in the approach previously taken on the question of timing. In the course of his judgment, Lord Woolf CJ, having sought to discourage the making of applications to stay in these sorts of cases, questioned whether it was helpful to make abuse applications in historical sexual offences type cases before any evidence had been given by the complainants. The court held that:

'If an application is to be made to a Judge, the best time for doing so is after any evidence has been called. That means that on the one hand the court has had an opportunity of seeing the witnesses, and, on the other hand the complainants have had to go through the ordeal of giving evidence. However, despite the latter point, which obviously is one of importance, it seems to us that on the whole it is preferable for the evidence to be called and for a judge then to make his decision as to whether the trial should proceed or whether the evidence is such that it would not be safe for a jury to convict. That is a particularly helpful course if there is a danger of inconsistencies between the witnesses …'.

1   [2004] 2 Cr App R 40.

10.137   Where trial Judges are following the *Smolinski* guidance, in these types of historic sexual offence type cases, the application to stay may be made part way through the prosecution's case, and after the complainant or complainants have given evidence. At this stage, the court recommended that there be a very careful scrutiny of the evidence by the judge.

10.138   Whilst this may be the proper approach for trial judges to adopt in the majority of cases, it is nevertheless submitted there will be cases where it will be entirely appropriate to hear an application to stay before the trial commences. Where there is no issue between the prosecution and the defence over the question of serious prejudice by virtue of the delay, for example (in the light of lost documentation, or missing witnesses), and no issue of apparent inconsistencies in witness accounts, leaving the argument to revolve around the appropriate remedy (stay or judicial direction on prejudice), then, in these circumstances, we submit it would be both inappropriate and unnecessary to put complainants through the ordeal of trial. On these occasions a sound exercise of judicial judgment may still be possible on the face of the papers, and agreed facts.

Must the trial judge conduct an inquiry into an abuse submission?

10.139   If, after hearing from the defence, the trial judge concludes that the submission has no justification or hope of success either because it is wrong in law or the facts appear very far from an abuse situation, it is submitted that the judge has no duty to conduct any inquiry.

10.140   In *R v Heston-Francois*[1] the question arose as to whether there was a general duty on the trial judge to conduct such an inquiry when it was *justifiably* requested by the defence. The facts were that the defendant was on bail awaiting trial and the police, in the course of conducting another investigation, searched his home and seized legally privileged documents (documents prepared for use in his defence to the trial he was already facing). These documents were not only seized but they were then handed to the investigators who were involved in the prosecution of the defendant's imminent trial. At this trial the defence submitted abuse arguing that the conduct of the officers had been oppressive and justified a stay. The trial judge however, declined to conduct any inquiry into this, ruling that all relevant matters could be adequately explored during the course of the trial, and so a ruling could be made later in the proceedings. Post-conviction, the defendant appealed to the Court of Appeal.

1   (1984) 78 Cr App R 209.

10.141   The Court of Appeal emphasised that in circumstances such as an abuse application, a trial judge should be the master of his own procedure and therefore enjoy a wide discretion as to how to conduct an abuse inquiry. If the trial judge exercised his discretion wrongly or behaved unfairly, then of course this could be reviewed subsequently by the Court of Appeal and, in the view of the court, it was well placed to conduct such a review.

10.142   A perusal of the judgment of Watkins LJ in this case reveals that the court was vexed by several policy considerations which clearly led it to reach the conclusion that it did. Watkins LJ suggested that if a trial judge was to have a duty always to conduct a pre-trial inquiry into allegations of abuse then this would tend to suggest that it was part of a court's duty to regulate the conduct of police officers. As no such duty existed then neither should there be a duty to always conduct a pre-trial inquiry. In relation to the trial process itself, Watkins LJ agreed with the trial judge's view that the trial was the best forum or procedure for eliciting facts relevant to an abuse application. Moreover, a trial judge having heard the relevant evidence had a variety of remedies available to him. Reprehensible conduct by the police could be dealt with within the context of the trial by judicial control over admissibility of evidence, the power to direct a verdict of not guilty and the ability of a jury having heard all the evidence to return a verdict of not guilty.

10.143   As a matter of practice Watkins LJ also pointed to several problems which would arise if a general duty on a trial judge was held to exist:

'... for example, (i) of defining the issues claimed to exist, which may be very complex, (ii) of providing for representation of persons whose conduct is impugned, (iii) of ensuring that the persons affected are sufficiently aware of the case they have to meet. Whilst these problems may be overcome, the issues referred to are best left, we think, to be dealt with during the course of the trial and; if necessary, later by the Court of Appeal.'

10.144   In relation to such problems Watkins LJ also observed that:

'A pre-trial inquiry such as the appellant contends the judge in this case was under a duty to embark on would itself be open to abuse by unscrupulous and dishonest accused persons. The criminal trial system would be placed in jeopardy'.

10.145   In *A-G's Reference* Lane CJ expressly approved the view of Watkins LJ expressed in *Heston-Francois*.[1] He held that the trial process is equipped to deal with most complaints of abuse, for example the ability to ensure that all relevant evidence of this is presented during the trial and the ability of the judge to give directions to the jury.

1   (1984) 78 Cr App R 209.

10.146 On the basis of these two authorities therefore, it appears that there is no obligation on a trial judge to hold a pre-trial hearing even when it is justifiably requested by the defence. It is however, submitted that both of these authorities have now largely been overtaken by subsequent developments and perhaps by the growth of abuse applications generally. Certainly it is the experience of the authors that where, for example, an allegation of mala fides is made against police officers, it would be extremely unusual for a trial judge to hold that this matter need not be investigated until the relevant officers gave their evidence in the ordinary way in the course of the trial. Furthermore, an increased awareness on the part of the judiciary as to their responsibility to ensure that abuses do not go uncorrected, together with the growth generally in our criminal justice system of pre-trial or preparatory hearings, means that there has been an increased focus away from the belief that the trial process is the best and most efficient manner for determining matters. Especially those which if decided in a particular way would result in the entire trial being stayed.

Voir dires

10.147 It is normal for applications concerned with the exclusion of prosecution evidence under PACE, s 78 or for a stay of the proceedings to be considered in a voir dire or a 'trial within a trial' held in the absence of the jury.[1] The usual procedure is for the prosecution to call witnesses to testify as to the circumstances about which the defence has made complaint, for the defence to cross-examine these witnesses and then for the defence to call any evidence it considers necessary. Judges will only expect the calling of live evidence in an abuse voir dire where it is absolutely necessary, however, for the parties will generally be encouraged to make the arguments on the face of the documentation, unless this is simply not possible. There is no obligation on the accused to give evidence although there is antiquated authority to the effect that he is not entitled to do so. However, it is submitted that if a fair determination of the issues makes it desirable for the accused to give evidence and he wished to do so, it would be wrong to refuse this. It should be borne in mind that if the accused does give evidence and the abuse application fails, the prosecution may lead evidence in the trial proper regarding this previous testimony. Prosecution cross-examination of the accused before the jury can be directed to expose any discrepancies and inconsistencies between the two testimonies in order to attack the credibility of the accused.

1   In *R v Barry Magistrates' Court, ex p Malpas* [1998] COD 90, DC, the Divisional Court acknowledged the Crown Court's use of abuse voir dires for dealing with disputed facts.

No power to order disclosure

10.148 The position of a trial judge conducting an abuse hearing was described by Watkins LJ in *R v Manchester Crown Court, ex p Cunningham:*[1]

'He is not in a trial situation nor is his role an inquisitorial one. He cannot compel any other evidential material to be provided'.

1   [1992] COD 23. This case is also known as *R v Manchester Crown Court, ex p Brokenbrow* (1991) Times, 31 October.

10.149   It was held in *ex p Cunningham* that a trial judge has no power to compel disclosure of documents from any party, including the prosecution, if such documents purely relate to the abuse application and do not fall under the prosecution's general duty of disclosure in relation to the trial. In relation to third parties, the trial judge has no power to issue a witness summons either for documents or for the giving of witness testimony pursuant to the Criminal Procedure (Attendance of Witnesses) Act 1965 (which has now been greatly amended by the Criminal Procedure and Investigations Act 1996, s 66). In *R v Gokal*[1] the Court of Appeal upheld the refusal of the trial judge to make orders under the Criminal Justice (International Co-operation) Act 1990 in relation to the seeking of foreign evidence in order to support a forthcoming abuse application to be made by the defence.

1   [1997] 2 Cr App R 266, CA.

Argument and giving of reasons

10.150   In practice, a considerable number of abuse applications tend to be made in circumstances where, at the appropriate hearing, the defence and prosecution present the facts and argument without the necessity of calling any evidence. This is largely because the dispute between the parties will generally lie over the proper inference to be drawn from the facts, as opposed to the facts themselves. Alternatively, the prosecution may contend that, even if the defence's arguments or allegations are made out, they do not in law amount to an abuse. Where the defence do contemplate calling evidence in a voir dire, as part of the abuse application, they need to be ever mindful of the inherent dangers of exposing their witnesses to prosecution cross-examination. Indeed, practitioners are cautioned against the calling of defence evidence, unless they are confident first, that it is necessary and secondly, that it would be of positive assistance to the application.

10.151   The burden of proving assertions as to the alleged abuse and/or establishing the evidential foundations rests on the defence. In *ex p Cunningham* the court considered how a judge should rule on an abuse application. Watkins LJ said: 'In rejecting or granting an application the judge need only deliver a short judgment showing his command of the law and a summary of the reasons for his decision'. While it makes for good practice for magistrates to similarly provide reasons, there is no legal obligation on them to do so.

Divisible indictments

10.152   In *R v Munro*[1] the Court of Appeal held that the power to stay proceedings exists in order to enable a court to regulate the efficient and fair disposal of criminal cases. Lord Justice Steyn went on to acknowledge the good sense in a court having an inherent jurisdiction to stay an indictment in part; whether that meant staying some counts and not others, or staying (in a multi-handed case) as against some defendants and not others. To that end, Steyn LJ held that it was 'an illusion to regard an indictment as an indivisible entity'.

1   (1993) 97 Cr App R 183.

Defendant giving evidence in committal proceedings

10.153   In *R v Clerkenwell Stipendiary Magistrate, ex p Bell*[1] the applicant, B, was alleged to have committed an offence of theft at some time before May 1987. He was charged with the offence on 26 September 1989. On 22 January 1990 at committal proceedings, it was contended on his behalf that given the delay the magistrate should not commit him for trial because of abuse of process. The magistrate proceeded to hear evidence from a police officer explaining the delay, in relation to B moving address, but refused to hear evidence from B himself. He committed B for trial, which decision was then subject to a judicial review application. The High Court granted the application and quashed the committal. It was held that the magistrate should have heard evidence from B, because any possible prejudice to B caused by the delay was a relevant matter and clearly B could give evidence as to this.[2] In short, the refusal to hear evidence from B amounted to a breach of natural justice.

1   [1991] Crim LR 468, QBD.
2   *R v Telford Justices, ex p Badham* was cited in support of this proposition.

Fairness to the prosecution

10.154   In *R v Derby Crown Court, ex p Brooks*[1] Sir Roger Ormrod in his famous dictum concerning the abuse of process said in relation to this subject as follows:

> 'the power to stop a prosecution arises when it is an abuse of the process of the court ... the ultimate objective of this discretionary power is to ensure that there should be a fair trial according to law, which involves fairness to both the defendant and to the prosecution ...'.

1   (1984) 80 Cr App R 164 at 168.

10.155   Lane CJ in *Attorney-General's Reference (No 1 of 1990)*[1] emphasised that the court's power to stay proceedings should never be used as a means of punishing the prosecution. This concern was similarly expressed in the course of the Lord Woolf CJ 2005 Protocol on the Control and Management of Heavy Fraud and Other Complex Criminal Cases.

1   (1992) 95 Cr App R 296, CA.

10.156   The issue of whether the prosecution have been fairly heard in answer to a defendant's abuse application usually rises in the context of a magistrate's decision to stay proceedings about which the prosecution subsequently seek judicial review arguing that this was irrational. In *R v Crawley Justices, ex p DPP*[1] the Divisional Court heard a prosecution application for judicial review arising out of a justice's decision to dismiss the charges against the defendant on the grounds of prosecution delay. The justices held that the delay was so protracted and unjustifiable that it constituted an abuse. For its part the prosecution, while it did not deny the facts concerning delay, submitted that it had not received a fair hearing because the magistrates had not directed themselves to the essential issue of whether the delay had in fact prejudiced a fair trial. Furthermore, the magistrates had not considered who was responsible for the delay, the prosecution arguing that some of the responsibility lay with the accused. It transpired that at the particular hearing complained of, the justices had refused to hear any submissions from the prosecution and immediately proceeded to dismiss the charges. Unsurprisingly, the High Court granted the application finding in effect that the tenets of natural justice have been broken and the prosecution had been treated unfairly.[2] Moreover, in the opinion of the court, had the magistrates heard all the facts they probably would not have decided that there was an abuse.

1   [1991] COD 365, DC.
2   See also *King v Kucharz* [1989] COD 469, DC.

10.157   In the case of *Director of Public Prosecutions v Ayres*[1] the prosecution also found themselves in some difficulty with the Justices. While the prosecution would appear to have rightly attracted certain criticism for failing to comply with various disclosure directions, nevertheless, the net result was that the Justices allowed a defence application that the prosecution not be permitted to respond to the abuse of process application, which application to stay succeeded. The High Court allowed an appeal by way of case stated by the prosecution. The Court held that, however serious a party's default had been in general terms in the course of a case, it was essentially unjust to deprive that party of the opportunity of putting forward an explanation for the default and/or of making submissions on the important issue of abuse of process.

1   See the report at [2006] Crim LR 62–63.

Fairness to third parties

10.158   Principles of even-handedness and fairness have also been held to apply, in the context of an abuse of process hearing where evidence is called, to the position of witnesses. In *A-G v Morgan; A-G v News Group Newspapers Ltd*[1] the Divisional Court held that where an application to stay had been founded on allegedly prejudicial publicity, it was irregular to have allowed the author of the criticised article (who was expecting to be a witness for the prosecution in the substantive trial) to be called as a witness on the application for a stay and then cross-examined at length as to his entire conduct vis-à-vis the article. The author should have first, been provided with an opportunity to take legal advice and second, having given evidence, should have been warned as to his privilege against self-incrimination.

1   [1998] EMLR 294, DC.

Third party abuse

1.159 In the light of the extensive disclosure obligations on the prosecution, in relation to third parties, and given the duties of disclosure incumbent upon the third parties themselves, it was not surprising to see judicial recognition of the concept of third party abuse in the decision of *R v Momodou*.[1] On the facts of the case, the third party who came in for criticism was a private company who ran an immigration detention centre, whose employees became prosecution witnesses in a criminal trial, there having been an arson and violent disorder at the centre. The abuse application arose from the fact that the third party employer had arranged for witness training for certain of its employees, some of whom were significant witnesses in the case. The Crown accepted that defence criticism of the witness training was justified.

1   [2005] 2 All ER 571.

1.160 The Court of Appeal found, on the facts of the case, that the trial judge properly dealt with the defence complaints by fully ventilating them before the jury, in the course of directions, which raised the potential difficulties they caused. In the course of his judgment Lord Justice Judge held as follows:

'The steady development of the abuse of process jurisdiction suggests that, notwithstanding that the prosecution or prosecuting authority may be blameless, as a matter of principle, the judge is vested with jurisdiction to order that proceedings should be stayed. The activities of third parties may constitute an abuse of process making a fair trial impossible, and if so, in an extreme case, this discretion is available to be exercised.'

1   See para 54 of the judgment.

The burden of proof

10.161 The applicant making the abuse of process submission has the burden of proving it, and the standard of proof is the balance of probabilities.[1] As Mann LJ commented, in *Telford Justices,* the manner in which the applicant discharges such an onus will depend on all the circumstances of the particular case. The applicant must carefully decide whether to make the submission on the papers, and agreed facts, or whether some initial calling of evidence, perhaps in a voir dire, is required.

1   *R v Telford Justices, ex p Badham*; *Attorney-General's Reference (No 1 of 1990)*; and *R v Cardiff Magistrate' Court, ex p Hole.*

10.162 It may well be essential for applicants to lay an evidential foundation for the intended submission. Indeed the Crown may take issue with the evidence presented, forcing the tribunal to make an initial determination as to the facts. The evidential burden would lie on the applicant. An example of such a situation might apply where a defence witness is called to testify to the effect that a number of important defence witnesses are unavailable by reason of the delay. The prosecution may challenge first, the assertion that they are important, second, the assertion that they are unavailable and third, that their alleged unavailability had anything to do with supposed prosecution led delay.

10.163 The *ex p Hole* decision provides clear guidance to applicants as to the manner in which the burden may be discharged. The Divisional Court there held that:

> 'If one is considering whether, on a balance of probabilities, the applicants are able to show that because of the delay they cannot fairly defend themselves against the charges, it is necessary to look at the charges and see exactly what defence it is that they are impeded from advancing'.

In essence, the burden is to specify the alleged prejudice or unfairness and whether or not it applies to oral or documentary evidence, for example, to directly relate such matters to the particular charge(s) against a defendant. In the above non-availability of evidence type submission, the burden would clearly be on the applicant to identify the witnesses he would have wished to call.

10.164 While the actual burden on applicants may in practice be less onerous in delay cases where there has been an exceptionally long delay, the burden of proof always remains on the applicant. In the *Tan v Cameron* decision[1] the Privy Counsel considered the vexed question as to whether there should be shifting burdens of proof, reversals of the burden of proof and rebuttable presumptions. The court held that the question as to whether proceedings ought to be stayed is a question to be considered 'in the round' and that nothing was to be gained by the introduction of shifting burdens of proof. The court was clearly not prepared to accept that in a case of substantial delay, prejudice was presumed to exist to the extent that the prosecution took on a burden to rebut such a presumption of prejudice.[2]

1   [1992] 2 AC 205, PC.
2   See also *R v Bow Street Magistrates, ex p DPP* (1989) 91 Cr App R 283.

10.165 What was described as a 'heavy' burden in the *Tan* decision, which was a delay case, may well be an even greater burden on the applicant who seeks a stay on the basis of alleged mala fides. In the case of *ex p Thomas*[1] the added evidential difficulties of proving dishonesty were considered by the Divisional Court. The essence of the defence case was an allegation that the prosecutor, who had unsuccessfully sought to extend custody time limits for defendants charged with a drugs importation offence, had dishonestly contrived to manipulate the prosecution process. The prosecutor had the defendants re-arrested, before they could leave the court building, on new charges of possession with intent to supply the self same drugs. The Divisional Court, remitting the case back to the magistrates, stated that the justices must bear in mind that the burden of establishing dishonesty lay fairly and squarely on the defence, and that it was a 'heavy' burden. Where the defence take on the mantle of proving dishonesty, as opposed to an error of judgment for example, the evidential hurdle is an obviously high one given the seriousness of the allegation.

1   See *R v Great Yarmouth Magistrates, ex p Thomas, Davis and Darlington* [1992] Crim LR 116; and *R v Rotherham Justices, ex p Brough* [1991] Crim LR 522.

The standard of proof

10.166   In cases where it is appropriate to consider the 'standard of proof', the applicant will have to satisfy a particular court or tribunal on the basis of the 'balance of probabilities' test. In *R (TP) v West London Youth Court*[1] the defence sought to judicially review an adverse ruling on abuse of process on the grounds that the District Judge should have applied a lesser standard of proof. In the context of an abuse application on fitness to stand trial, the defence contended that the judge should have asked himself whether there 'was a real possibility that the claimant would not be able to participate effectively'. The Divisional Court dismissed the application, and, in so doing, pointed out how 'It would be odd in the extreme if one species of abuse [referring to fitness to stand trial]... requires proof of a lesser standard'.[2] In the course of his judgment, Scott Baker LJ went on to make the important point that any trial judge who had concerns over a defendant's fitness to stand trial has a continuing jurisdiction, and that, should the stage be reached where it is apparent a defendant is unable to effectively participate, the proceedings may then be stayed.

1   [2006] 1 Cr App R 25
2   See Scott Baker LJ, p 408, at para 14 of the judgment.

Judicial discretion in delay cases

10.167   The language of burden and standard of proof has, however, been described as potentially misleading in relation to the exercise of judicial discretion in the case of applications to stay based on delay grounds. The Court of Appeal in the decision of *R v S (SP)*,[1] consistent with their approach in *Smolinski*, held that 'the discretionary decision whether or not to grant a stay as an abuse of process, because of delay, is an exercise in judicial assessment dependent on judgment rather than on any conclusion as to fact based on evidence'.[2] The court disapproved of the use of burden and standard terminology in these cases on the basis that such language was more apt to an evidence-based fact-finding process, which is clearly not necessarily the case in all delay abuse applications.

1   [2006] 2 Cr App R 23; 170 JP 434
2   See the judgment of Rose LJ (Vice President) at para 20.

Presentation

10.168   Before presenting the abuse arguments at court, the practitioner is well advised to have already taken specific client instructions on the matters raised. Certain species of abuse are clearly more directly connected than others to the clients' own particular recollection of a set of events; breach of promise or substantial delay cases being prime examples. Indeed the practitioner may also wish to question and take statements from defence witnesses in relation to abuse matters. Even if the client and his witnesses provide a long series of negative answers in relation to their ability to, for example, recall material events in the distant past, the same should be noted in their witness statements.

10.169   If an enquiry agent has, for example, also been used to investigate important aspects of a client's defence, the result of such investigation (if relevant to the abuse application) may also be reduced into an evidential format, possibly for use in a voir dire or in argument. Likewise, a compendious way of summarising the extensive efforts to prepare a client's case, which may have met with abject failure given the delay for example, could be for the solicitor in question to prepare a full, accurate and detailed witness statement..

10.170   In a sexual abuse delay case, for example, the solicitor could, in such a witness statement,, succinctly set out matters such as:

(1)   the names of defence witnesses who were to be traced; an outline of their relevance; the results of efforts to trace and proof the same;

(2)   details of the disclosure sought from the prosecution (such as unused material); an outline of its relevance; the results of efforts to receive the same and/or the availability;

(3)   details of efforts made to seek voluntary or other disclosure from third parties (such as social service files, medical records, educational records); an outline of the relevance of the same; the results of efforts to receive the same and/or the availability.

10.171   Such a solicitor could also annex to the statement the copy exhibits, such as letters or documents, which evidence the above-mentioned inquiries and their results. If the case has been thoroughly prepared and the solicitor's evidence is sufficiently relevant and material, such a document could clearly be of assistance to the court. Not only would it possibly save the court's valuable time, in terms of obviating the need for the calling of live evidence, it is presentationally more attractive, with more evidential weight than simple bland assertions in open court. If it is intended to contain certain disclosure from the clients' instructions, or from his witness statements (for example, re their inability to remember), the solicitor is advised to ask for the clients' specific consent to such a course.

10.172   The abuse of process Practice Directions make it clear that the practitioner is now expected to have his or her documentation well in order, be it a skeleton argument, bundle of trial documents and/or supplementary material, in readiness for such an application. In addition to the skeleton argument's submissions on law, possibly with a chronology of events and list of dramatis personae attached, it is sometimes helpful to annex copies of particularly pertinent abuse authorities. Having said that, practitioners are cautioned against the excessive citation of abuse authorities, which has been expressly disapproved of by the Divisional Court.[1]

1   See *R v Sheffield Stipendiary Magistrate, ex p Stephens* [1992] Crim LR 873.

Chapter 11

Confiscation proceedings

INTRODUCTION

11.01   That the court retains jurisdiction to stay an application for confiscation where it amounts to an abuse of the court's process is not in doubt. In *R v Mahmood and Shahin*,[1] Thomas LJ said this:[2]

> 'It was accepted on behalf of the Crown that a judge had in principle a discretion to stay proceedings if what the Crown was proceeding to do amounted to an abuse of process. We consider that that concession was rightly made by the Crown.'[3]

1   [2005] EWCA Crim 2168; [2006] Cr App R (S) 96, CA at 570.
2   At para 26.
3   See also *R v Farquhar* [2008] EWCA Crim 806 and *R v Nield* [2007] EWCA Crim 993.

11.02   However, in *R v Hockey*,[1] having acknowledged that the court can intervene if it concludes that the prosecuting authorities are abusing their powers, a clear note of caution was sounded:

> 'The Parliamentary intention is, in our judgment clear, and has been stated to be clear in decisions of the House of Lords and this court ... There is a borderline between legislative powers and judicial powers, and it is sometimes open to argument where that borderline should run. The intention of this statute is clear. It was not open to the judge to frustrate the intention of Parliament, as expressed in the statute, as he purported to do [by refusing to make a confiscation order].'

1   [2008] 1 Cr App R (S) 50, CA at para 18.

11.03   Nevertheless, it is clear that the court's power to stay is available as a remedy where a truly oppressive, and thus disproportionate, confiscation order would otherwise be made.

11.04   It is crucial for the practitioner to appreciate that factors that might well constitute an abuse of ordinary criminal proceedings would not necessarily do so in confiscation proceedings. The confiscation regime tolerates a large measure of harshness. The practitioner must understand the 'legislative intention' to which the Court of Appeal referred in *R v Hockey*[1] in order to identify circumstances in which an order will be oppressive, and not merely harsh. To do this, it is important to see the development of the law of confiscation.

1   Above para **11.02**.

PROCEEDS OF CRIME ACT 2002, PART 2

11.05   Part 2 of the Proceeds of Crime Act 2002 ('PoCA') is designed to provide a comprehensive system for the making and enforcement of confiscation orders. The PoCA regime replaces the previous legislation[1] and applies to offences committed on or after 24 March 2003. Although the focus of this chapter is the 2002 Act, the discussion below is equally applicable to the earlier confiscation regimes.

1   Drug Trafficking Offences Act 1986; Criminal Justice Act 1988; Drug Trafficking Act 1994.

11.06   A confiscation order is an *in personam* order made in the Crown Court requiring a convicted defendant to pay a sum of money within a given period of time, in default of which he must serve a term of imprisonment. Confiscation orders are not intended to be restitutionary measures; the term 'confiscation' is not used in the sense in which schoolchildren understand it.[1] A criminal who has benefited financially from crime but no longer possesses the specific proceeds will be deprived of assets of equivalent value, if he has them. The object is to deprive him, directly or indirectly, of what he has gained.

1   *R v May* [2008] 2 WLR 1131, HL per Lord Bingham at para 9.

11.07   If the prosecution asks the court to proceed with confiscation, it must do so (s 6(1)). Although the court was originally given a discretion as to whether to make a confiscation order, this was removed by Parliament[1] so the making of an order became a duty, and not just a power. A confiscation order became, in effect, a form of mandatory sentence; it goes without saying that the possibilities of injustice arising are greater in the case of a mandatory sentence.

1   By the amendments made to the Criminal Justice Act 1988 by the Proceeds of Crime Act 1995.

11.08   Throughout the complex legislative history, the essential structure of the confiscation regime introduced by the Drug Trafficking Offences Act 1986 has been retained. It requires the court, before making a confiscation order, to address and answer three questions:

(1)   Has the defendant (D) benefited from the relevant criminal conduct? If so;

(2)   What is the value of the benefit D has so obtained?

(3)   What sum is recoverable from D?

11.09   Although the method adopted by Parliament for calculating the amount of a confiscation order produces results which those subject to them doubtless consider grossly unfair, that method has repeatedly been upheld as fair and proportionate by the Court of Appeal, the House of Lords and the European Court on Human Rights. Proper application by the prosecution of what has been characterised as a fair system will not normally amount to an abuse of the process, even if the result for a defendant is harsh. Nevertheless, as we will see, the Court of Appeal has, very occasionally, invoked the abuse jurisdiction to quash unjust confiscation orders. If prosecuting authorities fail to exercise any judgment and instead continue to seek confiscation orders that bare no relation to the actual benefit to the offender, this trend has potential to become more widespread.

The 'intention of the statute'

11.10   Until legislative intervention beginning in 1986, the courts' powers of confiscation were narrow. So, in *R v Cuthbertson*[1] the House of Lords held[2] that the power of forfeiture and destruction conferred by s 27 of the Misuse of Drugs Act 1971[3] applied only to tangible property (including drugs, apparatus, vehicles and 'cash ready to be, or having just been, handed over for them') and did *not* attach to intangible property, or to property situated abroad. In particular, s 27 did not authorise the court to follow or trace assets which had been acquired with the property (e g cash) that could have been forfeited. As a means of stripping professional drug-traffickers of the profits of their unlawful enterprises (some £750,000 in that case), the powers of forfeiture were inadequate.

1   [1981] AC 470, HL.
2   With an expression of 'considerable regret' (at 479).
3   Under s 27 of the Misuse of Drugs Act 1971, 'anything shown to relate to the offence' is subject to forfeiture.

11.11   The decision in *Cuthbertson* prompted the establishment of a committee under the chairmanship of the Hon Mr Justice Hodgson.[1] The Committee's recommendations led to the enactment of the Drug Trafficking Offences Act 1986[2] which made provision for confiscation of the benefit of drug trafficking. Two years later, the court was given power to make a confiscation order against those convicted of crimes other than drug trafficking by s 71 of the Criminal Justice Act 1988. Parliament also gave effect to the UK's obligations under the Vienna Convention against Illicit Traffic in Narcotic Drugs and Psychotropic Substances (1988)[3] and the Council of Europe Convention on Laundering, Search, Seizure and Confiscation of the Proceeds of Crime (1991).[4] Part 5 of the Vienna Convention required parties to 'adopt such measures as may be necessary to enable confiscation of ... [the] proceeds derived from offences established in accordance with article 1, or property the value of which corresponds to that of such proceeds'. Article 5.7 provided for the reversal of the burden of proof.[5] Over time, the confiscation regimes were modified, extended (so as to include a distinct regime for terrorist offences: Terrorism Act 2000, Pt III) and tightened.

1   See Report of the Committee: *The Profits of Crime and their Recovery* (Heineman, 1984).
2   The Drug Trafficking Offences Act was repealed by the Drug Trafficking Act 1994 which extended the confiscation regime in relation to drug trafficking offences: see Pt 1.
3   United Nations Convention against Illicit Traffic in Narcotic Drugs and Psychotropic Substances (Vienna, 20 December 1988).
4   Council of Europe Convention on Laundering, Search, Seizure and Confiscation of the Proceeds of Crime (Strasbourg, 8 November 1990; ETS No 141). The convention aimed to facilitate international cooperation and mutual assistance in investigating crime and tracking down, seizing and confiscating the proceeds thereof.
5   'Each Party may consider ensuring that the onus of proof be reversed regarding the lawful origin of alleged proceeds or other property liable to confiscation, to the extent that such action is consistent with the principles of its domestic law and with the nature of judicial and other proceedings.'

'Draconian' statutory assumptions

11.12 Under each successive confiscation regime, in determining the value of the defendant's 'benefit', the courts have been able to assume that all property that passed through his hands during the six years preceding his conviction derived from the commission of criminal offences by him with which he has not been charged, still less convicted.[1] Thus the legislation, driven by international imperative, has reversed the burden of proof, requiring the defendant to show that his entire assets were not derived from criminal conduct.

1   DTOA, s 2(3); CJA, s72AA(4); DTA, s 4(3); PoCA, s 10. As Lord Bingham CJ explained in *R v Clarke and Bentham* [1997] 2 Cr App R (S) 99, CA at 102 (a drug trafficking case): 'The object of [the DTOA] is to strip drug traffickers of their ill-gotten gains, whether or not those gains are the product of the offence giving rise to the enquiry'.

11.13 It follows that the powers have not been restricted to confiscating the proceeds of the particular offence of which the defendant was convicted. The practical effect of the assumption is to require the court to presume that the defendant is a career criminal whose acquisitions and expenditure in the preceding six years represent the proceeds of his criminal activity. It is up to the defendant to prove (on the balance of probabilities) that it was not. The rationale of the confiscation regime was explained by Lord Woolf CJ in *R v Benjafield*[1] as follows:[2]

> 'The reason the legislation gives the courts the power to make confiscation orders and the reason why it creates statutory assumptions which interfere with the onus and burden of proof which normally exist in criminal proceedings is obvious and illustrated by the facts of these appeals. The provisions of the 1988 Act are aimed at depriving repeat offenders of the fruits of their crimes. The 1994 Act is aimed at achieving the same objective in relation to those who profit from drug trafficking. Both in the case of repeat offenders and drug traffickers, it is very much in the public interest that they are not able to profit from their crimes. If offenders are likely to lose their ill-gotten benefits, then this in itself will be a significant deterrent to the commission of further offences. In particular in relation to drug trafficking, justice requires that the profits made by the commission of those especially antisocial offences should be confiscated. Their profits are usually achieved at immense cost to those to whom the drugs are ultimately supplied. It is notoriously difficult to combat the traffickers' activities and the dangers that they create for society provide a justification for action out of the ordinary. In addition, those at whom the legislation is aimed, whether repeat offenders or drug traffickers, are usually adept at concealing their profits and unless they are called upon to explain the source of their assets, it will be frequently difficult and often impossible to identify the proceeds of their crimes.'

1   [2001] 3 WLR 75, CA.
2   At para 43.

11.14 In *R v Dickens*,[1] Lord Lane characterised the DTOA confiscation regime as follows:

> 'It is plain that the object of the Act is to ensure, so far as is possible, that the convicted drug trafficker is parted from the proceeds of any drug trafficking

which he has carried out. The provisions are intentionally Draconian. Since the amount of those proceeds and the size of his realisable assets at the time of conviction are likely to be peculiarly within the defendant's knowledge, it is not surprising perhaps if evidential burdens are cast upon him of a kind which are, to say the least, unusual in the area of the criminal law and this, despite the fact that the confiscation order and the penalties for failing to comply with it may be rigorous.'

1   [1990] 2 QB 102, CA.

11.15   Part 2 of the Proceeds of Crime Act is, if anything, intended to be more 'draconian'. Nevertheless, the confiscation legislation has, thus far, survived all challenges in the House of Lords and the European Court of Human Rights ('ECtHR'). Before considering specific situations where it may be possible to invoke the court's abuse of process jurisdiction, it is useful to consider the leading decisions as to the compatibility of the confiscation powers contained in the various Acts.

Draconian but ECHR compliant

11.16   There have been several challenges in the ECtHR to the confiscation regime directed at the compatibility of the assumptions. In the first of these, *Welch v UK*,[1] the court concluded that the confiscation regime amounted to a penalty, and so could not have retrospective application (cf Art 7(1)). However, the court made it plain that:

'... this conclusion concerns only the retrospective application of the relevant legislation and does not call into question in any respect the powers of confiscation conferred on the courts in a weapon in the fight against the scourge of drug trafficking.'

1   (1995) 20 EHRR 247.

11.17   *In Phillips v UK*,[1] following the applicant's conviction for a drug trafficking offence, a confiscation order was made under the DTA 1994 in the sum of £91,400. Although he had no declared taxable source of income, Phillips had deposited considerable sums of cash in his building society accounts in the period running up to his arrest; he had also purchased a property that he converted into four flats, invested in a newsagent's business and was the registered owner of five cars including a recently acquired BMW. He gave evidence at the confiscation hearing that the judge rejected as untruthful. In assessing the amount of the benefit, the judge applied the assumption in DTA, s 4(3). Before the ECtHR, Phillips claimed that the statutory assumptions breached his right to the presumption of innocence under Art 6.2. The UK Government argued that Art 6.2 was not engaged at all (though it conceded that Art 6.1 applied to confiscation).

1   European Court of Human Rights, Fourth Section: 5 July 2001.

11.18   The Court held that the purpose of the confiscation procedure was not the conviction or acquittal of the applicant for any other drug-related offence, but was 'to enable the national court to assess the amount at which the confiscation order should properly be fixed'.[1] Article 6.2 had no application, because the procedure, which was analogous to the determination of the amount of a fine or the length of imprisonment to be served, was part of the sentencing process and did not involve a new 'charge'. However, Art 6.1 applied throughout the entirety of the criminal proceedings and included a right to be presumed innocent and to require the prosecution to prove the allegations against the defendant (cf *Saunders v UK*[2]). The question of compatibility was not to be answered in the abstract, but rather by examining whether the way the assumptions applied in the applicant's case offended the basic principles of a fair trial procedure inherent in Art 6.1.[3] The confiscation process was fair because, although the application of the assumption[4] was mandatory, there were proper safeguards to protect a defendant: judicial proceeding; public hearing; advance disclosure; a measure of judicial discretion etc. In particular, a defendant had the opportunity to rebut the presumption by giving and calling evidence to show that the property in question was legitimately obtained. The applicant's complaint that the confiscation powers under the DTA 1994 were unreasonably extensive and in breach of the First Protocol was also dismissed. The interference with the applicant's right to peaceful enjoyment of property guaranteed by Art 1 was proportionate given the importance of the aim pursued by the legislation, namely the serious problem of drug trafficking.

1   At para 34.
2   European Court of Human Rights, Fourth Section: 17 December 1996, para 68.
3   At para 40.
4   In DTA, s 4(3).

11.19   Soon after *Phillips*, confiscation under both the CJA 1988 and the DTA 1994 was considered by the House of Lords in *R v Benjafield*; *R v Rezvi*.[1] Again, the issue was whether the statutory provisions which govern the making of confiscation orders under the DTA and CJA were compatible with the ECHR. The House of Lords (unanimously) held that the assumptions were not wider than was necessary to achieve the legitimate (and internationally recognised) aim in the public interest of depriving professional and habitual criminals of the proceeds of their criminal conduct and so were not incompatible with the defendants' Convention rights. It was a notorious fact that such criminals frequently take steps to conceal their profits from crime; putting a burden on the defendant was not disproportionate to the objective. Article 6.2 was not engaged because the confiscation proceedings did not amount to a 'charge' but were part of the sentencing process following a conviction for a relevant offence.[2] Parliament had devised 'a precise, fair and proportionate response to the important need to protect the public'.[3]

1   [2003] 1 AC 1099, HL. See also *McIntosh v Lord Advocate* [2003] 1 AC 1078, PC.
2   *Phillips v UK* (above para **11.17**) applied.
3   Per Lord Steyn at 1161.

11.20   Significantly though, Lord Steyn considered that one reason why the means adopted by the legislation to accomplish the legitimate aim were not wider than necessary was 'the role of the court in standing back and deciding whether there is or might be a risk of serious or real injustice and, if there is, or might be, in emphasising that a confiscation order ought not be made'.[1] However, as the Court of Appeal explained in *R v Ahmed*[2] and again *R v*

Neuberg[3], this remark is confined to the application of the assumptions and was not intended to suggest that the court has a surviving general discretion.

1   Per Lord Steyn at 1153..
2   [2005] 1 WLR 122, CA para 10.
3   [2007] EWCA Crim 1994, paras 29–30.

11.21   Once the court has determined the value of the defendant's benefit, it must assess the value of the realisable property available. The Court of Appeal has made it clear that, while the burden of proving benefit is on the prosecution, it is for the defendant to establish, on the balance of probabilities, that the amount that might be realised is less: if he fails to do so, the order should be made in the amount of the benefit as found by the court.[1] In *Grayson and Barnham v UK*[2] it was argued in the European Court of Human Rights that the fact that a legal burden was placed on a defendant to show he did not have realisable assets equivalent to the benefit figure offended the basic principles of a fair procedure in contravention of Art 6 and the 1st Protocol. The court concluded that the legislation did *not* violate the applicants' Convention rights. Noting the safeguards built into the system,[3] it was not unreasonable to expect a convicted person to explain what had happened to the money shown by the prosecution to have been in his possession any more than it was unreasonable at the first stage of the procedure (assessing benefit) to expect him to show the legitimacy of the source of such money or assets. Such matters fell within the applicants' particular knowledge and the burden would not have been difficult to meet had the accounts of their financial affairs been true.

1   *R v Barwick* [2001] 1 Cr App R (S) 445, CA.
2   European Court of Human Rights, Fourth Section: 23 September 2008.
3   Above para **11.18**.

11.22   Thus, each stage of the confiscation procedure has (so far) been found to be compatible with the Convention. A submission that the legislation is per se unfair is bound to fail. As Lord Steyn said in *Benjafield*:[1]

'The application by the Crown to apply primary legislation (subject to control by the court and subject to a full right of appeal on the part of the convicted defendant) could not amount to an abuse of the process of the court. The procedure is fair inasmuch as the sentencing court is duty bound not to make the assumptions if it might be unfair to do so.'

1   At para 20.

CONFISCATION AND JUDICIAL DISCRETION

11.23   In the passage from *Benjafield* quoted above,[1] Lord Steyn was referring to DTA, s 4(4), but PoCA, s 10(6) is in the same terms:[2]

'But the court must not make a required assumption in relation to particular property or expenditure if – (a)the assumption is shown to be incorrect, or (b)there will be a serious risk of injustice if the assumption were made.'

1   Above para **11.20**.
2   CJA, s 72AA(5) is also to identical effect.

11.24 It is by this method that the court is given a measure of discretion in relation to the assumptions. However, s 10(6)(b) does not give the court a general discretion not to make a confiscation order where it might cause hardship; rather, it applies only where a risk of injustice arises from the operation of the assumptions in the calculation of benefit. 'The purpose of the discretion is to ensure that there is a sensible calculation of benefit; it is not a discretionary exercise by the judge to determine whether or not it is fair to make an order against a particular defendant.'[1] What is contemplated is some unjust contradiction in the process of assumption (*e.g.* double counting of income and expenditure), or between an assumption and an agreed factual basis for sentence.

1   *R v Jones* [2007] 1 Cr App R (S) 71, CA at para 14.

11.25 So, in *R v Lunnon*,[1] where the defendant had submitted a detailed basis of plea and the prosecution had explicitly conceded that he had no prior involvement in drug trafficking, it was inconsistent with that concession for the court to assume all property that passed through his hands during the six years preceding his conviction derived from drug trafficking (s 4(3)). Accordingly, unless the concession was withdrawn, there would be an apparent injustice if the assumption was applied and s 4(4)(b) enabled the court to avoid the risk of injustice by disapplying the assumption. The Court of Appeal stressed that the obligation on the court under s 4(4)(b) to 'stand back' and make its own independent assessment was of fundamental importance, since this was what rendered the reverse burden of proof compatible with the requirements of Art 6 of the European Convention on Human Rights.

1   [2005] 1 Cr App R (S) 24, CA; c f *R v Lazarus* [2005] Crim LR 64, CA; *R v Threapleton* [2002] 2 Cr App R (S) 46 and *R v Olubutan*[2004] 2 Cr App R (S) 14.

CONFISCATION AND ABUSE OF PROCESS

11.26 Although this discretion is important, it is obviously limited. Once the Crown decides to invoke the confiscation process, the making of an order is mandatory and its amount is arithmetically determined. Apart from the discretion given by s 10(6)(b),[1] the amount cannot be moderated by judicial decision. The court cannot be criticised for applying the law, even if that law is draconian – it is meant to be (see above). Accordingly, the decision to invoke the confiscation process is a critical one, and one that is capable of being abused. It is for these reasons that the court has confirmed that it retains jurisdiction to stay an application for confiscation where it amounts to an abuse of the court's process.[2]

1   Above paras **11.23–11.25**.
2   Above para **11.01**.

Prosecutorial discretion

11.27 It will not be appropriate to seek confiscation in every single case where some benefit has been obtained by crime. The making of a confiscation order is not an automatic requirement whenever a person is convicted of a relevant offence; only if (i) the prosecution asks the court to proceed, or (ii) the court considers it appropriate must the court proceed to confiscation.[1] Accordingly there is an individual decision to be made by the Crown in *each case* whether to ask the court to apply the confiscation process. It is also open to the Crown, subject to the approval of the judge, to discontinue the confiscation proceedings at any stage.[2]

1   See DTA, s 2(1), CJA, s 71(1) and POCA, s 6(1) and (3).
2   *R v Shabir* [2008] EWCA Crim 1809 at para 22.

11.28   There is an individual exercise of judgment involved in each case. Plainly, the mere fact that the effect of a confiscation order will be to extract from a defendant a sum greater than his profit from his crime(s) is no basis to decline to seek an order; that will often be the effect of a confiscation order.

11.29   As we will see, the critical question is not whether it would be lawful to seek confiscation, but whether it would be oppressive. It is not open to the judge to refuse to make a confiscation order because he does not consider it necessary or appropriate, for to do so would frustrate the intention of Parliament,[1] but a judge can and should quash an application as an abuse of the court's process where the effect of the order when made would be oppressive. The well-known general observations of Lord Salmon in *DPP v Humphrys*[2] apply to a confiscation case as they do to any other application to stay on grounds of abuse of process:

> '... a judge has not and should not appear to have any responsibility for the institution of prosecutions; nor has he any power to refuse to allow a prosecution to proceed merely because he considers that, as a matter of policy, it ought not to have been brought. It is only if the prosecution amounts to an abuse of the process of the court and is oppressive and vexatious that the judge has the power to intervene.'

1   R v Hockey (above para 11.02).
2   [1977] AC 1, HL at 46.

R v Shabir

11.30   There will be situations where applying the law as it is would result in a confiscation order that is not merely harsh, but oppressive. The case of *R v Shabir*[1] is a recent example. The defendant was a pharmacist. He had to make a monthly claim to the appropriate NHS payment body for the cost of prescriptions dispensed. He dishonestly inflated several of his monthly claims by a small amount. He was paid monthly by way of BACS transfer; he was legally entitled to the vast majority of what he was paid, but had the payment body known that any monthly claim was inflated, he would not have been paid anything until his true entitlement was established.

1   Above para **11.27**.

11.31   He was indicted on counts of obtaining a money transfer by deception contrary to s 15A of the Theft Act 1968; the counts identified the full amount he had received in a particular month. He was convicted of six counts, not said to be 'samples'. Although the amount by which he inflated the relevant six claims was not precisely established at his trial, the calculation accepted by the judge for the purposes of sentencing was £464. Whilst not formally admitting the correctness of the precise figure, the prosecution accepted that the amount of the inflation involved in the six counts, taken together, did not exceed £5000 (indeed it was very much less); in other words, below the minimum amount required by s 75(4) before the assumptions can be applied. The total value of the six money transfers was £179,731.97. By statutory definition, the defendant had a criminal lifestyle, so that the various assumptions about his property which are prescribed by PoCA, s 10 fell to be made. In the event, the prosecution sought a confiscation order in a sum over £400,000. In the Crown Court, it was argued on behalf of the defendant that benefit should be calculated by reference to the amount he was *not entitled to*, rather than the total received.[1] That argument was rejected by the judge, following which agreement was reached between the prosecution and defence over figures.[2] The order made by the Judge was £212,464.17; on any view some hundreds of times the amount by which the defendant had inflated all his monthly claims taken together (£464).

1   Cf *R v Richards* [2005] EWCA Crim 491.
2   The fact that the defendant had agreed the benefit figure does not prevent him arguing that the confiscation order was unjust; *R v Hirani* [2008] EWCA Crim 1463 at para 35.

11.32   Although the counts on the indictment were appropriate as a matter of law, they failed to reflect what might be regarded as the 'true position'. The Court of Appeal concluded that it was patently oppressive to rely on the form of the counts (i) to bring the criminal lifestyle provisions into operation when they could not have applied if the charges had reflected the fact that the defendant's crimes involved fraud to an extent very much less than the threshold of £5,000, and (ii) to advance the contention that the defendant had benefited to the sum of over £179,000 when in any ordinary language his claims were dishonestly inflated by only a few hundred pounds.

11.33   On the very unusual and exceptional facts of this case, the Court was sure that, if application had been made to the judge to stay the confiscation application for abuse of process, it would have been granted. The confiscation order was quashed; a compensation order in the sum of £464 was substituted.

11.34   Although the Crown sought to apply the assumptions, this compounded, rather than caused, the unfairness. Had the court not applied the assumptions and considered only the defendant's *particular* benefit (s 6(4)(c)), the result (an order of not less than £179,000) would still have been oppressive. The court's statutory discretion not to apply the assumptions (s 10(6)(b)) would not have prevented an oppressive order being made.

Repayment by the defendant

11.35   Confiscation orders are not intended to be restitutionary measures. The victim may seek damages in the civil courts and, for this reason, Parliament has acknowledged that payment to the victim should have priority over a confiscation order. Although the making of a confiscation order is mandatory provided the conditions are met (s 6(1)), an exception is made where the victim of the offending has launched a civil claim to recover his or her losses (or intends to do so). In that event, the confiscation order is discretionary (s 6(6); below); the judge has a discretion as to whether to make an order and if so, in what amount (s 7(3)).

11.36 There is every reason, in the public interest, to encourage the prompt and voluntary repayment by the criminal of the benefit derived from the crime.[1] If before sentence, the defendant has made full restitution, there will be no occasion for the victim to make a civil claim. However, without either the fact or prospect of such proceedings, s 6(6) is not engaged; a person making full restitution in those circumstances has no protection. If the prosecution applies, a confiscation order will be made for the full sum of benefit obtained, up to the amount of the defendant's realisable/available assets. If the only benefit the defendant has obtained is the amount which he has already repaid to the loser, this has the inevitable consequence that there must be a confiscation order for the same sum again, so long as the defendant has assets to meet it. That means he pays up to double the benefit he has obtained from crime. A confiscation order sought in such circumstances is potentially abusive.

1   See *R v Mahmood & Shahin* (above para **11.01**); *R v Farquhar* (above para **11.01**).

11.37 In the conjoined appeals of *R v Morgan; R v Bygrave*,[1] exactly this issue was considered by the Court of Appeal. The facts of each case were highly material to the eventual outcome.

1   [2008] EWCA Crim 1323.

R v Morgan

11.38 Between July 2001 and his arrest in March 2004, Morgan cheated an elderly lady out of a total of £279,872.02. Adjusted for RPI inflation, his benefit from the offences was £306,913.93. Between his arrest and the confiscation hearing, he repaid about five-sixths of what he had obtained; he said that he stood ready to repay the balance. At the confiscation hearing, his benefit was assessed at £306,913.93; his realisable assets were found to be £106,259.46. The judge determined that a confiscation order was mandatory once the Crown had given notice invoking the confiscation procedure, and had to be made either for the full amount of benefit, or for the lesser sum of the defendant's realisable assets. Accordingly he made a confiscation order in the sum of £106,259.46, directing, pursuant to CJA 1988, s 72(7), that the outstanding loss suffered by the victim (£51,967.83) should be paid out of the sum confiscated.

R v Bygrave

11.39 Between January 2004 and October 2005, Bygrave stole a total of £12,768.17 from her employers by falsifying expenses and/or salary claims for herself. When interviewed, she admitted the thefts; she pleaded guilty at the first opportunity. She promised her employer that she would repay what she had stolen and she borrowed against her home to enable her to do so. In the event, the judge made a PoCA confiscation order in the sum of £12,768.17, but without directing (under s 13(6)) for compensation to be paid out of the confiscated monies (because he was not told he could do so). Because the defendant had said all along that she would repay them the whole of the loss, there had been no occasion for the employers to make any civil claim. As such money as she had went to satisfy the confiscation order, and thus disappeared into the coffers of the State, she was, in the event, unable to repay her employer; eventually they made a claim against her. So it was that about a year after sentence had been passed, the defendant sought leave to appeal the confiscation order.

The Court of Appeal

11.40   It was not asserted in either case that the Crown had given any form of undertaking or agreement not to seek it if repayment were made, so abuse of process was not established on the basis of it being unconscionable for the Crown to go back on a promise.[1] The Court held that it could amount to an abuse of process for the Crown to seek a confiscation order which would result in an order to pay up to double the full restitution which the defendant has made or is willing immediately to make, and which would thus deter him from making it. However, this would only be so where:

(a)   the defendant's crimes are limited to offences causing loss to one or more identifiable loser(s);

(b)   his benefit is limited to those crimes;

(c)   the loser has neither brought nor intends any civil proceedings to recover the loss; but

(d)   the defendant either has repaid the loser, or stands ready willing and able immediately to repay him, the full amount of the loss.[2]

1   Discussed in detail in **Chapter 2**.
2   It is likely to be difficult to establish abuse unless the defendant has either already made restitution in full or is in a position to tender it immediately in a guaranteed form, such as a banker's draft or funds in a solicitor's hands.

11.41   The Court made it absolutely clear that it is not sufficient to establish oppression (and thus abuse of process) that the effect of a confiscation order will be to extract from a defendant a sum greater than his profit from his crime(s). Even where there had been repayment (or the offer thereof), it might well be appropriate for the crown to seek confiscation if:

(a)   the defendant has significantly profited through use of the stolen money whilst it was in his hands and thus has obtained a benefit beyond the loss inflicted on the victim (as where stolen property had been invested in such a way that it had doubled in value); or

(b)   the Crown alleges that the statutory assumptions ought to be applied to demonstrate that the defendant has obtained a benefit beyond the loss inflicted upon the particular victim.

11.42   Similarly, if repayment in full is offered, but it is uncertain that it will be accomplished (as was the case for Morgan whose appeal was dismissed), there will be good reason for seeking a confiscation order, particularly given that the judge can direct that compensation to the victim be made out of the sum recovered (s 13(6)) – the actual result in the case of *Bygrave*.

HARSH BUT NOT ABUSIVE

11.43   Situations where a confiscation order may be regarded as harsh by the defendant, but is fair when judged according to the legislative intention (and so not an abuse of the process) might include the following.

Criminal property recovered by the authorities

11.44   There is nothing oppressive about a confiscation order made in the full value of the property obtained where the defendant has made no profit at all (and may have made a substantial loss) because the criminal property has been recovered from him by the investigators.[1]

1   See, for example, *R v David Smith* [2002] 1 WLR 54; HL.

Multiple recovery

11.45   Where two or more defendants obtained and shared the benefit of crime, each has obtained the full value of the benefit and each is liable to confiscation orders up to that full value.[1]

1   See, for example, *R v May* (above para **11.06**) at para 46.

'Hidden assets' orders

11.46   If the defendant fails to persuade the court that the value of his assets is less than the benefit figure, a confiscation order should be made in the amount of the benefit.[1] Although such orders are said to assume the existence of undeclared or hidden assets, the making of such an order is no more than a consequence of the burden of proof and will never amount to an abuse of the process.

1   *R v Barwick* (above para **11.21**); *Grayson and Barnham v UK* (above para **11.21**).

Benefit not profit

11.47   Criminals frequently incur considerable expense in the process of the crime which cannot be deducted when calculating the value of the benefit; the benefit is the value of gross receipts, not net profit.[1]

1   *R v Banks* [1997] 2 Cr App R (S) 110, CA.

Application of the assumptions

11.48   It is clearly not sufficient to establish oppression, and thus abuse of process, that the effect of confiscation will be to extract from a defendant a sum greater than his net profit from his crime(s). If it is a case in which the criminal lifestyle provisions of PoCA can be applied, it may be perfectly proper for a confiscation order to be vastly greater than the gain from the offences of which the defendant has been convicted. That is the whole purpose of the criminal lifestyle provisions and is inherent in the statutory scheme; they extend the reach of confiscation beyond the particular offences of which the defendant has been convicted. Moreover, the legislation provides a mechanism to disapply the assumptions where to do so might cause injustice.[1]

1   See above paras **11.23–11.25**.

CONCLUSIONS

11.49   These recent decisions represent a welcome development in this area of the law. As has been observed by the domestic courts and the ECtHR, confiscation achieves the legitimate (and internationally recognised) aim in the public interest of depriving professional and habitual criminals of the proceeds of their criminal conduct. Nevertheless, the courts have also recognised that an important element in the overall fairness of the regime is the existence of proper safeguards to protect a defendant, including judicial control over the proceedings. Even if the prosecution asks the court to proceed with confiscation, in which case it is mandatory for the court to proceed (s 6(1)), the court retains power to stay for abuse of process.

11.50   It should be remembered that confiscation was originally intended for cases of repeat offenders and drug traffickers; this is the reason for the assumption about property held in the six years preceding his conviction being derived from drug trafficking/the commission of criminal offences by him.[1] In cases that are far removed from the paradigm 'repeat offenders and drug traffickers' case, applying the assumptions may lead to great unfairness, not in the public interest.[2]

1   DTOA, s 2(3); CJA, s 72AA(4); DTA, s 4(3)); PoCA, s 10.
2   For trenchant criticism of the capacity of the confiscation regime to produce unfairness see the commentary in 'Criminal Law Week' in the following cases: *R v Mahmood and Shahin* CLW/05/34/9; *R v Farquhar* CLW/08/18/10; *R v Morgan*; *R v Bygrave* CLW/08/25/35; *R v Shabir* CLW/08/33/9.

11.51   These decisions also represent a timely reminder to the prosecuting authority that confiscation need not be sought in every case. On the contrary, as Lord Justice Hughes observed in *R v Shabir*,[1] there is an individual decision to be made by the Crown in *each case* whether to ask the court to apply the confiscation process. Even if the court has already been asked to embark upon confiscation, the prosecutor may discontinue the confiscation proceedings at any stage. Importantly, the Court expressly acknowledged the desirability of sensible give and take in anticipation of confiscation proceedings and that the Crown has a discretion whether to ask for an order, and if so, in what amount.

1   Above para **11.27**.

11.52   Whether an application for confiscation is or is not oppressive will fall to be considered by the trial judge individually on the facts of each case. Where abuse of process is relied upon, it is essential to make the application in the Crown Court; the Court of Appeal will not usually be in a position to make findings of fact that should have been made by the judge, and, save in a very clear case (like *Shabir*) will be assisted in knowing whether, as a matter of judgment ,the trial judge would have refused a stay.[1]

1   *R v Shabir* (above para **11.27**) at para 26.

Code for Crown Prosecutors

The Crown Prosecution Service is the principal public prosecuting authority for England and Wales and is headed by the Director of Public Prosecutions. The Attorney General is accountable to Parliament for the Service.

The Crown Prosecution Service is a national organisation consisting of 42 Areas. Each Area is headed by a Chief Crown Prosecutor and corresponds to a single police force area, with one for London. It was set up in 1986 to prosecute cases investigated by the police.

Although the Crown Prosecution Service works closely with the police, it is independent of them. The independence of Crown Prosecutors is of fundamental constitutional importance. Casework decisions taken with fairness, impartiality and integrity help deliver justice for victims, witnesses, defendants and the public.

The Crown Prosecution Service co-operates with the investigating and prosecuting agencies of other jurisdictions.

The Director of Public Prosecutions is responsible for issuing a Code for Crown Prosecutors under section 10 of the Prosecution of Offences Act 1985, giving guidance on the general principles to be applied when making decisions about prosecutions. This is the fifth edition of the Code and replaces all earlier versions. For the purpose of this Code, 'Crown Prosecutor' includes members of staff in the Crown Prosecution Service who are designated by the Director of Public Prosecutions under section 7A of the Act and are exercising powers under that section.

1 INTRODUCTION

1.1   The decision to prosecute an individual is a serious step. Fair and effective prosecution is essential to the maintenance of law and order. Even in a small case a prosecution has serious implications for all involved — victims, witnesses and defendants. The Crown Prosecution Service applies the Code for Crown Prosecutors so that it can make fair and consistent decisions about prosecutions.

1.2   The Code helps the Crown Prosecution Service to play its part in making sure that justice is done. It contains information that is important to police officers and others who work in the criminal justice system and to the general public. Police officers should apply the provisions of this Code whenever they are responsible for deciding whether to charge a person with an offence.

1.3   The Code is also designed to make sure that everyone knows the principles that the Crown Prosecution Service applies when carrying out its work. By applying the same principles, everyone involved in the system is helping to treat victims, witnesses and defendants fairly, while prosecuting cases effectively.

2 GENERAL PRINCIPLES

2.1   Each case is unique and must be considered on its own facts and merits. However, there are general principles that apply to the way in which Crown Prosecutors must approach every case.

2.2   Crown Prosecutors must be fair, independent and objective. They must not let any personal views about ethnic or national origin, disability, sex, religious beliefs, political views or the sexual orientation of the suspect, victim or witness influence their decisions. They must not be affected by improper or undue pressure from any source.

2.3   It is the duty of Crown Prosecutors to make sure that the right person is prosecuted for the right offence. In doing so, Crown Prosecutors must always act in the interests of justice and not solely for the purpose of obtaining a conviction.

2.4   Crown Prosecutors should provide guidance and advice to investigators throughout the investigative and prosecuting process. This may include lines of inquiry, evidential requirements and assistance in any pre-charge procedures. Crown Prosecutors will be proactive in identifying and, where possible, rectifying evidential deficiencies and in bringing to an early conclusion those cases that cannot be strengthened by further investigation.

2.5   It is the duty of Crown Prosecutors to review, advise on and prosecute cases, ensuring that the law is properly applied, that all relevant evidence is put before the court and that obligations of disclosure are complied with, in accordance with the principles set out in this Code.

2.6   The Crown Prosecution Service is a public authority for the purposes of the Human Rights Act 1998. Crown Prosecutors must apply the principles of the European Convention on Human Rights in accordance with the Act.

3 THE DECISION TO PROSECUTE

3.1   In most cases, Crown Prosecutors are responsible for deciding whether a person should be charged with a criminal offence, and if so, what that offence should be. Crown Prosecutors make these decisions in accordance with this Code and the Director's Guidance on Charging. In those cases where the police determine the charge, which are usually more minor and routine cases, they apply the same provisions.

3.2   Crown Prosecutors make charging decisions in accordance with the Full Code Test (see section 5 below), other than in those limited circumstances where the Threshold Test applies (see section 6 below).

3.3   The Threshold Test applies where the case is one in which it is proposed to keep the suspect in custody after charge, but the evidence required to apply the Full Code Test is not yet available.

3.4   Where a Crown Prosecutor makes a charging decision in accordance with the Threshold Test, the case must be reviewed in accordance with the Full Code Test as soon as reasonably practicable, taking into account the progress of the investigation.

4 REVIEW

4.1   Each case the Crown Prosecution Service receives from the police is reviewed to make sure that it is right to proceed with a prosecution. Unless the Threshold Test applies, the Crown Prosecution Service will only start or continue with a prosecution when the case has passed both stages of the Full Code Test.

4.2 Review is a continuing process and Crown Prosecutors must take account of any change in circumstances. Wherever possible, they should talk to the police first if they are thinking about changing the charges or stopping the case. Crown Prosecutors should also tell the police if they believe that some additional evidence may strengthen the case. This gives the police the chance to provide more information that may affect the decision.

4.3 The Crown Prosecution Service and the police work closely together, but the final responsibility for the decision whether or not a charge or a case should go ahead rests with the Crown Prosecution Service.

5 THE FULL CODE TEST

5.1 The Full Code Test has two stages. The first stage is consideration of the evidence. If the case does not pass the evidential stage it must not go ahead no matter how important or serious it may be. If the case does pass the evidential stage, Crown Prosecutors must proceed to the second stage and decide if a prosecution is needed in the public interest. The evidential and public interest stages are explained below.

The evidential stage

5.2 Crown Prosecutors must be satisfied that there is enough evidence to provide a 'realistic prospect of conviction' against each defendant on each charge. They must consider what the defence case may be, and how that is likely to affect the prosecution case.

5.3 A realistic prospect of conviction is an objective test. It means that a jury or bench of magistrates or judge hearing a case alone, properly directed in accordance with the law, is more likely than not to convict the defendant of the charge alleged. This is a separate test from the one that the criminal courts themselves must apply. A court should only convict if satisfied so that it is sure of a defendant's guilt.

5.4 When deciding whether there is enough evidence to prosecute, Crown Prosecutors must consider whether the evidence can be used and is reliable. There will be many cases in which the evidence does not give any cause for concern. But there will also be cases in which the evidence may not be as strong as it first appears. Crown Prosecutors must ask themselves the following questions:

Can the evidence be used in court?

a   Is it likely that the evidence will be excluded by the court? There are certain legal rules which might mean that evidence which seems relevant cannot be given at a trial. For example, is it likely that the evidence will be excluded because of the way in which it was gathered? If so, is there enough other evidence for a realistic prospect of conviction?

Is the evidence reliable?

b   Is there evidence which might support or detract from the reliability of a confession? Is the reliability affected by factors such as the defendant's age, intelligence or level of understanding?

c   What explanation has the defendant given? Is a court likely to find it credible in the light of the evidence as a whole? Does it support an innocent explanation?

d   If the identity of the defendant is likely to be questioned, is the evidence about this strong enough?

e   Is the witness's background likely to weaken the prosecution case? For example, does the witness have any motive that may affect his or her attitude to the case, or a relevant previous conviction?

f   Are there concerns over the accuracy or credibility of a witness? Are these concerns based on evidence or simply information with nothing to support it? Is there further evidence which the police should be asked to seek out which may support or detract from the account of the witness?

5.5   Crown Prosecutors should not ignore evidence because they are not sure that it can be used or is reliable. But they should look closely at it when deciding if there is a realistic prospect of conviction.

The public interest stage

5.6   In 1951, Lord Shawcross, who was Attorney General, made the classic statement on public interest, which has been supported by Attorneys General ever since: "It has never been the rule in this country — I hope it never will be — that suspected criminal offences must automatically be the subject of prosecution". (House of Commons Debates, volume 483, column 681, 29 January 1951.)

5.7   The public interest must be considered in each case where there is enough evidence to provide a realistic prospect of conviction. Although there may be public interest factors against prosecution in a particular case, often the prosecution should go ahead and those factors should be put to the court for consideration when sentence is being passed. A prosecution will usually take place unless there are public interest factors tending against prosecution which clearly outweigh those tending in favour, or it appears more appropriate in all the circumstances of the case to divert the person from prosecution (see section 8 below).

5.8   Crown Prosecutors must balance factors for and against prosecution carefully and fairly. Public interest factors that can affect the decision to prosecute usually depend on the seriousness of the offence or the circumstances of the suspect. Some factors may increase the need to prosecute but others may suggest that another course of action would be better.

The following lists of some common public interest factors, both for and against prosecution, are not exhaustive. The factors that apply will depend on the facts in each case.

Some common public interest factors in favour of prosecution

5.9   The more serious the offence, the more likely it is that a prosecution will be needed in the public interest. A prosecution is likely to be needed if:

a   a conviction is likely to result in a significant sentence;

b   a conviction is likely to result in a confiscation or any other order;

c   a weapon was used or violence was threatened during the commission of the offence;

d   the offence was committed against a person serving the public (for example, a police or prison officer, or a nurse);

e   the defendant was in a position of authority or trust;

f   the evidence shows that the defendant was a ringleader or an organiser of the offence;

g   there is evidence that the offence was premeditated;

h   there is evidence that the offence was carried out by a group;

i   the victim of the offence was vulnerable, has been put in considerable fear, or suffered personal attack, damage or disturbance;

j   the offence was committed in the presence of, or in close proximity to, a child;

k   the offence was motivated by any form of discrimination against the victim's ethnic or national origin, disability, sex, religious beliefs, political views or sexual orientation, or the suspect demonstrated hostility towards the victim based on any of those characteristics;

l   there is a marked difference between the actual or mental ages of the defendant and the victim, or if there is any element of corruption;

m   the defendant's previous convictions or cautions are relevant to the present offence;

n   the defendant is alleged to have committed the offence while under an order of the court;

o   there are grounds for believing that the offence is likely to be continued or repeated, for example, by a history of recurring conduct;

p   the offence, although not serious in itself, is widespread in the area where it was committed; or

q   a prosecution would have a significant positive impact on maintaining community confidence.

Some common public interest factors against prosecution

5.10 A prosecution is less likely to be needed if:

a   the court is likely to impose a nominal penalty;

b   the defendant has already been made the subject of a sentence and any further conviction would be unlikely to result in the imposition of an additional sentence or order, unless the nature of the particular offence requires a prosecution or the defendant withdraws consent to have an offence taken into consideration during sentencing;

c   the offence was committed as a result of a genuine mistake or misunderstanding (these factors must be balanced against the seriousness of the offence);

d   the loss or harm can be described as minor and was the result of a single incident, particularly if it was caused by a misjudgement;

e   there has been a long delay between the offence taking place and the date of the trial, unless:

- the offence is serious;

- the delay has been caused in part by the defendant;

- the offence has only recently come to light; or

- the complexity of the offence has meant that there has been a long investigation;

f   a prosecution is likely to have a bad effect on the victim's physical or mental health, always bearing in mind the seriousness of the offence;

g   the defendant is elderly or is, or was at the time of the offence, suffering from significant mental or physical ill health, unless the offence is serious or there is real possibility that it may be repeated. The Crown Prosecution Service, where necessary, applies Home Office guidelines about how to deal with mentally disordered offenders. Crown Prosecutors must balance the desirability of diverting a defendant who is suffering from significant mental or physical ill health with the need to safeguard the general public;

h   the defendant has put right the loss or harm that was caused (but defendants must not avoid prosecution or diversion solely because they pay compensation); or

i   details may be made public that could harm sources of information, international relations or national security.

5.11 Deciding on the public interest is not simply a matter of adding up the number of factors on each side. Crown Prosecutors must decide how important each factor is in the circumstances of each case and go on to make an overall assessment.

The relationship between the victim and the public interest

5.12 The Crown Prosecution Service does not act for victims or the families of victims in the same way as solicitors act for their clients. Crown Prosecutors act on behalf of the public and not just in the interests of any particular individual. However, when considering the public interest, Crown Prosecutors should always take into account the consequences for the victim of whether or not to prosecute, and any views expressed by the victim or the victim's family.

5.13 It is important that a victim is told about a decision which makes a significant difference to the case in which they are involved. Crown Prosecutors should ensure that they follow any agreed procedures.

6 THE THRESHOLD TEST

6.1 The Threshold Test requires Crown Prosecutors to decide whether there is at least a reasonable suspicion that the suspect has committed an offence, and if there is, whether it is in the public interest to charge that suspect.

6.2 The Threshold Test is applied to those cases in which it would not be appropriate to release a suspect on bail after charge, but the evidence to apply the Full Code Test is not yet available.

6.3 There are statutory limits that restrict the time a suspect may remain in police custody before a decision has to be made whether to charge or release the suspect. There will be cases where the suspect in custody presents a substantial bail risk if released, but much of the evidence may not be available at the time the charging decision has to be made. Crown Prosecutors will apply the Threshold Test to such cases for a limited period.

6.4   The evidential decision in each case will require consideration of a number of factors including:

●   the evidence available at the time;

●   the likelihood and nature of further evidence being obtained;

●   the reasonableness for believing that evidence will become available;

●   the time it will take to gather that evidence and the steps being taken to do so;

●   the impact the expected evidence will have on the case;

●   the charges that the evidence will support.

6.5   The public interest means the same as under the Full Code Test, but will be based on the information available at the time of charge which will often be limited.

6.6   A decision to charge and withhold bail must be kept under review. The evidence gathered must be regularly assessed to ensure the charge is still appropriate and that continued objection to bail is justified. The Full Code Test must be applied as soon as reasonably practicable.

7 SELECTION OF CHARGES

7.1   Crown Prosecutors should select charges which:

a   reflect the seriousness and extent of the offending;

b   give the court adequate powers to sentence and impose appropriate post-conviction orders; and

c   enable the case to be presented in a clear and simple way.

This means that Crown Prosecutors may not always choose or continue with the most serious charge where there is a choice.

7.2   Crown Prosecutors should never go ahead with more charges than are necessary just to encourage a defendant to plead guilty to a few. In the same way, they should never go ahead with a more serious charge just to encourage a defendant to plead guilty to a less serious one.

7.3   Crown Prosecutors should not change the charge simply because of the decision made by the court or the defendant about where the case will be heard.

8 DIVERSION FROM PROSECUTION

Adults

8.1   When deciding whether a case should be prosecuted in the courts, Crown Prosecutors should consider the alternatives to prosecution. Where appropriate, the availability of suitable rehabilitative, reparative or restorative justice processes can be considered.

8.2 Alternatives to prosecution for adult suspects include a simple caution and a conditional caution.

Simple caution

8.3 A simple caution should only be given if the public interest justifies it and in accordance with Home Office guidelines. Where it is felt that such a caution is appropriate, Crown Prosecutors must inform the police so they can caution the suspect. If the caution is not administered, because the suspect refuses to accept it, a Crown Prosecutor may review the case again.

Conditional caution

8.4 A conditional caution may be appropriate where a Crown Prosecutor considers that while the public interest justifies a prosecution, the interests of the suspect, victim and community may be better served by the suspect complying with suitable conditions aimed at rehabilitation or reparation. These may include restorative processes.

8.5 Crown Prosecutors must be satisfied that there is sufficient evidence for a realistic prospect of conviction and that the public interest would justify a prosecution should the offer of a conditional caution be refused or the offender fail to comply with the agreed conditions of the caution.

8.6 In reaching their decision, Crown Prosecutors should follow the Conditional Cautions Code of Practice and any guidance on conditional cautioning issued or approved by the Director of Public Prosecutions.

8.7 Where Crown Prosecutors consider a conditional caution to be appropriate, they must inform the police, or other authority responsible for administering the conditional caution, as well as providing an indication of the appropriate conditions so that the conditional caution can be administered.

Youths

8.8 Crown Prosecutors must consider the interests of a youth when deciding whether it is in the public interest to prosecute. However Crown Prosecutors should not avoid prosecuting simply because of the defendant's age. The seriousness of the offence or the youth's past behaviour is very important.

8.9 Cases involving youths are usually only referred to the Crown Prosecution Service for prosecution if the youth has already received a reprimand and final warning, unless the offence is so serious that neither of these were appropriate or the youth does not admit committing the offence. Reprimands and final warnings are intended to prevent re-offending and the fact that a further offence has occurred indicates that attempts to divert the youth from the court system have not been effective. So the public interest will usually require a prosecution in such cases, unless there are clear public interest factors against prosecution.

9 MODE OF TRIAL

9.1 The Crown Prosecution Service applies the current guidelines for magistrates who have to decide whether cases should be tried in the Crown Court when the offence gives the option and the defendant does not indicate a guilty plea. Crown Prosecutors should recommend Crown Court trial when they are satisfied that the guidelines require them to do so.

9.2   Speed must never be the only reason for asking for a case to stay in the magistrates' courts. But Crown Prosecutors should consider the effect of any likely delay if they send a case to the Crown Court, and any possible stress on victims and witnesses if the case is delayed.

10 ACCEPTING GUILTY PLEAS

10.1   Defendants may want to plead guilty to some, but not all, of the charges. Alternatively, they may want to plead guilty to a different, possibly less serious, charge because they are admitting only part of the crime. Crown Prosecutors should only accept the defendant's plea if they think the court is able to pass a sentence that matches the seriousness of the offending, particularly where there are aggravating features. Crown Prosecutors must never accept a guilty plea just because it is convenient.

10.2   In considering whether the pleas offered are acceptable, Crown Prosecutors should ensure that the interests of the victim and, where possible, any views expressed by the victim or victim's family, are taken into account when deciding whether it is in the public interest to accept the plea. However, the decision rests with the Crown Prosecutor.

10.3   It must be made clear to the court on what basis any plea is advanced and accepted. In cases where a defendant pleads guilty to the charges but on the basis of facts that are different from the prosecution case, and where this may significantly affect sentence, the court should be invited to hear evidence to determine what happened, and then sentence on that basis.

10.4   Where a defendant has previously indicated that he or she will ask the court to take an offence into consideration when sentencing, but then declines to admit that offence at court, Crown Prosecutors will consider whether a prosecution is required for that offence. Crown Prosecutors should explain to the defence advocate and the court that the prosecution of that offence may be subject to further review.

10.5   Particular care must be taken when considering pleas which would enable the defendant to avoid the imposition of a mandatory minimum sentence. When pleas are offered, Crown Prosecutors must bear in mind the fact that ancillary orders can be made with some offences but not with others.

11 PROSECUTORS' ROLE IN SENTENCING

11.1   Crown Prosecutors should draw the court's attention to:

- any aggravating or mitigating factors disclosed by the prosecution case;

- any victim personal statement;

- where appropriate, evidence of the impact of the offending on a community;

- any statutory provisions or sentencing guidelines which may assist;

- any relevant statutory provisions relating to ancillary orders (such as anti-social behaviour orders).

11.2   The Crown Prosecutor should challenge any assertion made by the defence in mitigation that is inaccurate, misleading or derogatory. If the defence persist in the assertion, and it appears relevant to the sentence, the court should be invited to hear evidence to determine the facts and sentence accordingly.

12 RE-STARTING A PROSECUTION

12.1 People should be able to rely on decisions taken by the Crown Prosecution Service. Normally, if the Crown Prosecution Service tells a suspect or defendant that there will not be a prosecution, or that the prosecution has been stopped, that is the end of the matter and the case will not start again. But occasionally there are special reasons why the Crown Prosecution Service will re-start the prosecution, particularly if the case is serious.

12.2 These reasons include:

a   rare cases where a new look at the original decision shows that it was clearly wrong and should not be allowed to stand;

b   cases which are stopped so that more evidence which is likely to become available in the fairly near future can be collected and prepared. In these cases, the Crown Prosecutor will tell the defendant that the prosecution may well start again; and

c   cases which are stopped because of a lack of evidence but where more significant evidence is discovered later.

12.3 There may also be exceptional cases in which, following an acquittal of a serious offence, the Crown Prosecutor may, with the written consent of the Director of Public Prosecutions, apply to the Court of Appeal for an order quashing the acquittal and requiring the defendant to be retried, in accordance with Part 10 of the Criminal Justice Act 2003.

CPS Legal Guidance on the Reinstitution of Proceedings

REINSTITUTION OF PROCEEDINGS

- Principle
    - o   Purpose of guidance
    - o   Fundamental principles
- Guidance
    - o   Fresh or further evidence
    - o   Special circumstances
- Procedure
    - o   Level of decision-making
    - o   Explaining the decision to terminate proceedings
    - o   Casework handling
- Relevant links
- Annex A

NOTE: This guidance should be read alongside the guidance on termination of proceedings.

Principle

Purpose of guidance

This guidance gives effect to the Attorney General's undertaking to Parliament of 31 March 1993 (at Annex A) concerning the exercise of the CPS discretion to institute, reinstitute or continue proceedings after a suspect has been informed by the police or CPS of a decision not to prosecute.

The undertaking does not affect a decision:

- to offer no evidence at committal proceedings; or
- to withdraw transfer proceedings because the court refuses an adjournment (see guidance on voluntary bills of indictment).

References in this guidance to 'reinstitution' cover the institution and continuation of proceedings after a suspect has been informed by the police or the CPS of a decision not to prosecute.

Fundamental principles

There is a presumption that once a suspect is informed of a decision not to prosecute, s/he is entitled to rely on that decision. Therefore, such a decision should not ordinarily be revoked. A decision to reinstitute proceedings can only be justified in those exceptional cases that fall into one of the following categories:

i. where the decision not to prosecute was taken, and expressed to be taken, on the ground that there was insufficient evidence and **further significant evidence** comes to light (see section 23(9) of the Prosecution of Offences Act 1985 for the residual power to reinstitute proceedings in this category); or

ii. where **special circumstances** exist that require the reinstitution of proceedings to maintain public confidence in the criminal justice system.

The accused should be informed promptly of any decision to reinstitute proceedings.

Guidance

i. Fresh or further evidence

'Evidence' in this context means all evidence and unused material received by the police by the final date for consultation, prior to discontinuance. The CPS should not discontinue a case until the final date for consultation with the police has expired. It also includes material of which the police are aware but do not have in their physical possession and evidence that is not in an admissible form.

'Fresh or further evidence' means significant evidence received by the police after the final date for consultation. It excludes evidence that the police knew about or had in their possession but did not forward to the CPS until after the expiry of the final date for consultation.

The CPS may consider reinstituting proceedings on receipt of further evidence, *unless*:

- the defendant has been acquitted;
- the case has been dismissed; or
- the offence is summary only and the statutory time limit has expired.

It is essential to consult the police before taking a decision to discontinue a case, in order to confirm that all of the evidence in the case has been communicated to the CPS (see guidance on termination of proceedings).

When a case is discontinued in order to obtain forensic evidence and the CPS expressly indicates that proceedings are likely to be reinstituted on receipt of that evidence, the case does not fall within this category but is instead classified as 'special circumstances'.

ii. Special circumstances

The following are examples of 'special circumstances' that may require the reinstitution of proceedings to maintain confidence in the criminal justice system:

- where **proceedings were terminated expressly to obtain evidence** that was likely to become available;

- where the **suspect knowingly contributed to the provision of misleading information** and that was a material reason for the decision to discontinue proceedings on public interest grounds; or

- where the original **decision to discontinue was unjustified** and a prosecution is required to maintain public confidence in the criminal justice system.

Cases involving **unjustified decisions to discontinue** are likely to be rare (see Attorney General's undertaking at Annex A). Discontinuance must never be approached on the basis that erroneous decisions can always be rectified by reinstitution.

In such cases, the decision-maker must be satisfied that:

- the prosecutor who originally discontinued the case made a significant error of law or fact in applying the evidential or the public interest test (although if the original error was on public interest grounds only, it may be inappropriate to reinstitute proceedings); **and**

- the decision was not one that a reasonable prosecutor could have made in the circumstances and so cannot be justified.

Factors to consider

Current law and policy should be applied when deciding whether to institute proceedings in order to maintain public confidence in the criminal justice system.

There is no definitive list of factors to consider when making such decisions; however, the following are potentially relevant:

- the views of witnesses;

- the views of the victim(s);

- delay; and

- potential abuse of process arguments (see guidance on abuse of process).

Serious offences are much more likely to demand reinstitution than low-level or summary only offences.

Procedure

Level of decision-making

The decision to reinstitute proceedings must be taken by a CCP (or ACCP in London).

Explaining the decision to terminate proceedings

i. Charging/reporting stage

The police must inform the CPS if they have told an accused that s/he will not be charged or reported for an offence.

The CPS should advise the police to explain to the suspect:

- that the decision was taken on the basis of available information; and

- whether the decision was taken on evidential or public interest grounds.

ii. Pre-court

If a case is discontinued before the case goes to court, the accused will be informed by notice under section 23 of the Prosecution of Offences Act 1985 (see Archbold paragraph 1–276). It is, however, advisable to consult a CCP before issuing a discontinuance notice or making an application to withdraw charges at court where it is intended to reinstitute proceedings at a later date.

The accused will then have a right to issue a revival notice (see guidance on termination of proceedings).

The accused should always be informed where proceedings have been discontinued with a view to reinstitution.

iii. Court

Prosecutors may apply to withdraw proceedings at court (refer to guidance on termination of proceedings). Prosecutors must, however, make a full endorsement of applications to withdraw and should invite the court clerk to make a full record on the court file.

The defendant must be told of the risk of proceedings being reinstituted.

Where the CPS is withdrawing proceedings because the requisite evidence is currently unavailable, prosecutors must make this clear to the court and defendant. The court and defendant must also be informed of any intention to reinstitute proceedings where proceedings are withdrawn.

Prosecutors should be able to explain to the court that the seriousness of the offence may require a future prosecution, notwithstanding the likely delay.

Proceedings cannot be reinstituted if the CPS offers no evidence and the case is dismissed in the magistrates' court.

Casework handling

A notice under section 23 of the Prosecution of Offences Act 1985 terminates proceedings for the purposes of time limits in section 127, Magistrates' Courts Act 1980. Summary proceedings must be reinstituted within the time limits specified in section 127, Magistrates' Courts Act 1980.

When proceedings are terminated in order to substitute charge(s), the new charge(s) should be laid before the original matters are terminated, to avoid the possibility of the substitute charge amounting to a reinstitution of proceedings.

Cases that are terminated with a view to reinstitution should be monitored and reviewed in order to avoid delay; otherwise these cases may be susceptible to abuse of process arguments.

Relevant links

Legal guidance on Termination of Proceedings

Prosecutors should also refer to the legal guidance on Private Prosecutions for advice on taking over private prosecutions – a form of reinstitution.

Annex A

Written Answers – House of Commons, 31 March 1993

ATTORNEY GENERAL

Mr Waterson:

To ask the Attorney General what amendment he proposes to make to the undertaking given by the Solicitor General on 25 April 1986 in relation to the reinstitution of proceedings which have been terminated, consequent upon the post of Deputy Director of Public Prosecutions being put into abeyance.

The Attorney-General:

The hon. Member refers to an assurance given during the course of the debate on 25 April 1986, at column 640, on prosecution policy.

The fundamental consideration remains that individuals should be able to rely on decisions taken by the prosecuting authorities. The policy of the Director of Public Prosecutions is that a decision to terminate proceedings or not to prosecute should not, in the absence of special circumstances, be altered once it has been communicated to the defendant or prospective defendant unless it was taken and expressed to be taken because the evidence was insufficient. In such a case it would be appropriate to reconsider the decision if further significant evidence were to become available at a later date – especially if the alleged offence is a serious one.

Special circumstances which might justify departure from this policy include:

(1) rare cases where reconsiderations of the original decision show that it was not justified and the maintenance of confidence in the criminal justice system requires that a prosecution be brought notwithstanding the earlier decision; and

(2) those cases where termination has been effected specifically with a view to the collection and preparation of the necessary evidence which is thought likely to become available in the fairly near future. In such circumstances the CPS will advise the defendant of the possibility that proceedings will be re-instituted.

In the circumstances described at 1 and 2 the decision will be taken at chief crown prosecutor level with effect from 1 April, 1993.

Attorney General's Guidelines on Disclosure

FOREWORD

Disclosure is one of the most important issues in the criminal justice system and the application of proper and fair disclosure is a vital component of a fair criminal justice system. The 'golden rule' is that fairness requires full disclosure should be made of all material held by the prosecution that weakens its case or strengthens that of the defence.

This amounts to no more and no less than a proper application of the Criminal Procedure and Investigations Act 1996 (CPIA) recently amended by the Criminal Justice Act 2003. The amendments in the Criminal Justice Act 2003 abolished the concept of 'primary' and 'secondary' disclosure, and introduced an amalgamated test for disclosure of material that 'might reasonably be considered capable of undermining the prosecution case or assisting the case for accused'. It also introduced a new Code of Practice. In the light of these, other new provisions and case law I conducted a review of the Attorney General's Guidelines issued in November 2000.

Concerns had previously been expressed about the operation of the then existing provisions by judges, prosecutors, and defence practitioners. It seems to me that we must all make a concerted effort to comply with the CPIA disclosure regime robustly in a consistent way in order to regain the trust and confidence of all those involved in the criminal justice system. The House of Lords in *R v H & C* made it clear that so long as the current disclosure system was operated with scrupulous attention, in accordance with the law and with proper regard to the interests of the defendant, it was entirely compatible with Article 6 of the European Convention on Human Rights.

It is vital that everybody in the criminal justice system operates these procedures properly and fairly to ensure we protect the integrity of the criminal justice system whilst at the same time ensuring that a just and fair disclosure process is not abused so that it becomes unwieldy, bureaucratic and effectively unworkable. This means that all those involved must play their role.

Investigators must provide detailed and proper schedules. Prosecutors must not abrogate their duties under the CPIA by making wholesale disclosure in order to avoid carrying out the disclosure exercise themselves. Likewise, defence practitioners should avoid fishing expeditions and where disclosure is not provided using this as an excuse for an abuse of process application. I hope also that the courts will apply the legal regime set out under the CPIA rather than ordering disclosure because either it is easier or it would not 'do any harm'.

This disclosure regime must be made to work and it can only work if there is trust and confidence in the system and everyone plays their role in it. If this is achieved applications for a stay of proceedings on the grounds of non disclosure will only be made exceedingly sparingly and never on a speculative basis. Likewise such applications are only likely to succeed in extreme cases and certainly not where the alleged disclosure is in relation to speculative requests for material.

I have therefore revised the Guidelines to take account of developments and to start the process of ensuring that everyone works to achieve consistency of approach to CPIA disclosure. The amalgamated test should introduce a more streamlined process which is more objective and should therefore deal with some of the concerns about inconsistency in the application of the disclosure regime by prosecutors.

A draft set of these revised Guidelines went out for consultation, and resulted in many thoughtful and detailed responses from practitioners, including members of the judiciary, who have to work with the scheme on a daily basis. The Group that was established to advise me on the revision of the Guidelines has taken account of the results of the consultation exercise. I give my warm thanks to all who have offered responses on the consultation and assisted in the revision of these Guidelines.

I am publishing today the revised Guidelines that, if properly, applied will contribute to ensuring that the disclosure regime operates effectively, fairly and justly – which is vitally important to the integrity of the criminal justice system and the way in which it is perceived by the general public.

DISCLOSURE OF UNUSED MATERIAL IN CRIMINAL PROCEEDINGS

Introduction

Every accused person has a right to a fair trial, a right long embodied in our law and guaranteed under Article 6 of the European Convention on Human Rights (ECHR). A fair trial is the proper object and expectation of all participants in the trial process. Fair disclosure to an accused is an inseparable part of a fair trial.

What must be clear is that a fair trial consists of an examination not just of all the evidence the parties wish to rely on but also all other relevant subject matter. A fair trial should not require consideration of irrelevant material and should not involve spurious applications or arguments which serve to divert the trial process from examining the real issues before the court.

The scheme set out in the Criminal Procedure and Investigations Act 1996 (as amended by the Criminal Justice Act 2003) (the Act) is designed to ensure that there is fair disclosure of material which may be relevant to an investigation and which does not form part of the prosecution case. Disclosure under the Act should assist the accused in the timely preparation and presentation of their case and assist the court to focus on all the relevant issues in the trial. Disclosure which does not meet these objectives risks preventing a fair trial taking place.

This means that the disclosure regime set out in the Act must be scrupulously followed. These Guidelines build upon the existing law to help to ensure that the legislation is operated more effectively, consistently and fairly.

Disclosure must not be an open ended trawl of unused material. A critical element to fair and proper disclosure is that the defence play their role to ensure that the prosecution are directed to material which might reasonably be considered capable of undermining the prosecution case or assisting the case for the accused. This process is key to ensuring prosecutors make informed determinations about disclosure of unused material.

Fairness does recognise that there are other interests that need to be protected, including those of victims and witnesses who might otherwise be exposed to harm. The scheme of the Act protects those interests. It should also ensure that material is not disclosed which overburdens the participants in the trial process, diverts attention from the relevant issues, leads to unjustifiable delay, and is wasteful of resources.

Whilst it is acknowledged that these Guidelines have been drafted with a focus on Crown Court proceedings the spirit of the Guidelines must be followed where they apply to proceedings in the magistrates' court.

General Principles

Disclosure refers to providing the defence with copies of, or access to, any material which might reasonably be considered capable of undermining the case for the prosecution against the accused, or of assisting the case for the accused, and which has not previously been disclosed.

Prosecutors will only be expected to anticipate what material might weaken their case or strengthen the defence in the light of information available at the time of the disclosure decision, and this may include information revealed during questioning.

Generally, material which can reasonably be considered capable of undermining the prosecution case against the accused or assisting the defence case will include anything that tends to show a fact inconsistent with the elements of the case that must be proved by the prosecution. Material can fulfil the disclosure test:

(a)   by the use to be made of it in cross-examination; or

(b)   by its capacity to support submissions that could lead to:

    (i)   the exclusion of evidence; or

    (ii)   a stay of proceedings; or

    (iii)   a court or tribunal finding that any public authority had acted incompatibly with the accused 's rights under the ECHR, or

(c)   by its capacity to suggest an explanation or partial explanation of the accused's actions.

In deciding whether material may fall to be disclosed under paragraph 10, especially (b)(ii), prosecutors must consider whether disclosure is required in order for a proper application to be made. The purpose of this paragraph is not to allow enquiries to support speculative arguments or for the manufacture of defences.

Examples of material that might reasonably be considered capable of undermining the prosecution case or of assisting the case for the accused are:

i.   Any material casting doubt upon the accuracy of any prosecution evidence.

ii.   Any material which may point to another person, whether charged or not (including a co-accused) having involvement in the commission of the offence.

Any material which may cast doubt upon the reliability of a confession.

Any material that might go to the credibility of a prosecution witness.

(iii)   Any material that might support a defence that is either raised by the defence or apparent from the prosecution papers.

(iv)   Any material which may have a bearing on the admissibility of any prosecution evidence.

It should also be borne in mind that while items of material viewed in isolation may not be reasonably considered to be capable of undermining the prosecution case or assisting the accused, several items together can have that effect.

Material relating to the accused's mental or physical health, intellectual capacity, or to any ill treatment which the accused may have suffered when in the investigator's custody is likely to fall within the test for disclosure set out in paragraph 8 above.

Defence Statements

A defence statement must comply with the requirements of section 6A of the Act. A comprehensive defence statement assists the participants in the trial to ensure that it is fair. The trial process is not well served if the defence make general and unspecified allegations and then seek far-reaching disclosure in the hope that material may turn up to make them good. The more detail a defence statement contains the more likely it is that the prosecutor will make an informed decision about whether any remaining undisclosed material might reasonably be considered capable of undermining the prosecution case or of assisting the case for the accused, or whether to advise the investigator to undertake further enquiries. It also helps in the management of the trial by narrowing down and focussing on the issues in dispute. It may result in the prosecution discontinuing the case. Defence practitioners should be aware of these considerations when advising their clients.

Whenever a defence solicitor provides a defence statement on behalf of the accused it will be deemed to be given with the authority of the solicitor's client.

Continuing duty of prosecutor to disclose

Section 7A of the Act imposes a continuing duty upon the prosecutor to keep under review at all times the question of whether there is any unused material which might reasonably be considered capable of undermining the prosecution case against the accused or assisting the case for the accused and which has not previously been disclosed. This duty arises after the prosecutor has complied with the duty of initial disclosure or purported to comply with it and before the accused is acquitted or convicted or the prosecutor decides not to proceed with the case. If such material is identified, then the prosecutor must disclose it to the accused as soon as is reasonably practicable.

As part of their continuing duty of disclosure, prosecutors should be open, alert and promptly responsive to requests for disclosure of material supported by a comprehensive defence statement. Conversely, if no defence statement has been served or if the prosecutor considers that the defence statement is lacking specificity or otherwise does not meet the requirements of section 6A of the Act, a letter should be sent to the defence indicating this. If the position is not resolved satisfactorily, the prosecutor should consider raising the issue at a hearing for directions to enable the court to give a warning or appropriate directions.

When defence practitioners are dissatisfied with disclosure decisions by the prosecution and consider that they are entitled to further disclosure, applications to the court should be made pursuant to section 8 of the Act and in accordance with the procedures set out in the Criminal Procedure Rules. Applications for further disclosure should not be made as ad hoc applications but dealt with under the proper procedures.

Applications for non-disclosure in the public interest

Before making an application to the court to withhold material which would otherwise fall to be disclosed, on the basis that to disclose would give rise to a real risk of serious prejudice to an important public interest, prosecutors should aim to disclose as much of the material as they properly can (for example, by giving the defence redacted or edited copies or summaries). Neutral material or material damaging to the defendant need not be disclosed and must <u>not</u> be brought to the attention of the court. It is only in truly borderline cases that the prosecution should seek a judicial ruling on the disclosability of material in its possession.

Prior to or at the hearing, the court must be provided with full and accurate information. Prior to the hearing the prosecutor and the prosecution advocate must examine all material, which is the subject matter of the application and make any necessary enquiries of the investigator. The prosecutor (or representative) and/or investigator should attend such applications.

The principles set out at paragraph 36 of R v H & C should be rigorously applied firstly by the prosecutor and then by the court considering the material. It is essential that these principles are scrupulously attended to to ensure that the procedure for examination of material in the absence of the accused is compliant with Article 6 of ECHR.

RESPONSIBILITIES

Investigators and disclosure officers

Investigators and disclosure officers must be fair and objective and must work together with prosecutors to ensure that disclosure obligations are met. A failure to take action leading to inadequate disclosure may result in a wrongful conviction. It may alternatively lead to a successful abuse of process argument, an acquittal against the weight of the evidence or the appellate courts may find that a conviction is unsafe and quash it.

Officers appointed as disclosure officers must have the requisite experience, skills, competence and resources to undertake their vital role. In discharging their obligations under the Act, code, common law and any operational instructions, investigators should always err on the side of recording and retaining material where they have any doubt as to whether it may be relevant.

An individual must not be appointed as disclosure officer, or continue in that role, if that is likely to result in a conflict of interest, for instance, if the disclosure officer is the victim of the alleged crime which is the subject of investigation. The advice of a more senior investigator must always be sought if there is doubt as to whether a conflict of interest precludes an individual acting as the disclosure officer. If thereafter a doubt remains, the advice of a prosecutor should be sought.

There may be a number of disclosure officers, especially in large and complex cases. However, there must be a lead disclosure officer who is the focus for enquiries and whose responsibility it is to ensure that the investigator's disclosure obligations are complied with. Disclosure officers, or their deputies, must inspect, view or listen to all relevant material that has been retained by the investigator, and the disclosure officer must provide a personal declaration to the effect that this task has been undertaken.

Generally this will mean that such material must be examined in detail by the disclosure officer or the deputy, but exceptionally the extent and manner of inspecting, viewing or listening will depend on the nature of material and its form. For example, it might be reasonable to examine digital material by using software search tools, or to establish the contents of large volumes of material by dip sampling. If such material is not examined in detail, it must nonetheless be described on the disclosure schedules accurately and as clearly as possible. The extent and manner of its examination must also be described together with justification for such action.

Investigators must retain material that may be relevant to the investigation. However, it may become apparent to the investigator that some material obtained in the course of an investigation because it was considered potentially relevant, is in fact incapable of impact. It need not then be retained or dealt with in accordance with these Guidelines, although the investigator should err on the side of caution in coming to this conclusion and seek the advice of the prosecutor as appropriate.

In meeting the obligations in paragraph 6.9 and 8.1 of the Code, it is crucial that descriptions by disclosure officers in non-sensitive schedules are detailed, clear and accurate. The descriptions may require a summary of the contents of the retained material to assist the prosecutor to make an informed decision on disclosure. Sensitive schedules must contain sufficient information to enable the prosecutor to make an informed decision as to whether or not the material itself should be viewed, to the extent possible without compromising the confidentiality of the information.

Disclosure officers must specifically draw material to the attention of the prosecutor for consideration where they have any doubt as to whether it might reasonably be considered capable of undermining the prosecution case or of assisting the case for the accused.

Disclosure officers must seek the advice and assistance of prosecutors when in doubt as to their responsibility as early as possible. They must deal expeditiously with requests by the prosecutor for further information on material, which may lead to disclosure.

PROSECUTORS

Prosecutors must do all that they can to facilitate proper disclosure, as part of their general and personal professional responsibility to act fairly and impartially, in the interests of justice and in accordance with the law. Prosecutors must also be alert to the need to provide advice to, and where necessary probe actions taken by, disclosure officers to ensure that disclosure obligations are met.

Prosecutors must review schedules prepared by disclosure officers thoroughly and must be alert to the possibility that relevant material may exist which has not been revealed to them or material included which should not have been. If no schedules have been provided, or there are apparent omissions from the schedules, or documents or other items are inadequately described or are unclear, the prosecutor must at once take action to obtain properly completed schedules. Likewise schedules should be returned for amendment if irrelevant items are included. If prosecutors remain dissatisfied with the quality or content of the schedules they must raise the matter with a senior investigator, and if necessary, persist, with a view to resolving the matter satisfactorily.

Where prosecutors have reason to believe that the disclosure officer has not discharged the obligation in paragraph 26 to inspect, view or listen to relevant material, they must at once raise the matter with the disclosure officer and, if it is believed that the officer has not inspected, viewed or listened to the material, request that it be done.

When prosecutors or disclosure officers believe that material might reasonably be considered capable of undermining the prosecution case or assisting the case for the accused, prosecutors must always inspect, view or listen to the material and satisfy themselves that the prosecution can properly be continued having regard to the disclosability of the material reviewed. Their judgement as to what other material to inspect, view or listen to will depend on the circumstances of each case.

Prosecutors should copy the defence statement to the disclosure officer and investigator as soon as reasonably practicable and prosecutors should advise the investigator if, in their view, reasonable and relevant lines of further enquiry should be pursued.

Prosecutors cannot comment upon, or invite inferences to be drawn from, failures in defence disclosure otherwise than in accordance with section 11 of the Act. Prosecutors may cross-examine the accused on differences between the defence case put at trial and that set out in his or her defence statement. In doing so, it may be appropriate to apply to the judge under section 6E of the Act for copies of the statement to be given to a jury, edited if necessary to remove inadmissible material. Prosecutors should examine the defence statement to see whether it points to other lines of enquiry. If the defence statement does point to other reasonable lines of inquiry further investigation is required and evidence obtained as a result of these enquiries may be used as part of the prosecution case or to rebut the defence.

Once initial disclosure is completed and a defence statement has been served requests for disclosure should ordinarily only be answered if the request is in accordance with and relevant to the defence statement. If it is not, then a further or amended defence statement should be sought and obtained before considering the request for further disclosure.

Prosecutors must ensure that they record in writing all actions and decisions they make in discharging their disclosure responsibilities, and this information is to be made available to the prosecution advocate if requested or if relevant to an issue.

If the material does not fulfil the disclosure test there is no requirement to disclose it. For this purpose, the parties' respective cases should not be restrictively analysed but must be carefully analysed to ascertain the specific facts the prosecution seek to establish and the specific grounds on which the charges are resisted. Neutral material or material damaging to the defendant need not be disclosed and must not be brought to the attention of the court. Only in truly borderline cases should the prosecution seek a judicial ruling on the disclosability of material in its hands.

If prosecutors are satisfied that a fair trial cannot take place where material which satisfies the disclosure test cannot be disclosed, and that this cannot or will not be remedied including by, for example, making formal admissions, amending the charges or presenting the case in a different way so as to ensure fairness or in other ways, they must not continue with the case.

PROSECUTION ADVOCATES

Prosecution advocates should ensure that all material that ought to be disclosed under the Act is disclosed to the defence. However, prosecution advocates cannot be expected to disclose material if they are not aware of its existence. As far as is possible, prosecution advocates must place themselves in a fully informed position to enable them to make decisions on disclosure.

Upon receipt of instructions, prosecution advocates should consider as a priority all the information provided regarding disclosure of material. Prosecution advocates should consider, in every case, whether they can be satisfied that they are in possession of all relevant documentation and that they have been instructed fully regarding disclosure matters. Decisions already made regarding disclosure should be reviewed. If as a result, the advocate considers that further information or action is required, written advice should be promptly provided setting out the aspects that need clarification or action. Prosecution advocates must advise on disclosure in accordance with the Act. If necessary and where appropriate a conference should be held to determine what is required.

The prosecution advocate must keep decisions regarding disclosure under review until the conclusion of the trial. The prosecution advocate must in every case specifically consider whether he or she can satisfactorily discharge the duty of continuing review on the basis of the material supplied already, or whether it is necessary to inspect further material or to reconsider material already inspected. Prosecution advocates must not abrogate their responsibility under the Act by disclosing material which could not be considered capable of undermining the prosecution case or of assisting the case for the accused.

Prior to the commencement of a trial, the prosecuting advocate should always make decisions on disclosure in consultation with those instructing him or her and the disclosure officer. After a trial has started, it is recognised that in practice consultation on disclosure issues may not be practicable; it continues to be desirable, however, whenever this can be achieved without affecting unduly the conduct of the trial.

There is no basis in law or practice for disclosure on a 'counsel to counsel' basis.

Involvement of other agencies

Material held by Government departments or other Crown bodies

Where it appears to an investigator, disclosure officer or prosecutor that a Government department or other Crown body has material that may be relevant to an issue in the case, reasonable steps should be taken to identify and consider such material. Although what is reasonable will vary from case to case, the prosecution should inform the department or other body of the nature of its case and of relevant issues in the case in respect of which the department or body might possess material, and ask whether it has any such material.

It should be remembered that investigators, disclosure officers and prosecutors cannot be regarded to be in constructive possession of material held by Government departments or Crown bodies simply by virtue of their status as Government departments or Crown bodies.

Departments in England and Wales should have identified personnel as established Enquiry Points to deal with issues concerning the disclosure of information in criminal proceedings.

Where, after reasonable steps have been taken to secure access to such material, access is denied the investigator, disclosure officer or prosecutor should consider what if any further steps might be taken to obtain the material or inform the defence.

Material held by other agencies

There may be cases where the investigator, disclosure officer or prosecutor believes that a third party (for example, a local authority, a social services department, a hospital, a doctor, a school, a provider of forensic services) has material or information which might be relevant to the prosecution case. In such cases, if the material or information might reasonably be considered capable of undermining the prosecution case or of assisting the case for the accused prosecutors should take what steps they regard as appropriate in the particular case to obtain it.

If the investigator, disclosure officer or prosecutor seeks access to the material or information but the third party declines or refuses to allow access to it, the matter should not be left. If despite any reasons offered by the third party it is still believed that it is reasonable to seek production of the material or information, and the requirements of section 2 of the Criminal Procedure (Attendance of Witnesses) Act 1965 or as appropriate section 97 of the Magistrates Courts Act 1980 are satisfied, then the prosecutor or investigator should apply for a witness summons causing a representative of the third party to produce the material to the Court.

1   The equivalent legislation in Northern Ireland is section 51A of the Judicature (Northern Ireland) Act 1978 and Article 118 of the Magistrates' Courts (Northern Ireland) Order 1981.

Relevant information which comes to the knowledge of investigators or prosecutors as a result of liaison with third parties should be recorded by the investigator or prosecutor in a durable or retrievable form (for example potentially relevant information revealed in discussions at a child protection conference attended by police officers).

Where information comes into the possession of the prosecution in the circumstances set out in paragraphs 51–53 above, consultation with the other agency should take place before disclosure is made: there may be public interest reasons which justify withholding disclosure and which would require the issue of disclosure of the information to be placed before the court.

Other disclosure

Disclosure prior to initial disclosure

Investigators must always be alive to the potential need to reveal and prosecutors to the potential need to disclose material, in the interests of justice and fairness in the particular circumstances of any case, after the commencement of proceedings but before their duty arises under the Act. For instance, disclosure ought to be made of significant information that might affect a bail decision or that might enable the defence to contest the committal proceedings.

Where the need for such disclosure is not apparent to the prosecutor, any disclosure will depend on what the accused chooses to reveal about the defence. Clearly, such disclosure will not exceed that which is obtainable after the statutory duties of disclosure arise

Summary trial

The prosecutor should, in addition to complying with the obligations under the Act, provide to the defence all evidence upon which the Crown proposes to rely in a summary trial. Such provision should allow the accused and their legal advisers sufficient time properly to consider the evidence before it is called.

Material relevant to sentence

In all cases the prosecutor must consider disclosing in the interests of justice any material, which is relevant to sentence (e.g. information which might mitigate the seriousness of the offence or assist the accused to lay blame in part upon a co-accused or another person).

Post-conviction

The interests of justice will also mean that where material comes to light after the conclusion of the proceedings, which might cast doubt upon the safety of the conviction, there is a duty to consider disclosure. Any such material should be brought immediately to the attention of line management.

Disclosure of any material that is made outside the ambit of Act will attract confidentiality by virtue of *Taylor v SFO* [1998].

APPLICABILITY OF THESE GUIDELINES

Although the relevant obligations in relation to unused material and disclosure imposed on the prosecutor and the accused are determined by the date on which the investigation began, these Guidelines should be adopted with immediate effect in relation to all cases submitted to the prosecuting authorities in receipt of these Guidelines save where they specifically refer to the statutory or Code provisions of the Criminal Justice Act 2003 that do not yet apply to the particular case.

Appendix D

CRIMINAL PROCEDURE AND INVESTIGATIONS ACT 1996 CODE OF PRACTICE UNDER PART II

PREAMBLE

This code of practice is issued under Part II of the Criminal Procedure and Investigations Act 1996 ('the Act'). It sets out the manner in which police officers are to record, retain and reveal to the prosecutor material obtained in a criminal investigation and which may be relevant to the investigation, and related matters.

INTRODUCTION

1.1   This code of practice applies in respect of criminal investigations conducted by police officers which begin on or after the day on which this code comes into effect. Persons other than police officers who are charged with the duty of conducting an investigation as defined in the Act are to have regard to the relevant provisions of the code, and should take these into account in applying their own operating procedures.

1.2   This code does not apply to persons who are not charged with the duty of conducting an investigation as defined in the Act.

1.3   Nothing in this code applies to material intercepted in obedience to a warrant issued under section 2 of the Interception of Communications Act 1985 or section 5 of the Regulation of Investigatory Powers Act 2000, or to any copy of that material as defined in section 10 of the 1985 Act or section 15 of the 2000 Act.

1.4   This code extends only to England and Wales.

Definitions

2.1   In this code:

–   *a criminal investigation* is an investigation conducted by police officers with a view to it being ascertained whether a person should be charged with an offence, or whether a person charged with an offence is guilty of it. This will include:

  –   investigations into crimes that have been committed;

  –   investigations whose purpose is to ascertain whether a crime has been committed, with a view to the possible institution of criminal proceedings; and

  –   investigations which begin in the belief that a crime may be committed, for

442

example when the police keep premises or individuals under observation for a period of time, with a view to the possible institution of criminal proceedings;

– charging a person with an offence includes prosecution by way of summons;

– *an investigator* is any police officer involved in the conduct of a criminal investigation. All investigators have a responsibility for carrying out the duties imposed on them under this code, including in particular recording information, and retaining records of information and other material;

– the *officer in charge of an investigation* is the police officer responsible for directing a criminal investigation. He is also responsible for ensuring that proper procedures are in place for recording information, and retaining records of information and other material, in the investigation;

– the *disclosure officer* is the person responsible for examining material retained by the police during the investigation; revealing material to the prosecutor during the investigation and any criminal proceedings resulting from it, and certifying that he has done this; and disclosing material to the accused at the request of the prosecutor;

– the *prosecutor* is the authority responsible for the conduct, on behalf of the Crown, of criminal proceedings resulting from a specific criminal investigation;

– *material* is material of any kind, including information and objects, which is obtained in the course of a criminal investigation and which may be relevant to the investigation. This includes not only material coming into the possession of the investigator (such as documents seized in the course of searching premises) but also material generated by him (such as interview records);

– material may be *relevant to an investigation* if it appears to an investigator, or to the officer in charge of an investigation, or to the disclosure officer, that it has some bearing on any offence under investigation or any person being investigated, or on the surrounding circumstances of the case, unless it is incapable of having any impact on the case;

– *sensitive material* is material, the disclosure of which, the disclosure officer believes, would give rise to a real risk of serious prejudice to an important public interest;

– references to *prosecution disclosure* are to the duty of the prosecutor under sections 3 and 7A of the Act to disclose material which is in his possession or which he has inspected in pursuance of this code, and which might reasonably be considered capable of undermining the case against the accused, or of assisting the case for the accused;

– references to the disclosure of material to a person accused of an offence include references to the disclosure of material to his legal representative;

– references to police officers and to the chief officer of police include those employed in a police force as defined in section 3(3) of the Prosecution of Offences Act 1985.

General responsibilities

3.1 The functions of the investigator, the officer in charge of an investigation and the disclosure officer are separate. Whether they are undertaken by one, two or more persons will depend on the complexity of the case and the administrative arrangements within each police force. Where they are undertaken by more than one person, close consultation between them is essential to the effective performance of the duties imposed by this code.

3.2   In any criminal investigation, one or more deputy disclosure officers may be appointed to assist the disclosure officer, and a deputy disclosure officer may perform any function of a disclosure officer as defined in paragraph 2.1.

3.3   The chief officer of police for each police force is responsible for putting in place arrangements to ensure that in every investigation the identity of the officer in charge of an investigation and the disclosure officer is recorded. The chief officer of police for each police force shall ensure that disclosure officers and deputy disclosure officers have sufficient skills and authority, commensurate with the complexity of the investigation, to discharge their functions effectively. An individual must not be appointed as disclosure officer, or continue in that role, if that is likely to result in a conflict of interest, for instance, if the disclosure officer is the victim of the alleged crime which is the subject of the investigation. The advice of a more senior officer must always be sought if there is doubt as to whether a conflict of interest precludes an individual acting as disclosure officer. If thereafter the doubt remains, the advice of a prosecutor should be sought.

3.4   The officer in charge of an investigation may delegate tasks to another investigator, to civilians employed by the police force, or to other persons participating in the investigation under arrangements for joint investigations, but he remains responsible for ensuring that these have been carried out and for accounting for any general policies followed in the investigation. In particular, it is an essential part of his duties to ensure that all material which may be relevant to an investigation is retained, and either made available to the disclosure officer or (in exceptional circumstances) revealed directly to the prosecutor.

3.5   In conducting an investigation, the investigator should pursue all reasonable lines of inquiry, whether these point towards or away from the suspect. What is reasonable in each case will depend on the particular circumstances. For example, where material is held on computer, it is a matter for the investigator to decide which material on the computer it is reasonable to inquire into, and in what manner.

3.6   If the officer in charge of an investigation believes that other persons may be in possession of material that may be relevant to the investigation, and if this has not been obtained under paragraph 3.5 above, he should ask the disclosure officer to inform them of the existence of the investigation and to invite them to retain the material in case they receive a request for its disclosure. The disclosure officer should inform the prosecutor that they may have such material. However, the officer in charge of an investigation is not required to make speculative enquiries of other persons; there must be some reason to believe that they may have relevant material. That reason may come from information provided to the police by the accused or from other inquiries made or from some other source.

3.7   If, during a criminal investigation, the officer in charge of an investigation or disclosure officer for any reason no longer has responsibility for the functions falling to him, either his supervisor or the police officer in charge of criminal investigations for the police force concerned must assign someone else to assume that responsibility. That person's identity must be recorded, as with those initially responsible for these functions in each investigation.

Recording of information

4.1 If material which may be relevant to the investigation consists of information which is not recorded in any form, the officer in charge of an investigation must ensure that it is recorded in a durable or retrievable form (whether in writing, on video or audio tape, or on computer disk).

4.2 Where it is not practicable to retain the initial record of information because it forms part of a larger record which is to be destroyed, its contents should be transferred as a true record to a durable and more easily-stored form before that happens.

4.3 Negative information is often relevant to an investigation. If it may be relevant it must be recorded. An example might be a number of people present in a particular place at a particular time who state that they saw nothing unusual.

4.4 Where information which may be relevant is obtained, it must be recorded at the time it is obtained or as soon as practicable after that time. This includes, for example, information obtained in house-to-house enquiries, although the requirement to record information promptly does not require an investigator to take a statement from a potential witness where it would not otherwise be taken.

Retention of material

(a) **Duty to retain material**

5.1 The investigator must retain material obtained in a criminal investigation which may be relevant to the investigation. Material may be photographed, video-recorded, captured digitally or otherwise retained in the form of a copy rather than the original at any time, if the original is perishable; the original was supplied to the investigator rather than generated by him and is to be returned to its owner; or the retention of a copy rather than the original is reasonable in all the circumstances.

5.2 Where material has been seized in the exercise of the powers of seizure conferred by the Police and Criminal Evidence Act 1984, the duty to retain it under this code is subject to the provisions on the retention of seized material in section 22 of that Act.

5.3 If the officer in charge of an investigation becomes aware as a result of developments in the case that material previously examined but not retained (because it was not thought to be relevant) may now be relevant to the investigation, he should, wherever practicable, take steps to obtain it or ensure that it is retained for further inspection or for production in court if required.

5.4 The duty to retain material includes in particular the duty to retain material falling into the following categories, where it may be relevant to the investigation:

- crime reports (including crime report forms, relevant parts of incident report books or police officer's notebooks);

- custody records;

- records which are derived from tapes of telephone messages (for example, 999 calls) containing descriptions of an alleged offence or offender;

- final versions of witness statements (and draft versions where their content differs from the final version), including any exhibits mentioned (unless these have been returned to their owner on the understanding that they will be produced in court if required);

- interview records (written records, or audio or video tapes, of interviews with actual or potential witnesses or suspects);

- communications between the police and experts such as forensic scientists, reports of work carried out by experts, and schedules of scientific material prepared by the expert for the investigator, for the purposes of criminal proceedings;

- records of the first description of a suspect by each potential witness who purports to identify or describe the suspect, whether or not the description differs from that of subsequent descriptions by that or other witnesses;

- any material casting doubt on the reliability of a witness.

5.5   The duty to retain material, where it may be relevant to the investigation, also includes in particular the duty to retain material which may satisfy the test for prosecution disclosure in the Act, such as:

- information provided by an accused person which indicates an explanation for the offence with which he has been charged;

- any material casting doubt on the reliability of a confession;

- any material casting doubt on the reliability of a prosecution witness.

5.6   The duty to retain material falling into these categories does not extend to items which are purely ancillary to such material and possess no independent significance (for example, duplicate copies of records or reports).

(b) Length of time for which material is to be retained

5.7   All material which may be relevant to the investigation must be retained until a decision is taken whether to institute proceedings against a person for an offence.

5.8   If a criminal investigation results in proceedings being instituted, all material which may be relevant must be retained at least until the accused is acquitted or convicted or the prosecutor decides not to proceed with the case.

5.9   Where the accused is convicted, all material which may be relevant must be retained at least until:

- the convicted person is released from custody, or discharged from hospital, in cases where the court imposes a custodial sentence or a hospital order;

- six months from the date of conviction, in all other cases.

If the court imposes a custodial sentence or hospital order and the convicted person is released from custody or discharged from hospital earlier than six months from the date of conviction, all material which may be relevant must be retained at least until six months from the date of conviction.

5.10   If an appeal against conviction is in progress when the release or discharge occurs, or at the end of the period of six months specified in paragraph 5.9, all material which may be relevant must be retained until the appeal is determined. Similarly, if the Criminal Cases Review Commission is considering an application at that point in time, all material which may be relevant must be retained at least until the Commission decides not to refer the case to the Court.

Preparation of material for prosecutor

(a) Introduction

6.1　The officer in charge of the investigation, the disclosure officer or an investigator may seek advice from the prosecutor about whether any particular item of material may be relevant to the investigation.

6.2　Material which may be relevant to an investigation, which has been retained in accordance with this code, and which the disclosure officer believes will not form part of the prosecution case, must be listed on a schedule.

6.3　Material which the disclosure officer does not believe is sensitive must be listed on a schedule of non-sensitive material. The schedule must include a statement that the disclosure officer does not believe the material is sensitive.

6.4　Any material which is believed to be sensitive must be either listed on a schedule of sensitive material or, in exceptional circumstances, revealed to the prosecutor separately. If there is no sensitive material, the disclosure officer must record this fact on a schedule of sensitive material.

6.5　Paragraphs 6.6 to 6.11 below apply to both sensitive and non-sensitive material. Paragraphs 6.12 to 6.14 apply to sensitive material only.

(b) Circumstances in which a schedule is to be prepared

6.6　The disclosure officer must ensure that a schedule is prepared in the following circumstances:

– 　the accused is charged with an offence which is triable only on indictment;

– 　the accused is charged with an offence which is triable either way, and it is considered either that the case is likely to be tried on indictment or that the accused is likely to plead not guilty at a summary trial;

– 　the accused is charged with a summary offence, and it is considered that he is likely to plead not guilty.

6.7　In respect of either way and summary offences, a schedule may not be needed if a person has admitted the offence, or if a police officer witnessed the offence and that person has not denied it.

6.8　If it is believed that the accused is likely to plead guilty at a summary trial, it is not necessary to prepare a schedule in advance. If, contrary to this belief, the accused pleads not guilty at a summary trial, or the offence is to be tried on indictment, the disclosure officer must ensure that a schedule is prepared as soon as is reasonably practicable after that happens.

(c) Way in which material is to be listed on schedule

6.9　The disclosure officer should ensure that each item of material is listed separately on the schedule, and is numbered consecutively. The description of each item should make clear the nature of the item and should contain sufficient detail to enable the prosecutor to decide whether he needs to inspect the material before deciding whether or not it should be disclosed.

6.10　In some enquiries it may not be practicable to list each item of material separately. For example, there may be many items of a similar or repetitive nature. These may be listed in a block and described by quantity and generic title.

6.11   Even if some material is listed in a block, the disclosure officer must ensure that any items among that material which might satisfy the test for prosecution disclosure are listed and described individually.

(d) Treatment of sensitive material

6.12   Subject to paragraph 6.13 below, the disclosure officer must list on a sensitive schedule any material, the disclosure of which he believes would give rise to a real risk of serious prejudice to an important public interest, and the reason for that belief. The schedule must include a statement that the disclosure officer believes the material is sensitive. Depending on the circumstances, examples of such material may include the following among others:

–   material relating to national security;

–   material received from the intelligence and security agencies;

–   material relating to intelligence from foreign sources which reveals sensitive intelligence gathering methods;

–   material given in confidence;

–   material relating to the identity or activities of informants, or undercover police officers, or witnesses, or other persons supplying information to the police who may be in danger if their identities are revealed;

–   material revealing the location of any premises or other place used for police surveillance, or the identity of any person allowing a police officer to use them for surveillance;

–   material revealing, either directly or indirectly, techniques and methods relied upon by a police officer in the course of a criminal investigation, for example covert surveillance techniques, or other methods of detecting crime;

–   material whose disclosure might facilitate the commission of other offences or hinder the prevention and detection of crime;

–   material upon the strength of which search warrants were obtained;

–   material containing details of persons taking part in identification parades;

–   material supplied to an investigator during a criminal investigation which has been generated by an official of a body concerned with the regulation or supervision of bodies corporate or of persons engaged in financial activities, or which has been generated by a person retained by such a body;

–   material supplied to an investigator during a criminal investigation which relates to a child or young person and which has been generated by a local authority social services department, an Area Child Protection Committee or other party contacted by an investigator during the investigation;

–   material relating to the private life of a witness.

6.13   In exceptional circumstances, where an investigator considers that material is so sensitive that its revelation to the prosecutor by means of an entry on the sensitive schedule is inappropriate, the existence of the material must be revealed to the prosecutor separately. This will apply only where compromising the material would be likely to lead directly to the loss of life, or directly threaten national security.

6.14   In such circumstances, the responsibility for informing the prosecutor lies with the investigator who knows the detail of the sensitive material. The investigator should act as soon as is reasonably practicable after the file containing the prosecution case is sent to the prosecutor. The investigator must also ensure that the prosecutor is able to inspect the material so that he can assess whether it is disclosable and, if so, whether it needs to be brought before a court for a ruling on disclosure.

Revelation of material to prosecutor

7.1   The disclosure officer must give the schedules to the prosecutor. Wherever practicable this should be at the same time as he gives him the file containing the material for the prosecution case (or as soon as is reasonably practicable after the decision on mode of trial or the plea, in cases to which paragraph 6.8 applies).

7.2   The disclosure officer should draw the attention of the prosecutor to any material an investigator has retained (including material to which paragraph 6.13 applies) which may satisfy the test for prosecution disclosure in the Act, and should explain why he has come to that view.

7.3   At the same time as complying with the duties in paragraphs 7.1 and 7.2, the disclosure officer must give the prosecutor a copy of any material which falls into the following categories (unless such material has already been given to the prosecutor as part of the file containing the material for the prosecution case):

–   information provided by an accused person which indicates an explanation for the offence with which he has been charged;

–   any material casting doubt on the reliability of a confession;

–   any material casting doubt on the reliability of a prosecution witness;

–   any other material which the investigator believes may satisfy the test for prosecution disclosure in the Act.

7.4   If the prosecutor asks to inspect material which has not already been copied to him, the disclosure officer must allow him to inspect it. If the prosecutor asks for a copy of material which has not already been copied to him, the disclosure officer must give him a copy. However, this does not apply where the disclosure officer believes, having consulted the officer in charge of the investigation, that the material is too sensitive to be copied and can only be inspected.

7.5   If material consists of information which is recorded other than in writing, whether it should be given to the prosecutor in its original form as a whole, or by way of relevant extracts recorded in the same form, or in the form of a transcript, is a matter for agreement between the disclosure officer and the prosecutor.

Subsequent action by disclosure officer

8.1   At the time a schedule of non-sensitive material is prepared, the disclosure officer may not know exactly what material will form the case against the accused, and the prosecutor may not have given advice about the likely relevance of particular items of material. Once these matters have been determined, the disclosure officer must give the prosecutor, where necessary, an amended schedule listing any additional material:

–   which may be relevant to the investigation,

–   which does not form part of the case against the accused,

- which is not already listed on the schedule, and

- which he believes is not sensitive,

unless he is informed in writing by the prosecutor that the prosecutor intends to disclose the material to the defence.

8.2   Section 7A of the Act imposes a continuing duty on the prosecutor, for the duration of criminal proceedings against the accused, to disclose material which satisfies the test for disclosure (subject to public interest considerations). To enable him to do this, any new material coming to light should be treated in the same way as the earlier material.

8.3   In particular, after a defence statement has been given, the disclosure officer must look again at the material which has been retained and must draw the attention of the prosecutor to any material which might reasonably be considered capable of undermining the case for the prosecution against the accused or of assisting the case for the accused; and he must reveal it to him in accordance with paragraphs 7.4 and 7.5 above.

Certification by disclosure officer

9.1   The disclosure officer must certify to the prosecutor that to the best of his knowledge and belief, all relevant material which has been retained and made available to him has been revealed to the prosecutor in accordance with this code. He must sign and date the certificate. It will be necessary to certify not only at the time when the schedule and accompanying material is submitted to the prosecutor, and when relevant material which has been retained is reconsidered after the accused has given a defence statement, but also whenever a schedule is otherwise given or material is otherwise revealed to the prosecutor.

Disclosure of material to accused

10.1   If material has not already been copied to the prosecutor, and he requests its disclosure to the accused on the ground that:

- it satisfies the test for prosecution disclosure, **or**

- the court has ordered its disclosure after considering an application from the accused,

the disclosure officer must disclose it to the accused.

10.2   If material has been copied to the prosecutor, and it is to be disclosed, whether it is disclosed by the prosecutor or the disclosure officer is a matter of agreement between the two of them.

10.3   The disclosure officer must disclose material to the accused either by giving him a copy or by allowing him to inspect it. If the accused person asks for a copy of any material which he has been allowed to inspect, the disclosure officer must give it to him, unless in the opinion of the disclosure officer that is either not practicable (for example because the material consists of an object which cannot be copied, or because the volume of material is so great), or not desirable (for example because the material is a statement by a child witness in relation to a sexual offence).

10.4   If material which the accused has been allowed to inspect consists of information which is recorded other than in writing, whether it should be given to the accused in its original form or in the form of a transcript is matter for the discretion of the disclosure officer. If the material is transcribed, the disclosure officer must ensure that the transcript is certified to the accused as a true record of the material which has been transcribed.

10.5 If a court concludes that an item of sensitive material satisfies the prosecution disclosure test and that the interests of the defence outweigh the public interest in withholding disclosure, it will be necessary to disclose the material if the case is to proceed. This does not mean that sensitive documents must always be disclosed in their original form: for example, the court may agree that sensitive details still requiring protection should be blocked out, or that documents may be summarised, or that the prosecutor may make an admission about the substance of the material under section 10 of the Criminal Justice Act 1967.

Disclosure: A Protocol for the Control and Management of Unused Material in the Crown Court

OUTLINE NOTE CONCERNING 'DISCLOSURE: A PROTOCOL FOR THE CONTROL AND MANAGEMENT OF UNUSED MATERIAL IN THE CROWN COURT' ('THE DISCLOSURE PROTOCOL')

1. INTRODUCTION

1.1 The Disclosure Protocol applies to all trials on indictment, including Very High Cost Cases [VHCCs], and will be effective from its date of publication (20 February 2006).

1.2 It was drafted by a team led by Mr Justice Fulford and Mr Justice Oppenshaw, which included representatives from the CPS, SFO and RCPO.

1.3 This outline note provides a basic guide to the Disclosure Protocol. There is an initial overview of the document, followed by the headline messages for each of the key CJS agencies, namely:

- police/investigators and disclosure officers;
- prosecutors;
- defence practitioners;
- courts;
- judges

2. OVERVIEW

2.1 The Disclosure Protocol is concerned with the management of issues relating to unused material in the Crown Court. Its main feature is a requirement for strict compliance with the disclosure provisions of the Criminal Procedure and Investigations Act 1996 (the Act), and the statutory Code of Practice laid under section 23 of the Act, where they apply to the proceedings.

2.2 In brief, the Act and Code together regulate the disclosure of unused prosecution material in cases which relate to a criminal investigation which commenced on or after 1 April 1997 (there are modified provisions which apply to investigations commencing on or after 4 April 2005).

2.3 The Disclosure Protocol sets out the 'overarching principle' in paragraph 4. The effect of the principle, in cases where the Act applies, is that material will fall to be disclosed if, and only if, it satisfies the statutory test for disclosure. Unless the material is capable of undermining the prosecution case or assisting the case put forward by the accused, it will not fall to be disclosed.

2.4 The protocol, consistent with the need for strict compliance with the Act, requires an end to free-standing orders for disclosure by judges otherwise than those properly made in the context of hearings conducted under section 8 of the Act and r25.6 of the Criminal Procedure Rules, following service of a defence statement by the accused. This means that ad hoc disclosure orders at 'mention' hearings and 'blanket' disclosure orders should no longer be made.

2.5 Regarding defence statements in particular, the Disclosure Protocol describes these as a 'really critical step' in the disclosure process and requires judges to conduct a 'full investigation' where they have not been served by the time of the PCHM.

2.6 The protocol also provides guidance on PII hearings and applications for 'third party disclosure', and provides an important additional source to the Attorney General's Guidelines in relation to the treatment of Government/Crown material.

3. POLICE/INVESTIGATORS AND DISCLOSURE OFFICERS

3.1 The Disclosure Protocol stresses the need for rigorous compliance with the provisions in the Code of Practice for the gathering of material, the assessment of it for 'relevance' (using the test in paragraph 2.1 of the Code), and the scheduling of material satisfying the latter test. (**Paragraphs 13, 14, 16**)

3.2 Schedules must be prepared timeously, so as to ensure that the prosecutor's duty to make disclosure under section 3(1) of the Act can be discharged 'as soon as practicable' after the matter has been committed or transferred to the Crown Court, or cases papers have been served following a section 51 Crime and Disorder Act 1998 'sending'. (**Paragraph 15**)

3.3 Where there are problems with providing case papers and/or disclosure schedules to the prosecutor within the normally permitted timescales, this information should be communicated promptly to the prosecutor so that an appropriate variation of the standard directions can be sought at the magistrates' court (or subsequent Crown Court hearing). (**Paragraph 23**).

4. PROSECUTORS

4.1 CPS duty prosecutors advising pre-charge at police stations should consider making a preliminary review of the unused material, where this is practicable. (**Paragraph 17**). There may be a need to provide early disclosure to the defence where R v DPP ex parte Lee (1999) applies. (**Paragraph 19**).

4.2 The prosecution cannot abdicate its statutory responsibility to apply the statutory test for disclosure by simply disclosing all non-sensitive unused material, irrespective of whether it satisfies that test. (**Paragraph 30**). This is particularly important in large and complex cases, where such disclosure may add considerably to the cost of proceedings. (**Paragraph 31**). Documents from a defence 'list' should only be disclosed if they satisfy the test for disclosure.

4.3   Where the prosecution seek an extension of time to serve papers, an appropriately detailed explanation must be given. (**Paragraph 28**).

4.4   Where the defence have defaulted on disclosure obligations, the prosecution should bring this to the attention of the court and seek an inference under section 11 of the Act, subject to any views expressed by the judge (**Paragraph 42**).

4.5   The prosecution must be mindful of its continuing duty to review disclosure. (**Paragraph 43**).

4.6   Guidance for prosecutors making PII applications is provided. (**Paragraph 51**).

5. DEFENCE PRACTITIONERS

5.1   Service of a defence statement on behalf of the accused is a 'really critical step' in proceedings. They are mandatory under section 5(5) of the Act, within 14 days of the prosecution making or purporting to make section 3(1) disclosure. (**Paragraph 32**) Applications for an extension of time must be made in compliance with the applicable regulations (**Paragraph 33**).

5.2   The defence need to be aware that the judge will undertake a full investigation, posing searching questions, where the mandatory requirement has not been properly complied with by the time of the PCMH (**Paragraphs 38 – 41**).

5.3   It will not be sufficient for the defence to say that insufficient instructions have been taken. The court will need to know why not, and what arrangements can be made to address the default (**Paragraph 28**). A PCMH may have to be put back for the defence statement to be served (**Paragraph 33**).

5.4   The defence statement cannot amount to a simple reiteration of the not guilty plea. There must be compliance with the formalities required by the Act (**Paragraphs 34 – 36**). There has to be a complete culture change in this respect (**Paragraph 37**). The accused should be warned of the real risk of a direction to the jury regarding a section 11 'adverse inference', where there is no justification for the defence default in disclosure. (**Paragraphs 39 and 42**).

5.5   Where the defence seek further disclosure of specific material, and the prosecution declines to make this, they will need to make an application under section 8 of the Act, complying with r25.6 CPR (written application, detailing grounds and giving the prosecution 14 days in which to respond and request a hearing). The defence need to be aware of any cut-off date set at the PCMH for such applications (**Paragraph 44**)

5.6   Regarding third-party disclosure, the defence should not sit back and expect the prosecution to make the running and must comply with any timetable set by the judge (**Paragraph 58**). The defence will need to prove that the material is admissible as evidence in the proceedings (**Paragraph 60**). The court will make a wasted costs order where applications are clearly unmeritorious and ill-conceived (**Paragraph 59**).

5.7   Unused material which has been gathered during the course of a criminal investigation and disclosed by the prosecution is received by the defence subject to a prohibition not to use or disclose the material for any purpose which is not connected with the proceedings for whose purposes they were given it, although neither statute nor the common law prevents use of such material if it has been displayed or communicated to the public in open court unless a reporting restriction is in place (**Paragraph 8**).

6. COURTS

6.1   Guidance is given regarding the listing of PCMHs (**Paragraphs 47 – 49**).

7. JUDGES

7.1   Judges must seize the initiative regarding disclosure issues, driving the case along to an efficient, effective and timely resolution, having regard to the CPR Part 1 overriding objective. It is the duty of every judge actively to manage disclosure in every case (**Paragraph 63**).

7.2   Judges should examine defence statements with care to ensure they comply with the formalities required under the Act (**Paragraph 37**). They must conduct a full investigation if no defence statement, or no sufficient one, has been served by the time of the PCMH (**Paragraph 38**). They must be ready to pose searching questions to the parties where either is in default and explore any reasons given before making appropriate directions (**Paragraph 41**).

7.3   Judges should set a timetable for matters such as section 8 applications and applications for 'third party disclosure' (**Paragraphs 43, 56, 58**). In respect of the latter, the judge should question whether inquiries with a third party are appropriate and, if so, identify who will make them (**Paragraph 56**). The judge should specifically inquire at the PCMH whether the defence intend to apply for a witness summons (**Paragraph 58**).

7.4   Where the defence seek material such as confidential medical records concerning the complainant, judges must balance the rights of victims against the real and proven needs of the defence. They must ensure that any interference with the victim's article 8 ECHR right to privacy is in accordance with the law and necessary in the pursuit of a legitimate public interest (**Paragraph 62**)

For further information concerning the Disclosure Protocol, please contact the Judicial Communications Office: 020 7947 6438.

February 2006

Index